INDIAN COUNCIL OF HISTORICAL RESEARCH MONOGRAPH SERIES 11

NETWORKS IN THE FIRST GLOBAL AGE 1400-1800

Networks in the First Global Age 1400-1800

Edited by

RILA MUKHERJEE

INDIAN COUNCIL OF HISTORICAL RESEARCH

in association with

PRIMUS BOOKS
An imprint of Ratna Sagar P. Ltd.
Virat Bhavan
Mukherjee Nagar Commercial Complex
Delhi 110 009

Offices at
CHENNAI KOLKATA LUCKNOW
AGRA BANGALORE COIMBATORE DEHRADUN GUWAHATI
HYDERABAD JAIPUR KANPUR KOCHI MADURAI MUMBAI PATNA

First published 2011

ISBN 978-93-80607-09-2

Published by Primus Books

in association with

Indian Council of Historical Research
35, Ferozeshah Road, New Delhi 110 001

Laser typeset by Digigrafics
New Delhi 110 049

Printed at Sanat Printers, Kundli, Haryana

To

ANDRE GUNDER FRANK

(Berlin, 24 February 1929 – Luxembourg, 23 April 2005)
Scholar and Friend Extraordinaire

This volume is dedicated to Andre Gunder Frank. Frank intellectually challenged the comfortable and self-serving assumptions of the wealthy and powerful about a superiority that results from their descent from European rationality, values, and institutions and about poverty that stems from the personal failures of the poor themselves and the backwardness of their 'cultures'. In focusing attention on the grossly disproportionate share of the world's economic and political resources controlled by a tiny minority of countries and furthermore by a tiny minority within those countries, he transformed academic disciplines, including history and the historical social sciences. In the final period of his life, he walked away from theoretical positions upon which much of his fame rested because 'the evidence has obliged me to do so', thereby providing a striking example of intellectual honesty and courage.

For Frank, the quest to understand the world so that greater equality and democracy could flourish would never end. For that example and quest, we honour his memory.

Pocatello, USA J.B. OWENS

Frank's last work, *ReORIENT: Global Economy in the Asian Age* (1998), compelled a whole generation of scholars to revisit traditional assumptions behind hegemony and counter-hegemony and asked us to rethink connections in the world economy. This volume is a modest venture in that direction.

Hyderabad, India RILA MUKHERJEE

To

ANDRE GUNDER FRANK

(Berlin 24 February 1929—Luxembourg, 23 April 2005)

Scholar and Friend Extraordinaire

This volume is dedicated to Andre Gunder Frank. Frank's intellectual challenge of the 'under-development' [illegible] assumptions of the wealthy and powerful about a superiority that results from their dedication to European rationality, values and institutions and about poverty that stems from the personal failures of the poor themselves and the backwardness of their cultures [illegible] focusing attention on the grossly disproportionate share of the world's economic and political power controlled by a tiny minority of countries and further more by a tiny minority within those countries. He transformed academic disciplines including history and the historical social sciences. In the [illegible] of his life [illegible] and [illegible] the correct positions upon which [illegible] of [illegible] because [illegible] obliged me [illegible] his [illegible] honesty and [illegible].

For Frank, the quest to understand [illegible] and to offer greater equality and democracy [illegible] world [illegible] we honour his memory.

[illegible] [illegible] Owens

Frank's life work [illegible] compelled a whole generation of scholars to revisit traditional assumptions behind hegemony and counter-hegemony and asked us to rethink [illegible] in the world economy. This volume is a modest venture in that direction.

Hyderabad, India [illegible] Mukherjee

Contents

Foreword

THE INDIAN COUNCIL OF HISTORICAL Research brings before the readers the present collection of essays with a sense of satisfaction. This is the second publication in the ICHR Monograph Series, coming close on the heels of the first one produced three months ago. In the past, from time to time the ICHR has published such monographs, numbering about ten over four decades, but the continuity of a series was lacking. It is now felt that there is need for a new ICHR Monograph Series to put together research contributions that possess a thematic focus. It is hoped that these monographs will provide bridgeheads into the frontiers of research today.

The theme of the present volume is the contemporary effort to question the traditional representation of world history as the story of the other parts of the world to catch up with Europe, the attempts in various areas of study to de-centre the writing of history from its Eurocentric focus, and to look at an alternative perspective on the growth of global networks from the fifteenth century to the nineteenth. Inevitably the reader would be reminded of Andre Gunder Frank and his last major work *ReORIENT: Global Economy in the Asian Age:*

> He argued that a 'horizontally integrative macro-history', a comparative historiography of the different parts of the global economy at the same time, was needed to understand the very long-term trends.... A radical revision of ideas was also implicit in the work *ReORIENT* in 1998. His new interpretative approach ... suggested that the capitalist system did not originate in the European metropolis,

that none of the characteristics of Europe was unique to Europe in the millennia before industrial capitalist imperialism, and that many of these characteristics were to be found in the Afro-Asian countries. In arguing thus he evidently questions what Braudel and Wallerstein, or Weber and Marx took for granted.... It was characteristic of Gunder Frank to challenge all received wisdom in his last major monograph.

The Economic and Political Weekly wrote thus on 7 May 2005, a few days after his death. I happened to be the author of this obituary article and at that time could not anticipate the outcome of the seeds of ideas he had planted—which are now in evidence in the present collection of innovative essays. I am glad that this monograph has been dedicated to the memory of Andre Gunder Frank.

The essays in this collection, ably edited by Professor Rila Mukherjee, project before us the implications of those ideas. The volume editor offers a perspicacious summing up and a review in the introductory essay. But even a casual reader glancing at these pages would note that in this collection one can see an innovative paradigm at work, continually questioning the received interpretation of history. When one situates these ideas and the historical evidence within the big picture, as one shuttles between the macro-perspective and the micro-history addressed in most of these essays, numerous questions arise. Perhaps the most important question is the one raised by more than one contributor: is it possible or useful to characterize a particular period as an age of 'cooperation' and following which, what exactly are the components of that category? Another set of questions relate to the perception of the 'global age' from the Afro-Asian point of view; one is reminded of the global awareness in the writings of ibn Khaldun (1332-1406) or even earlier al Idrisi (*c.*1100-65). The relationship between 'networks', local, regional, national and supra-national, also needs to be problematized. *Networks in the First Global Age: 1400-1800* raises many interesting questions and one looks forward towards further explorations and validation of the arguments presented here.

I would like to thank Dr Ishrat Alam, Member Secretary, Indian Council of Historical Research for having expeditiously piloted the book through the publication process.

Chairman SABYASACHI BHATTACHARYA
Indian Council of Historical Research
New Delhi

Preface

As the dedication suggests, this volume on global systems and networks was written as a response to the many questions that Andre Gunder Frank raised in *ReORIENT*, in particular on what constituted the chief driving force(s) in the world system in the First Global Age that lasted from 1400-1800.

Networks in the First Global Age: 1400–1800 is the result of an unbelievable, in fact a marvellous, cooperation between members of the academic community based in such diverse locations as Kolkata, Hyderabad, Paris, Pocatello, Mumbai, Dartmouth, Aix en Provence, Porto, Puduchcheri, Mallorca and Madrid. I wish to state my thanks to all the contributors here; they were gracious enough to respond promptly to my request for chapters (initially conceived of as articles for a special themed issue of the *Indian Historical Review*). They were agreeable to the changes suggested and, most importantly, were swift with the proofreading!

As regards the presentation of this volume, it was decided to have as little editorial control (or interference!) as possible beyond an adherence to a particular style format for the body texts and the notes. I would like to thank the contributors for adhering to the format and thereby making almost painless my task as the volume editor.

For members of the DynCoopNet family represented by J.B. Owens, Ana Crespo Solana, Amélia Polónia, Amândio Jorge Morais Barros, David Alonso García and Antoni Picazo Muntaner, my sincere gratitude, as several chapters in this volume grew out of an initial European

Science Foundation meeting in Budapest in the summer of 2007. For Timothy D. Walker, also a special thanks for his chapter here; we corresponded about the volume long before we met finally in Hyderabad in 2009. For Ernestine Carreira, my appreciation for a collaboration that started way back at Lyons in 2000 and continued at Aix and then India in 2004 and 2008. And for Rattan Lal Hangloo, my colleague at Hyderabad, whose work on Kashmir and Ladakh may be familiar to many readers, a special note of appreciation. Finally, to Srijan Sandip Mandal and Alex M. Thomas, my students of the 2008-9 batch of the Indian Ocean course at the University of Hyderabad, my thanks yet again, as their interventions in the Indian Ocean class enabled me to clarify many of the ideas presented in my chapter.

This book would have been impossible to put together without the support I received from several quarters. I am grateful to the Maison des Sciences de l'Homme, Paris, who made possible for me to consult the French archives at the C.A.O.M., Aix, France, and the many libraries in Paris over the last few years and also to the University of Hyderabad for providing a congenial atmosphere for research.

My thanks are also due to the Indian Council of Historical Research, New Delhi, for agreeing to publish this volume under their Monograph Series, to the Series Editor and the Chairman of the Council, Professor Sabyasachi Bhattacharya, to the Member Secretary Dr Ishrat Alam and to Dr Anup Taneja, Deputy Director, Publications, ICHR.

Hyderabad, India RILA MUKHERJEE

INTRODUCTION

The Many Faces of the First Global Age c. 1400–1800

Rila Mukherjee

NUMEROUS SCHOLARS HAVE QUESTIONED the assumption of a 'First Global Age' during the 400 years that Europe encountered the world. Consequently, the formulation of the First Global Age from 1400 to 1800, four centuries that coincided with Europe's domination over a large part of the world, has been regarded as a Eurocentric notion.[1] Certain scholars, therefore, have opted for earlier global ages; see, for example, the writings of Janet Abu Lughod or Philippe Beaujard.[2]

Nevertheless, it is certain that during these four hundred years the world saw unprecedented levels of trade both in scope and intensity; and previously marginal areas such as parts of Africa and Central Asia were drawn into a global trade system that surpassed all the earlier levels of mercantile activity and encompassed the greater parts of Central, South and South-East Asia, North and East Africa, Europe, and the North and South Americas.

The First Global Age also witnessed increased cooperation across different parts of the globe, involving a process of cultural sharing, of increased knowledge about others and a certain amount of hybridization as more and more people travelled to, and sometimes settled in, different parts of the world.

The System

DynCoopNet focuses on this First Global Age, while aiming to highlight networks hitherto neglected or marginalized in conventional history writing. Owens opens Chapter 1 in this volume by elaborating upon the nature of DynCoopNet and what kind of a 'system' it is a part of. He writes:

> I define the First Global Age, roughly 1400–1800, as an open, complex, dynamic, nonlinear system. Within this system, the self-organizing social networks studied by DynCoopNet are the sources of innovation and the emergence of new forms. I agree with Frank's position in *ReORIENT* that although the system was not global in the fifteenth century, that period was crucial for the development of the dynamics characteristic of the system for about four centuries.

We have taken the liberty, in this volume, of including the history of transregional trade in a landlocked state—Ladakh—to demonstrate that when the phase transition from the First Global Age occurs *after* 1800 the resulting system is largely unable to face the challenges of the Second Global Age.

SHIFTS AND TRANSITIONS WITHIN THE SYSTEM

Stepping away from the traditional methods of characterizing the transition as a European one, held in place between entities labelled 'Feudalism' and 'Capitalism' (*pace* Wallerstein), or adopting labels such as the 'Coming of the State', the 'Early Modern' period between 1500 and 1800, the 'Modern' period, the coming of the 'Individual' or the beginnings of 'Individualism' (linked with the so-called Protestant Ethic of Max Weber and the Burckhardtian thesis on the originality and individualism of the fifteenth century European Renaissance) and so on, Owens suggests an alternate apparatus to view the First Global Age. Given that these notions essentially describe the historical experiences of Europe thereby 'distorting the experiences of the men and women of the First Global Age and turning a three- or four-century-long period into the antechamber of the nineteenth and twentieth centuries', he opines that we may view the First Global Age in terms of an overall system stability, which in turn depended on only a few variables that were stable but near instability. These variables can be identified, according to Owens, by a careful examination of the system's nonlinear dynamics, which is one of DynCoopNet's tasks. A phase transition is initiated when these critical variables become unstable, leading the system to instability, chaos, and bifurcation, around which a new system organizes itself.

How do we then define the major shifts? Owens feels that major historical periods should be defined on the basis of such phase transitions and identifying and explaining these should become a major focus of research for the historical social sciences. '*History is seen here as an account characterized by complex, dynamic, nonlinear systems separated by phase transitions of instability, bifurcation, and reorganization*' [italics mine]. Owens concludes that the period 1400–1800 constituted an open, complex, dynamic, nonlinear system flanked by phase transitions that separated it from systems before in Afroeurasia and afterwards throughout the world. What then was the spatial framework of this system?

SPACE, SYSTEM AND SYSTEMS

Crespo Solana examines one such spatial framework—the Atlantic—and questions the very foundations on which a global model, such as the Atlantic model, rests by interrogating the notion of the 'Spanish Atlantic'. To quote her opening paragraph: 'In order to geographically depict this so-called Atlantic System, I always think of it as an immense space of frontier; a space which developed under an umbrella of common, and at the same time various enterprises. These enterprises were established between diverse societies via a network of centres under development and which, in turn, drew together various areas in different states of development.'

Crespo Solana continues: 'The Atlantic, then, appears to have constituted elements which were functionally bonded so that a series of rules led to total interdependence. This concept has been re-examined in the last decade and Renate Pieper and Peer Schmidt have concluded that it was a "deep reassessing of the category of space as a constituent of the action of history", a valuation of the space factor well above the temporal or chronological, a "spatial turn" that implies elaboration by the historian of "mental maps".' She concludes:

> To summarize, understanding the role played by the Iberian expansion in general, and by the Spanish expansion in particular, on the formation of this Atlantic, or even worldwide or global system will enable us to comprehend the various spatial and geographical sub-systems which derived from the different expansion models with which the Spanish empire had to coexist. Far from analysing the historic-political and social issues (widely discussed by their respective historiographies), this understanding will help us to comprehend why the current globalized world is absolutely not a homogeneous world.

Crespo Solana's perspective is significant insofar as it moves the discipline of history which has been, traditionally, organized around a temporal framework, away from time and toward space. The temporal scheme was a notion that was the outcome of nineteenth century scientific schemes in Europe of sequential and/or evolutionary development. In this schema economy, society and culture moved from one stage (or level) to another, attaining progressively higher levels at each move. Consequently, these levels were all linked to periods of time, categorized by historians as ancient, medieval, early modern, modern and so on. Within these slices, and especially in the last two, one could discern 'capitalism', 'individualism', 'nationalism', 'democracy', etc. This scheme enforced a terrible historicism.

Crespo Solana's Atlantic model urges us to think spatially instead. Her essay reinforces what has been labelled a 'spatial turn' in the social sciences and is particularly relevant for the discipline of history.[3] The 'spaces' investigated in this volume not only move out of national frames but are understood not to be physical given(s). In fact they are regarded as created and conditioned by historical events; see for example Barros' Atlantic and Indian Ocean worlds in Chapter 4.

Routes, Networks and Commodities

The next section, describing oceans, routes, ports and systems, contains two valuable chapters. Picazo Muntaner looks at the different trading models in the Indian Ocean and the South Seas to question whether these qualify to be component parts of a global system. Comparing the network models adopted by the English and Dutch companies and contrasting them to the Hispanic network model, Picazo Muntaner attempts an explanation, in terms of networks and models of capitalism, as to why the first two succeeded and the last failed in the Indian and Pacific Oceans.

From the eastern seas we reposition ourselves in the Atlantic world, but with a difference. Barros' essay introduces readers to the port of Porto, a northern Portuguese port that successfully linked the Atlantic and Indian Ocean trade circuits through, in the main, informal circuits and private initiative. The common theme linking the two chapters is the interrogation of the European experimentation with different models: the Atlantic model versus the Indian Ocean model as in Barros, and the English East India Company (EEIC) model as opposed to the Vereenigde Oostindische Compagnie (VOC) model and the first two as compared to the Hispanic model (Picazo Muntaner). These two essays affirm that systems in the First Global Age were inherently flexible and could readily adapt to new circumstances.

The third section on military, scientific and terrestrial networks contains essays by Carreira, Walker and Hangloo. Although not members of the DynCoopNet group, their discussions on alternative networks as included in this volume enhance the vision of DynCoopNet. Carreira's chapter on the French military in the service of the Portuguese Crown in India opens up a neglected, although immensely valuable, dimension not only of Europe's encounter with India, but also of encounters between Europeans in what used to be known as 'an age of empire' and what this volume terms instead the 'First Global Age'. To emphasize cooperation, Carreira focuses on the army rather than the navy, as has been conventionally the custom in accounts of the Portuguese at Goa. There is also a chronological significance. Carreira's intervention covers both the First Global Age as well as the period after 1800; this is significant because her account shows the gradual demise of the older cooperative networks as we move into the nineteenth century.

Walker's essay on indigenous plants and trade in medicinal commodities will be of much interest to readers of this volume because he too anticipates networks both within and beyond the Portuguese empire, as particularly evident in the circulation of commodities and cultures. Moreover, Walker's singular use of the archives in Goa, specifically the records of the Military Hospital and the Santa Casa da Misericórdia, illuminates social networks and complex scientific connections on the ground, so to speak. He also highlights a peculiar form of cultural sharing borne out of the reluctance of Portuguese physicians and surgeons to be posted to Goa. The import of scientific knowledge into the Portuguese medicinal corpus and the consequent hybridization is summed up succinctly:

> the practical commercial dimension of hybridized health care in Portuguese South Asia (Goa, Cochin, Bassein, Damãn and Diu) from the early sixteenth to the mid-seventeenth century . . . . the types of indigenous medicines commonly found in colonial missionary and state pharmacies—medicines that had been adopted by Portuguese medical practitioners, secular and ecclesiastic, and assimilated into use in official colonial medical institutions. During the time covered by this study, dozens of South Asian healing preparations were in common circulation within the Indo-Portuguese colonial medical sphere. Because of their centrality to the practice of healing arts in the colonies, much of the contemporary trade in, and dissemination of information about, indigenous Indian medical substances lay in the hands of Catholic missionary orders....

Walker concludes:

> Stocking colonial pharmacies in Portuguese India during the Enlightenment era was thus largely a matter of relying on local resources. To be sure, remedies and drugs did arrive to colonial hospitals and infirmaries in the *Estado da Índia* from the metropôle, China, Africa and Brazil. However, in the thoroughly hybridized healing culture of seventeenth-century Goa, Damãn and Diu, indigenous practitioners, even if Christianized and Portuguese-speaking, held most of the medical posts. Their natural inclination was to resort to familiar (and convenient) local medicinal plants of the kind extolled in India for millennia.

Hangloo's chapter takes us away from the seas into the landlocked region of Ladakh, an intermediate node on the Silk Route that transcended various state forms in Central Asia in the First Global Age. This region, linked through social, cultural and commercial networks that connected China and Persia, had its own dynamics; dynamics whose vitality was sapped once Ladakh was incorporated into British India. This resulted in its commercial networks being largely reoriented toward the port of British Calcutta. However, the reorientation toward British India did not result in new dynamic and cooperative networks; rather the purpose of Hangloo's essay is to demonstrate the malign effects when mobile and adaptive networks are forcibly reoriented toward new economic spheres.

The fourth section, on dynamic cooperative networks, contains four essays that indicate the diverse ways the system functioned over land and sea. To begin with, Owens describes the social networks of the Milanese merchants. He reminds us that the story of a global system and its component parts is not always necessarily about 'official' trade; piracy, and in Owens' case smuggling, constituted equally important parts of the system. Incisively making the point, he says:

> … the complicated ways that multiple networks interlinked with each other over expanding geographic spaces enhanced possibilities that cascading disruptions would affect ever larger portions of the world economic system and entail ever more elaborate efforts to repair damage and prevent such sizable disruptions in the future. Because as a consequence of the nature of complex systems, the sources of systemic instability would not be eliminated by such repairs, the increased network density and interlinking would make it ever more likely, in an event that could not have been predicted, that some disruption would cascade so widely that the system would enter a period of chaos and transition to a new system.

Such cascading effects can also be observed for Mukherjee's precolonial Kasimbazar in Bengal, India.

Alonso Garcia's account of the Fornari networks leaves us breathless with the scope and dimension of their manifold activities in southern Europe, Central America, North Africa and Europe, networks that united the Mediterranean and the Atlantic worlds. He writes:

> The activities of the Fornari are integral to the understanding of the degree of geographical integration which occurred in the sixteenth century. Most research on merchant communities, at least in relation to the Hispanic world, is based on a single framework. Such a perspective is very useful in order to gain knowledge of the evolution of merchant groups within a local ambit. However, merchants operated on different scenarios through their networks. The operations of a single trader were closely linked to those of the others, which rules out the study of an individual. In the case of the Fornaris, their involvement in America, North Africa and Italy made them powerful enough to become one the most influential intermediaries of the time. The Fornari were able to offer credit as this was backed by their tax collection business. They were capable of clothing the military, thanks to their

involvement in the textile trade in several countries. They engaged in the slave trade because this could be organized from Oran. To sum up, each individual business depended on all the other trading activities.

Mukherjee's essay also deals with networks but not of individuals per se. She charts the various shifts of Kasimbazar, a seventeenth century mart town in eastern India: one, from a regional node marked by Asian networks stretching from the Persian Gulf to the China Seas to an eighteenth century international silk market where European mercantile and financial networks met Asian networks; two, its transformation from a small river port to a royal maritime port in the eighteenth century in response to the forces emanating from the networks set in motion by the First Global Age; and three, its shift from a regional overland trade mart to an international mart town on the caravan routes. Using the 'small world network' model, Mukherjee shows that nonlinear, and somewhat random pathways of networks, accompanied the transformation of Kasimbazar from a relatively marginal Asian mart town and port, progressively integrated through commercial and transport networks to mainland South Asia, the Bay of Bengal and the eastern Indian Ocean, to one provisioning distant European markets through other ports from about 1660. In the latter phase Kasimbazar had neither presence nor control in terms of merchant networks, finance and shipping; the system collapsed soon after and Bengal was colonized by the EEIC in the second half of the eighteenth century.

We move on to Polónia's essay which introduces the readers to Vila do Conde, a small seaside port in northern Portugal, as a counterpoint to Barros' Porto. Polónia discusses the representations of the East, and particularly of 'the Indies', though an interlocking system of networks in Vila do Conde, a settlement that Polónia has studied extensively and where she took the DynCoopNet community one windy spring afternoon in 2008.

The last two essays are written by two research scholars who again are not members of the DynCoopNet community. Associated with the Departments of History and Economics at the University of Hyderabad, both Mandal and Thomas were students of the Indian Ocean course taught at the Department of History in 2009. They critically examine the applicability of a world systems theory and a comparative studies framework (such as mercantilism) to the First Global Age. Their dissatisfaction with such theories and concepts only highlights the virtues of network analysis over concepts that can work to the detriment of non European societies, such as the notions of world systems and mercantilism that Mandal and Thomas address. Can a system make a 'world'? Mandal opines that a world systems theory can be stretched too far, while Thomas is of the view that an Indian Ocean 'world' may be found, but not through the application of European mercantilist practices.

Discussion

COOPERATION

The primary conclusion one draws from the contents in this volume is that cooperation, going side by side with what Picazo Muntaner calls 'information accumulation', was a hallmark of the First Global Age. Picazo Muntaner succinctly discusses the changeover from the Hispanic mercantilist model to the more 'cooperative' EIC and VOC models by way of the somewhat more collaborative Portuguese model. The First Global Age therefore experienced significant shifts from mercantilism and the 'closed sea' models of the sixteenth century to the more cooperative models of the seventeenth century and then to the 'absolute control' model of the eighteenth century. Picazo Muntaner ends:

> In conclusion, the commercial strategies established by the VOC and the EIC in the seventeenth century were primarily based on the collaboration with the different institutions, merchants and local trade networks of South-East Asia, with vastly diverse connections with different ports throughout the region. Their first priority was to learn to control the market, through a subtle penetration model that enabled them to accumulate capital, and yet more importantly, know-how. Indeed, this was a prelude for the new capitalism that was emerging in Europe. Conversely, the Spanish Crown, which had its most important base in the Philippines, continued to depend exclusively on the Chinese market, hinging economic growth on a number of ports that supplied the islands: Canton and Amoy.

The more collaborative Portuguese model is highlighted in Barros', Polónia's and Walker's essays. The significantly mercantilist Portuguese *Estado da Índia* model, ruling from Lisbon via Goa over large parts of Africa, part of South America, the Atlantic islands and South and South-East Asia, also contained within it networks, commercial/financial as well as cultural, that were more malleable, much more collaborative, and essentially nonlinear in scope and action. They were, nonetheless, as effective as formal networks. Carreira's work introduces cooperation of a different kind: that of a European nation engaged in the service of another; this is distinct because the so-called Age of Empire is also taken to be the burgeoning age of nationalism. However, Carreira's essay, highlighting French commanders in the formal service of the *Estado da Índia* in Goa, suggests otherwise.

Mukherjee suggests that it may not be quite correct to label the seventeenth century wholly as one of collaboration/cooperation and the eighteenth century as one of total control. Although a century is an expedient unit of analysis, micro studies show that there was no convenient cut off point between cooperation and conflict in any one century. Frequently the two went together, as she shows in her study of seventeenth and eighteenth centuries Kasimbazar. Thomas suggests that it was precisely the dynamic cooperation between the state and different sectors of the economy in Mughal India that made the rise of a 'national' merchant class redundant in South Asia.

Discussing Ladakh, Hangloo demonstrates how age-old cooperative models become pallid and lifeless once they are incorporated within new systems. In his words:

> Ladakh was one of those principal regions on the silk route that acted as a major centre of an inter- and intra-regional exchange system, facilitating economic, cultural and political contacts between India on the one hand, and the Chinese, Tibetan, Russian and the wider central Asian worlds on the other, on the silk route, from very early times. My argument is that although part of the western Tibetan political, cultural and economic system, Ladakh also formed the western end of an economic network cutting through from Yunnan and Tibet in the historical period. However, in the course of the nineteenth century, through British expansion in the region, its economy was largely sundered from that of its Central Asian neighbours and reoriented toward the port of Calcutta. This was a heavy price for Ladakh as an economic and facilitating node to pay.

He adds: 'From the foregoing discussion it becomes clear that while putting forward a preparatory framework for understanding the nature of trade networks on the silk route, one realizes also the complexity of the political linkages and distances that the items of trade travelled both on land and sea.'

A MULTINATIONAL AND MULTIDIMENSIONAL WORLD

What are the other conclusions that we can draw from this collection? Owens', Alonso Garcia's and Carreira's chapters open up a multinational world, both within Europe and its imperial outposts, where Italians cooperated with the Spanish Crown and where the French worked alongside the Portuguese in Portuguese colonies. Indeed, commercial and financial cooperation *among* Europeans seems to be the hallmark of the First Global Age. This multinational world came under strain increasingly from the end of the eighteenth century and by the nineteenth century, when the DynCoopNet interrogation ends, 'national' characteristics, identities and destinies became immutably fixed.

The two essays by Barros and Polónia also open up multinational worlds in two small ports (three, if we count Vila Nova de Gaia that Barros mentions) that exist till today, a world where the 'world of the Indies' penetrated into the daily, lived, lives of its inhabitants. I had the privilege of visiting Porto, Vila Nova de Gaia and Vila do Conde in March 2008 and was struck by the commercial and intellectual vitality of these three port towns, a heritage no doubt from their networks that straddled the world in the First Global Age. What emerges clearly from both Polónia's and Barros' arguments is the involvement of the northern Portuguese ports in the India trade, an issue that has been neglected in the narrative of the first 'Portuguese empire' in the East.

Polónia's and Barros' interventions are exceptional in yet another way. Conventionally, the historiographic thrust of Portuguese history in the 'Indies' has tended to concentrate on the Lisbon-Goa route, thus, these two essays are particularly valuable in their highlighting of the *northern* Portuguese networks to the East. We now become aware, through their skilful handling of wills, notarial and *Misericórdia* records, that multiple networks from Portugal supported the trade to the East. This is a significant addition to our knowledge of the Portuguese expansion to the East.

The essays by Owens, Walker, Mukherjee and Barros bring out the multidimensionality in the system: smuggling networks complemented 'official' ones, medicinal and pharmacological knowledge went across continents, Asian networks supported European ones, and the Atlantic model nourished the Indian Ocean trade. These were truly dynamic cooperative networks!

THE PROBLEMS OF THE 'EARLY MODERN', AND 'MERCANTILISM' AS UNIVERSAL CONCEPTS AND OF A 'WORLD SYSTEMS' THEORY

A problem that plagues the historian of the First Global Age is the notion of the 'early modern'. This was a distinctly west European formulation that sought to encapsulate within it such diverse processes as the European renaissance of the fifteenth century, the European 'voyages of discovery' [*sic*] that commenced from the end of that century, the coming of capitalist agriculture in Great Britain in the sixteenth century, the start of the 'renaissance state' (frequently termed the 'early modern state' to include those countries in Europe that experienced neither capitalist development nor the European renaissance), the 'scientific revolution' of the sixteenth and seventeenth centuries, and the enlightenment, the birth of capitalism and the rise of colonial empires from the eighteenth century.

Despite the fact that these describe purely European experiences, the 'early modern' continues to be taught as the 'Rise of the West', the 'Transformation of Europe' and the 'transition from feudalism to capitalism' in classrooms around the world. These are patently western European experiences that not only neglect the greater part of the world *outside* Europe but also the central, southern and eastern parts *within* Europe. However, although this has been the dominant trend in the academy so far, Frances Amelia Yates attempted a corrective by documenting the neglected scientific history of eastern and central Europe in *The Rosicrucian Enlightenment* and Ian Hunter discerned 'rival enlightenments' in the same space.[4]

In 1993 and again in 1997 the journal *Modern Asian Studies* attempted to grapple with the chronology of the 'early modern' but the conclusion the contributors came to in the issue of 1997 was that different temporalities ruled South and South-East Asia, and indeed a great part of Asia as well.[5] When was the early modern in Asia? Was it in 1350? In 1400? Or around 1450? The conclusion was that while there was a kind of global modernity in view (this was never spelt out, however), no 'early modern' in terms of material processes such as agricultural expansion, consolidation of politics, commercial exchange, firearms, fiscal methods and functional ideologies could be found uniformly for this region, and particularly not in terms of national frames. But it could be found in terms of geographical redefinition, a hallmark of the so-called 'early modern age', and in millenarian symbols, faiths and ideologies whereby the region dubbed 'Eurasia' presented a coherent unit.[6]

Yet, this notion of the 'early modern' cannot be applied to the vast areas outside of Europe and Asia, and nowhere is this truer than in Hangloo's Ladakh. Is the 'early modern' then conceptually flawed? Goldstone argued that 'a rigorous review of evidence would show that the 'early modern' world was neither 'early', nor 'modern', although it was arguably, in its trade relations, a single 'world'.[7] What we are doing, by applying this term to non European societies, is ignoring that:

'Early Modern' derives from a particular sociological theory of history that privileges modes of production in characterizing and powering history, not from any 'natural' historical periodization, such as the rise and fall of major political units, or changes in styles of cultures, which are commonly used to periodicize history for other periods and societies than post-1500 Europe.[8]

Peter Van der Veer has pointed out, in the same issue:

modernity is a project and an ideology that originates in the Enlightenment. Modernity celebrates freedom from localized, hierarchical bonds, progress in terms of scientific knowledge and economic welfare, and rejects the past in so far it does not fit the story of progress. The paper also suggests that this project has multiple origins in Western Europe and the Americas and is itself partly the product of the European expansion. As such it has spread over the world and forced societies in different parts of the globe increasingly to come to grips with the project at least from 1800 onwards. The main argument here is that modernity should in the first place be understood as a *project, that is as a political notion which is realized in the nation-state* [italics mine].[9]

Quoting Hegel, Weber and Gellner, Van der Veer argued that 'the emergence of the European nation-state is commonly seen to depend on three connected processes of centralization: the emergence of supra-local identities and cultures (the "nation"); the rise of powerful and authoritative institutions within the public domain (the "state"), and the development of particular ways of organizing production and consumption (the "economy")'.[10]

The first volume of Wallerstein's *The Modern World-System*, attempted to escape both temporal framework and organization by placing the events described therein as the period of 'capitalist agriculture'. But his second volume was on mercantilism, which 'consolidated the European world economy', thereby placing European expansion, and consequently world history, solely within a European historical context.[11] Mandal and Thomas express their uneasiness with such explicitly European frameworks in their critiques of world systems analysis and mercantilism in the concluding essays of this volume.

This brings us, finally, to the problems associated with history writing. What are the pitfalls of History? In *Provincializing Europe* Dipesh Chakrabarty noted that History, a discipline that is a product of Europe, placed concurrent societies into different historical times via a historicist narrative that posited Europe as the 'sovereign, theoretical subject of all histories', including the ones we call 'Indian', 'Chinese', and so on.[12] In referring to this kind of historicism, Chakrabarty speaks of a notion prevalent in nineteenth century Europe, that to understand anything it had to be seen both as a unity and in terms of its historical development. Thereby notional entities could be mapped onto an actual material entity along a normative scale of development, one that was defined by Europe's *experience of history* [italics mine].

Chakrabarty buttressed his argument against this terrible historicism by examining in Marx that which he called 'two histories of capital'. He labelled these two histories as *History 1* and *History 2s* (or *Histories 2*).

History 1 is undeniably a universalizing history, 'capital's antecedent "posited by itself"'. In this universalizing history, capital takes a look back at those elements it sees as having been necessary for its own rise and *naturalizes* them, thereby ensuring the conceptual valourization of those components it requires in order to survive. For example, capital posits 'free labour' [as] both a precondition of capitalist production and 'its invariable result'. This is the universal and necessary history we always associate with capital. By identifying labour as requisite for its own rise, capital establishes a particular historical narrative that it puts forward as both naturalized and universal. Because capital posits itself as a universal, those locations, societies, and processes that do not include capital's necessary antecedents (free labour, for instance) are seen as being left 'behind', as containing a fundamental lack from which they will eventually transition. Thereby, a certain *kind* of history is privileged over others.

History 2s are also antecedents to capital, but according to Chakrabarty these 'do not lend themselves to the reproduction of the logic of capital'. As such, these allow for multiple possibilities (processes, subjectivities, desires, etc.) that 'could be central to capital's self-reproduction, and yet it is also possible for them to be oriented to structures that do not contribute to such reproduction'.

Chakrabarty's argument fits with our (re)construction of the 'early modern world' in terms of networks. Nonlinear, random, sometimes short-lived networks in the First Global Age that did not transition into a more durable system were a part of *Histories 2*. We see that *History 1* approximates the history of the 'early modern', of mercantilism, of the 'rise of the West', the 'age of empire', etc. In order to ensure its own reproduction, the universalizing *History 1* of capital must either subjugate the *History 2s* or destroy them.

This is the manner in which the history of the First Global Age has been traditionally understood and represented. Despite the interventions recorded here the contributors of this volume feel that notions of the 'early modern', as a precursor to globalization and the ideas of sequential development whereby non European societies are judged on a normative scale refuse to die. Such themes and labels, enabling a comparative history writing, will remain one-sided because we always compare the 'rest' with the 'best'. Will other parts of the world then have to write their histories by inserting themselves into these events and processes, an exercise that naturally works to the detriment of all non-western European peoples? This is what Mandal cautions us against. And where do we locate 'Islamic modernity', the Japanese, Indian or Chinese 'modernities'? Therefore, is it at all necessary or relevant to locate 'modernities'?

These questions haunt the current crop of researchers worldwide, but more so in the non European parts of the world. Hence this volume on global system(s), dynamic networks, cooperative strategies and coveted commodities in the First Global Age from 1400 to 1800 as an alternative window to the world.

Conclusion

This work is an attempt to encourage a rethink on structure, agency, and contingency and to urge for an analytical shift toward random, nonlinear pathways in the study of history.

The 'early modern' is the time frame that this volume addresses, but we label it as the First Global Age. It emphasizes networks, phase shifts and transitions rather than spatially contextualized labels and thus avoids the pitfalls connected with the 'early modern'. The ideas here offer a corrective to the conventional history of 'overseas expansion in the age of empire' by highlighting complexity, adaptability, contingency, randomness and nonlinear evolutionary pathways in which networks, although functioning simultaneously, were sometimes ruled by different temporal imperatives.[13]

Different *chronologies*, a subject this volume intends to show, were part of the same physical and temporal spaces in the First Global Age, something Crespo Solana suggested at the outset.

This vision presents a challenge because historians are usually comfortable with centuries. Centuries are marked by categories conceived of and decided by the historian. Events are thereby pigeonholed and are, subsequently, easier to analyse. Consequently, historians become anxious when they see randomness and nonlinear evolution because these defy all attempts at organization in appropriately linear and clearly defined spatial slots.

Connectivity rather than structure or agency has been emphasized as the key to understanding societies, events and their histories. Networks are deemed to be central. Multiple types of relationships can and do exist within the same network, i.e. one ruled by the same set of elements. A 'large' network need not necessarily imply length; it can also refer to a larger set of elements within it. This calls for more intensive interrogation on the part of researchers, especially difficult for economic and social historians given the paucity of data. As additional networks come to light the more we will know of our history.

One reason many historians remain uneasy with network theory is that they are trained to work within the archive to highlight *structure* and to interrogate *agency* within given *temporal and spatial frameworks*; this was a legacy of nineteenth century historicism. But what if we were to write a history of different spaces which were connected at a particular point in time? This would be a *connective* history and therefore the application of network theory, to study processes and events joined at a particular point in space and time, marks a paradigmatic shift in our understanding of history.

Duncan Watts has claimed that social networks exhibit structural characteristics that are basically *non local* [italics mine] so no local analyses can predict their global statistical features and behaviour.[14] Therefore, we need to step out of local contexts to study the global context at that particular point in time. The *qualitative* nature of a system's *connectivity* determines both its *structural* and dynamical properties [again, italics mine].[15] That is, it is the *nature of connectivity*, or the kind of network(s) we find in any investigation, that determines structure. This is problematic and involves a radical shift for historians. This shift is mostly random; changes in topology are consequences of what Watts calls 'random rewiring'.[16] Randomly connected systems do not exhibit the same features as systems connected like a 1-lattice.[17]

However, there are some reservations I end with: Watts himself pointed out in *Small Worlds* that certain features of networks have not been studied in the 'real' world: analytical difficulties rise with the *size* of the network, and it is still not certain where on the structural spectrum do real social networks lie. Also there has been no treatment of the properties of continuous families of networks, whose structural properties vary all the way from one extreme to the other, with the intention of determining the location and nature of any transitions that occur in between. Added to this confusion is the difficulty of determining in what kind of 'social space' a network exists because, as Watts notes, the notion of a social space is both theoretically and empirically slippery.[18] And hence the problem of determining, as Owens notes at the outset: what kind of a system it is.

In conclusion, let me reiterate that it was our association with Andre Gunder Frank and his ideas, notably as expressed in *ReORIENT* that inspired the DynCoopNet vision. This volume is a tribute to Frank's imagination. While the greater part of the essays in this volume was written by the DynCoopNet community, the contributions in this volume of those who are not members of the community have only served to enrich this book even more. This book is, therefore, an excellent example of cooperation within—dare I say it ?—a small world network!

Notes

1. See A.G. Frank, *ReORIENT: Global Economy in the Asian Age*, Berkeley-Los Angeles-London: University of California Press, 1998.
2. Janet Abu Lughod, *Before European Hegemony: The World System AD 1250–1350*, Oxford University Press, 1991; Philippe Beaujard, 'The Indian Ocean in Eurasian and African World-Systems before the Sixteenth Century', *Journal of World History*, vol. 16, no. 4, 2005, pp. 411–65.
3. Barney Warf, Santa Arias, eds., *The Spatial Turn: Interdisciplinary Perspectives*, Routledge, 2008; Denis Cosgrove, 'Landscape and Landschaft', lecture delivered at the 'Spatial Turn in History' symposium, German Historical Institute, 19 February 2004, *GHI BULLETIN*, no. 35, Fall 2004, pp. 57–71, available at <http://www.ghi-dc.org/publications/ghipubs/bu/035/35.57.pdf> (accessed on 10 May 2009). Cosgrove says: Across the humanities and social sciences, the past two decades have witnessed a shift away from the structural explanations and grand narratives that dominated so much twentieth-century scholarship, with its emphasis on universal theories and systematic studies, and a move toward more culturally and geographically nuanced work, sensitive to difference and specificity, and thus to the contingencies of event and locale. Variously referred to in the social sciences as the 'spatial turn' and the 'cultural turn', this move has reworked the relationship between the social sciences and traditionally hermeneutic fields within the humanities. Both sides increasingly privilege questions of culture, meaning, and identity over 'scientific' theories borrowed from economics, biology, psychology, or political 'science', p. 57.
4. Frances Amelia Yates, rpt, Routledge Classics; 2001; Ian Hunter, *Rival Enlightenments: Civil and Metaphysical Philosophy in Early Modern Germany* (Ideas in Context), Cambridge University Press; new edn., 2008.

5. Victor Lieberman, 'Local Integration and Eurasian Analogies: Structuring South-East Asian History, *c.*1350–*c.*1830', *Modern Asian Studies*, vol. 27, no. 3, July 1993, pp. 475–572; Victor Lieberman, ed., 'The Eurasian Context of the Early Modern History of Mainland South-East Asia, 1400-1800', Special Issue: *Modern Asian Studies*, vol. 31, no. 3, July 1997.
6. Sanjay Subrahmanyam, 'Connected Histories: Notes towards a Reconfiguration of Early Modern Eurasia', *Modern Asian Studies*, vol. 31, no. 3, July 1997, pp. 735–62. See also, David Ludden, 'History Outside Civilization and the Mobility of South Asia', *South Asia*, n.s., vol. 17, no. 1, 1994, pp. 1-23.
7. Jack A. Goldstone, 'The Problem of the "Early Modern" World', *Journal of the Economic and Social History of the Orient*, vol. 41, no. 3, 1998, pp. 249–84. See p. 249.
8. Ibid., pp. 253–4.
9. Peter Van der Veer, 'The Global History of "Modernity"', *Journal of the Economic and Social History of the Orient*, vol. 41, no. 3, 1998, pp. 285–94. See p. 285.
10. Ibid., p. 287.
11. Immanuel Wallerstein, *The Modern World-System: Capitalist Agriculture and the Origins of the European World-Economy in the Sixteenth Century,* vol. I, New York/London: Academic Press, 1974; *The Modern World-System: Mercantilism and the Consolidation of the European World-Economy, 1600-1750,* vol. II, New York: Academic Press, 1980; *The Modern World-System*, vol. III: *The Second Great Expansion of the Capitalist World-Economy, 1730-1840s,* San Diego: Academic Press, 1989.
12. Dipesh Chakrabarty, *Provincializing Europe: Postcolonial Thought and Historical Difference,* Princeton: Princeton University Press, 2000, pp. 6, 27, 63-4. I am indebted to Bascom Guffin, Ph.D. scholar, U.C. Davies, for this reference.
13. See Duncan J. Watts, *Small Worlds: The Dynamics of Networks Between Order and Randomness*, Princeton Studies in Complexity, Princeton: Princeton University Press, 2003.
14. Ibid., p. 21.
15. Ibid., p. 240.
16. Ibid., p. 16.
17. Ibid., p. 241. See pp. 34–5, 41, 53–4, 62, 67–8, and 70 for more on 1-lattice systems.
18. Ibid., pp. 21–2.

PART I

Situating the Agenda
The Many Systems of the First Global Age

CHAPTER ONE

What Kind of System Is It? The DynCoopNet Project as a Tribute to Andre Gunder Frank (1929–2005)

J.B. Owens

IN THIS CHAPTER, I WILL CONNECT some of the central concerns of the final stages of Andre Gunder Frank's research with a multinational, interdisciplinary project that I created after Frank's death and now help coordinate. The project has a long title, 'Dynamic Complexity of Cooperation-Based Self-Organizing Commercial Networks in the First Global Age', and is usually referred to by its acronym, DynCoopNet.

In 1994, I began serving as one of Frank's readers and commentators for a book manuscript on which he was working. Despite our differences, we were able to collaborate because we shared two assumptions: (1) the history of no place can be understood without an understanding as to how it has been connected to other places, and (2) a place is ultimately part of a global system that influences the history of all places, all of the time. It was probably in 1997 that Frank commenced pestering me with a question that was fundamental for the book.[1] He had begun to recognize that although he had argued that there existed in the period 1400–1800 a world system, he did not clarify the nature of the system itself. He asked me repeatedly, 'What kind of system is it, Jack?' We launched his book, *ReORIENT* with a brace of sessions that I organized for the annual meeting of the World History Association in June 1998,[2] followed by a session at the annual meeting of the American Historical Association in January 1999.[3] Even before his book was published, Frank managed to generate a debate about his views in May 1998 on several listservs by responding to William McNeill's review of David Landes' recently published *The Wealth and Poverty of Nations.*[4]

Frank's critics increasingly pointed out that nothing he said in *ReORIENT* explained why the centre of the world economic activity shifted in the period roughly 1750 to 1850 from one where the major centres were Asian to one centred on north-western Europe, including Britain. His explanation that this change simply represented an 'inclination' in a world system that had existed for thousands of years failed to satisfy critics. To respond adequately, especially in the book on the nineteenth century on which he was still working when he died, he needed to present a model of the system, but he did not have one to offer.[5]

I recognized the importance of his question to me, but other Frankian queries filled my time. In early drafts of *ReORIENT*, Frank again offered the three-legged stool metaphor to explain a holistic world history, which he originally suggested in 1993.[6] 'It rests equally on ecological/economic/technological, political/military power, and social/cultural/ideological legs.'[7] In any discussion of the metaphor, he was quick to admit that he did not know how to combine the 'legs' to achieve the holistic analysis he felt was necessary to understand world history, and he challenged me to discover a way to realize this combination. By the time *ReORIENT* appeared, I had plunged into an exploration of Geographic Information Systems (GIS) as a means of organizing, analysing, and visualizing data corresponding to all of the legs. Unsurprisingly, I could not focus on the nature of the world system of the First Global Age, 1400–1800.[8] With my colleague at Idaho State University, Laura Woodworth-Ney, I designed a GIS-based graduate programme in Geographically-Integrated History when it became apparent that there was no graduate education in the discipline of History that prepared students to carry out this type of research.[9] Frank followed my work in this area with interest, but on the day that we were to present our newly approved graduate programme at a large GIS conference, I learned from his younger son that Frank was dying and would never learn of this success. I turned our presentation into a tribute to him.

Although he defended the need for a holistic global history, Frank often expressed scepticism about the degree to which institutional and cultural environments shaped human action, and he challenged others, me included, to explain how they did so. This challenge related directly to a central question in my research on the 'Asian Age' of *ReORIENT*'s subtitle: How did small groups maintain a greatly disproportionate share of resources without adequate force to deal with potential resistance? In response to the challenge, I have published one book, but although he read several draft chapters, Frank passed away before the final version appeared in September 2005.[10]

Simultaneously, I was working on another manuscript, 'From Hostility to Affinity: Cooperation in the Construction of Oligarchy in Golden Age Spain' (working title), portions of which Frank also read. Both works reveal the great weaknesses of command and control systems and the need of the Castilian Crown for collaborative relationships for the effective exercise of political authority in the period 1400–1700 throughout its global domains. In the course of the research for this book, I discovered the records of a judicial investigation conducted in 1565 that revealed the existence of a geographically extensive smuggling network—the basis of my contribution elsewhere in this book and the creation of the DynCoopNet project.

DynCoopNet integrates the work of historians, geographic information scientists (GIScientists), and mathematical modellers in economics and geography. One of our principal goals is the creation of spatial-temporal GIS that will permit us to understand the dynamics at various scales of the cooperation-based self-organizing social networks, as manifestations of human agency, which knit together the first global economy. While accepting Frank's contention that as a complex system this world economy was greater than the sum of its parts, I always emphasized to him that the local parts interacted with and, therefore clearly influenced, the nature of the economy as a whole. And I desired a tool that allows me to deal with these social networks in the context of the world system of which they were a part. This spatio-temporal information management system requires new data models based on ontologies that express and link the social theories associated with the legs of Frank's metaphorical stool. To design DynCoopNet, I had finally to respond to Frank's persistent question about the First Global Age, 1400–1800: What kind of system is it? He would not have found my response compatible with his own assertion of the existence of a single world system over a period of 5,000 years.[11]

I define the First Global Age, roughly 1400–1800, as an open, complex, dynamic, nonlinear system. Within this system, the self-organizing social networks studied by DynCoopNet are the sources of innovation and the emergence of new forms. I agree with Frank's position in *ReORIENT* that although the system was not global in the fifteenth century, that period was crucial for the development of the dynamics characteristic of the system for about four centuries. Where we differ is in our understanding of the fourteenth century, which I view as a period of phase transition from an earlier system rather than as a fluctuation in a system common to both the thirteenth and fifteenth centuries, as Frank asserted. In my entrance into the 'House of Discontinuity',[12] my position is closer to that of Immanuel Wallerstein in the first volume of *The Modern World-System*. However, I agree with Frank that Wallerstein erred in concentrating on changes in northern Europe and in characterizing the transition as a European one between entities labelled 'Feudalism' and 'Capitalism'.

Rather than a mere inclination in the existing world system, the period (roughly 1750–1850) constituted a phase transition representing discontinuity between two different systems. This position places me at odds with both Frank and Wallerstein.[13] Because of the highly complicated nature of the First Global Age, how is one to explain this type of phase transition in the face of a large number of variables? In response, I accept the position of Hermann Haken and his Synergetics school that overall system stability (which does not mean that nothing happened for four centuries) depended on only a few variables that are stable but near instability. These variables can be identified by a careful examination of the system's nonlinear dynamics, which is one of DynCoopNet's tasks. A phase transition is initiated when these critical variables become unstable, leading the system to instability, chaos, and bifurcation, around which a new system organizes.[14] Thus, major historical periods should be defined on the basis of such phase transitions and identifying and explaining these should become a major focus of research for the historical social sciences.

There are some important implications of this view of history as an account characterized by complex, dynamic, nonlinear systems separated by phase transitions of instability, bifurcation, and reorganization.

- Because of the nature of nonlinear dynamics, predictability is extremely limited, just as it is in weather forecasting.
- With the emergence of a new system, people have different values and perspectives about the world, which makes it difficult for them to understand the peoples of the earlier system.[15]
- In their confusion and struggles to define the new system, European intellectual and political leaders of the Second Global Age, and those influenced by them, projected their ideological positions onto the First Global Age, which they characterized as an era experiencing the rise, in Europe beginning about 1500, of the State, Capitalism, and the Modern Individual or Individualism, thereby distorting the experiences of the men and women of the First Global Age and turning a three- or four-century-long period into the antechamber of the nineteenth and twentieth centuries.

- This European dynamism was erroneously contrasted to the presumed perpetuation of civilizations or cultures of non-Europeans everywhere.
- In the historical social sciences, it has unfortunately become increasingly fashionable to refer to the period 1500–1800 by the obviously teleological term 'early modern'.[16]
- In terms of DynCoopNet's focus on cooperation, because there was a phase transition at the end of the First Global Age, historians of that four-century period can say something important about cooperation that cannot be dealt with well by research on contemporary scenarios.

Although it comes too late to be of any use to him, my response to Frank's final question to me is that the period 1400–1800 constituted an open, complex, dynamic, nonlinear system flanked by phase transitions that separated it from the systems before in Afroeurasia and afterwards throughout the world. I miss the frequent, often long email messages and resulting debates that the response would have elicited from him if I had only formulated my answer sooner. Because of Frank's ability to expose the poorly developed aspects of others' arguments, DynCoopNet's design and results would have been much improved had he lived and participated in the project. However, if Frank had not written *ReORIENT*, there would have been no DynCoopNet project at all and, therefore, DynCoopNet really is my tribute to him and his work.

Notes

*This chapter was originally presented at the conference 'Andre Gunder Frank's Legacy of Critical Social Science', University of Pittsburgh, USA, 11–13 April 2008. Many of the contributions to this book are associated with the DynCoopNet project, as is the editor of this volume Rila Mukherjee. Without the continuous, vigorous prompting of Frank, I would not have arrived at a point in my own work where I could have conceptualized and designed such a project, and I, therefore, offer this chapter as a tribute to my late friend Gunder.

This material is based upon work supported by the US National Science Foundation (NSF) under Grant Nos. 0740345 and 09413371. Any opinions, findings, and conclusions or recommendations expressed in this material are those of the author and do not necessarily reflect the views of the National Science Foundation.

DynCoopNet is one of five multinational, multidisciplinary research projects within the European Science Foundation's EUROCORES (European Collaborative Research) Scheme programme 'The Evolution of Cooperation and Trading' (TECT). For my description of the project, see 'Dynamic Complexity of Cooperation-Based Self-Organizing Commercial Networks in the First Global Age

(DynCoopNet)', in *The Evolution of Cooperation and Trading (TECT)*, ed. Ronald Noë et al., Strasbourg, France: European Science Foundation, EUROCORES Programme, 2008, pp. 23–35, and <http://www.esf.org/activities/eurocores/programmes/tect.html> (accessed on 17 June 2010).

1. A.G. Frank, *ReORIENT: Global Economy in the Asian Age*, Berkeley and Los Angeles: University of California Press, 1998.
2. In order to reach a broad group of those in attendance, which included a large number of secondary school teachers, I focused the sessions on the implications of *ReORIENT* for teaching world history: 'ReORIENTing the Basis of World History Teaching' [involving papers by Mark S. Johnson, Marilyn A. Levine, and me (from the perspective of recent research on the global Hispanic Monarchy, 1400–1800), with a comment by Frank] and 'ReORIENTing the Teaching of World History' (involving papers by John A. Betterly, Ross Dunn, Deborah Smith Johnston, and William R. Zeigler, with an extended comment by Frank), Colorado State University, Fort Collins (19–20 June 1998).
3. 'Making Connections: The ReORIENTation of World History', 113th Annual Meeting of the American Historical Association, Washington, D.C. (9 January 1999), with papers by John Richards, David Ringrose, Martin W. Lewis, and me, and a response from Frank.
4. David Landes, *The Wealth and Poverty of Nations: Why Some Are So Rich and Some So Poor,* New York and London: W.W. Norton, 1998.
5. In one of the most valuable sessions of the Pittsburgh conference on Frank's scholarship, where a version of my paper was presented, Robert Denemark of the University of Delaware, USA, explained how he is piecing together as much of Frank's last book as possible from the surviving fragments of the manuscript and related documents. All of us who are interested in Frank's thought owe Prof. Denemark our gratitude for undertaking such a difficult task.
6. Andre Gunder Frank and Barry K. Gills, eds., *The World System: Give Hundred Years or Five Thousand?*, London: Routledge, 1993.
7. Frank, *ReORIENT*, p. 340. He would frequently vary the composition of the legs, attaching the social to the political for the second and leaving the cultural/ideological as the third.
8. I have written elsewhere about this intellectual adventure. See, J.B. Owens, 'What historians want from GIS', *ArcNews*, vol. 29, no. 2, Summer 2007, pp. 4–6, and <http://www.esri.com/news/arcnews/summer07articles/what-historians-want.html> (accessed on 17 June 2010); also available in *GIS Best Practices: Essays on Geography and GIS*, Redlands, California: ESRI, 2008, pp. 35–46, and <http://www.esri.com/library/bestpractices/essays-on-geography-gis.pdf> (accessed on 17 June 2010).
9. J.B. Owens and Laura Woodworth-Ney, 'Envisioning a Master's Degree Program in Geographically-Integrated History', *Journal of the Association for History and Computing*, vol. 8, no. 2, September 2005, available at <http://mcel.pacificu.edu/jahc/2005/issue2/articles/owenswoodworth.php> (accessed on 17 June 2010); J.B. Owens, 'Graduate Education in Geographically-Integrated History: A Personal Account', *Journal of the Association for History and Computing*, vol. 13, no. 1, May 2010, available at <http://hdl.handle.net/2027 spo.3310410.0013.105> (accessed on 17 June 2010).

10. J.B. Owens, *"By My Absolute Royal Authority": Justice and the Castilian Commonwealth at the Beginning of the First Global Age*, Rochester, New York: University of Rochester Press, 2005; abstract available at <http://www.boydellandbrewer.com/store/viewItem.asp?idProduct= 6555> (accessed on 17 June 2010).
11. For my overall assessment of Frank, *ReORIENT*, see J.B. Owens, 'Toward a Geographically-Integrated, Connected World History: Employing Geographic Information Systems (GIS)', *History Compass*, vol. 5, no. 6, October 2007, pp. 2020–2; doi: 10.1111/j.1478- 0542.2007.00476.x.
12. I take this phrase from J. Barkley Rosser Jr., *From Catastrophe to Chaos: A General Theory of Economic Discontinuities*, 2nd edn, vol. 1, Boston: Kluwer Academic, 2000.
13. For my understanding of system discontinuity, I rely heavily on my DynCoopNet colleague Tõnu Puu's *Attractors, Bifurcations and Chaos: Nonlinear Phenomena in Economics*, 2nd edn, Berlin and Heidelberg: Springer-Verlag, 2003, especially Chap. 12. Those interested in Puu's argument without the mathematics should consult his *Arts, Sciences, and Economics: A Historical Safari*, Berlin and Heidelberg: Springer-Verlag, 2006, Chap. 9. Immanuel Wallerstein has become interested in complexity theory as a way of understanding our current situation; see his *World-Systems Analysis: An Introduction*, Durham, North Carolina, and London: Duke University Press, 2004, Chap. 5 ('The Modern World System in Crisis: Bifurcation, Chaos, and Choices'). Although Wallerstein has apparently not used the bifurcation theory to reconsider the significance of the period 1750–1850, I find it interesting that in a recent fascinating essay, which he presented at the same conference in Pittsburgh where I presented this chapter, he discusses a series of circumstances that should provoke reflection on the possibility of a system transformation about 1800; see Immanuel Wallerstein, 'Remembering Andre Gunder Frank While Thinking About the Future', *Monthly Review*, vol. 60, no. 2, June 2008, available at <http://www.monthlyreview.org/080630 wallerstein.php> (accessed on 17 June 2010).
14. Hermann Haken, *Advanced Synergetics: Instability Hierarchies of Self-Organizing Systems and Devices*, Berlin et al.: Springer-Verlag, 1983. Rosser, *From Catastrophe to Chaos*, asserts, correctly I think, that Haken's synergetics provides a satisfactory synthesis for the various positions within the 'House of Discontinuity'.
15. My DynCoopNet colleague Michael Sonis of the Geography Department of Bar-Ilan University pointed out this consequence of bifurcation in complex systems in his lecture 'The Evolution of Complexity' for the Mathematics Colloquium of Idaho State University, 27 February 2007.
16. Although I was unsuccessful in my attempt to convince Frank to eliminate the phrase 'early modern' from the text of *ReORIENT*, I was able, early in 1998, to keep the term out of the title. Jack Goldstone was part of these cyber-enabled discussions and shortly afterwards published his valuable article 'The Problem of the "Early Modern" World', *Journal of the Economic and Social History of the Orient*, vol. 41, 1998, pp. 249–84.

[illegible] ... Emergent ... Waddington ... [illegible]

[illegible] ... Oxford University Press ... [illegible] ... Waddington [illegible]

CHAPTER TWO

Geostrategy of a System? Merchant Societies and Exchange Networks as Connection Centres in the Spanish Atlantic Trade in the First Global Age

Ana Crespo Solana

SPANISH EXPANSION IN THE ATLANTIC was not an isolated occurrence. On the contrary, it was part of a single system of expansion that globalized actions and interactions at economic, social, political and cultural levels. In order to geographically depict this so-called Atlantic System, I think of it as an immense space of frontier; a space which developed under an umbrella of common, and at the same time various enterprises. These enterprises were established between diverse societies via a network of centres under development and which, in turn, drew together various areas in different states of development. As described by Francisco de Solano, a space of *frontier* demanded long-term processes involving situations which not only divided mentalities and civilizations but also promoted new forms of exchange.[1] In such a space, one of the characteristic consequences was the growth and expansion of merchant communities which produced, as Fernand Braudel said, a wide area of exchange that spread in the vast field between the production and retail stages.[2]

In order to mentally visualize such a 'system', which was generated on the basis of the aforementioned exchange, seen in cooperation among assorted agents and which was affected by the divergence which occurred in the process of spatial integration, we must analyse it without losing sight of certain methodological parameters from both the General Systems theory and the spatial economic analyses from a methodological perspective. The Atlantic world had a systemic character that was derived from the expansion model created by merchant empires throughout the significant period between 1450 and 1800. The Atlantic, then, appears to have constituted elements which were functionally bonded so that a series of rules led to total interdependence. This concept has been re-examined in the last decade and Renate Pieper and Peer Schmidt have concluded that it was a 'deep reassessing of the category of space as a constituent of the action of history', a valuation of the space factor well above the temporal or chronological, a 'spatial turn' that implies elaboration by the historian of 'mental maps'.[3]

Traditionally, historiography on mercantilist empires in the Early Modern Age had barely studied this latter aspect. A new methodology more focused and stronger than traditional Atlantic history is a must. This complements the general understanding of the Atlantic System within a global and comparative study in an attempt to view the world as a single unit, where various systems and sub-systems form part of that unit, as well as observing the value of research into repetitive processes as is undertaken by empirical sciences.

Comparative study whether on spatial or on temporal-chronological issues would facilitate actually knowing whether a universality of human nature exists or whether a shift in the history of exchange can be traced back to a cause.[4]

Within this new historical and methodological context, the Spanish expansion appears to be a single system in itself that, to a certain degree, has a significant impact on, and is perfectly linked to and interdependent on, other processes of expansion in which other European countries are involved. Moreover, it constitutes a two-way route that interacts with the newly colonized lands. As stated by Braudel, 'there is no society without exchange': Spain's role in the Atlantic expansion is a checkerboard of those actions and interactions where the past and the future meet, influenced by assorted cultures and the forming of new realities. Spain's position in global trade has been depicted by a long historiographical tradition that has resulted in a wealth of information, however scattered. This information is, regrettably, largely unknown to specialists of the Atlantic world and global history. However, internal and external mechanisms which encouraged the expansion of the Spanish monarchy in the Atlantic and its connected areas, and which helped to consolidate it, are a clear example of how historical evolution in one location is heavily conditioned by events in other geographical locations. The spectacular Portuguese expansion is also a very clear example of this. This peculiar view of the Chaos theory can be helpful, as well as encouraging a shift in the historical analysis perspective.[5]

The discovery and colonization of America, the role played by Spanish travellers and merchants in the opening of new routes to diverse points on the planet and the impulse that accounts for the projection of the old European continent onto distant areas of America, Africa and Asia, have been analysed from disparate theoretical methodological perspectives coloured by different ideological views. Traditional historiography has carried out in-depth, extensive studies of the wide-ranging dimensions of the Spanish Atlantic expansion, focusing particularly on its relations with America and, to a lesser degree, with the Philippines and other colonies in Asia. Nevertheless, a more detailed analysis of this expansion in the light of new theoretical perspectives seems to highlight that the Spanish Atlantic system participated in various mercantile systems within its own world system, and that it had links with several regional economies, some of which were marginal to the Spanish system itself.

The marginalization of some of these regions, such as the West Indies or the production and trade centres in Asia where the Spanish settlers arrived, was largely encouraged by the arrival of other European powers that were in conflict with Spain. Those powers succeeded in settling in a number of those areas, thus turning them into major production zones linked to extensive international maritime routes. In the latter decades, a great deal of this historiography has become an important part of the latest research trend on the so-called 'History of the Atlantic System'. Until now, Atlantic specialists have covered only certain parts of this Hispanic expansion; cultural encounters, the promotion of new economic interests by the settlers and the natives, the measures taken by private individuals and institutions to establish a Spanish empire or, at least, to integrate, at several levels, the colonists and the colonized. These studies follow an old and oft-taken line of research that stems from a particular intellectual tradition. However, in the Spanish case, this area of study opens new perspectives which are still far from being thoroughly investigated.

Emphasis has been largely placed on continuous revisions of the formation of empires and the dynamics of interdependence between the metropolis and the colonies from a socio-political standpoint. The role of Europe, of Portugal and Spain at first, is fundamental to the articulated reasons and inherited attitudes of an old imperialistic tradition that was highly charged with territoriality, religious fervour and a search for wealth. Nevertheless—as stated by Fernández Armesto—from the sixteenth to the nineteenth centuries, a worldwide expansion occurred, where the old

Europe was only *a single thread of the hank* in a long and complex process of intercultural exchange. Outside this framework, the study of the formation of a Spanish colonial empire has been followed by a more polemic debate.

Discussions have been centred around the impact on the formation and consolidation of an authentic, centralized and highly bureaucratized Spanish state in order to harness both fiscal and military efforts for the defence of the empire outside its borders. Paradoxically, it was the defence of the territories of the Hispanic Crown in Europe which attracted the most economic and political efforts, which could have had a decisive influence on the crisis and decadence of the ultramarine colonies throughout the seventeenth century. In the eighteenth century, economic issues had a stronger impact on the transformation of the Spanish state, as the necessity to strengthen royal power (absolutism) became apparent and also due to the interests of the new mercantile and aristocratic elites that brought pressure to bear on the governments to create new laws and a new institutional framework that would be more in tune with the times.

Comparatively, the case of Spain was very similar to those of other colonial empires in the Early Modern Age. Despite inadequate documentation, the economic issues have been thoroughly discussed although there are still many areas worthy of greater research. It is also essential to increase our understanding of the other aspect of the Atlantic expansion and integration: the socio-cultural view. As a specialist, I beg to expand further the study of empires and colonies from a comparative perspective, although it is necessary to remember that such a task would not be possible without a previous and more thorough regional study which accepts a transnationalist perspective as well as—as stated by David Armitage—a cisatlantic viewpoint (i.e. a national or regional viewpoint from a perspective of the Atlantic context). We are also in great need of, especially, extensive studies of the connections linking places (towns, regions, economic spaces, states, etc.) in order to identify comparative cases and to ascertain the connections between the types of collaboration and cooperation among actors and factors involved in the process of integration and globalization. Thus, a cultural and socio-economic vision which transcends the essentially political and ideological aspects is required, in order to try to shed more light on the truly leading figures in this process of expansion.

With regard to the Hispanic monarchy's role in world trade, various studies have delineated related aspects: the main characteristics of the different processes in the formation of an empire, its ties with its colonies (whether close or otherwise) and the weaving across the Spanish Atlantic arena of a complex network, constituting both public and private interests. Both old and new research seems to underline (however differently in their theses and the issues studied) major aspects which would somehow condition the fate of the empire: its enormous size and the high-level of expansion reached in a relatively short time. From a political point of view, Spain comprised, when the extent of the empire was at its largest, a good part of the American continent from Alaska to Patagonia, including vast regions in North America, South America and the Caribbean. Spain also occupied territories on the Atlantic side of Africa.

In Asia, it governed the Philippines, and it also ruled over the Mariana and the Carolina Islands. The vast size of the Spanish empire at first forced other competitors in the colonial race (the Dutch, English and French) to begin an aggressive infiltration from the marginal areas of the Hispanic empire. This took place mainly in America, where the north European powers began to settle in areas that were marginalized by the Hispanic expansion, such as the Antillean Islands and other such locations in the Spanish Caribbean. To a large extent, this also conditioned the political and economic fate of Spain itself, which was centred around the notion of a 'composite state' and lacked administrative centralization in spite of efforts to effect an authentic institutional unfolding. This phenomenon thus paved the way for many cities in various Spanish regions to become central nodes in a complex network of horizontal interests that in turn caused the presence and intervention of foreign merchants. This was a decisive factor as may be seen in several conjunctures, such as in the so-called Iberian Union between Portugal and Spain (1580-1640).[6] Such a factor, during several historical periods, perpetuated a multiple identity in the Hispanic monarchy whence actions and intentions originated from diverse points and areas across the globe.

The composite monarchy was, in fact, a truly global monarchy, but, from an economic point of view, Spain played a major role in the emergence of a capitalist world economy, if one is to follow the classic lines set out by Wallerstein. The role of Spanish trade, during the seventeenth and the eighteenth centuries, in the emergence and consolidation of a global economic system, began before the institutionalization of the system of fleets and galleons. Overcoming the challenges posed by the marine space which were also interrelated with distant production areas creating large markets and strong links could only take place because of technological progress, the import of precious metals and migratory flows. Studies of Spanish trade since the discovery and colonization of America have evolved from the lines of a macro-economic investigation to the micro-history of companies and entrepreneurial families involved in Atlantic commerce. From the last decade, thanks to a truly interdisciplinary effort, emphasis was placed on perspectives that moved beyond the classic theses of centre and periphery and towards a broader context. Nevertheless, it is necessary to state that, methodologically speaking, such perspectives did not usually differ much from the Wallersteinian premises of the existence of a world economy or even from the theses of centre and periphery.[7] The difference lies in that studies of economic changes, institutional analysis and research on colonial cultures are now favoured.[8]

Although the economic impulse conflicted with both the social and the internal political system, the Hispanic expansion contributed to the formation of a first cycle of economic roles and shifting supremacy. The expeditions undertaken by Columbus and his successors opened routes which caused the economic axis to shift from the Mediterranean to the Atlantic. The increase of Spanish commercial activity in this Atlantic axis between Africa and America was aimed partly at neutralizing the advantages gained by the Portuguese seafaring merchants in their systematic occupation of diverse Atlantic enclaves and islands; especially, after having successfully circumnavigated the African continent and thereby opening new possibilities for European trade in Asia. Nevertheless, initial trips of colonization and trade, as well as various later commercial enterprises, remained greatly indebted to an earlier maritime and technological tradition, inherited from the Phoenicians, Greeks, Romans and Arabs. The conditions that could lead to this period of expansion were in existence prior to Christopher Columbus, especially those of a geographical nature, although expansion also stemmed from the existing link with Mediterranean maritime cultures which had previously strengthened the Hispanic colonizing impulse.[9]

Moreover, the marks left by Arab culture in large areas of the Iberian Peninsula (Andalusia or Valencia, for instance) caused these regions to become a kind of globalizing experiment. The Phoenicians, Romans and, later, the Arabs, brought into these areas their customs, vocabulary, technology and products, which in turn found their way to the Atlantic. In fact, Spain did likewise in other areas of the globe by introducing products and technology that had formerly been brought to Spain by the Arabs; this was apart from the seafaring and trading traditions inherited from ancient Mediterranean cultures. Those cultures somehow influenced the globalization of the Mediterranean well before the axis was moved to the Atlantic.[10] Such a heritage was a crucial and decisive factor in the role played by the Iberian Peninsula in this process. One also has to take into account those pre-existing determining factors in the society and economy in Spain with regard to its traditional relations to various market areas outside the country. Concomitantly these had helped to increase prosperity in several Spanish regions, such as the northern and the eastern coastal areas which enjoyed new momentum as they became involved in the expanding Atlantic economy. Thus, the process of expansion, which began in the fifteenth century, was merely the result of an accumulative process that allowed for the integration of market areas into a global, macro-level system.[11]

Another factor which contributed to Spain's singular role throughout the sixteenth century is that for various international circles of commerce, Spain had become the main centre and outlet for silver and other precious metals.[12] As a consequence, several Spanish cities became trade centres engaged in re-exporting colonial products along various maritime routes. This phenomenon also attracted merchants from different European and Mediterranean countries. Mercantile colonies were thus formed from which, the merchants in turn, directed their economies to the Atlantic. The Spanish regions, especially those on the seaboard, witnessed a constant flow of capital and merchandise that turned their cities into cosmopolitan centres attracting many foreign merchants and travellers.[13] If one momentarily disregards the line of research focusing on the formation and development of the colonial empires as well as Spain's role in this historical context, one must however, pay some attention to the importance of the research along a thread which provides us with more information on this complex and intricate cooperation network on which is based the consolidation of a truly worldwide, large-scale commerce. This specific thread will delve more deeply into the historical geosociology of the merchants and their associates as involved in the formation of the first worldwide economy.[14] In this particular aspect, the Hispanic monarchy of the fifteenth to the eighteenth centuries offers a valuable scenario for such research, as multiple commercial networks can be found operating within it.

The circuits of Spanish colonial trade made it possible for worldwide interests to be established in Spain, especially in Andalusia and coastal areas where port cities usually became trade centres for both natives and foreigners. A constant exchange of ideas, cultures, productive activities and trade turned Seville, and later Cadiz, into a 'Babylon with a hundred faces'.[15] A school of historians has analysed from diverging points of view these merchant communities, and such studies received special attention from the late 1980s when this historiographical line was enriched with socio-institutional, demographic, economic and cultural, all-embracing perspectives.[16] Consequently, these studies could well represent a fundamental chapter of what could be a global history formed by a number of interwoven regional studies where a global vision would mean a study based on a regional economy or a unit of analysis, i.e. the economy of the various interrelated spaces in Europe with diverging Atlantic areas: 'an interlocking network of trades shaped by public and private interests'.[17]

The fast growth of the Spanish colonial trade with America was favoured by a series of factors such as the geostrategic position of the Iberian Peninsula. One also has to take into account the economic needs and the historic bonds with several economic regions that went back to older links, maritime routes and political and cultural relationships, such as those with Flanders, with several Hanseatic cities and, on the other side, with the

Mediterranean ports and Asia Minor, as well as with the Far East. This led to circumstances and situations based on structures which characterized the nature of Atlantic trade during the centuries of mercantilism. In fact, the achievements of some of the centres in modern Europe which had become the driving force behind the European expansion in the world, such as Venice and other Italian cities, the Low Countries, the Hanseatic League and even England itself, can be accounted for by their relationships (either as allies or as enemies) with Spain.[18] For instance, the interest that 'maritime powers' had in their trade with the ports of call of the Iberian Peninsula in relation to the Baltic and the Mediterranean greatly conditioned the development of such market areas as well as their regular connections with the Atlantic area. In the case of the Baltic trade, France and England began to obstruct Dutch trade by means of strong protectionist measures, which made the Dutch Republic view Spain as an ally in the second half of the seventeenth century.

With regard to world trade, the Hispanic monarchy had several fronts, and the various Spanish regions were the keys to the relationships with various economic regions, especially during the seventeenth century, when the economic centres in Spain moved to the seaboard, and regions such as Catalonia or Galicia joined in Spanish foreign trade. One of the main European areas integrating into the Spanish Atlantic trade situation was the Baltic. I cannot stress enough the importance of the ports in the Iberian Peninsula for trade with other European countries such as England, France and the Low Countries. This situation lasted until the structural changes in the European economy took place, well into the eighteenth century. The route through The Sound (the strait between Denmark and Sweden) was one of the most important commercial maritime routes in the pre-industrial era, and several maritime powers traded in cereals and raw materials for construction purposes, such as timber and iron, bound for the south and west of Europe. The return cargoes were produce from the south and the Mediterranean, as well as products from the colonies in great demand due to the then contemporary social and economic life in northern Europe. A great deal of such merchandise arrived indirectly from the warehouses in Cadiz. Mediterranean markets influenced Atlantic expansion more than was previously believed, and their products were in high demand in the international market.

As Braudel claims, there is an investigation still pending into a great many of the products that arrived in Spanish cities from Asia Minor and Italy, and which were redirected to the Atlantic circuits. Certain goods, such as silk from Persia, fine fabric and glass as well as other merchandise from the East, such as dyes and spices that had traditionally arrived in Seville, began, from the sixteenth century, to be paid for with American gold and silver as these became international currency.[19] Not only did Genoese merchants settle in some Spanish port cities, but they also influenced important political and financial processes within the Spanish monarchy. Furthermore, the strategic position of the Iberian Peninsula as a link between the Mediterranean and the areas that had been strengthened since 1492 held a strong appeal for the commercial firms trading with the Mediterranean from other European regions. Dwindling Mediterranean trade in the sixteenth century now ceases to draw the attention of historians, although the investigation on the role of the *Mare Nostrum* in the Atlantic expansion has gained currency in recent years. In that respect, the role played by Genoese and Maltese merchants settled in Cadiz as middlemen between the Mediterranean and the Atlantic is highly relevant.[20]

From the outset of the Atlantic expansion, a great deal of Spanish foreign trade effort targeted the American markets. Between 1492 and 1600, Spain played a decisive role in the initial stages of the expansion, and consolidated, in these early years, its Atlantic position, while also having to face the first symptoms of its decline. This 'Spanish Atlantic system' and its colonial trade with America is called the *Carrera de las Índias* and has, from the outset, certain institutional and socio-political features that somehow determined the remaining European 'expansions'. In fact, the *Carrera de las Índias* did occur both in Portugal and in Spain. The term referred to maritime activity between the Iberian Peninsula and the American colonies as well as every business and other endeavours related to that activity. When a trader engaged in American trade by loading his merchandise onto the fleets and galleons, it was said that he was involved in the *Carrera de las Índias*. After all, this term defined a historical category that entailed the development of a definitive way of life, which was strongly linked or even subjected to, the evolution of a specific, but not limited, mercantile-geographical system, for this system was connected to other trading areas that did not belong to the Spanish empire but were intrinsically linked to it.

Some of the main characteristics of the Spanish colonial trade were laid down during Columbus' initial voyages. The beginning and favourable evolution of the Atlantic traffic, which commenced with the occupation of the Canaries and later focused on the American continent, offered new, unsuspected possibilities to the Andalusian region in southern Spain. In a relatively short period of time, the rest of the Spanish regions were integrated with varying degrees of success. In these decades Seville became the focus of the activities that set in motion the dynamics of the Spanish empire.[21] Spanish colonial trade has been extensively discussed and there have been significant historiographical contributions, mainly since the 1980s. Some topics, such as the structure of commercial capital and its functionality, the crucial connection between trade and production, the study of the market areas and the structure of the mercantile areas, as well as the analysis and social structure of those who made trade possible and who controlled commercial activities, have all been thoroughly documented.[22] The quantification of such high commercial traffic flow has defined this aspect of Spanish overseas trade, with the traffic characterized by a regular shipping flow both centralized and organized from a single port (first Seville, later Cadiz), and as a colonial mercantile system shaped by the State through certain governing organs [namely, the Spanish Board of Trade (La Casa de la Contratación)]. The Spanish Board of Trade, although consistently broken by the private commercial firms (whether foreign or otherwise), remained the chief agency involved in the trade.

In a sense, the nature of the Spanish misconceived capitalism (or false mercantilism), from the outset of the Catholic kings' regime, conditioned the economic structure of Spanish overseas trade to be biased to the export of raw materials in exchange for large amounts of gold and silver and other foreign products. Nevertheless, I agree with García-Baquero that there is a great difference between protectionism and other measures stipulated in Spanish laws, and the actual practices implemented since the intensification of Spanish foreign trade, both of which were totally different from the mercantilism implemented by other European countries.[23]

In recent times, a new lease of life has been given to the mechanics of Spanish colonial trade with innovative perspectives lent by Oliva Melgar.[24] New ideas about the basic mechanics have come to light, and these help to clarify the complex operation of the Spanish monopolist system that, for more than three centuries, concentrated legal trade with the Indies on the Seville-Cadiz axis, so to speak. The credit system, in the form of loans and policies of marine risk, was essential to maintaining trade, but the capital that fed the system came mostly from foreign financial centres. Behind the scenes the true monopoly was cached below the legal structure and this supported the men, ships and merchandise in the geographical landscape of the legal monopoly.

Discussions on the various elements, such as free trade, could only add reasons to confirm that, on the whole, the foreign financial conglomerate was able to control, to its own advantage, the exploitation of the American territories. When it comes to the Spanish crises (both internal and external) due to the wars waged by the Spanish Crown in Europe, the internal uprisings (such as that in Catalonia) and even the loss of Portugal, a new era began which was characterized by a situation of general crisis in the heart of the Hispanic monopoly. Seville as an economic centre was displaced by Cadiz, economically and socially from the 1640s.[25] There were also clear institutional changes that took place, especially as Cadiz assumed its central role in the Spanish reform programme related to America.[26] The relocation of the Board of Trade and the establishment of a *Consulado de Cargadores* (a body of registered merchants entitled to load their goods on the ships to Spanish America) in Cadiz was regarded by its counterpart in Seville as threatening competition in Spain in 1717, besides also being perceived as favouring foreign interests.

Various issues were involved with diverse economic and political consequences. In the first place, the reform of the institutional basis of the *Carrera de las Índias* and the revision of the Spanish mercantilist regulations responded, among other things, to the desires of those involved in the centralization of the new dynasty: the reinforcement of centralization would be one of the new Bourbon government's maxims. On the other hand, the idea of concentrating protectionist policies in an attempt to enrich the treasury, begin new industrial policies and protect colonial interests, was a widespread practice for statesmen and European thinkers from Colbert to Campomanes and led to the proliferation, in the whole of mercantilist Europe, of monopolistic commercial companies. In the case of Spain, the reforms to be implemented were a particularly complex issue since Cadiz had become a port city with great international maritime trade, as well as also being a strategic port of substantial scale for navigation and a centre for foreign commercial companies. This is the reason why Cadiz was a unique port, for trade with the Indies was the object of reforms which sought to introduce certain improvements as well as provide for the maintenance of the monopoly as the only means to save Spanish colonial trade.

It is worth highlighting the intrinsic relationship between colonial trade as a State business and the formation of a navy. Some similarities can be found between the Bourbon reform programmes and those carried out in other countries in relation to commercial reforms and naval policies. However, Spanish rule-making was crucial to the development of a symbiotic relationship between the European currents of the time and the Spanish politico-administrative tradition (as exemplified by the creation of the provincial *Intendencias* or Quartermaster Offices). Such a symbiosis became apparent in relation to three issues: permanent state financing of the navy, the politics of arsenals and the organization of authentic naval bases, such as those built in Cadiz, Cartagena, El Ferrol and various American port cities. In the case of Cadiz, the creation of a unique organism, i.e. the General Quartermaster Corps for the Navy, and its functions as an administrative and fund-collecting agency, constituted, in spite of the conflict with the Board of Trade due to some duplication of administrative duties, one of the most decisive episodes within the commercial and naval policies.

In the Atlantic context, from the late seventeenth century, Spain went on to play second fiddle in the political and economic fields, although, paradoxically, its role seemed to become more important as a centre that connected Euro-American migratory flows (whether free or forced) and the spread of a pan-Atlantic Hispanic culture. The relationship between Spain and its American colonies also shaped the expansion of European competitors, mainly the Low Countries and England. Well before ships from the Low Countries ventured into the Atlantic, Portuguese merchants had been carrying sugar and wood from Brazil and gold, ivory and other products from the Atlantic to Antwerp, mainly via Lisbon. This practice changed drastically after the decline of Antwerp in 1585. The relocation of Flemish trade to northern cities and the prominence of Dutch transport systems as the main link with the Atlantic production centres, determined the close relationship between Spain and the north European merchants who had played a leading role in their own colonies as well as in Spanish America, particularly since the middle of the seventeenth century.[27] Late in the seventeenth century, four trading networks were operating in the Atlantic and the degree of interrelation of the expansion carried out by assorted maritime powers competing with each other reached very high levels.

This system was based on: first, the consolidation of bilateral trade between Spain and its colonies. This was in turn based on a state monopoly imposed by the Spanish Crown. Second, Spain used to its own advantage the Portuguese expansion, a mutual sharing during the years of the Iberian Union. In spite of this union in 1580, both systems operated separately. Trade between Portugal and Brazil, carried out on a free basis by merchants and shipowners rather than on a system of monopoly, developed before and after this historic period. This development occurred in combination with the local and regional internal processes which were taking place in different areas of America, such as the Caribbean. Third, the Dutch, English and French became involved in this trade with America and integrated with the American markets. The fourth pillar of this system was represented by the Portuguese trade with the Western African coast and the slave traffic initiated after 1550 from Africa to America. Slave trade is a key factor in the involvement of Portuguese, Dutch, English and French monopolistic companies in the so-called triangular trade.

In this context, Spanish foreign trade, and the might of the Hispanic empire itself, faced fierce competition in an ever-increasingly belligerent landscape.[28] During the seventeenth century, European countries regarded trade with the Antillean islands essential as the latter were the main suppliers of certain tropical products which were in great demand since they could not be grown in Europe. Very often, another nation's colonies were more appealing than their own, as they played a role in the political and diplomatic arena, since they could be won as trophies and then used as bargaining tools. Unless they had a great strategic value, sooner or later they would be returned as a result of the political pressure exercised by the colonial elites who were keener on keeping their own monopolies than on pursuing national interests.[29]

A global viewpoint on Spain's Atlantic role allows us to analyse these very factors from the perspective of the space strategy devised by the merchants' networks, considering commercial exchange itself as an incentive for the growth of a region or economic area. From this point of view, it is necessary to consider issues such as the influence of the expansion abroad in the economic development of the Spanish regions themselves and to what extent such expansion conditioned the form of integration of different regions into territories or international economic circuits. In relation to the first point, it is necessary to emphasize that the formation of this empire and its overseas trade did not have the same impact on all Spanish regions. In fact, just as is stated by Marcos Martin in his outstanding work on Spain's socio-economic system between the fifteenth and seventeenth centuries, Spain's uneven development influenced the way in which the very same country, after having been the first economic power, gradually lost ground until the complete loss of its empire at the end of the nineteenth century.[30] Nevertheless, from the fifteenth century onwards several areas opened up to trade, while the Atlantic and the economic poles fluctuated and shifted throughout the following centuries until the end of the seventeenth century.

The integration of the various Spanish regions was heavily conditioned by activities carried out by foreign and native merchants. Certain Spanish regions stretched their links between the hinterland and the foreland, such as areas in northern and eastern Spain. Other areas, such as Andalusia, were bound to open up to foreign markets, leaving no chance for the profits gained to be invested in the development of local industries. The Catalan case followed a completely different pattern. The economy of inland Spain remained permanently active thanks to old complementary routes such as those stretching between Castile and Flanders which had been in operation since the Middle Ages. Other areas such as Aragon and Castile were also linked via trade fairs, ensuring an active financial world that was soon to connect to primary European financial centres such as Genoa or Antwerp. Eastern Spain thrived through times of great commercial activity, especially in the major port cities of the former kingdoms of Valencia and Murcia. Arab heritage in Valencia is still visible in agricultural techniques and trading practices on its fertile, irrigated areas and the growing of oranges, rice, etc.[31] Mediterranean cities were involved in coastal traffic, trebling the number of connections between ports. They provided a link between some inland areas such as the southern parts of the former kingdom of Aragon and the rest of Europe;[32] ships coming from the Atlantic bound for Italian ports and Asia Minor put in at these ports, as well as ships heading for the garrisons in northern Africa. They were the natural access points between Castile and the old *Mare Nostrum*.

In cities such as Alicante, there were important colonies of merchants engaging in various activities aimed at overcoming the threat from both Berber pirates and Ottoman expansionism. In short, in these Mediterranean ports very important, lucrative exchanges took place as they connected the Mediterranean economy with the Atlantic routes. Most of these activities were carried out by foreign traders while influential groups of native merchants were engaged in the exploitation and commercialization of regional or intraregional wealth. Goods imported, stored and sold by foreign merchants included British salted fish, cereal and manufactured goods, while local products were exported, such as wine from the Valencia region, nuts, dried fruit and esparto. Foreign ships were the main means of transportation.

Both the Canary and the Balearic Islands were central to the connection between America and the Mediterranean. The Canaries became an 'experiment' where colonization and trade were tested. They were the target of important migratory waves as well as a geostrategic connection on the route to the Antilles and the rest of America. The merchants from the Canaries had to face, in the fifteenth and seventeenth centuries, the monopoly of the Seville merchants, and were forced to fight to defend their interests because they were seen as a threat to peninsular trade, while the islands were regarded as an enclave of illicit trade. The economic activities of the island were very soon devoted to the production and commercialization of specialized agricultural produce. In spite of some opposition, the archipelago was granted a series of licenses of trade in selected years. In 1564, the Official Canarian Board of Trade to the Indies was created in Las Palmas and, during the seventeenth century, both foreign and Spanish ships were allowed to dock at the Canaries on payment of the relevant duty. In northern Spain, the seafront location of cities such as Santander or Bilbao determined their commercial function as ports.

In spite of evident regional contrasts, these cities experienced a population growth due mainly to the rise in employment which also attracted inhabitants from inland areas. The characteristics of this regional economy forced its inhabitants, who were mostly rural, to travel long distances in order to exchange their surplus of products for consumer goods. There was a remarkable growth in this mobile population that started in the middle of the seventeenth century. In the second-third of this century a cycle of economic growth began which was based on and driven by factors related to this mobile population and their agricultural activities. In the case of Santander, it was originally a town with a seafaring and trading tradition that harked back many years, although in the fifteenth century, with a very small population which experienced, in the seventeenth century, a new cycle of population growth. Bilbao, on the other hand, was an important port linking to the rest of Europe and from which local commercial firms operated in direct competition with other northern cities, as well as with foreign traders, especially the Dutch who tried to monopolize trade in iron and wool.

The complexity of the trade along the mercantile routes between Castile and the Galician, Cantabrian and Basque ports until early in the seventeenth century has hindered investigation though the topic has been thoroughly studied. Galician relationships with American trade greatly developed in the seventeenth century. The incorporation of Catalonia into the Atlantic routes was crucial to overcoming the problem of overseas trade, mainly with the colonies. Unlike what happened in Andalusia, the growth of overseas trade in Catalonia did produce an acceleration of capital growth crucial to its internal economic development.[33]

Andalusia, with its unmistakably Arab imprint, and, above all, its commercial cities (mainly Seville and Cadiz), had been for centuries the base for the institutional monopoly despite being on the very edge of the Spanish State. The Arab influence had been felt in Andalusia for a very long time both in the type of products that were the object of exchange and also in the production of certain products. Gradually, new Atlantic influences affected Spain by enriching the Spanish commercial structure, creating certain improvements as well as certain structural problems. Trade with the Indies attracted merchants from other Spanish provinces. Foreign colonies in practically all Andalusian cities, even in those far removed from the American trade, such as Cordoba, Malaga, Seville and, especially Cadiz, expanded their overseas economic activities and demographic conditions due to the enormous growth in the foreign population of largely temporary residents as well as a floating percentage. In these cities a form of mercantile life environment developed that was 'exported' to America where it duly adopted colonial features.[34]

To what extent did expansion influence the integration of space into international economic circuits? And, how did it influence their increase in strength? Apart from the measures taken by the Spanish regions and by the political and military institutional mechanisms that developed Spanish trade abroad and, especially, in its colonies, one of the most important aspects was the populating of those areas (through mechanisms of colonization, as well as trade and migration) that gave rise to a diversity of space structures created by different types of societies. In this respect, cultural extrapolation had always been an active factor to spatial economic processes, a fact that is rather obvious in the Spanish case. The Hispanic monarchy's role was fundamental in consolidating mercantile capitalism. From the fifteenth century, there was a quick rise in the integration of the economic activities in many Spanish regions which merged with different areas of the globe. Spatial economy helps us to understand this evolution, although the application of the models of spatial economic analysis have not been yet thoroughly developed for the study of the integration of spaces and societies existing before the nineteenth century.[35] Nevertheless, the simplified theoretical model of spatial economy can be suitably applied to the period between 1492 and 1828 (when free trade in Spain came to an end). This model consists of a set of consumers and a set of production settings within a specific space. Consumers—all the individuals—are mobile, while settings are fixed. Consumers moved in order to consume goods and services, although on occasions, it was the products which moved from the production place to the consumer. However, both products and consumers usually met at a fixed point: the marketplace.[36] The need to travel long distances to access products and markets, which is the norm in modern maritime economies, led to a broadening of interrelations between production (always fixed) and trade.

Merchants and their various colonies in many Spanish cities were the main figures of this intermingled exchange. Commercial activities, and the invaluable opportunity of gaining access to different markets, attracted a series of mercantile interests comprising mixed communities of merchants (whether Spaniards or foreigners) now settled in Spain. The process of a number of merchant communities settling in Spain occurred within a very confused political process set in a context of long periods of war and conditioned by diplomatic agreements between Spain and other European powers. Their presence in Spain was connected to Spain's interest in developing the logistics of international trade. The impact of their activities varied, depending on the regions and the internal economy that influenced and developed them. In eastern Spanish cities, such as Murcia, Cartagena, Alicante or Valencia, foreign colonies gained complete control over trade in certain products, especially agricultural produce. Italians, Genoese and French in Alicante, and merchants from Béarn in Cartagena, seemed to monopolize trade during the seventeenth century.[37]

In Catalonia and in the Cantabrian and Basque cities, depending on the situation, there was fierce competition between foreigners and locals. In Andalusia (especially in port cities such as Malaga, Cadiz and Seville), there were significant foreign colonies of various nationalities (German, Flemish, Dutch, French, Genoese, English, Irish, etc.) that developed strong integrative mechanisms and reached high levels of social cohesion. They controlled the export trade and a series of related activities, depending on the nature of the city itself. In Seville, the existence of many foreign communities led to internal disagreements and social conflicts that explained some of the court cases raised in the seventeenth century against foreigners and their offspring (the so-called *jenízaros*).[38]

It is obvious that Spanish trade held strong appeal for foreign merchants who were actively seeking new markets and could see the Iberian Peninsula as a key to accessing different maritime routes. During the sixteenth and seventeenth centuries, ongoing migration in some cities saved commercial relationships immediately after the wars, which interrupted trade in some historical conjunctures, ceased.[39] The latest investigations provided new, complementary viewpoints of the constant migration of manpower from the economically developed areas in Europe which experienced a constant process of demographic explosion in spite of the wars and politico-religious conflicts that spread across Europe throughout the fifteenth and seventeenth centuries. These migratory waves affected mainly large tracts of Atlantic and Mediterranean Europe. These groups, of diverse geographical origins, different political tendencies and religious confessions in the context of a troubled Europe, chose as destinations port cities that were gateways to the maritime networks of the Hispano-Portuguese Empire. It is a proven fact that these communities played a leading role in the maintenance of the mercantile system of their respective regions of origin.

Of all these colonies, one of the most active was the French. While we ignore whether they actually were the wealthiest and most powerful, yet they have been the most thoroughly studied in recent historiography. The reason could rest with the traditional relationship of Spanish historiography with the French school, and the wealth of available sources of information. As for the English, they settled in a few Spanish port cities. From the second half of the seventeenth century and during the early years of the War of Spanish Succession they were able to conquer certain places with a strategic value for their trade both with Spain and with other locations.

To summarize, understanding the role played by the Iberian expansion in general, and by the Spanish expansion in particular, on the formation of this Atlantic, or even worldwide or global system will enable us to comprehend the various spatial and geographical sub-systems which derived from the different expansion models with which the Spanish empire had to coexist. Far from analysing the historic-political and social issues (widely discussed by their respective historiographies), this analysis will help us comprehend why the current globalized world is absolutely not and least of all a homogeneous world.

Notes

*This work has been carried out within the Dynamic Complexity of Cooperation-Based Self-Organizing Commercial Networks in the First Global Age project, which is part of the EUROCORES Programme of the European Science Foundation (06-TECT-FP004). It has also been funded by the Spanish Ministerio de Ciencia e Innovación (AACC: SEJ2007-29226-E/SOCI). An earlier draft of this essay was published as Ana Crespo Solana, 'The Iberian Peninsula in the First Global Trade: Geostrategy and Mercantile Network Interests (XV to XVIII centuries) in Federico Mayor Zaragoza', *Global Trade before Globalization (VIII-XVIII)*, Madrid: Fondo Cultura de Paz, 2006, pp. 103-27. I am greatly indebted to Rila Mukherjee and Jack Owens for their comments have helped me to enrich this text. This essay has been translated by Ernie Alconchel and Robin Duff.

1. This definition of *frontier* is in: Francisco de Solano and Salvador Bernabeu, eds., *Estudios (Nuevos y Viejos) sobre la Frontera, Pérez-Lila, Estudios nuevos y viejos sobre la frontera,* Madrid: CSIC, 1999. Foreword by F. de Solano, p. 7.
2. Fernand Braudel, *La dinámica del capitalismo*, México: Fondo de Cultura Económica, 1986.
3. Renate Pieper and Peer Schmidt, eds., 'Latin American and the Atlantic World'/'El mundo atlánticoy América Latina (1500-1850)', *Essays in Honour of Horst Pietschmann*, Köln: Böhlau–Verlag, 2005, Introduction, pp. 9-15, 17.
4. On new methodological perspectives see: J.B. Jack Owens, Emery Coppola Jr. and Ference Sidra Szidarovsky, 'Fuzzy Ruled–Based Modelling of Degrees of Trust in Cooperation-Based Networks: Close Research Collaboration among Domain Experts (Historians) and Mathematical Modellers', essay presented in *Visualization and Space-Time Representation of Dynamic, Non-linear, Spatial Data in DynCoopNet and other TECT Projects*, ESF EUROCORES Workshop, TECT Strategic Workshop in Madrid, Spain, 25-26 September 2008; J.B. Jack Owens, 'A Multi-national, Multi-disciplinary Study of Trade Networks and the Domain of Iberian Monarchies during the First Global Age, 1400-1800', *Bulletin of the Society for Spanish and Portuguese Historical Studies*, vol. 33, no. 2, in press.
5. J.B. Jack Owens, 'Toward a Geographically-Integrated Connected World History: Employing Geographic Information Systems (GIS)', *History Compass*, vol. 5, no. 6, 2007, pp. 2014-40.
6. On the influence of the Portuguese Crown on the fate of the Spanish empire, see Valladares Rafael, 'Portugal y el fin de la hegemonía hispánica', *Hispania, Revista Española de Historia,* vol. 56, no. 193, 1996, pp. 517-39. See also Francisco Bethencourt and Diogo Ramada Corto, eds., *Portuguese Oceanic Expansion, 1400-1800*, Cambridge: Cambridge University Press, 2007. For some ideas towards a complete picture of the Spanish Empire in the Atlantic see Jerry Brotton, *Trading Territories: Mapping the Early Modern World*, London: Reaktion Books, 1997; Guillermo Céspedes del Castillo, *América Hispánica (1492-1898)*, Madrid: Marcial Pons, 2009; Phillip D. Curtin, *The World and the West: The European Challenge and the Overseas Response in the Age of Empire*, Cambridge: Cambridge University Press, 2000; Antonio García-Baquero González, *La Carrera de Indias: Suma de contratación y océano de negocios*, Sevilla: Universidad de Sevilla, 1992; Hugh Thomas, *El Imperio Español: De Colón a Magallanes*, Barcelona: Editorial Planeta, 2006; Manuel Lucena Giraldo, 'Tres décadas que cambiaron el mundo (sobre "El Imperio español de Colón a Magallanes" de Hugh Thomas)', *Revista de Occidente*, no. 276, 2004, pp. 191-4. About the term 'composite state' see H.G. Koenigsberger, *Politicians and Virtuosi: Essays in Early Modern History*, London and Ronccevette: Hambledon Press, 1986, p. 12; Raymond Fagel, 'España y Flandes en la época de Carlos V: Un imperio político y económico?', in Crespo Solana and Herrero Sánchez, *España y las 17 Provincias de los Países Bajos*, Una revisión historiográfica, Córdoba: Universidad de Córdoba, Fundación Carlos de Amberes, Ministerio de Asuntos Exteriores, 2002, pp. 513-33.

7. Immanuel Wallerstein, *El moderno sistema mundial III: La segunda era de gran expansión de la economía-mundo capitalista, 1730-1850*, Madrid: Siglo XXI, 1999; and *El moderno sistema mundial II: El mercantilismo y la consolidación de la economía-mundo europea, 1600-1750*, Madrid: Siglo XXI, 1984; Horst Pietschmann, ed., *Atlantic history: history of the Atlantic system, 1580–1830*, Göttingen:Vandenhoeck & Ruprecht, 2002; J.N. Ball, *Merchants and merchandise: The expansion of trade in Europe 1500-1630*, New York: St. Martin's Press, 1997.
8. Lauren Benton, 'From the World-Systems Perspective to Institutional World History: Culture and Economy in Global Theory', *Journal of World History*, vol. 7, no. 2, 1996, pp. 261-95.
9. Felipe Fernández-Armesto, *Before Columbus: exploration and colonisation from the Mediterranean to the atlantic 1229-1492*, 1st edn, London: Houndmills, Hamsphire, 1987; Anna Unali, *Ceuta 1415: los orígenes de la expansión europea en África*, Ceuta: Archivo Central, 2004; J.R.S. Phillips, *La expansión medieval de Europa*, México: Fondo de Cultura Económica, 1994.
10. Olivia Remie Constable, *Trade and traders in Muslim Spain: the commercial alignment of the Iberian Peninsula: 900-1500*, Cambridge: Cambridge University Press, 1994.
11. Regina Grafe, *Entre el mundo ibérico y el Atlántico. Comercio y especialización regional, 1550–1650,* Bilbao: Diputación Foral de Bizkaia, Departamento de Cultura, 2005, p. 25.
12. Pierre Chaunu and Huguette Chaunu, *Seville et l'Atlantique (1504–1650)*, Paris: S.E.V.P.E.N., 1955–6, 10 vols.; Dennis O'Flynn and Arturo Giráldez, 'Cycles of Silver: Global Economic Unity through the Mid-Eighteenth Century', *Journal of World History,* vol. 13, no. 2, Hawai, 2002, pp. 391–427; Dennis O'Flynn, Arturo Giráldez and Richard Von Glahn, eds., *Global Connections and Monetary History, 1470–1800*, Aldershot: Ashgate Publishing, 2003.
13. Alberto Marcos Martín, *España en los siglos XVI, XVII y XVIII*, Barcelona: Crítica, 2000; Hilario Casado Alonso, ed., *Castilla y Europa: comercio y mercaderes en los siglos XIV, XV y XVI*, Burgos: Diputación Provincial, 1995.
14. Jack Owens and Matthew Ciolek, 'Rutas: reuniendo datos sobre el tejido conector de una Monarquía Global', in J.M. Bernardo Ares and S. Gómez Navarro, eds., *Estudios de Historia Iberoamericana I: XXXIII Reunión Anual de la Society for Spanish and Portuguese Historical Studies* (SSPHS), Athens, Georgia, 11-14 April 2002, Córdoba: Universidad de Córdoba, 2003, pp. 39-56.
15. Michel Cavillac, *Pícaros y mercaderes en el Guzmán de Alfarache*, Granada: Universidad de Granada, 1994, p. 427.
16. Clear examples are: Ruth Pike, Javier Alfayam and Barbara Mc Shane, *Aristócratas y comerciantes: la sociedad sevillana en el siglo XVI*, Barcelona: Crítica, 1978; Nélida García Fernández, *Comerciando con el enemigo: El tráfico mercantil anglo-español en el siglo XVIII (1700-1765)*, Madrid: CSIC, 2006; Manuel Bustos Rodríguez, *Cádiz en el sistema atlántico: la ciudad, sus comerciantes y la actividad mercantil (1650-1830)*, Madrid: Sílex, 2005; Klaus Weber, *Deutsche Kaufleute im Atlantikhandel 1680-1830. Unternehmen und Familien in Hamburg, Cádiz und Bordeaux*, Munich: C.H. Beck, 2004 and Ana Crespo Solana, *Entre Cádiz y los Países Bajos: una comunidad mercantil en la ciudad de la Ilustración*, Cádiz: Fundación Municipal de Cultura, Cátedra Adolfo de Castro, 2001.

17. David Ormrod, *The Rise of Commercial Empires: England and The Netherlands in the Age of Mercantilism, 1650–1770*, Cambridge: Cambridge University Press, 2003.
18. Manuel Bustos Rodríguez, 'España en el desarrollo capitalista mercantil europeo (siglos XVI-XVIII): Historia y estado de la cuestión', *Anales de la Universidad de Cádiz*, nos. 3-4, 1986–7, pp. 215-28.
19. Pierre Chaunu, *Sevilla y América: Siglos XVI y XVII*, Seville: Universidad, 1983; Ferdinand Braudel, 'La economía del Mediterráneo del siglo XVII', *Mediterráneo e Historia Económica*, no. 7 'Colección Mediterráneo Económico', 2005.
20. Carmel Vasallo, *Corsairing to Commerce: Maltese Merchants in XVIII Century Spain*, Malta: University Publishers, 1997.
21. Carlos Martínez Shaw and José María Oliva Melgar, eds., *El sistema atlántico español (siglos XVII-XIX)*, Madrid: Marcial Pons, 2005.
22. Antonio García-Baquero González, *Cádiz y el Atlántico, 1717-1778,* Cadiz: Diputación Provincial, 1976, 2 vols. and Lutgardo García Fuentes, *El comercio español con América, 1650-1700*, Seville: Diputación, 1980, pp. 69-72.
23. Antonio García-Baquero González, *Andalucía y la Carrera de Indias (1492–1824),* Granada: Universidad de Granada, 2002.
24. José María Oliva Melgar, *El monopolio de Indias en el siglo XVII y la economía andaluza: La oportunidad que nunca existió*, opening lecture, academic year 2004-5, Huelva: Universidad de Huelva, 2005, pp. 261-83; and José María Oliva Melgar, 'Realidad y ficción en el monopolio de Indias: una reflexión sobre el sistema imperial español en el siglo XVII', *Manuscrits: Revista d'història moderna,* no. 14, 1996, pp. 321-58.
25. Manuel Bustos Rodríguez, 'De Sevilla a Cádiz: hacia el cambio de funcionalidad en el seno del monopolio andaluz con América (1600-1650)', *Estudios de la Universidad de Cádiz ofrecidos a la memoria profesor Braulio Justel Calabozo*, Cadiz: Universidad de Cádiz, 1998, pp. 487-98.
26. Antonio García-Baquero González, 'Comercio colonial y reformismo borbónico: de la reactivación a la quiebra del sistema comercial imperial', *Crónica nova: Revista de historia moderna de la Universidad de Granada*, no. 22, 1995, pp. 105-40; Antonio García-Baquero González, 'Cádiz y su Tercio de Toneladas en las flotas de Indias: Contribución al estudio de la pugna Sevilla-Cádiz en el interior del complejo monopolístico andaluz', *Gades*, no. 1, 1978, pp. 107-20; Ana Crespo Solana, *La Casa de la Contratación y la Intendencia General de Marina de Cádiz (1717–1730),* Cádiz: Universidad de Cádiz, 1996.
27. Johannes Postma and Victor Enthoven, eds., *Riches from Atlantic Commerce: Dutch Transatlantic Trade and Shipping, 1585-1817,* Leiden: Brill, 2003; Ana Crespo Solana, *El comercio marítimo entre Amsterdam y Cádiz (1713-1778)*, Estudios de Historia Económica, no. 40, Madrid: Banco de España, 2000.
28. Idelfonso Pulido Bueno, *Almojarifazgo y comercio exterior en Andalucía durante la época Mercantilista, 1526-1740,* Huelva, 1993; Kenneth R. Andrews, *Trade, Plumber and Settlement: Maritime Enterprise and the Genesis of the British Empire, 1480-1630,* Cambridge: Cambridge University Press, 1984; James D. Tracy, ed., *The Rise of Merchant Empires. Long-Distance Trade in the Early Modern World, 1350-1750*, Cambridge: Cambridge University Press, 1990.

29. María M. Alonso and Milagros Flores, *El Caribe en el siglo XVIII y el ataque británico a Puerto Rico en 1797*, Puerto Rico: National Park Service, Dept. of the Interior, 1998.
30. Alberto Marcos Martín, *España en los siglos XVI, XVII y XVIII*, Barcelona: Crítica, 2000.
31. Enrique Giménez López,'Dos décadas de estudios sobre el comercio valenciano en la Edad Moderna', *Revista de Historia Moderna*, nos. 6-7, Alicante, 1986, pp. 93-206; See also the summary by Alberola Romá,'La actividad comercial de los puertos de Valencia, Alicante y Cartagena durante la Edad moderna: Una aproximación historiográfica', in A.di Vittorio and C. Barciela López, (a cura di) *La Storiografia maritima in Italia e in Spagna in etá moderna e contemporanea. Tendenze, orientamenti, linee evolutive*, Bari: Caccuci, 2001, pp. 237-51.
32. Alberola Romá 'La actividad', p. 239.
33. Ramón Lanza, *La Población y el crecimiento económico de Cantabria en el Antiguo Régimen*, Cantabria: Universidad de Cantabria, 1991; Aingeru Zavala Uriarte, *La función comercial del País Vasco en el siglo XVIII: El comercio y tráfico marítimo del norte de España en el siglo XVIII*, San Sebastián: Diputación, 1983; L. Alonso Alvarez, *Comercio colonial y crisis del Antiguo Régimen en Galicia, 1778–1818*, La Coruña: Xunta de Galicia (Consellería da Presidencia), 1986; Carlos Martínez Shaw, *Cataluña en la Carrera de Indias, 1680–1756*, Barcelona: Crítica, 1981; Fernando Fernández González, *Comerciantes vascos en Sevilla: 1650-1700*, Vitoria-Gasteiz, Sevilla: Diputación de Sevilla, Area de Cultura y Deportes, 2000.
34. José María Oliva Melgar, 'Inmigración extranjera en la Andalucía del siglo XVII: la atracción de la plata americana', in Domingo L. González Lopo and Antonio Eiras Roel, eds., *Mobilidade interna e migraçoes intraeuropeas na Península Ibérica: Proceedings of the European Symposium,* Santiago de Compostela (8-9 November 2001, 2002), pp. 281-98; Bernd Hausberger and Antonio Ibarra, eds., *Comercio y poder en América colonial: los consulados de comerciantes, siglos XVII-XIX,* Madrid, Frankfurt am Main: Iberoamericana, 2003; Henry Kamen, *Imperio: La forja de España como potencia mundial*, Madrid: Aguilar, 2004; Jackie Robinson Booker, *Veracruz Merchants, 1770–1829: a mercantile elite in late Bourbon and early independent Mexico*, Boulder: Westview Press Co., 1993; Miguel Ángel Echevarria Bacigalupe, 'Sistemas productivos y espacios económicos: Los Países Bajos en la España Imperial, 1500-1621', in Crespo Solana and Herrero Sánchez, eds., *España y las 17 Provincias de los Países Bajo,* vol. 1, pp. 491-513; M. Fujita, P. Krugman and A. Venables, *Economía Espacial*, Barcelona: Ariel, 2000; David Ringrose, *Expansion and Global Interaction, 1200-1700*, Longman Worlds History Series, Series Editor, Michael Adas, 2001.
35. Based on Johann Heinrich von Thiunen's theories (circa 1828). See Horacio Capel, *Geografía humana y ciencias sociales*, Barcelona: Editorial Montesinos, 1987; R. Chorley and P. Haggett, eds., *La geografía y los modelos socio-económicos,* Madrid, 1967.
36. About the choice of the year 1828 as the end of Spanish free trade see Marina Alfonso Mola, '1828: el fin del Libre comercio', Martínez Shaw and Oliva Melgar, *El sistema*, pp. 312-49.

37. Vicente Montojo Montojo, 'Las relaciones comerciales entre el Sureste español y América a finales del siglo XVI y principios del XVII: el ejemplo de Cartagena', in Juan Bta. Vilar, ed., *Murcia y América,* Murcia: V Centenario, Comisión de Murcia, 1992, pp. 79-106; Vicente Montojo Montojo, 'Mercados y estrategias mercantiles en torno a Cartagena en el siglo XVI y primera mitad del XVII: Un microanálisis', in *Cuadernos del Estero*: *Revista de Estudios e investigación*, no. 7-10, 1992-5, pp. 143-202.
38. Enrique Otte, *Sevilla y sus mercaderes a fines de la Edad Media*, Sevilla: Diputación, 1996; Elisa Torres Santana, *La burguesía mercantil de las Canarias Orientales, 1600-1625,* Las Palmas de Gran Canaria: Cabildo Insular, 1991; Augustín Guimerá Ravina, *Burguesía extranjera y comercio atlántico: la empresa comercial irlandesa en canarias, 1703-77*, Santa Cruz de Tenerife, Madrid: CSIC, 1985; Ana M. Azcona Guerra, *Comercio y comerciantes en la Navarra del siglo XVIII*, Pamplona: Gobierno de Navarra, 1996; Ramón Maruri Villanueva, *La burguesía mercantil santanderina, 1700-1850: cambio social y mentalidad,* Santander: Universidad de Cantabria, 1990; José Ignacio Gómez Zorraquino, *La burguesía mercantil en el Aragón de los siglos XVI y XVII: 1516–1652*, Zaragoza: Diputación General de Aragón, Departamento de Cultura y Educación, 1987.
39. Vicente Montojo Montojo, 'Le Béarn et le Levant espagnol', *Revue de Pau et du Béarn*, no. 32, 2005, pp. 215-28, Proceedings of the 'Journées du Patrimoine' Échanges et rélations entre le Béarn et l'Espagne: Du Moyen-Âge à la Révolution Française', Olor on-Sainte Marie, 18 September 2004. A. Crespo Solana, 'La Gran Guerra del Norte y el comercio holandés con Cádiz y el Báltico en un período de crisis (1699-1723)', *Investigaciones de Historia Económica,* no. 8, 2007, pp. 45-76.

PART II

Oceans, Routes and Ports Systems and Networks

CHAPTER THREE

Ports and Commercial Networks in the Indian and Pacific Oceans Models and Flows of Capitalism

Antoni Picazo Muntaner

FREQUENTLY, AND PERHAPS TOO OFTEN, neo-liberal scholars have attempted to cast aside Marxist theories under the contention that certain concepts have been completely defeated or annulled by their theoretical inconsistencies. Nevertheless, the notion of 'capital accumulation' continues to be one of the most noteworthy and unresolved issues for research. The historiographical debates of the past on the transition from feudalism to capitalism served as valuable tools, offering us a closer view of the problem, however the approach to the issue was excessively Eurocentrist and the economic dynamics of South-East Asia had yet to be incorporated into the Old World-based models. Theories proliferated. From Europe, some scholars viewed the very market dynamics in cities and long-distance international trade as the foundations for the new capitalist model. From the Asian historiographical standpoint, researchers set out to ascertain whether the British had hindered the capitalist development of the Mughal Empire in India. Along these lines, the work of Chaudhuri[1] was an essential point of departure, both for its critique of the Marxist concept of the 'Asian production model' and for its hermeneutic study in itself.

Indeed, Asia not only upheld the classic mode of production that Marx established in his self-critique to elude his own Eurocentrism, but similar and identical conditions to the European structures (cities, market economy, the manufacture of everything from textiles to metal works, and long-range trade) were also booming, and post-1750 colonialism both distorted and restructured them. Fernand Braudel's notion of the coexistence of many 'world economies' that interacted thus becomes more than obvious.[2] The dynamics were surprising at the very least, as relations went from an initial phase of cooperation and collaboration to a later phase of domination.

Nevertheless, the problem at hand did not reside solely in distinguishing the driving force for change, but rather to investigate how such change itself gradually developed and improved through its own triumphs and errors. Over and above the need to 'accumulate capital', Europe also needed to 'accumulate information', cut operating costs[3] and learn to control the markets.[4] There is no doubt that overseas expansion was quick and thorough in facilitating this task, opening the doors to a spectacular boom in commercial capitalism. However, in the early centuries of the European presence in Asia this process was not yet totally complete.[5]

Europe's expansion was one of the underpinnings for such burgeoning capitalism, as well as for capital accumulation. Yet it also served as a catalyst for control over American, African and Asian markets, alike. For the first time, Europeans would attempt to dominate the world economy by availing themselves of the world's most important centres for trade and exchange. To do so, it was imperative for them to learn to control the main networks for trade and consolidate their presence at the most important ports around the globe. Though lengthy, this learning process would prove to be extremely lucrative, and cooperation was the only suitable means of acquiring information and know-how from the different Asian economic agents.

Such global dominance would set in motion different models. These included the Hispanic model, first in the Americas and later in Asia, based on both a comprehensive control of the region and the failed attempt to establish a rigid monopoly; and the Portuguese model, characterized by a far greater adaptation to the strategic determinants, its complete regional dominance in the Americas, its control over trade in the Indian Ocean, and other forms of hegemony.

If the sixteenth century was the century for Hispanic trade, the beginning of a European expansion that would upset the global economy, the seventeenth century could then be considered the epoch for major change. New ideas were taking root in the north of Europe, including a new understanding of the value of work and capital accumulation, a new theory of freedom of the seas that refuted the Hispanic notion of the 'closed sea', the penetration of large consortiums in the Asian market,[6] and the palpable fact that it was not the 'possession of territories' that was important, but rather selling to those that produced overseas.

The starting point for the era that marked the abandonment of the old 'closed' model[7] and the move into another more open and cooperative model was 1595, just a few years prior to the formation of both the Vereenigde Oostindische Compagnie (VOC) and the English East India Company (EIC). In 1595, different Dutch companies would begin to sell Asian products through direct trade. In scarcely a single decade, 96 Dutch ships with a cargo capacity of 34,810 tons gained access to several ports in the area. To be precise, they made 9 journeys to Enggano; 1 to Jaratan; 1 to Ternate; 56 to Bantam; 13 to Aceh; 3 to Ceylon; 1 to Madagascar; 1 to Cambodia and 11 to Johor.

On their part, the British merchants of the EIC[8] would begin to enter the region later on in 1601, theoretically using the large convoy technique. In 1601, they sent five ships to Bantam, with a total freight capacity of 2,330 tons, repeating the same journey in 1603 with four ships with a freight capacity of 2,200 tons. The system was indeed triggering a change.

Ports, Networks and Trade

The sixteenth century was an epoch of monopoly for certain powers, such as the Portuguese and the Spanish. In contrast, the seventeenth century began with the extension of commerce in South-East Asia to other nations, and primarily with the arrival of the Dutch and English to the region. Incipient capitalism undoubtedly needed information on the trade networks and on the main ports in the zone. Hence the implementation of different measures that would alternate and combine, giving rise to a considerable change in Europe's economic structures and in those of the areas that the Europeans entered, among them Africa and Asia.

The English and the Dutch opted for a two-pronged strategy, consisting of pressure on the one hand, and yet on the other, an element that would come to be essential in consolidating capitalism and controlling trade networks: cooperation. This was a cooperative model that greatly diverged from the first phase of trade, in which the Portuguese hired native navigators from the area to guide the ships to the chief ports of destiny. This strategy helped lower costs, as well as risks. In contrast, the English and Dutch system was a far more active model of collaboration. In certain cases, such as that of the small *patache* boat 'San Buenaventura',[9] such cooperation extended equally to all the members of the diverse crew, just as it extended to the merchants that held a share in each voyage. Indeed, the English and Dutch brought a new system to the Indian Ocean and the South Seas. Rather than aspiring to trade in the central hubs of exchange, the major commercial ports of the time, their modus operandi included keeping their boats in the area for an average of three to four years, actively taking part in the economic dynamics of the networks, specifically also in local and regional trade. Yet, in addition to such extended trade, representatives were gradually positioned in most of those ports, through pacts and agreements. Thus, representatives of the EIC and the VOC would settle in the South Seas Islands, Africa, India, China, Japan and Indonesia. Indeed, this system diverged greatly from the old mercantilist model that the Spanish had imposed in the Philippines.

Manila had become a key strategic component of Hispanic control, on the one hand, because it was a stronghold for the protection of the western coast of America. Yet its trade also facilitated a powerful economic vitality in New Spain. Indeed, the Spanish monarchy continued to uphold a truly mercantilist system. For the Spanish themselves there were serious restrictions that precluded any free trade with the ports of the region and even with the vast Chinese market. Given the demand for Asian products in the economies of the Philippines and New Spain, the entry of goods from the kingdoms of the region was permitted, though significantly limited. China was Manila's main supplier, albeit for a brief period entry was admitted to Portuguese ships coming from India, Goa, Cochin and Nagapattinam. Yet the problems caused by such global trade in the traffic of Spain's Atlantic monopoly would bring forth new changes, and obviously new limitations. Trade between America and the Philippines was reduced to the bare necessary minimum, with limitations on both freight and capital. Clearly, this model differs considerably from the English and Dutch approach. While it is true that the Spanish Crown made some efforts to enter into contracts and agreements with some kingdoms such as Makassar, such endeavours bore no resemblance to the complex economic understanding forged by the other powers of the time. It is also correct that the British and Dutch exercised force to defend their commercial interests in the region, eventually settling into strategically favourable areas. For their part, the Spanish also attempted to use force to control those geostrategic or productive regions. Instances of these were the cases of Taiwan, the Island of Formosa, which belonged to the Philippine authorities, and the Spanish imperialist attempts in the area of Cochin China, and particularly Cambodia. Moreover, the Spanish Court also had in mind more ambitious ideas, including the possible invasion of China.

One example of cooperation that cannot be ignored is that of the EIC. In the early seventeenth century, the Company would enter into countless new agreements. These included agreements with the King and Queen of Jakarta in 1618; with the King of Sohar in 1645; with the King of Makassar in 1614;[10] with Bantam, in 1603, and others. At the start of the century, the company would use the Bantam factory as a base[11] to erect and expand other factories in Sumatra, Borneo, Banda, Japan and Siam, yielding extraordinary profits. On 27 March 1621, Richard Weldem sent a letter from Banda to the English agent in Amboina stating that he was working on the island with the intention of reaching a favourable trade agreement.[12] In 1681, the EIC headquarters in London sent two letters to the King of Tonkin and the Emperor of Japan, in an effort to boost trade and the Company's presence in both countries, respectively.[13]

Stationed at each of the nodes that formed England's dense trade network in the Indian Ocean and the South Seas were business representatives, individuals responsible for trade and political connections with the different kingdoms of the region. In 1614 and 1615 the EIC had a large number of representatives in Japan. For example, the town of Hirado became the home of Richard Cocks, William Eaton, William Nealson, Andrea Dittis, Ralph Coppendale, John Osterwick and Edmund Sayers. From Hirado they controlled a network of smaller offices such as those of Osaka, Kyoto, Shizuoka, Naha (Okinawa), etc. This policy is patently illustrated in Figure 3.1 on the EIC's dealings in the Indian Ocean and the South Seas. The numbers of Company ships in the region grew slowly yet steadily, from a minimum of one ship to as many as 25 ships a year. The freight tonnage also increased considerably, with an average of 2,000 tons annually in the first half of the century, eventually peaking at a maximum tonnage of 5,000. In contrast, during the second half of the century, the average annual freight volume was 5,000 tons, and the maximum tonnage exceeded 10,000.

The implementation of a cooperative model in South-East Asia involved the acquisition of experience and know-how for the Europeans who had settled in the region. Market control was a slow process. Thus, if the sixteenth century was the era of the Spanish-Portuguese monopoly, the seventeenth century was a cooperative learning period, and the eighteenth century was the epoch of the Europeans' absolute control over the markets and trade networks.

The EIC Network Model

Both the EIC and the VOC implemented trade models in the Indian Ocean and South Seas that opposed diametrically the Spanish model. Initially, their methodology was based on the direct exploitation of the local and regional markets with the purchase of products for re-export to the main European markets, yet above all, they also sold such products within the Asian region itself. All of the Old World trade models implemented in South-East Asia faced a serious problem, as there was no demand at all for European-manufactured products in many of the region's centres. This meant that the capitalization of the circuit was very limited. As a result, they saw themselves forced to turn to the trade of local and regional items. Such was the case, for example, of textiles from India, as there was a high demand for them in the region of Indonesia. Thus, the EIC had direct business dealings not only with the primary trade centres in South-East Asia, but also with the secondary centres, through the purchase and sale of goods of all types. In a word, it was taking over the trade market and accumulating capital to purchase the goods that the European markets needed. In this stage, cooperation with the small local and regional trade networks was a key part of the entire process, as it gave the European traders the vital know-how and experience that they needed to control the entire network. As mentioned earlier, capitalism did not solely depend on 'primitive accumulation', but rather also on 'information accumulation'. The transmission of information among economic agents was a fundamental component of the capitalist enterprise. Moreover, the first 50 years of trade did not give the EIC enough time to 'accumulate capital' to reinvest in its expansion.[14]

According to the list of the primary ports (see Table 3.1) used by the East India Company in the 1600–50 periods and the number of journeys made by the Company, it is clear that key strategic ports such as Bantam and Surat, and Madras in around 1640 were the most frequently used. All the same, in the second half of the century, the primary nodes of exchange would diversify greatly and moreover change the geostrategic space. Between 1651 and 1700, the region most often used was India, though the trade impact on China and Japan also increased.

TABLE 3.1: PRIMARY PORTS OF THE EIC IN THE INDIAN OCEAN 1600–1750

Year	*Ships*	*Tonnage*	*Primary port 1*	*Trips*	*Primary port 2*	*Trips*	*Primary port 3*	*Trips*
1600	0	0						
1601	5	2,330	Bantam	5				
1602	0	0						
1603	4	2,200	Bantam	4				
1604	1	200	Bantam	1				
1605	0	0						
1606	3	1,715	Bantam	3				
1607	2	660	Aceh	2				
1608	1	320	Bantam	1				
1609	3	620	Bantam	3				
1610	4	2,196	Bantam	4				
1611	5	2,900	Bantam	5				
1612	1	320	Bantam	1				
1613	8	2,995	Bantam	7	Surat	1		
1614	6	2,603	Bantam	5	Surat	1		

(*Table 3.1 contd.*)

TABLE 3.1 (*continued*)

Year	*Ships*	*Tonnage*	*Primary port 1*	*Trips*	*Primary port 2*	*Trips*	*Primary port 3*	*Trips*
1615	8	3,122	Surat	7	Bantam	1		
1616	7	3,317	Surat	8	Bantam	1		
1617	8	5,362	Bantam	8	Surat	2		
1618	9	4,935	Bantam	6	Batavia	2	Aceh	1
1619	7	3,260	Surat	4	Batavia	2	Bantam	1
1620	3	1,600	Batavia	2	Surat	1		
1621	6	3,300	Surat	5	Bantam	1		
1622	6	3,086	Batavia	3	Surat	3		
1623	7	3,672	Surat	6	Bantam	4	Surat	4
1624	6	3,369	Surat	4	Batavia	2	Bantam	2
1625	6	3,300	Batavia	5	Surat	4	Bantam	2
1626	7	2,760	Bantam	3	Surat	5		
1627	3	1,120	Surat	1	Bantam	2		
1628	5	2,880	Bantam	1	Surat	4		
1629	4	2,700	Bantam	3	Surat	4		
1630	6	4,483	Bantam	4	Surat	2		
1631	7	3,380	Bantam	2	Surat	3		
1632	5	2,793	Bantam	3	Surat	2		
1633	5	2,400	Bantam	3	Surat	3		
1634	3	1,460	Surat	2	Bantam	2		
1635	9	3,160	Surat	2	Bantam	2		
1636	2	1,075	Machilipanam	1	Surat	1	Bantam	1
1637	1	500	Surat	1				
1638	3	1,900	Bantam	2	Surat	1		
1639	4	1,625	Surat	2	Bantam	3	Machilipatnam	1
1640	3	2,400	Bantam	1	Madras	1	Surat	2
1641	5	1,600	Bantam	2	Surat	2	Madras	1
1642	5	2,240	Bantam	2	Surat	5	Madras	1
1643	5	1,960	Bantam	3	Surat	2		
1644	2	710	Surat	2				
1645	6	2,450	Bantam	3	Surat	2		
1646	4	1,570	Bantam	2	Surat	3		
1647	3	1,200	Surat	2	Madras	1		
1648	2	600	Bantam	2				
1649	8	3,255	Bantam	6	Surat	3	Madras	2
1650	5	1,480	Surat	2	Bantam	1		

The use of the network was not limited to the primary trade centres alone, but also included secondary ports, thereby making it complete. If the primary nodes of the English network in the region were located essentially in three fundamental places, the secondary port network encompassed a far denser and more complex geographic area that included virtually all the ports in Africa, Arabia, Persia, India, Malaysia, China and Japan. Details regarding the traffic to these regions during the seventeenth century are given in Table 3.2. Of the entire trade space, both in the Indian Ocean and in the South Seas, a geographic region that accounted for the vast majority

TABLE 3.2: SEVENTEENTH-CENTURY TRAFFIC IN THE INDIAN OCEAN

Year	Secondary Ports									
	Port 1	*Trips*	*Port 2*	*Trips*	*Port 3*	*Trips*	*Port 4*	*Trips*	*Port 5*	*Trips*
1606	Socotra	2	Surat	1						
1607	Madagascar	1	Surat	2	Zanzibar	1	Mocha	1	Aden	1
1608										
1609	Socotra	3	Aden	3	Mocha	3	Makassar	3	Surat	3
1610	Socotra	3	Mocha	3	Surat	3	Aceh	2	Makassar	1
1611	Socotra	1	Mocha	1	Aceh	1	Surat	1	Hirado	1
1612	Dofar	1								
1613	Makassar	4	Socotra	4	Madagascar	4	Tikai	1	Bandar Abbas	1
1614	Surat	2	Socotra	3	Hirado	2	Aceh	2	Bandar Abbas	1
1615	Bantam	5	Machilipatnam	4	Macao	2	Aceh	1	Mocha	1
1616	Bantam	6	Machilipatnam	3	Batavia	2	Aceh	1	Mocha	1
1617	Batavia	7	Machilipatnam	2	Aceh	1				
1618	Batavia	5	Aceh	3	Tikai	1	Batavia	1	Makassar	1
1619	Batavia	6	Surat	5	Chaul	2	Aceh	2	Sohar	2
1620	Batavia	1								
1621	Bandar Abbas	4	Surat	4	Batavia	3	Mocha	2	Aceh	1
1622	Bantam	5	Surat	4	Socotra	5	Makassar	3	Bandar Abbas	2
1623	Bandar Abbas	5	Surat	5	Batavia	3	Mocha	1	Madagascar	1
1624	Batavia	3	Bandar Abbas	5	Surat	5	Mocha	1	Madagascar	1
1625	Bantam	4	Machilipatnam	4	Batavia	3	Surat	3	Bandar Abbas	1
1626	Bandar Abbas	2	Surat	5	Moheli	3	Batavia	1	Mauritius	2
1627	Surat	2	Makassar	1	Machilipatnam	1	Mozambique	1	Bandar Abbas	1

(*Table 3.2 contd.*)

TABLE 3.2 (*continued*)

Year	Secondary Ports									
	Port 1	*Trips*	*Port 2*	*Trips*	*Port 3*	*Trips*	*Port 4*	*Trips*	*Port 5*	*Trips*
1628	Moheli	2	Bandar Abbas	3	Mauritius	1	Mozambique	1	Bandar Abbas	1
1629	Madagascar	2	Bandar Abbas	3	Jambi	2	Mozambique	1	Pulicat	1
1630	Madagascar	4	Bandar Abbas	6	Machilipatnam	4	Makassar	1	Goa	1
1631	Madagascar	3	Bandar Abbas	5	Machilipatnam	3	Moheli	2	Surat	4
1632	Madagascar	2	Bandar Abbas	4	Mozambique	2	Honore	1	Bombay	1
1633	Machilipatnam	3	Goa	2	Bandar Abbas	3	Malacca	1	Aden	1
1634	Goa	1	Madagascar	1	Machilipatnam	2	Bandar Abbas	2	Machilipatnam	2
1635	Bandar Abbas	3	Madagascar	2	Machilipatnam	2	Goa	1	Macao	1
1636										
1637	Bandar Abbas	1	Surat	2	Mocha	1	Madagascar	1		
1638	Bandar Abbas	1	Surat	1	Madagascar	1				
1639	Machilipatnam	2	Madras	1						
1640	Madagascar	1	Goa	1	Surat	3	Bandar Abbas	1	Mocha	2
1641	Madagascar	2	Machilipatnam	2	Madras	1	Bantam	1	Cochin	1
1642	Machilipatnam	2	Surat	6	Goa	2	Malacca	2	Macao	1
1643	Madagascar	1	Madras	1	Bandar Abbas	1	Pegu	1		
1644	Bandar Abbas	2	Mocha	1	Jambi	1	Batavia	1		
1645	Madagascar	1	Bandar Abbas	1	Machilipatnam	1	Surat	2	Rajapur	
1646	Jambi	1	Madagascar	1	Madras	1	Goa	1	Bandar Abbas	1
1647	Machilipatnam	1	Goa	1	Rajapur	1	Madras	1	Surat	1
1648										
1649	Cochin	1	Machilipatnam	2	Bandar Abbas	1	Madras	2		

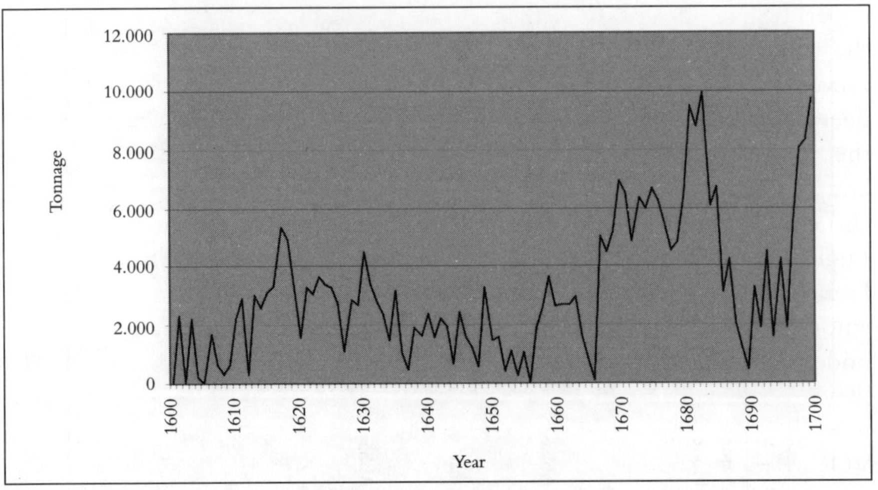

FIGURE 3.1: Trade, EIC

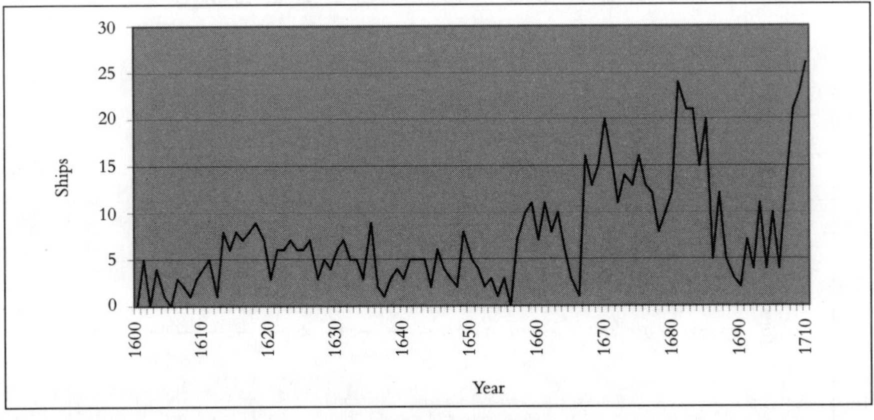

FIGURE 3.2: Trade, EIC

of the EIC's secondary journeys, it was India, which in the late seventeenth century and particularly in the eighteenth century became an essential component of the incipient British Empire, and naturally, of its industrialization process.

The VOC Network Model

Whilst the VOC and the EIC models were very similar, there also existed differences between them. Both had their major logistics bases centred in Java—one in Batavia and the other in Bantam—and both engaged in local, regional and of course global trade, buying and selling goods and acquiring information. Thus, both undertook to capitalize and sought to acquire the experience and know-how that would enable them to control all trade in the region. Hence the inevitable clash between the two companies. Nevertheless, the VOC always had both a higher freight capacity and a larger fleet than the EIC, particularly in the seventeenth century. What is more, the two companies had their fair share of hostilities, such as the conflicts of Java between 1616 and 1625. Interestingly, despite everything, there were also clear points of understanding between the two. To take a case in point, English fleets had authorization to dock in Batavia, as did those of the French, although the latter were far more apprehensively received. In fact, among the French ships, one recalls the incident of the *L'Esperance*, a vessel under the command of the Spanish navigator Diego de Molina. Though they managed to arrive at an agreement, it must also be noted that they were interrogated by the authorities. The major trading posts used by the VOC were still more varied than those of the EIC, in terms of both the number of journeys and the geographic zone. Like the EIC, the VOC focused on cooperative aspects, particularly with the kingdoms of the area, setting up and implementing trade agreements, creating bases and factories, using the local know-how to strengthen their knowledge and their own acquisition of strategic products. Table 3.3 describes the Dutch trade hubs in the Indian Ocean and South Seas.

TABLE 3.3: VOC Trade Hubs in the Indian Ocean

Year	*Ships*	*Tonnage*	*Primary port 1*	*Trips*	*Primary port 2*	*Trips*	*Primary port 3*	*Trips*
1600	8	4,210	Bantam	8				
1601	19	5,190	Bantam	12	Aceh	7		
1602	15	6,950	Bantam	9	Aceh	3	Colombo	3
1603	12	5,970	Bantam	9	Aceh	1	Madagascar	1
1604	1	260	Bantam	1				
1605	12	6,100	Johor	11	Bantam	1		
1606	8	4,460	Goa	7	Aceh	1		
1607	14	7,460	Goa	13	Malabar	1		
1608	2	330	Bantam	2				
1609	0	0						
1610	11	5,280	Bantam	10	Mauritius	1		
1611	13	5,210	Bantam	11	Pulicat	2		
1612	5	4,440	Bantam	5				
1613	12	7,000	Bantam	12				
1614	15	6,380	Bantam	8	Ternate	5	Pulicat	1
1615	7	2,610	Bantam	5	Ternate	2		
1616	8	4,690	Bantam	7	Makassar	1		
1617	12	4,100	Bantam	9	Pondicherry	1	Machilipatnam	1
1618	12	7,040	Bantam	7	Batavia	4		
1619	17	9,900	Batavia	10	Bantam	6	Negapatnam	1
1620	23	8,860	Batavia	20	Pulicat	2	Batavia	1

(*Table 3.3 contd.*)

TABLE 3.3 *(continued)*

Year	*Ships*	*Tonnage*	*Primary port 1*	*Trips*	*Primary port 2*	*Trips*	*Primary port 3*	*Trips*
1621	18	6,290	Batavia	17	Pulicat	1		
1622	3	1,240	Batavia	3				
1623	18	7,940	Batavia	16	Surat	1		
1624	5	2,720	Batavia	3	Surat	1	Pulicat	1
1625	11	5,560	Batavia	7	Surat	3	Pulicat	1
1626	14	4,260	Batavia	14				
1627	22	7,590	Batavia	17	Pulicat	5	Galle	2
1628	13	5,860	Batavia	10	Pulicat	2		
1629	18	7,200	Batavia	18				
1630	19	6,770	Batavia	19				
1631	8	4,300	Batavia	8				
1632	16	6,780	Batavia	16				
1633	10	4,530	Batavia	8	Bandar Abbas	2		
1634	16	6,580	Batavia	16				
1635	3	1,800	Batavia	3				
1636	21	8,960	Batavia	21	Bantam	1	Padaran	1
1637	14	5,520	Batavia	14				
1638	13	6,210	Batavia	13				
1639	21	8,230	Batavia	21				
1640	33	16,090	Batavia	33				
1641	10	6,640	Batavia	10				
1642	21	10,570	Batavia	21				
1643	17	12,180	Batavia	17				
1644	20	9,870	Batavia	20	Mauritius	1		
1645	17	9,840	Batavia	17				
1646	20	11,510	Batavia	20	Madagascar	1	Mozambique	1
1647	12	8,820	Batavia	12	Mauritius	1		
1648	14	12,170	Batavia	14				
1649	17	13,960	Batavia	17				
1650	11	8,550	Batavia	11				

Whilst the heart of the Dutch network was located in Batavia, the intensity of travel into the Indian Ocean regions was now growing at a considerable rate, and factories rapidly emerged in the main centres for production throughout South-East Asia. The VOC's main objective was to sell the native production directly and to reposition goods in both the regional and international markets. It is in this realm that the small but tremendously productive factories played their most essential role. Such was the case of the factories of Taiwan (1624–59), Siam (1625–90), Cambodia and Tonkin, among other areas. This strategy made it possible to purchase certain products that were chiefly brought into Holland (Texel). Spices accounted for the bulk of such products, with some minor imports of Chinese and Cambodian silk products.

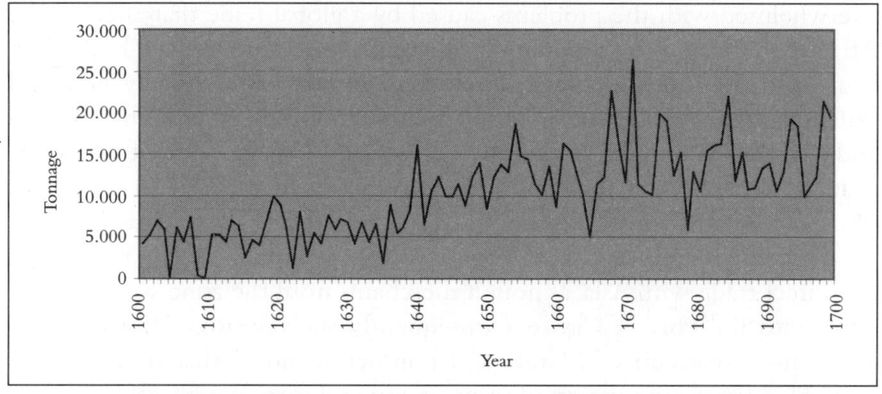

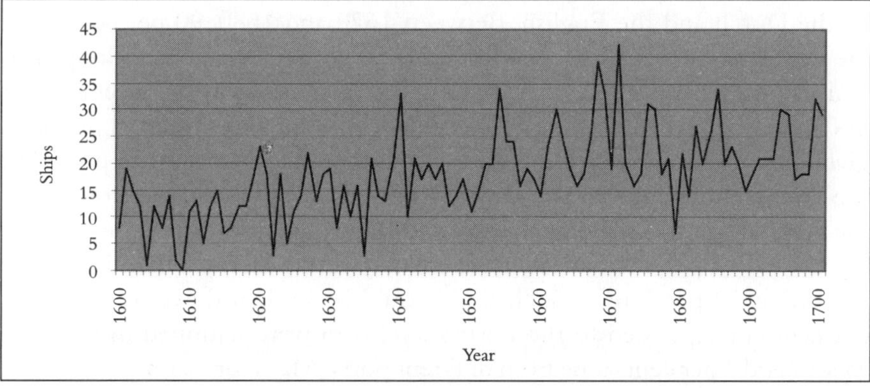

FIGURE 3.3: TRADE, VOC

If the EIC adopted a 'coalescent' and cooperative policy with the main authorities of the Indian Ocean and South Seas, particularly in the seventeenth century, the VOC followed the very same policy. Perhaps one of the most important initiatives of the time was the cooperative agreement between the VOC and Shogun Hidetada, which was signed in 1617. Through this agreement, the Dutch gained total freedom to trade in each and every one of Japan's ports. Further patent evidence of this cooperation can be seen in the letter of 1616, which the VOC representative sent to Matsuura, the Lord of Hirado, guaranteeing to the latter that they would not attempt to engage in any form of religious proselytism whatsoever and that their activities would be strictly centred on the treaty and trade agreement.

THE HISPANIC NETWORK MODEL

The Spanish Monarchy imposed strict mercantilist control over trade from Manila, and most particularly in its trans-Pacific dimension. In the first period of trade between the Philippines and New Spain, the Crown was overwhelmed with the problems caused by a global trade that affected the Atlantic traffic and the production of manufactured products in both New Spain and the mother country itself. The answer to this totally new and unfamiliar set of problems was absolute protection. Trade between Acapulco and Manila was limited to one ship per year, the capacity of that vessel was reduced to merely 500 tons, and strict measures were imposed on the export of capital. In addition to this control, which served to unite trade between the Philippines and Mexico, the Spanish were prohibited from engaging in any direct trade with Asia, although merchants from the zone were granted entry into the Port of Cavite. Consequently, such measures thwarted the economic expansion of Manila and imposed a model that by no means resembled the accumulation of information and market control established by the Dutch and the English. Between 1620 and 1680, 90 per cent of all the vessels that reached Manila from all the ports in the zone belonged to Chinese merchants. Hence, as we shall see later, any sort of retrenchment in China would obviously lead to a deep economic crisis in the Philippines, given the virtual monopolist nature of Chinese trade during this period of the seventeenth century. The scope of this commercial traffic encompassed the ports of Siam, Cambodia, Taiwan and Banda, and the Chinese accounted for up to 90 per cent of all trade with Japan. On the other hand, the remaining 10 per cent of such trade could be broken down as follows: 7 per cent corresponded to the Portuguese, who were stationed in Goa and Macao, and 3 per cent came from different ports (Makassar, Banda, Cambodia, Siam, Johor, Japan, etc.). For this very reason the Spanish would fruitlessly attempt to revive trade with Japan. An example of these attempts to recover commercial control and the inconsequential trade that that took place, is available in the details of the journey of a Japanese ambassador to Manila in 1600. The diplomat took advantage of the trip to sell a number of goods[15] including the following items: 200 *pikuls* of iron; 20 *pikuls* of lead; 2 *pikuls* of copper; 500 Japanese katanas; 2,000 reed mats; 36 large copper cauldrons; 100 small copper cauldrons; 460 dishes; 80 pounds of cotton thread; 10,500 cotton blankets; 688 pieces of clothing; 7,200 cotton sashes and 36 bundles of canvas. Though such a list does not mention the purchase and sale prices of these items, the facts speak for themselves. Moreover, bearing in mind that this was a single vessel with limited capacity, the amounts of the fabrics carried on board are undoubtedly noteworthy.

The direct trade situation with India was also very limited, as it was confined to the era in which Portugal was united with the Spanish monarchy, using the port of Cavite as a secondary stopover port. The list of goods transported by a Portuguese ship is also highly suggestive, as it enables us to compare the purchase prices in China and the sales prices in Japan with similar and sometimes higher prices in the Philippines.

On the way back to India, the same Portuguese vessel would complete its freight with purchases made in Japan and China for resale in the Portuguese enclaves and in the mother country. These goods included: 1,000 *pikuls* of white silk to sell in India at a rate of 200 Portuguese *cruzados*; 12,000 pieces of taffeta; 4 *pikuls* of gold with a 90 per cent profit; 600 *pikuls* of wrought brass (making a profit of 100 per cent); 6 *pikuls* of anise; 500 *pikuls* of vermillion with a 90 per cent profit; 100 *pikuls* of quicksilver; 1,000 *pikuls* of senna tree; 2,000 *pikuls* of brass handles that cost 5 *taels* in China and were sold in Bengal for 7 *taels*; 200 *pikuls* of camphor that would go to Portugal; a large quantity of crockery, as well as numerous pieces of furniture including beds, tables, desks and more, with profits exceeding 100 per cent.

This example not only gives us a notion of the profits obtained by the merchants and the goods most frequently exported, but also reveals the stringency of governmental management, as the latter paid rights in Malacca of 7.5 per cent and an anchorage fee in China at a rate of 10 *taels* per ton of freight.

Whilst the commercial transactions between Manila and Acapulco were limited to one ship per year, as noted earlier, the influx of goods into Manila was far higher. In the mid-seventeenth century, between 1620 and 1653, we observe a large volume of capital and vessels, yet at the same time three critical phases: the first between 1622 and 1624, the second between 1629 and 1631 and the third from 1637 to 1641. These phases marked a significant retrenchment of trade in Manila. Yet such retrenchment would become an absolute crisis as the one of 1643 when market lethargy set in, due to two circumstantial ruptures: the loss of connections with India, Malaysia and Macao following the Portuguese secession from the Spanish Monarchy and the economic retrenchment of the Chinese market, as a result of its own domestic situation.

Figures 3.4, 3.5 and 3.6 enable us to evaluate trade during the era of splendour, specifically between 1631 and 1639, at a time when the port of Manila received an average of 40 vessels per year, with an average annual freight worth 2 million Spanish pesos.

The commercial strategies established by the VOC and the EIC in the seventeenth century were primarily based on the collaboration with different institutions, merchants and local trade networks of South-East Asia, having vastly diverse connections with different ports throughout the region. Their first priority was to learn how to control the market, through a subtle penetration model that enabled them to accumulate capital, and yet more importantly, to acquire know-how. Indeed, this was a prelude for the new capitalism that was emerging in Europe. Conversely, the Spanish Crown, which had its most important base in the Philippines, continued to depend

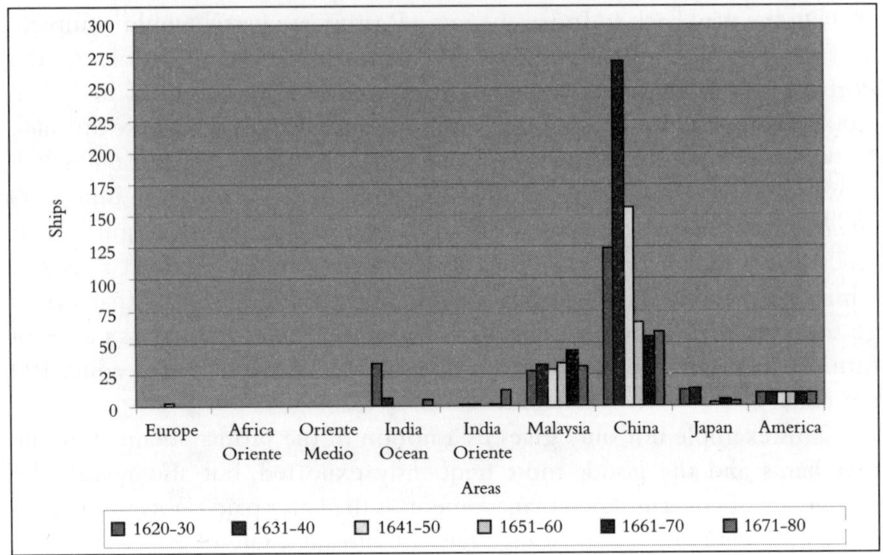

FIGURE 3.4: Trade areas with Manila

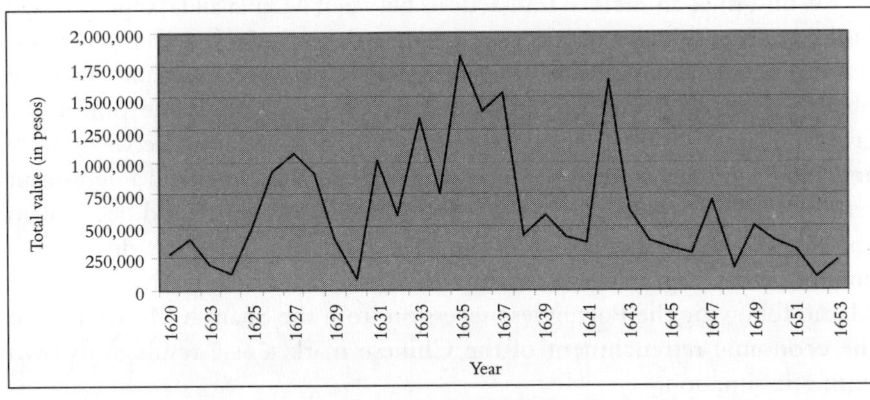

FIGURE 3.5: Trade, Manila

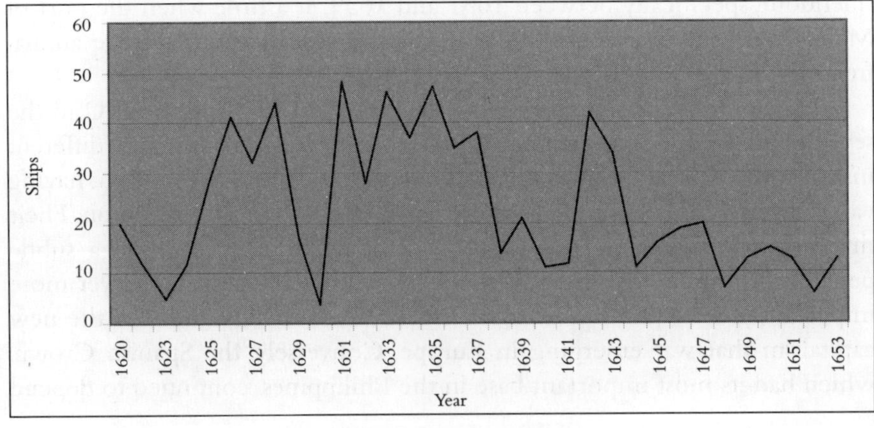

FIGURE 3.6: Trade, Manila

exclusively on the Chinese market, hinging economic growth on a number of ports that supplied the islands: Canton and Amoy.

Notes

*This article is funded by and forms part of the EUROCORES European Science Foundation research project, 'Dynamic Complexity of Cooperation-Based Self-Organizing Commercial Networks in the First Global Age (DynCoopNet)'. (06-TECT-FP-004), with the support of the Ministry of Education and Science SEJ2007-29226-E/SOCI.

1. K.N. Chaudhuri, *Asia before Europe: The Economy and Civilisation of the Indian Ocean from the Rise of Islam to 1750*, Cambridge: Cambridge University Press, 1990-91.
2. Fernand Braudel, *La dinámica del capitalismo*, Madrid: Ariel, 1985.
3. Oliver Volckart, *The Influence of Information Cost on the Integration of Financial Markets: Northern Europe, 1350-1560*, Institute of Economic History, Berlin: Humboldt University, 2006.
4. G. Knaap and H. Sutherland, in *Monsoon Traders*, Leiden: Kitlv Press, 2004, explain that the full development of capitalism required a complete and in depth understanding of long-distance trade, and of Asian trade in particular.
5. For a classic study that displays the importance of Asian trade, see J.C. Leur, *Indonesian Trade and Society*, New York: Institute Pacific Relations, 1955, which explores the keys to precolonial Indonesia.
6. See particularly Om Prakash's work, 'International Consortiums, Merchants Networks and Portuguese Trade with Asia in the Early Modern Period' in *XIV International Economic History Commerce*, Helsinki, 2006.
7. It would be appropriate here to underscore the utility of 'models' not so much to provide final solutions but rather as a tool to interpret, compare and evaluate the interrelations among the different patterns for the establishment of trade in the South-East Asia.
8. E. Erikson and P. Bearmann, *Routes into Networks: The Structure of English Trade in the East Indies, 1601–1833*, Columbia: Columbia University Press, 2004. Here the authors propose three major cycles in the dynamics of the EIC in South-East Asia. The first, formation, which took place between 1600 and 1680; the second, consolidation, corresponding to the period 1681–1764; and the third, total control, between 1765 and 1835.
9. See Antoni Picazo Muntaner, 'Comercio y colaboración en el Mar del Sur: El ejemplo del Patache San Buenaventura', in *X Reunión Científica de la Fundación Española de Historia Moderna*, Santiago de Compostela, 2008. This was a boat under the command of members of the EIC, with a multi-ethnic and multi-religious crew (including Armenian, English, Indonesian, Portuguese, Hindu, and other nationalities) which alongside private parties, shared the ship's freight, and thus the profits of the voyage.
10. Makassar was the heart of a commercial network that connected merchants from China and the Indian Ocean with Europeans. From Makassar, *patache* and *champan* boats would make their way to Mindanao, Manila, Macao, Cebu, Cambodia, Aceh, Sukadana, and other ports.

11. National Archives (NA), IOR/G/21 'East India Company, Records of Java'. In 1616, the Company's representatives in Bantam included John Jourdain, George Ball, Richard Westby and Hernando Ximenes, who was of Portuguese origin.
12. NA, IOR/G/40/25 (4) 'Richard Welden at Banda to George Muschamp at Amboina', pp. 17–19.
13. NA, IOR/G/12/17, p. 300 and subsequent pages.
14. See Patrick J.N. Tuc, *The East India Company*, 1600–1858, London: Routledge, 2001.
15. Archivo General de Indias (AGI), Seville, Philippines 7-R-7-N-88 'Memoria de las mercancías del embajador japonés'.

CHAPTER FOUR

Linking the Atlantic and Asian Worlds Porto and the Indian Trade Dynamics in the Sixteenth Century

Amândio Jorge Morais Barros

THE DIRECT CONNECTION BETWEEN Europe and Asia, that started in the beginning of the Early Modern Age by the Portuguese, represented a serious boost for commercial capitalism and for the history of international relationships. As had occurred in the Atlantic, the reinforcement of standards for the new relationship depended to a large extent on the efficiency of maritime action—a factor that was very decisive for Portuguese expansion.[1]

What held the attention of researchers for long was the Portuguese interference in the spice trade during the sixteenth century, whereby they were able to obtain a dominant position on the market, held until then by the Republic of Venice. It has been said that the establishment of the Portuguese Rota do Cabo (Cape Route or India Run) eliminated the mediators, a notion that is incorrect. The Rota do Cabo *replaced* the mediators and implemented a group who are nowadays termed *middlemen* in modern economic terminology. This term defines an active group, promoting cooperation strategies, from which it also gathers benefits. This is quite an important role, enacted since then by the Portuguese involving several areas, sometimes functioning under the framework defined by the central state but also, simultaneously and actively, outside the governmental framework.

Consequently, an immense circuit developed in trade between Europe and *India*—the latter used in the sixteenth century to define the vast territory from the eastern African coast up to China and Japan. This circuit implied considerable logistic effort, annually made due to the will of the Portuguese Crown. Spices were just part of a bigger set of goods.[2] The success of this eastern maritime enterprise depended on the results of this circuit, which were also dependent on the amount but primarily on the quality of the logistic equipment, that is to say, the ships involved and the competence of the naval technicians.

Since the very beginning of the route, the northern ports of Portugal were involved in the circuit and in all the practices around it; specially the city of Porto through its entrepreneurs and port features. The attention drawn to Porto is justified by the human resources involved (as also coming from other northern towns), but mainly because of its naval construction; also, although at a minor level, due to the existence of local vessels on the route. These contributions are generally unknown to the research community.

Therefore this study focuses on the analysis of the participation of the city and ports related to it in its dealings with India. Different levels are analysed: naval logistics, as also commercial action in the way that it involved positions and business strategies which new historical tendencies put in place. For example; the trade organizational skills or the method of implementing relationship models which resulted in what we nowadays call the *global world*.

Porto: An Atlantic Port in Asian Trade

The opening of the Indian circuit could not be missed by Porto, a structured mercantile centre since the Middle Ages. This Indian circuit meant a new world of opportunities for many people. Those circumstances meant, as usual, the beginnings of a large-scale emigration, which left evidence not only in the economy but also in society. A great part of the population felt the impact directly or indirectly: many were emigrants; others had relatives who had emigrated or were familiar with individuals who had emigrated. They went after a far, unknown world and the promise of wealth. This was the very beginning of the so-called 'cultural exchange' that is evident in the First Global Age. As will be seen, significant means and resources were necessary for this activity, putting into action self-organized groups that should be recognized due to the importance of the role they took.

A central question arises when we focus on the impact that the East had on the economy of Porto and its port activity: Was the Indian circuit and the relationship with India real factors of development? That is, what did India really mean to the port activity of Porto, assuming it as an economic endeavour? What were the kinds of resources needed? How many vessels were involved? Were there any vessels from Porto in the Rota do Cabo? Who were the merchants involved in the business and in which routes of that trade, assuming that it is not correct to consider it as a single circuit?[3] What kind and quantity of activity did the merchants promote in that endeavour?

Issues like these make sense when one looks at the bigger picture: on the one hand, one must keep in mind the intricacies surrounding trade with India, namely, the policy of royal monopoly over the Cape Route. And on the other hand, the life of this particular port town by itself, i.e. the fundamental Atlantic tendency of this town, that, in this essay, opens an 'Indian' arm.

However, when sifting through the evidence, this referred Atlantic tendency does not really seem to be a problem. In fact, it might even have been an advantage. Considering the resources it offered, could not the Atlantic have presented a means of development for eastern trade? American silver also played a key element once it imposed European participation on the eastern economic and trade circuits, as for example, those of spices and textile products which demanded considerable money resources.

These issues cause a complete reformulation of the chronology involved. For the northern Portuguese seaports the Atlantic prosperity did not occur before the late sixties of the sixteenth century, with the discovery of the potential of sugar from Brazil. This asset is one of the reasons whereby the northern Portuguese merchants were strengthened and were able to penetrate into the circuits of the Spanish Indies, mainly in the silver circuits. There they somehow gathered enough resources which enabled them to 'survive', be successful and set course towards the more demanding Indian Ocean trade. Therefore the need to distinguish between Porto's emigration before and after the middle of the sixteenth century. If the first wave mostly comprised soldiers serving in the armadas or in the military forces that supported the first Portuguese settlements in India, the second mainly included merchants, most of who were organized in trade networks. There was a specific movement towards India departing from Porto during the last decades of the sixteenth century; and the stories of some of the men that departed clearly reveal the connections between the two systems: the Atlantic and the Asian.

The Atlantic Model Remodelled for the Cape Route

The essay will focus on the ways the town took part in the logistics of the Cape Route, providing data on naval construction, maritime intervention and the provisioning of fleets. Considering the migratory movements mentioned earlier, I will focus on organizational standards introduced in the East by the Portuguese, and examine how they coped with them. Some successful cases demonstrate that the ability of achieving integration or the ability to adapt to strategies or of reorganizing strategies considering special contexts were significant. In conclusion, I will deal with another subject-matter: the characterization of trade networks and how far they extended.

The theses I wish to examine are as follows: how did a small Atlantic port participate in the Indian trade, and in particular, how was the wealth that was generated in the Atlantic by its agents while participating in the Asian dynamics eventually managed? Did the organization in the Atlantic fit in within the Asian routes and circuits and into the working practices of traders and businessmen? On the other hand, I intend to demonstrate that throughout the informal trade networks, which most of the time operated outside the Portuguese Crown framework, it was possible to develop an extremely interesting and widespread economic activity. Finally, I will evaluate the impact—if there was one—of these activities in the general economy of the port.

To elucidate the analytic subjects proposed here, this essay will make use of a set of documents collected both from the archives and published data. The most important documents retrieved from the archives are notary records which constitute a unique testimony of seaport social and economic life. It is only recently that Portuguese historians realized the value and the potential of such documentary sources for social and economic studies.[4] Notary services were used by many of those who intended to depart, for ordering representation acts/procurations (*procurações*), writing their wills, closing accounts and deeds—activities which were suggestive of the kind of people they were and how they were interested in India.

There were about four-hundred legal acts that were issued by the town's notaries, and they were complemented by other papers/rolls from other institutions such as the local Crown administrative section, whose account books kept royal benefits granted for services overseas, for instance, in India; these are also complemented by records produced by the city's municipality that, from time to time, had to deal with the shipping and fleet provisioning regarding the India Route; and, finally, the documentation produced by charitable institutions such as the powerful *Misericórdia* of Porto, the most important confraternity in the city, which was regularly financed by emigrants in India. The legacies, heritage and donations in favour of the *Misericórdia* confraternity originating in India, China, Japan, and other eastern Portuguese outposts, are good indicators of measuring the extent of Porto's presence in the oriental world. Besides, the *Misericórdias'* networks and the role they performed in terms of money and commodity circulation also provide key data to illuminate the mechanisms of trade used by the merchants. As far as the published data is concerned, several collections of India's documentary sources have long been printed: from log-books to account papers, voyage literature to chronicle narrations, as we will see, they provide excellent information to be examined and enlighten us on various aspects of Portuguese daily life in that region.

PORTO'S RESOURCES IN ASIAN TRADE SHIPS, MEN AND VICTUALS

A detailed analysis of the Portuguese maritime structure at the beginning of the sixteenth century, reveals, not surprisingly, the heavy involvement of the northern Portuguese ports in the discoveries and expansion logistics, particularly in the designated Cape Route. Nautical and economic performance, and the projection of maritime hubs such as Aveiro, Porto/ Gaia/Matosinhos/Leça, Azurara/Vila do Conde, Esposende/Fão, Viana, Caminha, were decisive factors to boost a national economy which was becoming increasingly based on international maritime trade.[5] These were supported by an extremely strong and innovative shipbuilding industry, as well as by fairly old nautical tradition. These two components were utilized by the Portuguese Crown when specific navigation and exploratory needs posed by such a demanding intercontinental route as the Cape Route were imposed.

The participation of Porto's shipyards was noted from the time that circuit began to develop. The *Saint Gabriel* and the *Saint Rafael*, the two headships of Vasco da Gama's armada were built in Porto. They were the result of a technical knowledge accumulation process, achieved in the northern Portuguese ports, which manifested in the creation of the most important type of ship used in the sixteenth century, the *nau*.[6]

As seen in Table 4.1, the work carried out in Porto's shipyards upholding the Crown's armadas reached a significant level regarding the supply of new vessels.

TABLE 4.1: SHIPS BUILT IN PORTO FOR THE INDIAN ARMADAS (1496-1511)

Year	*Model*	*Name of the ship*	*Local officer in-charge*	*Observations*
1496	*nau*	*S. Gabriel*	supervision of João de Figueiró	
	nau	*S. Rafael*	supervision of João de Figueiró	
1497	*nau*	*Flor de la Mar*		
	nau	*Cirne*		
	caravel	unidentified		

(*Table 4.1 contd.*)

TABLE 4.1 (*continued*)

Year	*Model*	*Name of the ship*	*Local officer in-charge*	*Observations*
1499	*nau*	*S. Mateus*		
1501	*nau*	*S. Pedro*		made before this year
	nau	*Leitoa*		
	nau			property of the account officer of Madeira Island
1504	*nau*	*S. Vicente*	contract of André Afonso	
	nau	*S. Gabriel*	contract of André Afonso	
	nau	*S. Rafael*	contract of André Afonso	
1506	*nau*	*S. João*	contract of André Afonso	
	caravel	*S. Simão*	contract of André Afonso	
	caravel	*S. Brás*	contract of André Afonso	
	caravel	*O Salvador*	contract of André Afonso	
	ship	unidentified		
1511	*nau*	unidentified	contract of Diogo de Bustamante	made in Quebrantões
	nau	unidentified	contract of Diogo de Bustamante	made in Quebrantões

Sources: Torre do Tombo (hencefort TT), *Chancelaria de D. Manuel*, liv. 1, fl. 28v; liv. 5, fl. 18; liv. 14, fl. 28v; liv. 30, fl. 91v, 122; Arquivo Historico Municipal do Porto (henceforth AHMP), *Cofre dos bens do concelho*, livros 2-5; Francisco Marques de Sousa Viterbo, *Trabalhos Nauticos dos Portuguezes nos Seculos XVI e XVII*, vol. II, 4-5; Gaspar Correia, *Lendas da Índia* I, 1, 269, 271, 3, 660, and the archive documents cited in this essay.

These data allow us to understand that the contract for Vasco da Gama's ships was just one among others. Despite all the symbolic effects of the expedition, which were promoted by traditional Portuguese historiography, the contract was accepted by the shipyard as a matter of course; besides, it was not the first time the shipmaker was required to build ships for the king.[7] Table 4.1 shows how these shipbuilding commissions continued to be made after da Gama's journey, and that the practice had to be interpreted as complementary to the shipbuilding activity of Lisbon's *Ribeira das Naus*, which became pivotal to the oriental enterprise.[8] Furthermore, we also realize that other ships, no less emblematical in the Cape Route were built in Porto: like the *Flor de la Mar* which set sail to India in 1502 with the second armada of da Gama, and to which she returned in 1505 with Francisco de Almeida, entering the service of India's fleet until she was wrecked in 1511 while returning from an expedition with Afonso de Albuquerque.[9] As for the *Cirne*, of the same size as the former, and owned by the Cirne family that was made famous by the future Flanders factor Manuel Cirne from Porto, we know that she departed to India in 1506, and stayed in service until she was dismantled around 1512 or 1513.[10] At the same time—and probably also integrated with the 1506 armada with *Flor de la Mar* and *Cirne*—one of the *Leitoas* mentioned in the Cape Route lists of ships, was also constructed in Porto.[11]

Caravels that were built for the same purpose are another item to be considered. These also become an additional expression of the accumulated technical knowledge in the northern Portuguese shipyards that was offered on behalf of the oriental expansion. They are, most probably, the well known round *caravels*, bulky ships that could be used both for transportation and naval war, in a long line of vessels built in fifteenth century Porto.[12] Different from the old and revolutionary medieval *caravels*,[13] these were predominantly propelled by round sails, no less than of 80 tons, and continued to stay at service throughout the sixteenth century.[14]

The first phase of service rendered by Porto's shipyards could be said to be due to two reasons: on the one hand, because of the technological innovation capacity revealed by this port, generated and generating a process that touched the whole of the Portuguese coast since the Middle Ages; those structures were recognized as top technological centres, and, in consequence, the ships produced were appreciated and reordered time and again. And on the other hand, also because the biggest Portuguese shipyard, the Lisbon *Ribeira das Naus* in which the main shipbuilding efforts were about to be concentrated, was, at that time, still in a phase of consolidation. By the beginning of the sixteenth century, the Crown was giving the finishing touches to the huge structure needed for the novel Portuguese expansionist reality for which, in fact, the contributions of the northern Portuguese technicians (carpenters and caulkers, etc.) requested by the king's officers in Porto, Vila do Conde and Caminha were decisive. This appears to be a knowledge transfer phenomenon which I will also examine as taking place in Goa's shipyard, comprising the participation of shipbuilders from the north of Portugal.[15]

This said, it may also be observed, at this level, the existence of a system of *informal networks* that was responsible for the technological resource transference throughout the Portuguese overseas world and which was crucial once naval capacity was recognized as one of the greatest assets that allowed the Portuguese to prevail in the Indian Ocean routes and participate extensively in the oriental maritime economy.[16]

After 1511, the references to ships delivered to this route by Porto's shipyards are very scattered. We only hear about the vessels made in Porto for India's armadas in 1537 when two shipowners, Francisco da Rua and João de Deus, ordered a *nau* of 550 tons and sold her to the king. Mentioned thereafter as *Nau do Porto* (*Nau* from Porto) she was sent to the service of the Oriental fleets.[17] In 1538, André Afonso, a shipowner from Porto had sold in Lisbon his *nau S. Tomé*, nicknamed *A Estirada* (*The Stretched*), of 150 tons to Cristóvão Pires, a master of the India Route.[18] Finally, it is difficult to know if the *nau* owned by João Fernandes, also from Porto, sold in Lisbon (with a slave sailor included in the sale) ever departed to India in 1569.[19]

The presence of private shipowners in the Route was conditioned by the monopolistic regime decreed by the Portuguese Crown in 1506 and which was effective until 1570. Even though ships from any port could furnish the fleets, this took place in a regime of requisition which allowed licensed contractors to hire the vessels they needed. There was the general interdiction of free shipping to any open regime permitting private businessmen to participate in the circuit in the early years of the Route, a procedure that was studied by Vitorino Magalhães Godinho.[20] However, it was usual to hire private ships available in any port given the non-existence of a Crown naval fleet.

The integration of Porto's ships with the Cape Route remains unknown. In 1523, Francisco de Sá, royal treasury officer in Porto, sailed to India in a ship charted in the city which he armed and supplied in Lisbon.[21] In 1538 is documented the requisition of the *naus Cício* and *Boquiqua* (these are the names of their owners), both of over 150 tons, to join that year's armada.[22] Later, in 1568, the *nau Santo António*, with master Gonçalo Pires, was also chartered to sail to India.[23]

One wonders whether the cessation of the royal monopoly (1570) caused Porto to intervene in this circuit in a bigger way. It does not seem so. The city and its mercantile agents had already defined the main maritime interventionist strategies which consisted in the exploration of the Atlantic world once they recognized the wealth of potential offered by the Brazilian economy and the slave trade to the Spanish West Indies. With this set-up the oriental trade was left to individual/single agents and to informal trade networks. However, this did not mean that it did not have any manifestation at all; despite not having generated a solid and extended economic flow, large amounts of fortunes were accumulated in India by several isolated and informally organized merchants, connected, somehow, with the consolidated trade networks existent in Porto. Besides, some of them operated both in the Atlantic and in the Indian world—a significant factor which I will discuss later.

However, the Indian trade failed to mobilize naval resources and to generate visible naval and port dynamics;[24] that is why the isolated cases of Porto's ships departing to India are relevant, since they were exceptional and document an interesting face of the city's navigation, and furthermore they were indicators of attempted investments in the Cape Route made by some local shipowners. Inconsequent and isolated, certainly not continuous in fact, because there are only two cases that indicate probable voyages to India: in 1574, just a few years after the lifting of legal restrictions, a *nau* belonging to the Alvo family, carrying on board the brothers and merchants Estêvão and Manuel Alvo, was likely set to sail to India;[25] over two decades later, in 1596, the owners of the *Bravo's ship* (again, the name of the master) contracted a loan in the city to finance an expedition to India.[26]

If such examples appear meaningless in terms of the city's naval commitment to the Cape Route, the logistical support she offered to it was much more solid and significant; specifically, this support meant the diversion of human contingents for the oriental possessions, and also the magnitude of the fleet's supply of provisions.

Regarding human resources, one has to consider the well known requisitions of soldiers and sailors for the armadas, besides the emigration flows, which first, from time to time during the sixteenth century, disturbed the life of the northern Portuguese maritime communities. In 1501, a letter from King Manuel I dated 28 March ordering troops to embark, reached Porto.[27] In 1538 (15 January), a letter from King João III ordered every spare sailor from all the commercial ships of the northern Portuguese ports to be enlisted with the king's representative at Porto, João Rodrigues de Sá, and to join the armadas 'of the Coast, Islands, Flanders, and India'.[28]

As far the supplies are concerned, some aspects deserve more attention, starting with the meat delivery to the navy. To talk about meat provisioning (barrelled dried meat) is to comprehend how the Indian expansion became a national enterprise and how various regions were summoned to participate in the process. The *Entre Douro e Minho* province was one of the premier cattle raising regions in the Portuguese kingdom. During the Middle Ages, the meat industry was concentrated in front of Porto (in Vila Nova de Gaia), where the herds were conducted, the cattle slaughtered and the meat was prepared[29] or, in the words of the old manuscripts, 'where the meats were done'. Such activity (which was complemented by the medieval and early modern trade in leather) meant a lot to the city's economy; and, not surprisingly, in the early days of the Route, the Porto authorities systematically refused or were reticent to cooperate with the 'Indian' ship contractors, even when they lived, or were born, in the city.[30] That could have compromised the Crown's planning and therefore the king resolved the problem by appointing a royal officer in-charge of the management of the slaughterhouses, and to be responsible for the annual shipping of vessels to Lisbon loaded with the 'king's meats' in the eve of the Indian armadas departure.

In a parallel development, the demand for barrels and for other cooperage products made in Porto and its surroundings saw an increase. This can be explained by the role of wine entrepôt performed by this city since the Middle Ages; the navy's requests were an extremely important incentive for this economic segment: in 1566, the Crown's officers bought 4,000 barrels for the Cape Route armada, and throughout the Filipine dynasty (1580–1640, i.e. during the period the crowns of Portugal and Spain were united under Philip II) consecutive and massive cooperage buying was done.[31]

This said, between the acquiescence and the hesitations to cooperate with the contractors, a certainty remains: the significant contribution of

Porto's historical documentation to fully understand the navigation history of the India Run.[32] In fact, even if their own ships barely participated in it, although they did, the integration of nautical technicians of all hierarchies on board was firm and is largely referred to. And in consequence we become aware that an important chapter of the Cape Route's history is not yet written: news about ships' commands, officers and shipmasters, sailors and specialized technicians (carpenters, caulkers, rope-makers, gunmen, cabin and sea-boys), daily life on board, shipwrecks, rescues of shipwrecked sailors and castaways, cargoes and salvaged goods, the rectification of travel and expedition dates, schedules of the armadas missions; information on these are abundant and await a systematic study.

Ships, equipment, provisions, and men were the main logistic support to the migratory movement towards Asia. A social analysis reveals how complex this phenomenon was in the Portuguese sixteenth century. It is inaccurate combine at the same level all of those that at a given moment of their lives decided to go to India, because the motivations behind that decision were dissimilar; linked as they were to the social and economic conditions of those who departed. Moreover, the motivations of the different social types were very complex and diverse. The differences were wide between the nobleman and elite members on the one hand, and the simple workers: the traders, the sailors, the individual/isolated merchants on the other. Importantly, these differences dictated their integration into the organized networks. There was a whole world of connections and specificities. Reis Thomaz wrote: 'The true social history of the Portuguese expansion in the East Indies is still not done';[33]—a statement that continues to remain valid. Therefore, this essay contributes to our knowledge of the social dimensions of the Portuguese expansion. By rescuing from the archives such an extended group of emigrants I intend to give a name and a face to the many Portuguese who participated in this process: the elite who were the Indian Ocean administration officials,[34] but above all people who reinforced the contingents of troops, and sailors and merchants that one day resolved to try their luck in those faraway places. Most of them never actually got rid of the misfortunes that tormented their lives at home, and died in far worse disgrace; but some certainly succeeded.

The Emigration Pattern from Porto and its Hinterland

This is also a history of relations and social types in which geographic provenance counted. It is a history that gives us data about port centrality and functionality, about the city's maritime projection, its capacity to attract individuals, and the potentialities and destinations it offered to its users. Therefore we have Porto, an Atlantic maritime centre, but also a passage to the Oriental world. Certainly a middle point—as we know that ships actually departed from the Tagus River—but also an exit point for those who felt tempted to leave the city. From the outset, the Route's departure point from Lisbon, and Porto's hinterland and inland provinces, both spaces structurally linked the seaport of Porto.

Map 4.1 clearly indicates Porto's role as a point of emigrational flows to India, as also depicting the influence of its port structure over an extended region of more than 120 km. As mentioned earlier, this is significant for India's social history in the early modern age, and somehow must be linked with the reports of chroniclers. To cite an example would be of Couto saying about Ceylon that 'for the most part, our people in this land come from Beira, Trás-os-Montes, and Entre Douro e Minho' provinces, precisely the ones represented in Map 4.1.[35]

Regarding when they left there is good archival material to explore in order to answer this question, and to propose a chronology; in fact, more than one chronology if we think in terms of the Route's logistics,[36] for the ships and the businessmen participating in the Route, and for the emigration.

In sum, this port is linked with two kinds of emigrants: first, the group which includes those who were competent to perform administrative and

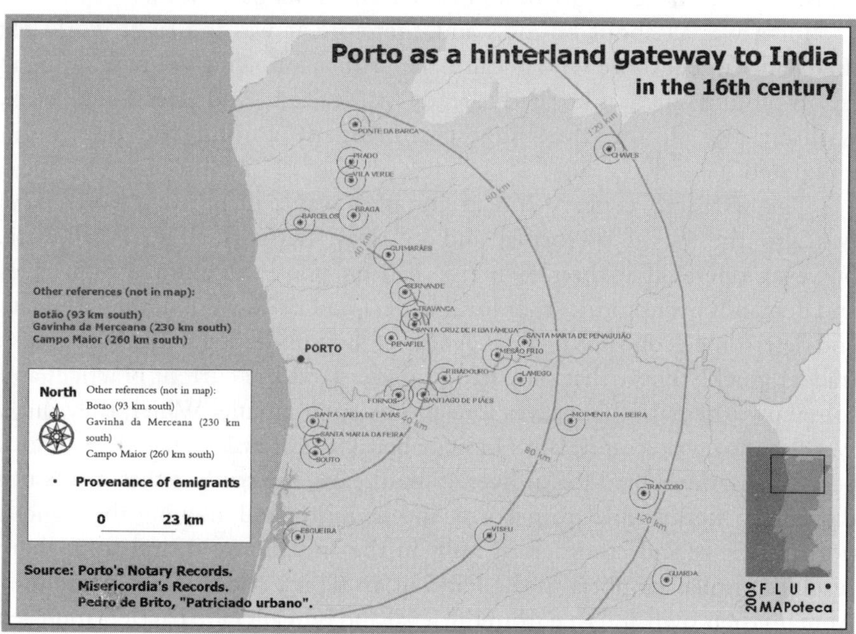

MAP 4.1: Porto as a Hinterland Gateway to India in the Sixteenth Century

Sources: Porto's Notary Records, Misericordia's Records and Pedro de Brito, 'Patriciado Urbano'.

governmental functions, and, at some point, were able to participate in the trade organization, and second, a large group of emigrants whose activity was carried out no matter who was in charge.

As for the elites concerned one wonders if the large-scale departure of relatives of the families who ran the city's administration did not have a historic parallel with the process of the renewal of the nobility in Europe at the end of the feudal era, when many European noblemen were 'dislodged' from the impoverished feudal system and had to seek their fortune elsewhere. The bourgeoisie of late medieval Porto, although they undisputedly ruled the city, faced a similar dilemma at the outset of the early modern age. Predisposed to adopt standards laid down for the nobility since time immemorial, owning lands around the city, and, in some cases, withdrawing from trade and business, the bourgeoisie seemed to be out of sync. With the beginning of a maritime mercantile economy, with the increasing role of money and floating capital, and the consequent overseas expansion, the nobility suffered the competition of newcomers such as the New Christian merchants and their commercial activities. The way out of the crisis for the old elite appeared in the shape of State commissions to India,[37] acting as ship captains, army officers or administrators of fortresses and factories which, curiously, enabled some of them to re-acquire the ancient commercial skills that had made the fortunes of their ancestors back home.

India was all about business and, therefore, it was the right world for merchants and of those who became merchants, following the path of many fellow countrymen who had already succeeded. And merchants were, without any doubt, the biggest contingent among the men who emigrated.

The sixteenth century Indian complex was a merchant's world. This was also the world of formal and informal networks. The Portuguese, however, operated at their own risk, had no power to enforce their rules and demands over producers or local traders, and neither could they stipulate and determine economic policies. Aware of their underdog status, Portuguese traders quickly knew that they had to understand the current practices and somehow integrate themselves into pre-existing circuits. Which they did; I was about to write: *easily*. But I hesitate because that *easiness* had tremendous costs, many times paid for in lives. Nonetheless, the truth is that it was not difficult to find people from Porto, and its hinterland, moving throughout ports, markets, and commercial hubs in the Indian world, and from there reaching similar emporia in the Far East, in China and in Japan. Here they were on their own and free from the legal and bureaucratic barriers imposed by the Portuguese authorities, which meant, of course, that these were very appealing locations of trade for anyone who wished to succeed in business. Examining the careers and the pathways covered by these men, one understands Boxer's description: that the bankruptcy of the Portuguese

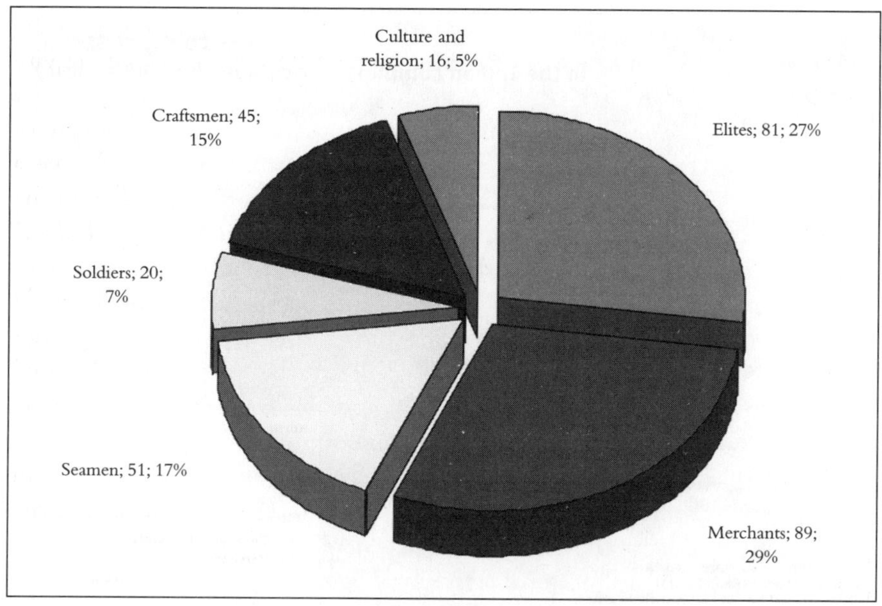

FIGURE 4.1: List of Professional Occupations of Emigrants from Porto to India (1548–1600)

Source: Porto's Notary Records.

imperial plan did not compromise the individual trader's projects,[38] that they easily adapted to the schemes they had to deal with; and that these were often and mostly *self-organized*, based on private funding. And, as modest as this financing was it had always run parallel with the public investments made by the Portuguese Crown.[39]

Merchants, elites, seamen, soldiers, craftsmen, and clergymen—these were the predominant types amongst the emigrants who fought battles and supported the Portuguese presence in the Asian system. However, all of them, at some point, entered the world of business and for most of them trade prevailed over any activity.

The Rise of Informal Networks

Despite all the organizational schemes imposed by the Crown such as monopolies, factories, military and naval forces, the merchants had to deal with an intricate reality on the ground[40] which revealed an immense territory, different spaces, multiple practices and resources that could only be in controlled ones dreams.[41]

When that reality was disclosed, especially in terms of the resources and riches available, a number of plans had to change, if not theoretically, at least

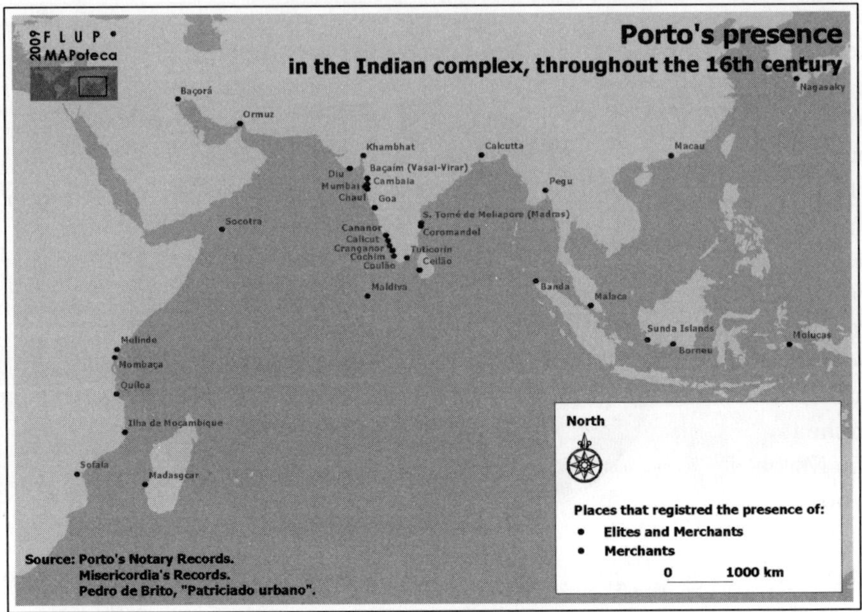

MAP 4.2: Port's Presence in the Indian Complex, throughout the Sixteenth Century

Sources: Porto's Notary Records, Misericordia's Records and Pedro de Brito, 'Patriciado urbano'.

in practice. First, it irresistibly attracted many people who understood that they had at their disposal a wide space to navigate, frustrating one of the basic principles for survival of a state: the cohesion of a given human group in a given territory.

Moreover, there was not one unique model or rule to follow but several. Those in search of fortune had to be part of one of the three existent regimes already acknowledged in the sixteenth century by João de Barros as: 'from lord to vassal' in the territories under Portuguese jurisdiction; by privilege or appointment in the territories embraced by commerce treaties; and under local law and according to custom in the places where there were no such treaties and jurisdictional statutes, which was the situation in the vast majority of cases.[42]

Taken together the activities of the northern Portuguese emigrants in India fitted these three arrangements. But it seems particularly relevant that the percentage of those dedicated to their own businesses chose to submit themselves to local rule and local market dynamics, in order to be integrated, as one more partner amongst many others, in the traditional trading system of the region. That seemed to be a successful formula and, in a certain way, it was the reproduction of the strategy adopted by Porto's medieval merchants when they were trading in the northern European markets.

Consequently, the Portuguese traders in India developed self-organized commercial practices, by aiming at cooperation more than confrontation.

The formula followed often dictated the stance that these merchants took. The written sources give us to understand that they managed to bend bureaucratic procedures and the monopolistic tendency of the factories; first of all, by taking advantage of the extensive and populated territory in which it would not be difficult for a merchant to circulate in and out of the 'official' circuits. Some of the trading routes were efficiently monitored by the Portuguese state: 'the demands of the first captains and governors are very well known concerning the monopolistic acquisition of products, namely, pepper in the Malabar region, as well as the price-fixation by the Portuguese authorities, which were strange to the relative freedom of commerce existent in the Indian Ocean'.[43] Moreover, in 1527 the merchants complained against the Malacca factory, denouncing the abusive demands of officers in-charge who controlled their movements and imposed on them the delivery of the merchandise at the factory at low prices. This was an expression of the opposition to official commercial policy.

Maria Emília Madeira Santos refers to the existence of an informal 'mercantile party' which did everything to thwart the State factories' network and somehow dis-organize the official trade system.[44] It was the onset of a dispute with manifold consequences: one, it undermined the statute of the factories as commercial posts and turned them into mere reception centres for those who arrived in India; and two, it neutralized the State's commercial supervision role. This outcome was predictable because 'the Portuguese, both royal officers and individuals, felt at ease to care less about the distant India's governor or even the Malacca captain'.[45] Portuguese commercial behaviour in India hovered between two standpoints:

- A permanent mercantile State;
- A strong group that intended to get rid of the impediments imposed by that State and steer clear of its strategies.

Such perspectives explain the concealed or open rivalries between the 'king's officers—as executors of royal policies—and private merchants'.[46] The interpretation of Portuguese business in Asia should not be reduced and limited merely to state intervention, but instead should keep in perspective the private, self-organized, dimension. Romero Magalhães begins his examination of the Portuguese dynamics in the Indian Ocean with a chapter entitled 'The official Portuguese trade in India' which is immediately followed by another that he significantly calls 'The Portuguese in the traditional Asian trade'.[47] This is the recognition of the two commerces, the two ways of doing business, the two attitudes;[48] and the willingness as well to understand the reasons why many Portuguese preferred to lay down arms and dedicated themselves instead to trade and smuggling, to get involved in commercial networks and well known circuits, always bending and ignoring prohibitions, and as this case study intends to prove, still being successful.

In fact, it appears that they did not have any other alternative: 'in this land', a chronicler once wrote, 'there is nothing but drugs (i.e. vegetable substances used in medicine, industry, and food) and merchandise'. In other words, in Asia the option was not to colonize, to plow the soil, and to establish large domains which were the options in the Atlantic islands and in Brazil. In India, the way out was to deal with fine goods and spices; the only option was simply to trade at an entirely new level. And for Couto this way out was obvious: 'to leave the king's service and to become a merchant'. Vitorino Magalhães Godinho says that 'the interests generated in the "Portuguese-Oriental complex" were many times opposed to the ones of Lisbon'.[49] Precisely; because this was a private kind of interest which was defined by the members of port communities: 'the constitution of Portuguese communities beyond royal authorities control indicates that the private trade was getting stronger all over the years'[50] by the reinforcement of positions and ties within the Indian Ocean circuits. Wealthy emigrants like the northern Portuguese Manuel Fernandes de Calvos, Domingos Monteiro, or Vicente Novais provide good examples of this evolution.

This is not just about breaking organizational barriers, and the immense geography involved; but also concerns overcoming obstacles in what we nowadays define as *commercial ethics*, as summarized by Reis Thomaz. First, the concept of *trust* under which commercial relations were based, second, the *religious factor* within which trust was laid down, which made it very difficult, if not impossible, for Portuguese and Arab competitors/cooperationists to function;[51] and worse still to function when becoming conscious that behind these were projects of domination. One might wonder how the individual agents could avoid such embarrassments; but, in a certain way and at some point, good sense prevailed and, resembling the 'Levant Scales' a kind of lively, cosmopolitan, and polite mercantile ambience helped, in some Asian ports, to minimize the religious issues and inspire a very particular ethics. It was once again the merchant's universe that was able to deal with these civilizational canons: this universe disregarded limitations, interfered with convictions and with group identities, and counterpointed 'the business ideology' against the 'official ideology'.

A Blend of Formal and Informal Networks?

I do not know if a renewed interest in India existed in Porto in the last decades of the sixteenth century; in fact, some existent indicators from other ports tell us otherwise.[52] Nevertheless, after a relative 'silence' during the

1560s and the 1570s, the notary records present evidence about some new emigrants departing on a regular basis towards India. Of course this renewed flow did not affect the structural pattern of Porto's emigration, shipping, and business which was overwhelmingly Atlantic; but I do believe Porto reflected the new conditions of trade with definite consequences.

In my opinion, this new interest regarding Asia benefited from the Atlantic-oriented vocation of the city and its merchants. In the second half of the sixteenth century, the northern Portuguese ports were firmly anchored in the Atlantic, mainly exploring the Brazilian sugar economy, and interfering in the Spanish West Indies trade, given their role as slave suppliers. For the merchants, at the head of who were the influential New Christian traders and their networks, the political situation after 1580 (when Portugal and Spain became one empire under the same king) somehow opened a way through the West Indies. This meant good access to the silver, or, at least, the possibility of smuggling Spanish silver.[53] And the silver was an asset to sustain the east Indian trade which was very bullion based and usually required payments in kind. Silver pieces provided more possibilities to the traders, and reinforced their position as middlemen in the oriental economies and, when the time arrived, even as intermediaries, between the newcomers from northern Europe, and the local Asian economies.

The articulation of these two systems awaits further research.[54] It is possible, in the archival records, to discover the trajectories, behaviour, and trade achievements of individuals within the Atlantic and the Indian complexes. It is also evident from the archival sources that thanks to private initiative, within isolated or informal networks, it was possible to promote the globally structured economy. Finally, through the same records, we realize that the role of middlemen performed by the Portuguese was for more important then previously considered, and was performed in spite of the evident difficulties of the Portuguese *Estado da Índia* (the State of India by which the overseas Portuguese empire was known), and furthermore despite the Dutch activities there.

I will now discuss a few examples of Porto's merchant activities in the Atlantic and in the Indian Ocean. In 1552, Cristóvão Pais carried out business in India by collecting the profits in the *Casa da Índia*, in Lisbon,[55] and at the same time by leasing the Azores customs house rents.

One of the most distinguished of Porto's traders was Vicente Novais; he owed a big part of his wealth to the business he conducted in India, and he became the in-charge of Porto's *Misericórdia* confraternity administration.[56] Novais is one the best examples of the articulation between the two systems: after a few successful years in India, he dedicated himself, at least between 1565 and 1585, to the Atlantic trade selling Brazilian sugar, African slaves and cotton, while he maintained, at the same time, a significant network in India.[57]

Another merchant was Gaspar Gonçalves, a wealthy shoemaker in Porto who became rich by his involvement in the slave trade between Africa, Spanish America, and India where he died in 1557.[58]

Another example is the family of Lucrécia Aranha, a businesswoman from Porto that was in the forefront of a network dealing in the Atlantic (mainly in the Azores) and in India where one of her brothers died before 1591.[59] I will have occasion to mention a few more important cases further on.

These examples denote a solid intervention that fits a more extended context: that of the Iberian expansion. Flynn and Giráldez propose an exact date to frame it: 1571, the year when Manila was founded. Why Manila? In their opinion it was because that port in the Philippines would soon become the steady platform of connection between America and Asia.[60] This is unquestionable; however we must mitigate their statement by saying that there was not a direct link between the two systems before that date;[61] as there was between the Atlantic and the Indian Ocean as can be proved by the cases mentioned above of Porto's merchants dealing in both systems. Of course we can speculate about the volume of trade and about what those businesses truly represented; but that is another history. Moreover, it is a matter of scale.

What seems interesting and meaningful in the context of the chronology I propose is that the capacity to plan and to schedule things as revealed by these men: the relationships they promoted, their integration in networks, and their role (especially in the Atlantic), revealed that the late sixteenth century emigration to India was anything but random. On the contrary, it was the result of a careful and previous evaluation. This is one of the fundamental characteristics of the merchants' action, when active individuals in this sixteenth century globalizing movement included merchants from northern Portugal. When we look at a merchant like Marcos Cardoso, as early as in 1557 establishing a small network that operated in the Spanish West Indies, Africa, and India, and furthermore connecting with a powerful individual such as the contractor Lucas Giraldo, we immediately comprehend the great extension and the tremendous influence of the business in the frame of the Iberian overseas trade. Such a conviction is reinforced when one realizes that the connection between Cardoso and his sons Jorge and Manuel de Morais passed first by Peru (where Jorge was settled) and followed through India (where Manuel remained).[62]

The same goes for the intervention of Fernão Ribeiro de Almeida, the son of another businesswoman, Inês Chamorra, involved in trade between Cap Vert, S. Jorge da Mina, Mozambique, and India.[63]

In sum, these merchants, by acting as middlemen, were promoters of connections that influenced international trade before the 1570s. They moved on through the 'middle passage' by supplying African human labour to the Spanish West Indies. From there they managed to obtain considerable means of payment that was vital to all the Asian circuits.[64]

However, the truth is that with Manila, the Philippines island complex and the commercial movement around it, it was easier to develop new commercial articulations. This also explains the consistent Portuguese intervention in the complex called 'Maluco', i.e. the Moluccas.[65] Once again, the northern Portuguese traders were involved. Besides Belchior Pais, there was the clove and cinnamon business conducted by a powerful man such as Aníbal Cernige in Banda and the Moluccas in 1531,[66] soon after the Saragossa treaty (1529).[67] And also, the expeditions towards China and Japan (not by accident one of the greatest silver producers in the sixteenth and seventeenth centuries)[68] where we can find men like the clergyman/trader André Coutinho doing business. Or, in the 1570s, Francisco Garcês (1571), Vasco Rebelo, who was a Malacca factor (before 1572), and Cristóvão de Figueiroa (between 1572 and 1574), all of them examples of a presence that would be increased at the end of the century.[69]

Reassessment of Global Systems

Examples such as those mentioned in the earlier section justifies the need for a reassessment of some of the celebrated historiographical interpretations. Since Wallerstein's[70] and A.G. Frank's theorizations,[71] notions of centralities (centre, semi-periphery, and periphery), development, intrusion, empire and domination, which I believe are very reductive, or even theories about the economic role of regions within the world system, have remained untouched. The information presented in this essay is clear. The Iberian Peninsula and its agents were organized, involved in the global circuits and able to adapt themselves to the contexts where commercial dynamics occurred and even to influence these dynamics.[72] Obviously they were very far from being secondary in the international trade organization. Heirs of a long line of medieval merchants, they were in the front line of business in the early modern age—a position where they struggled to stay. We must keep in mind that in terms of the Hispanic Monarchy, the Dutch never seized the silver circuits. Moreover, until the nineteenth century, against all odds, the Portuguese continued to send ships to the Indian Ocean, and they succeded to hold on to the South American positions that the Dutch never were able to neutralize.[73] Also, one needs to keep in mind the crucial role performed by the New Christian Portuguese merchants in the United Provinces at the outset of their commercial expansion.

Thus, a better understanding of the sixteenth century tendency to globalization, can lead one to conclude that the operative roles were distributed, each zone had a function and that mitigates the linearity of such notions as superiority, dependence, centre and periphery. Undoubtedly there existed leading roles, but around them, and interacting with them, there were supporting roles (that changed according to contexts and chronologies) performed by the Portuguese, Spanish, Dutch, Italian, English, French, and of course, the Indian, Malay, Chinese and Japanese merchants, without whom it was impossible to talk about a global trade, and a world economy. It is with this perspective that the DynCoopNet project gathers significance because it brings forth new interpretations and also introduces the theme of cooperative mechanisms—in fact the strategy that was adopted by the Portuguese individual merchants in Asia[74]—as the motor of the so-called 'First Global Age'.

Strategies of Cooperation

The history of Manuel Fernandes de Calvos, citizen of Porto born in Vila Nova de Gaia, is a good example of an emigrant's trajectory in India.[75]

This is a short account of a long life passed in the East Indies, which turned this man into a very successful trader. It is the story of a man who one day left his homeland and arrived in India where, after 43 years of a life dedicated to business (between 1549 and 1592), he died with the unofficial title of 'The Rich of Ormuz'. Porto's *Misericórdia* confraternity, inheritors of his huge fortune, never forgot him.

From his trajectory in the eastern seas one can recover facts that portray other lives, other livings, and varied practices of many others like him who prospered at their own cost by the paradigmatic mechanisms of intervention and by way of their own initiative.

Manuel Fernandes de Calvos was one of the seven children of Pedro Fernandes' first marriage with Isabel Anes, resident in Vila Nova de Gaia, situated on the south bank of the Douro River opposite Porto.[76] Calvos reached Goa in 1549 on board the ship *S. Boaventura* and enlisted with the company of D. Álvaro de Noronha, son of D. Garcia de Noronha who was the viceroy of India.[77] There is much information like this one in Porto's records: to attach dates and events to ships, armadas, battles and officers would be a guarantee for a correct service calculation and payment; and Calvos would have benefited from it since he was a soldier. Very soon he entered the service of D. Jorge Cabral, the governor. At his service he participated in the embassy Gaspar Correia entitled 'Interview with the Pepper King' in Chembe.[78] We do not know how long he stayed in the army; but probably not very long. Soon after he got involved in more peaceful enterprises, although his military career gave him knowledge about the land, markets, merchants, and perhaps also his first useful commercial contacts.

He moved to Ormuz where he became a frontiersman ('fronteiro')[79] and where he embraced mercantile activity. From Ormuz he travelled through Asia doing business in Goa, Cochin, Chaul (modern jurisdiction of Mumbai), in the Bay of Bengal, expanding his operations until he reached China. And he succeeded. His patrimony was composed, among others, of horses and stables, and a fortune of more than 1,00,000 *cruzados*.[80] He managed to gather such a large fortune by diversifying his activities; amid which moneylending was one of the most important. Money, as noted earlier, meant a lot in India's trade. Those who possessed cash to invest and to lend could earn good profits. Calvos was not alone in such dealings; among those who did the same was, for instance, Ferdinand Magellan, the circumnavigator and also a renowned moneylender in Cochin in the first decade of the century.[81] In a parallel move, Calvos dedicated himself to trade at the highest level: with Indian cloth in Asia and in Portugal,[82] and with spices, especially pepper.

By analysing Calvos' heritage we come to know what kind of commodities the merchants of Porto dealt with in India.[83] Besides slaves[84] and spices, they worked with high quality textiles, particularly silk fabrics and drapery and cotton tissues, precious stones, gold, silver, and jade jewellery, and also musk, presumably from China and Japan. Duarte Barbosa and Tomé Pires, chroniclers of the Portuguese expansion in Asian waters, and who travelled throughout Asia, reported the extreme rarity and high price of this last item.[85]

As discussed earlier, the Calvos businesses were spread all over an extensive geographical area, and they were made through an agent's network which would have been more than merely formal. There were ships at the service of this organization which were often crucial in succeeding in the Bay of Bengal trade;[86] at least there were two ships: one owned by Amador Tavares, a *ship*, and another possessed by António Ferreira, a *nau*.[87]

Among the members was Simão Leal *casado* (married, i.e. with the marriage arranged by the Portuguese authorities to a local Indian woman), settled in Goa, João Dias de Matos and Manuel da Silva, both from Ormuz, as well as António Fernandes and Gaspar do Vale, 'frontiersmen' in the same place. Tomé Braz was the itinerant merchant in-charge of commercial relations with China, and Bento da Veiga used to do the same throughout the Bay of Bengal until 'he was drowned in the *nau* of D. Diogo de Meneses coming from "Bengal"' with the Calvos' firm's merchandise. Fernão Machado Soares, from Barcelos in the Minho province, Luís Borges, resident in Vila Real in the Douro province, Domingos Ferreira, resident in Esgueira near Aveiro, and Domingos Ribeiro, who lived in Vila Nova de Gaia, used also to be members of the network before they returned to Portugal.[88] Perhaps the fact is relevant that amongst the Calvos employees (and relatives) there was one Venetian, Marcos de Melim[89] who married Calvos' daughter, and lived in Cyprus in the beginning of the seventeenth century.[90]

As in Europe, the support of State officials in India was indispensable to success; this network influenced some important officers who benefitted from loans they contracted with Calvos, like India's *alguazil* (officer in-charge of the fiscal accounts), and the Indian *reixarato* (with similar functions to those of the *alguazil* within one of the local states), both owing 1,000 *pardaus* to the company, and also with Simão da Costa, who was in debt of more than 11,000 *pardaus*.

Another way to succeed consisted in the use of influential institutions such as the *Misericórdias*. Organized in networks, running parallel to the Portuguese circuits of penetration in Asia, *Misericórdias* were a fundamental support for the Portuguese settlers/emigrants and very soon turned into effective political centres.[91] To integrate them and, more importantly, to administer them meant prestige, esteem and influence. The *Misericórdia* was ruled by a powerful *provedor* (i.e. a purveyor, administrator), mandatorily 'a noble brother of authority, prudence, temperance, virtue, reputation, and age, in such ways the rest of the brothers could recognize him as head of the institution'.[92] The case of Manuel Fernandes de Calvos, a man born into a family of merchants and seamen from Porto, who came to be *provedor* of the Ormuz *Misericórdia* for several years, can only be understood as an example of a social promotion and an influence gained through commerce. Incidentally, Calvos' situation was extremely similar to the success of Vicente Novais, already mentioned, who was also *provedor* and treasurer of the wealthy and powerful *Misericórdia* of Porto in the years 1569 to 1570, and again from 1575 to 1576.[93]

Misericórdias display a particular settlement pattern in Asia:'the *Misericórdias* began very soon to "travel" the paths of the expansion and the overseas business circuits. The rich legacies inherited from merchants in frantic motion throughout the Indian Ocean and South China Sea economies, forced the *Misericórdias* to perform intricate operations in favour of heirs placed in different areas of the overseas empire or for those waiting in the homeland for the fortunes gathered by their relatives overseas',[94] as took place with the Calvos legacies which were collected by the *Misericórdias* confraternities of Cochin, Chaul, Ormuz, Goa, Lisbon and Porto.[95]

Formal and Informal Financial Networks

Within the Asian mercantile complex, working parallel with the *Misericórdias* and other religious congregations like the Jesuits,[96] and articulated with them through their information and contact circuits, one must also mention the finance networks which were a fundamental support to the merchants' activities. Frequently, in Asian business, big transactions were largely dependent on the role performed by the banking houses from the most relevant financial centres: Lisbon, Porto, Madrid, Medina del Campo and Lyon. Through these trading and exchange centres there circulated the capital and the letters of exchange/credit which guaranteed the safety and the viability of the transactions. From the correspondence of the *Misericórdias* one gets an accurate evaluation of the factors at stake; for these informal schemes of trade organization the existence of merchant bankers willing to finance or support business was crucial. The amount of capital required, the risks, the distance, the regimes of trade participation, and later the competition of the Dutch and the English, sometimes discouraged investments; often simply because there was no money: 'pepper here and in Coulão is as much as straw', Rui Gonçalves de Caminha wrote; 'however', he added, 'money is very scarce and from Goa they only sent me 10,000 *pardaus* when I was expecting 30,000'. This led him to uncomfortable situations that revealed the weakness of a monarchy that had presented itself in India as powerful: 'when I arrived here', said Caminha, 'I found out that António Correia had asked the King of Cranganor for a loan of 6,000 *pardaus* and I blamed him very harshly because borrowing money from pagan kings is to reveal the needs of our lord King of Portugal'.[97]

The capital shortage was noted by the representatives of Porto's *Misericórdia* when they referred to the trouble of finding merchants capable of accepting money 'by letter as usual because of the risks there are in this Route'. Therefore, the informal channels and merchant-to-merchant relations were so important and are a subject that requires further research. The business was always lucrative despite all the risks when undertaken with proven safety measures, such as, the distribution of cargo in more than one ship. The correspondents had to decide whether it was better to send the money invested in merchandise, 'at risk', because 'even if some *naus* were lost, God forbid, the cargo of the ones that arrived safely would be more than enough to cover all the losses'. They were also advised to distribute insurance and merchandise by ships and merchants and told that they should not give more than 3,000 or 4,000 *pardaus* each.[98] In these circumstances it is important to emphasize the support provided by the financial firms from Lisbon and Porto represented by the Elvas and Anaia (or Anhaia) families from Lisbon, and Simão Vaz, Diogo Henriques or Melchior Mendes, from Porto. And, it is thanks to the intervention of these firms, their contacts, information channels, credit, money transfer, and exchange capabilities, that the commercial relations with India acquired the status of transactions integrated in networks dynamics.

Besides, the commercial contacts related to India kept in Porto's archives reveal this double facet of individual acts performed by individual and sometimes isolated agents that took advantage of their occupation as soldiers or sailors in the armadas, or else as emigrants, to deal on their own, carrying out small business operations or acting as 'representatives of people who have family in there',[99] or, in a different manner, acting as individual agents but benefiting from the organization of the informal networks on the ground.

The interpretation of this subject can be a little more accurate. At a first glance we come across individual merchants and informal networks. However, as informal they were, these networks existed and were radically interventionist in Asia. Whenever we come across a notary procuration one observes that there were always merchants and emigrants acting as someone's representatives in India and that they were recommended to someone settled there. Therefore, these documents reveal the constitution of mercantile and business associations,[100] looking after cooperation, providing mutual help, undertaking mediation strategies, in short, framing the organizational trade system by using the models they were accustomed to in Europe and in the Atlantic.

It is time to close this essay in the month of May in 1498, Vasco da Gama's armada anchored in front of Calicut. His ships were built in Porto, and some of his crew members were born in that same city. From that moment on, a new era of relations between Europe and Asia began, preparing for the emergence of a global trade. Born from a medieval context, the trade with Asia was dominated by luxury goods and spices, seen as special assets by the Iberian merchants. From this point of view the Portuguese India Route was very successful. Forcing their way up to the Indian Ocean trade networks, the Portuguese seized a vast quantity of commodities and then they moved into the European markets.

For a long time this process was interpreted as a result of imperialistic schemes planned in Europe. This interpretation, however, disregarded the individual/private nature of a good deal of the relations that took place through self-organized initiatives. In this essay, India is looked at from a European point of view, but by avoiding Eurocentric prejudicial conceptions. The essay attempted to offer a new perspective about the relations between the two continents.

From an Atlantic port with an Atlantic vocation and an Atlantic strategy, it was possible to evaluate how the Asian expansion influenced the life of its merchants. India, on the contrary, without any significant expression in terms of navigation and shipping dynamics, attracted numerous northern Portuguese emigrants. It is due to this emigration that we find those northern Portuguese men in every circuit, of an Indian Ocean port, alongside other Portuguese who chose the same destinations. Consequently, one comprehends that other projects existed beyond the ones promoted by the State. We also recognize the need to oppose cooperation strategies that seem to have been predominant to an imperial conception. And so, to the circuits generated by the Crown's factories and their representatives one must add individual initiative; the work of private men that generated multiple relations and multiple processes of mercantile intervention in which the middleman's function was of the utmost relevance. These allowed the middlemen to survive the troubles that adversely affected Portuguese presence in Asia.

From Porto's point of view, the Asian expansion revealed:

- the city's participation in the Cape Route logistics providing ships, provisions, and human resources;
- the reinforcement of the role of what we can call the merchant-entrepreneur;
- the promotion of the strategic connection between the Atlantic and the Indian Ocean systems;
- the development of emigration flows, the chronology of which is crucial to understanding their impact on Porto's society.

We must, however, be cautious about interpreting the extent of the effects, e.g. about the impact emigration had on Porto's dynamics. With the exception of the first decades of the sixteenth century, the impact on the local shipbuilding industry was insignificant.

Second, the Asian expansion never generated a shipping industry in Porto directed to Indian trade because the naval structures of the Cape Route were already in place at Lisbon.

Also, despite all the significant examples described in this essay, it is important to keep in mind the fact that the number of merchants who departed to Asia was insignificant when compared to the number of merchants committed to the Atlantic enterprise. Identical assertions can be made about the level of investment applied in the two trades.

Finally, fabulous fortunes were gathered in India and immense capital circulation was mention of throughout this essay, however it is necessary to keep in mind that both occurred at a private level. Therefore the impact on Porto's economy is impossible to assess at our present level of knowledge.

However some things are certain; when examining the hundreds of wills, heritages, legacies, donations, procurations, etc., we immediately perceive that India was very much present in the lives of a large group of people in a far away northern port. For many of them, India provided a way to ascend in the social scale. It is significant that the majority of those entitled 'fidalgos'[101] served in India or had relatives in India. However, there was also a group of more humble people who improved their way of life thanks to a parent, or a relative who returned wealthy from Asia, or who received an unexpected legacy from a long forgotten relative deceased in India.

In the sixteenth century many men from Porto crossed two oceans to find a better life in India. From elite members to simple workingmen, they usually ended up being involved in business and trading in all the Asian ports. And, by the resources they mobilized, the relations they generated, the exchanges they promoted, as well as by the extent of their commitments, they made a contribution to the construction of the global economy.

Appendix

Elite Members from Porto's Society in Sixteenth-Century India

Year	Name	Place	Function	Other	Observations
1500	Pero Vaz de Caminha	Calicut			
1512	Manuel de Castro Alcoforado		Captain	*Nau*	
1530	Fernão Camelo		Captain	*Nau* Santiago	
1537	Henrique Homem Carneiro				
	Tristão de Mesquita			*Nau* S. Roque	
1538	Manuel Carneiro				
	Diogo Pires de Figueiroa				
	Pero de Mesquita			*Nau* capitânea	Commanding ship of the fleet
	João Pires de Figueiroa			*Nau* S. Filipe	
1540	Álvaro Rodrigues de Azeredo	Bassein			
1548	João Martins Ferreira	Goa	Custom House Judge		
	António Monteiro			Macau	
1550	Fernão Álvares Cernache	Ormuz	Captain	Cananor	
1551	João de Caminha		Captain	*Armadas*	In several armadas
1553	Fernão Vieira				
1571	Duarte Carneiro Rangel		India's General Attorney		
1584	Matias Leite Pereira		Captain	*Nau*	
1597	Fernão de Valadares Carneiro			*Nau* S. João	
	Baltasar Carneiro				sixteenth century
	Miguel Carneiro				sixteenth century
	Vicente Carneiro				sixteenth century
	Frei António Brandão				sixteenth century
	Francisco Ferraz				sixteenth century
	Fernão Brandão	Chaúl	Captain		sixteenth century
	João Cirne				sixteenth century
	Gaspar de Andrade				sixteenth century
	Diogo de Sousa Soares				sixteenth century
	Francisco Soares de Albergaria	Cochin			Married Lucrécia de Figueiroa
	Francisco Carneiro				sixteenth century
	Jerónimo de Figueiroa				sixteenth century
	One sort of Cristóvão de Madureira				sixteenth century
	Bartolomeu da Rua Magriço				sixteenth century
	Gaspar Leite				sixteenth century
	Estêvão Pereira				sixteenth century
	Sebastião Leite				sixteenth century
	Rui de Pina				sixteenth century

(*Appendix contd.*)

APPENDIX (*continued*)

Year	*Name*	*Place*	*Function*	*Other*	*Observations*
	Cristóvão de Cernache				sixteenth century
	Gonçalo Vaz de Cernache	Moluccas			sixteenth century
	Diogo de Mesquita				sixteenth century
	One brother of Diogo de Mesquita				sixteenth century
	Another brother of Diogo de Mesquita				sixteenth century
	Baltasar Ferreira	Calicut			sixteenth century
	Brás Baião				sixteenth century
	Afonso Vaz de Caminha				sixteenth century
	João de Castro Pinheiro				Fryer João de Santo António
	Francisco de Sousa				sixteenth century
	Rui Mendes de Sousa	Chaúl			Married Jerónima de Meneses
	João de Sousa Alcoforado				sixteenth century
	One relative of Brandão Sanches				sixteenth century
	One relative of Brandão Sanches				sixteenth century
	Another relative of Brandão Sanches				sixteenth century
	Another relative of Brandão Sanches				sixteenth century
	Vasco Rebelo	Malacca	Crown Factor		sixteenth century
	António Rebelo Bravo	China		Macau	Married Antónia Nasi
	Miguel de Sousa Pimentel	Bassein	Captain		Married Maria Rebela
	Luís de Brito de Melo	Goa			Married Isabel Rebelo
	Vicente Novais				sixteenth century
	Belchior Malheiro				Married Catarina de Figueiroa
	Francisco da Rua				sixteenth century
	Luís de Valadares	Achin	Crown Factor		sixteenth century
	Luís Álvares de Madureira				Married with cousin
	Brás de Araújo		India's Commercial Delegate		Married Brites de Sousa
	Lourenço Mendes de Carvalho				sixteenth century
	Mateus Mendes de Carvalho		India's Chancellor		sixteenth century

(*Appendix contd.*)

APPENDIX (*continued*)

Year	*Name*	*Place*	*Function*	*Other*	*Observations*
	Gonçalo Leite	Ceylon			With Capt. Rui Vaz Pereira
	António Brandão Pereira	Moluccas	Captain	Monomotapa	sixteenth century
	Francisco Pereira de Miranda	Chaúl	Captain		Married Guiomar Pereira
	Francisco de Almeida	Ormuz	Captain		Married Isabel Brandão
	Frei Cristóvão de Cernache				sixteenth century
	Miguel de Castro Ferreira				sixteenth century
	Gonçalo Ribeiro Pinto	Cananor	Captain		Married Luísa de Paiva
	Cristóvão da Costa de Sá	Goa	Court's Judge		sixteenth century
	Fernão Martins de Sousa		Chaplain		sixteenth century

Source: Pedro de Brito, *Patriciado urbano Quinhentista: as famílias dominantes do Porto (1500–1580)*, Porto, 1997.

Notes

1. See the interpretation of this phenomenon in George Modelsky and William R. Thompson, *Seapower in Global Politics, 1914–93*, London: Macmillan, 1988.
2. See M.N. Pearson, *Spices in the Indian Ocean World*, Sydney: Ashgate/Varorium, 1996.
3. In this essay the expression *India* embraces all the regions between the Cape of Good Hope and the Filipinas and beyond, as it was used in Porto in the sixteenth century. The many articulations, routes, trades, and ways of facing trade are very well explained by Sanjay Subrahmanyam, *Comércio e conflito: A presença Portuguesa no Golfo de Bengala, 1500–1700*, Lisboa: Edições 70, 1994, pp. 9-11.
4. For instance, as a good documentary source to the mercantile activities study, giving notice about credit, investment, corporations, organization of trade, etc. A good example is provided by Amélia Polónia, *Vila do Conde um porto nortenho na expansão ultramarina quinhentista*, 2 vols., Porto: s.n. Ph.D. dissertation, 1999.
5. About these ports, see Amândio Barros, *Porto: a construção de um espaço marítimo nos alvores dos Tempos Modernos*, 2 vols., Porto: Faculdade de Letras, 2004; Amélia Polónia, *Vila do Conde*; Manuel A.F. Moreira, *O porto de Viana do Castelo na época dos descobrimentos*, Viana do Castelo: Câmara Municipal, 1984; Sara Pinto, *Caminha no século XVI: estudo sócio-económico, Dos que ganhão suas vidas sobre as águas*, Porto: Faculdade de Letras, 2009.
6. Amândio Barros, *Construção naval e cronologia das embarcações do Rio Douro*, Ílhavo: Musen Marítimo, 2009, pp. 84-7.
7. Between December 1483 and January 1484 King João II was in Porto where he observed the construction of a *nau* for the Duque of Bragança which he

would come to use when he ordered the stone transport from Porto during the opening of the Main Street of Lisbon. Iria Gonçalves, 'Uma realização urbanística medieval: o calcetamento da rua Nova de Lisboa', in *Um olhar sobre a cidade medieval*, Cascais: Patrimonia, 1996, pp. 127-8.

8. Recent research (for example Amândio Barros, Amélia Polónia, Leonor Freire Costa Augusto Salgado) proves that in the sixteenth century many ships started to be built in Porto or in Vila do Conde, and were finished in Lisbon for logistical motives or because of the financial incentives the king reserved for the shipbuilding industry.
9. See the history of this 400 ton ship in Quirino da Fonseca, *Os Portugueses no Mar*, Lisboa: Tipografia do Comercio, 1926, pp. 227-30. It is both necessary and desirable that we are aware of an important detail about the commands of these ships because it also gives us information about the port's involvement in this history of commercial and naval contacts. One of the captains of this ship since 1506 was João da Nova, whose origins were in Galicia and whose family was living in Porto for a long time. There are other similar cases.
10. Ibid., pp. 182-4.
11. Ibid., pp. 219-20.
12. About these ships' specifications, see Francisco C. Domingues, 'Os navios de Cabral', in *Oceanos*, no. 39 (July-September 1999), pp. 70-80, and *Os navios dos Descobrimentos*, Lisboa, 1991.
13. The first reference to medieval *caravels* appear in the Vila Nova de Gaia (in front of Porto) municipal chart of 1255. About the *caravel* and its significance for the Portuguese discoveries, see Francisco C. Domingues, *Os navios dos Descobrimentos*.
14. Amândio Barros, *Porto: a construção de um espaço marítimo*, pp. 236, 578.
15. For instance, the presence of João de Braga, in India since the first expedition of Vasco da Gama; he was involved in the construction of the da Gama ships; then there was his son-in-law João Álvares, who died in India, and António de Braga who died during the return trip to Portugal (1512) after a service commission in the Goa shipyard. Arquivo Distrital do Porto (Porto's District Archive), *Contadoria da Comarca do Porto*, liv. 2 (0007), fls. 196-196v.
16. Which was noted, amongst others, by A.G. Frank, *World Accumulation, 1492–1789*, New York: Monthly Review Press, 1978, pp. 37–8. In the works of Barros, and Polónia that have been referred to, particular attention is devoted to these 'knowledge circulation networks' particularly lively in the northern Portuguese shipyards.
17. Torre do Tombo (Portugal's National Archive), *Gavetas*, XV, maço 18, doc. 13. Referred to in Leonor F. Costa, *Naus e galeões na Ribeira de Lisboa. A construção naval no século XVI para a Rota do Cabo*, Cascais: Patrimonia, 1997, p. 140.
18. Arquivo Distrital do Porto, *Po1º*, 3ª série, liv. 2, fl. 106v.
19. Ibid., liv. 31, fl. 22-22v.
20. *Os Descobrimentos e a economia mundial*, III, Lisboa, 1987, pp. 53-69.
21. Luciano Ribeiro, *Registo da Casa da Índia*, vol. I, Lisboa, 1954, p. 23.
22. The names of these ships use the name of their owners, a common practice in the maritime world of that time. They went to India in the same armada where

the referred *nau do Porto* was, or in the next year's armada; Torre do Tombo, *Gavetas*, XV, maço 18, doc. 13.

23. Arquivo Histórico Municipal do Porto (Porto's Historical Archive), *Livro do despacho das naus*, fls. 24-24v.
24. The enterprise was very expensive, and there was always the possibility of using the State logistics.
25. In fact, we know that the two Alvo brothers stayed in India for some years after that date. Manuel Bravo would have died in the return trip to Portugal, perhaps in the same ship, Arquivo Distrital do Porto, *Po1º*, 3ª série, liv. 76, fls. 45-46.
26. Arquivo Distrital do Porto, *Po2º*, 1ª série, liv. 5, fls. 183v-185. The Bravo were Porto's merchants; the more distinguished maybe were António Gonçalves Bravo, already dead by this time, and Hércules Bravo. They had a relative, António Rebelo Bravo, who was deeply involved in the commercial route between Malacca and China, associated, since 1585, with Manuel Ribeiro, from Vila do Conde; Arquivo Distrital do Porto, *Po1º*, 3ª série, liv. 77, fl. 91v.
27. At first, those soldiers were prepared to depart to the northern African garrisons with the king, and as the plans changed it was decided to send them in a 'crusade against the Turks'; finally they embarked on the India's armadas. Arquivo Histórico Municipal do Porto, *Provisões*, liv. 1, fl. 8.
28. Arquivo Histórico Municipal do Porto, *Provisões*, liv. 1, fl. 339. In the mind of the shipowners there was no such thing as 'spare sailors'; many times these men simply refused to embark and deserted. About the armadas' recruitment problems, see Eulália Paulo; Paulo Guinote, *Problemas de recrutamento para as armadas da* 'Carreira da Índia', available at <www.nautarch.tamu.edu/shiplab/index>.
29. Curiously, these slaughterhouses were functioning in the place where the old early medieval galley arsenals were located.
30. In 1501 the municipal rulers refused to deliver meat suppliers to the owners of the newly built *nau Leitoa*, even if one of them, Afonso Leitão, was a citizen of Porto, with the excuse that there was not enough meat available, and the existent few were for the city's consumption. This attitude can be in part explained by the relative lack of interest in this new route, when there were more tested and profitable circuits like the ones which directed the city's ships to northern Europe, mainly Flanders. See Arquivo Histórico Municipal do Porto, *Vereações*, liv. 7, fol. 98.
31. Francisco Ribeiro da Silva, *O Porto e o seu termo (1580–1640): Os homens, as instituições e o poder*, vol. I, Porto, 1988, p. 204.
32. And also military history since it provides information about naval engagements.
33. Luís F.R. Thomaz, *De Ceuta a Timor*, Lisboa, 1998, p. 205.
34. For example, see the amount, quality, and diversity of the services accomplished in the Eastern Indies by the various Sá family members, which was an elitist family in Porto since the Middle Ages, in Luciano Ribeiro, *Registo da Casa da Índia*, vol. II, Lisboa, 1955, p. 81.
35. And Couto said that they are so brave defending the land, that he would not spare paper to write about them; Diogo do Couto, *Década 8ª da Ásia*, vol. I, ed. Maria Augusta Lima Cruz, Lisboa, 1993, p. 34.

36. In which, as we saw, the city's participation occurred in the first years of the sixteenth century as far as the supply of ships is concerned.
37. See the appendix to this essay about Porto's elite participation in the Indian trade complex.
38. Charles R. Boxer, *O império colonial Português (1415–1825)*, Lisboa, 1981, pp. 77, 153-4. This interpretation contradicts, or at least mitigates, A.G. Frank's opinion according to which the Dutch installed an effective monopoly in the Indian Ocean. Porto's records seem to be in concord with Boxer's view. See Frank, *World Accumulation,* p. 86.
39. The Crown, as we know, was always in difficulty keeping those investments, and in most times depended on loans from external and internal investors to survive in the exchange game.
40. K.N. Chaudhuri, *The Trading World of Asia and the English East India Company, 1660–1760*, Cambridge: Cambridge University Press, 1978, pp. 204-5.
41. Albuquerque was, perhaps, the greatest dreamer of them all.
42. Referred by Luís F.R. Thomaz, *De Ceuta a Timor*, p. 223. Reis Thomaz believes that the last two were incompatible with the project of absolute control of trade and navigation planned by the Crown (which I think gives proof of the intense work done by private merchants who embraced that identity to succeed). He also thinks that even the adoption of naval policies, such as the 'cartazes' regime (licences granted by the Portuguese authorities to 'friendly' ships), which certificated the origin of ships, was determined by that same structural incompatibility.
43. Francisco Bethencourt, 'A administração da Coroa', in *Nova História da Expansão*, vol. 1, Lisboa: Circulo de Leitores, 1998, p. 394.
44. Maria Emília Madeira Santos, 'Afonso de Albuquerque e os feitores', in *II Seminário Internacional de História Indo-Portuguesa*, ed. Luís de Albuquerque and Inácio Guerreiro, Lisboa: Instituto de Investigação Cientifica e Tropical/Centro de Estudos de Historia e Cartografia Antiga, 1985, pp. 201-26.
45. Joaquim R. Magalhães, 'Açúcar e especiarias', in *Nova História da Expansão*, vol. 1, p. 305.
46. Luís F.R. Thomaz, *De Ceuta a Timor*, p. 201.
47. Joaquim R. Magalhães, 'Articulações internacional-regionais e economias-mundo', in *Nova História da Expansão*, vol. 1, pp. 327 e 331.
48. We do not know yet if they were opposite or complementary.
49. That means: of the Crown. The chroniclers' references and this statement are in his excellent work *Os Descobrimentos e a economia mundial*, vol. III, Lisboa, 1987, p. 133.
50. Joaquim Romero Magalhães, *Nova História da Expansão*, vol. 1, p. 333. Reis Thomaz refers that to elude the state surveillance, especially in times when the strategies of control were weak, 'a great number of small Portuguese traders chose to abandoned the Portuguese hubs and established themselves beyond official range', trying to be fortunate in ports and territories less affected by the royal monopolies, and also to escape the license system attribution, which was always a matter of discontent. See, Thomaz, *De Ceuta a Timor*, p. 230.
51. *De Ceuta a Timor*, pp. 174–5.

52. Amélia Polónia, *Vila do Conde*, I, Porto, 1999, p. 634.
53. 'Which then [the silver bars from the New Spain colonial mining] were either delivered to royal mints for assaying, taxation, and coinage or clandestinely from the producing colony'. Stanley J. Stein; Barbara H. Stein, *Silver, Trade, and War: Spain and America in the Making of Early Modern Europe*, Baltimore and London, 2000, pp. 22-3. One possibility to explain the huge difference between the registered silver and the actual amount entered through merchant's channels in the early seventeenth century, offered by Morineau, is simply 'massive under-registry, so extraordinary fraudulent, it was no longer fraud'; Michel Morineau, *Incroyables gazettes et trésors merveilleux: Les retours des trésors américains d'après les gazettes holandaises (XVIe-XVIIIe siècles)*, London, 1985, pp. 238, 267, Table 44, cited by Stein and Stein, p. 25.
54. The arrival of the 'new silver' in the Indian Ocean at the end of the sixteenth century had a great impact on the Asian economy; one of the consequences was the significant 'production frontiers enlargement' and the other was, inclusively, the population growth. See Dennis O. Flynn, *World Silver and Monetary History in the 16th and 17th centuries*, Aldershot: Ashgate/Varorium Press, 1996.
55. Arquivo Distrital do Porto, *Po1º*, 3ª série, liv. 6, fl. 94.
56. Ibid., liv. 8, fls. 17-18v.
57. His brother, António da Silva, remained in India in 1572. Novais was there before 1548. About his Atlantic business services, see for example, Arquivo Distrital do Porto, *Po1º*, 3ª série, liv. 21, fls. 144v-146v.
58. Ibid., liv. 14, fl. 34.
59. Ibid., liv. 100, fls. 58v-62v.
60. See the excellent interpretation given by Luke Clossey, 'Merchants, migrants, missionaries, and globalization in the early-modern Pacific', in *Journal of Global History*, vol. 1, London, 2006, pp. 41–58.
61. About this subject, see Dennis O. Flynn and Arturo Giráldez, 'Born with a "Silver Spoon": The Origin of World Trade in 1571', in *Journal of World History*, vol. 6, no. 2, University of Hawai'i Press, 1995, p. 201.
62. Arquivo Distrital do Porto, *Po1º*, 3ª série, liv. 14, fls. 70–71.
63. Ibid., liv. 50, fl. 117v. Some of these cases are related to the elite's involvement in the Cape Route. For those who started by serving in the military or in the administration and then moved to trade; this involvement in trade was always very connected with the city's commercial dynamics. This can be noticed by the numerous exchange and payment letters at various points of the empire. Porto even had a permanent representative Manuel Leitão in the 'House of India', to deal with the business related to Asia, all of those mentioned here had dealings with him.
64. About the importance of Portuguese slave supplying activities to Spanish America's mining regions, see Stanley J. Stein; Barbara H. Stein, *Silver, Trade, and War*, p. 36.
65. Porto's intervention in 'Maluco' started earlier and meant a lot. Already in 1535 is documented the presence of a Porto merchant, Belchior Pais, in the 'clove islands' promoting the connection between Malacca (he was clerk secretary

in the Malacca factory), Goa (he had business with several merchants sited there), Patan, Borneo, and Maluco. Belchior Pais can be considered one of the pioneers of this new maritime route promoted by the Portuguese from 1525. See A. de Magalhães Basto, *História da Santa Casa da Misericórdia do Porto*. 2nd edn, vol. I, Porto, 1997, pp. 378-79. About the new 'clove route' called the 'voyage through the Borneo path', see F. Thomaz, *De Ceuta a Timor*, p. 556; see also the chapter 'Maluco e Malaca' in the same book, pp. 537-65.

66. In a letter from Maluco (8 June 1531) the arrival of a ship 'of your Highness returned from Banda with clove, and for captain came Dinis de Paiva because in Banda rested Aníbal Cernige that had been send there from Maluco' is referred to in *As gavetas da Torre do Tombo*, vol. VII, Lisboa: Centro de Estudos Históricos Ultramarinos, 1968. With the Cernige it is also possible to talk about a network of influence, which is very interesting given that one of Anibal's brothers, Jerónimo Cernige, was archpriest in the Lisbon Cathedral; Arquivo Distrital do Porto, *Po1°*, 3ª série, liv. 14, fl. 148.
67. This treaty ended the dispute raised by Magellan's circumnavigation. The information I mentioned reveals that Aníbal Cernige was the commander of the first Portuguese expedition to the Moluccas after the treaty was signed. Cernige was a great promoter of one of Porto's maritime neighbourhoods, Massarelos. He was prominent in a very interesting meeting in which were present all the neighbours living in Massarelos, including seamen and fishermen who protested against impositions ordered by Porto's Customs House; Cernige, a noble, was the lord of the place. See Arquivo Distrital do Porto, *Po1°*, 3ª série, liv. 14, fls. 147-148v.
68. Ward Barrett, '"World Bullion Flows", 1450–1800', in *The Rise of Merchant Empires: Long-Distance Trade in the Early Modern World, 1350–1750*, ed. James D. Tracy, Cambridge, 1990, pp. 225, 245-7.
69. See A. de Magalhães Basto, *História da Santa Casa*, vol. I, p. 455; Arquivo Distrital do Porto, *Po1°*, 3ª série, liv. 41, fl. 193 and, Arquivo Distrital do Porto, *Po1°*, 3ª série, liv. 41, fl. 198.
70. Immanuel Wallerstein, *O sistema mundial moderno*, 3 vols., Porto, 1974–99.
71. Frank, *World Accumulation*, p. 37; *Asian-based world economy 1400–1800: A horizontally integrative macrohistory*, Amsterdam, 1995, and *ReORIENT: Global economy in the Asian Age*, Berkeley: University of California Press, 1998. See the reassessment of Frank's thoughts in Ricardo Duchesne, 'Between Sinocentrism and Eurocentrism: debating Andre Gunder Frank's *ReOrient*: Global Economy in the Asian Age', *Science & Society*, vol. 65, issue 4, Winter 2001, pp. 428-63.
72. This is a very debatable judgement; in fact, almost all of Wallerstein's chapter about the Portuguese presence in Asia is, at least, very arguable. See, Wallerstein, *O sistema mundial moderno*, vol. I, pp. 318-33.
73. They even failed to seize some Portuguese posts in Asia; for instance in the minor Sunda Islands the local communities offered them strong resistance; and, in other places 'the Dutch were not very pleased when they realized that the Indian merchants were more favourable to the Portuguese than to any other nation' as happened with the pearl catchers of Tuticorim, which allowed the

Portuguese to maintain a very interesting position in the trade. See Charles R. Boxer, *O império colonial Português*, pp. 120-1, 130-5.

74. That seems to have been much more effective than any other hypothetically imperial project that, in India never occurred before the mid-eighteenth century.
75. The essentials of Manuel Fernandes de Calvos' biography were analysed by Eugénio de Andrea da Cunha Freitas, *História da Santa Casa da Misericórdia do Porto*, vol. III, Porto: Santa Casa da Misericórdia, 1995, pp. 7–47. There are those that I will follow in this chapter.
76. Arquivo Distrital do Porto, *Po1º*, 3ª série, liv. 63, fls. 98v–100v. This document reveals very useful information which is repeatedly mentioned in several records. It is referred that it had been 25 years since Calvos had left for India, and nobody knew 'if he was dead or alive'—for his family he was presumably dead. Another 15 years would pass before the family knew something about him (in fact, they only received the news of his death and legacy). It is easy to understand that this kind of situation could have tremendous consequences for the existence of the relatives who remained at home.
77. The armada was also composed by the *naus S. Bento* and *Zambuco* (or *Santa Cruz*), and the *Burgalesa*, the last was lost. The *Zambuco* would sink later with sailors and emigrants from Porto. See *Relação das naus e armadas da Índia*, ed. Maria Hermínia Maldonado, Coimbra, 1985, pp. 61-2.
78. Gaspar Correia, *Lendas da Índia*, vol. IV, p. 736.
79. About the notion of *fronteiro*, from which derived the *casado* condition, see Sanjay Subrahmanyam; Luís F.R. Thomaz, 'Evolution of empire: The Portuguese in the Indian Ocean during the sixteenth century', in *The Political Economy of Merchant Empires*, Cambridge, 1991, p. 298.
80. He left to Porto's *Misericórdia* more than one hundred and fifty thousand *cruzados*.
81. Amândio Barros, *A naturalidade de Fernão de Magalhães revisitada*, Porto, ed. Afrontamento, 2009.
82. The records discuss the *business of the lanios*, i.e. of wool textiles.
83. Which were, mainly, commercialized in Lisbon, the pivotal port of the Indian Route trade, although a part of it, a small one, could sometimes reach Porto and other northern Portuguese ports. *See Nova História da Expansão*, vol. I, pp. 321-9. See also Artur T. de Matos, 'Some aspects of the Portuguese trade in the Malabar Coast: Cochim and the "mercadorias meudas"', *Indica*, vol. 26, nos. 1-2, 1989, pp. 93–102.
84. There are a few references to 'slaves from India' bought by emigrants in Goa or Malacca, or even from China, these were referred to as 'Indians from China'.
85. José Manuel Vargas, 'Almíscar', in *Dicionário de História dos Descobrimentos*, vol. I, Lisboa, 1994, pp. 56-7. In 1592 a round *caravel* called *Assunção* arrived in Porto; it was said she returned from Mina (west coast of Africa) but it is possible she had returned from India; she brought slaves, gold (which in fact are commodities from Africa), and musk, and then went to Lisbon (to the House of India, which

was also ('Mina and India warehouse') from where she was chartered in favour of India's contractor João Baptista Rovellasca. See Arquivo Distrital do Porto, *Cabido*, *Sentenças*, liv. 768, fls. 297–306.

86. In a letter to D. Álvaro de Castro (5 December 1547), Pedro de Ataíde regrets the failure of an expedition to the Bay of Bengal which he considers was caused by the lack of adequate number of ships. See *Colecção S. Lourenço*, vol. II, Preface and notes by Elaine Sanceau, Lisboa, 1975, p. 27.
87. And, as mentioned, also the *nau* of one of India's governors D. Diogo de Meneses, was used by this company until she sunk. The ship of Tavares needed an anchor which was paid for by the firm, and while *nau* of Ferreira caused a lawsuit after Calvos' death.
88. One of Calvos' brothers, Brás de Calvos was also an emigrant in India where he died; we don't know if he ever crossed with his brother or if he ever worked for him in Asia. See Arquivo Distrital do Porto, *Po1º*, 3ª série, liv. 63, fl. 99.
89. Or Lomelim, which is the Portuguese way to refer to Lomelini. However, this is the name normally attributed to the Genoese (there is an important banker-merchant family with this name; they operated in Portugal); the long distance and the years between the facts (this was a piece of a court process lasting more than 20 years after Calvos' death) could explain some of the blurry details and mistakes.
90. *História da Santa Casa da Misericórdia*, vol. 3, p. 30.
91. The more important ones of Cochim and Goa started to be founded since the beginning of the sixteenth century; an extensive roll of more than 20 followed. See Laurinda Abreu, 'O papel das Misericórdias dos "lugares de além-mar" na formação do Império Português', in *História, Ciência, Saúde: Manguinhos*, vol. VIII, no. 3, September-December 2001, pp. 591–611, and the excellent synthesis by Isabel dos Guimarães Sá, *Quando o rico se faz pobre: misericórdias, caridade e poder no Império Português*, Lisboa: CNCDP, 1997.
92. Ivo Carneiro de Sousa, 'As Misericórdias de Lisboa a Manila: Muito poder e alguma caridade', in *Campus Social*, no. 2, Lisboa, 2005, p. 116.
93. *História da Santa Casa da Misericórdia*, vol. II, pp. 419, 478. It should be mentioned that he was engaged in a business in the Atlantic (buying and selling sugar) involving the considerable amount of one million Portuguese *reais*; Arquivo Distrital do Porto, *Po1º*, 3ª série, liv. 80, fls. 93–95.
94. Ivo Carneiro de Sousa, *As Misericórdias de Lisboa a Manila*, pp. 116-17.
95. In the one of Cochim there were 28,000 *pardaus*, in that of Ormuz, 40,000 *pardaus*; the money (another amount remained in the Goa *Misericórdia*) would be sent to the *misericórdia* of Lisbon, where the brothers of Porto would collect them. See *História da Santa Casa da Misericórdia do Porto*, op. cit., vol. III, p. 7.
96. In the records collected to support this essay there are 24 references to the interventions of the *misericórdias*, 6 to Jesuits, 1 to Franciscans, and 9 attributed to 'religions'.
97. Letter of 6 December 1547, *Colecção São Lourenço*, pp. 96, 100.
98. All this information is available in *História da Santa Casa da Misericórdia*, vol. III, pp. 18–20. In a certain way, this is an adaptation of the mid-sixteenth century

Venetian merchant Andrea Berengo's thoughts, whose correspondence was published by Ugo Tucci in which he recommended to trust in God but, at the same time, a good insurance contract.

99. Which is a reality in almost every northern European port; see Amélia Polónia, *Vila do Conde*, p. 634.

100. There are numerous examples of people from Porto and northern Portuguese ports moving between Portugal and India as a result of these procurations: Arquivo Distrital do Porto, *Po1º*, 3ª série, liv. 1, fl. 129v, Gaspar de Sequeira, António Mendes and Cristóvão Mendes, who were Vicente Novais' cousins, got procuration to take care of his business in India; Arquivo Distrital do Porto, *Po1º*, 3ª série, liv. 13, fl. 94, Álvaro Mendes, a merchant from the maritime neighbourhood of Miragaia was always in contact with India thanks to his brothers-in-law, António, Afonso and Gonçalo Gil, 9 years after he had returned from India; Arquivo Distrital do Porto, *Po1º*, 3ª série, liv. 43, fl. 160, business between Gaspar Nunes Barreto, António Lobo and Estêvão Gonçalves de Bulhão, ended in court in 1572; Arquivo Distrital do Porto, *Po1º*, 3ª série, liv. 96, fl. 122v, Simião Pinto, stepson of Filipe da Silva, Porto's citizen, recommended this one to the heirs of his brother António da Silva, in India in 1590 (a procuration that he renewed in 1595, adding his son Duarte Mendes de Vasconcelos, who was ready to depart to Asia), proving that the family ties and commercial relations were very connected; Arquivo Distrital do Porto, *Po1º*, 3ª série, liv. 105, fl. 14v.

101. A sort of 'noble' rank attributed to the city's bourgeois elite.

PART III

Other Networks
Military, Scientific and Terrestrial

CHAPTER FIVE

The French Military Network in the Service of the Portuguese in India

Ernestine Carreira

ALTHOUGH THE GLORIOUS MARITIME past of Portugal is often recognized, one hardly questions the conditions of the survival of its empire over the centuries.

After the famous trip of Vasco da Gama, who arrived in India via the Cape of Good Hope in 1498, in a few decades the Portuguese succeeded in not only monopolizing the shipping between the Atlantic and the Indian Ocean but also in dominating the waters of the Asian seas from the Persian Gulf to Japan, and in creating a network of big trading posts in which the most famous were Ormuz (Persia), Goa (India), Malacca (Malaysia), and Macau (China).

Portugal and its empire came under Spanish domination in 1580 and were not liberated until 1640, thanks to the help received from the French state, and then from the British Crown. The fight for independence in Europe mobilized all sorts of means and energies. The new king D. João IV was unable to prevent the Dutch from conquering his entire overseas territories. He then chose to save the Atlantic, and succeeded in re-conquering Brazil. João IV occupied it for several years, as well as the

Angolan coast, which was the usual reservoir of slave labour for the American plantations.

On the other hand, the sovereign had neither the troops nor the necessary financial means to save the eastern empire, which was going to sink rapidly. Between 1640 and the end of 1660, the area of the Cape of Good Hope, the majority of the Indian ports, Ceylon, the rich islands of Sumatra, Java, and Malacca, along with the trading posts of Japan, were lost to Portugal and passed under the domination of Batavia. The British, present in the Indian Ocean since the beginning of the century, helped the Shah of Persia expel the Portuguese from Ormuz (before obtaining the latter by a treaty signed in 1661). They had also succeeded in obtaining Tangier (Morocco) and Bombay (India) in exchange for military protection to the Portuguese, which however never materialized. Neither did the military help, offered by the English under the terms of the treaty, to enable the Portuguese to reconquer the Indian ports lost to the Dutch. Therefore, Bombay was lost to the Portuguese and neither did the promised military help materialize from the English side.[1]

Even worse, from a commercial point of view, the expansion of the port of Bombay quickly relegated the port of Goa to a secondary, indeed marginal, position. In Africa, the Muslim reaction against the presence of the Portuguese came from the Sultanate of Oman, causing them to lose the entire coastal zone to the north of Cape Delgado, and in particular, the flourishing port of Mombassa, the centre of ivory and slave exchange. Simultaneously, in India, the creation of the Maratha Empire in 1739 brought to the Marathas the very rich *Província do Norte*, the coastal zone between Bombay and Daman, which represented a rice storehouse/granary and which had been in the possession of the Portuguese beyond the Cape of Good Hope. The former 'Magestoso Estado da Índia', the 'sub-empire', whose jurisdiction formally extended from the Indian Ocean to the Sea of Japan, was then reduced to three small territories in India (the ports of Goa, Daman, and Diu—which were hardly 800 sq. km. in extent), a coastal strip in East Africa (what was later to be Mozambique), a port in Macau, and the islands of Timor and Solor, although the western part of Timor was occupied by the Dutch from the beginning of the eighteenth century.

The sub-empire struggled to find a political balance and a relative economic agreement, a process commencing from the return of peace in Europe and the end of the hostilities in India in the 1670s, the loss of Mombassa, then the *Província do Norte*, and in 1752, the management of East Africa, the true colony of Goa over the centuries. From the middle of the eighteenth century, its governors were forced to entirely restructure the military and economic organization of what remained of the *Estado*. In order to survive against the other European nations and the Indian states, the

Estado now endeavoured to become a regional 'Asiatic' and continental power rather than remain a European maritime power in the East, thanks to the skilful policy of territorial conquests around Goa, from which they would eventually quadruple the extent of their territory between 1744 and 1788.[2] At that moment, Portugal was flourishing, thanks to the exploitation of the mineral and agricultural richness of Brazil. Furthermore, the Crown provided the required means: men, material, and money for the realization of these projects, not counting a favourable political evolution in the Indian subcontinent.

It is at this time that one should note the presence of an important French military group in the service of the *Estado*. They contributed to the formation of the army, made use of skills their Portuguese fellow-members did not have, intervened successfully at the time of decisive expeditions, and sometimes managed to be integrated into the higher ranks of the Goan military hierarchy.[3] The term 'French' is used here to describe not only people of French nationality but also the descendants of French families settled in Portugal or Asia, who had acquired Portuguese nationalities for professional reasons.[4]

The collapse of Portugal's navy and the growth of the maritime might of the remarkably well equipped European powers are documented but Portuguese historians still neglect the history of the armed forces in favour of the navy, which was indeed more spectacular. Nonetheless, this does not clarify what became of the Portuguese East after the seventeenth century.

Service of the Empire

Contrary to a well known fact concerning the other Asian and European states at that time in India, the French soldiers of the *Estado* were very seldom deserters or refugees in the French establishments, mercenaries grouped in 'partis' to serve the highest bidder.[5] The majority of the officers came from Portugal where they had often served lengthy military careers.

Their presence in Goa continued a tradition founded in the seventeenth century. In order to face Spanish hostility, João IV signed with France the treaty of 7 September 1655 by which the latter undertook to provide troops, artillery officers, and war material to the new Portuguese army.[6] In 1666, his successor D. Afonso VI married a French princess, Marie-Francoise of Savoy, entrusted by Louis XIV to counter the British influence in Lisbon to the advantage of the French. Gradually a small influential military community formed around the young queen.

Her success initiated a big wave of arrivals after the War of Succession in Spain. Indeed, the warmongering policy of the Sun King had enabled the French army not only to employ nearly all of the noble candidates, but also obliged them to promote locals to the rank of officers. After the death of Louis XIV, there followed a series of restrictive measures which limited the recruitment of nobles.[7] To this discrimination was added the mediocre pay given to the minor nobility who, most of the time, occupied secondary ranks (lower than that of Captain). A few, who were badly neglected, tried their luck in the colonies or other European countries.

However, this option coincided with a high demand for qualified Portuguese professionals. The new sovereign, D. João V, rich, thanks to the revenues from the gold mines freshly discovered in Brazil, wished to modernize his army, which required the creation of a corps of officers familiar with the new techniques of combat and artillery. Compared to France, Portugal had not invested in training schools and so the foreign officers were welcome.[8] Several young nobles and a few well-trained locals, with no career prospects back home or hope of acquiring a fortune in their homeland, now found room for their ambitions and generally ended up by settling permanently in their host country.[9]

The service to the Crown also being seen as service to its empire, some were requested, others volunteered, to join postings in Brazil or India. Most chose the first option on account of personal enrichment and Brazil's relative geographic proximity to Europe. Service in Africa was hardly ever an option, and in fact often the consequence of a disciplinary measure. To my knowledge, no French officer was sent to East Africa in the eighteenth century. Only a few Italian volunteers worked there.

The *Estado* and its Army

While the presence of French officers in Goa was effective from the end of the seventeenth century, they acquired significant importance only after 1740, at the time of the organization of an army, which was indispensable for the survival of the *Estado*, as well as for safeguarding its conquests.

Until the close of the seventeenth century, the navy was capable of defending the various territories because danger had always approached from the sea. The viceroys had a free hand in managing their armadas. The ships were manufactured in Bassein or Daman, thanks to the vast teak forests in the upcountry, and Portugal provided equipment and artillery.[10] In the beginning of the eighteenth century, in spite of catastrophic territorial losses, these armadas continued to dominate the other European fleets and countered coastal piracy on this western coast of India.

The emergence of the Maratha Empire created a historical break for the *Estado*. Due to the loss of the North, the Portuguese were deprived of shipbuilding areas and the Maratha progress in Goa at the end of 1730 required an urgent land response. The authorities of Goa were forced to conceive of a new defence system and finally opted for the constitution of a land army.

In fact, according to Charles Ralph Boxer, until the emergence of Maratha power from the 1660s, no one had ever formed regular troops in Goa. There were merely small units, called 'companies', which were mobilized or demobilized depending upon the circumstances.[11] The latter were composed of deported or exiled Europeans with an unsavoury reputation, ready to desert, and even to join the enemy! The recruitment of local volunteers hardly enhanced career prospects due to the discriminatory rights and regulations in force until the 1760s: only metropolitan promotions were favoured rather than those of the Christian Indians and the Luso-descendants (Eurasians). The Indian troops of neighbouring princes dependent upon the Portuguese also helped them occasionally, but they demanded high salaries for their services and the *Estado* did not always have the means.[12] When there was danger, generally the Christian inhabitants (militia) and the religious monks of the numerous convents were mobilized.

The first regiment of the infantry, later known as *regimento velho* was created only in 1671. The king sent the French captain Pierre Joseph du Verge as counsellor for its organization; the latter died in Goa in 1697. But, due to the lack of means, this military formation remained in an embryonic form for a long time while the Maratha army, on the contrary was equipped with munitions, the same as the Europeans, due to the covert supplies of European material provided by the East India Company.[13] This disparity was one of the major causes of the fall of the North.

Still unaware of the disaster, Portugal finally ended up reacting to the desperate appeals for help sent by the Goan authorities. In 1740, they dispatched substantial reinforcements: six warships and four battalions of veterans as well as artillery. The expedition arrived far too late to rescue the North, but constituted the base of its new army, and substantially reinforced the manoeuvring capacity of the regiment.[14] From 1742 to 1746, the regiment passed under the command of one of the most dynamic and experienced veterans from Lisbon, Louis de Pierrepont,[15] who completely reorganized it with the Viceroy's support. Its European manpower of the pre-war period was maintained (approximately 1,000 men divided into small infantry companies and grenadiers), but the new financial means enabled 1,000 *sepoys* and a cavalry company to join the regiment.[16] Modernization, which then affected all the European armies, also followed here: from 1746 to 1752, two artillery companies (150 men) were entrusted to the engineer Christophe de Saint Martin.[17] Soon, the strategic position of the Portuguese saw an alteration. The latter passed from a series of humiliating defeats to some glorious conquests against the neighbouring princes, allies of the

Marathas. The most famous conquest was that of the powerful Alorna Fortress where, in 1744, the major part of the attack was carried out by Pierrepont and Saint Martin. This victory guaranteed to the Portuguese not only the border-security of the Bardez Province, but also ensured the pacification of hostilities on the trade route between Goa and its mountainous up-land (the Ghats).[18] This was a source of worry for the Marathas as well as the British, but it especially impressed Dupleix, the then French Governor in India, who noticed the revival of Portuguese power in India and, on several occasions, tried to convince the directors of the French East India Company to negotiate an alliance treaty with Goa.

Significantly, it was back in Portugal that this achievement, advantageously publicized by the Crown, had the biggest impact. In military circles, people started believing in the possibility of career prospects and enrichment in India. The example of Louis de Pierrepont—who was rewarded with lifetime revenue, and with the military command of the Salcette Province this added to a significant promotion—gave rise to more than one ambition. Hence, at the end of 1740, about 10 young French soldiers, infantry or artillery experts, arrived in Goa.

The Continental Intervention

The accession to power of Marquis de Pombal (1756-77), the chief minister of King D. José I, initiated a new phase in the military history of the *Estado*. At that time, India was going through great upheavals, punctuated by significant international conflicts, which led to the beginning of the decline of the Maratha Empire in north India, and the emergence of the Empire of Mysore, which dominated the south from the 1760s. In 1761, the European situation had also undergone major changes since the fall of the French in India. Despite the restitution of French trading posts in 1765, the influence of the English East India Company continued to grow. On the verge of bankruptcy, the French *Compagnie des Indes* was unable to restore itself and was forced to surrender its territories to the Crown in 1769. But, the latter never recovered its riches of yesteryears, and between 1778 and 1785 (the War of Independence in the United States) a second British occupation destroyed them again.

In this context, Portuguese military policy was also going to change. In his instructions to the Count of Ega, Pombal, the Viceroy who joined his duty in 1758, again ordered him not to intervene with the army beyond the *Estado* boundary due to the Maratha threat as well as due to the conflict between the French and English since 1756 (The Seven Years War). He recommended caution because the Portuguese Crown had opted for neutrality. Instead, all efforts were to be focused now upon economic development.[19]

Following the Portuguese model, where French officers were employed at all levels of the army including the highest ranks,[20] before his departure to Lisbon, the governor, Count of Ega recruited a few qualified officers. In addition to infantry and artillery professionals, he was the first one to choose a surgeon from this nation, whereas in India, in this field, the Portuguese had a very strong reputation, and sometimes even treated certain Maratha leaders. Following Pombal's orders, during the first years of his government service, that governor built a network of economic and political contacts with the Maratha leaders in an attempt to decrease the risk of war. In September 1759, he appointed Jacques Philippe de Landreset to go to Poona and negotiate a treaty of free trade.[21] The diplomatic discussions quickly took a political turn and led to the signing of the Luso-Maratha Treaty on 20 March 1760, which established regular and durable relations between the two capitals.[22]

However, since 1763, the conquests of Haydar Ali, Sultan of Mysore, extended to the Kingdom of Kanara, then that of Sunda, which was dependent upon the Portuguese. His belligerent intentions towards Goa were certain and military intervention became crucial in the face of this threat. The decision was taken to protect the unoccupied territories of the king of Sunda (in the south and east of Goa) which consisted of creating a security zone between the troops of the Nabab and Portuguese territories. The operation was entrusted to two experienced men: Landreset and Frei António sa Purificação, a former monk who had previously joined the army in the service of Dupleix. With a group of 700 men, they had no difficulty in occupying the provinces of Pondá and Zambaulim, the troops of Sunda offering no resistance.[23] In reward, Noronha was appointed 'general' (military commander) of the conquered provinces, and Landreset, colonel of his regiment.[24]

New Conquests and New Structures

From the 1760s, one notices the first military setbacks that the Marathas faced: the aggressive expansion of Mysore, the rising power of the British, and the various conflicts, which opposed these three powers. All these events altered Pombal's position. In 1774, his instructions to the new Governor (D. Pedro da Câmara) specified that the various territories still under Sunda sovereignty, but actually already under the Portuguese army's 'protection', were to be annexed for good. In addition to this strategic angle, Haydar Ali was growing much more powerful everyday; in his domains were rich farming lands which produced rice and pepper, goods which the Goan traders were finding increasingly difficult to obtain, as Haydar Ali had also annexed the Malabar Coast. Moreover, the king of Sunda was not going to fight back, and negotiated his kingdom in exchange of a personal annual pension.

On the other hand, from the end of the seventeenth century, in the north and east of Goa, the Sawants from Waddi (known as the Bhonsles), Maratha princes dependent upon Goa and Poona, were to become a cause of worry. Their incursions into Bardez Province were frequent and often the cause of plundering. While the Portuguese hold on Alorna had somewhat weakened this dynasty, it still strongly desired to recover its independence through collaborating with Maratha troops against Goa. The British had also started infiltrating dangerously into this zone in order to develop trade. It was thus necessary to put an end to this threat by mastering this turbulent tributary. Consequently, what began as a defensive position turned into a true project of annexation of the principality. In a few years' time, 'new conquests' (2,800 sq. km. of the Sunda and Bhonsle territories) were going to be added to the 'old conquests' (800 sq. km.).

To implement these projects, a bigger army was needed, and especially, a more effective one. From 1774, Pombal ordered the reorganization of the *Estado* military structure. He chose to promote the development of artillery and native recruitment.

In 1762, the Count of Ega had created a small regiment of *sepoys*. From 1774, Pombal set it up as a 'legion', designed to supervise the territories originally derived from the old Sunda Kingdom. Its 1,200 members would be recruited from among the soldiers and traditional chiefs (the *Dessays*) of the king's army. It was made up of Christian, Indian, and European officers and based in Pondá, the ancient stronghold of Sunda.[25] Autonomous in nature, it included corps of the artillery, infantry, and cavalry. A 'general brigadeiro'—the highest military rank of the colony after that of Governor—would command the unit, while each corps would be under the command of a colonel.[26] The legion was going to revive a vocation among the Goan Christian Brahmins because the *regimentos* continued to keep them under control in subordinate posts.[27] For a number of French officers, it was also in the colony that the best prospects for promotion were to be found. An example to be cited could be of Henri Claude of Anjes Tonnelet,[28] who organized and directed the cavalry corps for more than 30 years.[29]

Very efficient in fighting on land against the neighbouring princes as well as against the Mysore troops, Tonnelet's corps continued to expand and promotions followed. A cadet on his arrival had in 1774, Tonnelet had become Lieutenant Colonel by 1792. In 1818, he directed the entire *sepoy* cavalry, with a special honorary rank created for him, namely the cavalry *brigadeiro*. As a reward for his engagement in India, Antoine Sauvage, his compatriot, was appointed Infantry-Lieutenant.[30] A career spent wholly in the service of the Legion, it was therein that he gathered renown for his defensive actions against Tipu Sultan's troops. In 1810, he rose to the rank of colonel. At this time, he had command over the entire Legion.[31]

The second Pombaline innovation was the creation of an artillery regiment. The latter would be composed of three companies: artillery, minors, and gunpowder manufacturing experts who were previously in the infantry regiments. According to the minister's decree, only soldiers and officers of Portuguese nationality were allowed to join this new regiment. However, this clause was never enforced due to lack of experts, and thus was finally abolished in 1792.[32]

Moreover, since the time of D. João V (1706-50) artillery and even the production of arms had always been a foreign business. Besides the absence of adapted coaching, the declaration of the French Ambassador in Lisbon in 1786, stated that the Portuguese nobility quit this Corps of Engineers, which ultimately came to be dominated entirely by foreigners, including at the highest positions of command.[33] One of the most representative examples is that of the Chermont family, coming from the Champagne province's minor nobility. Jean Alexandre de Chermont, an engineer and an expert in artillery, arrived in Portugal in the 1730s after a few years of service in the French army.[34] He quickly made his career in the province of Alentejo, where he settled with his family. His son, Gustave Adolphe Hercule de Chermont, followed in his father's footsteps and had already gained the military stripes of an officer when D. José Pedro da Câmara, a family friend and newly-appointed Governor of India, asked him for assistance.[35] He was entrusted with the creation and organization of the new artillery regiment. His indisputable skills were going to make him essential, and he ultimately remained there for the last 14 years of his service in India. He occupied all the major military positions, which required technical skill. As a result, from 1775 to 1786, he was in-charge of the artillery regiment, the powder depository, and the Agricultural Office. Organizing the artillery regiment was not an easy task due to the lack of arms and rudimentary knowledge of its 520 men.[36] But, against the imminent threat from Mysore, the Governors ended up complying with his requests and took no action on the numerous complaints against his authoritarian character. His mission regarding the powder depository was more 'scientific'. He was to improve the quality of this locally manufactured product, and make it comparable to the European one.[37] Appointed Governor of Diu between 1786 and 1787, he also organized the artillery regiment of this fortress as he did that of Daman.

From 1774 onwards, the attempts at army reform were going to bear fruit during the Portuguese annexation projects in later years thanks to a very favourable international context (diverse conflicts between the various great powers). With the Marathas having neither the opportunity nor the will to intervene in Bhonsle's favour, the latter was at the mercy of the troops of Goa.

In August 1781, a large-scale military operation, mobilizing more than 1,000 men, facilitated the annexation of 130 villages in the territories of Bicholim and Sanquelim.[38] In this expedition, only the sepoy corps and the artillery regiment intervened. At headquarters, the 'general brigadeiro' Luis Carlos Henriques, commander of the operation, was in-charge of almost exclusively French officers and non-commissioned/warrant officers.[39]

In 1782, the Portuguese government wished to coordinate the workings of the various regiments designed for rational action, and more specifically for a better defence ability, against Mysore. Hence, it sent to Goa a 'marechal de campo', charged to supervise all the troops. Generally, this function was always assigned to the Viceroy, which explains why Francisco António da Veiga Cabral, the selected official, a veteran who had directed colonial troops during his service in Brazil was so unwelcome, not only by the Governor Frederico Guilherme de Sousa, but also by all the French officers, with whom there was always going to be discord. At the time of Cabral's departure from Portugal, he was accompanied by another experienced officer, the Lieutenant Colonel Diogo Jacques Miles de Noyers, promoted especially to the position of infantry 'brigadeiro'.[40]

The 1783 campaign mobilized all the regiments, i.e. more than 5,000 men. The province of Pernem was eventually annexed by Tonnelet, Sauvage, and Chermont, all of whom proved to be particularly talented, as revealed by their immediate promotion to headquarters.[41]

However between 1783 and 1788, the annexation operations ceased because of Tipu Sultan's direct threat upon Goa. The latter had just succeeded his father Haydar Ali at the head of the Mysore Empire. His intent of invading Goa was clear and the Pondicherry authorities, who were on good terms with the Nabob, continued to menace Frederico Guilherme de Sousa. But, at that time, the army was going through a period of total confusion in Goa. Veiga Cabral was put in prison by the Governor's order; Cabral accused the Governor of undue support to the French officers at the expense of the Portuguese.[42] The two officers just below him in rank (caporals) died in 1785. As a result, the most highly graded officers were two Frenchmen, Noyers and Chermont. F.G. de Sousa then took command of all the troops, and directly under him, Noyers was appointed Commander of one of the two infantry regiments, while Chermont commanded the artillery.

If Chermont proved to be worthy of his mission, Noyers, ill and senile, was unable to take even the smallest decision. But, fortunately, Tipu resumed war against the Marathas and moved away from the Goa area in 1786. The State Secretary, Martinho de Mello E. Castro, disapproved of F.G. de Sousa's decisions and arranged for his replacement. He also ordered Noyers' retirement.[43]

The last military expedition against Bhonsle took place in 1788. The Government of Poona had signed a peace treaty with Tipu in 1787 and started demanding, in the name of Bhonsle, who also remained the latter's tributary, the restitution of the territories annexed in 1781 and 1783. A quick intervention was needed in order to consolidate the Portuguese position. A military campaign ensured the Portuguese control over Pernem. In order to avoid deportation from his own territories, Bhonsle agreed to give up his rights to Alorna, Bicholim, Pernem and Sanquelim (the Treaty of 29 January 1788).[44] Tonnelet was the only French officer to take part in this operation.

From 1793 onwards, the influx of French officers into Goa began to cease when Portugal joined the war against France in addition to its military requirements in the Atlantic. In India, neither Mysore nor the Maratha Empire, now in absolute decline, represented anymore a threat for Goa. Therefore, only key officers were retained for maintaining terrestrial law and order as well as for maritime safety: Tonnelet and Sauvage in the Legion, the Mondotéguy brothers in the Daman Regiment, and Jean-Baptiste Gigault[45] and Jean-Baptiste Verquin[46] in the few warships which the *Estado* still owned.

Specificities of the French Military Group

PROMOTIONS AND HEADQUARTERS

Studying the promotions of soldiers of French origin, not-withstanding the exceptional circumstances referred to previously, does not reveal any peculiarities as compared to the body of the military corps of Goa.

In all the cases encountered, the commissioned/warrant officers and officers who departed voluntarily for India systematically obtained career advancement and doubled their pay. Any promotion subsequently granted by the military authorities of Goa was to be approved of by the Crown if the beneficiary wanted to receive payment matching his rank. The process of file examination then became a matter of well-placed contacts. Thus, Tonnelet, promoted to Lieutenant Colonel in 1792, had his rank validated only in 1799.[47] It should also be specified that overseas service led to promotions much faster than in Portugal. Except in particular cases, each renewal of voluntary enlistment in India (every three years) included a promotion. But, once they returned, the soldiers were granted only the grade which they could have held with seniority benefits. This encouraged more than one to settle in India, which was precisely the goal of this legislation.

One notes however, with certain French officers, a rate of promotion much slower than their Portuguese fellow-members. These were the cases of Tonnelet and Sauvage. The former took 18 years to pass from the rank of Second Lieutenant to that of Lieutenant Colonel (while Landreset took scarcely 8 years!) and was not assimilated as Staff Officer (as 'brigadeiro') until 1818, i.e. after 44 years of service in India. However, all the governors commended his performance, particularly the fine behaviour of his cavalry, and readily entrusted him the headquarters. Initially appointed as Lieutenant in 1780, Sauvage was going to take 20 years to be promoted to the rank of a Lieutenant Colonel, and approximately 10 more years, to become a Colonel in spite of the quality of his service, which was more than satisfactory.[48]

Several explanations exist for these circumstances. Their regiment was the least prestigious in Goa, and was indeed ranked behind that of the Portuguese infantry officers. In addition, since 1793, the monies of the Crown were low because of the war and the situation evened out only after 1815. Finally, they did not benefit from any particular protection from the governors of Goa. In fact, one can note that even the most brilliant careers, like those of Pierrepont, Saint Martin, Landreset, or even Chermont, reached their zenith under governors known for their sympathy towards the French community and culture: Le Marquis d' Alorna (1744-50), the Count of Ega (1758-65), Dom Pedro da Câmara (1774-9) and Dom Frederico Guilherme de Sousa (1779-86). The comprehensive study of the French group from Lisbon (40 persons) enables us to note that the majority of its members trained in India precisely during the very same government rules. Theirs was not the case of Tonnelet and Sauvage who, from 1786 to 1794, had over them as direct Senior Superior, someone who strongly opposed promotions to foreign officers: Veiga Cabral. To crown it all, Cabral was appointed Governor of Goa from 1794 to 1807!

In addition to promotions within regiments, service in India also included service within a series of infantry headquarters: fortresses, provinces, and harbour cities along with their districts. These responsibilities also required administrative and political skills, crucial, because they brought income. Indeed, these executives were expected to ensure customs control, navigation passport supervision and, from the sixteenth century, were offered a series of commercial benefits. Assigning these posts was one of the Viceroy's privileges. Either it concerned prerogatives within the regiment, or regularly the covert offer of a lump sum of money as reward for services rendered. In the eighteenth century, several foreign officers, almost all of them French, occupied these posts.

The position of fortress commander was most advantageous insofar as it ensured the safety of the border posts on the continent or the coasts. Hence, the fortress became a regular passageway of ships and goods. Most of them were situated in the Northern Province. With the majority of French soldiers having trained in India only from the 1740s, only a few could achieve this honour. However, mention could be made of Mathias Renaudier who, in 1713, commanded one of the fortresses facing Bombay, the Island of Caranja, a site threatened jointly by British and Maratha ambitions. Perhaps one should also note the short-lived commandment of the Aguada Fort, one of the two fortresses protecting the Mandovi River, on which the old city of Goa and Panaji were built by Miles de Noyers in 1783. The latter, opting for the role of courtier rather than that of lord of manor, resigned after 8 days, excusing himself on the grounds that the climate there was bad for his health and thereafter made for the Governor's palace.[49]

Four French officers also joined the Government of the Provinces in Goa territories. In the old conquests, the rich province of Salcette, which was generally the prerogative of those who commanded the First Regiment of Infantry, this was of course entrusted to Pierrepont between 1746 and 1752, then to Miles de Noyers in 1785 and 1786.[50] As sepoy officers, they were charged with the military organization of the 'new conquests'. On account of services rendered to the State, Tonnelet and Sauvage were granted the command of several new provinces. Sauvage controlled Canacona from 1800 onwards, and Tonnelet controlled Bicholim and Sanquelim, from 1818.[51]

At the top of the commanding hierarchy were the major cities, together with the dependant jurisdictions, i.e. the entire territory under Portuguese control. Four French officers were granted this honour but without gaining any recognition.

In October 1783, Frederico Guilherme de Sousa appointed Miles de Noyers as Governor of Diu. Arriving in January 1784, the latter did not stay for more than a year. At that point in time, the old cosmopolitan island was verily declining and scarcely had any European residents; it had a garrison of about 600 deportees. Coastal piracy prevailed and the powerful local commercial class (banias) expected beneficial reforms. Noyers was noticed for his lack of initiative, as revealed by his detractors, because he was readily corruptible.[52] Old and ill, in fact this officer had come to India to gather the funds needed for his daughters' marriage in Portugal without too much effort. What is more, he himself asked to be called back to Goa after having tried to tactfully sell to a colleague, the two remaining years of his government service.

Gustave Adolpe Hercules de Chermont succeeded him from December 1786 to December 1787.[53] Extremely dynamic and enterprising, he tried to get involved in military defence, the Navy, in addition to the health and economy sectors. But, his deliberately authoritarian attitude and his refusal to consult people concerned with his decisions—particularly in connection with the hospice managed by the monks of the island, whom he accused of incompetence—made a series of enemies for him. He disciplined and organized the regiment, repaired the fortress and condemned piracy, but due to moderate funds at his disposal, he was unable to obtain convincing results. After direct intervention of the Archbishop of Goa, he was dismissed and returned to Goa to await his departure for Portugal.[54] Indeed, in 1786, his appalling behaviour towards his superior Veiga Cabral negated all hope or prospect for command or promotion.[55]

In sequential order comes Captain Jean-Baptiste Verquin, who had joined the *Estado* Navy in 1784, and quickly obtained promotions and excellent recommendations from his superiors. Appointed Governor of Timor in 1793, he joined the post in January 1794. Verquin proved to be particularly inefficient at the time of his first mandate, but with the war prevailing in the Indian Ocean, Veiga Cabral could not find a substitute. Given the situation, Verquin's posting was renewed until January 1800; under the blow of a legal enquiry about his disastrous management, he left the island and took refuge in Macao where he died two months' later.[56]

The very last to be appointed was George Frederic Lecor whose family had left France in 1737 for Portugal and had acquired a Portuguese nationality in 1762.[57] He governed Daman in 1810 and 1811, during a period when Portuguese India was under British military occupation and practically devoid of economic or political activity.

This network of French officers working for Portuguese India was actually—it must be emphasized—integrated into a larger scheme, the Empire. Very often, these prestigious positions obtained in India were the result of the influence of the family concerned in Lisbon and the participation of this family in the army in Brazil. Brazil was where the Lecor and the Chermont families had shone and in turn had brought to their families both honour and noble titles.

Local Recruitments

This study will conclude with the discussion of a minor phenomenon but nevertheless an existing one: that of the French mercenaries who offered their services to the *Estado*. One cannot use the term 'parti' for them insofar as the Goan army did not include this kind of formation. They were integrated into the other corps during their stay in Portuguese-speaking territory, without being allowed to benefit from the advantages and promotions given to their compatriots who had come from Portugal and been appointed by the king. The decline of the *Estado* in the seventeenth century, and especially the absence of prospects for enrichment, explains why this community was so small, and there were rare cases of permanent settlement. Goa was always viewed and opted for as more a refuge than a choice. Besides, the higher degree of the arrivals took place during the Seven Years War, after the eventual decline of the French presence in India in 1761.

Indeed, some rare cases are recorded beforehand. Jean-Baptiste Tavernier, traveller and diamond merchant, was one of the rare person as to state that he had met several younger members of the French nobility in Goa in 1648, who had served the Dutch a few years prior, when the latter drove out the Portuguese from Ceylon. Disappointed because of the non-existence of remuneration promised by the Government of Batavia, many of them offered their services to Goa, where they remained for a few years.[58]

The most famous case, and the only notable exception, is no doubt that of Mahé de la Bourdonnais, future Governor of the Mascareignes Islands. The latter had left the Compagnie des Indes in 1727. He then devoted himself to commercial navigation and in 1728, started visiting the port of Goa frequently. At that time, the Viceroy planned to recover Mombassa from the Sultanate of Oman. So, Mahé de la Bourbonnais joined the navy of Goa. It is not known whether he took part in the disastrous expedition of 1729 against Mombassa, but his competence was greatly appreciated by the authorities because at the end of 1730 he was promoted *capitão de mar-e-guerra* (highest rank of that navy) and was granted the command of a warship. He took this opportunity to plan a new attack on Mombassa and even went to Pondicherry in order to negotiate the purchase of a ship and arms with the French Governor. King D. João V, however, no longer wished to get involved on this coast. Disappointed, Mahé de la Bourbonnais then left the *Estado* service in September 1732. Indeed, his actions in Goa had been restricted to the struggle against coastal pirates.[59]

At the time of the government of the Count of Ega and after the fall of Pondicherry, several French soldiers, who had initially taken refuge in the neutral port of Tranquebar (Danish) or with the House of Haydar Ali, then a young war leader in the service of the Rajah of Mysore, decided to leave India for I'lsle de France. They left with their families by land routes towards Goa, at that time the only neutral European port on the Western coast. The Viceroy willingly offered them a pension,[60] and they were able to leave Goa in September 1761 on a ship coming from Port Louis.[61]

The Knight of Mouhy disembarked from the same ship and had to cross the peninsula in order to join Haydar Ali's camp in the Coromandel to advocate an alliance. Haydar Ali refused, and it is highly probable that a part of the officers who were in his service then decided to leave. Mouhy returned to Goa with 8 officers; there all of them stayed on for several months thanks to the subsidies granted by the Count of Ega.[62] Several then left the territory by land routes for unspecified destinations. Meanwhile, the small community of refugees had significantly grown. In July 1762, Louis Laurent Federbe, Comte de Modave was part of it, returning from a mission ordered by Haydar Ali. The Comte de Modave managed the funds allotted by the Viceroy for the group's survival.[63] Between August and October, tens of soldiers as well as several families of officers in turn arrived. The majority of these people embarked in November 1762 on another ship sent from Port Louis.

Although the Portuguese documentation is rather brief on this subject, it is known that several officers and a number of soldiers decided to stay in the Portuguese territory and earn their living by joining the Portuguese troops. Indeed in 1762, after the declaration of war by Portugal to France, the Count of Ega on 25 January 1763 ordered all French officers who were not yet naturalized to leave Goa. Before departure, De Forges, on behalf of all, came to thank the Count for his hospitality.[64] Next, they certainly passed on into Haydar Ali's service. Indeed, by the end of 1763, a part of the Nabob's army, commanded by Haibut Jang (usually known as Fazal Ulla Khan), seized the territories of the king of Sunda, and laid siege on the fortress of Cabo da Rama at the gates of Goa. Among his troops was a European Elite Corps formed by 275 men, commanded by a so-called Yele. The majority were refugees from Pondicherry.[65] A group of Frenchmen, disappointed by the way they had been treated, and refusing to defy the Portuguese, ended up deserting and was welcomed in Goa in January 1764. A few of them declared having already resided in Goa earlier. Led by Captain Hughel, this group stayed in Goa for 4 months, providing to the Portuguese vital strategic information for defence, besides being incorporated into troops of Salcette province, the one most exposed to Haibut Jang's attacks. Hughel took an active part in the occupation of the kingdom of Sunda province, which had not yet been invaded by Mysore.

Of the entire group, the majority had left the territory by 1764 and numbers dwindled until hardly three or four families decided to stay permanently in Goa. The most famous being that of Mondotéguy, who later settled in Daman and pursued their career in the army for many generations. Some worked until the restitution of the French territories and then joined Pondicherry and Mahé in 1765.

Today it is difficult to quantify the number of French soldiers in the whole of the Portuguese Empire, and more especially to determine the real impact of their actions. Indeed, one still does not have comprehensive quantitative and analytical studies about the Portuguese armies between the seventeenth and nineteenth centuries. On the other hand, this community acted within a larger unit: Europeans serving the Portuguese Crown. To isolate this fact could lead to a much-overstated image of its achievement. In this sense, the case of Portuguese India is an exception because today there is sufficient archival knowledge to identify the entire European group. One can now bring to light, without error, the domination of the French on the rest of the community in the eighteenth century, both in number and in quality. But for the future, any attempt to understand the actions of the European armies in India, must not avoid a study on the role of foreigners in the French and English armies in India during that period. Similarly for the French group, it was obvious that service to the king of Portugal was to be a family affair for several generations. One can only hope to appreciate the role of the overseas service within the constitution of family patrimony and heritage, as well as their role in the process of social integration.

Notes

1. Ernestine Carreira, 'Un empire à vendre: stratégies d'appropriation des ports de l'Estado da India par les compagnies britannique et française', in *L'empire portugais face aux autres empires*, Paris: Maisonneuve et Larose, 2008, pp. 80-5.
2. Cf. Ernestine Carreira, 'O estado português no Oriente, aspectos políticos (1660-1815)', in *Nova História da Expansão Portuguesa*, Lisboa, 2006, Chap. 1.
3. Two studies were devoted to the French soldiers in Portuguese India. Not confronting the various sources, A.C.G. da Silva integrates in the French group all surnames with French-sounding names, which ends up including Italian, Swiss, and even Irish soldiers. See A.C.G. da Silva, 'Os Franceses Na colonização portuguesa da Índia', in *Studia*, Lisbon: C.E.H.U., 1959, p. 105 and H. Moura, 'Dois franceses, castelães de Diu', in *O Oriente Português*, vol. 2, Goa, 1905, pp. 405-22.
4. This group includes a French-speaking soldier of Switzerland, Jacques Philippe de Landreset de la Tour because of his very close links with France.
5. European groups and mercenaries who commanded troops of the sepoys formed elite corps in the Indian armies. Among the most famous, one can quote the 'parti' of the nabob, Rene Madec, in the service of the Mughal emperor, as well as the 'Swiss parti', formed after 1761, which served successively Nizam Ali, and then Haydar Ali, from 1779.
6. J. F. J. Biker, *Colecção de Tratados*, vol. 9, Lisboa: Imprensa Nacional, 1880, pp. 86-93.
7. E.G. Leonard, *L'armée et ses problèmes au 18e siècle*, Paris: Librairie Plon, 1958, p. 101.
8. The creation of the first artillery school in La Fère in 1719. G. Cabourdin and G. Viard, *Lexique historique de la France d'Ancien Régime*, Paris: Armand Colin, 1978, p. 115.
9. L.A. de O. Ramos, *Franceses em Portugal nos fins do século XVI*, Lisboa: Instituto de Alta Cultura, 1968, p. 21.

10. Cf. Ernestine Carreira, 'From decline to prosperity: shipbuilding in Daman, 18th–19th centuries', in *Indo-Portuguese encounters: journeys in science, technology and culture*, vol. 2, ed. Lotika Varadarajan, New. Delhi: Indian National Science Academy, Aryan Books International, 2006.
11. C.R. Boxer, *O Império colonial português, 1415–1825*, Lisboa: Edicões 70, 1981, p. 284.
12. C.R. Boxer, *Realções raciais no império colonial português 1415–1825*, ed. Afrontamento, Porto, 1977, 1988, pp. 84-128.
13. C.R. Boxer, 'Asian Potentates and European artillery in the sixteenth-eighteenth centuries', *Journal of the Malayan Branch of the Royal Asiatic Society*, vol. 38, 1965, pp. 156-72.
14. M.A. Norton, *D. Pedro Miguel de Almeida Portugal*, Lisboa: Agência Geral do Ultramar, 1967, p. 154.
15. Coming from a family of minor nobility, Norman, Louis de Pierrepont was born in 1680. Portugal favoured Pierrepont's career path. After 12 years of service in India, he set out again towards Portugal. Aged 70, and having suffered from many wounds, he died at sea, offshore of Brazil. See Desbois and Badier de la Chenaye, *Dictionnaire de la Noblesse*, t. 15, Chez Schlesinger Frères, 1869, p. 991 and 'Livros das Monções', vol. 116, f. 19r, Historical Archives of Goa (LMHAG).
16. Indigenous soldiers recruited among the elite of the troops of the princes dependent upon Goa.
17. Saint Martin, of whom little is known, especially of his origins, but who had a French nationality, also achieved a brilliant career in the Portuguese army before leaving for India in 1740. Ambitious and qualified, he was approached on several occasions by the East India Company, as well as by Mahé of Bourdonnais, which obliged the Viceroys to promote him quickly and to offer the wages that he asked. Married, and father of a family in Portugal, he decided to set out again in 1752 and died during the trip. LMHAG, vol. 146, f. 31 rv.
18. Biker, *Colecção de Tratados*, vol. 6, pp. 27-295.
19. A. de S. Saldanha and V.S. de Saldanha, *As cartas de Manuel de Saldanha: Conde da Ega e 47 Vice-Rei da India a Sebastião José de Carvalho e Melo e seus irmãos (1758–1765),* Lisboa: Gabinete Português de Estudos Humanistícos, 1984, p. 15.
20. R. Carvalho, 'O recurso a pessoal estrangeiro no tempo de Pombal', in *O Marquês de Pombal e o seu tempo*, vol. 1, *Revista de História das ideias*, Lisboa: Faculdade de Letras, 1982, p. 106.
21. The family of Jacques Philippe of Landreset de la Tower hailed from Freiburg. Of Swiss nationality, Jacques had spent his childhood and his adolescence in Paris, as page to the ambassador of Portugal. Second Lieutenant of the infantry, he left for the first time to India in 1749. He returned to Lisbon in 1757, having already reached the rank of Lieutenant Colonel. He set out again the following year for Goa with the Count of Ega, and returned with him to Lisbon in 1765. He rejoined the army in 1773. He became Governor of the town of Faro in 1789, before leaving for Morocco as the ambassador for Portugal. He died in

Lisbon in 1798. At the beginning of the 1760s, in Goa he married Marie Catherine Michele Bourquenod, daughter of a member of the High Council of Pondicherry. Saldanha, *As cartas de Manuel de Saldanha*, p. 49. Arquivo Nacional da Torre de Tomo, Arquivos das Ordens militares, Ordem de Cristo, Lisbon (ANTT), vol. 12, doc. 17.

22. Biker, *Colecção de Tratados*, vol. 7, p. 139.
23. LMHAG, vol. 147A, ff. 507r–08v.
24. *Regimento Velho* had been divided into two infantry regiments at the beginning of the 1750s. Landreset then commanded one or both until 1765.
25. C.L.M. de Barbuda, *Instruçoes com que El-Rei D: José mandou passar ao Estado da Índia o Governador, e Capitão General, e o Arcebispo Primaz do Oriente no ano de 1774* (publicadas e anotadas por), Lisbon: Imprensa Nacional, 1903, p. 85.
26. Barbuda, *Instruçoes com que El-Rei D*, pp. 30–1.
27. Ernestine Carreira, 'Portuguese India in the reign of Tipoo Sultan', *Moyen Orient & Ocean Indien*, vol. 6, 1989, pp. 111–14.
28. Born in Lisbon in 1747, Henri was the son of Claude Tonnelet, who had left France in 1718 in order to join the Portuguese cavalry corps. He joined the army in 1766 as a cadet in the cavalry regiment of Lisbon and did not obtain any promotion until his departure to India, where he settled permanently. He was made a naturalized Portuguese in 1788, which enabled him to become a member of the city council. Single, he died in Goa in 1821. J.A.I. Gracias, *Catálogo dos livros de assentamento da gente de guerra que veio do reino para a Índia*, Goa: Imprensa Nacional, 1893, p. 26.
29. In 1787, the legion comprised approximately 1,500 men, including nearly 120 in the cavalry. 'Maços da Índia', 11 February 1787, M. 151, O. 157, Arquivo Histórico Ultramarino, Lisbon (AHU).
30. Originating in Lyon, he was a warrant officer in the Portuguese army before his departure for Goa. He served the first period in India (1779–86) then he returned to Portugal, where his hopes to further his career were quickly disappointed. He finally departed for Goa in 1789, to settle down and start a family there. He asked for Portuguese naturalization after 1793. See Silva, 'Os Franceses Na colonização', p. 91.
31. LMHAG, vol. 180B, f. 492r.
32. AHU, 5 October 1792, M. 160, O. 145.
33. Marquis of Bombelles, *Journal d'un ambassadeur de France au Portugal 1786–1788*, Paris: Editions P.U.F., 1979, p. 36.
34. The engineer was at the same time the manufacturer of engines of war and specialized in fortifications.
35. The Chermonts were a family from Champagne whose ennoblement commenced in the first half of the sixteenth century. Gustave was born around 1742, in Alentejo. He joined the artillery regiment, which his father commanded. In 1762, he reached the rank of Captain, thanks to his knowledge of mathematics, engineering, and artillery. He left for India with the title of Lieutenant Colonel. C.A. de M. Sepulveda, *História orgânica e politica do exército português*, vol. 15, Imprensa da Universidade, 1928, p. 191.

36. LMHAG, vol. 159A, ff. 278v-279r.
37. The 'Superintendent of Agriculture' was a Pombaline creation whose objective was to rationalize agricultural production, particularly that of the 'new conquests', and to develop, as in Brazil, agriculture generating exports which would generate finance for the colony. AHU, 18 March 1784, M. 143, O. 128.
38. AHU, 24 August 1781, M. 142, O. 127.
39. Jacques Philippe of Mondoteguy, Jacques Goeticer, François Joseph Latte-Sagon, Antoine Sauvage, Henri Claude des Anges Tonnelet, Antoine Naron, and Gustave Adolphe Hercule of Chermont.
40. Diogo Jacques Miles of Noyers belonged to the very old, noble family of Yonne, of which one of the ancestors had been a Marshall of France. Born about 1715, he conducted the major part of his career in Portugal, where his family had followed. In 1781, Noyers ended his career with the rank of Lieutenant Colonel. He probably died in Goa about 1787. H.M. dos Santos, *Catálogo dos documentos secretos do extinto Conselho de Guerra*, vol. 4, Lisboa, 1963, p. 253.
41. LMHAG, vol. 190A, ff. 65r-66v.
42. Arrested in September 1785, he recovered his post and freedom only in March 1786.
43. AHU, 17 March 1786, M. 149, O. 155.
44. S.K. Mhamai, *The Sawants of Wadi and the Portuguese*, New Delhi: Concept Publishing Company, 1984, p. 105.
45. Gigault came from a family of French merchants who had been settled in Lisbon from the beginning of the eighteenth century. His low family origins undoubtedly played a part in him not pursuing a military career. Instead he opted for the navy. In 1756, he became a soldier of the marine regiment, only rising after 17 years of service to the rank of Second Lieutenant. He embarked for India in 1774 and saw service as a naval officer. J.F. Labourdette, *La nation française à Lisbonne de 1669 à 1790: Entre Colbertisme et Libéralisme*, Paris: Fondation Gulbenkian, 1988, p. 474.
46. Originating in Lille, he commenced service in Goa in 1784 as frigate under-officer. Frederico Guilherme de Sousa and his successor promoted him quickly. In 1793, he was 'capitão de mar e guerra'. Gigault and Verquin probably demanded their naturalization in 1793.
47. AHU, 2 April 1798, M. 170, O. 163.
48. LMHAG, vol. 190C, f. 1006v.
49. AHU, 16 February 1787, M. 154, O. 154.
50. Norton, *D. Pedro Miguel de Almeida Portugal*, p. 137.
51. LMHAG, vol. 191D, f. 1219r.
52. AHU, 16 February 1787, M. 154, O. 154.
53. LMHAG, vol. 170C, f. 848v.
54. Moura, 'Dois franceses, castelães de Diu', p. 407.
55. One cannot miss emphasis, through a chance of circumstance that at the time when Gustave Adolphe left India never to return, his first cousin Dominique Prosper de Chermont, officer with the service of the French army, was a colonel of the regiment of I'Isle de France (now Mauritius Island). He controlled the

Bourbon Island in 1790 and was named Governor of Pondichery in 1791. However, he took over command only in February 1793 because of the revolutionary disorders which disturbed the city. At the time of the launch of the war, he was unable to resist the enemy and signed the capitulation of French India on 23 August 1793. He died in Pondicherry, prisoner on parole, in 1798. Centre des Archives d'Outre-Mer, Aix-en-Provence, Colonies C2 (CAO), vol. 304.

56. LMHAG, Correspondência of Macau, vol. 35, f. 106r.
57. ANTT, Junta do Comércio, Registos Gerais, vol. 108.
58. Jean-Baptiste Tavernier, *Les six voyages*, vol. 3, Paris: Gervais Clouzier, 1681/2, pp. 128-38, 140-53.
59. Philippe Haudrère, *La Bourdonnais: Marin et aventurier*, Paris: Editions Desjonquères, 1992, pp. 32-35; Silva, 'Os Franceses Na colonização', p. 35.
60. Statement of account that the Company of the Indies had been engaged in honour after the war.
61. To quote among them Talbovet de Severac, Lalauzier, and Deverinne. Saldanha, *As cartas de Manuel de Saldanha*, pp. 254-6.
62. These officers were: Regard de Mulseau, Dagey de Mouhy, De Changeac, De Cantons (or Chatons), La Violette (M. de la Vilote?), Kracht (Crachet), De Palmas, and Henaud. The documents are not very readable. Silva, 'Os Franceses Na colonização', pp. 60-1.
63. CAO, C2, vol. 97, f. 96; LMHAG, vol. 147A, f. 119rv.
64. LMHAG, vol. 135B (166-1763), f. 437v; Saldanha, *As cartas de Manuel de Saldanha*, p. 65.
65. Ph le Treguilly, *Les français en Inde au temps de la guerre d'indépendance américaine (1778–1788)*, Paris: Thèse pour le doctorat ès-lettres, 1992, p. 61.

CHAPTER SIX

Stocking Colonial Pharmacies: Commerce in South Asian Indigenous Medicines from their Native Sources in the Portuguese *Estado da Índia*

Timothy D. Walker

PORTUGUESE COLONIAL EXPANSION INTO Asia during the sixteenth and seventeenth centuries had a profoundly important scientific dimension, the impact of which far outlasted the economic ascendancy of their Eastern empire. In the South Asian colonies, Portuguese healers encountered a radically different sphere of natural knowledge, one that they would explore, exploit, expropriate and export for more than three centuries. In a remarkable, unprecedented feat of scientific dissemination, Portuguese colonials popularized Indian drugs and spread information about South Asian healing methods to European territories over four continents. Portuguese colonial agents (administrators, medical practitioners, maritime officers, merchants and missionaries) undertook this activity consciously for commercial and scientific ends, as well as to further Portuguese imperial ambitions. Indian medicines thus played a significant role in the state-sponsored health care institutions of the disparate global Portuguese colonies. Traditional Indian medicinal preparations and healing techniques in particular, became widely known in Portuguese-controlled enclaves in the Atlantic and Pacific Oceans, far from their indigenous roots, and were deeply inculcated into the lexicon of tropical medicine in the Lusophone colonies.[1]

By the close of the seventeenth century, 200 years of Portuguese colonial endeavour in India had resulted in the founding of numerous medical institutions to care for garrison troops, colonial officials, missionaries and European settlers. Yet in the late 1600s Goa, the capital and administrative hub of Portugal's Asian territories, had become a colonial backwater, a mere shadow of its former commercial and demographic predominance. Only a century before, Goa had been a thriving mercantile metropolis of 300,000 people, one of the largest and richest cities in all Asia.[2] By the mid-seventeenth century, though, the economic focus of the Portuguese empire had shifted to Brazil and, without a professional incentive or strong expectation of profit, few European officials could be induced to serve in the fading *Estado da Índia.*[3] The European-born population of Portuguese in India had shrunk to just a few hundred souls, most of whom were illiterate convict soldiers.[4] The day-to-day activities of maintaining the colonies—carrying on the commerce, administration, health care, missionary work and defence measures that made the enclaves viable—were carried out mainly by mixed-race descendents of earlier Portuguese settlers, along with Luso-acculturated indigenous peoples whose ancestors had long ago converted to Christianity.[5]

Reticence to serve in the Indian colonies naturally extended to licensed Portuguese physicians and surgeons, as well. Reduced social and economic circumstances in the *Estado da Índia* after the mid-seventeenth century had significant implications for Indo-Portuguese medical services, and led to increased hybridization, or cultural sharing, of healing knowledge. For lack of European-trained medical practitioners to staff them, hospital installations in the *Estado da Índia* were gradually forced to rely on local healers who were also trained locally and, typically used a blend of Indian and imported medical plants to treat an illness. As European medical influence waned in the Asian colonies during the seventeenth and eighteenth centuries, the remedies prescribed in Indo-Portuguese hospitals and infirmaries were increasingly of native origin and applied by native practitioners.[6]

Portuguese colonialism in India depended on an active Catholic missionary effort, and most ecclesiastical orders considered caring for the sick—whether European colonists or newly-converted indigenous peoples—to be an integral part of their activities. In the course of their ministrations, European missionaries inevitably encountered and experimented with native medicinal substances. Thus, Portuguese India had a old addition of supporting medical facilities that blended Western and Eastern influences.

In the Portuguese-held enclaves of India, medical facilities could be either state-run hospitals or infirmaries operated by missionary orders, but religious brotherhoods generally administered the colonial government hospitals, as well. From the earliest days of the Portuguese conquest, missionary priests had played a central part in facilitating medical hybridization. The Dominicans who accompanied Vasco da Gama and Alfonso de Albuquerque understood that their spiritual mandate to minister to the men of these expeditions of conquest included an explicit directive to comfort the sick and wounded, of which there were of course many. Having exhausted their medical supplies from Europe and being long-used to procuring efficacious healing plants or simples from local populations along the African coast, Portuguese priests began, already in the opening decades of the sixteenth century, the gradual but wholly natural process of inculcating South Asian drugs into their own healing lexicon. A rich cultural sharing of medical lore would follow, developing over the next three centuries and achieving a high state of hybridization as European medical influences diminished in Lusophone India, concurrent with the downturn of Portuguese economic and political power after approximately 1600.[7]

However, two questions arise: what medicines did these ecclesiastical and secular practitioners use, and from where did they procure their stocks of drugs and remedies? This essay will discuss the practical commercial dimension of hybridized health care in Portuguese South Asia (Goa, Cochin, Bassein, Daman and Diu) from the early sixteenth to the mid-seventeenth century. Specifically, I will describe the types of indigenous medicines commonly found in colonial missionary and state pharmacies—medicines that had been adopted by Portuguese medical practitioners, secular and ecclesiastic, and assimilated into use in official colonial medical institutions. During the time period covered by this study, dozens of South Asian healing preparations were in common circulation within the Indo-Portuguese colonial medical sphere. Given their centrality to the practice of the healing arts in the colonies, much of the contemporary trade in, and dissemination of information about, indigenous Indian medical substances lay in the hands of Catholic missionary orders (Jesuits, Franciscans, Dominicans and Augustinians).[8]

This essay will address the following questions: What caused the Portuguese to adopt certain Indian remedies, and on what specific indigenous medicines did they rely? Moreover, what benefits did the Portuguese missionaries believe such medicines provided? Also, from what sources were the Portuguese supplied with indigenous medicines? And finally, what were the characteristics of the South Asian drugs market at this time? This essay will analyse the problem of stocking colonial pharmacies to best meet the imperial exigencies of the Portuguese in their Eastern empire.

Contemporary evidence (missionary field reports, infirmary diaries of treatments given to patients, official medical reports and, pharmacy stock lists) demonstrates that, generally speaking, the subtleties and rationale of Indian healing philosophies were not of interest to most Portuguese colonizers—neither evangelical priests nor professional medical practitioners took much notice of venerable South Asian healing systems, beyond the practical application of diverse native remedies for the specific diseases or illnesses they were prescribed to address.[9] The Europeans were interested primarily in the medical efficacy of applied substances, an efficacy that could be exploited either for healing or as a marketable commodity. Therefore, early modern Portuguese merchants and missionaries typically sought portable, profitable and above all practical remedies that could be marketed and sold for application to specific maladies. So, while Portuguese medical practitioners often mimicked indigenous medical procedures in the application of drugs in an effort to reproduce their efficacy, the practitioners in the colonies usually did not absorb, replicate or disseminate the broader, codified philosophical context of traditional indigenous Indian healing systems.

I will focus on the European colonizers who received, interpreted and ultimately disseminated indigenous South Asian medical knowledge, rather than on native sources of colonial medical knowledge. My primary goal is to explore how the Portuguese in India interpreted indigenous medical practices: what they gleaned, made use of and eventually disseminated.

Almost from their inception, Portuguese efforts to establish colonial enclaves in India included the founding of health care institutions. Establishing new medical facilities was, of course, a pragmatic state policy—a logical response to the shocking mortality rates Europeans experienced in Monsoon Asia. That is, the exigencies of personnel survival in the colonial military sphere helped foster European inquiries into native medicine. Typically during the sixteenth to eighteenth centuries, new conscript arrivals to the eastern colonies from continental Portugal numbered from a few hundred to as many as 3,000 annually,[10] but their ranks shrank rapidly due to tropical diseases. The sixteenth-century Dutch traveller John Huyghen van Linschoten observed that, in the Royal Military Hospital of Goa, 'every yeare at the least there entered 500 live men, [who] never come forth till they are dead.'[11] According to a contemporary estimate, in the three decades between 1604 and 1634, Portuguese military deaths exceeded 25,000 men in the Hospital Real Militar alone.[12] Until the early nineteenth century yearly mortality rates of 25 to 50 per cent were common for newly disembarked European soldiers in Portuguese colonial enclaves.[13]

By the first quarter of the seventeenth century, Goa could boast of two hospitals operated by the charitable Santa Casa da Misericordia (Holy House of Mercy): those of Nosso Senhora da Piedade and Todos-os-Santos. The latter, older by a century, had been founded in about 1524 and was open to persons of any race. For reasons of financial expediency, these two were amalgamated in 1681. Also in Goa there existed the famous military hospital (mentioned earlier), the Hospital Real Militar do Espírito Santo, founded in the early sixteenth century and widely praised for its cleanliness and quality.[14] Its facilities were reserved, however, mainly for Portuguese soldiers and for officials of the India garrison.[15]

The Hospital Real Militar in Goa was a major medical facility, the most important Portuguese colonial health installation in Asia. Except for a very few brief periods of hiatus, brothers of the Society of Jesus administered this hospital from 1579 until 1760. Although on several occasions during their long tenure the Jesuits had petitioned the king and Overseas Council to be released from these duties, the king's firm royal will, citing the Jesuits' superior medical skill and pharmaceutical knowledge, kept them in their managerial posts.[16]

Not only did the Royal Military Hospital of Goa treat some 3,000 patients per year, on average, during the seventeenth century but,[17] to provide medicines for so many invalids, the hospital boasted a grand pharmacy staffed by more than 25 apothecaries and their assistants.[18] In fact, many of the indigenous medicinal plants used to treat the soldiers interned in the Hospital Real Militar were home-grown, having been raised in the spacious botanical gardens just outside the institutional walls, near the Mandovi River in old Goa. According to the hospital's official regulations, it was the head pharmacist's duty to oversee the cultivation, harvest, drying and conservation of these medicinal plants.[19] Such healing herbs as could not be grown in the hospital gardens the head pharmacist was authorized to buy from native or international merchants and indigenous 'herbalists', but only upon having approved the purchase with the chief physician, who was ultimately responsible for all hospital operations.[20] Of course, surplus medicinal plants from the garden could be sold for a profit in the hospital pharmacy, or exported to regions of need within the *Estado da Índia.*

From the earliest years of colonization in India, Portuguese commanders, appalled at the ineffectiveness of European remedies against previously unknown tropical diseases and desperate to preserve the fighting effectiveness of their garrisons, turned to native healing practitioners to treat their men.[21] Information about the efficacy of any local remedy that appeared to save soldiers' lives soon passed unofficially from ship to ship and garrison to garrison before being adopted for regular use by colonial forces in state-run military hospitals.[22]

For their part, native healers along the Malabar and Coromandel coasts rapidly learned to cater to the particular health concerns of the Portuguese troops and administrators posted to their shores. Responding pragmatically to a demand for indigenous healing substances and remedies, Indian merchants set up apothecary markets in garrison towns to vend native medicinal preparations specifically to the foreign colonizers.[23] Their stocks of medicines drew from pre-existing South Asian trade routes for medical substances and included all manner of curative derivatives common to ayurveda, unani and localized healing systems in the regions where the Portuguese established themselves.[24]

Moreover, the Portuguese garrisons, political authorities, missionaries and traders made use of local medical practitioners simply because of the scarcity of Portuguese *médicos* (physicians) in Goa and the other colonial enclaves. Elite Indian ayurvedic healers, called vaidyas, quickly came to enjoy the patronage of their new rulers largely because these native doctors better understood the effective treatment of local tropical diseases. Several vaidyas are known to have held important posts in Goa through the sixteenth and seventeenth centuries, serving as personal physicians to at least one governor (António Moniz Barretto in 1574), a viceroy (the Conde de Aveiras in 1644) and other members of the Portuguese aristocracy. Besides, Indian doctors could also be found treating patients at the Jesuit College of São Paulo and the Convent of Madre de Deus; one even served as the *físico-môr* (chief physician) of the *Estado da Índia* in the 1640s.[25] These contacts naturally helped to introduce native Indian medicines and the healing arts into Portuguese colonial usage. In these early exchanges we see the roots of a broadly hybridized healing culture within imperial medical institutions that would steadily expand within the Portuguese Indian enclaves during the sixteenth and seventeenth centuries, and continue to grow as the European-born Portuguese presence diminished.

Exchanges of medical knowledge in the missionary context were substantially more complex—and intellectually more profound—than those effected between sick Portuguese soldiers or administrators and the native vaidyas whom they patronized. Catholic priests and missionaries often found themselves, like their martial coreligionists, desperately in need of indigenous cures to treat their own tropical maladies contracted in the service of the Church.[26] Clearly, as outsiders in a South Asian disease environment, the Europeans often found themselves at a loss for understanding of pertinent medical knowledge and, indeed, dependent on the assistance of local medical practitioners.[27]

Missionaries soon recognized that native cultures harboured a great store of folk knowledge about highly efficacious local medicinal plants. The same intellectual proclivities that led missionaries to study indigenous languages and customs (as a form of strategic knowledge for winning conversions) led them to gather detailed information about native healing arts: remedies and their ingredients. Within a generation of the initial Portuguese conquest, missionaries began to write and circulate protracted descriptions of indigenous healing plants, including advice about how to identify, prepare and apply native drugs.[28] As a core component of their evangelical activities, missionary organizations founded infirmaries and apothecaries in colonial enclaves to treat the sick and win conversions. There they dispensed imported and local drugs, and sold prepared remedies using ingredients from Europe, India and other Portuguese imperial regions, as well.[29] Taken together, such remedies represented a gradually developing hybridized Indo-Portuguese medical culture.

The missionary brotherhoods in time also developed the primary European body of expertise about indigenous medicine in the Portuguese colonies. Missionary orders, recognizing the potential for profit from commercializing native drugs, quickly became the principal disseminators of these healing commodities—and the specialized knowledge of how to prepare and use them—throughout the Portuguese maritime world. The Jesuits in particular systematically gathered empirical and practical ethnobotanical information, beginning almost from the moment of their arrival in colonized regions in the sixteenth century. Their numerous extant field manuals detail indigenous healing plants and remedies with striking precision and respect for local knowledge.[30] As near monopolists in the global trade of indigenous medicinal substances during the sixteenth, seventeenth and eighteenth centuries, missionary orders relied on this revenue to support their evangelical operations in the Portuguese overseas territories.[31]

Contrary to what is often supposed, the Jesuits and other missionary orders were not bound by a strict prohibition on engaging in commerce. On the contrary, canon law stipulated only that ecclesiastics could not purchase objects produced by others with the intent to sell them for profit; they *could*, however, vend goods that they had made, grown or developed themselves.[32] In the case of trade goods like medicines—wares that the missionaries directly gathered and blended, and the profits from which commerce contributed to their evangelical mission—Church and state authorities had no official grounds for objection (though many colonial merchants complained that the Jesuits took advantage of their position to glean large revenues).[33] This is precisely why the Jesuits dealt so aggressively and widely in medical drugs; theoretically they were barred from profiting on virtually any other type of trade that involved the buying and selling of finished goods.[34]

Archived South Asian missionary medical records mainly consist of commercial and inventory documents about what drugs or prepared remedies the missionary orders bought and sold. Extant missionary medical institution records also describe in detail the daily remedies that were prescribed and administered to patients—but somewhat counter-intuitively, they generally do not ascribe any overt religious or thaumaturgic philosophical significance to these drugs.

In fact, during the later period under consideration here (after *c.* 1575), the medical trade carried on by religious organizations in the colonies seems to have been carried out primarily as a pure revenue-earning enterprise. The Jesuit, Dominican and other brothers do not discuss any religious meaning attributed to the particular indigenous drugs or remedies that they adopted and employed. On the contrary, the documentation shows a very practical, empirical approach to healing, assigning efficacy and curative properties to medicinal substances based on observation of native practice and experimentation. In their zeal to locate effective new medicinal products within expanding European colonial spheres of influence, the Jesuits in particular showed themselves to be dismissive of thaumaturgic significance attributed to native plants within indigenous belief systems, preferring instead in their field notes to describe native plants in practical empirical terms, focusing on a given plant's traditional use or proven efficacious application (and thus its marketability, or viability as a product of sale) without reference to any supposed exterior divine cause for that effect.

Further, the Jesuits in particular showed a quite marked—even cynical—propensity to sell artificial or manufactured 'exotic Asian remedies' to customers in Europe or Brazil, primarily because such substances produced handsome profits that in turn supported the brotherhood's far-flung evangelical missions. Indeed, it was precisely because the Jesuits were restricted from trading in conventional commercial commodities that they turned to medicines and drugs as a source of revenue. Because healing was a recognized, approved dimension of their missionary activities and because, by long precedent, infirmaries and dispensing pharmacies had been part of the missionary establishment, evangelical brotherhoods were able to employ their global networks of pharmacies to generate revenue in a way that was perceived to be spiritually legitimate, orthodox and legal.

By the early seventeenth century, then, missionaries in Goa, Daman and Diu actually had few if any purely 'religious' motivations to gather information about Indian medicines (aside from the general imperative fundamental to all missionary orders—attempt to heal the sick and give comfort to the dying); instead, they were monopolizing trade in these substances to make money to support and perpetuate their activities. True, the operation of missionary infirmaries and hospitals was done out of requirement to provide Christian charity and made in an attempt to heal the sick, but their approach to medicine by 1600 and into the seventeenth and eighteenth centuries was far more commercial and scientific than it was spiritual.

Through such missionary commerce, medicines originating in India came to play a particularly significant role in the state-sponsored health care institutions of the Portuguese colonies around the world (though remedies from China, Brazil and Africa also found their place in the global Portuguese drugs market). Over time, colonial medical authorities in Goa produced a number of official reports about Indian medicines at the request of the Portuguese *Conselho Ultramarino* (Overseas Council, the royal body responsible for colonial administration) in Lisbon.[35] Such reports became an important conduit of information to crown officials in the metropôle and to medical practitioners in other parts of the empire; they provide a way to gauge the state of contemporary knowledge about certain medicinal substances from South Asia, and about the commercialization of—and market demand for—these medicines.

Additional insights about the acquisition and circulation of indigenous Indian medical knowledge within the Portuguese colonial empire can be gleaned by examining records of consignments of medicines shipped from Goa to such destinations as Macau, Timor, Mozambique, Brazil, São Tomé and continental Portugal. Colonial health officials generally supplied drug consignments to stock shipboard medical chests or regional colonial hospital facilities within the *Estado da Índia* and beyond.[36] Merchants and missionaries in Portuguese India, China and Brazil also supplied consignments of indigenous drugs for trade in the active global market for medicinal substances.[37]

Markets and Trade Routes for Drugs within the *Estado da Índia*

Early modern travellers from other European maritime powers occasionally described drug markets and medicines in the *Estado da Índia* for the commercial and scientific edification of their countrymen back home. One of the most vivid descriptions of indigenous medicinal drug use in Portuguese India comes from the account published in Amsterdam in 1596 by John Huyghen van Linschoten, who lived in Goa from September 1584 to January 1589. As a retainer of the Archbishop of Goa's household, he gathered detailed information about Portuguese colonial society and trade in India and around the Indian Ocean rim.[38]

Describing the market at 'Cambaia' (Khambhat, formally the port and mainland native kingdom of Cambay, east of Diu Island in present-day Gujarat) at the end of the sixteenth century, John van Linschoten wrote that the Portuguese, Persians, Arabs and Armenians 'go there to lade many kinds of drugs, as Amfiom, or Opium, Camfora [camphor], Bangue [*bhang*, or cannabis], and Sandalwood'.[39] He wrote that opium came mostly from Cambay and the Deccan plateau, further inland, but that it was also shipped from Ormuz, at the mouth of the Persian Gulf, Portuguese-controlled from 1515 until 1622 when they capitulated to a joint Anglo-Persian assault. Linschoten also noted that the inhabitants of the Malabar Coast, whereon the Portuguese held many of their Indian trading enclaves, consumed opium and other native medicinal substances in great abundance.[40] By the 1520s, Portuguese-licensed traders had taken over this lucrative commerce; much of the Indian Ocean drugs trade would remain in their hands for the next two centuries.

Soon after the Portuguese occupation of Goa and other parts of the Malabar Coast, opium rapidly found its way into use in colonial medical facilities. Most of the best-quality opium originated on the Indian Deccan Plain, to which the Portuguese had relatively easy access through their ports in Gujarat.[41] Clearly, opium was one of the most important products that the Portuguese (or any other merchants operating in Indian port towns) shipped throughout the Asian trade routes. Opium was unique among available contemporary drugs because it alone would effectively and reliably ease pain from traumatic injury.[42]

Other contemporary European travellers observed the use of various indigenous medicines being traded on the Malabar Coast, as well. In an account published during the third quarter of the seventeenth century, Philipus Baldaeus, a Dutch Protestant clergyman, noted the continued use of opium in Goa. In his detailed description of Goa, 'its Traffick and Manners, and Way of Living of the Portuguese there...', Baldaeus observed that Goa's main street had abundant rich shops 'well-stor'd with ... drugstery wares ...'[43]

Of course, commerce in opium also existed outside the framework of religious missionary orders. Portuguese army surgeons procured opium for their medicinal requirements; naval ships carried chests of medicines stocked with opium and other Indian medicines; and labour overseers or slave drivers in the Atlantic and Indian Ocean spheres occasionally bought opium in sufficient quantity to give to their hard-suffering workers.[44]

In the *Estado da Índia*, to make bulk opium purchases government military facilities (be it a garrison fortress, naval warship or a hospital), as well as private plantations or labour contractors, naturally had access to sources other than the religious orders' institutional pharmacies. Wholesale merchants or port markets in Gujarat could just as easily have supplied large consignments of opium at an attractive price. However, details about this commerce are largely un-documented.

Fiscal documents in Portuguese India reveal that the colonial government typically expended large sums annually to outfit state-owned vessels with appropriate medicines against tropical disease. A chart of colonial revenues and expenditures for 1762, for example, records that the apothecary of the Hospital Real Militar in Goa distributed drugs that year worth 5,287 *xerafins* (a substantial government expenditure) to the medicine chests of various vessels of the Portuguese fleet bound for other destinations in the maritime empire.[45] Most of these medicines, of course, originated in India.

After 1579, when the Jesuits took over administration of the Hospital Real Militar of Goa, the funds they spent on drugs and other medical expenses derived from a colony-wide excise tax levied on soap, opium and victuals. In turn, from these sources the Jesuits received some 14,000 *xerafins* per year to run the hospital. In addition, the hospital was to receive a royal subsidy of 25,000 *pardaus* per year (but this emolument was frequently left in arrears or remained unpaid).[46]

During the sixteenth and seventeenth centuries, some Indian medicinal stocks for Portuguese colonial apothecaries and pharmacies were gathered at Diu or Daman and shipped on to Goa, where the main stores of drugs were collected for use or re-export.[47] Often, though, consignments of drugs were supplied directly by Hindu merchants—wholesalers of medicinal plants—who procured bulk quantities of native remedies for Portuguese medical facilities in the Indian colonies.

Evidence of Hindu merchants providing regular deliveries of indigenous medicinal substances to Portuguese-run medical institutions can be found in the financial records of the Convents of São João de Deus and Nossa Senhora de Graça, both missionary confraternities located in Goa. This commercial procurement pattern continued well into the eighteenth century. For example, in 1758 a Hindu merchant named Varaná Camotim received cash for a variety of 'remedies' to be used in the São João de Deus infirmary.[48] Four decades later, two Hindu pharmacists, Rama Xandra Camotim and Segunam Camotim, received very large sums of cash for medicines and services rendered to the Graça Convent Hospital.[49]

Regular payments to Hindu drug merchants [identified by their names, such as 'Camotim' (i.e. the modern Kamat) or 'Ragunate' (Raghunath), spelled phonetically in the Portuguese texts] were also common in the sixteenth and seventeenth centuries. Indeed, medicinal purchases are consistently some of the largest disbursements recorded in the Nossa Senhora de Graça Hospital expense accounts. A single consignment of drugs and medicinal plants typically cost between 300 and 800 *xerafins*, a princely sum at the time.[50] (To give a sense of the value of these drug transactions, the chief physician of the Hospital Real Militar in Goa, the highest medical authority of the *Estado da Índia*, earned an official salary of only 25 *xerafins* per annum in the seventeenth and eighteenth centuries).[51]

From Goa, Indian medicinal substances were trans-shipped and widely distributed; coasting vessels carried consignments of the popular medicines to Portuguese-held ports along the Konkan and Malabar Coasts, or north to Bassein, Daman and Diu, as well as to Sri Lanka and destinations in eastern India. The Europe-bound ships of the annual Portuguese India fleet carried cargos of opium and other Indian drugs to Mozambique, Brazil and Lisbon. Meanwhile, Indian medicines travelled eastward in Portuguese-licensed vessels to imperial colonies at Timor and Macau, among others.[52]

For example, in 1682, after the Portuguese Overseas Council (*Conselho Ultramarino*) decided to restructure the colonial hospital at Mozambique, in part as an aid station for the crews and passengers of the India Fleet (*Carreira da Índia*), a very large consignment of medicines originating from Europe, Brazil and India was forwarded from Goa to stock the facility's pharmacy. Imperial officials included a range of South Asian remedies, many containing opiates, in this initial shipment.[53] Colonial medical authorities made sure that the new Mozambique hospital would have a stock of the popular *pedras cordeais* ('cordial stones') in the pharmacy—a mercury and opium-based 'panacea' in pill form.[54] Missionary apothecaries in Goa and Macau produced *pedras cordeais* using a variety of exotic Asian ingredients and shipped them great quantities, along with a printed sheet of dosage instructions, to destinations all over the Portuguese world—their particular use was to combat syphilis.[55] Besides opiated painkillers, other Indian medicines shipped in the consignment for Mozambique include rhubarb leaves and pills; medical pastes and unguents prepared with tamarind or aloe; althea ointment; asaetida root and the curiously named 'Hindu Pearls' (*Pirullas Hindoos*), a prepared medicine apparently manufactured with ingredients of Indian origin, if not indeed copied from a traditional Malabar Coast bolus.[56]

Over a century and a half later, in 1838, various Indian medicines, including opiates and healing balms, pastes and lotions, were still being shipped from Goa to imperial locations like East Timor as part of a consignment of drugs requested for the Military and Public Hospital in Dili. Several of these medical preparations had equivalents in traditional Indian ayurvedic methods: an unguent made from althea, pain balms including camphor and the roots and leaves of asaetida are salient examples.[57] Hospitals, pharmacies and infirmaries situated throughout the *Estado da Índia*, as well as medical facilities located in the Atlantic colonies, ordered and consumed a steady supply of traditional Indian medicinal substances from at least the 1550s into the mid-nineteenth century.[58]

In the sixteenth and seventeenth centuries, Portuguese pharmacies in Macau and Goa became practiced in the manufacture of artificial 'bezoar stones', a mystical Asian remedy that had been highly valued in the West since the Middle Ages. To meet overwhelming European demand for this esteemed panacea (believed to be able to immediately staunch the flow of blood from wounds and cure almost any illness), Jesuit apothecaries blended exotic ingredients from India and China, including 'unicorn horn shavings', emeralds, rubies, sapphires and topaz, and of course a bit of genuine bezoar stone (in actuality a naturally occurring concretion found in the stomachs or entrails of sheep and goats).[59] The sole, truly efficacious ingredients included opium and camphor. Shipments of artificial bezoar stones, packaged in Macao and Goa, arrived in Lisbon as late as the 1760s, after which the suppressed Jesuit order was forced to cease this lucrative (if somewhat deceptive) trade.

Such practices underscore the Jesuits' role as savvy marketers. In their shrewd trafficking of 'hindoo pills' and bezoar stones to European pharmacy retail outlets, the Jesuits cynically traded on the exotic nature of these remedies. Thus, it could be understood that their supposed effectiveness had nothing to do with the missionaries according sincere faith in the effectiveness of their products. Instead, the medicines were sold on the merit of their strange and exotic names. The Jesuits earned hefty profits through clever merchandising but, as the manufacturers, they were well aware that the implied source of potency of the drug was false. This clearly amounted to fraudulent sales practices.

Missionary Control of the Pharmaceutical Trade Within the Portuguese Maritime Empire

In continental Portugal at the beginning of the seventeenth century, the great majority of pharmacies were in the hands of that nation's numerous monasteries and operated by the often highly trained brothers of those institutions, be they Jesuit, Dominican, Franciscan, Augustinian, Benedictine or Carmelite.[60] Only in the larger cities, like Lisbon, Oporto, Coimbra or Évora, were secular pharmacies to be found. These, however, were generally modest concerns; secular pharmacists complained frequently to crown authorities that they could not compete with the monopolistic practices of the great missionary orders, whose purchasing power, established trade and procurement networks throughout the overseas empire and superior professional reputations combined to impoverish lay pharmacies in the metropôle.[61]

Hence, a virtual monopoly of the lucrative trade in medicinal substances in continental Portugal during the early modern period was controlled by missionary orders or monastic institutions and the colleges associated with them. In the case of medicines arriving from Brazil and the *Estado da Índia*, Jesuit druggists or apothecaries (*boticários*) in particular enjoyed a clear advantage, as they could rely on their co-religionist associates in Goa, Macau and Salvador da Bahia to procure and ship consignments of medicinal plants or prepared medications, such as the prized opium-and-mercury-containing *pedras cordeais*, to their brethren in Portugal.[62] Remedies of all kinds, from cheap tamarind paste to expensive bezoar stones, were common substances in which the Jesuit brothers trafficked on a truly global scale, sending consignments of drugs from India and China to Africa, South America and Europe.

Moreover, the missionary orders relied to a large extent on this trade for revenue that supported their proselytizing work. The Jesuits and other missionary orders sold medicines directly to the public through their networks of pharmacies in India, China, Brazil and other colonial locations, as well as in Portugal, earning considerable profits for their coffers. The market for colonial medicines in continental Portugal was largely their bailiwick for over two hundred years.[63]

Traditional South Asian Medicinal Substances Purchased for Use in the Pharmacies, Hospitals and Infirmaries of Portuguese India (*c.* 1530–1650)

We will now look at the actual indigenous medicinal substances and drugs found to be in use in Indo-Portuguese medical institutions between 1530 and 1650. First, it will be instructive to consider what the term *droga* ('drug') connoted to the early-modern Portuguese mind. It was a word of great imprecision, having a far broader meaning than simply 'drug' as it is understood today. The word included medicinal substances derived from animals or plants, but covered consumer goods like spices, dye woods, and tobacco, as well. Resins, gums, oils, balsams, and roots: all were categorized as *drogas* on the manifests of merchant ships of the *Carreira da Índia*.[64]

What follows is a brief catalogue of just some of the typical indigenous plant substances utilized in the hospitals and infirmaries of Portuguese India between 1530 and *c.* 1650 (but widely available in the Lisbon market, as well). Collectively, they give a good general overview of the type of substances the Portuguese obtained for medical applications in their Asian colonial holdings.[65] Each of these substances was also commonly employed in contemporary ayurvedic medicine, as well as other indigenous medical systems of the Malabar Coast. Given the hybrid nature peculiar to Indo-Portuguese colonial medical culture, in official state medical installations these drugs were being applied to counteract the same general maladies or symptoms for which classical ayurveda or local healing systems would prescribe them.

1. Aloe (in Portuguese *aloes*; also known as *azebre*): The general name for the sap of diverse species of genus *Aloe*, found in the environs of India, on the island of Socotra (at the mouth of the Gulf of Aden), and near

the Cape of Good Hope. In Europe it was used in concert with other drugs for the mixture of medicinal plasters or poultices, or as a topical external ointment. The substance was also attributed with powers as a purgative to clear the bowels or emetic to induce vomiting; it was further employed topically as a cooling agent to treat fevers. This latter use was taken directly from Indian practice: native healers on the Malabar Coast employed the fresh pulp of aloe leaves as a cooling compress.[66]

2. Altea (in Portuguese *althea*): A plant of the genus *Malva*, also known as *sida* or 'marsh mallow'. A small shrub, *althea* grew all over India as a common weed. There is considerable disagreement among historians regarding exactly which plant—among several possible candidates—this might be. The plant's seeds saw use as an aphrodisiac and to increase sexual potency; in combination with ginger (as a decoction) it was applied for certain fevers (an analogous use is documented in ayurvedic texts); the powdered root bark of *althea* was given with milk to women for nervous disorders; the root juice was used topically to help heal wounds.[67] A dose of *althea* was a common daily treatment for patients in some Indo-Portuguese healing facilities in the middle of the seventeenth century.[68]
3. Asafoetida (in Portuguese *asafétida*): A preparation made from the leaves and gum resin obtained from crushing parings from the roots of diverse plants of the genus *Ferula*, which was native to the Persian Gulf and adjoining regions. This plant was used popularly in India as an agent to ward off evil spirits. Contemporary usage often combined this plant with *arruda*, known in English as the herb rue.[69] Trained and licensed European *médicos* recommended *asafétida* as an anti-spasm agent; in India it was known as an aphrodisiac, drunk as an aperitif to stimulate the appetite and used as a treatment for hysteria.
4. Benzoin (in Portuguese *benjoim*; also known as *assadulcis*): This balsam or salve was made from sap obtained through incisions cut in the trunk of the *Styrax Benzoim Dryander*, which is a native plant of Sumatra, the Persian Gulf and eastern India. The raw sap could also be dried into a powder for transport and then mixed into a balm once it arrived in Europe.[70] In India, where it was very abundant, according to Garcia da Orta, eating it was thought to strengthen the limbs and calm stomach disorders.[71]
5. Cardamom (in Portuguese *cardamomo*): This is a common medicinal plant that grows wild in south India and has long been known to ayurveda and other indigenous healing systems. The drug consists of the dried fruits and seeds of the plant. Often used in combination with cloves, ginger or caraway seeds, Indian vaidyas saw it as effective for indigestion, or administered with a purgative to relieve digestive problems.[72] Portuguese colonial pharmacies stocked this *droga* commonly from the mid-sixteenth century onward.

6. Cashew Feni (in Portuguese *vinho de cajú*): A medicine, the basis of which was a fermented or distilled alcoholic beverage made from the fruit of the cashew tree, it was administered at home as an infusion and decoction. Feni was also served in colonial hospitals as a heated medicinal beverage. The Portuguese, of course, introduced cashew trees into India from Brazil, but indigenous medicine along the Malabar Coast soon embraced 'cashew wine' and spirits as a painkiller, decongestant, and for relief of respiratory ailments. This is a clear instance, then, when Portuguese practice added to the medical lexicon of Konkani-speaking peoples in Goa.[73]
7. Cinnamon (in Portuguese *canela*): In Indian antiquity this plant was credited with curative qualities. The drug was prepared from the husk or shell of the cinnamon plant, a plant native to Ceylon (modern Sri Lanka) and the Malabar Coast. In the sixteenth and seventeenth centuries, the Portuguese in India used cinnamon as a stimulant and as an agent to calm nervous stomachs. It was much sought as a stimulating tonic and aphrodisiac, and also used, of course, as a food additive, or as a spice in soured wine.[74] The plant was ground into powders, used as a base for perfumed oils, combined with other substances in solutions, or sold as a dried plant cutting which was then soaked in a beverage or medicine.[75] Classical ayurveda assigned cinnamon with similar healing qualities.[76]
8. Cloves (in Portuguese *cravos*): These are dried flower buds of the tree which in Hindi is known as *jambuh* or *jambol*, a large evergreen found in the humid, deciduous forests of Kerala and Goa. Cultivated by natives and colonists alike, cloves were common along the Malabar Coast water channels. Its application among ayurvedic practitioners, as well as in Portuguese colonial hospitals, included use for anti-nausea and vomiting; indigestion; as a stimulant; an antiseptic and preservative (clove oil); an anti-spasmodic; and a carminative.[77]
9. Ginger (in Portuguese *gingebra*): A 'universal remedy', according to classical ayurveda.[78] This plant is widely cultivated throughout south India and has been central to ayurvedic principles long before the arrival of the Europeans. As an acrid, heat-inducing food, it was valued as an anti-rheumatic, carminative, diuretic and aphrodisiac. Ginger root, dried and powdered, is thought to cure cardiac disorders, stop vomiting and coughing, and help liver inflammation. It addresses such conditions as constipation, fever, swelling, flatulence and colic. Ginger is also applied to stop diarrhoea, to treat cholera, for dyspepsia and to cure eye diseases.[79] Portuguese colonial medical facilities procured large quantities and made extensive use of ginger during the sixteenth and seventeenth centuries.
10. Opium (in Portuguese *opio*): Cultivated in India for medicinal purposes since at least the fifteenth century, opium, sometimes called *amfiam*, found

a niche in ayurvedic practices. Useful as a strong painkiller and sedative, it was also a popular aphrodisiac.[80] Sixteenth-century Portuguese physician and medical author Garcia da Orta was well aware of the addictive dangers of this drug, but described its attraction and value as an item of trade. In Portuguese colonial hospitals and infirmaries of the sixteenth and seventeenth centuries, opium was sometimes administered mixed with wine, or as a component of the alcoholic tincture.[81]

11. Pepper (in Portuguese *pimenta*): Originally from the Spice Archipelagos of the Pacific Ocean and the Malabar coast, this *droga*, like cinnamon mentioned earlier, was a food condiment but also credited with medicinal powers. Used as a tonic or general stimulant, this plant also was employed as an aperitif to stimulate the appetite, and as an aid to digestion. Popularly, it was considered an aphrodisiac, or at least as an agent to attract the affection of a desired mate. Typically, pepper was ground into a powder, but in Portuguese India it also formed the base of medicinal oils, unguents or syrups, or as an ingredient in specially-prepared *águas* ('waters').[82]
12. Rhubarb (in Portuguese *ruibarbo*): A tall herb with very stout stems and roots; its primary application was as a purgative, ingested in considerable quantities to cleanse the bowels. It is found at high altitudes in the Himalayas in Kashmir, Punjab, Uttar Pradesh and Nepal, but conventional wisdom amongst medical practitioners in Goa held that the best variety was grown in Persia or elsewhere in Central Asia and shipped from the Safavid realm through Ormuz. Rhubarb is valued for its healing properties all over India; hence it was especially cultivated. Because of its obscure habitat, it is very expensive to gather and distribute. The Portuguese, like Indian practitioners, used this plant as a purgative, but the plant has tannins, which act as an astringent, causing constipation after the purging effect. Therefore, rhubarb was an effective agent both against constipation and diarrhoea.[83] Such results served the Portuguese well, since many of their European conscript soldiers suffered from cholera and other gastro-intestinal diseases.
13. Sandalwood (in Portuguese *sandalo*): A middle-sized evergreen tree, common in the Deccan; called *chandan* or *sandhan* in the Hindi and Malayalam languages, respectively. The oil of the plant, as well as the ground, powdered wood, is considered medicinal. Sandalwood oil is applied for urinary tract problems or difficulty in urination; bladder infection; gonorrhoea; cough; tuberculosis and other respiratory ills; and gall bladder ailments. The seed oil of sandalwood is considered a treatment for skin diseases. Sandalwood pulp or paste is used in a poultice for inflammations, as a fever reducer and as a treatment for skin diseases.[84] Indo-Portuguese practitioners used sandalwood paste to treat seasonal fevers in the Royal Military Hospital of Goa.[85]

14. Sarsaparilla (in Portuguese *sarsaparilha*): A perennial climbing vine that is found throughout India, ayurvedic healers have long employed this plant drug as a substitute for true Sarsaparilla. The woody root, powdered and mixed with water or other plant juice, constitutes the drug. Sarsaparilla is useful as a fever reducer and anti-rheumatic; it can also be used to treat skin diseases, syphilis, and urinary disorders. Finally, ingested, its diuretic effect was used to purify the blood.[86] Indo-Portuguese surgeons and physicians prescribed sarsaparilla for the same maladies and made sure that colonial pharmacies were well stocked with the substance.[87]
15. Tamarind (in Portuguese *tamarindo*): A pulp made of the body and seed pod of the tamarind plant, a leafy, vegetable-like tree of the tropics. Alternatively, this preparation could consist of the stems, roots and bark of the plant, reduced to a consistent paste. As a medicine, it was used for its qualities as a digestive, as a laxative, and to reduce fever. Indo-Portuguese practitioners often mixed *tamarindo* paste with other plants. It is rich in organic acids (citric and tartaric), as well as sugars and pectins.[88] This preparation was also a common ingredient in medicinal *águas*, preserves and syrups.[89]
16. Zedoaria (in Portuguese *zedoária*): It is the root of the *Curcuma Zedoaria*, originating in India and the Molucca islands. Associated with the root of *angélica* and diluted in vinegar, this plant was used by Europeans and South Asians to perfume the mouth during times of plague or epidemic, or to ward off disease. This bitter substance was also used in a balm, together with licorice and gentian, to soothe and protect burns or used popularly to deflect the evil eye; the drug was also considered a stimulant and an anti-spasmodic.[90]

Since the number of European physicians and surgeons in the *Estado da Índia* were so few, practical need dictated that medical attention for the indigenous population within the Portuguese Indian colonies had to be met by native practitioners and apothecaries. Over time, especially following the stark decline of Golden Goa, the colonial government began to acquiesce to that reality and recognize officially contributions made by Hindu health care providers. For example, in 1687, the local director (*provincial*) of the monastery of Madre de Deus wrote a letter to the Portuguese Viceroy in India, citing examples of service and aid provided by Hindu healers in his region during times of epidemic disease. The *provincial* recounted numerous episodes when vaidyas had served alongside his ecclesiastical brethren in the hospitals and infirmaries of Mormugão (south Goa), and reminded the Viceroy that Hindus had contributed to Portuguese efforts from the beginning of the colonial period. On the strength of these contributions, the *provincial* advocated that the colonial government continue to formally cultivate native healing talents.[91] Eventually, as several local Goan healers found their way into Portuguese service, the widespread introduction and use of indigenous medicine in Goa's medical institutions became inevitable and the hybridization of Indo-Portuguese medical culture was complete.

Stocking colonial pharmacies in Portuguese India during the Enlightenment era was thus largely a matter of relying on local resources. To be sure, remedies and drugs continued to arrive at colonial hospitals and infirmaries in the *Estado da Índia* from the metropôle, China, Africa and Brazil. However, in the thoroughly hybridized healing culture of seventeenth-century Goa, Daman and Diu, indigenous practitioners, even if Christianized and Portuguese-speaking, held most of the medical posts. Their natural inclination was to resort to familiar (and convenient) local medicinal plants of the kind extolled in India for millennia. Colonial pharmacy stock lists and purchasing records clearly reflect the contemporary predilection for medicines that were of local Indian origins. Considering the overwhelmingly native composition of the colonial population at that time, this revelation should come as no surprise.

Notes

*I wish to thank the American Institute of Indian Studies, the United States National Endowment for the Humanities, the Wellcome Trust Center for the History of Medicine at University College, London and the University of Massachusetts Dartmouth Center for Portuguese Studies and Culture; this research was completed with grants provided through these organizations. For logistical support in Goa, I am grateful to the Xavier Centre for Historical Research and the Portuguese Fundação Oriente.

1. Timothy Walker, 'Acquisition and Circulation of Medical Knowledge within the Early Modern Portuguese Colonial Empire,' in *Science, Power and the Order of Nature in the Spanish and Portuguese Empires*, ed. Daniela Bleichmar, Kristin Huffine and Paula De Vos, Stanford: Stanford University Press, 2009, pp. 250-60.
2. M.N. Pearson, *The Portuguese in India*, Cambridge: Cambridge University Press, 1987, pp. 133-7.
3. *Estado da Índia* is the term used to describe the Portuguese Empire across Asia, from Mozambique to Macau.
4. In 1791, for example, the population of all territories in Portuguese India was reported as 201,919; barely over one thousand (under 0.25 per cent) were Portuguese natives. See HAG MR 173, f. 227. For detailed 1788 population statistics, see HAG MR 169A, ff. 305-7. See also Timothy J. Coates, *Convicts and Orphans: Forced and State-Sponsored Colonization in the Portuguese Empire, 1550–1755*, Stanford: Stanford University Press, 2002, pp. 35, 69-71.

5. See Maria de Jesus dos Mártires Lopes, *Goa Setecentista; Tradição e Modernidade (1750–1800),* 2nd edn, Universidade Católica Portuguesa, 1999, pp. 90-4, 115-23.
6. For further discussion on this point, see Walker, 'Acquisition and Circulation', pp. 257-8, 260.
7. Ibid., pp. 260-8.
8. Ibid., and José Pedro Sousa Dias and Rui Pita, 'A Botica de S. Vicente e a Farmácia nos Mosteiros e Conventos da Lisboa Setecentista', in *A Botica de São Vicente de Fora,* Lisbon: Associação Nacional das Farmácias, 1994, pp. 19-20.
9. Representative examples include, respectively, HAG 865, 'Doentes do Hospital Real do Baçaim'; HAG 831, Livro da Receita e Despeza de Medicamentos do Hospital do Convento de São João de Deus', HAG 8032, 'Botica do Convento do Santo Agostinho', HAG MR 175, ff. 219-30 and HAG MR 178B, ff. 644-64.
10. See, for example, HAG MR Nr. 181A, ff. 9-45; HAG MR Nr. 181B, ff. 370-98.
11. Arthur Coke Burnell and P.A. Tiele, eds., *The Voyage of John Huyghen Van Linschoten to the East Indies...,* vol. I, London: The Hakluyt Society, 1885, p. 237.
12. Alberto C. Germano da Silva Correia, *La Vieille-Goa,* Bastora: Rangel Press, 1931, pp. 274-5; F.P. Mendes da Luz, 'Livro das Cidades', *Studia* 6, 1960, f. 8. The author is grateful to Professor M.N. Pearson for this reference.
13. See, for example, HAG MR Nr. 181A, ff. 65, 194-201; HAG MR Nr. 212A, f. 200v.
14. François Pyrard de Laval, *The Voyage of François Pyrard of Laval to the East Indies,* vol. II, London, 1888, pp. 3-7.
15. Charles R. Boxer, *Portuguese Society in the Tropics,* Madison: University of Wisconsin Press, 1965, pp. 25-6.
16. Charles J. Borges, *The Economics of the Goa Jesuits, 1542–1759,* New Delhi: Concept Publishing, 1994, pp. 27-8.
17. For figures of the annual number of patients treated at the Hospital Real Militar, see HAG MR 173, fol. 168; HAG MR 176B, fol. 436; HAG MR 176B, fol. 448; and HAG MR 177A, fol. 218.
18. HAG MR 115 (1742), fols. 88-9.
19. HAG 646, fol. 39.
20. Ibid., fols. 40-1.
21. For examples, see HAG MR 52, fol. 191r/v, and HAG MR 115, fols. 88r-89r.
22. See M.N. Pearson, 'The Portuguese State and Medicine in Sixteenth Century Goa', in K.S. Mathew, Teotonio R. de Souza and Pius Malekandathil, eds., *The Portuguese and Socio-Cultural Changes In India, 1500–1800,* Goa: Fundacao Oriente, 2001, pp. 401-19.
23. See J.B. Amâncio Gracias, *Médicos Europeus em Goa e nas Cortes Indianas nos séculos XVI á XVIII,* Bastora: Rangel Press, 1939, pp. 10-11 and 30-5. See also M.N. Pearson, 'The Thin End of the Wedge: Medical Relativities as a Paradigm of Early Modern Indian-European Relations', *Modern Asian Studies,* vol. XXIX, no. l, 1995, pp. 141-70.

24. Maria Bernadette Gomes, *Ethnomedicine and Healing Practices in Goa,* Unpublished Ph.D. dissertation, Department of Sociology, University of Goa, India, 1993, introduction.
25. João Manuel Pacheco de Figueiredo, 'The Practice of Indian Medicine in Goa During the Portuguese Rule, 1510–1699', *The Luso-Brazilian Review*, vol. IV, no. 1, June 1967, pp. 51-2.
26. See the Shembaganur Province Archives, Sacred Heart College, Kodaikanal, Tamil Nadu, India; Annual Jesuit Missionary Letters of the Malabar Province; Shelf 211, Book 34 (1606-1643), pp. 30-44, 47-50, 52-3 and 78. See also Shelf 211, Book 102 (1655-66), pp. 87-91 and 221-7.
27. Ibid., and Borges, *Economics of the Goa Jesuits,* pp. 27-8, 86-8 and 106.
28. See, for example, the Biblioteque National du France (Paris), Department of Manuscripts, Fonds Portugais No. 59, Breve compendio de varias receitas de medicina (1598), fols. 2-79v; also Biblioteca Nacional do Rio de Janeiro (BNRJ, Brazil), Manuscripts Division; Nr. I-15, 02, 026, Curiosidade; un libro de Medicina escrito por los Jesuitas en las Misiones del Paraguay en el año 1580 (1580), fols. 1-280; and Archivum Romanum Societatis Iesu (ARSI, Rome, Italy), Opp. NN. 17, Colecção de Varias Receitas e Segredos Particulares das Principais Boticas da Nossa Companhia de Portugal, da India, de Macao e do Brazil (1766), fols. 1-688.
29. See HAG Nr. 9477, fols. 43, 58, 90 and 141. See also HAG 7887, fols. 2v, 7r, 9v and 40-3.
30. Refer to the manuscripts cited in Note 29.
31. Dias and Pita, 'A Botica de S. Vicente', pp. 19-20.
32. See Dauril Alden, *The Making of an Enterprise: The Society of Jesus in Portugal, Its Empire, and Beyond, 1540–1750*, Stanford: Stanford University Press, 1996, p. 529, main text and footnote 2.
33. Borges, *Economics of the Goa Jesuits,* pp. 41, 86.
34. In practice, of course, the Jesuits often did engage in various types of commercial activity, often with crown consent, but usually in modest volume. See Alden, *The Making of an Enterprise,* pp. 529-31 and 540-4; see also Borges, *Economics of the Goa Jesuits,* pp. 41, 86.
35. See Central Library of Panaji, Goa, India, Manuscripts No. 18: Notícias Particular do Commércio da Índia, fols. 2-58; HAG MR 175, fols. 219-30 and HAG Monções do Reino 178B, fols. 644-64. See also Bibliotheque Nationale du France (Paris), Department of Manuscripts, Fonds Portugais No. 59, Breve compendio de varias receitas de medicina (1598), fols. 2-79v.
36. See, for example, HAG MR 46A, fols. 96r-97v; and HAG 7926, fols. 56r-56v, 'Relação de Medicamentos que vão da Botica do Hospital Real [de Goa] para a Fortaleza de Diu'.
37. Brazil, for example, supplied large quantities of 'Jesuits Bark', or quinine derived from the chinchona tree; see HAG 8030, fol. 28 and HAG MR 180B, fols. 444-5v. Meanwhile, the Jesuit pharmacy in Macau supplied Chinese medicinal preparations to India; see A.M. Amaro, *Introdução da Medicina ocidental em Macau e as receitas de segredo da botica do Colégio de São Paulo,* Macau: Instituto Cultural de Macau, 1992, pp. 7-11.

38. Burnell and Tiele, *The Voyage of John Huyghen*, vol. I, pp. xxiii-xl.
39. Ibid., p. 61.
40. Ibid., vol. II, pp. 113-14.
41. Carlos Xavier, 'Daman Port and Shipyards', in *Purabhilekh-Puratatva*, Journal of the Directorate of Archives, Archaeology and Museum, vol. III, no. 1, January-June 1985, Panaji, Goa, pp. 10-12.
42. HAG Volume 9477; Despezas do Convento da Graça (1726-1733), fols 6-18.
43. Philip Baldaeus, *A True and Exact Description of the Most Celebrated East-Indian Coasts of Malabar and Coromandel, and also of the Isle of Ceylon*, facsimile edition, New Delhi: Asia Educational Services, 2000, p. 608.
44. HAG MR 85, fol. 59v.
45. HAG MR 135B, fol. 489v.
46. Borges, *Economics of the Goa Jesuits*, pp. 27, 86-7.
47. Burnell and Tiele, *The Voyage of John Huyghen,* vol. II, pp. 113-14.
48. HAG 7887, 'Despeza do Convento de São João de Deus' (1758-71), f. 2v.
49. HAG 8031, fol. 4r/v.
50. Ibid., fols. 10r-17v.
51. HAG 4508, 'Pessoal do Hospital Militar' (1777-79), fol. 5r.
52. See CLP, Manuscripts No. 18, fols. 2-58. A similar document describing commercial transfers of medical substances, dated 1779, is held in the AHU in Lisbon, but has been published in Afzal Ahmad, *Os Portugueses na Ásia*, Lisbon: Imprensa Nacional/Casa da Moeda, 1997, pp. 51-118.
53. HAG MR 46A (1681-82), fols. 96r-97v.
54. Borges, *Economics of the Goa Jesuits,* pp. 87 and 106 (endnote 5); Alden, *The Making of an Enterprise,* p. 543.
55. Manoel Rodrigues Coelho, *Farmacopeia Tubalense Chimico-Galenica*, Lisbon: Officina de Antonio de Sousa Sylva, 1735, pp. 845-6.
56. Ibid.
57. HAG 1346, f. 183.
58. Fátima da Silva Gracias, *Health and Hygiene in Colonial Goa, 1510-1961*, New Delhi: Concept Publishing Company, 1994, pp. 105-6.
59. Amaro, *Introdução da Medicina ocidental em Macau,* pp. 100-2.
60. Dias and Pita, *A Botica de São Vicente de Fora,* p. 19.
61. ANTT, Ministério do Reino, Maço 469 (no date); cited in José Pedro Sousa Dias, 'Inovação Técnica e Sociedade na Farmáci da Lisboa Setecentista', doctoral dissertation of the Universidade de Lisboa, Faculdade de Farmácia, 1991, vol. II, pp. 638-9. See also Dias and Pita, *A Botica de São Vicente de Fora*, p. 20.
62. Dias and Pita, *A Botica de São Vicente de Fora*, pp. 19-20.
63. Ibid.
64. A.J.R. Russell-Wood, *The Portuguese Empire: 1415-1808,* Baltimore: The Johns Hopkins University Press, 1998, p. 129.
65. See José Pedro Sousa Dias, 'O Odor e o Sabor da Farmacologia Galénica', in Inácio Guerreiro, ed. *A Epopeia das Especiarias*, Lisbon: Instituto de Investigação Científica Tropical and Edições INAPA, 1999, pp. 90-103.

66. Garcia da Orta, *Coloquios dos Simples e Drogas de Índia*, Goa: Rachol Seminary, 1563, pp. 4-9 and 38, 40, 42; Maria Benedita Araújo, 'A Medicina Popular e a Magia no Sul de Portugal', doctoral dissertation of the Universidade de Lisboa, Faculdade de Letras, 1988, vol. III, p. 144.
67. S.K. Jain, *Medicinal Plants*, New Delhi: National Book Trust, India, 1999, pp. 160-1; and V.V. Sivarajan and Indira Balachandran, *Ayurvedic Drugs and Their Plant Sources*, New Delhi and Bombay: Oxford & IBH Publishing Co. Pvt. Ltd., 1994, pp. 71-9.
68. HAG 831 (Livro da Receita e Despeza de Medicamentos do Hospital do Convento de São João de Deus), f. 3r (18 May 1733), and many subsequent days.
69. Ibid., p. 149.
70. Araújo, 'A Medicina Popular...', vol. III, pp. 152-3.
71. da Orta, Colloquy IX.
72. Jain, *Medicinal Plants*, pp. 72-4. Sivarajan and Balachandran, *Ayurvedic Drugs*, pp. 398-9. See also da Orta, Colloquy XIII.
73. HAG 831, fol. 72r (27 July 1735).
74. HAG 8030, fol. 28 (November 1832).
75. Frei Caetano de Santo António, *Pharmacopea Lusitana Reformada*, p. 41; Frei Caetano de Santo António, *Pharmacopea Lusitana*, p. 69.
76. Jain, *Medicinal Plants*, pp. 56-8.
77. Jain, *Medicinal Plants*, pp. 172-4; Sivarajan and Balachandran, *Ayurvedic Drugs*, pp. 188-9. See also da Orta, Colloquy XXV.
78. Robert E. Svoboda, *Ayurveda: Life, Health and Longevity*, New Delhi, London and New York: Penguin Books, 1993, pp. 130-1.
79. Sivarajan and Balachandran, *Ayurvedic Drugs*, pp. 50-1. See also da Orta, Colloquy XXVI.
80. Svoboda, *Ayurveda*, pp. 215-16. See also da Orta, Colloquy XLI.
81. For use in an Indo-Portuguese medical facility, see HAG 831, fol. 7r (21 June 1733).
82. Araújo, 'A Medicina Popular…', pp. 204-5.
83. Jain, *Medicinal Plants*, pp. 150-1. For application of rhubarb in an Indo-Portuguese medical facility, see HAG 831 ('Livro da Receita e Despeza de Medicamentos do Hospital do Convento de São João de Deus'), fol. 2r (6 May 1733).
84. Jain, *Medicinal Plants,* pp. 154-5; Sivarajan and Balachandran, *Ayurvedic Drugs*, pp. 111-12.
85. See Bernadette Gomes, 'Ethnomedicine and Healing Practices in Goa', unpublished Ph.D. dissertation, Department of Sociology, University of Goa, India, 1993, Chapter 2; and Jain, *Medicinal Plants,* pp. 154-5. For evidence of use in Portuguese medical facilities, see HAG volume 7887 ('Despezas do Convento do São João de Deus'), fols. 197r, and HAG MR 46A, fol. 96.
86. Jain, *Medicinal Plants*, pp. 96-7. Sivarajan and Balachandran, *Ayurvedic Drugs*, pp. 434-8.
87. See, for example, HAG 8030, fol. 37.

88. Ibid., p. 214.
89. Frei Manuel Azevedo, *Correcçam de Abusos*, Tome III, Lisbon: 1680, p. 292; Brás Luís de Abreu, *Portugal Medíco*, pp. 192-3; 386; da Orta, p. 203; Frei Caetano de Santo António, *Pharmacopea Bateana*, Lisbon, 1713, p. 105.
90. Araújo, 'A Medicina Popular...', vol. III, pp. 217-18.
91. HAG MR 52, fol. 191r/v.

CHAPTER SEVEN

Between South and Central Asia Networks in the Himalayan Region of Ladakh

Rattan Lal Hangloo

> But we know of course that urban development does not happen of its own accord, it is not an endogenous phenomenon produced under a bell jar. It is always the expression of society, which controls it from within, but also from without, and in this respect our classification is, I repeat, too simple. That said, how does it work when applied outside the narrow confines of Western Europe?
>
> —Fernand Braudel,
> *Structures of Everyday Life,*
> *vol. 1: Civilization and Capitalism*, p. 520.

Ladakh was one of those principal regions on the Silk Route that acted as a major centre of an inter- and intra-regional exchange system, facilitating economic, cultural and political contacts between India on the one hand, and the Chinese, Tibetan, Russian and the wider Central Asian worlds on the other, on the Silk Route itself, from very early times.[1] My argument is that although part of the western Tibetan political, cultural and economic system, Ladakh also formed the western end of an economic network cutting through from Yunnan and Tibet.

However, in the course of the nineteenth century, through British expansion in the region, its economy was largely sundered from that of its Central Asian neighbours and reoriented toward the port of Calcutta. This was a heavy price for Ladakh as an economic and facilitating node to pay.

The spatial history of Ladakh can be envisaged in many ways: as the westerly point of the Tibetan cultural world, as a part of Central Asia, as part of the South Asian Himalayan world and as a point on the Silk Route. While in particular a transnational region, it is also a landlocked one with no access to the sea except through the networks that connected it to ports throughout its history. Therefore, it would be incorrect to consider Ladakh in terms of the national frames that exist today.

The Silk Route, embracing the Takla Makan desert, was one of the most important highways linking the trading world from the coasts of the Indian Ocean to the Bosporous, to Trapenzut on the Black Sea to the Volga and the Siberian Rivers, to the Baltic Sea, to Manchuria, Korea, Japan, the Chinese coast, to Indonesia, India and Ceylon. These linkages took root two thousand years before the German researcher Baron Ferdinand Von Richthofen gave it the name of Silk Route in the nineteenth century.[2] Ladakh as a trading mart on the Silk Route was significant in pre-modern times both as a mart as well as a pivot: 'Upper Indus (i.e. Ladakh) as a centre of gold producing country has been known to the world since the times of Herodotus.'[3]

Situated in the Western Himalayas, the region of Ladakh represents a specific geographical type, bound by physical conditions that are far more restrictive. From the north-eastern side it is separated by the Karakoram Mountains from China, located to its north and north-west are Central Asia and Russia. The Indian state of Himachal Pradesh falls towards the southern side of Ladakh. On its west lies Baltistan (at present in Pakistan) and Kashmir. The immense barrenness and the strong parallelism of its mountain ranges constitute the prominent feature of its geography.[4] Amidst these mountain ranges lie uniform river valleys along the headwaters of the Indus, the Sutlej and the Chenab where human society forms a componential part of the organic world. The sparsely populated valleys of Nubra, Zanskar and Suru are situated in some of the most elevated regions of the world.[5]

Ladakh was not an insular region; rather it formed part of a long and distinguished chain of economic exchange from early times located as it was on the Silk Route. The Silk Route was not just a horizontal cultural and commercial route, various, vertical, trading routes and networks also connected with it at specific junctures thereby bringing together the worlds of the mountains and the seas.

The interaction between the people of Ladakh and the region's overall nature of elevation, ecosystem, irrigation potential, climatology, soil qualities and other geographical and geological specificities, produced a material culture unsuitable for agriculture. Therefore, the features of the social formation that evolved in Ladakh from early times were not only accompanied by inert socio-economic processes that were dependant on meagre agricultural incomes but were also supplemented by craft production and pastoral produce, derived by the herding of sheep, goats and yak. This mix represented two complementary forms of production, i.e. pastoralism and agriculture. This in turn facilitated a primitive exchange economy which acquired regular, formalized processes with the passage of time.[6] A.H. Franke appropriately remarks,

> ...the irrigable valleys of Western Tibet (i.e. Ladakh) had been brought under cultivation by the Aryan tribes of Mons and Dards and the latter especially exhibited an extraordinary skill in construction of water courses along almost inaccessible cliffs. The products of the fields were as welcome to the Tibetan nomads as were the produce of flocks to the Dard peasants, and the lively barter which took place between the two tribes apparently led to many matrimonial 'bargains' as well, and so a race grew up which combined the agriculturist and the nomad.[7]

It was against this background that the early societal transition took place in Ladakh. This process involved a gradual dissolution of kinship forms among the Mons and Dards with increasing interaction with the people of Tibet, China, Central Asia, Kashmir and other surrounding regions, who

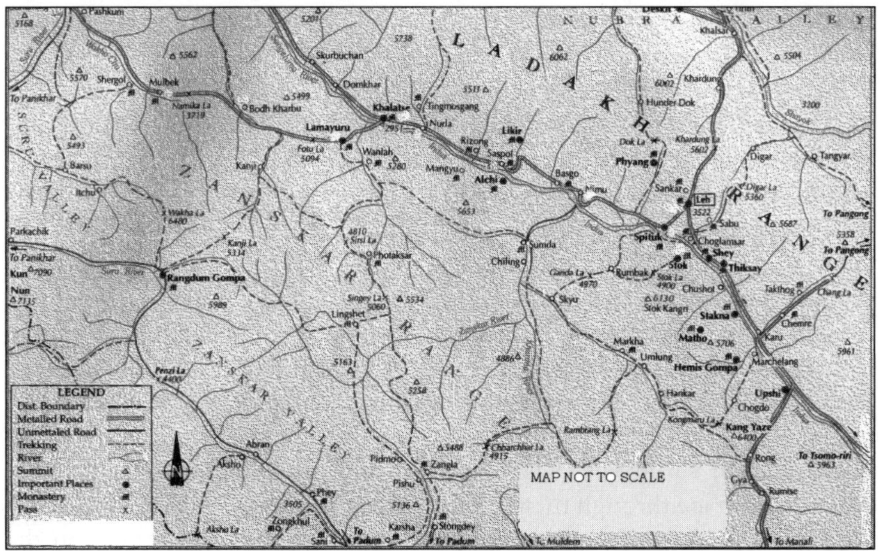

MAP 7.1: MAP OF LADAKH

Source: http://members.rediff.com/travel_ladakh/maps.htm

traversed the Silk Route accompanying Buddhist monks and trading caravans from early times.[8] This transition was also accompanied simultaneously by the appearance of a rudimentary division of labour, including ceremonial labour and the establishment of Buddhist monasteries and *viharas* from the first century AD along the Silk Route.[9] From this period onwards Buddhism played a significant role in influencing the wandering nomadic tribes of the region by establishing monasteries, which dotted the entire landscape of Ladakh in course of time. During this phase, from the first to the sixth century AD, Buddhism spread in western Central Asia and in several other places like Peshawar, Balkh, Sogdian, Herat, Kandahar, Bactria, Samarkand, Khotan, Kashgar and Yarkand, all of which developed as important centres of religious and market activity on the Silk Route.[10] These developments influenced the Ladakh region where many settlements came up: 'The almost empty land attracted more and more colonists, and the religious settlements grew into villages and towns in course of time.'[11]

From the sixth century AD onwards, when the forces of urbanization and spread of Buddhism received a serious setback in western Central Asia, the focus shifted to eastern Central Asia, i.e. the Tibetan plateau, and for the first time the formation of a unified Tibetan empire took place, of which western Tibet (i.e. the Guge Kingdom which also included Ladakh) was an integral part.[12] In the tenth century AD, after the persecution of Buddhists in Tibet by Lang Darma, the unified Tibetan empire broke up. The revival of Buddhism started in the Western Tibetan kingdom of Guge under the patronage of Yesho Od. Under his patronage Tholing, the capital of Guge, became the main centre and 108 Buddhist *gumpas* (monasteries) were established all over the Western Himalayas by Rinchen-Zangpo.[13]

King Lha chen Palgyigon Rgyalpo (AD 1100-25) built the first real *lamasery* at Likir near Saspol in Ladakh, establishing a brotherhood of *lamas* to settle down there because Likir was also an urban node on the trade route.[14] In most of the Ladakhi small towns located at critical junctures, trading patterns continued to grow. With that grew the general populations' interest and appetite for luxuries and other avenues that trading could provide. King Lha chen Utpala (AD 1125-50) united the forces of upper and lower Ladakh, subjected all the vassal chiefs and extracted tributes from them to safeguard the trade routes. The chiefs of different localities competed with each other to divert trade routes through their territories knowing that their political and economic fortunes were dependent upon these routes. The Dard chiefs of Khaltse of Ladakh built an additional bridge to facilitate the diversion of trade through their territory. King Lha chen Naglung (AD 1150-75) built a palace at Wanla, a castle at Bragnag as well as a bridge on the Indus to divert trade and secure taxes through his territories.[15] These efforts saw the proliferation of various trade marts in the region and resulted in the real beginnings of urbanization. King Jamyang Namgyal (AD 1560-90) gave a tax exemption to those merchants who preached Buddhism while trading on the Silk Route, because by this period Buddhism had emerged as a vital political ideology for the State. Buddhism was also viewed as a powerful force for integrating local communities, particularly when a large number of merchants from various regions visited Ladakh frequently.[16] Buddhism was especially favoured by traders as it preached non-violence and peace, both preconditions for trade to thrive in such mountainous regions.[17]

The interface between such forces indicates how closely linked were the urban and religio-political systems of Ladakh. The Buddhist monasteries functioned both as institutions of the State and as urban centres. In this process the monk-and-the-merchant nexus served to strengthen the bonds between the town and the countryside. The twin roles of monks as spiritual leaders and as traders-cum-political agents provided both an ideological and a real basis for the creation of strong personal ties between the rulers and their followers. The town of Leh became the headquarters of the monk and the minister and served as the centre of cultural, socio-economic and political activities. Similarly, monasteries in other parts of Ladakh also became more institutionalized and absorbed the surplus population by attaching one child from each family as a monk for services in the monasteries. This became an established custom which continues till date.[18] These establishments combined the religio-political authority and were regularly in receipt of surpluses from peasants, pastoralists and labourers. The monasteries also facilitated urban influences. Monumental buildings such as the castles of Bragnag, Khaltse, Shaskar, Basgo, Tingmogang, Likir and various monasteries which were constructed in the Ladakh region symbolized the concentration of social surplus.[19]

The monks constituted the religio-political elite of the region on account of their superordinate social status that was reinforced by their economic strength as they controlled the surplus. Religious and political expediency facilitated reading, writing and record-keeping. The bulk of documentation thus produced is still available in most of the monasteries of the region. Lahor Gyal, also known as King Lha chen Kungra Namgyal (AD 1250-75), promoted and popularized Lamaist literature. He gave orders for two voluminous Lamaist works to be copied on gold and indigo tinted paper.[20] King Dngosgn (AD 1300-25) commissioned two copies of a colossal Tibetan encyclopaedia of Lamaism of 108 volumes. During his reign he also reconstructed monasteries, refurbishing and adorned them with costly items of gold, silver, copper, coral, beads and pearls.[21]

These slew of developments initiated a new socio-cultural and politico-economic pattern which included the growth of the institutional basis of the monasteries and the delegation of powers by the state to the monasteries to administer and mediate the relations between state and society. The material resources were then redistributed by the monasteries. The monks invested their accumulated surplus from the *labrangs* (personal property of monks) into long distance trade by sponsoring caravans. Surpluses from land and pastoral products were exported. Some of the monastic centres like Hemis became big complexes and were considered 'mother monasteries', attracting students and pilgrims from far-off places.[22] As a major consumer of agricultural, pastoral and artisan production items of prestige, such as precious stones and other articles, for everyday ritual activities, the monasteries developed into urban complexes. These monastic establishments trained and employed specialists who gave new direction to artistic expression by processes of carving or drawing, according to the styles dictated to them by the monks themselves. Festivities like Saga Dawa (Budh Purnima) and other periodic festivals witnessed large-scale participation of subjects, which translated into economic activities and in turn reinforced the urbanization process from time to time.[23]

Sources suggest that people attained a fairly high degree of prosperity during this period. During King Lha chen Jopal's reign (AD 1275-1300) it was said, 'people wore hats of gold and their mouths never became empty of tea or beer (*chhang*). Masters and servants alike spent their days in frolic and merriment.' Although such statements may not be free from exaggeration they are nevertheless indicative of growing urban influences. Eventually various centres of a proto-urban nature developed and expanded in due course of time.

Another important reason for these settlements being located on trade routes was to facilitate the military supervision of the routes. The diffusion of urban settlements in areas as widely disposed like Leh, Likir, Basgo, Tingmogang, Mutadar in Nubra, Karmar in Rutog, Tseshogyari, Nizung in Purang, etc., were the striking features of this process. In fact, Buddhism gave the Ladakhis a greater tradition, which coalesced with their local tradition and merged into a worldview that fitted the requirements of the state. Thus, Buddhism can be said to have provided the necessary impetus to urbanization, as well as the ideological accompaniment to state-formation in this region. It also establishes how the growth of an exchange economy as the earliest symptom of urbanization and the political formation both evolved as aspects of the same process in Ladakh from a very early time.

Urbanization and polity formation in Ladakh were also influenced by the nature of the region's geographical or locational centrality because Ladakh was surrounded by prosperous civilizations like the Chinese, Russian, South Asian and the Central Asian. Therefore, its topographical centrality bestowed on this region the status of a neutral junction to facilitate inter-regional commerce.[24] Table 7.1 details the articles imported into and exported from Ladakh to various countries in the nineteenth century.[25]

The Silk Route trade in the goods (mentioned in Tables 7.1 and 7.2) passing through Ladakh became another integral feature of the urbanization process in the region and also determined the social position of the region's political elite. In these early civilizational stages, though the critical variable was economic, yet the region's polity was also seriously influenced by its interaction with people from surrounding regions. Ladakh did not produce standard market towns like the rest of medieval India or medieval agrarian China, because of the lack of a prosperous agrarian economy which could have supplemented relatively dense, organized populations and a prosperous village life—an essential sub-structure for developed polity. That, however, does not deter us from recognizing or identifying the ingredients of a traditional urban system specific to this region of the Himalayas in the precolonial period.

The frequent visits of traders and pilgrims from various countries provided opportunities for the local people to interact with mainstream influences from India, China, Tibet, Russia and Central Asia.[26] These visits

TABLE 7.1: Goods Imported into Ladakh from Various Countries

Countries	*Goods imported into Ladakh*
Russia	Iron caps, tea trays, iron boxes, lamps, locks, cotton, lanka, plain brocades of coarse quality, Russian leather also known as Bulgar, tables.
China	Tea, teacups, hemp, linseed black and green, medicinal herbs, roots, momiran (a drug), China silk (plain flowered and brocaded), felts.
Yarkand	Gold in Turkish coins of Khokand, Bokhara, grain of Khotan, jade, horses, skins, green dyed skins, jackfruits, anklet or boots, soap, goats' down, ponies, dates.
Iran	Silver in Chinese ingots, cuttings of turquoise.
Turan	Drugs, tongza, gharikum, chintz, cotton, arms.
	Broad cloth, lining (used for carpets made in Iran and Turan) felts, Moroccan hides, skins.
India	Pearls, corals, opium, lime syrup. Preserved fruits, ginger, sugar, sugar candy, indigo, spices, drugs, European cotton cloth. Broad cloth, lining, Indian cotton, turbans, embroidered silk and clothes, cotton Chikan, mint silk, Indian shawls, looking glasses, lac dyed goat skins of Nurpura. Skins from feathers of Kashmiri Inomel, treated leather of pheasants, girdles, cardamoms, cooking utensils, fire stands, ammonia.
Kashmir	Rice, saffron, bastard saffron, crocus petals, opium, sugar, raw tobacco, tobacco snuff of Kashmir and of Peshawar, pepper, dry pot herbs, spinach, meta lotus, mast, almonds, oil (chiefly of walnuts), clarified butter, meal of parched rice, kulcha, or Kashmiri biscuits, coarse white cotton and cotton clothes, chintz mostly blue, burkas, patchwork shawls in white, carpets, hashish, hashia lining, Pashmina (plain and coloured), horse gloves, woollens, soap, pepper, ink, coarse sealing wax, Eastern fire pots, wicker frames, iron horseshoes with nails, needles, wooden hair combs, finger rings, trinkets, brass locks and shells of India.

TABLE 7.2: Goods Exported from Ladakh to Various Countries

Countries	*Goods exported from Ladakh*
Russia	Broad cloth, Pashmina, shawls, sal ammoniac, alum, leather, *charas* and spices.
China	Musk, crystal, jade, fine wool, Pashmina shawls molasses, *charas*, silver, cotton piece goods, opium, lak, spices, saffron, brocades and clothes.
Yarkand	Pearls, corals, opium, preserved fruits, ginger, lime syrup from India, sugar, sugar candy, indigo, spices, drugs, European cotton cloth and cotton clothes, goat skin dyed in red from Nurpur, cotton flowed chikan, chintz of all kinds, Indian kimkhab, silk, coarse shawls, jamawar shawls, looking glasses, feathers of Inomel, bulk pieces of leather, heron plumes, *Etlas* (a kind of special cloth) and spices.
Iran	Silk, embroidered cotton, Etlas, Gulbadan (a kind of cloth) mint silk, Indian kimkhab, Kashmir shawls, Punjab clothes, heron, rhubarb root and spices.
Turan	Alum, sal ammoniac, gold, copper, cotton, sheep wool, fruit, madder asafoetida, woollen fabrics and silk.
India	China silk, lining for shawls, coarse shawls, Russian and Bulgarian hides, China rhubarb root, China seaweed, hemp drug, gold, silver, salt and apricots.

laid the foundation of a unique economic system associated with the Ladakhis, one which provided them the means through which the pastoralists, craftsmen, peasants, priests and political elements could be supported on a year-round basis. Concomitantly, this opened up new vistas of exchange. In Ladakh, marketing took place in a domestic market which could be described as extremely underdeveloped, and in which the technology deployed was primitive but where the production of wool, human and animal labour and exotic items always exceeded local requirements.[27] It was the passage of the trans-Himalayan commerce through the area that enabled the people of this region to maintain a permanent residence and support their physical needs through the exchange of necessary resources like wool, salt, animals and personal labour. The trade passing through Ladakh was mainly in the hands of Central Asian and Indian merchants.[28] The Ladakhis stepped in to transit goods from one caravan to another. 'The people of Nubra live on for the most part on the caravans.'[29]

During precolonial times, when political conditions in the surrounding regions were far from being conducive to urban growth and political stability, Ladakh's frequent battles with its neighbours represented a slight setback for urban growth in the region. Despite this uninterrupted trade continued between India and Central Asia as it was backed by popular demand. When King Tsewang Namgyal I (AD 1530–60) defeated the vassal chiefs of Ladakh, the importance of the region as a centre of international trade was not allowed to diminish even amidst this turmoil. To put an end to the warfare that was going on for some time between King Tsewang Namgyal and the Turks, when King Tsewang Namgyal wanted to proceed against the Turks, the people of Nubra province foresaw the harm that this step could bring in jeopardizing the trade passing through Ladakh and so petitioned the ruler to abandon the project.[30] The desperate struggle and turmoil that followed is not of our concern here. But what is of significance is that it shows us once more that a political power base was crucial to the growth and continuity of Ladakh, particularly to maintain and perpetuate its identity as a centre of the intra- and inter-regional exchange economy. Otherwise the desire to trade unsupported by political power would not have guaranteed the survival of individual centres like Leh, Nubra and others. Significantly, during this process, Ladakh could never assert itself as a separate political entity and gain political expression as a strong regional state in the Himalayas because of a lack of domestic products to trade within its economic linkages with its strategically located neighbours.

Before getting incorporated into the mighty Mughal Empire, the region's polity was strongly influenced by Tibetan polity. Whatever was the nature of its economic potential, the major share of its benefits as derived from the wool trade went to Tibet and Kashmir. Although the Mughal conquest of Ladakh in 1683 strengthened the nature of the political power structure in the region, by bringing various chiefs under a centralized control through tribute relations and direct administrative links with the *subah* (province) of Kashmir, Mughal economic policy did not operate for the advancement of the indigenous population. The Mughals in fact concerned themselves with seeking a monopoly over the wool trade of Ladakh.[31] This was because, by this time the famous Kashmiri shawls, which were made of pashim and other varieties of wool brought from Ladakh, had established their identity as an important economic item in the world economy. With increasing challenges to Mughal rule in various regions of its dominion, the peripheral regions also witnessed the growth of powerful and rebellious tendencies.[32] In Ladakh, Pun Tsog Namgyal (AD 1740–60) seized the government through treachery, but soon-after his uncle Tarashi, who controlled a part of the kingdom, i.e. Purik, declared war on Kashmir and among other moves also terrorized traders—rather a rare phenomenon. This war enveloped the entire region of Tibet until 1780, when Tswang Namgyal's son Tsistan Namgyal became king and regulated the trade again.[33] However, by this time Mughal economic and political structures had been incorporated into the colonial polity and the economy of Ladakh also began to attract the attention of colonial adventurers for the specificities of its geography. The last was convenient for adventurers to pursue their colonial and counter-colonial ambitions in the trans-Himalayan territories.[34]

By this time period (of the eighteenth century) the Industrial Revolution had provided the British colonial empire with an automatic route to economic supremacy in the world.[35] From 1780 a fundamental change began to take place. The export of manufactures grew rapidly and Britain began to be pushed into novel cosmopolitan commercial relations outside her area of influence. She responded to this problem by attacking markets in the weaker peripheries of Europe.[36] This strategy had worked in the seventeenth century, in the eighteenth century, however, her success was undermined by the French in northern and southern Europe. Such problematics within Europe resulted in circumstances which led to more intense development of distant peripheries across the Atlantic and in Asia.[37] It was for the first time in the eighteenth century that the British had a product that gave them a competitive edge in the world market. For Britain the question that now arose was whether she could maintain and more importantly perpetuate her monopoly on resource pools and markets that were outside her political control. Given such circumstances more forceful policies were necessary, collaboration alone could not be relied upon to sustain the economic base and markets were specially needed. Besides, the early nineteenth century witnessed an acute measure of the domestic depression, with Chartism reaching its climax further accompanied by a more frequent use of the political arm of overseas expansion in many areas other than China. Such an economic and social crisis reared its head in Britain when the Russian influence was advancing and forces of protectionism were expanding from the Mediterranean to Central Asia, an extensive area of strategic and economic importance.[38] It was at this juncture that the British colonial masters realized the significance of the Himalayas in general and of Ladakh in particular. Ladakh appeared as the most appropriate location from where they tried to push back the Russian influence while extending British trade connections in the Central Asian markets. Simultaneously, the British also had opportunity to exploit the region's wool trade.[39]

This aggressive trade-cum-colonial diplomacy got entangled in the political ramifications of the Himalayan region from the beginning of the nineteenth century up to the end of the first half of the twentieth century. By the first quarter of the nineteenth century three political powers emerged on the scene in the Western Himalayas, all of whom influenced the politics and economy of Ladakh. In 1819, when Kashmir passed into the hands of Sikh rulers, they extracted tribute from the ruler of Ladakh while continuing to enjoy trade privileges—a practice that was carried on from the Mughal occupation of the region.[40] Raja Gulab Singh who controlled the hills of Jammu and Kishtwar as a feudatory of the Sikhs was also keeping track of these developments in the neighbourhood. And when he became the Maharaja of Jammu and Kashmir in 1846 his interests grew further in this direction.[41] The English already controlled the hilly areas between the rivers Kali and the Satluj, the boundaries of which were also coterminous with the region of Ladakh.[42] These powers rapidly became interested in the shawl wool of Ladakh and western Tibet, apart from the strategic centrality of the region. We should note that even though Ladakh acted as a trading mart for various countries, it was Kashmir alone which had the monopoly over shawl wool from 1684 onwards when the Mughals obtained this monopoly under a special treaty.[43]

With the penetration of the colonial economy into the Himalaya region, the Ladakhis discovered that shawl wool was a great source of income to the local ruler and his subjects. The Ladakhis promptly monopolized the major portion of trade of the shawl wool from Tibet under strict treaty terms. From the last quarter of the eighteenth century the English Merchant Company and officials had also become interested in shawl wool products. 'In 1774 while commissioning George Bogle to Tashilhunpo, Warren Hastings, the Governor-General of India, had requested him to send one or more pairs of animals called Tus, which produce the shawl wool'.[44] In 1799 the Board of Agriculture also asked the Court of Directors, 'if they could secure samples of shawl bearing sheep of Tibet with a view to breeding it in England.'[45] Initially the Tibetans were against selling it to the Europeans because Ladakh had a monopoly over this commodity. Any one caught doing so was supposed to be given the death penalty. However, when William Moorcroft entered this region in 1812 and offered more money to the Governor of Tibet than was usually offered to him by the Ladakhis—who, as a practise, passed on the supplies exclusively to the Kashmiris for manufacturing—the Ladakhis and Tibetans were encouraged to sell it to the Europeans. Thereafter, with the help of the British government the Europeans diverted the wool trade of Kashmir through their territories.[46] This was the manner in which the extension of British colonialism to the Western Himalayas came to facilitate the transformation of a traditional trade and simultaneously also subverted traditional commercial networks in the region. New networks now rose. This was naturally a cause of concern to both the regions of Ladakh and Kashmir and affected their respective economies. Many merchants abandoned Ladakh. Even though Russia was watching these developments and sending their emissaries to the Raja of Ladakh,[47] the British government, on behalf of the English merchants was able to enter into an agreement with the authorities in Ladakh on 4 May 1821. This arrangement not only gave the British access to the Ladakh trade but also facilitated the expansion of their trade networks in Chinese Turkistan and other parts of Central Asia.[48] This was clearly stated by Moorcroft to Lord Minto in one of his letters.[49]

These economic and diplomatic considerations emerged as major factors in the contest for supremacy between Russia and England. Although the Dogra rulers of Kashmir brought the region of Ladakh under their political control from 1842 when they were still ruling Jammu and Kashmir on behalf of the Sikhs, this did not undermine the growth of British influence in the region.[50] During this period Ladakh trade received a setback and the merchants abandoned Ladakh. The population of Ladakh fell from 1,65,000 to 1,50,000.[51] The British authorities posted a Resident-cum-Trade Commissioner at Leh to regulate the commerce and facilitate its advance into Central Asian markets under British aegis.[52] Several European visitors and officials entered the region from time to time to comprehend the mechanics of the colonial economy at such a critical juncture. As a result, Ladakh again played an effective role as a trading mart of international commerce on the Silk Route until the first half of the twentieth century.

Marco Pallis has portrayed the scene of the town of Leh in the second half of the nineteenth century in the following words:

> … in the summer, when caravans from India and Turkistan enter or leave Leh almost daily, the scene in the bazaar is most picturesque. Here can be seen tall, thin, hawk-nosed Kashmiris in their unbecoming Buro-Indian rags. Across the way are seen stocky Baltis in thick grey brown homespuns and close-fitting caps. Tall Turks, fair as Englishmen, but with narrow slits of eyes and rather unintelligent faces, stalk about the market clad in white shirts, sheepskin caps and high Cossack boots. Some of them add a Bolshevist touch in their drab Russian semi-uniforms, probably exported from the factories of five-year plans. Their women wear fine orange or rose embroidered dresses and are closely veiled; while their Ladakhi sisters move about freely, for their position is high in society and stand in no need of protection. A few red-cloaked lamas are always to be seen and occasionally a true Tibetan or an Afghan youth of great beauty, with skin and long eyelashes and oval face, an amorous prince from the Bush of Persian Bihsal came back to life.[53]

Similar views were expressed by Venkof who visited Ladakh in 1875. He states,

> Leh town has only 3,000 to 4,000 permanent inhabitants but on the other hand there are always many merchants and servants of caravans who are more numerous … extending almost exclusively along the only one street, Ladakh has only good Bazars and the climate is distinguished in spite of the snowy winter by an unusual salubrity and hence visitors from north and south hardly make it a resting point. The English government maintains at Ladakh a special agent whose duty is to protect the interests of Indian subjects and of the government of Calcutta because at Ladakh the officials of Maharaja of Kashmir value goods on transit from India to Central Asia and Calcutta according to their valuation the custom duty which the English pay to the Kashmir treasury.[54]

All these details give a clear picture of Ladakh's existence as a growing urban centre although its indigenous production was only in shawls, wool and salt. Ladakh stood at the crossroads of long distance overland commerce, and therein lay the source of its wealth.

Figure 7.1 and Table 7.3 show the volume of trade carried through Ladakh during the period from 1878 to 1882.[55]

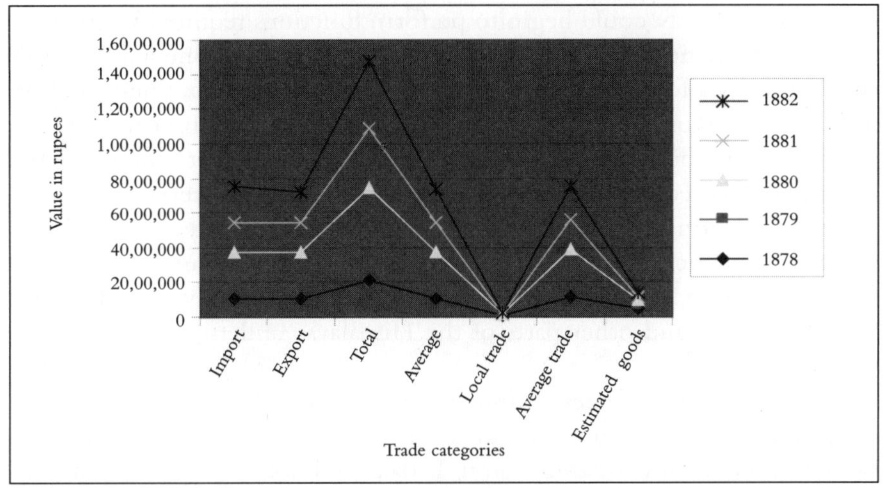

FIGURE 7.1: LADAKH TRADE FIGURES (1878-82)

TABLE 7.3: ANNUAL TRADE FIGURES AT LEH TRADING MART (1878-82)

Category	*1878*	*1879*	*1880*	*1881*	*1882*
Import	1050152	1236018	1479847	1712343	2061272
Export	1079351	1179401	1454238	1713972	1785886
Total import and export	2129503	2415419	2934085	3426315	3847158
Average import and export	1064751.8	1207709.8	1467042.8	1713157.8	1923529
Local import and export	42675	45609	36191	47263	35941
Average trade	1107426.8	1253318.8	1503233.8	1760420.8	1959520.8
Estimated value of goods at Leh at the end of the year	4,53,968	3,36,618	2,16,425	1,20,608	2,82,646.8

This growth in trade was consolidated chiefly by the British colonial masters by cashing in on the locational potential of Ladakh, remaining the mainstay of the region's prosperity almost up to the middle of the twentieth century. It enabled Ladakh to evince its dominance over neighbouring towns across the political boundary before the independence of India.[56] Undoubtedly there were variations in the pattern of urban development and in the different parts of the Himalayas but the common driving force was the British colonial interest. These initiatives operated with varying degrees of intensity and generated different forces necessary for the propulsion of urbanization to a new stage. The region's mountainous nature and other geographical problems did not allow the developing of a transport network which would have allowed for an efficient functioning of the colonial spatial economy and helped usher in a new era in the development of human settlements in Ladakh. But before this externally-oriented commercial and exchange economy could begin to perform functions required by the new economic activities, the process was scuttled when on the one hand, British colonialism was forced to withdraw from the Indian subcontinent, and on the other, the Russian revolutions of 1905 and 1917, the absorption of the political futures of the Central Asian *khanates* into the Soviet Union and the anti-imperialist consciousness in China took place. The territorialization and consolidation of countries surrounding the Himalayan region of Ladakh as nations restricted the region's status as a centre of an international exchange system. Consequently, economic activity not only in Ladakh but also in Kashmir and other parts of the Himalayas underwent a significant transformation.[57]

The interplay of forces within and outside the Himalayas portrays the indigenous urban system of Ladakh as one of uncoordinated development. Because traditionally urbanization in Ladakh did not evolve in response to merely socio-economic needs of the indigenous population alone but its creation in a landscape originally barren of urban settlements was largely facilitated by the corridor of foreign commerce which endowed the settlements in the Ladakh region with a permanent nature, Ladakhi society seems to have been akin to those folk societies of the mountains which were incorporated into states as regionally specialized sub-cultures and which underwent an urbanization of a different type from the Indian mainland. In Ladakh the urbanization was of an adaptive type rather than a transformative one, because the process of urbanization did not begin with an assumed goal, rather was one that advanced irregularly, adapting itself to immediate needs. Though one notices the urban symptoms in Ladakh produced by inter-regional commerce much before the birth of the world economy in the seventeenth century, the lack of extensive agriculture and a large concentration of population worked against it. These were inherent weaknesses, which failed to maintain the growth and correspondence between the region's socio-economic and political structures and the changing nature of external forces—a problem that continues until today. Despite the region's long historical contacts with various civilizations of the world, Ladakh did not experience the benefits of a land-based centralized political power, strong and durable enough for individual centres to perpetuate themselves, and less still for nodal regions of settlement to emerge. The kingdom of Ladakh also exemplifies the difficulties encountered by lesser political units during the scramble for this region by the surrounding polities, both within and outside the Himalayas and the impediments to the development of an indigenous urban system down to present day.

In the postcolonial era, the mountainous society in the Himalayan region of Ladakh was largely bypassed and the sparse settlements were more often than not left out by mainstream developments. Though modern Ladakh was established with the creation of the Indian Union, the region no more enjoyed the topographical centrality which was an asset in precolonial and colonial times. Unlike other landlocked countries, viz., Nepal, the Central Asian states or Afghanistan that have preferential access to seaports which serve as compensation for their landlocked status, Ladakh cannot claim such a status as it is part of the Indian Union. The Buddhist monasteries which were once important trading houses in the area also fell into decline because of the land reforms that deprived them of the state's patronage as well as of surplus produce and labour. In time the salt trade with Tibet and Kashmir also disappeared.

It thus becomes clear that while putting forward a preparatory framework for understanding the nature of trade networks on the Silk Route, one realizes the complexity of the political linkages and distances that the items of trade travelled both on land and sea. There has never been any doubt about the central importance of sea routes for facilitating trade on the Silk Route. Even as early as the first century AD when enterprising Roman merchants wanted to bypass the Parthian merchants, they imported bales of silk and many other items from China through the sea route from India.[58] The postcolonial restructuring of territorialities and the making and unmaking of nation-states brought an end to the trade on the Silk Route and the accompanying diverse benefits in terms of information and technology that the countries sharing the Silk Route enjoyed both on land and sea. In the contemporary economic and political scenario it forms an important component but has lacked definitive study.

In the post-Cold War era when globalization has touched new heights and the growing transnational capitalism has spread its tentacles everywhere, several avenues of research have to be pursued if significant change has to be brought about to make its relevance eminent. The new technologies, new political patterns and large multinational and corporate enterprises are certain to greatly facilitate the growth and development of regions such as Ladakh that have followed serious neglect. It shall also undermine the conflicts surrounding these regions, though not without cost.

Notes

*Apart from the sources referred to in this chapter, I have also conducted extensive fieldwork in Ladakh and its surrounding regions, upon which I have based my arguments. I am thankful to Prof Dietmar Rothermund, University of Heidelberg, Prof J.L. Chavanne, University of Paris, Sorbonne, Prof Rila Mukherjee, Dr M.N. Rajesh, University of Hyderabad, and my wife Dr Sharika Kaul for valuable suggestions, as well as to Temjenwabang, Research Scholar, Department of History, University of Hyderabad, for editorial assistance. Sections of this paper were presented at the XIII International Economic History Congress, Buenos Aires, Argentina, 22–26 July 2002, Session 33.

1. A.H. Francke, *Ladakh, the Mysterious Land: History of Western Tibet* (hereafter *Ladakh*), London, 1907, pp. 27-37. See also D.C. Sircar, 'Text of Puranic List of Peoples' in *Indian Historical Quarterly*, no. 21, Calcutta, 1945, p. 303. See also by the same author, *Studies in Ancient and Medieval Geography of India*, Calcutta,1960, p. 25.
2. R. Sanakrityayana, *History of Central Asia*, Delhi, 1964, pp. 25, 34, 55, 99 and 145.
3. Francke, *Ladakh*, pp.1-4. See also for details J. Rizvi, *Trans-Himalayan Caravans: Merchant, Princes and Peasant Traders in Ladakh*, Delhi: Oxford University Press, 1999, p. 21.
4. F.M. Husnain, *The History of Jammu, Kashmir, Ladakh and Kishtwar*, Delhi, 1972, pp. 4-12. See also A. Cunningham, *Ladakh: Physical, Statistical and Historical* (hereafter *Ladakh: Physical*), London, 1854. See also Fredrick Drew, *The Jammu and Kashmir Territories,* London, 1875; and H. Strachey, *Physical Geography of Western Tibet,* London, 1854.
5. De Terra, 'Himalayan and Alpine Orogenies', in *Report of the XV International Geological Congress,* vol. 2, 1936, pp. 859-72. In Ladakh, agriculture depended mainly on natural conditions, viz., sufficient warmth of the climate, alluvial soil, and rivulets for irrigation. The first of these confined the areas below 14,000 ft. though agriculture was carried out even up to 15,000 ft. above sea level. However, it was less profitable than pastoralism. The highest agricultural villages in Ladakh are Nyema and Mut in the upper Indus at 14,000 ft. Even in these areas the inhabitants found pastoralism more profitable. According to Sir John Strachey's estimate in 1850-5, there were only 37,000 acres under cultivation in a 30,000 sq. km. area; See for details, Political Consultation Nos. 151-52, dated 12 September 1851, pp. 465-87. (Unpublished document in the National Archives of India, New Delhi).
6. L. Petech, *The Kingdom of Ladakh* (hereafter *The Kingdom*), Roma, 1977, pp. 1-24. See also H. Osmaston, 'The productivity of agricultural and pastoral system in Zanaskar (North West Himalayas),' in Claude Dendaletche, ed., *Ladakh, Himalaya Occidental: Ethnology, Ecology,* Recent research no. 2, France, 1985, pp. 75-88.
7. A.H. Francke, *Ladakh*, pp. 28, 47-8. It was in remote antiquity that Mons and Dards migrated to various parts of Himalayas. First they came to Western Himalayas and settled down along the Indus Valley. In course of time many of them migrated to Ladakh. Ethnologically the Dard tribes were of Indo-Aryan stock. Interestingly, it is also believed that the Dards are the survivors of Alexander's troops who settled near the Indus Valley between Kullu and Dardistan and established their colonies at Skardu, Dras, Skurbuchan and Kh-la-che village in Ladakh after their Genlissimo's departure. After the fourteenth century they accepted Islam. F.M. Husnain, 'The Brokpa Dards of Dah, Hanor and Gakun', in *Ladakh: Life and Culture*, ed., K.N. Pandita, Srinagar, 1986, p. 29. See also Francke, *Ladakh*, pp. 28, 47–8, also E. Jolden, *Harvest Festival of Buddhist Dards of Ladakh and other Essays*, Srinagar, 1985, p. 15. In Tibetan sources Mons are believed to have possessed Kirata-like characteristic and inhabited the area between Tibet and the upper levels of the Nepal Himalayas, northern Bhutan, upper Assam,

Kullu and Lahoul. See Sikander Khan Kachow, *Kadeem-Ladakh-Ki-Tawarikh-va-Tamadun* (Urdu), 1987, p. 40. Chinese historians believe that Mons were barbarians, settled at the border of Tibet and West Asia. See Francke, *Ladakh*, pp. 20-5.

8. Francke, *Ladakh*, pp.12-39; See also R.Vohra, 'Sogdian Inscriptions from Tangtse in Ladakh' in P. Kvaerne, ed., *Tibetan Studies: Proceedings of 6th Seminar of the International Association for Tibetan Studies,* Fagernes,1992, vol. 2, pp. 20-9. See also, S.Turner, *An Account of an Embassy to the Court of Tessholame in Tibet*, 1800, pp. 381-4; S. Camman, *Trade through the Himalayas*, Princeton, 1951, pp. 58-9; J.P. Vogel, *Archaeological Survey of India Report*, 1906, p. 32; and Petech, *The Kingdom*, pp. 5-13.
9. According to Francke it would have been difficult to influence wandering nomadic tribes without Buddhist teachings, temples and monasteries. Francke, *Ladakh*, pp. 19-25.
10. Mircea Eliade, *Encyclopaedia of Religion*, New York, 1987, vol. 16, pp. 400-14. See also, Geoffrey Samuel, 'Tibet as Stateless Society and Some Islamic Parallels', *Journal of Asian Studies,* vol. XLI, no. 2, February 1982, pp. 215-21. See also Sir Charles Bell, *The People of Tibet*, Oxford: Clarendon Press, 1928; Karl Jettmar, *Between Ghandhara and Silk Roads*, Wiesbaden, Germany, 1987, pp. 28-9.
11. Francke, *Ladakh*, p. 21.
12. Deb-Ther-Son-Po, *Gos-lostba (Tibetan)*, English translation by G.N. Roirich, *The Blue Annals*, part I, Calcutta, 1947 pp. 68-74; See also Vidya Deheja, 'The Collective and popular basis of Early Buddhist patronage: Sacred Monuments 100 BC-250 AD', Barbara Staler Miller, ed., in *Powers of Art,* Delhi, 1992, pp. 35-9.
13. Ibid.
14. Francke, *Ladakh*, p. 62.
15. King Lha chen Naglung also stated, 'I will employ any means that may serve towards the propagation of religion of Buddha and make it spread. But as the religion of Buddha for its propagation is entirely dependent on the people, I will on my part, relieve them from taxation and trust them like my own children.' This reaffirms the relevance of trade to the region's sustenance and how religion and economy were made to reinforce each other. Ibid., p. 94.
16. Ibid. See also Barbara Staler Miller, *Powers of Art*, pp. 35-9. For details on this aspect, see also, Xinru Liu, *Silk and Religion*, Delhi, 1996, pp.49-72.
17. Drew, *The Jammu and Kashmir Territories*, p. 256; E.F. Knight, *Where Three Empires Meet*, London, 1895, p. 128; P.S. Nazarof, *Moved on*, London, 1935, p. 250; See also William Moorecroft and George Trebeck, *Travels in Himalayan Provinces of Hindusthan and the Punjab, in Ladakh and Kashmir, in Peshawar, Kabul, Kunduz and Bokhara 1819-1982* (hereafter *Travels*), 2 vols., London, 1841, vol. I, p. 23.
18. J.B. Lyall, *Kangra Settlement Report*, Lahore, 1889, p. 129; See also Francke, *Ladakh*, pp. 64-5, 80.
19. Francke, *Ladakh*, pp. 84-7.
20. Ibid.

21. H.L. Ramsay, *Western Tibet: A Practical Dictionary of the Language and Customers of the Districts included in Ladakh Wazaret*, Lahore, 1890, p. 83; See also C.L. Dutta, *Ladakh and Western Himalayan Politics (1819-1847),* Delhi, 1972, pp. 25-7, 32, 59, 197.
22. Francke, *Ladakh*, p. 67.
23. Prem Singh Jina, 'Monasteries in the Economy of Leh-Ladakh', paper presented at the All-India Conference on Buddhist Monasteries of Himalayan Region: Various Aspects, Leh, 9-13 August 1988.
24. Petech, *The Kingdom of Ladakh*, pp. 5-13.
25. The details have been collected from the bulk of published and unpublished sources. Some of them are: *Foreign secret proceedings*, 27 December 1850, no. 629, pp. 1567-8 (National Archives of India, New Delhi)*;* Foreign Department, Political A, 9 September 1876; *Ladakh: A Trade Report*, National Archives of India, New Delhi, pp. 1-47 (unpublished); See also A. Cunningham, *Ladakh: Physical,* pp. 238-56.
26. Foreign Department, Political A, March 1882, nos. 149-54, *Diary of British Joint Commissioner*, National Archives of India (unpublished document). See also Cunningham, *Ladakh: Physical*, pp. 239-61.
27. Lt. Col. T.E. Gordon, *The Roof of the World*: *Being a Narrative of Journey over the High Plateau of Tibet to Russian Frontiers and the Oxus; sources on Pamir*, Edinburgh, 1876, pp. 5-22, 28, 49, 87, 96 and 148; See also, M. Venkof, *A Brief Sketch of English Dominion in Asia* (Russian) (hereafter *A Brief Sketch*), St. Petersburg, 1875; English translation by F.L. Dankes, Simla, 1876, pp. 10-11 and also Appendices XXIII to XXVII in the same book.
28. Foreign Department, Political A, *Ladakh Diary, 1880,* nos. 67-77, National Archives of India (unpublished document).
29. *Political Consultations,* 12 September 1851, no. 154. National Archives of India (unpublished document), pp. 546-50.
30. Francke, *Ladakh*, p. 86; See also Karl Marx, 'Three documents relating to the History of Ladakh', *Journal of the Asiatic Society of Bengal*, n.s., LX, 1891, part I, p. 126.
31. *Indian Historical Quarterly*, vol. XV (Supplementary), 1939, pp. 142-5; See also L. Petech, 'The Tibetan-Ladakhi-Mughal War 1681-1683' in, *Indian Historical Quarterly,* no. 23, 1947, pp. 169-99.
32. Dutta, *Ladakh and Western Himalayan Politics*, pp. 56-65; See also *Indian Historical Quarterly,* vol. XXIII, 1947, pp. 183-5. Irfan Habib, 'Agrarian Aspects of the Revolt against the Mughal Empire', *Agrarian System of Mughal India*, Bombay, 1957.
33. Francke, *Ladakh*, pp. 126-30.
34. George H. Hodson, ed., *Hodson of Hodson's Horse*, London: Keagan Paul Trench and Co., 1883, p. 90; See also William Napier, *The Life and Opinions of General Sir Charles James Napier*, 4 vols., London: John Murray, 1857, vol. 4, p. 287; Margaret W. Fisher, Leo E. Rose and Robert Huttenback, *A Himalayan Battleground*, New York, 1963, pp. 61-3.
35. R. Davis, *The Industrial Revolution and British Overseas Trade*, Leicester, 1979, pp. 9-10, 55-6; See also by the same author, *Industrial Revolution,* pp. 13-24,

75-6; S.B. Saul, *Studies in British Overseas Trade, 1870-1914*, Liverpool, 1960, Chap. 3.

36. S. Sideri, *Trade and Power: Informal Colonialism in Anglo-Portuguese Relations*, Rotterdam, 1970, Chaps. 3-5; For details see H.S.K. Kent, *War and Trade in the Northern Seas: Anglo Scandinavian Economic Relations in Middle Eighteenth Century*, Cambridge 1973.
37. R. Davis, 'English Foreign Trade 1700-74' in, W.E. Minchinton, ed., *The Growth of English Overseas Trade in the Seventeenth and Eighteenth Centuries,* London, 1969, p. 108. Also by the same author, *The Rise of the English Shipping Industry in the Seventeenth and Eighteenth Centuries,* London, 1962, pp. 300-1; See also R.T. Rap, 'The Unmaking of the Mediterranean Trade Hegemony: International Trade Rivalry and the Commercial Revolution', *Journal of Economic History,* vol. XXXV, 1975, pp. 499-525.
38. D.R. Gillard, *The Struggle for Asia 1828-1914: A Study in Russian and British Imperialism*, London, 1977, Chaps. 1-3.
39. E. Ingram, *The Beginning of the Great Game in Asia: 1828-34*, Oxford, 1979, pp. 7-11, 332; See also H.B. Bayley, *Letters to John Hob, House President of the Company's Board of Control*, on 11 January 1841, Research Department, Miscellaneous Correspondence, no. 836, pp. 184-5. (Unpublished document in India Office Library, London).
40. Dutta, *Ladakh and Western Himalayan Politics*, pp. 84-92.
41. Herbert Benjamin Edwards and Herman Merivale, *Life of Sir Henry Lawrence*, 2 vols., London: Smith Elder and Co., 1872, 3rd edn. in single volume, 1873, p. 388n.
42. A. Lamb, *British and Chinese Central Asia: The Road to Lahore 1767-1905,* London, 1960, p. 58.
43. Dutta, *Ladakh and Western Himalayan Politics*, p. 87.
44. C. Markham, *Narratives of the Mission of George Bogle to Tibet and of the Journey of Thomas Manning to Lhasa*, London, 1876, p. 8.
45. Bengal Commercial Despatches of 31 October 1799; See also Lamb, *British and Chinese Central Asia*, p. 58.
46. W. Moorecroft, *Letters to Traill*, no. IV, *Asiatic Journal*, XXI, 1836, p. 217.
47. Moorecroft, *Travels*, 1841, vol. I, pp. 384-6.
48. National Archives of India, Foreign Department, Political A, March 1882, nos. 149-50, *Diary of British Joint Commissioner,* National Archives of India (unpublished document); See also Foreign Political proceedings, 26 July 1822, no. 56 (unpublished document).
49. Moorecroft, *Travels*, 1841, vol. I, pp. 384-6.
50. Foreign Department, Political Consultation, 10 October 1823, nos. 23-5 (unpublished document in National Archives of India); See also John Keay, *When Men and Mountains Meet: The Explorer of Western Himalayas 1820-75,* London: John Murray, 1977, pp. 241-58.
51. Cunningham, *Ladakh: Physical*, pp. 287-9.
52. *India Papers,* 1864-71, pp. 3-24.
53. Marco Pallis, *Peaks and Lamas*, London, 1939 and 1940, p. 292. Foreign Department A, Political E, May 1883, nos. 8-25, Ladakh Trade Statistics (unpublished document, Jammu Archives).

54. Venkof, *A Brief Sketch*, p. XXVII.
55. Foreign Department A, Political E, May 1883, no. A-25, *Ladakh Trade Statistics* (unpublished document, Jammu Archives).
56. Dutta, *Ladakh and Western Himalayan Politics*, pp. 72-6.
57. Veena Bhasin, *Tribals of Ladakh: Ecology, Human Settlements and Health,* Delhi, 1999, pp. 28-113.
58. P. Hopkirk, *Foreign Devils on the Silk Route,* Oxford, 1980, pp. 20-1.

PART IV

Dynamic Cooperative Commercial, Financial and Cultural Networks in Europe and Asia

PART IV

Dynamic Cooperative Commercial, Financial and Cultural Networks in Europe and Asia

CHAPTER EIGHT

Social Networks of Milanese Merchants in Sixteenth-Century Castile

J.B. Owens

In *the world of the Merchant-Smuggler*, which is the working title of a book I am writing,[1] I have examined how individuals constituted for themselves multiple social networks that intersected irregularly with each other. As such, the term 'network' may call to mind an image of a railroad or airline network,[2] but in fact, the social networks discussed in this essay consisted of multidimensional interactions that if visualized, would not look anything like such transportation networks. Researchers commonly express social networks in terms of the hub-and-spokes metaphor, if the focus is on a place such as the sixteenth-century Castilian commercial and manufacturing centre of Cuenca, the subject of this essay, or if the research focuses on an individual, in terms of the nodes-and-ties metaphor. Some researchers suggest using the 'rhizome' metaphor, which suggests a visualization of the multiple strands, without any central core, that looks like a maze whose overall shape changes as its parts grow or die in response to multiple factors. Although those embracing the rhizome metaphor wish to keep the focus on the dynamic and temporal elements of networks,[3] their analyses often appear too homogeneous in that they fail to recognize the importance of different types and strengths of connections.

The take-away message of this essay is that if we are to grasp the nature of complex human communities, we must understand social networks as far more complicated phenomena than these metaphors indicate. As described in the work of Harrison C. White, individuals constitute their lives within multiple social networks that intersect irregularly at different nodes. They present their social identity with some fluidity, in multiple ways, depending on the network in which they are trying to interact with others.[4] Moreover, the various networks often have quite different spatial extents, and their points of intersection often involve different geographic loci. From this perspective, the assumption that the elites' networks formed the basis of the global Hispanic Monarchy is likely to be erroneous.[5] This essay presents an analytic approach that combines two different research streams—on complex, dynamic, nonlinear systems and on social networks—which are not often brought together.

My focus here will be on social networks involving merchants from the Duchy of Milan who were resident in the Kingdom of Castile in the mid-sixteenth century. This important group has received scant attention from historians of Spain who have instead preferred to concentrate on the Genoese when examining the economic, social, and cultural roles of Italians. I have chosen to illustrate my points with information largely drawn from 1559. The year prior to that, the royal high commissioner (*corregidor*) of the city of Cuenca arrested a large number of the Genoese and Milanese merchants resident in Cuenca for their failure to register, and thus pay taxes on their wool exports from Castile. Therefore, although the smuggling continued after the merchants paid the Crown relatively small compensation fines, it seems likely that they recorded more of their transactions before notaries while officials were scrutinizing their activities.[6]

However, I cannot discuss all of the Milanese social networks because of inadequate evidence about some of them concerning the purpose being taken up here. For example, one of the most important of these merchants, Borsio Cavitello from Cremona, petitioned the Crown in 1567 to have two daughters legitimized. However, I have found no information about their mother or mothers or about the social network through which Cavitello was able to establish a relationship with the woman or women who bore him these children.[7] On 26 September 1565, Pedro de Alegría, citizen (*vecino*) of the town of Pareja, acknowledged payment by the Milanese Juan Pedro de Anón, Julián Castellón, Juan Pablo Dada, and Jusepe Vila for the years that Alegría's daughter Juana had served in the house that the Milanese shared in Cuenca.[8] However, my data reveal almost nothing about the networks that connected servants and journeymen to their employers.[9] There also exists a third type of network again about which I have inadequate information. During 1565–6, Cavitello, who had shifted the locus of his activities from Cuenca to Madrid after the Royal Court established itself in the latter town in 1561, used his political network there to block further investigation, arrests, and trials of smugglers by the royal high commissioner (*corregidor*) of Requena and Utiel, Dr. Valencia, whom King Philip II had secretly appointed as an investigating justice after the killing of a royal mounted border guard.[10] However, there is no record of those whose influence he sought or even whether his efforts were responsible for the Council of Castile's attempts to rein in Dr. Valencia and force him to stop his investigation and return to his *corregimiento* after he had tried to arrest Cavitello's younger Milanese colleague, Juan Pedro de Anón, in Cuenca.

Therefore, the major examples of Milanese networks I discuss will be those involving their commercial activities. The commodity of major interest during the period was Castilian wool, which they were exporting to northern Italian manufacturing centres. However, they also diversified into other economic activities, and their smuggling operations involved not only wool but also precious metals. The capacity of merchants to smuggle large quantities of silver, for example, was demonstrated dramatically in the aftermath of the Crown's suspension of payments in 1607 and the arbitrary conversion of short-term debt instruments into long-term bonds.[11]

* * *

Five broad categories of networks are manifested in the documents I have been able to use:

- An enclosed network of the Milanese themselves.
- A broader network of merchants who assisted each other in different commercial centres and who pooled capital to undertake large operations.
- A network of agents.
- A network of those who handled transportation.
- A network of workers skilled in washing wool for export.

I will offer some examples of each and elaborate on why each possesses a special importance for understanding of the 'reach' of social networks. As I shall explain later in this essay, social networks provided the basis for innovation and the emergence of new forms within the First Global Age. In general terms, this process increased network density and made the system more robust or stable. However, the complicated ways that the multiple networks interlinked with each other over expanding geographic spaces enhanced possibilities that any cascading disruptions would in turn affect ever-larger portions of the world economic system. Thereby, such cascades would also entail ever more elaborate efforts to repair damage and prevent such sizable disruptions in the future. However, the stability of complex systems depends on one or a few 'control' variables, which are always close to instability. Because these sources of potential systemic instability would not be eliminated by such repairs, the increased network density and interlinking would make it ever more likely, in an event that could not have been predicted, that some disruption involving a 'control' variable would cascade so widely that the system would enter a period of chaos and transition to a new system.

One of the more obvious networks involved those from the Duchy of Milan, either from the city itself or from Cremona. Contraband formed an important component of their business activities and, therefore, they required a network held together by high levels of trust and one that was impervious to information leaks. As seen in the Alegría example, the Milanese in Cuenca sometimes shared a residence. Networks were well-suited for organizing the corruption of hierarchical organizations and organized criminal activity.[12] Given the need to keep clandestine economic activities sealed off from the view of others, these networks required a much higher level of trust than others.[13] For the historian, these 'dark networks' left few documents for research. We see Milanese working together, often from different places (for example, Cuenca, Medina del Campo, Seville, Toledo, Valencia), but have scant information about what sustained their tight organization. For example, on 19 October 1559, Juan Pablo Dada, a Milanese who was an inhabitant of Cuenca, authorized Gerónimo Tetón, a Milanese who was an inhabitant of the Castilian financial and manufacturing centre of Toledo, to collect from Juan Angelo Cernúsculo (Cerniscolli), a citizen (*vecino*) of Toledo and the major Milanese businessman there, 16,000 *reales* (544,000 *maravedís*) owed to Dada by virtue of a letter of exchange from Nicolás Oliginate (Nicolo Olginate), an inhabitant of Valencia. Smugglers used this type of flexible financial instrument to pay for contraband from Castile to Valencia. However, we know nothing about what transactions this payment sustained or anything specific about the business relationships among these individuals.[14] On 2 May 1559, Borsio Cavitello followed instructions he had received in a letter of 15 April from Jerónimo Lita, a Milanese inhabitant of Medina del Campo. As instructed, Cavitello paid 4,000 *ducados* (1,500,000 *maravedís*) to Felipo (or Filippo) Raverta, a frequent business associate of the Milanese, who may have been Milanese himself. Raverta was then living in Cartagena, but he was present in Cuenca for the transaction. The 4,000 *ducados* had come from an unnamed source in Seville, and Lita wanted Cavitello to pay the money to Raverta for silk cloth that he had purchased in the 'Kingdom of Murcia and Province of Cartagena'. Three witnesses signed the document that recorded the payment, testifying that they knew Raverta; they were Juan Pedro de Anón, Julio Castellón, and Alfonso Mozón, all Milanese.[15]

The Affaitadi formed one of the most successful Milanese financial networks in Europe with bases in Antwerp, London, Lisbon, Medina del Campo, Valladolid, Seville, and their original family home in Cremona in the Duchy of Milan.[16] Therefore, it is not surprising to find the Milanese in Cuenca interacting with the Affaitadi in Castile. Just three days after the payment to Raverta, Borsio Cavitello and Julio Castellón jointly received from Juan de Ortega, a merchant who was a citizen of the town of Ocaña, 60,600 *reales* (2,060,400 *maravedís*), which was sent to them by the company of Juan Bautista de los Afeytates (Affaitadi) and Nicolau Giraldi in Seville and Tomás Raso, resident in Seville. In both Seville and Lisbon, the Affaitadi formed companies over a long period with the Giraldi, a major Florentine financial house. Of this amount, 48,000 *reales* were received on the account of Juan Agustín Lita, Milanese of Medina del Campo, and 22,000 *reales* on that of Juanote Castellón, also a Milanese of Medina del Campo. This largely Milanese network of businessmen arranged the payment on behalf of the 'judges and deputies' of Seville's public granary. Ortega received 500 *reales* for his efforts, and I assume that the remaining amount was used to pay for the documents. Of the three witnesses, one was Felipo Raverta, and another was Juan Bautista Sitón, another Milanese inhabitant of Cuenca.[17]

Although this transaction was a largely Milanese affair, it did involve connections with others, including the administrative and political officials of Seville's granary. The information available to those in networks linked only among family and close friends is often inadequate.[18] One potential danger for the strongly connected networks was that they were vulnerable to disruption if crucial figures were removed.[19] Therefore, if the degree of trust has to be higher in a network engaged in clandestine economic behaviour, such a network would need other activities to supply the weaker contacts necessary for information about the larger world of business and political affairs and about the activities of local judicial officials throughout a wide geographic area. These contacts in turn involved connections to otherwise separate networks. This need for interactions beyond a tight Milanese network is the reason why their ties, often through loans that were unrecorded by notaries, to revenue collectors (*dezmeros*) and judicial officials (*alcaldes mayores*) were so important, and why they sought positions as Inquisition *familiares*.[20] As an example of a relationship with a judicial official who was supposed to supervise Milanese wool exports, on 17 September 1559, Borsio Cavitello empowered Pedro de Mena, citizen of Cuenca to collect a debt of 200 *reales*, which had been established by oral agreement with Juan de Villaroel. Villaroel was the constable (*alguacil*) of the judge,

Licenciado Villanueva, responsible for investigating fraud at the frontier customs stations (*puertos secos*) with the Kingdom of Valencia through which Cavitello and the other Milanese were smuggling wool and other products.[21]

Not surprisingly, at one level removed from exclusively Milanese interactions were those with businessmen from other Italian polities (as in the case of the close association between the Milanese Affaitadi and the Florentine Giraldi), and there is much more documentation of these relationships in the notarial registers. For example, on 8 March 1559, Juan Pedro de Anón and Julio Castellón purchased wool for the Florentine Vicencio Ambrosi, resident of Valladolid, while Ambrosi was away in Florence. For this wool, Ambrosi paid Anón and Castellón 19,800 *reales* (673,200 *maravedís*). Since the payment does not indicate the amount of wool involved, there is no way of knowing if the payment included any commission or if Anón and Castellón simply acted to maintain a valuable relationship with an Italian merchant based near the major financial centre of Medina del Campo whose active business contacts extended to Florence.[22] An even more complicated interaction among Italians from different political entities is suggested by a document of 7 November 1559. Juan Pablo Dada, Milanese, and Lorenzo Guideti (or Guidetti), Florentine, both inhabitants of Cuenca, authorized Juan Ángelo de Nomboa, inhabitant of Toledo, and Juan de Comendro, Dada's servant, to collect from Agustín and Esteban Imperiale, Genoese inhabitants of Toledo, 31,000 *reales* (1,054,000 *maravedís*). The amount collected was to be based on a payment order (*cédula de cambio*) of 26 October 1559 from Juan Bautista Vivaldi and Lucián de Oria, inhabitants of Valencia, to repay a debt incurred with Juan Antonio de Reinaldo (Rinaldo) Dada, inhabitant of Valencia. From the surviving record, there is no way ascertain if Reinaldo Dada had conducted a transaction on behalf of the Imperiales or if he was simply using money that the Imperiales had agreed to pay in Toledo for some other reason.[23]

The Milanese maintained connections with other network levels through agents they authorized to collect debts and contract obligations. These contacts in turn involved a bewildering variety of networks. Since the export of wool was the major component of Milanese business activities, agents engaged in collecting the sheared wool (individuals whom the Milanese had contracted) formed a special component of trusted collaborators. Some of the authorizations to these agents were quite broad, indicating a high degree of trust. For example, on 14 July 1559, Juan Pedro de Anón, authorized Pedro de Albendea, citizen of the town of Albendea, and Pedro de Alegría, citizen of the town of Pareja (also father of the girl who served in the Milanese joint household in 1565), both towns north-west of Cuenca, to collect all of the wool and other things owed to Anón.[24] Still broad, although a bit more specific, was the authorization issued to Alonso de Canalejas, citizen of Pliego (Murcia), south-east of Cuenca, who was described as their wool collector (*percibidor de lanas*), by Julio Castellón, acting in his own name and that of the company he had with Juan Pedro de Anón. Canalejas was to collect all the wool and anything else owed to the company, and in particular the wool owed to them by two citizens of Povo Fuentemolina (a place unknown to me), which they had sold to Damián del Carpio, who was acting on their behalf.[25] A larger number of authorizations involved a single collection, such as that of 13 June 1559 by Juan Pedro de Anón and Julio Castellón. They authorized Juan López Abad, citizen of the town of Zaorejas (Guadalajara), and Pedro de Agreda, citizen of Cuenca, to collect the contracted amount of 100 *arrobas* of white wool from Alonso Castellar, citizen of Zaorejas.[26]

Given the diversity of their business activities, the Milanese also required the collection of other types of debt. Once again some of these authorizations were quite broad. For example, on 3 July 1559, Juan Pablo Dada empowered Gaspar de la Torre, citizen of Cuenca, to collect all the money, livestock, wool and other things was owed to him by any financial instruments, contracts, or verbal agreements.[27] Borsio Cavitello, perhaps as a form of repayment for his participation in one of the loans to the Crown, was entitled to payments from the collection of a tax known as the *cruzada*, which had been granted to the Crown by the Papacy. For the Bishoprics of Sigüenza and Osma, he authorized Diego de Cortinas, a citizen of Valdemorrillo in the Marquesado de Moya, east of Cuenca, to collect what was owed from the *cruzada* treasurers there. While he was at it, Cortinas was also to collect what was owed by six other clients on royal contracts, letters, and accounts or in their own names.[28] Cortinas was clearly a much-trusted individual because the people named lived in a number of widely separated municipalities. We have seen that in early May, Felipo Raverta, inhabitant of Cartagena, was in Cuenca, and Borsio Cavitello authorized him to collect a number of debts, including *cruzada* revenues, not only in Cartagena but also in widely separated places in the Murcian region (for example, Hellín and Lorca). Some of these debts were not recorded before a notary or in any other official document.[29]

Significantly, some of the collections suggest interactions with complicated local networks in the areas from which were obtained wool, carters, and workers in their wool-washing houses. On 18 September 1559, Borsio Cavitello empowered Juan Martínez, citizen of the town of Beamud to the east of Cuenca (but an inhabitant of Cuenca), to collect 80 *reales* from Julián López, citizen of Beamud, for an orally contracted debt,[30] and a few weeks later, on 1 October 1559, he authorized Julián Artero and Juan del Olmo, citizens of the town of Pareja, north-west of Cuenca, to collect from five fellow citizens similar debts for amounts between 17 and 100 *reales*.[31] The range of potential collaborators was quite broad. For example, Borsio Cavitello used Melián de la Coba, Vicar of the town of Iniesta, to collect 1,000 *reales* that Cavitello had lent to Isabel de Espinosa, inhabitant of Iniesta.[32] Iniesta served as a node on the routes used to move products to the border smuggling centres of Ves (now Villa de Ves) and Carcelén. Similarly, another way to connect with other networks was by serving as a collector for others. Thus, Cosme Moreno, a citizen of Cuenca, authorized Borsio Cavitello and his servant Cristóbal de Beteta, both inhabitants of Cuenca, to collect 30 *arrobas* of wool in the town of Armallones (Guadalajara), north-west of Cuenca. This wool had been seized judicially from Licenciado de la Fuente, former Vicar of Armallones, and Moreno was commissioned to hold the wool on deposit.[33]

Naturally, another network or set of networks to which the Milanese would connect when necessary was that of the carters who hauled sheared wool to Cuenca and carried washed wool and other products to the Kingdom of Valencia. For example, Juan Pedro de Anón and Julio Castellón made a contract with Antón Martínez, citizen of the village of Pajarocillo in the jurisdiction of the town and Marquesado de Moya, east of Cuenca, to use Martínez's four ox carts to bring to their wool-washing house in Cuenca the wool Anón and Castellón had purchased in the *sierra* of Cuenca and in the villages of the Uclés *común*, south-west of Cuenca. Each cart was to carry approximately 42 *arrobas*, and Martínez received 44 *maravedís* per league (*legua*) for the more difficult trip from the *sierra* and 34 *maravedís* from the plain of Uclés.[34] On 4 December 1559, Anón and Castellón contracted with Juan Esteban and Antonio López, citizens of San Clemente, at the residence of the governor of the large royal seigneurie of the Marquesado de Villena, south of Cuenca, to haul 9 sacks of washed wool (approximately 90 *arrobas*) to the Valencian port of Alicante where they were to deliver the cargo to Juan Pablo Graso. They had 15 days to make the delivery and would be paid 112 *maravedís* per league, plus all of the normal tolls on the route. Anón and Castellón paid the carters 88 *reales* (2,992 *maravedís*), and they were to get the rest of their money from Graso when they delivered the wool.[35]

Finally, the Milanese had to maintain contact with the networks that provided workers and supplies to the wool-washing establishments in the river valleys outside the walls of Cuenca. Some of these were local men, such as Bartolomé Ortega, a citizen of Cuenca who agreed, on 9 December 1559, to wash wool for Gerónimo Tetón, Milanese, by then an inhabitant of Cuenca, during the following year for 60 *reales* a month (2,040 *maravedís*) and his food.[36] To supply the meat required by their wool washers, on 3 May 1559, Borsio Cavitello and Juan Agustín Lita paid Pedro González, citizen of the village of Villanueva de los Escuderos, in Cuenca's jurisdiction,

245.5 *reales* (8,347 *maravedís*) to purchase livestock for what remained of 1559.[37]

* * *

The commercial networks in which the Milanese merchants were involved were sustained by high levels of cooperation among participants regardless of origin or ethnic identity. Based on the application to published sources about medieval trade of game experiments involving social dilemmas, Avner Greif has argued that cooperation among merchants was sustained because of the development of coercive institutions capable of compelling adherence to agreements.[38] However, smuggling continued to remain a widespread phenomena in the commercial life of the First Global Age. Given the persistent stereotype about the lack of 'efficiency' and 'rationality' of Iberian trade monopolies relative to those of northern Europe, I note, for example, that even in an apparently well-run commercial organization such as the English East India Company (EIC), authorities could not control smuggling. Although Chinese tea was marketed through a single point in East Asia, and therefore provided a product that was supposedly easier to control than most, in mid-eighteenth-century England three times more tea entered the country through clandestine networks than through the legal tea trade.[39] A recent analysis of the routes taken by EIC vessels throughout the company's history from 1601 to 1833 helps explain the astonishing volume of clandestine commerce in even a difficult-to-smuggle product. The routes of voyages were predominately determined by the illegal private trading of the ships' captains rather than by EIC orders.[40] No court adjudicated violations of cooperative agreements among smugglers, and there seems to have been little of the kind of violence that coerces compliance within the smuggling networks of the present global economy.[41] My current research explores the paradox of how such high levels of relatively uncoerced cooperation in the commercial networks on which the developing world economy depended could exist when those involved in moving contraband were clearly unable to seek recourse from commercial or other judicial bodies set up by municipal or Crown governments.

* * *

Beyond this specific purpose, we must understand social networks. The First Global Age, 1400–1800, was a complex system characterized by nonlinear dynamics. Within this system social networks served as the locus for the emergence of new forms. This emergence of new forms sustained the system by dealing with weaknesses that would otherwise have led to a system collapse. For example, the fifteenth-century expansion of the system could have produced its collapse, but this did not happen.[42] To take a European example of new forms emerging in social networks, the doctoral dissertation of Jessica Roitman at the University of Leiden explains how the more successful 'Sephardim', the term she uses to cover all those of the 'Portuguese nation' regardless of whether they were Jews or New Christians (converts to Christianity whether sincere believers or crypto-Jews), engaged in a form of 'group augmentation'[43] by which they incorporated themselves into networks involving non-Sephardim. The clearest cases of the way that such group augmentation altered existing networks were those involving Jews who embraced such networked interaction with non-Sephardim, eventually resulting in an important transformation of aspects of Jewish social and cultural environments in north-western Europe and overseas areas of European influence such as the city of New York. By augmenting their networks, these merchants avoided the fragile nature of the narrower networks involving only the Sephardim, and especially only Jews.[44]

Although the emergence of new forms could come to compensate for weaknesses in the system, these weaknesses remained, and the complex, dynamic, nonlinear system of the First Global Age eventually entered into a period of as yet poorly understood systemic chaos, phase transition, and bifurcation during the period 1750–1850. Out of this transition appeared a new system, characterized by new forms of world interaction, institutional forms, values, and perspectives on the world.[45] The new system manifested itself in the greater importance of the firm and its role in reducing the transaction costs, which were presumably associated with the cooperation-based commercial networks of the First Global Age.[46] Simultaneously, throughout the world, leaders placed greater emphasis on vertically integrated institutions in general in the economy and in the so-called 'nation-states' with their bureaucratic hierarchies.[47] Cooperation-based commercial networks have hung on in the Second Global Age, but they have had a more marginal role. The most prominent examples are the *havala* or *hawala* networks that remain a component of the economic life of the Indian Ocean basin.[48] In the last few decades, some economists have begun to recognize the existence and importance of collaborative networks within and between firms, but the meaning of such networks changed within the different context of the Second Global Age.[49]

Also, networks of the Second Global Age held new values and perspectives on the world. In defence of their moral and political positions, elites projected their ideologies onto the First Global Age to justify their assessment of the importance of the rise of the 'State', 'Capitalism', and the 'Modern Individual' or 'Individualism', in Europe. With the creation of the modern discipline of History in nineteenth-century Europe, chronologically lengthy metanarratives became the basis for the periodization of a linear myth-history of ancient, medieval, modern (or early modern), and contemporary (or modern) eras. A shift to periodization based on nonlinear dynamics should therefore seek to undermine this linear myth-history, and especially the use of the teleological term 'early modern'.

Rather than use such a linear and Eurocentric approach, this essay is based on the view that historical periods, such as the First Global Age are complex systems characterized by nonlinear dynamics. Such systems admit of only a limited predictability, and research on them should not be directed to the study of long strings of linear causation but to identifying the system's characteristics for the understanding of it and of the transition to a different system.[50] This perspective also points to significant opportunities for new research on the phase transition at the beginning of the First Global Age, likely in the period 1250–1350, which will produce a new understanding of the poorly named 'Middle Ages' or 'medieval' period, a terminology that should be replaced.[51]

Contrasting the view of periodization presented here with two well known positions based on the 'world system' analysis will clarify what is at issue. Immanuel Wallerstein argued that a new world system, specifically a capitalist one, began in Europe about 1500 and continued to embrace the globe until our time. In the 1990s, A.G. Frank challenged Wallerstein's position by asserting the existence of an Asian-centered, 5,000-year-old world system of Afroeurasia, which expanded from the fifteenth century to become the global system of our time, with an inclination toward the centrality of north-western Europe about 1800. Wallerstein drew heavily on the nineteenth-century linear and Eurocentric historiography and accordingly placed a major dividing point both chronologically and geographically, and as presented in his three-volume treatment, he recognized no major transition in the period around 1800. Frank, however, argued for the continuity of a world system whose chronological periods should be marked by the pulsations of expansion and contraction within the system, which he sometimes characterized as Kondratieff cycles. However, his approach did not position him to offer an explanation that satisfied his critics of the inclination or inflection of the system about 1800, and he died in 2005 before he could complete a book on the global economy of the nineteenth century in which he intended to offer a response to those critics. In recent years, Wallerstein has become interested in nonlinear dynamics and the bifurcation (or chaos) theory because he feels that the world may have entered a phase transition to a new world system.[52]

The emergence of new forms, led to an enhanced and increased network density throughout the First Global Age. Through this process the networks became more 'robust' or stable, but they also became more vulnerable to a global cascade that would transform the system as a whole. The global cascade of system instability depended on the irregular linkage of different social networks so that the sources of instability could be propagated before any system-saving repair was possible. In complex systems, system stability depends on a small number of variables, sometimes only one, which are always near instability.[53] In general, the emergence of new forms compensated for the weaknesses associated with these variables. However, sometime in the eighteenth century, one or more of these variables became unstable. This situation led to system instability and the development of a period of bifurcation around which a new system came to be organized. The sudden weakness of a variable could be propagated throughout the system from a cluster of individuals who could spread their influence through social networks by their impact on individuals who were near them in the nodes of these networks.[54] Researchers may not be able to comprehend the dramatic suddenness, in relative terms, of this process unless they grasp how individuals were involved in multiple social networks and how this involvement required them to shape their social identities depending on the variable contexts of their interactions with others.

Those interested in social networks, particularly within mathematical sociology, have tried to understand these processes through computational thinking, but so far, those engaged in this type of research have not been able to arrive at any effective means to model the phenomenon. Often they err by trying to follow physicists' ways of modelling network behaviour.[55] To cite the example posed in this essay, cooperation-based social networks present grave difficulties for mathematical modellers and those who rely on digital database management systems because the relationships between cooperating individuals involve subjective characteristics such as trust, which are based on human perception and expressed in a natural language that is open to variant interpretations of meaning.[56] Understandably, researchers in history and the humanities want to conserve for analysis the nuances and ambiguities of the information they discover about trust, reputation, adherence to social norms, and other variables of cooperation. In turn they become frustrated by the demands of database systems that insist data be squeezed into artificial categories requiring precise or 'crisp' numerical values.[57] However, when the body of information is large, the networks are dense and overlapping, and the networks' spatial extent is vast, some sort of information management system, such as Geographic Information Systems (GIS), must be used for the adequate organization, querying, and analysis of the data.[58]

* * *

To bridge the gulf between the frustrations of those who study human systems with their pervasive imprecision and uncertainty but need some way to manage information, we are using data about Milanese merchant networks in the period 1550–70 and the trust involved in maintaining various levels of necessary cooperation to experiment with the use of fuzzy logic (or fuzzy set theory)[59] in which the interpretive role of the humanistic domain expert (historian) continues throughout the recording, querying, and analysis of the available information, even for modelling and simulation. Complex systems present researchers with high levels of imprecision. Fuzzy logic offers considerable advantages both for researchers and for subsequent debates of research results: data can be imprecise or vague; a researcher can use linguist variables that are subjective in nature (for example, trust); the rules to determine the degree of membership in a linguistic variable (for example, low trust, medium trust, high trust) are transparent and are thus readily understood and evaluated; and these rules can bound the expected range of system behaviour under different conditions so that data are restrained to real world conditions. For those who might be interested in quantitative approaches, it must be stressed that fuzzy logic is not the same as statistics because it is often employed to deal with situations where information about the world is vague, ambiguous, incomplete, or otherwise 'messy' and where researchers cannot know much about the universe of data to which known information can be compared in order to derive any sort of proportional estimates. However, fuzzy logic can be used with statistics if the research requires that be done.[60] While this experiment with fuzzy logic will be dealt with in the future,[61] for such research to produce useful results, the historian as a domain expert must grasp something about the human system under study. In the case of social networks, such an attempt by the historian requires an understanding of the human capacity to be involved in multiple networks and to shape personal identity on the basis of the contexts of such complicated negotiations of multiple interactive contexts. Further, complex analyses require the use of multiple concepts (for example, hierarchy, institution, social network, business cycle, climate change), and historians have not as yet defined effectively how such common concepts fit together. Therefore, to make effective use of information management systems, it is the task of the historians to conduct ontological research to define conceptual interaction. Such research requires the expression of axioms that take the researcher from an incident to a concept. The use of fuzzy logic will guide researchers on human systems to the derivation of such axioms.[62]

For those who are interested in cooperation, which is the research context out of which the investigation of Milanese networks comes, the detailed examination of individual intentions in establishing and maintaining trust takes on an even greater importance. In a recent article, Laurent Lehmann and his colleagues review the research carried out on cooperation, briefly summarizing the debates among game theorists and economists. The authors highlight the importance of research on the neglected area of individual intentions, advocating the creation of games that will expose the potential importance of this variable.[63] However, designing new games need not be the only avenue to be able to investigate this crucial aspect of cooperative relations among humans. Historians possess a great deal of empirical evidence about individuals within cooperative networks and movements, which they can effectively bring into debates about cooperation. Moreover, historians generally express their understanding of their data through narrative, and narrative is a special form of human knowledge not well represented within the various spheres of cooperation research.[64] Researchers within the DynCoopNet project are now working to implant narrative within Geographic Information Systems (GIS) in order to understand the dynamics of cooperation-based commercial networks and other phenomena within geographic domains to elucidate on debates about human cooperation.[65]

All individuals are involved in multiple networks that link irregularly only at certain nodes. It is obvious from even the limited examples in this essay that social networks serve the needs of participating individuals in different ways. Some of the broader, more open networks provided the Milanese merchant-smugglers greater access to information, both on a broader geographic scope and in terms of contacts with different institutions, while others required higher degrees of trust, ultimately culminating in those networks used for smuggling. Using social network software packages permits researchers to manage a large quantity of information about network participation, but the available packages embrace the node and tie metaphor to such an extent that they show poorly the impact on individual action and self identity of multiple networks. Moreover, the designers of the network analysis software have not recognized the potential importance of the connections between the networks and their geographical context.[66] When the social networks in question engage in commerce, and especially in smuggling, their geographical context sits near the head of factors that must be considered to understand human action within the networked relationships, and it is toward crafting such an analysis that future research will be directed.

Notes

*This essay is based on a paper I presented as part of the session 'Networking in Cuenca: Youths, Adulterers, and Merchants', organized by DynCoopNet 'Associated Partner' Sara T. Nalle, for the annual meeting of the Society for Spanish and Portuguese Historical Studies, Kansas City, Missouri, USA, 2–5 April 2009. This material is based upon work supported by the US National Science Foundation (NSF) under Grant Nos. 0740345 and 09413371. Any opinions, findings, and conclusions or recommendations expressed in this material are those of the author and do not necessarily reflect the views of the National Science Foundation.

1. Research for the book has been supported by a Summer stipend in 2000 from the U.S. National Endowment for the Humanities (NEH), consecutive fellowships from NEH (2004–5) and the John Simon Guggenheim Memorial Foundation (2005–6), several small, internal research grants from Idaho State University, and currently a grant from the U.S. National Science Foundation (NSF Award No. SES-0740345; US$394,000; 2007–10). The NSF award also supports my role as co-leader of the project I created, 'Dynamic Complexity of Cooperation-Based Self-Organizing Commercial Networks in the First Global Age' (DynCoopNet).
2. For example, see Albert-László Barabási, *Linked: The New Science of Networks*, Cambridge, Massachusetts: Perseus, 2002. For a good introduction to debates about the nature and analysis of social networks, see Gernot Grabher, 'Trading Routes, Bypasses, and Risky Intersections: Mapping the Travels of "Networks" between Economic Sociology and Economic Geography', *Progress in Human Geography*, vol. 30, 2006, pp. 163–89. Also useful is Mark Newman, Albert-László Barabási, and Duncan J. Watts, *The Structure and Dynamics of Networks*, Princeton, New Jersey: Princeton University Press, 2006, which constitutes a type of textbook in which selected papers are presented and discussed.
3. The 'rhizome' metaphor is prominent in the actor-network theory (ANT). On this subject, see the discussion in Grabher, 'Trading Routes', pp. 178–9. For specific presentations, see Michel Callon, 'The Sociology of the Actor-Network: The Case of the Electric Vehicle', in *Mapping the Dynamics of Science and Technology*, ed. M. Callon, J. Law, and A. Rip, London: Macmillan, 1986, pp. 19–34; Gilles Deleuze and Félix Guattari, *Rhizome: Introduction*, Paris: Éditions de Minuit, 1976; Alan Latham, 'Retheorizing the Scale of Globalization: Topologies, Actor-Networks, and Cosmopolitanism', in *Geographies of Power, Placing Scale*, ed. Andrew Herod and Melissa W. Wright, Malden, Massachusetts: Blackwell, 2002, pp. 115–44; Bruno Latour, 'On Recalling ANT', in *Actor-Network Theory and After*, ed. John Law and John Hassard, Oxford, UK, and Malden, Massachusetts: Blackwell/Sociological Review, 1999, pp. 15–25; Bruno Latour, *Reassembling the Social: An Introduction to Actor-Network-Theory*, Oxford and New York: Oxford University Press, 2005; Jonathan Murdoch, 'The Spaces of Actor-Network Theory', *Geoforum*, vol. 29, 1998, pp. 357–74; Nigel J. Thrift, 'Rhizome', in *The Dictionary of Human Geography*, ed. Ronald J. Johnston et al., Oxford, UK, and Malden, Massachusetts: Blackwell, 2000, pp. 716–17.
4. For full expositions of the views on social networks of Harrison C. White, see his works, *Identity and Control: A Structural Theory of Social Action*, Princeton, New Jersey: Princeton University Press, 1992; 'Social Networks Can Resolve Actor Paradoxes in Economics and in Psychology', *Journal of Institutional and Theoretical Economics*, vol. 151, 1995, pp. 58–74; and *Markets from Networks: Socioeconomic Models of Production*, Princeton, New Jersey: Princeton University Press, 2002. Also, see G. Reza Azarian, *The General Sociology of Harrison C. White: Chaos and Order in Networks*, New York: Palgrave Macmillan, 2005.

5. This assumption appears to underlie the contributions to the valuable book edited by Bartolomé Yun, *Las redes del imperio: Élites sociales en la articulación de la Monarquía Hispánica, 1492–1714*, Madrid: Marcial Pons, Universidad Pablo de Olavide, 2009. Many of the chapters do, however, illustrate nicely the expansion of social networks toward greater density, which is a phenomenon of great importance for an understanding of the First Global Age.
6. I am writing an article based on the extensive documentation that resulted from the indictment of many of Cuenca's major Italian businessmen for failure to register their wool exports. One Milanese company of Juan Pedro de Anón and Julio Castellón, agreed to settle for the payment of the required tax on 36 sacks of washed wool exported through the 'dry port' of Yecla (an agreement reflected in a contract of 8 March 1559; Protocolo [henceforth P] 170, 1559, fols. 231r-231v, Protocolos Notariales, Archivo Histórico Provincial, Cuenca, Spain [henceforth AHPC]. Another Milanese company, that of Juan Agustín Lita and Borsio Cavitello, created a paper trail during the fall of 1559 to suggest that the wool to be registered for export had been lost somewhere along the way by irresponsible carters (on wool for Burgos, Yecla, and Alicante see pp. 170, 1559, fols. 377r, 379v, and 381v, AHPC).
7. Madrid, 5 March 1567, fol. 88, 1567-March, Registro General del Sello, Archivo General de Simancas (Valladolid), Spain.
8. P 176, 1565-66, fols. 578r-578v, AHPC.
9. DynCoopNet 'Associated Partner' Sara T. Nalle has undertaken research that will reveal many of these connections.
10. I have in progress an article on this investigation and its impact on the smuggling networks that moved contraband across the border between the kingdoms of Castile and Valencia, which were then separate countries with a common monarch.
11. Thomas Kirk, 'The Apogee of the Hispano-Genoese Bond, 1576-1627', *Hispania*, vol. 65, no. 1, 2005, pp. 58–9. Silver may have flowed out of Castile for a few years prior to the suspension as a result of the Crown's devaluation of the currency, which was met by sharp attacks within the kingdom; see Juan E. Gelabert, *La bolsa del rey: Rey, reino y fisco en Castilla (1598–1648)*, Barcelona: Crítica, 1997, p. 41.
12. Wayne E. Baker and Robert R. Faulkner, 'The Social Organization of Conspiracy: Illegal Networks in the Heavy Electrical Equipment Industry', *American Sociological Review*, vol. 58, 1993, pp. 837–60; H. Richard Friman, 'The Great Escape? Globalization, Immigrant Entrepreneurship and the Criminal Economy', *Review of International Political Economy*, vol. 11, 2004, pp. 98–131; Diego Gambetta, 'Mafia: the Price of Distrust', in Diego Gambetta ed., *Trust: Making and Breaking Cooperative Relations*, New York: Basil Blackwell, 1988, pp. 158–75; Jörg Raab and H. Brinton Milward, 'Dark Networks as Problems', *Journal of Public Administration Research and Theory*, vol. 13, 2003, pp. 413–39.
13. Pino Arlachi, *Mafia Business: The Mafia Ethic and the Spirit of Capitalism*, tr. Martin Ryle, London: Verso, 1986.
14. P 170, fol. 383v, AHPC; one of the witnesses to this document was another Milanese, Juan Pedro de Anón, who may already have been sharing a residence

with Dada. The *maravedí* was a money of account that was not in circulation. A *real*, a silver coin, was equal to 34 *maravedís* or *maravedíes*; the value of a *ducado*, another money of account, was generally stated as 375 *maravedís*. Both the stated amount of a transaction and its amount in *maravedís* are given in this essay for the benefit of readers who have a better sense of the actual value of the latter compared to goods and services in the mid-sixteenth century.

15. P 170, fols. 329r-329v, AHPC.
16 *Inventaire des Affaitadi: Banquiers italiens a Anvers de l'année 1568*, ed. Jean Denucé, Anvers: Éditions de 'Sikkel' and Librairie Ernest Leroux, 1934.
17. P 170, fols. 332r-332v, AHPC.
18. Yoram Ben-Porath, 'The F-Connection: Families, Friends, and Firms in the Organization of Exchange', *Population and Development Review*, vol. 6, 1980, pp. 1–30.
19. Réka Albert, Hawoong Jeong, and Albert-László Barabási, 'Attack and Error Tolerance in Complex Networks', *Nature*, vol. 406, 2000, pp. 378–82; Duncan J. Watts, 'Networks, Dynamics, and the Small-World Phenomenon', *American Journal of Sociology*, vol. 105, 1999, pp. 493–527.
20. On the importance of such weak ties for obtaining necessary information, see David Constant, Lee Sproull, and Sara Kiesler, 'The Kindness of Strangers: On the Usefulness of Weak Ties for Technical Advice', *Organizational Science*, vol. 7, 1996, pp. 119–35; Mark S. Granovetter, 'The Strength of Weak Ties', *American Journal of Sociology*, vol. 78, 1973, pp. 1360-80; Joel M. Podolny and James N. Baron, 'Relationships and Resources: Social Networks and Mobility in the Workplace', *American Sociological Review*, vol. 62, 1997, pp. 673–93; Ray Reagans and Bill McEvily, 'Network Structure and Knowledge Transfer: The Effects of Cohesion and Range', *Administrative Science Quarterly*, vol. 28, June 2003, pp. 240–67. Relations with various types of administrative officials are discussed in J.B. Owens, 'Smuggling through Spain: A Neglected Sixteenth-Century Commercial Connection between the Mediterranean and the Atlantic', in *Comunicaciones del VIII Congreso de la Asociación Española de Historia Económica, 13-16 de septiembre de 2005, Galicia (Santiago, A Coruña, Vigo)*, Sesión B24; available at <http://www.usc.es/es/congresos/histec05/b24.jsp> (accessed on 14 March 2009).
21. P 170, fol. 378r, AHPC.
22. P 170, fols. 230r-230v, AHPC.
23. P 170, fol. 384r, AHPC.
24. P 170, fol. 371r, AHPC.
25. P 170, 22 June 1559, fol. 368r, AHPC.
26. P 170, fol. 367r, AHPC.
27. P 170, fol. 369r, AHPC.
28. P 170, fol. 348v, AHPC.
29. P 170, fol. 362r, AHPC.
30. P 170, fol. 378v, AHPC.
31. P 170, fol. 381r, AHPC.
32. P 170, 21 January 1559, fol. 351r, AHPC.
33. P 170, 20 September 1559, fol. 379r, AHPC.

34. P 170, fols. 236r-236v, AHPC.
35. P 170, fols. 478r-478v, AHPC.
36. P 170, fols. 480r-480v, AHPC.
37. P 170, fols. 330r-330v, AHPC.
38. Avner Greif, *Institutions and the Path to the Modern Economy: Lessons from Medieval Trade*, Cambridge, UK and New York: Cambridge University Press, 2006.
39. William J. Ashworth, *Customs and Excise: Trade, Production, and Consumption in England, 1640-1845*, Oxford: Oxford University Press, 2003, pp. 176–8; Anne E.C. McCants, 'Exotic Goods, Popular Consumption, and the Standard of Living: Thinking about Globalization in the Early Modern World', *Journal of World History*, vol. 18, no. 4, 2007, pp. 443–4; Hoh-Cheung Mui and Lorna Mui, 'Smuggling and the British Tea Trade before 1784', *American Historical Review*, vol. 74, 1968, pp. 44–73.
40. Emily Erikson and Peter Bearman, 'Malfeasance and the Foundations for Global Trade: The Structure of English Trade in the East Indies, 1601–1833', *American Journal of Sociology*, vol. 112, no. 1, July 2006, pp. 195–230.
41. For a summary of a detailed analysis of the potential role of violence in a major sixteenth-century smuggling network, see J.B. Owens, 'Violence and Smuggling in Sixteenth-Century Eastern La Mancha', *Society for Spanish and Portuguese Historical Studies: Bulletin*, vol. 32, nos. 1 & 2, Fall 2007, pp. 70-1. Although I initially felt that I would uncover some sort of violence-prone, hierarchically organized criminal cartel like the Mafia or South American narcotics smugglers, my subsequent research revealed no such organization. The subtle shift in my own research about these smuggling networks can be seen in the titles of two early, unpublished papers I presented about my research on the 1565 investigation: 'The "Villena Cartel": Organized Crime and International Smuggling in Philip II's Spain', unpublished paper presented to the annual meeting of the Society for Spanish and Portuguese Historical Studies, Santa Fe, New Mexico, USA, April 2001; 'The Political-Economic Anatomy of a Criminal Organization Connecting America and Philip II's Western Mediterranean Domains', unpublished paper presented as part of the session I organized, entitled 'Smuggling, Clandestine Political Economies, and Public Authority in the First Global Age: Iberian Monarchies, Sixteenth to Eighteenth Centuries', at the annual meeting of the American Historical Association, Washington, D.C., 10 January 2004.
42. This aspect of systems theory was clarified for me by the lecture of Eörs Szathmáry, Professor of biology at Eötvös Loránd University and fellow of the Collegium Budapest, Hungary, at the TECT-INCORE summer school in Obernai, Alsace, France, 1 September 2008.
43. The leader of DynCoopNet's Portuguese team, Amélia Polónia da Silva and I picked up the concept of group augmentation through cooperative relationships from a presentation by Hanna Kokko of the University of Helsinki, entitled 'Group Augmentation', at the TECT 'launch conference' in Budapest, Hungary, 6 July 2007. On our use of the concept, see Owens and Polónia da Silva, 'Scientific Report: TECT Networking Workshop' (University of Porto, Portugal), 26–9 March 2008; "Trust, Reputation, Defectors, and Sustaining

Social Norms: Studying spatially complex cooperative relationships in ways that connect TECT projects'", prepared for the European Science Foundation's EUROCORES (European Collaborative Research) Scheme's programme 'The Evolution of Cooperation and Trading' (TECT), Strasbourg, France (1 June 2008), pp. 10–11, 19–20, 23 (available at <http://idahostate.academia.edu/JBJackOwens/Papers> accessed on 17 June 2010), henceforth Owens and Polónia, 'Scientific Report'. See, Hanna Kokko, Rufus A. Johnstone and T.H. Clutton-Brock, 'The Evolution of Cooperative Breeding through Group Augmentation', *Proceedings of the Royal Society of London B*, vol. 268, 2001, pp. 187–96, doi 10.1098/rspb.2000.1349; and Hanna Kokko, 'Commentary, Cooperative Behaviour and Cooperative Breeding: What Constitutes an Explanation?', *Behavioural Processes*, vol. 76, 2007, pp. 81–5.

44. Jessica Roitman, 'Us and Them: Inter-cultural Trade and the Sephardim, 1595-1640', unpublished Ph.D. thesis, University of Leiden, 2009; supervised by P.C. Emmer.

45. On the characteristics of such a system, see Tönu Puu (a DynCoopNet 'Associated Partner'), *Attractors, Bifurcations and Chaos: Non-linear Phenomena in Economics*, 2nd edn, Berlin and Heidelberg: Springer-Verlag, 2003, and J. Barkely Rosser, Jr., *From Catastrophe to Chaos: A General Theory of Economic Discontinuities*, vol. I, 2nd edn, Boston: Kluwer Academic, 2000. A simplified version of Puu's argument, without the mathematics, is available in the final chapter of his book *Arts, Sciences, Economics: A Historical Safari*, Berlin and Heidelberg: Springer-Verlag, 2006. The point that after a phase transition to a new human system, the cultural environment would be dominated by new values and perspectives about the world, impairing the ability of people to understand their ancestors in the earlier system, was emphasized for me by the lecture of Michael Sonis (a DynCoopNet 'Associated Partner') of Israel's Bar-Ilan University, entitled 'The Evolution of Complexity', for Idaho State University's Mathematics Colloquium, 27 February 2007. My understanding was also enhanced by a talk given by DynCoopNet 'Associated Partner' Shahriar Yousefi, director of the Centre for Advanced Research in Nature and Society (CARINAS); for details on this talk, see Owens and Polónia, 'Scientific Report', pp. 5–6.

46. Although probably overstressing the issue of transaction costs, Ronald Coase contributed to an understanding of the Second Global Age of the nineteenth and twentieth centuries by pointing out that too much activity takes place within institutions for markets to play their theoretical role in the allocation of resources. See, Coase, 'The Nature of the Firm', *Economica*, n.s., vol. 4, November 1937, pp. 386–405; Coase, *The Nature of the Firm*, Oxford, UK: Oxford University Press, 1991; and Oliver E. Williamson, *The Economic Institutions of Capitalism: Firms, Markets, Relational Contracting*, New York and London: Free Press and Collier Macmillan, 1985. The best-known proponent of the stress on institutions is Douglas C. North; see his *Institutions, Institutional Change, and Economic Performance*, Cambridge, UK and New York: Cambridge University Press, 1990, and the bibliography therein of his earlier works. Although moving in a useful direction, those who embraced this 'institutional economics' failed to provide, through their emphasis on an ideal of hierarchical

coordination and planning in contrast to the market as an ideal type, an adequate framework to understand innovation and entrepreneurship in economic activities. In this area, social network analysis has been a more fruitful line of research. On this issue, which is crucial for an understanding of the First Global Age, see the editors' Introduction (and bibliographic references) in *Spinning the Commercial Web: International Trade, Merchants, and Commercial Cities, c. 1640-1939*, ed. Margrit Schulte Beerbühl, and Jörg Vögele, Frankfurt am Main et al.: Peter Lang, 2004, pp. 11–23. Schulte Beerbühl is a DynCoopNet 'Cooperating Partner', whose leadership has directed DynCoopNet members to pay greater attention to social network analysis.

47. Of course, hierarchies existed in the First Global Age, but they tended to be segmented ones in which the ties within each level or segment were usually far stronger than any vertical ties. To achieve their goals, authorities had to elicit the cooperation of those at other levels. On this predicament, see J.B. Owens, *"By My Absolute Royal Authority": Justice and the Castilian Commonwealth at the Beginning of the First Global Age*, Rochester, New York: Rochester University Press, 2005.
48. See Roger Ballard, 'Coalitions of Reciprocity and the Maintenance of Financial Integrity within Informal Value Transmission Systems: The Operational Dynamics of Contemporary *Hawala* Networks', *Journal of Banking Regulation*, vol. 6, no. 4, 2005, pp. 319–52. For additional papers by Ballard on the *hawala*, see <http://www.casas.org.uk/papers/hawala.html> (accessed on 17 June 2010).
49. For example, see David C. Stark, 'Heterarchy: Distributing Authority and Organizing Diversity', in *The Biology of Business: Decoding the Natural Laws of the Enterprise*, ed. John H. Clippinger III, San Francisco: Jossey-Bass, 1999, Chap. 7.
50. On the limits of predictability in complex, dynamic, nonlinear systems, I follow the views of Puu, *Attractors*, and Rosser, *From Catastrophe*. Elsewhere, Puu has shown that about 1960, economists moved away from nonlinear and spatial models; see Tönu Puu, 'Introduction to Mathematical Economics', in *Mathematical Models in Economics: UNESCO Encyclopaedia of Life Support Systems*, ed. Wei-Bin Zhang, Oxford, UK: Eolss Publishers, 2007, pp. 78–117. Within the DynCoopNet project, there is disagreement about prediction within such systems because Shahriar Yousefi believes that if we only knew enough, we would have the capability for longer-term predictions, which are essential for him to justify the forecasting of future conditions such as petroleum prices. See Shahriar Yousefi, Ilona Weinreich, and Dominik Reinarz, 'Wavelet-based Prediction of Oil Prices', *Chaos, Solitons and Fractals*, vol. 25, 2005, pp. 265–75.
51. A good place to begin such transformative research would be China, which was home to 20-25 per cent of the world's people. By the late eleventh century, commercial centres began to emerge in China, which were often geographically separate from administrative centres. Some of the implications of this development are captured by Peter Bol, *'This Culture of Ours': Intellectual Transitions in T'ang and Sung China*, Stanford, California: Stanford University Press, 1992; see also

his suggestive articles, 'The Rise of Local History: History, Geography, and Culture in Southern Song and Yuan Wuzhou', *Harvard Journal of Asiatic Studies*, vol. 61, no. 1, 2001, pp. 37–76, and 'Neo-Confucianism and Local Society, Twelfth to Sixteenth Century: A Case Study', in *The Song-Yuan-Ming Transition in Chinese History*, ed. Richard von Glahn and Paul Smith, Cambridge, Massachusetts: Harvard University Asia Center, 2003, pp. 241–83. The spread of a huge Mongol empire, which included China, served to diffuse developments in the Eurasian social and cultural environments and encourage greater social network density. Greater connectedness across Afroeurasia supplied the means for the diffusion of epidemic disease, beginning in China in the 1320s, with disastrous consequences.

52. Immanuel Wallerstein, *The Modern World System*, 3 vols., New York and San Diego, California: Academic Press, 1974, 1980, 1989; A.G. Frank, *ReORIENT: Global Economy in the Asian Age*, Berkeley and Los Angeles: University of California Press, 1998. Frank defended his hypothesis of the 5,000-year-old world system in his contribution to *The World System: Five Hundred Years or Five Thousand*, ed. A.G. Frank and Barry K. Gills, London: Routledge, 1993. Wallerstein offered a concise discussion of his application of the bifurcation theory in Chapter 5 of his *World-Systems Analysis: An Introduction*, Durham, North Carolina, and London: Duke University Press, 2004.
53. Hermann Haken, *Advanced Synergetics: Instability Hierarchies of Self-Organizing Systems and Devices*, Berlin et al.: Springer-Verlag, 1983. Rosser, *From Catastrophe*, pp. 54–61, argues, after a thorough review of theories of complex systems, that Haken provides the most satisfactory understanding of them and, therefore, a point of synthesis for the theories.
54. See Duncan J. Watts, *Six Degrees: The Science of a Connected Age*, New York and London: W. W. Norton, 2003, pp. 229–44 and 250–2. Also relevant is Per Bak, *How Nature Works: The Science of Self-Organized Criticality*, New York: Copernicus Press for Springer-Verlag, 1996. Malcom Gladwell, *The Tipping Point: How Little Things Can Make a Big Difference*, Boston: Little, Brown, 2000, suggests that it is adoption by the influential and highly connected that leads to a cascade. However, Watts' current work shows that such elite influence probably does not exist. For example, see Duncan J. Watts and Peter S. Dodds, 'Influentials, Networks, and Public Opinion Formation', *Journal of Consumer Research*, vol. 34, no. 4, December 2007, pp. 441–58.
55. For introductions to social network analysis, see *Models and Methods in Social Network Analysis*, ed. Peter J. Carrington, John Scott, and Stanley Wasserman, Cambridge, UK, and New York: Cambridge University Press, 2005, and David Knoke and Song Yang, *Social Network Analysis*, 2nd edn, Los Angeles: Sage, 2008. An overview of the literature that is useful for economic historians is Grabher, 'Trading Routes'.
56. For a panoramic treatment of the importance of trust in social networks, see Charles Tilly, *Trust and Rule*, Cambridge, UK, and New York: Cambridge University Press, 2005, which is dedicated to Harrison White whose work on network complexity stimulated my present essay.

57. This problem is exposed by those who attempt to apply to large data sets the Actor-Network-Theory (ANT) of Bruno Latour and often fail to evaluate in any way the variable strength of interactions. See Latour, *Reassembling*.
58. See J.B. Owens, 'Toward a Geographically-Integrated, Connected World History: Employing Geographic Information Systems (GIS)', *History Compass*, vol. 5, no. 6, October 2007, pp. 2014–40; doi: 10.1111/j.1478-0542.2007.00476.x.
59. The best introduction to fuzzy set theory and why one should use it as a way of organizing information about humanistic systems can still be obtained by reading some of the major papers of Lotfi Zadeh, who first proposed this extension of set theory. A list of these papers can be found in Lotfi A. Zadeh, 'Toward a Theory of Fuzzy Information Granulation and its Centrality in Human Reasoning and Fuzzy Logic', *Fuzzy Sets and Systems*, vol. 90, 1997, pp. 111–27.
60. See Charles C. Ragin and Paul Pennings, 'Fuzzy Sets and Social Research', *Sociological Methods & Research*, vol. 33, no. 4, May 2005, pp. 423–30, and other articles in this special issue of the journal, especially Michael Smithson, 'Fuzzy Set Inclusion: Linking Fuzzy Set Methods with Mainstream Techniques', pp. 431–61.
61. I presented an early version of what we are writing to the TECT Strategic Workshop 'Visualization and Space-Time Representation of Dynamic, Non-linear, Spatial Data', Technical University of Madrid (Universidad Politécnica de Madrid), Spain, 25–6 September 2008: Emery A. Coppola, Jr., J.B. Owens, and Ference Szidarovszky, 'Fuzzy Rule-Based Modeling of Degrees of Trust in Cooperation-Based Networks: Close Research Collaboration Among Domain Experts (Historians) and Mathematical Modelers', available at <http://mapas.topografia.upm.es/Dyncoopnet/presentations/Madrid_fuzzy_owens.pdf>(accessed on 17 June 2010). A brief, general treatment of the subject is Michael Smithson and Jay Verkuilen, *Fuzzy Set Theory: Applications in the Social Sciences*, Thousand Oaks, California: Sage, 2006.
62. See the brief definition of ontology and its constituent parts in John Davies, Rudi Studer, and Paul Warren, *Semantic Web Technologies: Trends and Research in Ontology-Based Systems*, Chichester, UK, and Hoboken, New Jersey: John Wiley & Sons, 2006, p. 4. Historians will make significant contributions to a knowledge-based economy through serving as domain experts in the creation of ontologies. In addition to the book cited, those interested will gain an understanding of the subject by readings selected articles in *Ontologies: A Handbook of Principles, Concepts, and Applications in Information Systems*, ed. Raj Sharman, Rajiv Kishore, and Ram Ramesh, New York: Springer-Verlag, 2007, especially Chaps. 1–6.
63. Laurent Lehmann, Kevin R. Foster, Elhanan Borenstein, and Marcus W. Feldman, 'Social and Individual Learning of Helping in Humans and Other Species', *Trends in Ecology and Evolution*, vol. 23, no. 12, 2008, pp. 664–71.
64. A partial recognition by animal ecologists of the value of narrative knowledge resulted in the popular television series 'Meerkat Manor', about a species that engages in cooperative breeding. The programme is aired in Australia, the United Kingdom, and the United States. See Tim Clutton-Brock, *Meerkat*

Manor: Flower of the Kalahari, New York et al.: Simon and Schuster, 2008; Nobuyuki Kutsukake and Tim H. Clutton-Brock, 'The Number of Subordinates Moderates Intrasexual Competition among Males in Cooperatively Breeding Meerkats', *Proceedings of the Royal Society B*, vol. 275, 2008, pp. 209–16, doi:10.1098/rspb.2007.1311.

65. Leadership in this area has been provided by DynCoopNet 'Associated Partner' May Yuan. See particularly her 'Adding Time', in *Handbook of Geographic Information Science*, ed. John Wilson and A. Stewart Fotheringham, Malden, Massachusetts: Blackwell, 2007, pp. 169–84; 'Dynamics GIS: Recognizing the Dynamic Nature of Reality', *ArcNews*, vol. 30, no. 1, Spring 2008, pp. 1, 4–5, and <http://www.esri.com/news/arcnews/spring08articles/dynamics-gis.html> (accessed on 17 June 2010). On the unique contribution of narrative knowledge, see Jerome Bruner, *Actual Minds, Possible Worlds*, Cambridge, Massachusetts: Harvard University Press, 1985; J.H. Hexter, *The History Primer*, New York: Basic Books, 1971.

66. For an introduction to this software, see Mark Huisman and Marijtje A.J. Van Duijn, 'Software for Social Network Analysis', in Carrington et al., eds., *Models and Methods*, Chap. 13.

CHAPTER NINE

Between Three Continents: The Fornari Networks and their Businesses at the Beginning of the First Global Age

David Alonso García

IN 1523 DOMINGO DE FORNE—ALSO known as Fornari—signed an agreement with other Genoese merchants whereby the sum agreed in a letter of exchange worth 167,407 *maravedis* was to be delivered in Seville.[1]

The contract was signed at a fair in Medina del Campo, near Valladolid, a place, several hundred miles away from the area of delivery. Domingo de Forne acted as an intermediary. The money was to be handed to Benito Doria, an important Seville-based merchant who was originally from Liguria. Silvestre Brina and Franco Leardo were Forne's agents in Seville. However, this transaction, despite being backed by several important businessmen, did not come to fruition. Castile, just as other European regions, was in the middle of a deep financial crisis and capital was not easy to raise.[2] The Fornari, therefore, were unable to make the agreed payment.

Such temporary exigencies did not affect the extraordinary commercial and financial period Europe had entered into in the first third of the fifteenth century. New products and new dictates of fashion had encouraged a fresh period of exchange all over Europe as well as between Europe and other parts of the world. A new world system had been born into a First Global Age. A growth in population and the availability of a surplus of capital boosted commerce. Trade had been growing from a continent-wide scale to a worldwide scale. Nevertheless, at the time, short-distance trade continued to remain more important than intercontinental commerce.[3] The development of non-monetary exchange instruments and a proliferation of international exchange centres, such as Lyon, Bruges and later Antwerp, Medina del Campo itself and even Constantinople, as well as several centres in Asia had a great effect on the growth of commercial enterprise and the manner in which it flowed.

The structural basis for this transformation is well documented. I will not deal with it in great detail as my area of interest lies in the study of the figures involved in this change. Incidentally, this is the trend today, as far as research into merchant communities is concerned.[4] In this particular instance, the Genoese together with inhabitants from other areas of northern Italy, were spearheading new methods of navigation, commerce, education, lending and tax collection that would ultimately become the foundation of the economy during the Renaissance. It was mainly the Genoese that led trade in London, Flanders, the Iberian Peninsula, Africa and America.[5] Their networks, together with those from other *nations*, came to be deciding factors in the subsequent economic progress, along with the proviso that this progress was based on individuals who were capable of generating goods, raising capital and capitalizing on personal connections and influence. In fact, Genoese influence was so great that Giovanni Arrighi claimed it was they who led the first stage of systematic accumulation of capital for they possessed the ability and skill to initiate a strong capitalist impulse, which, even today, is perceived as the key to understanding the current economic model.[6] Undoubtedly, the Genoese played key roles in the closing phase of the Middle Ages where economic strategies, with the purpose of obtaining profits, rose to the forefront.

Paradoxically it was the family structure and the family ability to adapt to new circumstances that made possible such systemized shifts—to use Arrighi's terminology. Such shifts did not arise from fresh perspectives on understanding the economy but rather from the aggregation of, or evolution through, small day-to-day details which, when combined, led to a new economic order. For this reason for us to apprehend the nuances involved and to discover new interpretations, we are obliged to turn to new microhistorical works which permit us to recreate that particular sector of history which focuses on merchant families, their practices, wishes, capabilities, education, as well as the manner in which these were adapted to relations of any nature, including the economic.

We will analyse the behaviour of the Fornari and their position in the beginning of the sixteenth century. The Fornari were not one of the prime families within the Genoese economic fabric, but they managed to become notably influential in the court of Charles V. Though their family name was far less well known than the Grimaldos, Vivaldos, Dorias or Centurions, among others, yet several of these families were dependant on the Fornari activities because of the latter's favourable relations with Charles V. The Fornari were therefore able to maintain a position of high privilege when it came to the exchange of commodities from other countries. This included merchandise, capital and influence in Castile, Genoa, Milan, Africa and Central America. The fact that Domingo de Fornari was chosen as the financial intermediary for the letter of exchange mentioned in the opening paragraph of this essay is not a coincidence. The Fornari were moneylenders to the Emperor and therefore participated in the collection of taxes. Such a role gave the family access to sources of credit, this activity being of a social rather than of an economic nature.[7] Domingo de Fornari was also an 'estante en corte',[8] i.e. he moved and mingled in the Emperor's most intimate circles. Given this access to power he became an important and very influential figure for all merchants. In addition to this, the Fornari could speak Spanish, Latin and Italian—a linguistic ability that provided them with opportunities to play unique roles as intermediaries between Liguria, Spain and America. They boasted of an elevated social standing from the late fourteenth century, and, although not one of the top Genoese families, they were nevertheless able to build their own *albergo*, i.e. a social network formed by a new Genoese nobility that went beyond their own family.[9] This network in turn provided mutual protection and influence. It is not unusual then that several members of the Fornari family became Genoese Consuls in Palermo (1473), Tunis (1472) and Malaga.[10] These dates depict the Fornari's deep involvement in the Mediterranean trade during the second half of the fifteenth century.

The Fornari and America

The Fornari soon realized the possibilities offered by trade with the Indies. It could also be said that by 1521 they had become interested in the trade of sugar, pearls, gold and other goods, always in collaboration with other Genoese merchants.[11] However, slave trade soon became their main interest. In 1517, Domingo and Tomás de Fornari, Fernando Vázquez—an important financier from Toledo—and Agustín de Vivaldo, established a business with a licence to deal in slaves. Their profits amounted to 30,000 *ducados*. In time further distinguished merchants became involved: Juan Fernández de Castro, the Centuriones and Alonso Gutiérrez de Madrid, the latter eventually becoming Treasurer of Castile.[12] At this point one can observe a fixed feature of the Fornari business—their close relationship with the various political powers of the time. In 1529 Domingo de Fornari joined forces with Esteban de Pasamonte—Royal Treasurer for the island of Santo Domingo—and Juan de Samano, with an order to transport 150 slaves from one place to another within a period of one year.[13] The ultimate destination was to be the gold mines in Central America. Pasamonte undertook most of the burden of the operation as he committed himself to purchasing two-thirds of the slaves. Fornari and Samano were to simply buy them in Castile or Portugal, look after them and then ship them in the name of the treasurer of Santo Domingo, to Central America.

Commerce and Finance in Oran

Esteban de Pasamonte had commissioned Fornari to obtain the slaves in Europe or Africa. Such a move was not mere coincidence for he recognized that the Fornari were in an ideal position to ensure the acquisition and shipment of such human cargo. The Fornari were responsible for Oran becoming a strong commercial operations base. From there they were able to take care of trade with Europe and Sub-Saharan Africa and this inevitably included the slave trade. The fact was that the North of Africa and the Alboran Sea was an established and ideal route for both short and long-distance trade. It was part of the commercial route into inland Africa as well as to Asia Minor for it was based on coastal trade along the northern shores of the African continent. North Africa was a frontier zone between cultures, religions and civilizations. First, the Catholic kings of Spain, then the Austrian monarchs, realized the political, religious and commercial advantages offered by this region. The 'International Money Republic' was not prepared to waste opportunities offered, which would enable them to furnish their armies and garrisons as well as provide for their towns and kingdoms plus the added bonus of heavy goods traffic in the area. Soon, merchants became regular visitors to North Africa which provided opportunities to negotiate truces and to become involved in the rescue operations of prisoners.[14]

In 1509 Oran was conquered on an initiative perpetrated by Cardinal Cisneros. This campaign was funded by the Vivaldos—at least partly.[15] There was an important, well populated Jewish colony in Oran which grew as a result of the repopulation plans devised by Cisneros.[16] Oran soon became an important commodity-exchange centre where cereals, wine, footwear and fabric of diverse quality, price and origin were traded. Trade activities were essential to maintain the Christian population in the town.

North African Muslims provided the remainder of the goods, which included meat, dried fruit and nuts, soap, vegetables and legumes. As well as produce, Oran of course also became an enormous market for slaves who had been taken as enemy booty.[17]

Table 9.1 shows the fiscal records for January 1523 where the wealth of commercial traffic in Oran becomes apparent.

TABLE 9.1: IMPORT TRADE IN ORAN, JANUARY 1523

Product	*Merchant*
Sheepskin	Pedro Resal
Varied produce	Pedro de Viles, Tomás de Nápoles
Soap	Alonso Travado, Diego de Villarreal, Bautista de Málaga, Mateo Veneciano, Luis Lanzarote
Wool and fabric cloth (various qualities)	Diego de Villarreal, Fernando de Baeza, Lequi Arasio
Silk	Diego de Villarreal, Francisco Fornari (gauze), Juan de Lunel (floss silo)
Almond	Diego de Villarreal, Juan de Tordesillas
Cumin	Diego de Villarreal
Aniseed	Diego de Villarreal
Linen	Diego de Villarreal, 'one Moorish man'
Mustard	Diego de Villarreal
Pearls	Juan de Lunel
Dutch stockings	Fernando de Baeza
Raisins	'one Moorish man from Mostagan'
Olive oil	'one Moorish man from Mostagan', Bautista Spínola
Cowhide	'one Moorish man from Mostagan', Mosse Harraz
Goat leather	Mosse Harraz
Cotton	Francisco Fornari, Lequi Arasio
Bonetes (a kind of hat)	Francisco Fornari
Caracol (purple dye from a sea snail)	Lequi Arasio
Grana (red dye from a worm)	Salomón de Lera
Bordates	Glao de Bondillo

Source: AGS, C(ontaduría) M(ayor) de C(uentas), 1ª Ép(oca), leg. 841, exp. 16.

TABLE 9.2: EXPORT GOODS FROM ORAN, JANUARY 1523

Product	*Merchant*
Leather	Francisco de Fornari, Antón Octavián, Joan Reyner
Lavender	Yan Tocaça [*sic*], a Jew
Paper	Joan Reyner
Raisins	Pedro Resal
Soap	Juan de Lunel
Feathers	Juan de Lunel, Francisco Fornari
Fat	Glao de Bondillo

Source: AGS, CMC, 1ª Ép., leg. 841, exp. 16.

According to Francisco Fornari, the key to such a strong economy was maintaining peace with the neighbouring kingdoms as this guaranteed a profitable exchange between Jews, Muslims and Christians.[18] The data in Table 9.2 confirms the role played by Oran as a redistribution centre in the area. Not only were those goods imported which were necessary for the sustenance of the population, but shipments also left the town bound for Canastel, Mazalquivir and Mostagan. Export goods included highly valued staple food such as almonds or mustard as well as clothes, fabric and highly valuable goods such as silk and pearls. This merchandise was sourced from a variety of locations. From Marseille came the *bordates*, a kind of fabric that was highly valued in the area. English cloth was also highly appreciated as at that time it was of extremely fine quality.[19]

Several merchants, who were based in Oran, were attached to the major companies of the time: Spinola Rayner—a name with an unmistakeable central European flavour—or Diego de Villareal. These names represented but the tip of a conglomerate of agents which was directly responsible for Oran becoming a central business base.[20] It is not surprising then that the Fornari chose Oran as the centre of operations. Here in Oran, the Fornari became a family of reference for several decades. Their status within the fabric of trade in Oran was created rather differently to that of other families, for they based their dominance in commerce on their status as royal tax collectors.[21] Following the conquest of the city, the Spanish monarchy established a system for the collection of customs duties. Merchants of all genres nominated themselves for these tax collector appointments in an attempt to strengthen their commercial positions.[22] While also selling their goods, the Fornari simultaneously began to trade in money and local connections. The Fornari had an edge over others in this because being the tax farmers of royal taxes established the capacity for greater control and intervention as well as handling information and direct commercial operations. Transaction costs were reduced by moving into the fiscal business itself, which entailed providing the political powers with much-coveted funds. In return, the political hierarchy guaranteed the royal tax collectors the kind of conditions which ensured ease of facilitation. Such double dealing was not odd or unusual in this era since taxation, finance and trade constituted the three facets of the same world—business. All three aspects were very closely related. Businessmen, obviously, tried to find protection under the umbrella of political power, and understandably so in a world which, at this stage, could barely conceive of free exchange. However, as it has since become apparent, in other parts of Europe, behind a tax-collection agreement three-pronged initiatives were also in place, which were equally useful for the purposes of tax collection. This was also a financial and commercial operation linked to the focus on successful strategies against competitors and, finally, which allowed for brilliant political manoeuvres at a regional level or at the king's court.[23]

The Fornari brothers, Francisco and Esteban, signed a contract as tax farmers of the customs duty collection of Oran between 1523 and 1527. Several other residents of Oran and two merchants from Savoy—whose names are unknown to us—followed in their footsteps as guarantors or *abonadores.*[24] The two brothers shared their duties so that Francisco stayed in Oran in order to oversee the implementation of the agreement while his brother remained in Castile, usually at court, in order to obtain and sustain necessary contacts and influences which were essential in ensuring that the operation was successful. Esteban also saw to it that the right documents were duly issued. The Fornari had all the connections they needed, particularly in the Marquis of Comares, Governor of Oran, the latter endorsing the lease contract by his mere presence. This was one of his prerogatives as Governor as this specific action had been agreed to with the King when the Marquis was appointed for the position.[25]

The clauses of the tax collection contract stipulated that:[26]

- 8,000 *ducados* were to be paid to the King every four months. If hostilities started with the King of Tremecen, the sum agreed would fall to 7,000 *ducados*.
- Half that amount would be paid in cash and the other half would be in the form of clothes that Franciso Forne would import into Oran.
- The Fornari would hold the monopoly in the sale of *bordates*.
- All trade carried out in the Alboran Sea had to be registered in Oran.

Being the tax farmers of the customs duty collection operations had many commercial advantages as well as a considerable impact on the family's trustworthiness and reputation as perceived by other inhabitants in the town. The Fornari were regarded as not only people of substance, but also as people with privileged connections and access to the political powers. One of the first measures taken by the Fornari was to subcontract the monopoly trade in *bordates* to Glao de Bordillo, who had to pay an annual sum of 3,000 *ducados.*[27] In other words, the Fornari took care of the monopoly so that they could transfer it to someone with whom they desired to have a good relationship. The specific aim was to create a network of connections that was favourable to their interests in the region. The Fornari increased their prestige and popularity by signing an agreement with the king whereby any resident in Oran and Mazalquivir was able to sell any goods produced or manufactured by him without having to pay customs duty.[28] To the observer, it seems obvious that the Fornari were more interested in obtaining the support of the inhabitants than in levying as much duty as was possible.

Thus, the Fornari were in an excellent position to reap handsome profits. It was clear to everyone that they were the tax collectors and therefore enjoyed certain favours bestowed by the king. This particular operation was not notorious for its profits, but in fact, the idea of paying in clothes rather than in cash actually reaped more profit. An accusation filed by a royal agent reads:

There is great swindle here as they receive their wages in clothes which are overvalued and they will not receive a single cash payment in a whole year.[29]

In clear breach of contract the Fornari would pass low quality clothes off as high quality to make more money when paying the tax farming. The Fornari themselves were also responsible for importing these garments and therefore once again had leverage to use the system to their own advantage. The tax farming allowed for smoother coordination between the markets of Europe and North Africa. The Fornari also imported other goods into Oran on which they made considerable financial gain and for which they had to pay the corresponding customs duties to themselves! Another advantage to the Fornari clan. Despite complaints and accusations, the Fornari maintained their right to pay wages with clothing. However, on this second contract they imposed upon themselves an order to deliver English cloth, i.e. cloth of exceptionally high quality. As a result of the complaints from inhabitants and soldiers, the new contract stated that the quality of the garments was to be superior and that their price had to be fair. Charles V wished the city to be maintained and well provided for, so he took advantage of the tax system and its inherent conditions.

Not only did the tax farming contract provide the Fornari with direct advantages, but also, and most significantly, because of their control over the customs affairs, they were always aware of events that occurred in the area in relation to commerce. The monopoly and the resulting control over the flow of commercial information were included in the clauses of the tax farming contracts which were ratified by royal decrees. The Fornari's privileged position was not only an actual fact but also perfectly legal under the protection of the law. The legal documents stated that all goods imported into Africa from Spain had to be registered with the Fornari's agents:

We have commanded that all things brought from our kingdoms into those areas in Africa are to be registered in the city of Oran, and all duties and taxes are to be paid there, so they can then be forwarded where they are wished to be finally delivered.[30]

Such a clause held a further, very advantageous feature for the Fornari family—this specific law applying to the registration of goods gave tax farming the ability to decide who was allowed to trade in the area and who was not. It was Francisco Fornari himself who, because of his privileged position of being able to make such decisions, had the right to issue corresponding licences of trade which were necessary for those wishing to act within the law. A law established by the king but directly controlled by the merchants. Importantly, such licences could only be obtained once the merchandise had been registered with the Fornari family. This order was proclaimed in all the squares and marketplaces of the towns in southern Spain where everybody would in turn become familiar with the Fornari name. Furthermore, the family also kept their own agents in Seville and Malaga; this was Nicolás Fornari, the tax farmer cousin, who acted under direct instructions from Oran, instructions which involved monitoring and ensuring correct procedures and progress of their businesses.[31] Finally, Francisco Fornari maintained, under his direct supervision, a network of agents and frontmen in all North African ports, the object being to ensure that the clauses of the tax farming contract were duly complied with. Incidentally, Venetian merchants, always in fierce competition with the Fornari, had been banned from selling their goods in Oran: their products could only be distributed elsewhere.

Fortune was not always on the Fornari side during their tax farming period. First, trade and therefore the tax collection business was badly affected by the breaking of the truce with the king of Tremecen.[32] Second, the Fornari encountered great difficulties when attempting to enforce compulsory registration of all goods on board ships trading in the western Mediterranean. A number of merchants ignored such regulations. For instance, Blasio de Basiniana, a Genoese merchant who, after several setbacks, was able to come to an agreement with the Fornari in order to avoid more serious difficulties.[33] A lawsuit filed for the same reason, was one lodged against Antí Cornete from Barcelona. 'He went to Xarxel, within the kingdom of Tunisia in northern Africa. He intended to load his vessel with a capacity quantity of goods without having secured the necessary licence beforehand thus flying in the face of the "specific order issued by me, Francisco de Forne".'[34] Fornari's reaction in this particular case was swift and absolute. Cornete was reported, charged and found guilty. His merchandise was confiscated and shared by the Fornari and Martín de Vargas, the governor of the prison of Algiers.[35] It is curious to note, though, that the Fornari's share was collected by Juan Vázquez de Campillo, one of the king's treasurers, head of the council of Murcia, paymaster of the army as well as royal provider in Bougie and Algiers.[36]

The Fornari's appointment as tax collectors in Oran ended in 1527. Alonso Alemán became the new tax farmer. He was a prominent merchant from Seville and obtained similar privileges to those enjoyed by the Fornari.[37]

FROM TRADE TO INFLUENCE: THE FORNARI INVOLVEMENT IN THE FINANCIAL WEALTH OF THE SPANISH MONARCHY

The figure of Vázquez del Campillo now becomes important to examine in order to access the terrain where the Fornari were more successful: the financial wealth of the monarchy during the reign of Charles V. Vázquez del Campillo was a renowned figure in the court because he had been appointed by the all-powerful Francisco de Vargas, General Treasurer of Castile between 1507 and 1523.[38] The Fornari were ushered into the rarefied world of opportunity provided by the royal credit business and soon became one of the families which lent money to Charles V.[39] Tomás and Esteban de Fornari, cousins of the tax collectors in Oran, were those primarily responsible for furnishing the royal treasury with funds. This relationship went beyond the usual family ties, for Domingo Fornari was the guarantor for transactions in the North African garrison.[40] This fact highlights how the Fornari's family worked on a variety of fronts while sustaining a sense of family solidarity.

From the year 1514 and in association with Adán de Vivaldo, Tomás Fornari was involved in the provision of funds. Vivaldo was Fornari's partner in the slave trade business with America.[41] During this period, Cardinal Cisneros was the key political figure and it was Fornari and Vivaldo who were responsible for supplying the Cardinal with the necessary finance for his ostentatious sepulchre in Alcalá de Henares.[42] A few years later, Tomás de Fornari became involved in the tax collection affairs of the Bishopric of Cuenca—ecclesiastical rent—where, once again, one observes the advantages that fiscal interests had in private businesses. The greatest advantage of such taxes was that they were paid in kind rather than in money. Fornari was in-charge of collecting the grain used as this form of payment, storing it and later selling it for the benefit of his own treasury. In order to ensure the success and progress of the business, Tomás was appointed as the bishop's accountant. He even succeeded in obtaining several prominent ecclesiastical figures as guarantors, a fact which demonstrated the good relationship he enjoyed with the ecclesiastical community in the area. This good relationship however, was not able to withstand the later difficulties encountered when certain discrepancies resulted in a lawsuit.[43]

The particular platform from which our merchant amassed a large fortune was the king's court. Wherever the king set foot, the Genoese merchant's influence immediately received a boost. At court he bonded with the highest officials of the treasury and through such connections was able to lend 1,000 *ducados* for a second time in 1521, again with assistance from the Vivaldos.[44] The total figure of such loans rose to 10,000 *escudos* and 30,000 *ducados* in 1523.[45] This amount had to be paid in Genoa, Milan and Antwerp with a 14 per cent interest plus a profit of 2 *maravedis* for each *ducado.*[46] The overall profits obtained totalled 3,000 *ducados*.[47] In 1524 and 1526 both brothers signed several other *asientos* with the royal treasury.[48] From 1527 they then resumed their business with Esteban Centurion, not surprisingly, since the latter was the brother-in-law of Tomás Fornari.[49] Once again, this verifies the fact that family and business went hand in hand. Juan Bautista Fornari, brother of Tomás and Domingo, also participated in the business of lending money to the king for a number of years.

The situation changed in 1527–8 when the French invaded the city and capital for the loan business became difficult to raise. The Fornari, as well as other Genoese families, were aware of the cash flow shortage. Fornari stated that 'money is so short here and everywhere else that everybody shies away from accepting any cargoes'.[50] A way out of this situation was arrived at through an agreement signed between Charles V and Andrea Doria in which military protection to the Republic of Genoa was agreed to in exchange for ships and capital. Such reform was framed within a context of shifts designed to develop an oligarchy in Genoa.[51] This relationship was central to the survival of the Spanish monarchy for more than 150 years. Within this context, the Fornari roles in the financial market progressed even more. They moved from being just moneylenders to how becoming intermediaries, brokers between Charles V and various Genoese suppliers. The Fornari were renowned for their role as mediators in the business with Ansaldo de Grimaldo, one of the most prominent moneylenders at the time. Ansaldo led his company from Genoa with a firm hand. By then, Tomas de Fornari had already acquired the ability to thrive well, thanks to his experience at the king's court. Now he began to work towards ensuring that the Genoese would not neglect the emperor's finances during the final stages of the war which the latter was waging against France. While the Diets of Spira and Augsburg with the Lutherans were under preparation, Gómez Suárez de Figueroa, ambassador to Genoa, stated with a certain degree of irony:

> He goes there to ensure that all negotiations are done through his direct involvement as he intends to reap more profits from his dealings with the court than by any other business.[52]

Tomás de Fornari was extraordinarily conversant with the Italian, Spanish and Flemish markets. According to details from his own correspondence, Tomás was engaged on business trips between Spain, Milan and Genoa in order to speed up his negotiations with the Genoese agents.[53] He relied on his brother Domingo, who remained in Castile, and whose responsibility it was to liaise with treasury officials with assistance from Fernando de Almonacid, a court agent specializing in the management of official documents.[54] The Fornari had major advantages as brokers for not only were they expert negotiators thanks to their profound knowledge of the very technical world of the finances of the Austrians, but they were also able to operate as collaterals for the transactions they arranged.

Futhermore, Tomás was in a position to assist Charles V and his family. The ambassador to Genoa asked Tomás to provide several ships for a trip that Charles V himself was to make. Fornari was able to ensure that three vessels were at the emperor's disposal, one of which was brand new.[55] The Fornari clan were also prepared to supply the army with uniforms, as we have seen in the case of Oran. Tomás de Fornari, as stated in a letter dated October 1536, offered to outfit 10,000 German soldiers who were part of Charles V's army.[56]

Not only were the Fornari regarded by Charles V as a family capable of supplying him with capital, clothes and ships, but more importantly they were also recognized as a family willing to use their correspondence and communication abilities in Italy for diplomatic purposes. The Fornari had become specialists in dealing with restricted information. The letters of Tomás Fornari were littered with fragments of commercial information interspersed with political news. In this manner he was able to advise, in 1529, of an imminent assault on Milan by the League of Cognac, although 'we only see a very weak force'.[57] One gathers from these details that not only was Tomás aware of the possibility of an assault but that he was also capable of assessing the enemy's actual strength. In 1532 he was the bearer of more promising news: 'The situation in Italy is one of peace with the exception of Piedmont, Saluce and Monferrato.'[58] Therefore, not only did Fornari trade in merchandise but he also dealt in information and intelligence for these had become very useful tools in his dealings with political powers. Hence, it is worth noting that the merchants' interests lay not only in commercial operations but were also engaged in other activities connected to the nobles they were serving. This aspect of their labours appears to have passed unnoticed in historiography yet it was perhaps more important than the mere trading of goods. The opportunities offered to merchants by Charles V's empire ensured their profound commitment to serving their lord, at least certainly in the case of both the German and Genoese businessmen. These aspects confirm that the emperor relied on privileged sources of information which came directly from families such as the Fornari. These key sources allowed the former to know, almost as they occurred, news of what was happening in his particular areas of interest. The diplomatic corps would cover such need to a degree but merchants did indeed play a major role in this respect.[59]

Therefore, from a certain perspective, diplomatic relations and business were not as separate from each other as might initially appear. Ambassadors to Rome, Milan or Genoa would first have to find someone in a position to advance the necessary finance for the maintenance of the embassy, and then, to negotiate the terms of such agreements, especially when it came to funds being transferred to the army. This requirement alone highlighted the necessity for a permanent contact from among the businessmen.

Ambassadors also had to watch over the punctuality of payments and the proper management of funds, although in this respect they were not always successful. The ambassadors in Italy played key roles in the important financial circles, which were specifically established in the area for the transfer of capital. It was the ambassadors, through their relationships with the Genoese, who ensured the continuum of the imperial structure, at least in relation to political intelligence and financing.[60] Therefore, Tomás de Fornari, as an intermediary, was not able to neglect his relationship with the ambassador to Genoa. When Fornari announced that Figueroa had arrived at the embassy, he was prompt in adding that 'all persons at the king's service will work as we are expected to'.[61]

Ambassador Figueroa would not be the only prominent connection in the Fornari portfolio. The role played by the family as intermediaries was also linked to the political rise of Francisco de Cobos.[62] Cobos was secretary of the treasury, secretary of Indian affairs, secretary of Castile, secretary of the court and, finally, prime minister. In fact, Cobos became the most prominent official in Spain at the time. By holding a series of such elevated positions he had access to very sensitive information, with particular emphasis on fiscal matters and Indian affairs—areas which were of major interest to the Fornari. In exchange, Tomás de Fornari would keep Cobos informed of every occurrence in Italy, whether at a political level—including details about Barbarossa or Don Álvaro de Bazán—or at a strictly economic level.[63] Apart from Tomás de Fornari's close relationship with such a high-ranking official, other facts confirmed that the Fornari were one of the most influential families in that discreet world of high finance. Tomás de Fornari would be in direct correspondence with Charles V. The privilege of very few, such an elevated position also highlights the considerable measure of trust placed in Tomás by Charles V, the leading European head of state at the time. Not only did they exchange letters, as their correspondence shows, but they also held discreet meetings which was a common occurrence within circles of power. Obviously, Fornari would cultivate this relationship carefully by presenting the emperor with all sorts of financial confidences and, especially, political secrets.[64] Fornari acted as a crucial intermediary for Charles V in matters central to the emperor's military interests in northern Italy. Tomás de Fornari even took it upon himself to deliver diplomatic correspondence to Ambassador Figueroa: Fornari stated at the end of 1529 that 'on arrival I handed the letters from your Majesty and in words advised him of everything I had spoken with your Majesty'.[65]

Therefore, not only did Charles V have an important source of information or capital in the Fornari but, since they were brokers, the latter also represented the tip of a solid mercantile and financial iceberg. They headed a network which served the Emperor as well as their own objective of increasing their profits and influence on the various stages in the world. In 1532, Fornari advised Francisco de los Cobos of an advance payment of 39,000 *ducados*, of which more than 3,000 had been raised in exchange for letters of credit from friends.[66] Friendship was capitalized upon for monetary favours. It is no surprise that the Fornari position as intermediaries appealed to many of Tomás de Fornari's relations. His Genoese friends were securely ensconced under the umbrella of a figure that was extremely well positioned in the highest circles of the monarchy. Several loans from Ansaldo de Grimaldo, Juan Bautista Usodimare, the Centurions and even Tomás' brother, Juan Bautista Fornari, were agreed upon as a result of the negotiations led by Tomás between the Emperor's court and the businessmen in northern Italy.

Good connections, however, did not always necessarily ensure the success of such negotiations. In fact, being on good terms with highly influential people was the consequence rather than the cause of these enjoyable relations with the king. The Fornari gathered prominence with the Genoese merchants for several reasons. First, they managed the 'know-how' of both financial and commercial matters of the Spanish monarchy. Second, they were able to maintain or to increase their connections with other people of different parts of Europe, America and Africa. And finally, proficient in several languages, they were thus able to strengthen with this ability, their position as brokers of other merchants.

In the kingdom of Charles V, which constituted several nations, the ability to communicate in several different languages was considered a major asset and presented a competitive edge in relation to other businessmen. Once again the Fornari's had the upper hand. Tomás de Fornari was able to speak, write and translate from and into Latin, Spanish and Italian. His decades-long experience in Spain in various contexts where a command of the native language was essential, such as in business and at the court, meant that he had mastered well the Spanish language. This was a significant asset at a time when merchants, apart from being informally trained in their trading skills with direct involvement by their relatives and friends, would also be formally educated with help from specific textbooks conducive to their learning. They were taught the four arithmetic rules as well as the origin and value of the main currencies at the time.[67] Ansaldo de Grimaldo, one of the major moneylenders to Charles V, used to write his letters to Fornari in Italian. The latter would then translate them into Spanish and send them on to the court. On occasions, the information contained in these letters was very sensitive; in one letter dated April 1532, Ansaldo informed Charles V—through Tomás' translation—of a split in his own family and the possibility of the dissident group taking to the hostile French side.[68] The trust placed on Fornari, obviously, had to be beyond any doubt given the nature of this kind of private, sensitive correspondence that passed through him.

Incidentally, Grimaldo, in this letter, did not miss the opportunity to request the bishopric of Majorca in favour of his nephew. Such a position would also guarantee the loyalty of all his family.

It was not an isolated, chance occurrence, that Fornari was chosen and responsible for translating this letter. Being a validated broker, he was not only important to Charles V in this respect, but thanks to his mediation, the Genoese were able to communicate their aspirations with a reasonable degree of certainty in the assurance of attaining a positive response. Tomás had never failed them since his family's position in the republic—and in various other businesses—hinged on the good relations they held with the other clans. Accordingly, he advised Francisco de los Cobos, in October 1532, of the opportunity to gain access to royal silver from Spain, Sicily and Naples despite the royal prohibition. Although this was a necessary condition for the agreement to be signed, the clause was not upheld despite the Grimaldos obtaining other economic compensations in Naples.[69] In conclusion, Tomás' privileged position was hugely advantageous to both Charles V and to a particular group comprising numerous Genoese suppliers and contractors.

From 1536, the relationship between the Fornari and the monarchy entered a different phase as the bond between Charles V and Tomás de Fornari became stronger. Tomás even became known as Charles V's proxy for he was authorized to sign contracts on behalf of the Emperor.[70] He arranged a loan worth 100,000 *escudos* with Benito, Augustín Centurion and Francisco de Grimaldo at an interest rate of 14 per cent combined with a licence to obtain 25,000 *ducados* in Naples. In return for his services, Fornari now began to receive direct payments from the royal treasury.[71] His link with political powers had reached an all-time high. Tomás then tried to expand the areas in which he was active by ambitiously attempting to obtain the tax farming of all the tax collection affairs in Milan through a joint venture with other financiers. By this time, he was promoted to Treasurer of the Army in Italy.[72] From his new position he continued to facilitate access to funding by the Emperor as may be seen in a further agreement with Ansaldo de Grimaldo worth 60,000 *escudos* for the wages of the soldiers in Lombardy and Piedmont. Tomás de Fornari had achieved for his family that which was the wildest dream of any merchant family. The Fornari were to become the most prominent family at the service of the most powerful European king at the time, thus holding the highest political and commercial positions. It is clear that the merchant status was more or less an intermediate step for that purpose. Everything, from the slave to the textile trade, was a means to such an end.

The close relationship Charles V and the Fornari shared was not unusual. From 1528, a genuine symbiosis existed between Genoa and the Spanish monarchy. The former would supply funds and provisions, particularly for naval stores, whereas Charles V and his successors provided a political regime that was the perfect setting to cultivate the interests of the major merchant clans. Thus was formed a Hispano-Genoese imperial system, as M. Herrero reminds us, to which thanks were owed when the Austrian family won guaranteed access to credit and the ability to allocate it.[73] In return, the Genoese became the major players in the markets of the territories that belonged to the Spanish monarchy. Thus, there was a reciprocal flow between the political and the economic powers, where the interests of the former were closely linked to the status of the latter.

The relationship between the Spanish Monarchy and the Fornari reveals that an analysis of the merchants and their lifestyles cannot be separated from that of the politics surrounding them. Suffice to say that economics is the governance of a home in an Aristotelian sense. Therefore, the activities of the traders were not purely economic, the purpose of economics therefore being not to obtain maximum profit but to utilize profits in order to achieve social and political recognition. The affiliation with a great power such as Charles V's empire ensured that this aim was well on the way to being fulfilled. In turn, this meant a great deal to Genoese families who were ever ready to trade, collect, negotiate, lend, inform or arm ships for those who were, on the other hand, interested in protecting them to guarantee the continuity of such collaboration. It was, in short, a relationship based on vassalage that led to the formation of circuits where the profits for some also had a positive snowballing effect for others. In this context, tax collection and trade were symbiotic and it is therefore not possible to separately analyse one sector without also addressing the other.

Examining the activities of the Fornari are integral to an understanding of the degree of geographical integration which occurred in the sixteenth century. Most research on merchant communities, at least in relation to the Hispanic world, is based on a single framework. Such a perspective is very useful in order to gather information on the evolution of merchant groups within a local ambit. However, merchants operated in different scenarios through their networks. The operations of a single trader were closely linked to those of the others. Such circumstances rules out the study of only an individual. In the case of the Fornari, their involvement in America, North Africa and Italy made them powerful enough to become one the most influential intermediaries of the time. They were able to offer credit as this was backed by their tax collection business. The Fornari were capable of clothing the military, thanks to their involvement in the textile trade in several countries. They engaged in the slave trade because this could be organized from Oran. To sum up, each individual business depended on all the other trading activities. They were intrinsically linked. It seems appropriate to recreate the particular stories of these families based on the information presented here as it places us in a better position to gain a deeper knowledge and insight into the history of trade yet still recognizing that the history of trade is but a part of the history of power.

Notes

*This essay is part of the Project 'Dynamic Complexity of Cooperation-Based Self-Organizing Commercial Networks in the First Global Age', European Science Foundation, FP.004 DynCoopNet (Project Leader, Ana Crespo Solana).

1. Archivo de la Real Chancillería de Valladolid (henceforth ARChV), *Pleitos Civiles, Fernando Alonso (Fenecidos)*, leg. 1294, no. 3.
2. David Alonso García, *El erario del reino: Fiscalidad en Castilla a principios de la Edad Moderna, 1504–525*, Valladolid: Junta de Castilla y León, 2007.
3. There is a wealth of bibliography regarding this matter. I am merely citing here certain classic works such as Immanuel Wallerstein's *The Modern World-System: I. Capitalist agriculture and the origins of the European world-economy in the sixteenth century*, New York, London: Academic Press, 1974; and Fernand Braudel's *Civilization and Capitalism, 15th-18th Century*, specially, vols. 2 and 3, New York: Harper and Row, 1979-84. The centre-periphery structure proposed by Wallerstein has been widely contested. See Patrick O'Brien, 'European Economic Development; The Contribution of the Periphery', *Economic History Review*, no. 35, 1980, pp. 1–18; Bartolomé Yun Casalilla, 'Entre la economía mundo y el crecimiento polinuclear (los rasgos generales de la economía europea en el tránsito del siglo XVI (1490-1530)', in *De la unión de coronas al Imperio de Carlos V*, ed. E. Belenguer, Madrid: Sociedad Estatal, 2001, vol. 1, pp. 29–46. A idea opposed to the alleged economic supremacy of Europe before the Industrial Revolution is available in A.G. Frank, *ReORIENT: Global Economy in the Asian Age,* Berkeley-Los Angeles-London: University of California Press, 1998.
4. P.D. Curtin, *Cross-Cultural Trade in World History*, Cambridge: Cambridge University Press, 1984; Kenneth Pomeranz and Steven Topik, *The World that Trade Created: Society, Culture, and the World Economy, 1400 to the Present*, Armank-London: M.E. Sharpe, 1999. The anthropology of merchants as a specially important economic factor has been widely discussed in 'Acteurs et pratiques du comerse dans l'Europe Moderne', *Revue d'Histoire Moderne et Contemporaine*, vol. 45, no. 3, 1998 and 'Réseaux marchands', *Annales: Histoire, Sciences Sociales*, no. 58, May-June 2003.

5. Jacques Heers, *Gênes au XVe Siècle: Civilisation méditerranéenne, grand capitalisme, et capitalisme populaire*, Paris: S.E.V.P.E.N., 1971.
6. Giovanni Arrighi, *The Long Twentieth Century: Money, Power, and the Origins of Our Times*, London: Verso, 1994.
7. Craig Muldrew, *The Economy of Obligation: The Culture of Credit and Social Relations in Early Modern England*, New York: St. Martin's Press, 1998; Laurence Fontaine, 'Pouvoir et cultures dans les circulations financières sous l'Ancien Régime', in *Pourvoir les finances en province sous l'Ancien Régime*, ed. Françoise Bayard, Paris, Comitè pour l'histoire économique et financièere de la France, 2001, pp. 415–21.
8. Archivo General de Simancas, *Escribanía Mayor de Rentas* (henceforth AGS, *EMR*), box 186–1.
9. Arturo Pacini, *La Genova di Andrea Doria nell'Impero di Carlo* V, Florence: Leo S. Olschki, 1999, pp. 82-3. On the concept of *albergo*, See Heers, *Gênes*, pp. 383–90.
10. Giovanna Petti Balbi, *Negoziare fuori patria: nazioni e genovesi in età medievale*, Bologna: CLUEB, 2005, pp. 118, 152 and 168.
11. Ruth Pike, *Enterprise and Adventure: The Genoese in Seville and the Opening of the New World*, Ithaca: Cornell University Press, 1966, p. 67; Enrique Otte, 'Il ruolo dei Genovesi nella Spagna del XV e XVI secolo', in *La Repubblica Internazionale del denaro tra XV e XVII secolo*, ed. Aldo de Maddalena and Hermann Kellenbenz, Bologna: Il Mulino, 1986, p. 31; Ildefonso Pulido Bueno, *La familia genovesa Centurión (mercaderes diplomáticos y nombres de armas), al servicio de España*, Huelva, 2004, p. 91.
12. Pulido, *La familia*, p. 171.
13. Archivo General de Indias, *Patronato,* leg. 18, N. 1, R. 17.
14. About the rescue of captives, see José Antonio Martínez Torres, *Prisioneros de los infieles: Vida y rescate de los cautivos cristianos en el Mediterráneo musulmán (siglos XVI-XVII)*, Barcelona: Bellaterra, 2004.
15. Alonso, *El erario*, p. 272.
16. Jean-Frédéric Schaub, *Les juifs du roi d'Espagne: Oran, 1509–1669*, Paris: Hachette Litérratures, 1999.
17. On trade between Oran and Castile, see Chantal de la Veronne, 'Población del presidio de Orán en 1527', *Revista de Archivos, Bibliotecas y Museos,* vol. LXXVI, no. 1, January-June 1973, pp. 69–108; José Enrique López de Coca, 'Relaciones mercantiles entre Granada y Berbería en época de los Reyes Católicos', *Baética: Estudios de arte, geografía e historia,* no. 1, 1978, pp. 293–311; 'Orán y el comercio genovés en la transición a los tiempos modernos' (henceforth 'Orán'), *Anuario de estudios medievales,* no. 24, 1994, pp. 275–98; María Teresa López Beltrán, 'Fiscalidad regia en los puertos españoles del reino de Tremecén: Datos para su estudio', *Baética: Estudios de arte, geografía e historia*, no. 5, 1985, pp. 301–10; Manuel Espinar Moreno, 'Precisiones sobre el avituallamiento de la ciudad de Orán (1510–12): La contratación de Diego de Espinosa, regidor de Almería', in *Actas del II Congreso Internacional 'El Estrecho de Gibraltar'*, Madrid: UNED, 1995, vol. IV, pp. 5–70; Beatriz Alonso Acero, *Orán-Mazalquivir, 1589–1639*, Madrid: CSIC, 2000, pp. 388–98. Miguel Ángel de Bunes Ibarra, 'Relaciones

económicas entre la Monarquía Hispánica y el Islam', *Revista de Historia Económica*, año XXIII, Special Issue, 2005, pp. 161–77.

18. AGS, *EMR*, leg. 177.
19. López de Coca, 'Orán', p. 277.
20. Ibid.
21. David Alonso García, 'Los *Fornari* y las rentas de Orán a comienzos del siglo XVI: Financiación del rey y negocio familiar', in *Los extranjeros en la España Moderna*, ed. M.B. Villar and P. Pezzi, Málaga: Universidad de Malaga, 2003, vol. II, pp. 101–12.
22. López de Coca, 'Relaciones mercantiles'; López Beltrán, 'Fiscalidad regia'.
23. Matthew Vester, 'The Political Autonomy of a Tax Farm: The Nice-Piedmont Gabelle of the Dukes of Savoy, 1525-1580', *The Journal of Modern History*, no. 76, 2004, pp. 745–92.
24. Alonso, 'Los *Fornari*', p. 109.
25. AGS, *EMR*, leg. 177. On the government system in Orán at the time, see Rafael Gutiérrez Cruz, *Los Presidios españoles del norte de África en tiempo de los Reyes Católicos*, Melilla: Consejería de Cultura, 1997.
26. AGS, *EMR*, leg. 177. Alonso, 'Los *Fornari*', pp. 105–6.
27. AGS, *CMC, 1ª Ép.*, leg. 841, exp. 16.
28. Ibid.
29. AGS, *EMR*, leg. 177.
30. Ibid.
31. Ibid. In 1524 we find Nicolás Fornari in Seville. ARChV, *Pleitos Civiles*, leg. 1294, exp. 3.
32. AGS, *EMR*, leg. 193–2.
33. Ibid., leg. 177.
34. Ibid. On trade between Catalonia and northern Africa, Eloy Martín Corrales, *Comercio de Cataluña con el Mediterráneo musulmán (siglos XVI-XVIII): El comercio con los "enemigos de la fe"*, Barcelona: Bellaterra, 2001.
35. AGS, *EMR*, leg. 191.
36. AGS, *Cámara de Castilla* (henceforth AGS, *CC*), leg. 139, no. 218; *CMC, 1ª Ép.*, leg. 382, *Expedientes de Hacienda*, leg. 712, exp. 5. Vicente Montojo Montojo, 'Las oligarquías de Murcia y Cartagena en el reinado de Carlos V: formación y perpetuación de su memoria', in *Carlos V: Europeísmo y Universalidad*, Madrid: Sociedad Estatal, 2001, vol. IV, p. 489.
37. AGS, *EMR*, leg. 191.
38. About this important official, see Carlos Javier de Carlos Morales, *Carlos V y el crédito de Castilla: El tesorero general Francisco de Vargas y la Hacienda Real entre 1516 y 1524*, Madrid: Sociedad Estatal, 2000; Alonso, *El erario*.
39. In relation to this matter, see James D. Tracy, *Emperor Charles V, Impressario of War: Campaign Strategy, International Finance, and Domestic Politics*, Cambridge: Cambridge University Press, 2002.
40. AGS, *EMR*, leg. 186–1.
41. AGS, *CMC, 1ª Ép.*, leg. 375.
42. Alonso, *El erario*, p. 272.
43. AGS, *CC*, leg. 131, no. 10.

44. Ramón Carande, *Carlos V y sus banqueros: 3. Los caminos del oro y de la plata*, Barcelona: Crítica, 1990, p. 124.
45. Carande, *Carlos V*, p. 128.
46. AGS, *CMC, 1ª Ep.*, leg. 115.
47. Carande, *Carlos V*, p. 128.
48. Ibid., pp. 130 and 132.
49. Richard Ehrenberg, *Le siècle des Fugger*, Paris: S.E.V.P.E.N., 1955, p. 164.
50. AGS, *Estado Génova*, leg. 1362, no. 145. Such difficulties have been highlighted by Carlos Javier de Carlos Morales, 'Carlos V en una encrucijada financiera: las relaciones entre mercaderes-banqueros alemanes, genoveses y españoles en los asientos de 1529–1533', in *Carlos V y la quiebra del humanismo político en Europa (1530–1558)*, ed. José Martínez Millán, Madrid: Sociedad Estatal, 2001, vol. IV, pp. 405–61.
51. Vicente de Cadenas y Vicent, *El protectorado de Carlos V en Génova. La 'Condotta' de Andrea Doria*, Madrid, 1997, pp. 77–126; Edoardo Gredi, *La repubblica aristocratica dei genovesi: Política, carità e commercio fra Cinque e Seicento*, Bologna: Il Mulino, 1987, pp. 105–38.
52. AGS, *Estado Génova*, leg. 1362, no. 43.
53. Ibid., no. 144.
54. AGS, *E(xpedientes) de H(acienda)*, leg. 878, no. 14.
55. AGS, *Estado Génova*, leg. 1362, no. 142.
56. AGS, *Estado Génova*, leg. 1369, no. 38.
57. Ibid.
58. AGS, *Estado Génova*, leg. 1365, no. 239.
59. The Tassis—another Italian family engaged in moneylending—acted as official couriers for the monarchy, whereas the Fuggers also became diplomatic couriers between Poland and Spain. See, furthermore other previous references, Jacques Botin, 'Négoce et circulation de l'information au debut de l'Époque Moderne', in *Histoire de la poste: De l'administration à l'enterprise*, ed. Michel Le Roux, Paris: Éditions Rue d'Ulm, 2002, pp. 41–54. Antonio Fontán and Jerzi Axer, eds., *Españoles y polacos en la Corte de Carlos V: cartas del embajador Juan Dantisco*, Madrid: Alianza, 1994.
60. Carande, *Carlos V*; Pacini, *La Genova*; David Alonso García, 'De crédito y mercaderes: los circuitos financieros entre Castilla e Italia en los orígenes de la Monarquía Hispánica'. Unpublished paper presented at the VIII Congreso Internacional de la Asociación Española de Historia Económica, Santiago de Compostela, 2005.
61. AGS, *Estado Génova*, leg. 1362, no. 142.
62. Hayward Keninston, *Francisco de los Cobos: secretary of the Emperor Charles V*, Pittsburg: University of Pittsburg Press, 1958; Henar Pizarro Llorente, 'Francisco de los Cobos', in *La Corte de Carlos V*, ed. J. Martínez Millán and C. J. de Carlos, Madrid: Sociedad Estatal, 2000, vol. III, pp. 87–94.
63. See as an example AGS, *Estado Génova*, leg. 1365, nos. 239-41; leg. 1375, no. 21.
64. AGS, *Estado Génova*, leg. 1365.
65. Ibid., no. 243.

66. Ibid., no. 239.
67. Betsabé Caunedo del Potro, 'Comercio y hombres de negocios castellanos en tiempos de los Reyes Católicos: Técnicas y aprendizaje', in *Comercio y hombres de negocios en Castilla y Europa en tiempos de Isabel la Católica*, ed. H. Casado Alonso and A. Garcio-Baquero, Madrid: Sociedad Estatal, 2007, pp. 251–77. Scholars propose the existence of a 'collective, professional know-how among merchants', see Giorgio Doria, 'Comptoirs, foires de changes et places étrangères: les lieux d'apprentissage des nobles négociants de Gênes entre Moyen Âge et Âge Baroque', in *Cultures et formations négociantes dans l'Europe Moderne*, ed. F. Angiolini and D. Roche, Paris: Editions de l'EHESS, 1995, pp. 321–47.
68. AGS, *Estado Génova*, leg. 1365, no. 243.
69. Carande, *Carlos V*, pp. 112–13.
70. AGS, *Estado Génova*, leg. 1369, nos. 5 and 10. Pulido, *La familia*, pp. 105 and following.
71. AGS, *Estado Génova*, leg. 1369, no. 38.
72. AGS, *Estado Génova*, leg. 1369, no. 38. Arturo Pacini, 'I mercanti-banchieri genovesi tra la Reppublica di San Giorgio e il sistema imperiale hispano-asburgico', in *L'Italia di Carlo V. Guerra, religione e politica nel primo Cinquecento*, ed. F. Cantù e M.A. Visceglia, Roma: Viella, 2003, p. 585.
73. Manuel Herrero Sánchez, 'La república de Génova y la Monarquía Hispánica (siglos XVI-XVII): Introducción', *Hispania*, no. 219, 2005, pp. 9–20.

CHAPTER TEN

The 'Small World' of the Silk Merchant at Kasimbazar, India

Rila Mukherjee

HOW DOES ONE STUDY THE WORLD of the Indian merchant? Although frequently mentioned in historical accounts as 'substantial merchant(s)' and despite references to his being involved in great volumes of trade, he remains essentially a one-dimensional figure. Conventionally, the world of the Indian merchant has been studied with reference to his role as shipowner, trader, or financier.[1] Consequently there is little idea of the social and political world of the Indian merchant. Likewise, the knowledge about the formal and informal networks established by him remains vague at best.

Apart from a lack of sources, there is also a historiographic problem. Given that the eighteenth century Indian merchant was a transient figure in the transition to colonialism, and because he functioned within an economy that would eventually face both a rupture and the coming of a radically different political and economic order, the received history is that he was weak in terms of financial and mercantile organization.

Typically, therefore, the story of the Indian merchant has been told within a background of decline.

The time-period studied in this essay is that immediately preceding the transition to a colonial economy, at a time when the decline in question was not evident. To tell this story I will study the Indian merchant's world with reference to the multiple networks he created to conduct his business: political, social, economic and religious, at Kasimbazar, a place that to this day exists as a suburb of Murshidabad town in the present West Bengal state in India (see Maps 10.1 to 10.4). This chapter will thereby try to understand the South Asian commercial economy through an examination of networks at a time when the economy was stable and functioning.

Method

small world networks

In *The Enchantress of Florence,* Salman Rushdie talks of the networks embracing sixteenth century Asia, Europe, and America. In his story of the Mogol dell Amore, Rushdie describes networks of war, of adventure, of desire and of avarice that ultimately created a world marked by the circulation of commodities and cultures, of men and money. Such networks demonstrate *links* between multiple worlds rather than establishing *comparisons* between them. I use here the Small World Network (SWN) model to narrate the story of the merchant at Kasimbazar, and suggest how a graphical model of links between the Asian and European mercantile worlds may be constructed in the future with Kasimbazar as node.[2]

What is the SWN? It is something that functions in between random and regular (ordered) networks; here 'small' need not necessarily imply smallness of size or scale. Girvan and Newman write:

> any system take the form of networks, sets of nodes or vertices joined together in pairs by links or edges. Examples include social networks such as acquaintance networks and collaboration networks, technological networks such as the Internet, the Worldwide Web, and on power grids, and biological networks such as neural networks, food webs, and metabolic networks. Recent research on networks among mathematicians and physicists has focused on a number of distinctive statistical properties that most networks seem to share. One such property is the 'small world effect'.[3]

Such networks also display: (1) clustering, (2) hierarchical clustering (a notion that is important for studying mercantile and financial communities), and (3) a marked community structure.

Watts writes, 'Many social metrics, such as status and power, and social processes, such as the diffusion of innovations and transmission of influence, are usefully represented in terms of networks of relationships between social actors, be they individuals, organizations, or nations.'[4] For Watts, '"small" means that almost every element of the network is somehow "close" to almost every other element, even those that are perceived as likely to be far away.'[5] The SWN is numerically large, almost random, yet clustered, and is generally sparse and decentralized. By testing his model, Watts was able to show that the small-world phenomenon was not just the property of an abstract class of hypothetical graphs, but that it arose in real networks as well.

Watts also elaborated on structure, system, and dynamics. He continued:

Having established that a set of relatively tiny perturbations to the local structure of a highly clustered graph can have a dramatic impact upon its global structural properties, it is natural to ask whether or not the same changes can also affect the behaviour of dynamical systems that are coupled according to such a graph. This is a topic that is *directly relevant to the social sciences* [italics mine]: the role of social structure in generating globally observable, dynamical features. So far, structure has been treated as an autonomous feature of networks and defined narrowly in terms of sparse, undirected graphs. This has paid off by yielding some robust statements about the small-world properties of a general class of graphs that are partly ordered and partly random, and that seem to reflect some of the features of real networks. However, a greater issue is to understand the relationship between structure and dynamics.[6]

Watts concluded that shorter path lengths (small, global-length scale) and smaller time scales made for dense clustering by noting 'an interesting role for small-world architectures, which by virtue of their short characteristic path length and high clustering coefficient, can support the rapid dissemination of information without necessarily compromising behaviour that is individually costly but beneficial when reciprocated'.[7]

It is clear from this account that networks that are somewhat random may not always operate with 'official' (political or systemic) sanction. In which case, how do networks organize themselves? Kogut—citing F.A. Hayek's *The Fatal Conceit: The Errors of Socialism*—feels that while a market is the engine, it is knowledge, with its specialization-creating value, which underlies efficient networks.[8]

Can networks coordinate in the absence of authority? Networks can, and do, organize themselves in the absence of a coordinating authority. Here specialization and knowledge are key factors. The technical, financial (accounting) and organizational knowledge of the silk merchants of Kasimbazar, who were born into the business and nurtured within it, created this value, felt the Vereenigde Oost-indische Compagnie (VOC) in 1687: 'The merchants . . . are exceptionally quick and experienced. When they are still very young . . . they already begin to be trained as merchants. They are made to pretend to engage in trade while playing, first buying *cauris*, followed by silver and gold. In this training as money changers, they acquire the capacity of large scale trade.'[9] The English East India Company (EEIC) and the French East India Company (FEIC) made similar observations on the social and commercial capital that the merchants acquired since childhood, by noting that they had been bred in the business since infancy.[10] Their technical knowledge was therefore a community-based and historically acquired knowledge that no modern knowledge system could hope to compete with. The East India Companies frequently clashed with this knowledge system as they sought to introduce their own ways of doing business at Kasimbazar.

SMALL WORLD SYSTEMS

Kasimbazar was initially a 'small world' economically and physically. At its inception it seems to have had limited commercial impact within a similarly limited spatial extent. When founded in the seventeenth century by Kasim Khan, a Mughal official,[11] soon after the Mughal conquest of Bengal, possibly in 1618 or 1628, it was only a small mart town. Situated near the future capital of Bengal, Rajmahal, a town and port to the north towards Patna in Bihar, Kasimbazar became a rich agricultural area in the 1630s (see Maps 10.1 and 10.4). Kasimbazar was always far from the other capital, Dhaka, which lay in the south-eastern delta and became capital from the 1660s. Its only access was to north Indian urban centres, which too was quite restricted. However it is known that Kasimbazar textiles were sold in Patna in the 1620s.[12]

But while its commercial networks may have been limited in its beginnings, some sort of a transport network was already in place. Goods to and from Bengal already moved through Bihar, up to Agra and Lahore or down to the Bay. Ralph Fitch (1583–91) sailed from Agra to Saptagrama in Bengal with a fleet of 180 boats, laden with salt, opium, lead, carpets, etc.[13] Salt was much prized in Bengal and had to be obtained from far. Teixeira wrote around 1600 that ships from Cochin arrived at Hormuz to pick up salt destined for Bengal.[14] Jourdain noted in 1611 that 10,000 tons of salt in barges of 400 or 500 tons moved from Agra to Bengal annually; this was echoed by Peter Mundy who noted vessels between 300 and 500 tons plying between Agra and Bengal as far as Dhaka, carrying salt and other merchandise.[15] It was recorded by the EEIC in the 1630s about a ship's voyage that 'From Gombroon she is to be sent with a cargo of salt to Masulipatam and Bengal, and thence to bring to Surat a return cargo of sugar, gum-lac, wax, etc.'[16]

Saltpetre, which was much in demand by the EICs was bought by them in Bihar and then transported to Europe from the Bengal coast. The saltpetre came into Bengal via Rajmahal, the fluvial frontier between Bengal and Bihar: saltpetre was first mentioned as a commodity in English records as early as in 1621, in Kerridge's letter to the EEIC.[17]

Bihar therefore played a very crucial role in connecting the Mughal north with the plains of Bengal, while Kasimbazar lay on the major land and water routes.[18] Kasimbazar's main trading partners were the north Indian markets and the caravan trade networks that passed through Patna into both Bhutan and Central Asia. Access to north Indian markets improved by mid century and it seems that Kasimbazar's financial and mercantile networks became more integrated to those of Agra, a great centre for provisioning both the Mughal court and the caravan trade. John Kenn of the EEIC, while emphasizing the close links between the silk and money markets in Kasimbazar and north India wrote in 1661, 'According as this silk sells in Agra, so the price of silk in Kasimbazar riseth and falleth. The exchange of money from Kasimbazar to Patna and Agra riseth and falleth as the said silk findeth a vent in Patna and Agra.'[19] Other northern destinations were Mirzapur, Lahore, Multan, Benares, and Delhi. In the south Aurangabad was an important destination, as was Gujarat to the west. Ispahan, or New Julfa, whose network was controlled by the Armenians, was another westward destination for Kasimbazar silk.

The shift toward more extensive networks began to take place from the middle of the seventeenth century—an important point to which I shall return later. It is worth noting that both Bernier and Tavernier visited Kasimbazar (although not together) in the 1660s; in fact Shaista Khan, then Mughal *subahdar* at Dhaka, gave Tavernier at Dhaka a bill of exchange drawn on Kasimbazar. This last fact suggests that Kasimbazar was gradually gaining importance as a trade mart and financial centre from the middle of the seventeenth century.

As with its northern networks, initially Kasimbazar's links with the south-western Bengal delta were few; the ports of Saptagrama and Hugli were its main outlets to the Bay of Bengal. English Calcutta had not yet been founded (it was founded in 1690). Kasimbazar's links with the south-eastern delta were negligible; because when the capital was shifted to Dhaka in the south-eastern delta in the 1660s the chief trading items exported from the ports in the south-eastern delta were still mainly the cottons and muslins manufactured in the Dhaka region, as well as grains, oils and foodstuff. One finds little or no mention of Kasimbazar silks in the trade of the sixteenth century *sultani* state of the Husain Shahis in Bengal with South-East Asia. The *Suma Oriental*, the accounts of Duarte Barbosa and Ludovico Varthema, Frederici's and Fitch's narratives, the main sources for the sixteenth century, list mainly cottons, sugar and rice as exports from Bengal.[20]

This was therefore initially a little world system marked by a limited transmission of information and an equally restricted exchange of goods, mainly of the luxury kind, from Kasimbazar and its neighbourhood, such as silks and silk and cotton mixes. These were destined primarily for the markets of the north and beyond. Rice to sustain this mulberry land came from nearby Bardhaman district.

And it was a water world! Deloche quotes Greenhill, 'during the South-West monsoon and for months after it is finished Bengal becomes a world of water. . . . It is the world of men who live three thirds of their lives on the water, a world of men who make voyages taking many months but who never sail the open sea . . . this world has songs and poetry of its own.'[21] One can see from Map 10.5 that Kasimbazar lies on a branch of the Ganga that is partially navigable throughout the year, and this channel links up with the main branch that is not very far and is fully navigable through the year. Ralph Fitch sailed from Agra to Saptagrama in Bengal by this route.[22]

This water world was subject to the fluvial shifts that ravaged the province from the fifteenth century onwards. Travellers from the sixteenth century have testified to these shifts. The sixteenth century 'first city' of Gaur was abandoned when the river changed its course, and a new capital—the second city of Gaur—had to be constructed on the opposite bank of the river. Tavernier wrote that Rajmahal, the splendid capital and flourishing port of the 1630s, was a wasteland in the 1660s due to the Ganga having changed its course. He added that Bernier was forced to go over land from Rajmahal to Kasimbazar as the Bhagirathi River too had dried up.[23] John Marshall travelling here in 1670 commented on the shallowness of the river at Rajmahal.[24]

This water world was sometimes disrupted by other, more serious, natural catastrophes. In October 1737, a terrible cyclone ravaged Bengal; English and French journals reported that many ships and lives had been lost. *The Gentleman's Magazine* (Historical Chronicle, June 1738, vol. 8, p. 321) reported that:

> the Storm reached 60 Leagues [300 km] up the River *Ganges*, it is computed that 20,000 Ships, Barks, Sloops, Boats, Canoes, &c. have been cast away. A prodigious Quantity of Cattle of all Sorts, a great many Tygers, and several Rhinoceroses were drowned; even a great many Caymans [crocodiles] were stifled by the furious Agitation of the waters, and an innumerable Quantity of Birds was beat down into the River by the Storm. Two English ships of 500 Tons were thrown into a Village above 200 Fathom [309 m] from the bed of the River *Ganges*, broke to Pieces, and all the People drowned pell-mell among the Inhabitants and Cattle. Barks of 60 Tons were blown two leagues [10 km] up into the Land over the tops of the trees. The Water rose in all 40 Foot higher than usual. The *English* ships drove ashore and broke to Pieces were the *Decker*, *Devonshire* and *Newcastle*; and the *Pelham* is missing.

A *French* Ship was drove on Shore, and bulged; after the Wind and Waters abated they opened their hatches, and took out several Bales of Merchandize &c., but the Man who was in the Hold to fling the Bales suddenly ceased working; nor by calling to him could they get a Reply; on which they sent down another, but heard nothing of him, which very much added to their Fear; so that for some time no one would venture down. At length one more hardy than ye rest went down and became silent and unactive as the two former, to the Astonishment of All: They then agreed by Lights to look down into the Hold, which had a great quantity of water in it; and to their great surprise, they saw a huge alligator staring as expecting more Prey: it had come in thro' a Hole in the Ship's Side, and 'twas with Difficulty they killed it; when they found the three Men in the Creature's Belly.[25]

This water world was not just an unstable world; it was also a calamitous one.

Having established that Kasimbazar was ecologically a small world and economically even more so, one largely dependent on the rhythm of the monsoons and the north-westerly winds, I would like to emphasize that this small world was also uncommonly vulnerable to political disturbances. This was evident from the Maratha invasions of Bengal from 1742 and the Afghan rebellion in Bihar, and particularly at Patna, from 1745, both of which sandwiched Kasimbazar from the west and the north. The first effectively deprived Kasimbazar of its rice supply from Bardhaman in the west as the Marathas proceeded into Bengal and the second meant that trade was stopped on the Ganga at Patna for almost a year. The passage of goods from north India into Bengal and from Bengal to Agra was disrupted and many of the networks fragmented in the 1740s, leaving the Kasimbazar merchants with little option but to undertake more orders from the EICs.

I shall adopt here the ingenuous model created by Chase-Dunn and Mann when they narrated the story of the Wintu, a small community in northern California with a 'small world system', in terms of a world systems perspective but with certain differences.[26] They claimed that world systems were 'intersocietal networks', ruled by a particular mode of accumulation, an exchange pattern that was 'local centric' and then moved up, rather than moving both top-down and horizontally as in conventional world systems theory, marked by four networks: (1) Information Networks (INs), (2) Prestige Goods Networks (PGNs), (3) Political/Military Networks (PMNs), and (4) Bulk Goods Networks (BGNs). This world system was marked by both a core-periphery hierarchy and differentiation.

Somewhat later, Chase-Dunn and Jorgenson expanded the model. According to Chase-Dunn and Jorgenson:

The largest networks are those in which information travels. Information is light and it travels a long way, even in systems based on down-the-line interaction. These are termed Information Networks (INs). A usually somewhat smaller interaction network is based on the exchange of prestige goods or luxuries that have a high value/weight ratio. Such goods travel far, even in down-the-line systems. These are called Prestige Goods Networks (PGNs). The next largest interaction net is composed of polities that are allying or making war with one another. These are called Political/Military Networks (PMNs). And the smallest networks are those based on a division of labour in the production of basic everyday necessities such a food and raw materials. These are Bulk Goods Networks (BGNs).[27]

Chase-Dunn and Jorgenson also distinguished between core/periphery *differentiation* and core/periphery *hierarchy*, thereby melding the world systems theory with cluster differentiation in network theory. Again according to Chase-Dunn and Jorgenson:

Core/periphery differentiation exists when two societies are in systemic interaction with one another and one of these has higher population density and/or greater complexity than the other. The second aspect, core/periphery hierarchy, exists when one society dominates or exploits another. These two aspects often go together because a society with greater population density/complexity usually has more power than a society with less of these, and so can effectively dominate/exploit the less powerful neighbour. But there are important instances of reversal (e.g. the less dense, less complex Central Asian steppe nomads exploited agrarian China) and so this analytical separation is necessary so that the actual relations can be determined in each case. The question of core/periphery relations needs to be asked at *each level of interaction* [italics mine] designated above. It is more difficult to project power over long distances and so one would not expect to find strong core/periphery hierarchies at the level of Information or Prestige Goods Networks.[28]

This model can be used to chart the transformation of Kasimbazar from a little 'place' to a big 'space' at the end of the seventeenth century. The initial 'small world' phenomenon that is discussed for Kasimbazar here was very similar to the small world system of the Wintu. The pattern of exchange was initially 'local centric' and then moved up, as one see from an English report of the 1620s.[29] Routes were simple, mainly radiating to north India through Patna in Bihar. The shift from the local to the global is documented in maps of the period, as I show, and readings of contemporaneous texts confirm this shift.

This little world system underwent a change from the mid-seventeenth century and, as commercial networks intensified in scope, it changed further when Murshidabad became the capital of Bengal from around 1704. The transportation benefits, from the fluvial network that ran through it and connected it to Murshidabad and Patna, were rediscovered. It was through the fluvial network and proximity to the new capital that Kasimbazar now catapulted itself into the uppermost rank among silk marts in the subcontinent.

In 1733, this world expanded further as Bihar became a part of the nawabi province of Bengal. This integration proceeded to open up new transport networks and simultaneously, new commercial and financial networks. The Mughal emperor Jahangir had connected Patna in Bihar to Agra in the seventeenth century, now by virtue of Bihar's integration with Bengal in 1733 the latter too became connected to Agra by way of Bihar. The road from Malda near Kasimbazar linked the commercial areas of Tirhut and Chhapra in Bihar, and Chhapra was only 10 *kos* (approximately 3.2 km.) away from Patna. It will be seen later that the Armenians had substantial business interests in the commercially rich region of Chhapra. The older Lucknow-Benares link now joined Murshidabad and Patna to this northern overland route.[30]

Merchants from other parts of the subcontinent now based themselves in eighteenth-century Kasimbazar: they were first and foremost the Gujaratis, subsequently came the merchants from Lahore, Multan, Benares, Gorakhpur, Delhi (Calwars) and Agra from the north, from Hyderabad in the Deccan, as also merchants from Jangipur in Murshidabad district, probably these last acted as *gomastas* or agents of Benares merchants.[31] In April 1712, there is a reference in the EEIC records of merchants from Lahore meeting Manickchand, the founder of the house of the Seths.[32] By the middle of the eighteenth century this list expanded to accommodate even more merchants from the subcontinent: 'Cashmeerians, Multanys, Patans, Sheiks, Sunniasys, Paggayahs, Betteeas and many others used to resort to Bengal in Caffeelas or large parties of many thousand together with troops of oxen for the transport of goods.'[33] This is clearly evidence of the overland trade within India that in turn connected to the great caravan routes of Asia.

It has been argued that the European merchants were not the chief trading partners of eighteenth-century Bengal. The networks of the little studied *sannyasis*, Gosains, etc., who controlled the silk trade between Benares, Mirzapur, Bengal, Bihar, and the Deccan, and who traded to the north-east between Bengal and Bhutan, are of immense value for the understanding of the organization of silk and other trades carried on throughout South Asia by such mobile groups.[34] The *sannyasi* network combined two identities: religious and commercial. Because of the former identity they could travel unhindered all over the continent and a large part of the internal circulation was in their hands. It was recorded that the Gosains numbered 10,000 in Benares alone, and in times of pilgrimage (and trade) their numbers swelled to 35,000.[35] Chaudhury writes that:

> the supremacy of the Asian merchants (over the Europeans) is also confirmed by one Sadananda Bandopadhyay who was the gomasta of a Gujarati merchant in Kasimbazar and was himself in the silk business for 30 years, who stated, referring

to the 1750s in all probability, that there were 10 merchants in Murshidabad who exported Bengal raw silk to the tune of 13,000 to 20,000 maunds annually. It was Louis Taillefert, the Dutch Director in Bengal, who clearly pointed out in 1763 that the procurement of raw silk by the gomastas of traders from Lahore and Multan had gone up to a great extent since the beginning of the eighteenth century.[36]

Silk was now neither a prestige commodity nor a bulk good, as in the Wintu model, but a commodity in the true sense of the term. It was obtained through a long information pathway and organizational chain where various grades of agents, brokers, banias functioned. The information networks (INs) show the longest pathway in both phases of Kasimbazar's history, and largely contributed towards both the expansion of trade and the integration of markets.

Other than the Asian merchants, there were the Armenians with a large house and garden, at Saidabad, a suburb of Kasimbazar. The Armenians had entrenched themselves in the trade marts and production centres of interior Bengal and Bihar, dealing in silk, opium and saltpetre, from possibly the end of the sixteenth century. The Armenians had networks stretching from New Julfa to Manila, and in the seventeenth century, the EEIC established close links with them for trade, financial remittances, and access to the court in Bengal.[37] Armenian trade in Bengal was charged less than the usual duty of 5 per cent by the nawabs. Goods from Bengal, mainly textiles, were taken to Madras by the Armenians from where they entered the Madras-Manila-New Spain network of the Armenians.[38] A church dedicated to the Virgin was built at Saidabad.

THE PHASE TRANSITION AT KASIMBAZAR

But this enormous change in Kasimbazar's trading networks was reflective of another shift, one perhaps little understood at the time. This shift took place within North-West Europe and spread over the Indian Ocean. From the seventeenth century, European merchants were present in Asian waters, either as individual traders or as traders under a national flag. Here they collaborated with Asian merchants (e.g. the Armenians who, represented by Khoja Panos Calendar in London, signed in 1688 the Treaty of East India Company with the Armenian Nation for cooperation in maritime commerce) and Asian states and gradually inserted themselves into maritime routes and financial and commercial networks (see Chapter 3 of this volume). In the eighteenth century, this cooperative model was gradually abandoned in favour of a more dominant model. The world of Kasimbazar, in the process of transition in the seventeenth century, was integrated into global networks that spanned Europe, Africa and Asia, thereby transcending its earlier networks. The Armenians too were progressively marginalized by the EEIC.

The new networks were increasingly governed by financial and political power emanating from Western Europe; it to here where the networks were different from those described for the Wintu. Kasimbazar now revealed the transformation of exchange patterns from an initial bottom-up trajectory to a top-down path.

Kasimbazar was full of various networks of financiers and traders by the eighteenth century, its growth as an urban centre was fuelled by two geographic networks that initially collaborated with each other, one Asian, the other European. Kasimbazar was born through Asian demand, as discussed here, but reinvented in the eighteenth century through *European maritime* demand, as the Kasimbazar Factory Records on the *dadni* merchants shows. It is important to note that the networks I dub here as 'Asian' and 'European' were never 'formally' so, nor were they single networks, the terms 'Asian' and 'European' refer to the dominant geographical features of each network.

It is not yet known what happened when these two networks met each other, but what is known is that when they initially intersected there was a trade boom at Kasimbazar, visible from the end of the seventeenth century and very apparent in the eighteenth century. Production rose to meet increased demand, there was a greater amount of money in circulation and merchants made fortunes overnight. This period of expansion ended from the 1730s, as reflected in the data from Kasimbazar, and the system entered into a period of crisis.[39] Between the 1740s and the 1750s the various components in the system started to crumble, this translated into a cascading crisis as Owens discusses in Chapter 8. The crisis was visible in price rise, late deliveries, inferior quality, deviation from the samples shown, subsequent imprisonment of *dadni* merchants for non-payment of dues, complaints of both parties to the nawab's court at Murshidabad, increasing impotence of the nawab in the face of the growing power of the EEIC and, ultimately, the bankruptcy of the *dadni* merchants at Kasimbazar.[40]

More significantly for purposes here, it seems that the EEIC demand had diverted production not only from the home (Asian) market but also from other European markets; witness the FEIC plea that fine quality *baftas* destined for royalty in Asia and in demand in France were no longer manufactured by the weavers at Jugdia because the EEIC only wanted medium quality or coarse *baftas*.[41] Even more significant, the old unitary production model was breaking down; earlier cloths were spun, woven, and washed (to ensure the quality of the dye) in *one place*. The Bengal merchants had total control over the production process as well as choice of place to carry on production; moreover, the price asked reflected this concentration of production in the hands of the merchants. Now, due to EIC exigencies of timely deliveries and the worry of additional financial charges due to late deliveries (much like credit card charges in the present!), cloths were transported to be washed at the regional EIC HQs; either because the ponds under the merchant's control were thought to be polluted or because the deliveries were late and so the ships already waiting at the regional harbours would have to depart for their outward journeys without their consignment if the cloths were not delivered 'finished' within a certain period.[42] New productive nodes thus came into existance due to the failure of older networks.

By the late 1760s, the foundations of the early colonial economy were taking shape, underlining the phase transition to the colonial economy of the nineteenth century. Transport routes were breaking down, there was decline in law and order, large numbers were dying from famine and lawlessness, and the textile investment could not be procured in either Bengal or Bihar.[43] It was precisely at this time that the EEIC and the FEIC sought to bypass 'interference' at the older Mughal mart towns and set up new market towns instead. Here they attempted to draw buyers and sellers and thereby denied the Mughal order the customs and transit duties due to it.

So, the new networks were clearly visible by the 1770s. In 1770, a terrible famine ravaged Bengal and Bihar, caused mostly by the reckless revenue farming policy adopted by the EEIC once it gained control over Bengal's revenues in 1765. Mughal poets, scholars, and philosophers in Kasimbazar, Patna, and Calcutta started lamenting the alien regime of the 'hat wearers'; they spoke of a revolution (*inquilab*) and remembered fondly an earlier golden age.[44] The phase transition must have been brutal.

Of particular note here are two events that moulded the peculiar conditions of the time: the terrible Bengal famine of 1770 which signalled the role of European capital and EEIC greed in the breakdown of the old order, and the Permanent Settlement of the Bengal revenues by Cornwallis in 1792 which signalled the demise of the old and the passage to the new. Both events saw the end of the old social networks that are studied here. The old silver and gold standard now yielded way to paper money printed by the EEIC. The old financial order too was declared defunct.

THE ROLE OF EUROPEAN FINANCIAL NETWORKS IN THE ECONOMY OF BENGAL

This account emphasizes the disruptive role of European capital in the economy of Bengal. But, were Europeans the main importers of bullion as well as the chief trading partners of Bengal? Received history gives this impression but they may not have been the case. Chaudhury writes:

> As far as the total value of the raw silk exported by the Europeans and Asians is concerned, the European share was thus only between $\frac{1}{5}$ and $\frac{1}{4}$ of the Asian share.

As such, and considering the fact, attested by many contemporaries including the Dutch Directors and English Officials in Bengal, that the Asians too had to bring in silver/cash to Bengal for buying raw silk, textiles and other commodities, the assertion that the Europeans were the major importers of bullion into Bengal in the pre-Plassey period can hardly be tenable.[45]

The fact that there may have been other, and perhaps more significant, sources of bullion into eighteenth-century Kasimbazar, as well as the presence of merchants from other parts of the empire and beyond, suggests that there may have been other networks in place and that one may have to revise the notion of the EICs being the principal importers of bullion into the economy, and hence, of being primarily responsible for the decline of the old order.[46] But, this needs more clues for research—something Chaudhury tantalizes us with, but does not offer.

The Many Networks of Kasimbazar

KASIMBAZAR AS CENTRAL NODE IN THE GLOBAL SILK TRADE NETWORK

Kasimbazar may have been a smallish place on the seventeenth century global map but it evolved into a central node in the commercial and financial networks in the eighteenth century. These were in turn connected with much larger networks emanating from India, Central Asia and Europe. Kasimbazar was now synonymous with the silk trade and unimaginable riches in the eighteenth century European imagination.[47]

Initially a seventeenth century mart town that supplied the markets of Patna via the river port of Rajmahal,[48] it was 'discovered' by the Europeans once the capital of Bengal was established at Maksudabad in the first decade of the eighteenth century.The capital was subsequently renamed Murshidabad by Murshid Quli Khan, a Persian Shi'ite Muslim who was the diwan and then the first nawab of Bengal. Maps support the hypothesis that Kasimbazar did not hold much importance in European perception in the first part of the seventeenth century or was perhaps too small to be depicted. I have found few representations of Kasimbazar on seventeenth century maps (one exception is Map 10.1), but plenty in the eighteenth century, emanating largely from the middle of the eighteenth century (Maps 10.2–10.4). As to why Murshid Quli Khan effected the actual shift of the capital as well as the shift in nomenclature around 1704-5 is not known but one may assume that it was designed to tap the resources and routes of this potentially rich and still unexplored region.

Kasimbazar was known in the eighteenth century as the great market town whose streets never saw the light of the sun, filled as it was with magnificent buildings.[49] As a mart town, Kasimbazar was the collection centre for silks produced further inland. Here too, the received history says that European demand was a major factor in according Kasimbazar a central place on the mercantile map of Bengal. In 1813, this magnificent city came to a decline as the Bhagirathi changed its course. Soon the area became swampy and malarial and was abandoned.

New commercial imperatives had decided Kasimbazar's fate. It was no longer important as a port for the English who were located further downstream at Calcutta complete with a port and harbour facilities. Its exports of silks had long ceased as Chinese silk fed the British market by the end of the eighteenth century. Cheap cotton textiles from the mills of England flooded the Indian market throughout the nineteenth century. Today Kasimbazar is a backwater. It is a suburb of Murshidabad, but remnants of its past grandeur remain and the arch over the port betrays vestiges of its former royal past.

Three periods in Kasimbazar's history reveal significant shifts in its economy: the first, from 1680 to 1704 when the town became increasingly important in Asian and Gulf trades; the second, from 1704 to 1733, i.e. from the time of the establishment of the capital at nearby Maksudabad to the incorporation of Bihar into the Bengal *subah* (province), when Asians and Europeans entered Kasimbazar in large numbers due to better transport and information networks and when the Asian and European networks operated simultaneously; and the period from 1733 to 1754, which saw a phase shift and the EEIC impose total control over silk production and trade. There were corresponding shifts in networks as the players adapted to changed conditions.

KASIMBAZAR AS CENTRAL NODE IN POLITICAL, FINANCIAL, AND COMMERCIAL NETWORKS

Kasimbazar's proximity to the mint and the royal capital at Murshidabad allowed the dynamics of trade to be conducted in a relatively uncomplicated manner from the beginning of the eighteenth century. It was advantageous for the Europeans to base themselves there because easy access to both the mint and court facilitated their trade interests. Moreover, Kasimbazar housed many prominent moneylenders, financiers, and bankers, which was an added bonus as both European official and private trade in Bengal was largely financed by local financiers.[50] One shall see here that the financial network emanating from Murshidabad was spatially wide and economically significant and that these networks ultimately went beyond north India.

If one studies any eighteenth century map of Kasimbazar such as those displayed at the end of this essay, one will notice that it is situated in a triangle caused by the Bhagirathi, Jalangi and Padma Rivers: these riverways facilitated communication with marts and production centres throughout the province. The Bhagirathi along this stretch was called the Cossimbazar River. This island exists no more; the Jalangi has dried up. The easily navigable fluvial highways to Patna in the north and Hugli in the south, made the transport of goods easy, both north to the great caravan routes or south to the Bay of Bengal. Because of Kasimbazar's propinquity to the production centres of Kumarkhali in Nadia district (in the present state of West Bengal, India) and Rangpur (in present Bangladesh), both of which could be easily accessed by good transport networks (both road and fluvial systems), as well as for having its own silk producing area around Jangipur, Gonatea, Rangamati, and Shantipur, the merchants of Kasimbazar were in a particularly advantageous position to furnish textiles of all kinds, but particularly silks, to the EICs. The locational and transport dynamics ensured that Kasimbazar occupied the foremost position as a trade mart in Bengal, the other being Dhaka in the east of the province.

Kasimbazar's advantageous location therefore greatly facilitated its position as the foremost silk mart of Bengal. Its central location supported a hierarchy of numerous mart towns and production centres. Map 10.3 shows that eighteenth-century Kasimbazar lay in a densely urbanized zone with numerous urban and rural markets to which it was connected both spatially and economically.[51] These markets were also connected via a social network; they were often established and controlled by the royal family and favoured courtiers, financed by local moneylenders (*sarafs*) and powered by local merchants who transported the goods to the markets.

The ruling class took the lead in establishing markets. Murshid Quli, the first nawab, constructed the Katra Masjid at Murshidabad; this functioned as the central royal market place and subsequently his tomb. Murshid Quli also established the Bhagwangola (wholesale market) near Murshidabad in his grandson Sarfaraz Khan's name; he also founded, in Murshidabad, J'afarganj, in 1708. Murshid Quli constructed simultaneously the *chowk* at the secondary capital in the east, Dhaka, to facilitate transactions, and established there the Bazaar Kartalabh Khan. The next dynasty of Alivardi Khan established even more bazaars; in Bihar, the bazaar of Hajiganj was owned by Haji Ahmad, who had substantial commercial interests in Bihar and Bengal, and who happened to be the brother of Alivardi Khan, the nawab from 1740 to 1756.[52]

THE CONVERGENCE OF POLITICAL, COMMERCIAL AND TRANSPORT NETWORKS AT KASIMBAZAR

Sarfaraz Khan, the grandson of Murshid Quli Khan and the founder of the *nizamat* of Bengal, became nawab of Bengal in 1739-40. But, courtiers and financiers such as the Seths, Alamchand, and Chin Ray at Murshidabad, as well as a handful of less powerful courtier merchants ultimately switched loyalties and deposed him in favour of Alivardi Khan from Bihar. The point worth noting here is that the more powerful landlords (*zamindars*) of Bengal also supported this move to topple the House of Murshid Quli and welcome a nawab from Bihar instead, possibly because most *zamindars* had become alienated through Murshid Quli's harsh revenue measures. This social network would rule Bengal until 1757, when Alivardi's grandson Siraj-ud-daulah, nawab of Bengal from 1756 to 1757, was killed and Bengal became a province administered by the EEIC.

It shall be seen later that this move obviously helped the commercial and financial interests of the courtier-merchant combine at Murshidabad. Bihar had become a part of Bengal *subah* in 1733, and it was deemed suitable, and advantageous, to have a nawab from that region. Alivardi himself had entered the Bengal nawab's service; he became the *faujdar* of Rajmahal around 1728 and in 1732-3, he was appointed as deputy governor (*subahdar*) of Patna. A year later Bihar became part of Bengal and it seems likely that Alivardi Khan was the architect of this annexation.[53]

Why was Patna (and Bihar) so important to eighteenth-century Bengal? The overland routes through Patna that connected Bengal to north India, through the Ganga, have already been mentioned, now let us look at maritime outlets. In the seventeenth century, when it was a Mughal province, Bengal's two main royal ports were Hugli in the west of the province and Dhaka in the east. The port that faced north, and connected Bengal with north India, was the Gangetic port of Rajmahal, sometime capital in the 1630s. This was a port that experienced 'great trade' in the seventeenth century but it was a secondary port, far from the Bay and functioning only as a transit point in communications and trade between Agra and Bengal. In the eighteenth century, when the rich province of Bihar became a part of Bengal province, the annexation was of immense strategic value because Bengal now had easy access to the markets of Awadh, Delhi, and Agra through Bihar's capital and port Patna, which lay on the Ganges. New transport networks, and along with them new commercial and financial networks, were set up linking Bengal with Bihar and northward with Mughal India, or, conversely, Mughal India with the Bay of Bengal.[54] The four ports of Bengal were now Hugli (under an official named *Baksh Bandar*), Dhaka under the *Shah Bandar*, Murshidabad under the *Pachotra Bandar* (or *Pachotra Daroga* as referred to in the Kasimbazar Factory Records of the EEIC), and Patna under the *Budrekha Bandar*. This last controlled all duties from trade from the upper and middle Gangetic routes and ports, so one can imagine the enormous profits accruing to Bengal with the incorporation of Bihar into the province.

Moreover, the export of Bihar's many products, namely saltpetre, sugar, rice, poppy, and cotton cloths, now acted to the financial advantage of Bengal. It is no accident that one finds a number of 'upcountry', i.e. Bihari and north Indian merchants operating from Kasimbazar; these merchants brought their financial expertise and business acumen to Bengal and enriched trading possibilities there. Among these, the houses of Jagat Seth and Alamchand were the most successful. By expanding their operations to the east, west, and north of the province and beyond, they organized a mercantile and financial web through the system of *hundis* (bills of exchange) that guaranteed payment against goods anywhere in north India and the Deccan. To this day there exists a Hiranand Shahu ki Gali in Patna; Hiranand was the founder of the house of Jagat Seth.[55] Such is the manner in which networks live on in public memory.

There were now put in place highly complex social and transport networks that linked a production centre to the market and the mart town to the port via *ghats* (a landing place on a river or lake), roads, and bridges.[56] Traffic regulations ensuring the safety of peoples and goods, the building of forts in border areas for protection and the setting up of *serais* helped sustain these transport networks. Enforcement of contracts and the protection of property nourished commercial relations within the province and beyond.[57] A postal system set in motion by the Mughals and then by the nawabs, both from Hugli by sea and overland through Patna and Surat, facilitated communication beyond the state. Map 10.4 shows Kasimbazar's riverine links with the north and the north-east of the subcontinent; these fluvial networks ensured reasonably safe and low transport costs facilitating both communication and trade.

The port administration, especially the nearby ports at Hugli and Kasimbazar/Murshidabad were controlled by the Bengal nawabs and their favourites from 1711, bypassing the emperor's nominees from Delhi.[58] De Gennes de la Chancelliere writes that in 1743 the office of the *faujdar* (chief port official, under whom the various *bandar* officials worked) of Hugli was held by the nephew of Alivardi Khan, the then nawab.[59] Local networks were becoming significant and the nawabs, by controlling the selection of port officials, sought to control the resources of the province to their advantage. By buying into bazaars, by establishing new markets and thereby diverting production and sales from older centres, by initiating roadways and bridges, and by putting their relatives in-charge of port administration, the nawabs sought to control the commercial and transport networks in the province by land, river and maritime routes. Other than thus securing the trade channels of the province to their own advantage, the Bengal nawabs also entrusted the administration of sensitive border areas, such as Purnia, to favourites or relatives. To keep prices low, the export of grain was prohibited;

an official checked the amount of grain carried on board in ships departing from Bengal against the number of crew every time a ship sailed from any of the ports of the province.[60] Bengal in the first half of the eighteenth century was a coherent political unit. It was also economically sovereign through networks set in motion by its own needs and which worked to its own advantage.

THE *DADNI* MERCANTILE NETWORK AT KASIMBAZAR

A particular type of merchant was domiciled at Kasimbazar; known as the *dadni* merchant. These were primarily local merchants, with local, 'small world' networks, who acted as intermediaries for merchants of diverse 'nationalities'. The *dadni* merchants were mostly upcountry Marwari merchants, Jain by religious persuasion, though there were also many Hindus: Bihari Hindus, Bengali Brahmins as also diverse Bengalis of the Hindu *Saivite*, *Shakta* and *Vaishnavite* sects worshipping, variously, Shiva, Kali and Vishnu. These merchants furnished textiles (mainly silk, silk piece goods, and cottons) for the European (Dutch, English, French, Danish and Belgian) investments in Bengal on the basis of a *dadan* or advance. The *dadan* worked out to about 80 per cent of the total sum contracted for each type of textile.[61] These merchants were, then, essentially brokers.[62]

Although brokers, these were no modest merchants. At the top of the list of brokers were the Treasurer General of Bengal and Controller of the Mint, controlled by the Seths of the House of Jagat Seth (literally banker to the world) and represented by Fatehchand, Kushalchand, Mahtab Rai and Surupchand, successive heads of the house from the 1730s to the 1750s. These lent the EEIC *Sicca Rupees* (*SR*) 42,32,278 between 1733 and 1750, i.e. approximately 4,23,227.8 (4,23,228) British pounds at the then rate of exchange;[63] and at the bottom of the ladder lay native Bengali lower cotton trading castes such as Kapris (from *kapar* in Bengali, literally meaning cloth), who scored a 8 per cent share in the total EEIC silk investment at Kasimbazar in 1744 (the total EEIC investment amounted to *SR* 1,368.58, so the Kapris' share was *SR* 10,94,864 or 1,09,486.4 British pounds) and a 10 per cent share in the total EEIC silk investment at Kasimbazar in 1745 (the total was *SR* 1,594.78, so the Kapris' share came to *SR* 1,59,47,800 or 15,94,780 British pounds).[64]

In other words, though the merchants at Kasimbazar may have been a motley group in terms of degree of access to political power, they were certainly equal in terms of the value of goods handled by them. Moreover, one sees from the trade figures of the Kapris in 1744 and 1745 that their volume of trade exceeded the 4,23,228 British pounds lent to the EEIC by the Seths between 1733 and 1750.

These merchant-brokers were politicians, courtiers, customs officials, revenue farmers, moneylenders, bankers, and the heads of large financial houses. They were frequently patrons of temples and large religious endowments in Bengal and Bihar. Their financial strength can be estimated from Tables 10.1 and 10.2 which give an idea of the amounts handled by them and the loans they and their family members made over to the EEIC. It must be kept in mind that these merchant-families also financed the FEIC and the VOC, as well as the Danish Company at times. These tables indicate the amount of ready cash at their disposal; testimony to the immense financial networks encircling Bengal.

THE COURTIER-MERCHANT AT KASIMBAZAR

As elsewhere in the First Global Age, the courtier sometimes acted as merchant at Kasimbazar. The most famous courtier-merchants were the big four: Fatehchand, the first Jagat Seth, his nephews, Mahtab Rai and Surupchand jointly the third Jagat Seths and Kushalchand, son of Mahtab Rai and the second Jagat Seth. Fatehchand, then somewhat under the shadow of Manickchand his father and one of the chief financiers of Bengal, is mentioned in the EEIC records of 13 August 1711, as offering to provide the entire EEIC investment at Kasimbazar *without advance.* On 21 August 1711 such a contract was made with Fatehchand.[65]

The family were given the title Nagar Seth (Chief Banker to the City) around 1713 by the then Mughal emperor Faruksiyar. Enjoying the confidence of the Mughals in Delhi and loaning considerable sums of money to Faruksiyar's successor, the Mughal emperor Muhammad Shah at Delhi, they were subsequently recognized as Jagat Seth (Banker to the World) in 1722.[66] The first Jagat Seth, Fatehchand, was estimated by de Gennes de la Chanceliere in 1743 to be worth 750 million French *sols*, not an insignificant sum.[67] Apart from being the Controller of the Mint and Treasurer General of the greater province of Bengal at Murshidabad, the Seths participated not only in trade with Europeans as brokers, but had significant shares in the caravan trade from Peking to Constantinople and in the maritime traffic between Japan and Mozambique, i.e. an area covering almost the whole of the Indian Ocean.[68] Therefore, brokers were not necessarily minor merchants.

Other courtier-financiers also participated in the textile trade at Kasimbazar as brokers. Alamchand, mentioned as *dadni* merchant in the raw silk and silk piece goods investments between 1748 and 1750 and as a 'principal merchant' of the EEIC in 1755,[69] was first the Diwan (finance minister) of Bengal and then Ray-Rayan, or Chief Minister, of Bengal in the 1730s. Alamchand, along with Fatehchand, was the power behind the throne.

From 1740, the destinies of Bengal and Bihar became firmly joined and provided an impetus to the formation of new financial networks; this was evident from Alamchand's financial career. Although Alamchand himself died in the battle of Giria in 1740 and could not personally profit from the accession of Alivardi Khan, his firm's financial interests evidently prospered thereafter because the various firms of Alamchand-Gainchand and Alamchand-Nimchand established offices in Kasimbazar, Patna, and Dhaka. Thus, the latter were able to establish a presence in three of the four ports of the province (the only exception being Hugli, perhaps because the EEIC were too close at Calcutta). Alamchand's son Raja Kirti Chand, diwan to the new nawab Alivardi Khan, also had considerable business interests in Patna. The career of the Chand family indicates that a uniform financial realm now prevailed in the whole of the province while the career of the Seths suggests that uniform financial markets were now appearing, linking Bengal to the Mughal north and beyond.

I will now analyse how these networks corresponded with the world of production.

THE *ARANG* NETWORK IN THE PRODUCTION SPHERE IN BENGAL

By the eighteenth century, a group of *arangs* (manufacturing centres) came up near Murshidabad, where silks and silk goods were produced for the market. Simultaneously, royal *arangs* were established for the consumption of the nawab and the ruling elite.[70] The second type of manufactory also furnished textiles for trade; both courtiers and the *harem* frequently dabbled in trade. These *arangs* acted as nodes in a production network of which Kasimbazar was at the centre. The catchment area of an *arang* could be up to 350 villages—a very large area.

It seems evident, going through French and English company records, that both types of *arangs* existed side by side and the lines dividing them were not always distinct. One was the so-called 'royal' *arang*, mainly for provisioning the household needs of the ruling elite as well as their varied mercantile interests. The other was the *arang* near mart towns and ports; these latter provisioned both the rural market as well as supplying port towns and merchants engaged in both the *dadan* and overseas trades. *Arangs* therefore had become bifurcated by the eighteenth century, but it is not known who or what organized them. Nor is it clear as to whether there was 'ownership' of *arangs*. It seems that they were set up both due to royal initiative as well as being natural outcome of the needs of the market. Some may have been controlled by the more powerful *dadni* merchants.

The courtiers had access to both kinds of *arangs*. They could thus engage in a 'royal trade', but by furnishing the EEIC investment in silk, instead of going to the trouble of engaging ships and captains and thereby also avoiding organizing the channels of trade and finance from *arang* to ultimate destination. But their role as 'controllers' of the trade from the *arang* would be undermined increasingly from the 1730s, as would the monopoly position of the *dadni* merchant at around the same time, when the EEIC as well as the VOC, in clear violation of their treaty obligations with Bengal, started penetrating the inland marts by virtue of their control over the waterways of Bengal.

THE MERCHANT AND THE MARKET

Given the various universes of the merchant of Kasimbazar, it is not surprising that he was directly involved, indeed integrated, with markets from the local to the regional, and that many of the merchants invested in markets, set them up on their own initiative, or bought their way into a share of the profits generated. As Bengal's economy began to become further integrated with the rest of northern India, and as the financial world permeated even remote villages, the periodic bazaars and haats of the seventeenth century crystallized into two kinds of markets: regular everyday markets and wholesale markets.

The latter, called *ganj* and *gola*, was a striking innovation from the late seventeenth century. It is a fact that many urban centres with the suffix *gola* or *ganj* appeared in eighteenth century Bengal. Bhagwangola at Murshidabad, established by the first nawab, Murshid Quli, for his family, is a case in point, Backergunge south of Dhaka in present Bangladesh is yet another. Both were grain (mainly rice) markets that provisioned Bengal from west and east, Backergunge was older, being mentioned by Fitch at the end of the sixteenth century.[71] J'afarganj and Hajiganj, already mentioned, were others. The point to note here is that the seasonal or weekly markets of the seventeenth century now gave way to *regular* markets.

Not only were markets daily now, they were firmly linked to the world market. In the eighteenth century, rural markets had one or more stalls for moneychangers.[72] This indicates how far global transactions had penetrated the province of Bengal. As had European tastes: European goods such as felts and velvet were to be found in smaller mart-towns.[73] The circulation of goods had reached immense proportions in eighteenth-century Bengal, long before the colonial changeover. The merchant was thus the chief architect of this change.

But, these were not the only markets. Roques writes that a larger market for foreign demand also existed in every city or production centre. This was not an actual physical market. This was a commodity against cash market, based on samples and prices agreed upon earlier and to be delivered anywhere within north, west and eastern India. And this was not a transparent market as far as the Europeans were concerned. The 'machinations' of the brokers, of which there were two kinds—the public or bazaar broker (who specialized in particular types of goods) and the European's private broker—ensured that much of the profit was skimmed off by them.[74] The broker was no less an important figure at the market than the merchant. Frequently, they were one and the same.

INFORMATION NETWORKS

But this was also an open market! Information circulated freely, people came and went, and strangers were welcomed as long as they came with letters of introduction or vast sums of money. Frequently there was news of the impending arrival of a ship or a convoy of merchants, and this would push prices up. Roques mentions that a kind of an informal 'post office' existed at the bazaars for banias to get news of coming arrivals and departures of foreign merchants, their caravans or vessels as the case may be, their credit worthiness, etc. The banias also acted as couriers and generally helped the newcomer to settle in.[75] The 'spying' by the banias that Roques also makes mention of can therefore also be interpreted as part of an open information network that enabled both buyer and seller to meet on an equal and transparent status.[76]

Aslanian refers to the indispensable roles of *hamvab* (information/news) and *fama* (public opinion/gossip) in long distance trade networks of the Armenians in the First Global Age.[77] This was equally valid for all merchant communities and this kind of information, what Chase-Dunn and Mann and Chase-Dunn and Jorgenson dubbed as the IN, travelled very long distances. Reputation, honour, trust, contracts, and the commercial laws of the different merchant communities travelled and prevailed over enormously long distances. For the Armenians, to sustain their extensive networks, 'portable courts' on the New Julfan Kalantar headed Assembly of Merchants, were established wherever there was a sizeable New Julfan community of merchants.[78] These 'portable courts' acted as financial and legal nodes in a network that primarily reinforced an Armenian economic identity.

Yet there are indications that this identity was soon to change; from the late 1740s, Alivardi Khan, the nawab of Bengal, named Khwaja Wajid as *Fakhru'l Tujjar* (Pride of Treasure or Pride of Merchants), suggesting that the latter was identifying himself with the court and local politics in the host society.[79] Wajid was one of the merchants who profited from the integration of Bihar's economy with that of Bengal, he had substantial saltpetre interests there and was a personal friend of the *faujdars* of Hugli and Chhapra from the 1740s.[80] I have already mentioned that Chhapra was a potentially commercially rich area from which all traders profited. Khwaja Wajid was friendly with Deepchand, the *faujdar* of Chhapra and he was reputed to have 2,000 boats in Bihar which plied regularly all over the fluvial network between Bengal and Bihar.[81] Deepchand was the brother of Umichand, a powerful merchant at court; this is how the networks organized themselves in Bengal just before the colonial takeover.

Armenian documents refer to two postal systems in existence from Bengal: the first a maritime one from Hugli to Surat, then on to Basra, Bandar Rig and so forth into the Gulf and then overland to New Julfa, and the second route was overland through Patna into Surat and then by sea up the Gulf.[82] Both networks were dependent upon a natural network—that of the *mausim* (monsoon), and together these networks ruled the circulation of merchants, commodities, information, and missionaries. Multiple copies of the same document were sent through different couriers to minimize the risks of being robbed or killed en route.[83]

Information networks are significant because they helped prepare the grounds for long distance trade and sustained such trade when it got underway. In a recent study on medieval Europe, Oliver Volckart wrote that he isolated 'information costs as a component of transaction costs which has central importance, then to split information costs into their constitutive components, and finally to measure one of these, namely transmission costs, i.e. the costs of transmitting information between different localities'. Volckart concluded that 'transmission costs were essentially labour costs, and hence dependent on the labour supply' and that 'transmission costs had a clear and positive influence on the integration of financial markets'.[84]

THE MERCHANT IN GLOBAL FINANCIAL NETWORKS

How did the financial market function? At one level, it spanned a whole network of financial centres in northern India, at another it undertook the transactions of the home state. The financial networks at Kasimbazar spanned continents and had the longest pathways, being part of larger (and longer) information networks that circulated between Asia and Europe. As Controller of the Mint and Treasurer General of the greater province of Bengal at Murshidabad, the Seths acted as catalysts in linking Bengal to the world economy through their financial acumen and fiscal measures. The Seths not only lent money to the court and the various EICs, they also changed all foreign currencies brought in by the EICs to Bengal into *Sicca Rupees*.

There were also other financiers in Bengal as mentioned and the financial structure, dealings, contacts, and networks of these firms linked the Mughal economy with the world. That trade was enmeshing Bengal and attaching it to the world economy is evidenced by the fact that interest rates came down from between 15 per cent and 18 per cent in the seventeenth century to 12 per cent in 1700 and then was firmly fixed at 9 per cent by mid century.[85] This is not only an example of more trade within India but also of cooperation between the market, the various agents, and financiers which powered the market and the various categories of *sarafs*, *podars*, or *mahajans* involved in moneylending in both rural and urban areas.

At the top of the financial pyramid were the Seths who also determined the rates of exchange in Bengal: EEIC bullion was fixed at 202 and $\frac{1}{2}$ per 250 *sicca* weight in 1741, in 1745 *ducatoons* were fixed at *SR* 2-7 *annas*-3 *pies* and the French Crowns, Pillar Dollars and Mexican dollars at 203 for *SR* 240.[86]

To enable the fixing of the rates of exchange some knowledge of world financial markets and their fluctuations were necessary. Through a web of informants, and through their active participation in the caravan and maritime trade networks, the Seths maintained a sound working knowledge of the relative strengths of the world's currencies. This was borne out in 1741 when the Seths refused the EEIC the same rates as the old Pillar Dollars for the new Pillar Dollars. Fatehchand, then in charge, insisted that the new Pillars were equivalent to the Mexico dollars and not to the old Pillars.

This is an example of how financial networks were part of the larger information pathways. Fatehchand was correct and the Calcutta Council of the EEIC noted: 'They (the new Pillars) might be inferior to what the pillar dollars used to be some time ago, and that about the year 1730 it was found in Europe that this specie was greatly debas'd where coin'd.'[87]

Merchants, Finance and Trade

The Merchant-Courtier Network at Kasimbazar

If not an actual courtier himself, most *dadni* merchants had close links with the court in nearby Murshidabad through a complex web of patronage and protection. They operated through the patronage of courtiers. The patronage took two forms: either through actual holding of office or through having a 'godfather' who acted as surety (guarantor) in the merchant's commercial dealings. This same godfather also acted for the merchant if the latter was wrongly imprisoned by the EICs for non-delivery of goods or non-payment of money.[88]

But, patronage was also necessary to organize production and supply and to enforce contracts. Until 1752, the *dadni* merchants of Kasimbazar controlled a vast mercantile pyramid with a hierarchy of underlings: gomasthas, banias, under banias, dalals, and pykars, along with a whole host of salaried employees who actually organized the production and sale from *arang* to company warehouse. Many merchants were now entering the productive sphere as entrepreneurs and mercantile organization, in this case, paralleled the financial organization just noted.

Obviously, activities of such economic and spatial magnitude that necessitated both control and precise organization could not be effected without some kind of patronage from the court. The merchants usually preferred as patrons the *Pachotra Bandar* (the port authority), the Diwan, and the Rai Rayan (chief minister) as these were the most powerful courtiers who had direct dealings with the economy.[89]

THE MERCHANT AS FINANCIER

The EICs in Kasimbazar were often short of capital for commercial operations, as ships carrying the desired quantity of bullion often did not arrive on time. Similarly, the private trade of the Europeans needed ready cash. Both needs were met by financiers at Kasimbazar, often by the *dadni* merchants themselves or members of their families who specialized in banking. The Seths lent *SR* 42,32,278 (or 4,23,228 British pounds) to the EEIC between 1733 and 1750.

Other than the Seths there are also the figures as indicated in Table 10.1 of the families of the *dadni* merchants lending money to the EEIC:

TABLE 10.1: AMOUNTS FINANCED BY THE MERCHANT BANKING FAMILIES TO THE EEIC AT KASIMBAZAR, 1733-50[90]

Merchant Banking Families	*Amount (in Sicca Rupees or British Pounds)*
Katma family	1,92,481 or 19,248
Achargee family	1,37,650 or 13,765
Das family	1,04,692 or 10,469
Pandit family	80,000 or 8,000
Tagore family	75,250 or 7,525
Dutt family	32,350 or 3,235
Kapri family	25,000 or 2,500
Sarkar family	25,000 or 2,500
Poddar family	23,665 or 2,367
Surma (Sharma) family	7,500 or 750
TOTAL	Pounds 70,359 (i.e. an average of around 3,909 pounds a year)

Table 10.1 shows that the *dadni* network contained financial networks, organized independently and in parallel to commercial dealings, but at the same time they were embedded within them. These networks were based on the community and kin group, in most cases the family itself. The data in Table 10.1 also demonstrates that those merchant families that had bankers within the family financed the EEIC investment to a large extent.

THE *DADNI* MERCHANT AS BANKER

Table 10.2 provides figures for merchant-bankers at Kasimbazar providing money to the EEIC:

TABLE 10.2: FINANCES PROVIDED BY THE *DADNI* MERCHANTS TO THE EEIC AT KASIMBAZAR, 1733-50[91]

Names of merchants	*Amount (in Sicca Rupees)*
Sachi Katma	1,83,536
Chakoo Katma	80,000
Preet Katma	25,000
Hatoo Katma	20,000
Hariballabh and Brajballabh Das	58,756
Kushalchand, the second Jagat Seth	1,30,000
Natmal-Rupchand	30,000
Natmal-Anandchand	1,25,000
Hiranath-Nani	6,000
Govindaram	35,000
Ramsing	5,000
Saulput (?)	2,500
Prankrishna Katma	20,000
TOTAL	Pounds 72,079 (i.e. an annual average of pounds 4,004)

Both Tables 10.1 and 10.2 illustrate that the mercantile and financial networks financed the EEIC, on average, for around the same amount of money each year. Further, Table 10.2 shows that it was the *dadni* financial network that underpinned much of the investment of the EEIC at Kasimbazar. If one considers the sum provided by the Seths (4,23,228 British pounds) and the sums the two financial networks (illustrated in Tables 10.1 and 10.2) offered the EEIC (1,42,438 British pounds) one sees that the total, over the period 1733 to 1750, comes to 5,65,666 British pounds, a not inconsiderable sum. These figures also give an idea of the enormous amount of money that was circulating in Kasimbazar until mid century, i.e. just before the colonial takeover of Bengal, and why Kasimbazar had to be throttled, to make way for Calcutta as port and commercial capital of colonial India.

SOCIAL NETWORKS

THE MERCHANT AS POLITICIAN

Were the manifold activities of the Indian merchant a reflection of 'portfolio capitalism?'[92] Subrahmanyam suggested that the amorphous body referred to as 'merchants' in pre-colonial South Asia contained within it various categories combining commercial interests with differing access to political power. The career of Harish Chowdhury (in EEIC records mentioned as 'Hurris Chowdree'), an important *dadni* merchant at Kasimbazar who supplied mainly silk piece goods (SPG) and was mentioned as a 'principal merchant' by the Kasimbazar council of the EEIC in 1752,[93] at a time when the *dadni* system was smashed by the EEIC, gives an appropriate picture of the political networks of the *dadni* merchant. Chowdhury is a title in use today in Bengal and there is a good chance that these Chowdhurys were native to Bengal. The first name, Harish, suggests that the family was Hindu by religion.

Of a well established family supplying SPG at Kasimbazar (there were as many as 11 members between 1733 and 1750), Harish made the transition from an SPG merchant to one specializing in such diverse textiles as raw silk (RS), SPG, and *garahs* and *dusuties* (G&D). *Garahs* were coarse cloths, usually painted and frequently blue in colour, and in popular demand in eighteenth century markets. Bengal was a significant supplier of *garahs*, which were sent by the EEIC to places as diverse as England and Australia. *Dusuties* refer to cottons with a two-by-two weave. Both the RS and G&D investments were more profitable than the SPG investment as the EEIC never invested over 32 per cent in the latter, while the other two amounted to as high as 82 per cent and 54 per cent respectively in the years between 1733 and 1750.[94]

Table 10.3 shows the activities of the Chowdhury family at Kasimbazar, although substantial in number, the members of this family invested only in SPG. Harish was the first to diversify, trading in RS, which fetched greater profits and was easier to supervise; being produced in bales rather than the various assortments of piece goods that frequently diverged from the samples shown. He also traded in the coarser G&D.

More important, Harish, possibly the son of Rasik, another substantial SPG merchant who traded between the time of 1733 to 1745, although the relationship is by no means certain, shot to prominence in 1744, the year that the EEIC invested the largest amount in silk at Kasimbazar until then (13,68,58,000 British pounds, this was only topped by 15,94,78,000 in 1745).[95] In 1744, Harish broke with family tradition and supplied RS as well; the next year, 1745, another year of abnormally high investment by the EEIC at Kasimbazar, he supplied all three items: RS, SPG, and G&D.

Was Harish privy to inside information that the investment would be hiked from 1744?[97] In 1743, the investment was only 5,19,09,000 British pounds, Alivardi Khan also having forbidden all EEIC commerce between July and September 1743,[98] due to the Maratha raids in Bengal that intensified from that year as well as due to disputes with the EEIC over river traffic rights.[99] Moreover, in 1744, Alivardi Khan also forbade all trade

TABLE 10.3: THE TEXTILE TRADING CHOWDHURY FAMILY OF KASIMBAZAR[96]

Name	*Year*	*RS*	*SPG*	*G&D*
Rasik	1733, 1736, 1737, 1739, 1740, 1742, 1743, 1744, 1745		1733, 1736, 1737, 1739, 1740, 1742, 1743, 1744, twice in March and May 1745	
Bekul	1733		1733	
Sadashib	1738, 1739, 1742		1738, 1739, 1742	
Kisanchand	1739, 1740		1739, twice in April and May 1740, twice in February	
Shibaprasad or Sriprasad	1743, 1744, 1745		1743, 1744, 1745	
Mohan	1744		1744, twice in March and May	
Ram	1743, 1744, 1745		1743, 1744, 1745	
Indranaran	1738		1738	
Radha	1739, 1742		1739, 1742	
Harish	1744, 1745, 1748, 1749, 1750	1744, 1745, 1748, 1749, 1750	1744, 1745, 1749, 1750	1745, supplied G&D thrice

in *garahs*[100] and Harish was one out of only two merchants who undertook to supply that item in 1745.[101]

Why he never furnished any cloths in 1746 and in 1747 is not known. But, Harish was also a political animal. He was a favourite of Hukum Beg, the *Pachotra Bandar* (the port authority) of the royal port at Murshidabad. In 1756, he was noted as Hukum Beg's diwan, i.e. the official in-charge of revenues and accounts. By virtue of his political connections, he was able to corner the EEIC investment at Kasimbazar and in 1748 and 1750, scored above the average annual investment; in 1744, 1745, and 1749, he scored the same as the average annual investment.[102] Once he became a courtier, Harish's activities as trader ceased, or one can conjecture that perhaps he carried on by another name. In 1769, when the *dadni* system was resumed at Kasimbazar, one finds a lone member of the Chowdhury family, Gour Chowdhury, going back to the family business of furnishing the SPG investment.[103] By the 1760s, the prominent *dadni* merchants had been rendered bankrupt.

THE MERCHANT AS RELIGIOUS AND SOCIAL PATRON

Numerous merchants at Kasimbazar were Jain, of the Digambara sect. The Seths built, in the eighteenth century, many temples in the environs of Murshidabad, at Jiaganj and Azimganj and Kushalchand, the second Jagat Seth, is said to have endowed the Jal Mandir at Parasnath in present Bihar—a fact corroborated by a travel account of 1802, which refers to endowments by the Jain merchants of Murshidabad on the route from Murshidabad to Gaya in Bihar.[104] There were also 10 Shiva temples in Kasimbazar.

The Murshidabad-Kasimbazar area also seems to have been an eclectic place in terms of religious beliefs. Maharaja Manindrachandra Nandy's palace at Kasimbazar, although he was Hindu, is reported to have had 24 Jain temples in the front courtyard of the palace. These temples commemorated all the *tirthankaras* of the Jain religion. Kiriteswari, although an ancient Hindu goddess and one of the *upapithas* of Sati, became the royal cult of the nawabs of Murshidabad; the last independent nawab, Mir Jafar Ali Khan, is reported to have drunk the holy water from her *puja* on his deathbed. By adopting Kiriteswari as the royal cult, the Muslim nawabs forged an enduring link with the merchants and financiers who were primarily Hindu. The terracotta temple of Kiriteswari in Murshidabad was rebuilt in the nineteenth century and exists to this day.

A MARKETPLACE OF LANGUAGES

In his analysis of the songs of the *bauls*, the *kartabhajas*, and the *sahebdhanis* groups in Bengal, Hugh Urban noted that the notion of market as *world* as also market as *journey* was very present.[105] This rich imagery of the market and the use of economic terms showed how far the market had penetrated the lives of the people of Bengal.

The coming of the market, the new economic conditions, and the consequent cultural shift was visible by the end of the eighteenth century. The cultural shift was the result of the long period of interaction with foreign trade that culminated with colonial control. A careful content analysis of the Bengali language shows the hidden presence of foreign loan words. These words testify not only to the existence of foreign networks in Bengal, but also indicate how far they had penetrated the host society.[106]

What is noticeable from Table 10.4 is that the English words had penetrated the furthermost, not surprising in view of colonial rule. Administrative and repressive institutions of governance are represented in the words for office, bank, jail, and school, as well as mechanisms of control: police, for example, as compared to loan words from other languages describing emotions, objects of everyday life, or objects of natural history.

DISCUSSION

In this section, I shall try to address those issues that are still unclear. Some of the questions that emerge from a reading of activities at Kasimbazar are:

TABLE 10.4: LANGUAGE NETWORKS

Particulars	*Arabic*	*Persian*	*Turkish*	*Portuguese*	*English*	*French*	*Chinese*
	kamiz (shirt)	Aena/arshi (mirror)	Kañchi (scissors)	almari (closet or cupboard)	kap (cup)	kartuj (cartridge)	
	jinish (thing)	kagoj (paper)		gamla (bucket)	plate (dish)	shemiz (chemise)	
	boi (book)	chôshma (eyeglasses)		chabi (key)	glash/glas (glass)		
		chador (blanket)		toale (towel)	chear (chair)		
Object		degchi (pot)		balti (pail)	tebil (table)		
				bashon (dish)	baksho (box)		
				botol (bottle)	lônthon (lantern)		
				botam (button)			
				boma (bomb)			
				shaban/sapon (soap)			
	môshola (spice)			anarôsh (pineapple)			cha (tea)
Foodstuffs				peñpe (papaya)			chini (sugar)
				peara (guava)			lichu (lychee)
				Pauruti/pau (bread)			elachi (cardamom)
Vocations			baburchi (cook/ chef)	mistri (mechanic/ artisan)	daktar (doctor)		
					pulish (police)		
	akkel (wisdom)	aoaj (sound)	chôkmôk (sparkle)	girja (church)	apish/ôfish (office)	añsh (plant fibre)	
	alada (separate)	adalat (court/ assembly)	thakur (lord or master)	janala (window)	inchi (inch)	ingrej (English)	

(*Table 10.4 contd.*)

TABLE 10.4 (*continued*)

Particulars	*Arabic*	*Persian*	*Turkish*	*Portuguese*	*English*	*French*	*Chinese*
	ashol (real)	andaj (guess)	Dada (paternal grandfather) (in Bangladesh)	tamak (tobacco)	khrishtan (Christian)	restorañ (restaurant)	
	elaka (area)	aram (comfort)	dadi (paternal grandmother)	baranda (verandah)	jel (jail)	Olondaj (Dutch)	
	elaka (area)	aste (softly)	nana (maternal grandfather)(in Bangladesh)		phut/fut (foot)		
	kôbor (grave)	kharap (bad)	nani (maternal grandmother)(in Bangladesh)		bêngk (bank)		
	ojon (weight)	khub (very)	begom (lady)		bhot (vote)		
	khôbor (news)	groom (hot)	lash (corpse)		ishkul/skul-(school)		
General	khali (empty)	chakri (job)			station (station)		
	gorib (poor)	jan (dear)			hashpatal (hospital)		
	khêal (consideration)	jaega (place)					
	jôbab/jôoab (answer)	dôm (breath)					
	jôma (collect)	deri (late)					
	tarikh (date)	dokan (store)					

(*Table 10.4 contd.*)

TABLE 10.4 (*continued*)

Particulars	*Arabic*	*Persian*	*Turkish*	*Portuguese*	*English*	*French*	*Chinese*
	dunia (world) nôkol (fake) fokir (poor person) bôdol (exchange) baki (remaining) shaheb (sir) hishab (calculation) hukum (order/ ruling, verdict)	bôd (bad) bagan (garden) bachcha (child) môja (fun) rasta (road) roj (everyday) shôsta (inexpensive) tadbir (to dispose, manage administer, regulate)					

WHAT WAS THE RELATIVE STRENGTH OF THE INDIAN MERCHANT VIS-À-VIS HIS EUROPEAN COUNTERPART?

It is the received impression that the Indian merchant was not as highly 'evolved' as his European counterpart; and that, in many respects, the Indian merchant of the eighteenth century was closer to his medieval European counterpart than to the new face of the mercantilist European merchant who had appeared with the coming of the English, Dutch and French merchants into India in the seventeenth and eighteenth centuries. Such a line of thought is a typical example of the attempt at comparative history. Naturally, therefore, this line of thinking anticipates the argument that the market in eighteenth century Bengal was still a medieval market. The Indian merchant then could not possibly have coped with the new strategies introduced by the European companies in the First Global Age.

However, this study on Kasimbazar shows various networks often intersecting with one another. And, on the contrary, the various chapters in this volume demonstrate that Europeans in the First Global Age adopted various flexible and dynamic strategies to trade with India. They established informal networks to organize trade and often inserted themselves into existing mercantile niches to trade in India. In Kasimbazar, the networks show similar clustering, activity, and dynamism.

HOW FAR DID THE INDIAN MERCHANT AT KASIMBAZAR TAKE ADVANTAGE OF THE NEW STRATEGIES FOR TRADE AND COOPERATION?

To answer this one has to move out of the world of official company archives into the private papers of merchants. Unfortunately, these are almost non-existent in the case of the merchants of Kasimbazar with the exception of those of Krishna Kanta Nandy.[107] However, it seems that most merchants preferred to retain conventional ways of doing business; and until there is more information about the business strategies of the very small merchants, those that Roques (discussed later) calls the bania, one cannot give a definitive answer on this point.

But, the enormous amounts of money available in eighteenth century Bengal, also borne out by the information in Tables 10.1 and 10.2, surely suggest that the merchants were adapting to new ways of business? And that business must have been very great in eighteenth-century Bengal. Despite Sushil Chaudhuri's assertion that the EICs did not import significant amounts of bullion into eighteenth-century Bengal, the figures available of EIC bullion imports are staggering: James Grant estimated in 1784 that 'during the century succeeding 1582 Bengal received twenty lacs [of rupees] out of the Manila treasure, and surely thirty more may be thought rather a scanty allowance for the direct commerce with Europe'. Much of this added specie perhaps came after 1650 with the advent of European houses in Bengal trade. F.S. Gaastra added another dimension to this flow by studying the inflow of Japanese silver that the Dutch Company increasingly poured into Bengal in exchange of silk from the mid-seventeenth century onwards. It stood, according to Om Prakash, at the equivalent of 12.8 tons each year during the 1660s, 20 tons during the 1690s, and 28.7 tons during the 1710s. Om Prakash found that during 1660-1720 the Dutch import consisted of 87.5 per cent bullion and the rest in goods.[108]

Table 10.5 in Indrajit Ray shows that there was a steady spurt of bullion import in Bengal by the English Company. It rose from £71,252 during 1708-17 to £1,33,153 during 1718-27 and culminated at £2,03,959 during 1748-56. Harry Verelst, the Governor, estimated in 1772 that the annual inflow of specie in Bengal prior to 1757 amounted to eight million pounds sterling. The Dutch Company annually imported £3,00,000, the English Company £2,50,000, the French Company £2,00,000 and the Danes £30,000. Bengal's trade with Persia and the Red Sea brought in additionally £1,80,000 per annum in that period.[109] Surely, these additional amounts must have impacted the networks within and without Bengal?

HOW FAR DID THE MANY NETWORKS OF THE KASIMBAZAR MERCHANT HELP TO CONSOLIDATE HIS MERCANTILE POSITION?

There is no doubt that these networks helped a great deal, enabling the merchant to integrate himself vertically with the economy from the *arang* to the port via the rural market. Simultaneously, it also ensured his prestige and the survival of his name through endowments that created a spatial web of piety, finance and charity. Nicholas de Graaf spoke in the seventeenth century of uncertain conditions at Murshidabad, quoting the case of a merchant travelling with his wife, children and slaves being killed by dacoits.[110] Therefore, such networks of piety, charity and prestige would have safeguarded merchants from such violent attacks on life and property somewhat. Religion, charity, and pilgrimage must have helped the merchant a great deal to earn social sanction. His networks also enabled the merchant to align himself horizontally with political power through a network of courtiers and, ultimately, the court.

WHICH GROUP REPRESENTED THE CATEGORY OF 'MERCHANTS FROM BENGAL'? WERE THEY NATIVE BENGALIS?

The documents show that the ideas of merchants from Bengal need not refer only to Bengali merchants; they could just as well be Bihari merchants trading from Bengal. And they could also refer to Muslim (Mughal, Arab, Persian, Turk Tajik and Turkic speaking) merchants based in Bengal or Bihar.

Pires noted for the sixteenth century: 'A large number of Parsees (Persians), Rumes (from Byzantium), Turks and Arabs . . . live in Bengal'.[111] Fitch mentioned that the chief merchants in Bengal were the 'Moores and the Gentiles'.[112]

HOW MANY TYPES OF MERCHANTS WERE THERE IN A TYPICAL MARKET?

The *dadni* merchant of Kasimbazar was not the only type of merchant one comes across in documents. There were other, bigger, merchants in Bengal who did not act as brokers. There are references in the sixteenth century to merchants in Bengal who stayed in Saptagrama and welcomed buyers, rarely venturing out themselves.[113]

It seems likely therefore that there were at least three categories of merchants: those who stayed at home as has been mentioned by Pires, possibly acting as wholesalers; others who acted as brokers as seen in the case of the *dadni* merchants; and those who voyaged overseas, represented by the large 'Bengali' community mentioned by Pires at Pasai and Melaka in the sixteenth century or the Bengali community at Achin (Dutch Atjeh) in the seventeenth century mentioned by Lombard.[114] Traders from sixteenth-century Bengal journeyed to other ports in the archipelago as well: two ships were sent from Cambay and Bengal to Pedir in the Indonesian archipelago.[115]

Roques' memoir, so vividly translated by Indrani Ray, however, presents a different categorization. Roques writes that there were three categories of merchants in western India in the seventeenth century: banias (those he calls hagglers and *colporteurs* at bazaars), the higher banias who contracted with the Turk, Persian, and Armenian merchants as well as European companies, and at the very top the Muslim merchants who maintained their distance from the banias whose trade practices they despised.[116] How far this stratification applied to eastern India is not certain.

HOW SIGNIFICANT A SHARE OF THE BAY TRADE DID MERCHANTS FROM BENGAL CONTROL?

A considered reading of the *Suma Oriental*, gives the impression that Bengal was prominent in the eastern Indian Ocean in the early part of the sixteenth century and these networks remained in place until the beginning of the eighteenth century, barring minor variations. Traders and ships from Bengal circulated this area, bringing commodities and ideas and departing with equivalents from the Chinese and South-East Asian worlds. Just as in sixteenth century Malacca there were *shahbandars* from each of the four main trading zones: Gujarat, the Coromandel/Bengal/Pegu region (the people were collectively called Kelings), the South-East Asian countries symbolized by Java and finally, at the extreme East, China,[117] here, too, at seventeenth century Achin, there were three main channels or 'canals' of trade that functioned as smaller networks once the Melaka network system was destroyed: these three canals were Surat, Melaka (Malacca), and Bengal.[118] It seems, therefore, that Bengal's trade was flourishing, it was carried on by traders from Bengal in their own or chartered ships. De Graaf noted in the seventeenth century: 'Bengale est la seconde Place du Commerce de la Compagnie apres les Isles Molucques, puisqu'il y va tous les ans de Batavia dix, douze, quinze vaisseaux'.[119]

And this circulation continued until the 1720s. Luillier wrote that in 1701 the Bengal Achin trade was still flourishing; ships left Bengal around October or the beginning of November and reached Achin in December/ beginning of January.[120] Other routes from Bengal in 1701, Luillier writes, radiated to Surat, to the Maldives (the *cauri* trade), to the Coromandel, to Persia, and to China.[121] The Bengal-Achin trade however would soon end: Vincens' trade report of the 1730s informs that this route, 'once the best trade in India', was almost over and that other networks had also disintegrated by then.[122] But, he refers to the Bengal-Maldives *cauri* run as still existing,[123] a network that connected the Bay and the Indian Ocean to Yunnan.[124]

HOW WAS PRODUCTION ORGANIZED?

While discssing the big merchants in 1701 Luillier wrote:

> chez les gros marchands on y trouve de toutes les marchandises qui se fabriquent en ce pais . . . ces marchands, outré leurs grands correspondances, entretiennent encore un grand nombre d'ouvriers, qu'ils font travailler pour tres peu de chose . . . .Il ne faut donc pas s'etonner si les marchandises y sont a si bas prix, ny du gain qu'on fait en ce commerce.[125]

Luillier's statement contains four important points: one, that there were wholesale merchants who held their position at the top of the mercantile pyramid, two, that these merchants organized their own production, employing a great number of workers at low wages, three, that because of low wages, goods were very cheap in Bengal, and four, because of this cycle great profits could be made. Roques noted equally wretched conditions for weavers and cotton workers in the seventeenth century.[126]

WERE THE LOW WAGES IN BENGAL REFLECTIVE OF LOW PRICES?

Every traveller in seventeenth century Bengal commented on the low price of provisions. Moreland noted that around the mid-seventeenth century,

Bengal could evidently afford rice, butter, oil, and wheat 'all at half the price or little more that they are in other parts [of India]'. Moreland concluded, therefore, 'The only reasonable answer seems to be that the prime cost of provisions in Bengal must have been so much lower as to cover the increased charge for transit.'[127]

Because of cheaper provisions, Bengal artisans, especially those totally dependent on this craft, could supply their produce at lower prices. The family-based structure of the textile industry in Bengal and its location in rural areas, as opposed to its location in urban areas as in the case of Surat, for example, also meant lower production costs. These made Bengal a very attractive node for the mercantile networks in the seventeenth century. The hypothesis of cheaper provisions was also corroborated by Bengal's regular export of those commodities to other provinces as well as to Sumatra, Makassar, Celebes, the Moluccas, and the Sundas and other ports in South-East Asia.

This state of affairs was soon set to change. The figures for silk given by K.N. Chaudhuri leads one to surmise that the silk price in Bengal rose steadily for 39 years during 1669-1708, then stagnated over 1708-43 with a slight upward tilt, and finally accelerated its momentum during 1743-60.[128] This rise is also reflected in Indrajit Ray and Mukherjee.[129]

Luillier had noted around 1701 that silks and rice from Bengal sold on the Coromandel at a profit of between 30 and 40 per cent.[130] This changed when financial markets moved toward greater integration in the eighteenth century, as seen from the study of the various firms linking Bengal and Bihar to the north. An integration of financial markets meant that transport networks had witnessed vast improvement, that information networks travelled ever-greater distances, and that, most importantly, markets were becoming more transparent. Consequently, price differentials soon ceased to exist.

There was consequently a shift toward facilitating more cash crops in Bengal, a hypothesis explored in the section 'Some Hypotheses' of this essay.

CAN ONE ACQUIRE, FROM THIS ACCOUNT, AN IMPRESSION OF THE RELATIVE STRENGTH OR WEAKNESS OF THE INDIAN MERCANTILE ECONOMY?

If taking into consideration EIC records, as this chapter has for the most part, one gets a one-sided picture. Yet even this offers an impression of the strength of the mercantile economy when the EICs arrived.

Chaudhury noted that there were two categories of merchants in Bengal: one operating on a large-scale with a substantial dealer network, the other composed of smaller merchants, operating on commissions.[131] This study has shown that there were many more categories of merchants in Bengal.

Chaudhury also wrote that the EEIC and the VOC preferred to deal with the first group in the eighteenth century. This may be incorrect:[132] as early as the 1670s the EEIC at least was beginning to consider the second group as a viable alternative to the first group. The smaller merchants would be easier to control. On 15 December 1676, Clavell (in Streynsham Master's Council in Bengal) referred to this practice as contracting with the 'Town Merchants'.[133] In this way, the EICs created a whole new group of contract merchants or brokers, who would furnish, in theory, the exclusive investment for an EIC and not contract with any other European company or Asian merchant. When William Hedges succeeded Master in 1681, a new category of merchants was in place at both Kasimbazar and Hugli.[134] Many shared surnames with the *dadni* merchants of Kasimbazar—Hari Kisen Katma, Gyan Chand Shah and Mathura Shah—are some examples of names of merchants at Hugli.[135]

And the 'Town Merchants' were not the only group! Hedges' consultations at Hugli reveal: 'Yesterday a certain number of Merchants came to me and offered to undertake ye providing what goods we shall have occasion for this year, to be paid for when the goods were brought in, and at as cheap rates as if money were given out beforehand.'[136] Such a statement indicates that this was yet another group, possibly composed of more substantial merchants, who could afford to undertake the investment *without the advance*. In Dhaka, the EEIC preferred not to deal with the substantial merchants such as the 'Dacca Dellols'.[137] The decision to bypass older, well established commercial networks to seek out and create smaller categories of merchants, already well versed in the textile trade and who would be loyal to the EEIC, suggests that networks of cooperation (as with the Armenians in London, represented by Khoja Panos Calendar, who signed the 1688 Treaty of East India Company with the Armenian Nation for cooperation in maritime commerce) as well as networks of control were both pursued by the EEIC from the end of the seventeenth century.

Chaudhury highlighted the link between the big merchants and the EICs because his archive at that time concerned largely the big *sarafs* in Hugli and Balasore (Chintaman Shah, Khemchand Shah and Mathuradas) who provided both cash and goods.[138] Such activity suggests that the mercantile and financial networks were perhaps not very clearly delineated at the end of the seventeenth century, or perhaps that the big merchants also doubled as financiers, as Chaudhury seems to suggest. But, more important from our perspective, it also suggests that different mercantile groups in Bengal were jockeying for large contracts, indicative of the mercantile stratification that had already occurred in urban Bengal at the end of the seventeenth century.

Some Hypotheses

SEVENTEENTH CENTURY SHIFTS

From Rice and Sugar to Silk

There are indications that rice, sugar, and grain, which formed export staples from sixteenth-century Bengal, were becoming dear from the second half of the seventeenth-century. Fitch had noted a booming trade in rice and grain from Bengal at the end of the sixteenth century.[139] Cesare Frederici, at the same time, noted the large-scale export of sugar from Bengal to different parts of the empire.[140]

There seems to have been a break in this commerce from the middle of the seventeenth century. *The English Factories in India* refers to sugar, beeswax, gum lac, and cottons being staple, 'coarse' exports from Bengal in the 1630s,[141] but from thereon one hears less of these staples, and more of cash crops as export items. Indeed cash crops seem to have dotted the province: Bowrey and de Graaf noted the shift to the production of saltpetre and opium.[142] Yet another cash crop was silk and it seems certain that the Bengal nawabs wanted to promote silk as an export commodity in the eighteenth century. Mulberry lands were taxed higher than rice lands in eighteenth-century Bengal, indicative of the great change that had taken place in the commercial landscape.[143] The Armenians were granted commercial privileges that reduced their export duties from 5 per cent to 3.5 per cent. Aslanian, however, is of the opinion that the Armenians traded in a portfolio of commodities rather than concentrating on a single item (email of 27 April 2009).

Why did this shift occur? Were Bengal staples still lower in price as compared to other parts of the Mughal Empire? If not—it is seen that to keep prices low, the export of grain by Europeans was prohibited in eighteenth-century Bengal; and an official checked the amount of grain carried on board ships departing Bengal (discussed earlier)—was the shift to capitalist agriculture a reflection of rising prices which made for unfavourable conditions of trade in these staples? Moreover, was the prohibition put in place to ensure that prices of grain and daily items remained accessible to all in Bengal? This seems to have been the case.

The Shift from Silk to Saltpetre

Saltpetre became a very significant export commodity from the end of the seventeenth century. It should be noted that this was due to European demand; resulting from the frequent wars in Europe in the seventeenth century. There was little or no Asian demand for this item. In the first half of the century, the little known Portuguese East India Company traded in saltpetre from Bengal, but it was reported that the costs were high, as it had to be transported to Goa. Saltpetre was obtained through contract in Bengal and Bihar and the names of two contractors there are available: Oliveira de Morses and Fernao Carvalho.[144]

Saltpetre increasingly rivalled silk as an export commodity from Bengal from the end of the seventeenth century. The VOC and the EEIC were major traders in saltpetre. Saltpetre also served as ballast on ships.[145] Regarding the boats called the *patella*, Thomas Bowrey wrote: '[these are boats] that come downe from Pattana with saltpeeter or other goods built of an exceedinge strength and are very flatt and burthensome', each carrying down 4, 5, or 6,000 Bengal maunds of 82 lb. each.[146]

From the 1740s silk prices rose steadily at Kasimbazar and alternative sources of taxation had to be found.[147] Therefore the saltpetre trade was promoted almost as a royal monopoly at first and then through revenue framing. The English records state that Umichand, a merchant-courtier with close links to the court at Murshidabad, was one of the monopolists in the trade of saltpetre from Bihar in the eighteenth century. His brother, Deepchand was the *faujdar* of Chhapra in Bihar, and the major part of Bihar saltpetre came from there. Umichand and Deepchand were courtiers and royal favourites, linked with the Nawab Alivardi Khan and with his brother Haji Ahmad who managed the royal commercial interests in Bihar.

Saltpetre concessions were sold off to courtiers by the nawabs. The Armenians monopolized a large part of the saltpetre trade from Bihar in that century, as seen from Khwaja Wajid's career. As part of a social-commercial-political network (Umichand, Deepchand and Khwaja Wajid) with direct access to the courts at Murshidabad and Patna, Khwaja Wajid virtually monopolized the Bihar trade, particularly in saltpetre, from the 1740s, through an annual payment of Rs. 25,000 to the Nawab Alivardi Khan.[148]

A Shift from Saltpetre to Opium?

While Bowrey referred to the trade in saltpetre De Graaf referred, at the same time as Bowrey, to the great production and trade of opium. One maund of opium in Bengal costing Rs. 70 or Rs. 75 was sold at Batavia at between Rs. 210 and Rs. 225, De Graaf adding however, regretfully, that this profitable trade was not open to the Dutch.[149] Luillier echoed this at the start of the eighteenth century, noting that there was great trade in opium, it being much in demand in the Levant,[150] adding that 'on peut dire que Bengale est le magasin de toutes les Indes'.[151] Incidentally Luillier also claimed that the EICs were denied participation in this trade.

Who, then, organized this trade? Was the opium trade also in the hands of 'upcountry' merchants? In seventeenth century Achin, merchants from

Bengal brought raw cotton, textiles, *ghi* (clarified butter used as oil in cooking) and opium into that port.[152] Until the middle of the eighteenth century, both the opium and saltpetre trades functioned as almost 'royal' monopolies. The Armenian Khwaja Wajid was active in this trade too, acting almost as a monopolist; he was reported to have cornered the market in Bihar opium in 1749.[153]

SALT

Salt became an increasingly lucrative commodity in eighteenth-century Bengal. One reads that salt came down from Agra, but was also obtained from far. Teixeira wrote in *c.*1600 that ships from Cochin arrived at Hormuz to pick up salt destined for Bengal, where it was much prized as Bengal, apart from the island of Sandwip, suffered from a scarcity of salt.[154]

Khwaja Wajid obtained the more lucrative monopoly of the salt trade, which was farmed by him in 1752 for a mere payment of Rs. 25,000 to Rs. 30,000 a year to the nawab. An estimate of 1773 put the annual revenues of salt production and sale in Bengal at Rs. 10,00,000. It thus becomes apparent how much Khwaja Wajid earned from the virtual monopoly of the salt trade in the 1750s.[155]

NEW COMMODITIES AT THE MID CENTURY BREAK

One sees that the Bengal nawabs experimented with a portfolio of export commodities in response to foreign demand. The traditional exports of rice, sugar, and cotton were supplemented with, and then supplanted by silk, saltpetre, opium, and salt. From 1711, the EEIC investment in saltpetre was immense.[156] By 1718, the EEIC in Bihar was contracting 10,000 maunds for the Madras factory as well.[157] Attempts at royal monopolies in saltpetre, opium, and salt around the middle of the eighteenth century could not survive the mid century break.

Were the networks for these newer, more controlled by outsiders and, therefore, more susceptible to a takeover by outsiders?

SOCIAL SPACE, SMALL WORLDS AND NETWORKS

In this study of Kasimbazar through an analysis of social networks, I applied the concept of social space and small world to Kasimbazar. However, one must take into account that there is a certain amount of scepticism in academic circles regarding what constitutes a 'social space'. Watts points out that:

> A number of social network theorists have utilized the concept of a 'social space' in which people exist as points separated by distances that can be measured according

to some appropriately defined metric. Unfortunately, this approach often runs into treacherous waters due to the inherent difficulty both of characterizing the space (which is all but unknown) and defining the metric (equally so). The following three assumptions avoid these difficulties: (1) All networks can be represented solely in terms of the connections between their elements, assuming that whatever combination of factors makes people more or less likely to associate with each other is accounted for by the distribution of those associations that actually form. (2) All connections are symmetric and of equal significance. That is, a definition of what is required in order to 'know' someone is defined such that either two people know each other or they do not. (3) The likelihood of a new connection being created is determined, to some variable extent, by the already existing pattern of connections.[158]

From social space, I moved on to an examination of SWN for Kasimbazar, a 'small world' interacting with a larger world, bound by networks that rendered it equally small. The motivation for the 'small world phenomenon' and the consequent formation of SWN comes from social networks, but as Watts notes:

it . . . [is] a much more general effect that arises under quite weak conditions in large, sparse, partly ordered and partly random networks. Its existence is not predicted by current network theories, yet it seems likely to arise in a wide variety of real networks, especially in social, biological, and technological systems. One consequence of this result is that it is highly likely that the phenomenon exists in the real social world—a notion currently supported by only limited data but consistent with anecdotal experience.[159]

Jackson and Rogers interrogate the economics of 'small worlds'. By marrying real world social networks to mechanical models they are able to show that in the real world,

in some situations, distant nodes greatly benefit (in terms of net utility) from forming links precisely because of the distance, which provides an answer as to why such shortcuts might be formed. The fundamental intuitions that emerge from the economic side are: (i) high clustering results from low costs of attachment to similar (nearby) nodes, and (ii) low diameter results from the large benefit of attaching to dissimilar (distant) nodes because of the substantial indirect access they provide to other distant nodes. A limited number of such distant links emerge due to the high costs, but in concert with the high interconnection rate at the local level, these distant links substantially decrease networks diameter and average path length.[160]

Here,

agents benefit from their direct connections and also from indirect connections. That is, friends of a friend generate value and so on. The departure from that model is that we describe a simple geographically based cost structure to forming links. This cost structure captures heterogeneity in link costs in a simple manner: agents are grouped on 'islands', and costs of connection are relatively low within an island and relatively high across islands. This cost structure, together with the indirect benefits structure of the connections model, generates the small world characteristics.[161]

Although the 'small world phenomenon' can apply over far larger spaces than Kasimbazar, one observed the networks at Kasimbazar eventually stretched to northern India and beyond. The Armenian network from their base at Saidabad, a suburb of Kasimbazar, connected Kasimbazar with the Levant, the Mediterranean, and the Persian Gulf (New Julfa) on the one side, and with Manila on the other in the seventeenth and eighteenth centuries. This network was truly global, and existed from the time the Armenians established themselves at Kasimbazar in the seventeenth century.[162]

This 'small world' then interacted with a global world system emanating from Europe. These were characterized mainly by random, somewhat irregular, networks in that they were transient and did not translate into a different and more durable system that was able to combat the colonial takeover. Perhaps this was so because these networks remained multinational networks. The Armenian network from Bengal, which comprised within it informal French, Portuguese and Muslim traders and courtiers based at Bengal, for instance, used Armenian colours to sail from Bengal to Cochin and Portuguese colours to sail from Cochin to the Persian Gulf.[163] Shifting nationalities denied the Armenians any political support, more so because at the time they did not have a state of their own. This system took on definitive contours in the eighteenth century, effectively foretelling the future, when Kasimbazar, Bengal, and indeed large parts of India, would come under EEIC rule by the nineteenth century.

Picazo Muntaner, in this volume, pointed to the collaborationist strategies adopted by the EEIC in the seventeenth century. Nowhere is this strategy so marked as in the EEIC's dealings with the Armenians in Bengal in the seventeenth century.[164] This collaboration turned hostile when the EEIC attempted to impose its hegemony on this network in the eighteenth century: see Aslanian's account of the Santa Catharina trial of the mid-eighteenth century when the EEIC accused the same network of piracy.[165]

One must remember, however, that these different networks showed different chronologies, just as the same space evinced different temporalities. Some networks retained collaborationist strategies into the eighteenth century: for instance, as revealed in the financial networks at Kasimbazar. Therefore, it is sometimes difficult to talk of the seventeenth century solely in terms of collaboration and the eighteenth wholly in terms of conflict and control.

MAP 10.1: KASIMBAZAR IN ROBERT MORDEN, *A DESCRIPTION OF THE WORLD*, LONDON, 1688.

This is one of the earliest maps showing Kasimbazar ('Casanbazar'). While important enough to be shown on a map of the world it is, however, wrongly placed near the Orissa coast, just above Ouguli; in actual fact, it is situated further to the north of Bengal, near to where 'Gouro' is marked.

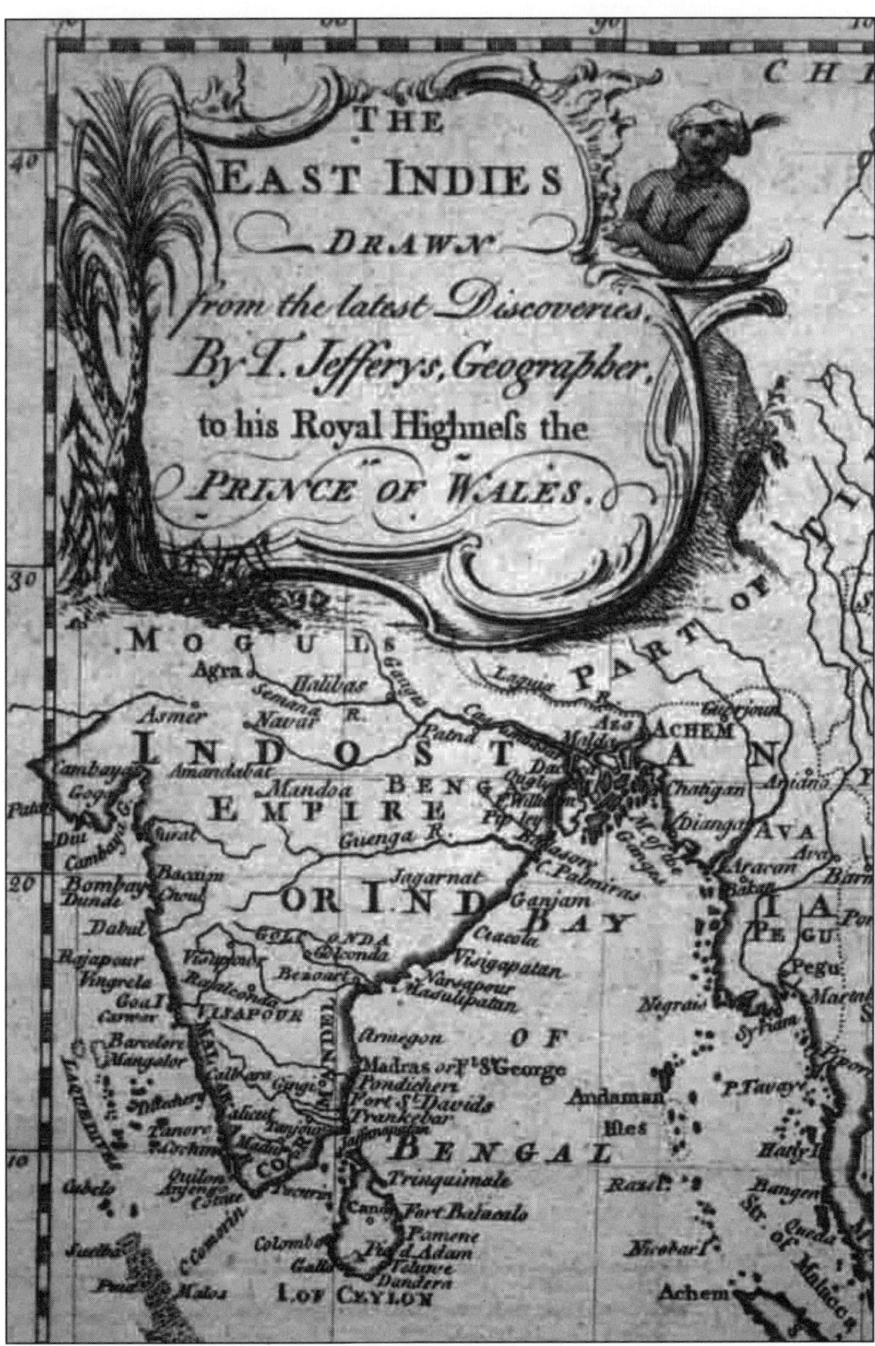

MAP 10.2: KASIMBAZAR IN THE 'ROYAL' *EAST INDIES* BY THOMAS JEFFERYS, LONDON, 1748.

In this particular map Kasimbazar's links with the delta are emphasized.

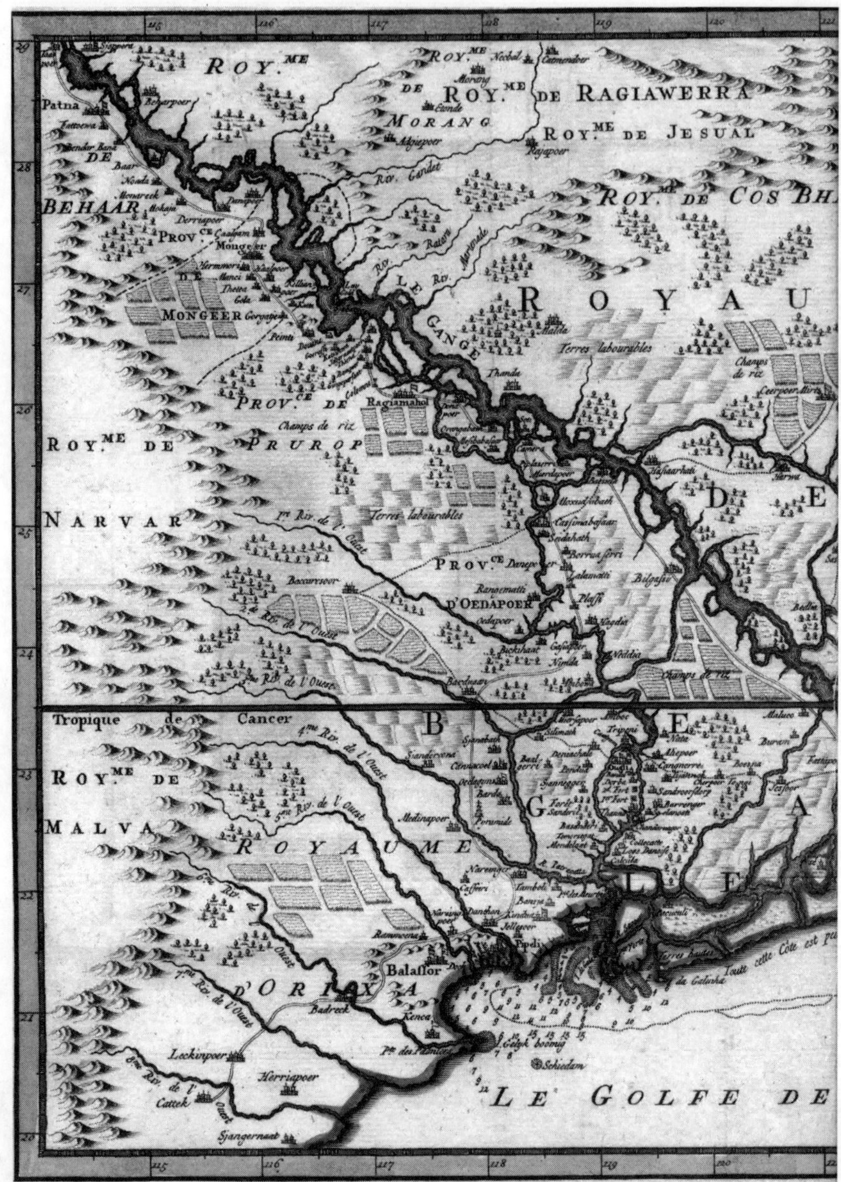

MAP 10.3: Kasimbazar in the urban and commercial networks of Bengal from Jacques Nicholas Bellin, 'Nouvelle Carte du Royaume de Bengale, 1747-61', in Prevost's *Histoire Generale des Voyages*, Amsterdam/Leipzig, *c.*1750.

This is a beautifully detailed map. Notice the urban and fluvial networks of Kasimbazar, lying roughly to the middle here, as also the intensely cultivated area it is centred on.

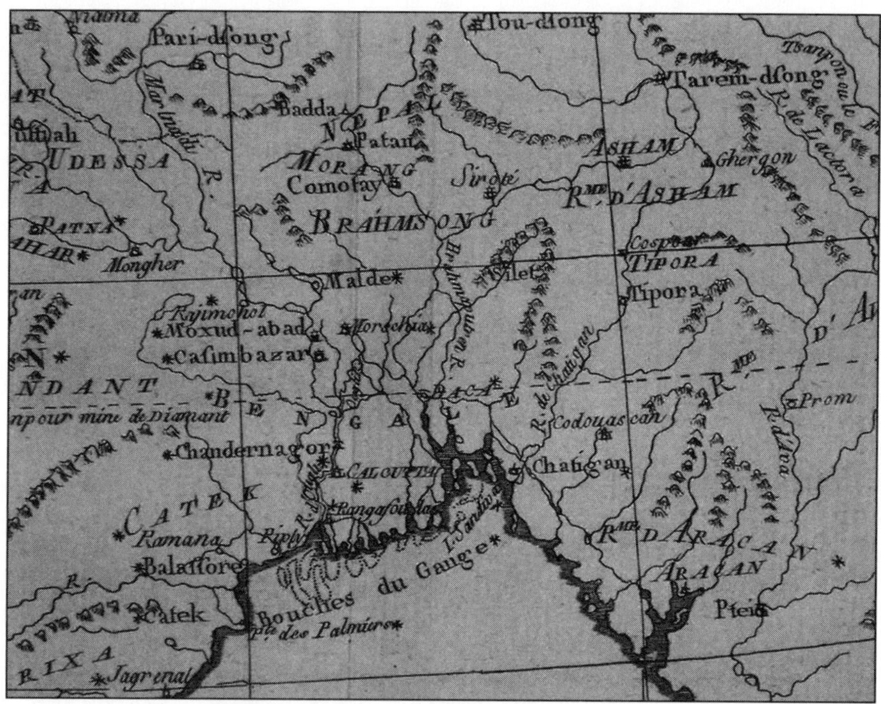

MAP 10.4: Rigoberto Bonne's map of India, 1780, Showing the Position of Kasimbazar within the North-Eastern Part of the Subcontinent from Rigoberto Bonne, 'Carte de la Partie Superieure de l'Inde en Deca du Gange Comprise entre la Cote du Concan et celle d'Orixa, avec l'Empire du Mogol, le Bengale etc.', in Guillaume Reynal's *Atlas De Toutes Les Parties Connues Du Globe Terrestre*, 1780.

Note the fluvial gateway to the north of India, as also Kasimbazar's (here as 'Casimbazar') southward links to the delta. The ports of Calcutta (EEIC) and Chandernagore (FEIC) are marked, Chandernagore somewhat more prominently that Calcutta, not surprising given the nationality of the cartographer. Interestingly, the Dutch port of Chinsura (Chunchura) is not marked on this map, nor is Serampore (Srirampur), the port and settlement of the Danish company, marked. Not surprisingly, Bankibazar of the Ostend Company (Belgium) is ignored as it hardly functioned as port and factory by that time.

MAP 10.5: RENNELL'S MAP OF INLAND NAVIGATION OF BENGAL FROM *BENGAL ATLAS*, LONDON, 1779-83, TAKEN FROM JEAN DELOCHE, 'BOATS AND SHIPS IN BENGAL TERRACOTTA ARTS', *BULLETIN DE L'ECOLE FRANÇAISE D'EXTRÊME-ORIENT*, VOL. 78, NO. 1, 1991, P. 4.

How were networks harnessed by a society or a corporation? A recent study of EEIC private initiative (composed largely of malfeasance, smuggling, corruption and free riding) in transforming routes into networks in the East Indies trade between 1680 and 1764 emphasizes private traders piggybacking on the official EEIC structure by showing 'that the emergence of a densely embedded and tightly coupled trade network in the East—under EIC control—played the critical role in shaping EIC commercial hegemony. This structure enabled the EIC to harness and increase information on prices, terms of trade, and commodities'[166] and 'by the middle of the eighteenth century, the EIC was in the position to control a densely connected and tightly coupled trade network'.[167]

Frank too has emphasized the role of free riding by European companies in *ReORIENT*, but in his account, this piggybacking was on 'Asian shoulders'. This chapter too emphasizes the role of Asian financial and commercial networks in creating a durable base for free riding by the EEIC, and attempts to explain why these remained essentially random, short path networks. A study of these networks is of value because such a study helps re-examine many of the formulations that were elaborated in the section entitled 'Discussion', whereby historians attempt to explain non-European processes in terms of Western experiences and thereby form parallels that work to the detriment of the history of capital accumulation and mercantile practice in non-European societies.

Maps are from Frances Pritchett's remarkable collection hosted at: <http://www.columbia.edu/itc/mealac/pritchett/00maplinks/index.html#index> (accessed on 21 April 2009). They have been reproduced here with her kind permission.

Notes

1. Tome Pires, *Suma Oriental of Tome Pires, An Account of the East, From the Red Sea to China, written in Malacca and India in 1512–1515 and the Book of Francisco Rodrigues, Pilot Major of the Armada that Discovered Banda and the Moluccas,* ed. Armando Cortesao, London: Hakluyt Society, 1944, p. 88; Ashin Das Gupta, *Indian Merchants and the Decline of Surat, 1700-1750,* Wiesbaden: Steiner Verlag, 1979; Ashin Das Gupta, *Malabar in Asian Trade, 1740–1800,* Cambridge: Cambridge University Press, 1967; S. Arasaratnam, *Merchants, Companies and Commerce on the Coromandel Coast, 1650–1750,* New Delhi: Oxford University Press, 1986; see also <www.data-archive.ac.uk/doc/5254/pdf> (accessed on 25 March 2009).
2. See M.E.J. Newman, D.J. Watts and S.H. Strogatz, 'Random Graph Models of Social Networks', *Proceedings of the National Academy of Sciences of the United States of America,* vol. 99, no. 3, 2002, pp. 2566–72.

3. M. Girvan and M.E.J. Newman, 'Community Structure in Social and Biological Networks', *Proceedings of the National Academy of Sciences of the United States of America*, vol. 99, no. 12, 2002, pp. 7821-26, see p. 7821.
4. Duncan J. Watts, 'Networks, Dynamics, and the Small-World Phenomenon', *The American Journal of Sociology*, vol. 105, no. 2, 1999, pp. 493-527, see p. 494.
5. Ibid., p. 495.
6. Ibid., p. 517.
7. Ibid., pp. 523-4.
8. Bruce Kogut, 'The Network as Knowledge: Generative Rules and the Emergence of Structure', *Strategic Management Journal*, vol. 21, no. 3, 2000, pp. 493-527, see p. 409.
9. Quoted in Om Prakash, *The Dutch East India Company and the Economy of Bengal, 1630–1720*, New Delhi: Oxford University Press, 1988, pp. 104-5.
10. Kasimbazar Factory Records (K.F.R.), 28 February 1744, India Office Records, London; Indrani Ray, *The French East India Company and the Trade of the Indian Ocean: A Collection of Essays by Indrani Ray*, ed. Lakshmi Subramanian, New Delhi and Calcutta: Munshiram Manoharlal and Centre for Studies in Social Sciences, 1999.
11. There was a Kasim Khan, Mughal *subahdar* of Bengal in 1613 and another named Kasim Khan Jang in 1628. Walter Hamilton, *East India Gazetteer*, 2 vols., London: Parbury Allen & Co., 1828. See vol. 1. It is not clear, however, which one of them established the town.
12. 'Report of Hughes and Parker 1620-25', in *The Diaries of Streynsham Master 1675-1680 and Other Contemporary Papers Relating Thereto,* 2 vols., ed. R.C. Temple, London: John Murray, 1911.
13. Benoy Kumar Sarkar, *Inland Transport and Communication in Medieval India*, Calcutta: Calcutta University Press, 1925, p. 12.
14. W.F. Sinclair and D.W. Ferguson, eds., *The Travels of Pedro Texeira, etc.*, London: Hakluyt Society, 1902.
15. Sarkar, *Inland Transport*, pp. 12-13.
16. William Foster, *The English Factories in India, 1618-1669*, vol. 5, Oxford: Clarendon Press, 1906-27, p. 212.
17. Balkrishna, *Commercial Relations between India and England, 1601-1757*, London: George Routledge and Sons, 1924, p. 100.
18. Anand Yang, *Bazaar India: Markets, Society and the Colonial State in Bihar*, Berkeley and Los Angeles: California University Press, 1988.
19. 'B. M. Addl. Mss.', 34, 123, f. 42; C.R. Wilson, *Early Annals of the English in Bengal*, vol. 1, Calcutta, 1895, p. 376, cited in Sushil Chaudhury, 'International Trade in Bengal Silk and the Comparative Role of Asians and Europeans, circa 1700-1757', *Modern Asian Studies*, vol. 29, no. 2, 1995, p. 375.
20. Pires, *Suma Oriental*; Duarte Barbosa, *The Book of Duarte Barbosa*, tr. M.L. Dames, London: Hakluyt Society, 1921; Ludovico Varthema, *The Itinerary of Ludovico Varthema*, tr. R.C. Temple, London: Hakluyt Society, 1928; 'Narrative of Ralph Fitch 1583-91', in *Early Travels in India 1583-1619*, ed. William Foster, London, 1921; 'Cesare Frederici', in Richard Hakluyt, *The Principal Navigations, etc.*, ed.

Edmund Goldsmid, vol. 9, pt. 2 of *F.R.H.S.*, 2006. <http://ebooks.adelaide.edu.au/h/hakluyt/voyages/> (accessed on 13 May 2009).

21. B. Greenhill, *Boats and Boatmen of Pakistan*, Newton Abbot, 1971, p. 35, cited in Jean Deloche, 'Boats and Ships in Bengal Terracotta Arts', *Bulletin de l'Ecole Française d'Extrême-Orient*, vol. 78, no. 1, 1991, pp. 1-49.
22. Sarkar, *Inland Transport*, p. 12.
23. Jean Baptiste Tavernier, *Travels in India*, book 1 of 2 vols., ed. and tr. Ball and Crooke, 1889, rpt, New Delhi: Asian Educational Services, 2001, pp. 102-3.
24. Shafaat Ahmad Khan, ed., *John Marshall in India: Notes and Observations in Bengal (1668-1672)*; rpt, Read Books, 2006, p. 69.
25. Quoted in Roger Bilham, 'The 1737 Calcutta Earthquake and Cyclone Evaluated', *Bulletin of the Seismological Society of America*, vol. 84, no. 5, 1994, p. 2; A.K. Sensarma, 'The Great Bengal Cyclone of 1737—an enquiry into the legend', *Weather*, 1994, pp. 90-6. I am indebted to Prof. Ranjan Chakrabarti of the Department of History, Jadavpur University, Kolkata, for the second reference.
26. Christopher Chase-Dunn and Kelly M. Mann, *The Wintu and Their Neighbors: A Very Small World-System in Northern California,* Tucson, Arizona: University of Arizona Press, 1998.
27. Christopher Chase-Dunn and Andrew Jorgenson, 'Regions and Interaction Networks: a World-Systems Perspective', Paper presented at *Interactions: Regional Studies, Global Processes, and Historical Analysis*, Library of Congress, Washington D.C., 28 February–3 March 2001. Available at <http://www.historycooperative.org/proceedings/interactions/chasedunn.html> (accessed on 8 April 2009).
28. Ibid.
29. 'Hughes and Parker Report'.
30. Kumkum Chatterjee, *Merchants, Politics and Society in Early Modern India, Bihar 1733-1820*, Leiden: Brill, 1996, p. 15.
31. Chaudhury, 'International Trade', p. 375.
32. C.R. Wilson, *The Early Annals of the English in Bengal being the Bengal Public Consultations for the First Half of the Eighteenth Century*, vol. 1, London: Thacker, 1900, p. 48.
33. Chaudhury, 'International Trade', p. 383. Grose mentions a host of Asian traders in Bengal at mid century. John Henry Grose, *A Voyage to the East Indies, etc.*, vol. 2 of 2 vols., London, 1772, p. 234.
34. Bernard S. Cohn, 'The Role of the Gosains in the Economy of Eighteenth and Nineteenth Century Upper India', *Indian Economic & Social History Review*, vol. 1, no. 4, 1964, pp. 175-82.
35. H.R. Ghosal, *Economic Transition in the Bengal Presidency (1793-1833)*, Patna: Patna University, 1950, pp. 183-4.
36. Chaudhury, 'International Trade', p. 382.
37. Sushil Chaudhury, 'Trading Networks in a Traditional Diaspora: Armenians in India circa 1600-1800' in *Diaspora Entrepreneurial Networks: Four Centuries of History*, 2nd edn, ed. Ina Baghdiantz McCabe, Gelina Harlaftis and Ioanna Pepelasis Minoglou, Berg Publishers, 2005, pp. 53-4.

38. Bhaswati Bhattacharya, 'Making money at the blessed place of Manila: Armenians in the Madras–Manila trade in the eighteenth century', *Journal of Global History*, vol. 3, 2008, pp. 1-20, see pp. 13-14.
39. Rila Mukherjee, *Merchants and Companies in Bengal: Kasimbazar and Jugdia in the Eighteenth Century*, New Delhi: Pragati Publications, 2006.
40. Ibid.
41. Ibid.
42. Ibid.
43. Rila Mukherjee, 'The Last Commercial Frontier: French and English Presence in South Eastern Bengal and Beyond', *Indian Historical Review*, vol. 35, no. 1, 2007, pp. 167-86.
44. Yang, *Bazaar India*.
45. Chaudhury, 'International Trade', p. 380.
46. Sushil Chaudhury believes that there were other sources of bullion in Bengal and while he holds this as one of the most important indicators of what he terms 'prosperity', he does not explain why there was then an economic breakdown. Sushil Chaudhury, 'The Inflow of Silver to Bengal in Global Perspective *c.*1650-1757', in *Global Connections and Monetary History, 1470-1800*, ed. Dennis O'Flynn, Arturo Giraldez and Richard von Glahn, Ashgate, 2003, pp. 159-68.
47. Mukherjee, *Merchants and Companies*.
48. 'Hughes and Parker Report'.
49. Hamilton, *East India Gazetteer*, 2 vols., London: Parbury Allen & Co., 1828, vol. 1.
50. P.J. Marshall, *East Indian Fortunes: The British in Bengal in the Eighteenth Century*, Oxford: Oxford University Press, 1976; Temple, *Streynsham Master Diaries*, vol. 1, pp. 53-4.
51. Ray, 'Journey to Cassimbazar and Murshidabad: Observations of a French Visitor to Bengal in 1743', in *The French East India Company*, pp. 144-76.
52. Mukherjee, *Merchants and Companies*, pp. xxxii-v.
53. Jadunath Sarkar, *Bengal Nawabs*, Calcutta: Asiatic Society, 1952.
54. Chatterjee, *Merchants, Politics and Society*.
55. Ibid., p. 22.
56. Tilottama Mukherjee, 'The Co-ordinating State and the Economy: The Nizamat in Eighteenth-Century Bengal', *Modern Asian Studies*, vol. 43, no. 2, 2009, pp. 389-436.
57. Rila Mukherjee, 'The Nawab's Business: Agricultural and Commercial Practices in Eighteenth Century Bengal' in *Business History of India*, ed. Chittabrata Palit and Pranjal Bhattacharyya, New Delhi: Gyan Books, 2006.
58. Wilson, *The Early Annals of the English*, vol. 1.
59. Ray, 'Journey to Cassimbazar', p. 151.
60. Mukherjee, *Merchants and Companies*, p. 158. See fn. 79.
61. Ibid., p. 21.
62. Brokers were an indispensable feature of medieval markets and helped negotiate the non-transparency of unknown markets. Lars Boerner and Dan Quint, 'Medieval Matching Markets', Mimeograph, 2007.

63. Mukherjee, *Merchants and Companies*, p. 61; the French archives tell us that between 1773 and 1775 the Seths approached the French government in Paris and succeeded in forcing thereby the defaulting French in Bengal to pay their debts to the Seths. See Entry Nos. 2548, 2570, 2584, 22MI41, C.A.O.M. For *Sicca Rupee* (*SR*) rates and equivalences, see <www.data-archive.ac.uk/doc/5254/pdf> (accessed on 25 March 2009). The equivalence is quoted at 10 *SR*=1 pound sterling or 2.25 *SR*=1 Spanish Dollar. In the nineteenth century, when the EEIC issued its own *SR* after the conquest of Bengal, the new *SR* was greatly debased, reflecting both the condition of Bengal as colony and EEIC policies there: about 2 shillings or 0.1 pound=1*SR*. See 'Note on East India Company Coinage', in Matthew Edney, *Mapping an Empire: The Geographical Construction of British India, 1765-1843*, Chicago: University of Chicago Press, 1997, p. xvii. Alain le Pichon's *China Trade and Empire: The Letters of William Jardine and James Matheson and the Origins of British Rule in Hong Kong, 1827-43*, Oxford: Oxford University Press, 2006, p. 249, gives the same rates, i.e. 2 shillings or 2sh1d.=1 *SR*. For more on Indian currency systems under British rule, see G.L. Molesworth, 'Indian Currency', *Annals of the American Academy of Political and Social Science*, vol. 4, 1894, pp. 1-36.
64. Mukherjee, *Merchants and Companies*, Table 15, Important Merchant Families and their Share in the EEIC Silk Investment at Kasimbazar: 1733-1750 (per cent of total investment), p. 54. For caste affiliations, see Table 8, Caste Affiliations among Dadni merchants at Kasimbazar, pp. 38-9, and for the total EEIC investment at Kasimbazar between 1733 and 1750, see Table 11, p. 43, in the same. The figures in Table 11 refer to thousands of rupees.
65. Wilson, *The Early Annals of the English*, vol. 1, pp. 20-1, 23.
66. J.H. Little, *The House of Jagat Seth*, Calcutta, 1967.
67. Ray, 'Journey to Cassimbazar', pp. 165-6.
68. Ibid., p. 166.
69. K.F.R., 12 and 20 May 1755.
70. Mukherjee, *Merchants and Companies*, p. xxxi.
71. 'Narrative of Ralph Fitch'.
72. K.M. Mohsin, *A Bengal District in Transition: Murshidabad 1765-93*, Dacca, 1973.
73. Rila Mukherjee, *Strange Riches: Bengal in the Mercantile Map of South Asia*, Delhi: Cambridge India/Foundation, 2006, p. 187.
74. Ray, 'Of Trade and Traders in the Seventeenth Century India: An Unpublished French Memoir by George Roques', in *The French East India Company*, pp. 1-62.
75. Ibid., pp. 33-4.
76. Ibid.
77. Sebouh Aslanian, '"The Salt in a Merchant's Letter": The Culture of Julfan Correspondence in the Indian Ocean and the Mediterranean', *Journal of World History*, vol. 19, no. 2, 2008, pp. 127-88, plus references, p. 152.
78. Sebouh Aslanian, 'Social capital, "trust" and the role of networks in Julfan trade: informal and semi-formal institutions at work', *Journal of Global History*, vol. 1, 2006, pp. 398-400.

79. Chaudhury, 'Trading Networks in a Traditional Diaspora', p. 59.
80. Ibid., p. 60.
81. Chatterjee, *Merchants, Politics and Society*, p. 50.
82. Aslanian, "The Salt in a Merchant's Letter", pp. 163-5.
83. Ibid., pp. 171-2.
84. O.J. Volckart, 'The Influence of Information Costs on the Integration of Financial Markets: Northern Europe, 1350-1560', in *Information Flows: New Approaches in the Historical Study of Business Information*, ed. Leos Mueller and Jari Ojala, Helsinki: Finnish Literature Society, 2007, pp. 31-62.
85. Mukherjee, *Merchants and Companies*, p. 59; *Streynsham Master Diaries*; Luillier, *Voyage du sieur Luillier aux Grandes Indes, avec une instruction pour le commerce des Indes orientales*, Paris: Claude Cellier, 1705.
86. Mukherjee, *Merchants and Companies*, p. 60.
87. K.F.R., 17 June 1741.
88. In the 'Davypersaud' case of 1753, when the merchant Debi Prasad was imprisoned by the EEIC at Kasimbazar for non-payment of debts, his security Ramkrishna Babu was also arrested. The latter was the adopted son of Raja Chin Rai, once Alamchand's agent in Bengal and the Chief Minister of Bengal at the time. All the rajas, including Kirti Chand, Alamchand's son, and Umed Rai, protested at the court in Murshidabad on Ramkrishna's and Debi's behalf. Debi Prasad was a member of a prominent merchant family supplying silk at Kasimbazar. By 1748 the family handled 22 per cent of the total amount invested by the EEIC at Kasimbazar, see Mukherjee, *Merchants and Companies*, pp. 83-4. It is not known what happened to him ultimately; because of the sensitivity of the matter, the EEIC agreed that Kisendeb Podar, their trusted *vakil* (interpreter and agent) from the 1750s, should handle the matter at court. Earlier Podar, as the favourite of Hukum Beg, the *Pachotra Daroga*, was the latter's diwan. From the K.F.R. cited in Mukherjee, *Merchants and Companies*, pp. 83-4.
89. K.F.R.
90. K.F.R. cited in Mukherjee, *Merchants and Companies*, Table 17, p. 64.
91. Ibid., pp. 64-6.
92. Sanjay Subrahmanyam and C.A. Bayly, 'Portfolio capitalists and the political economy of early modern India', *Indian Economic Social History Review*, vol. 25, no. 4, 1988, pp. 401-24.
93. K.F.R., 12 November 1752, cited in Mukherjee, *Merchants and Companies*, p. 96.
94. Table 18, ibid., p. 81.
95. Table 11, ibid., p. 43.
96. Table 7, ibid., pp. 23-35.
97. The investment was hiked that year and the next due to a price rise attending the Maratha raids. Ibid., p. 78.
98. Table 11, ibid., p. 43.
99. The EEIC controlled the riverways of Bengal by the 1730s, long before they actually 'conquered' the province. This control made it easier for them to smash

the *dadni* system and replace it with the agency/*gomastha* system in 1753, whereby the EEIC could enter the *arangs* directly and procure goods. This is also hinted at in P.J. Marshall, *The Making and Unmaking of Empires: Britain, India and America, c.1750-1783*, Oxford: Oxford University Press, 2005, p. 243.

100. Mukherjee, *Merchants and Companies*, p. 78.
101. Table 9, ibid., pp. 40-1.
102. Tables 12 and 13, ibid., pp. 47-8, 50.
103. B.P.C., R.I., vol. 44, 14 August 1769, cited in ibid., p. 91.
104. James Burgess, 'Extracts from the Journal of Col. Colin Mackenzie's Pandit on his Route from Calcutta to Gaya in 1820', *Indian Antiquary*, vol. 31, 1A, 1902, pp. 65-75.
105. Hugh B. Urban, 'The Marketplace and the Temple: Economic Metaphors and Religious Meanings in the Folk Songs of Colonial Bengal', *The Journal of Asian Studies*, vol. 60, no. 4, 2001, pp. 1085-114, especially pp. 1088-9, 1094-5, 1107-8.
106. <http://bangla.com/Wikipedia/bangla.htm>.
107. S.C. Nandy, *Life and Times of Canto Baboo: The Banyan of Warren Hastings*, 2 vols., vol. 1, Bombay: Allied Publishers, 1987; vol. 2, Calcutta: Dev-ALL Pvt. Ltd., 1981.
108. Indrajit Ray, 'Long Waves of Silk Price in Bengal during 16th-17th Centuries', pp. 1-33, 18. Available at <http://www.lse.ac.uk/collections/economicHistory/GEHN/GEHNPDF/PUNERay.pdf> (accessed on 28 April 2009).
109. Ibid., p. 19.
110. *Voyage de Nicolas de Graaf aux Indes Orientales, etc. 1639-87*, Amsterdam: J.F. Bernard, 1719.
111. Pires, *Suma Oriental*, p. 88.
112. 'Ralph Fitch' in Hakluyt, *The Principal Navigations*, vol. 10, pt. 3.
113. Pires, *Suma Oriental*; See also the *Mangalkavya* genre of medieval literature in Bengali.
114. Pires, *Suma Oriental*, pp. 93, 142. Bengalis at Pasai were deemed by Pires to be the 'most important' group and Pires notes that there were numerous instances of intermarriage. Moreover, he says that the Bengalis imposed their own king at Pasai (p. 142), but this is not verifiable. Denys Lombard, *Le Sultanat d'Atjeh au temps d'Iskandar Muda 1607-1636*, vol. 61, Paris: EFEO, 1967, p. 47.
115. Pires, *Suma Oriental*, p. 139.
116. Ray, 'Of Trade and Traders', pp. 15-16, 45.
117. Pires, *Suma Oriental* cited in Luis Filipe F.R. Thomaz, 'The Malay Sultanate of Melaka', in *South-East Asia in the early Modern Era: Trade, Power and Belief*, ed. Anthony Reid, Ithaca: Cornell University Press, 1993, pp. 69-90.
118. Lombard, *Le Sultanat d'Atjeh*, p. 42.
119. *Voyage de Nicolas de Graaf*, p. 306. 'Bengal is the second-largest trading partner of the Dutch after the Moluccas. Each year, ten, twelve, fifteen ships go to Bengal from Batavia' (my translation).
120. Luillier, *Voyage du sieur Luillier*, pp. 242-3.

121. Ibid., pp. 244-51.
122. Ray, 'India in Asian Trade in the 1730s: A Discussion by a French Trader', *The French East India Company*, p. 190.
123. Ibid., pp. 191-2.
124. Bin Yang, *Between Winds and Clouds: The Making of Yunnan, Second Century* BCE *to Twentieth Century* CE, New York: Columbia University Press, 2008; Bin Yang, 'Horses, Silver and Cowries: Yunnan in Global Perspective', *Journal of World History*, vol. 15, no. 3, 2004.
125. Luillier, *Voyage du sieur Luillier*, pp. 112-13.
126. Ray, 'Of Trade and Traders', pp. 17-18, 23-4.
127. Moreland quoted in Ray, 'Long Waves of Silk Price', p. 6. Ray concludes that Bengal silk was cheap at the beginning of the seventeenth century and then became cheaper as the century progressed. In the eighteenth century, it rose steadily due to the bullion imported into Bengal by the EICs.
128. K.N. Chaudhuri, *The Trading World of Asia and the English East India Company, 1660-1760*, Cambridge: Cambridge University Press, 1978.
129. Ray, 'Long Waves of Silk Price'; Mukherjee, *Merchants and Companies*.
130. Balkrishna, *Commercial Relations between India and England*, p. 171.
131. Sushil Chaudhury, *Trade and Commercial Organisation in Bengal, 1650-1720*, Calcutta: Firma KLM, 1975, p. 147.
132. Mukherjee, *Strange Riches*, pp. 224–6.
133. *Streynsham Master Diaries*, vol. 2, p. 86.
134. William Hedges, *Diary of, During His Agency in Bengal: 1681-87*, 2 vols., ed. R. Barlow and H. Yule, London: Hakluyt Society, 1880.
135. Ibid., vol. 1, p. 73.
136. Ibid., p. 76.
137. Ibid., p. 152.
138. Chaudhury, *Trade and Commercial Organisation*.
139. 'Narrative of Ralph Fitch'.
140. 'Cesare Frederici'.
141. Foster, *The English Factories in India*, vol. 5.
142. Thomas Bowrey, *A Geographical Account of the Countries Around The Bay of Bengal 1669-1679*, ed. R.C. Temple, Cambridge: Hakluyt Society, 1905, pp. 225-9; *Voyage de Nicolas de Graaf*, pp. 307-8.
143. Prakash, *The Dutch East India Company*, p. 25; Mukherjee, *Merchants and Companies*, p. xxxii.
144. Chandra Richard de Silva, 'The Portuguese East India Company 1628-1633', *Luso-Brazilian Review*, vol. 11, no. 2, 1974, pp. 187-8.
145. Chatterjee, *Merchants, Politics and Society*, pp. 26-8.
146. Bowrey, *A Geographical Account of the Countries*, pp. 225-9.
147. Mukherjee, *Merchants and Companies*.
148. Chaudhury, 'Trading Networks in a Traditional Diaspora', p. 56.
149. *Voyage de Nicolas de Graaf*, pp. 307-8.
150. Luillier, *Voyage du sieur Luillier*, p. 79.
151. Ibid., p. 69.
152. Lombard, *Le Sultanat d'Atjeh*, p. 116.

153. Chaudhury, 'Trading Networks in a Traditional Diaspora', p. 57.
154. Sinclair, *Travels of Pedro Texeira.*
155. Orme, Mss. OV 134, ff. 21-2, cited in Chaudhury, 'Trading Networks in a Traditional Diaspora', p. 57.
156. Wilson, *The Early Annals of the English*, vol. 1, pp. xxii, lviii, lix, 15, 29, 141.
157. Ibid., p. 305.
158. Watts, 'Networks, Dynamics, and the Small-World Phenomenon', pp. 502-3.
159. Ibid., p. 524.
160. Matthew O. Jackson and Brian W. Rogers, 'The Economics of Small Worlds', *Journal of the European Economic Association*, vol. 3, nos. 2 and 3, 2005, pp. 617-27.
161. Ibid.
162. Sebouh Aslanian, 'Trade Diaspora versus Colonial State: Armenian Merchants, the English East India Company, and the High Court of Admiralty in London, 1748–1752', *Diaspora: A Journal of Transnational Studies*, vol. 13, no. 1, 2004, pp. 37-100.
163. Ibid., p. 60.
164. M.S. Seth, *The Armenians in India*, New Delhi: Oxford & IBH Publishing Co., 1983.
165. Aslanian, 'Trade Diaspora versus Colonial State', p. 51.
166. Emily Erikson and Peter Bearman, 'Routes into Networks: The Structure of English Trade in the East Indies, 1601-1833', *ISERP Working Paper 04-07*, 2004, pp. 3-4.
167. Ibid., p. 5.

CHAPTER ELEVEN

Global Interactions: Representations of the East and the Far East in Portugal in the Sixteenth Century

Amélia Polónia

THIS ESSAY WILL DISCUSS THE WAYS BY which the most occidental kingdom of Europe, Portugal, could be connected in the sixteenth century with a faraway, exotic and much larger universe, the East and the Far East,[1] located on the other side of the globe. The observations made here intend to provide some representations of that world, including those produced and interiorized by a small maritime community, Vila do Conde, actively involved in the overseas dynamic.

I will first attempt to identify the ways by which the East and the Far East were represented in the Western European world, namely, through written accounts. Second, I will try to identify the agents and the networks involved in the connections established between Portugal and that world totally new to the common European. And finally, I will take up for consideration the representations of this distant and exotic world in the daily life of a specific community: people, commodities, iconography, architectural styles and material culture, are some of the selected items to check the connections between a very small world, located in the extreme west of Europe, and a distant and unknown universe, of which representations were created in the sixteenth century. Through diplomatic connections, warfare and piracy, navigation and trade, evangelization and cultural exchanges, the local connects with the global, touching a universe located, in geographical, as well as in civilizational terms, at its antipodes. This essay deals with the concept of cultural representation as presented and elaborated upon by Robert Chartier, i.e. the way in which a cultural agent, at a specific time and in a specific place, noticed, understood, interiorized and represented to others a particular reality. To develop this understanding, the status of the agents, their intentions and the active functions the representations were meant to fulfil, become central analytical variables.[2]

The representations of this other world took the form of political, diplomatic, geographical, historical, anthropological, cartographic or literary accounts. However, they could also be transmitted by oral registers, oral narratives or even find expression in merchandise, commodities, iconographic patterns or architectural achievements or human beings and material culture, which became real materializations of that alternate world.

In order to understand the formal and informal representations of such a world in a small maritime town, namely through the presence, in its daily life, of slaves, commodities, furniture, iconography and aesthetic references, this essay will focus on the agents, the networks and the mechanisms that enabled transferences and exchanges between these two distinctive, distant worlds: navigation, trade, evangelization and emigration flows will thus emerge as phenomena to be explored.

To gather an understanding of the 'periscope' through which these cultural transfers are going to be analysed, the community's profile will be presented and characterized, from geographical, demographic, economic and social points of view.

It is vital to analyse a broad set of documental sources, namely municipal records, notary records, *Misericórdia*[3] records, wills, inventory of assets, and inquisition proceedings to identify the testimonies and the impact of the exotic Eastern world on a local community, that of Vila do Conde, a small Portuguese port located in northern Portugal. The architectural features of Vila do Conde's urban landscape will also be examined to identify lasting material testimonies to those Eastern references and the corresponding aesthetic values.

East and the Far East: Representations in Portugal

The intersection between the local and global, between East and West, between Europe and other worlds was, for Europeans, a new experience which structurally framed the Early Modern age.[4] Old and even ancient worlds became 'new worlds' to the Europeans, whose perception was spread by a large group of common and anonymous historical agents. A motley group of Crown officers, merchants, sailors, soldiers and adventurers became, thus, responsible for massive cultural exchanges. These agents built networks, frequently informal and unrecognized by the European powers, particularly the Portuguese Crown, emerging as the very first people to establish contact and to interact with this 'new world'. Fernão Mendes Pinto,[5] an adventurer who became a central figure in political, economic and military dynamics in the Far East, as a soldier and as an unofficial trader, is a good example of those whose actions were central to these dynamics of global transferences, even though they were not recognized as official representatives of the Portuguese Crown.

Manifold representations resulted from these connections between worlds, some official (political, diplomatic), produced from the perspective of the central power and its administrative structures in the East; some geographic, territorial, or cartographic. Others were anthropological, ethnographic or historical, produced following the chronicle genre; and some were literary, such as the *Lusíadas,* by Luís de Camões,[6] the epic account of Portuguese expansion; still others were scientific, mathematical, cosmographical and pharmacological, such as the work by Garcia da Orta, a New Christian (i.e. a converted Jew) Portuguese doctor who discovered a whole new universe in the pharmacological powers of oriental botany and the therapeutic approaches of oriental medicine.[7]

Those are written records, all of them shaped by the profiles of the agents who interiorized and transmitted their perspectives, their accounts, realistic or fantastic, to others. Incidentally some of these narratives were even written by people who had not had direct contact with the reality they represented. Their readings or what they heard from the testimonies of others were the filters through which they represented a reality they did not actually know.

In fact there are a great number of literary sources and a considerable body of technical literature which help to see this other world which is, for the Europeans, the East. The sources can be split into several groups. Chronicles tend to be indirect evidence of the events that they narrate and may consist of information gathered directly by the author, or through third parties. When analysed, authors such as Duarte Barbosa, Tomé Pires, Damião de Góis, João de Barros, Diogo de Couto, Fernão Lopes de Castanheda, Gaspar Correia or the Father Luís Fróis[8] we see that their discourses are memorialist and serve as apologia and, therefore, as sources and viewpoints tend to take a traditional approach.

Descriptions of countries and travel journals are the main genres within what is known as travel literature. The descriptions of countries and regions are generally provided by direct testimony and personal travel experiences and events. They achieve a discourse notable for accuracy, with a tendency to quantify and measure, for detail and, possibly, for rigour. They rarely contain learned citations or hints of bookishness and academic knowledge. Written by travellers, merchants, missionaries, crew members of ships, they embody the values, mentalities, experiences, life paths and the various—and widely disparate—socio-professional status of the chroniclers. Travel journals are similar in some ways to route guides and ship's logs since they link the description of the itinerary of a voyage with an account of experiences en route and with testimonies of civilizational encounters and confrontations. Even though they may also include details of journeys overland, their authors are mostly seafarers or government officers linked to shipping and navigation.

The accounts of shipwrecks may be seen as a subgenre of this form of travel literature. Sometimes circulating as single printed pamphlets, they appeal to the imagination with their often exaggerated descriptions of dramatic seafaring episodes. They are thus largely written by crew members, missionaries or travellers and passengers. The Cape Route was so dangerous and so reliant on the monsoons that accidents were common, and they appeared frequently in records of this type.[9]

There was information on the East in nautical literature, as well, though its content was more technical in nature.[10] These included ship's logs, routes and nautical guides. Their technical content and strong geographic character (distances, latitudes, depths) sometimes required expert deciphering. Whereas the first two groups were more likely to be written by sailors and other nautical officers, the authors of the works in the third group were primarily cosmographers, mathematicians and specialized pilots. Works on navigation were another sub-group of this genre and took the form of notebooks in which mariners jotted down nautical information for their own use.

Geographical literature was another source of information for representations of the East, though this focused on territorial dimension and landscape, including descriptions of local fauna and flora, which obviously highlighted the exotic. They may have stemmed from direct observation or from accounts and records by third parties. Geographers and cosmographers were the main authors of these works, which were related to and supplemented by a vast cartographic output, which also contained spatial and figurative images of these other worlds.[11]

Technical and scientific treatises on many subjects, like botany, zoology, pharmacopoeia and cosmography, were characterized by the association of empirical knowledge, derived from observation, and scientific knowledge, from learning and academic study. Written by cosmographers, mathematicians, physicians and surgeons, they conveyed more specialized images of the East. Garcia de Orta and D. João de Castro topped the list for output in this field, with reference works: the *Diálogos dos simples e drogas e coisas medicinais da Índia;*[12] and the *Tratado da Sphaera,*[13] respectively. One should also mention the work of Francisco Faleiro, the *Tratado de la Esphera y del arte del marear,*[14] and Cristóvão da Costa's *Tratado de las drogas y medicinas de las Índias Orientales.*[15]

The ethnographic and anthropological literature provided additional important observations about the East. This was the work of missionaries, travellers, men of letters and culture who described peoples, customs, religions, languages, cultures and even mentalities (often with distortions), based on direct records of their own observations, or on stories related by third parties. Generally imbued with values which were clearly Western in emphasis in relation to the Eastern situations and circumstances depicted, this literature portrayed a reality that was filtered through the focus of the observer and was quite resistant to the notion of otherness. A great number of the records produced by missionaries, in particular the Franciscans and Jesuits, in the form of letters sent to Portugal and Rome, played a large part in providing an overall knowledge of peoples and civilizations with whom they came in contact, which was also an essential tool in evangelical work.[16] This literature did not have, however, a significant diffusion and dissemination.

Literature of a mostly political, diplomatic and commercial nature also has to be mentioned. Letters by merchants and trading agents; by diplomats based in Lisbon; by royal representatives of Portugal in Rome and other European courts; or even by Portuguese monarchs themselves, telling other rulers and the Pope about the 'discovery of new lands' and the contact with new peoples,[17] emerged as representations of the East which also need to be considered. In the official royal epistolography a political perspective of the East can be identified, which is steered by power strategies and by European political and diplomatic schemes. Alongside, attention should be drawn to the dispatch from D. Manuel's embassy to Rome, in 1513–14,[18] which tried to materialize, visualize and make tangible to the multitudes who watched the parade, the zoological, botanical and anthropological picture of these alternate worlds that Europe was keen to get to know and supposedly dominate.

Diverse genres of literature conveyed equally disparate representations. The literary and fictional works reflecting episodes such as travels, military exploits, or even the social types, values and emerging behaviours associated with the expansionist dynamic, now became common. Poets such as Luís de Camões and dramatists like Gil Vicente[19] were the leading creators of works of this kind.

There is no way to actually know the true extent of the diffusion of these written records, their actual dissemination or the public they reached. They do not seem to have been very well known in Portugal. Only a few printing houses were available, besides those founded by universities, some monasteries, the Crown or the members of the royal family. There were very few businessmen in Portugal involved in a large-scale publishing industry,[20] and among those, some were foreigners, such as Valentim Fernandes.[21]

The specific historical frameworks which might explain this phenomenon are not the focus of this essay. They have already been partially explained and studied by a few Portuguese historians.[22] The result is, nevertheless, surprising. The relative weight of the specific publication of records on Portuguese expansion, in its various expressions and forms is not conspicuous: it is only about 7 per cent of the total published books in Portugal in the sixteenth century, and 96 references in a total of 1,312 records correspond to those registers.[23] At the same time, published travel or nautical literature seemed to be predominant in the early decades of the century, when overall publishing activity was on a smaller scale. They are associated with 'unofficial' and foreign printers, such as Valentim Fernandes.

On the contrary, Portuguese chronicles, maritime routes and other travel books were printed, read and 'consumed' all over Europe by an élite group of intellectuals and politicians, attracted by the accounts of these unimaginable worlds. The spread of humanist ideals throughout Europe, although not so widespread in Portugal, also explains the popularity of these epic accounts, comparable in many ways to those of the Greeks, the Romans or the conquests of Alexander the Great. These accounts were, thus, printed and circulated in Italy, Germany, The Netherlands; they were written in Latin or translated into local languages, thus becoming more widely available, more publicized and more well known abroad than in Portugal, where first editions were not printed until the eighteenth, nineteenth or even the twentieth centuries. There seems to be a shift in this situation during the seventeenth century, when the Portuguese press, mostly located in Lisbon, became more active, responding to the need for more widespread news and coverage of Portuguese achievements overseas. However, these followed mostly chronicle standards.[24] This tendency can be understood as a strategic need to defend the historical rights of the Portuguese to overseas territories in times when they were being contested politically, commercially and militarily at sea and in every overseas territory, mostly in the East and Far East, by the Dutch, British, French and even the Spanish.

The increasing number of writings by foreigners about those Portuguese settlements and the Eastern world under the influence of Portugal should be noticed in the same context. The interest in these distant lands, principally the Eastern ones, of travellers and mapmakers from the various European political regions during the last decades of the sixteenth and the early seventeenth centuries is indisputable. The reports and cartographical representations of the East and the Far East gave the Europeans detailed information about the trade, geography, politics and customs of these regions. The French and, more particularly, the Dutch, took the lead in these representations. After spending 13 years in Goa, Jan Huygen van Linschoten returned in 1589. In 1596 he published his *Itinerarium ofte Schipvaert van J.H. van L. naer Oost ofte Portugaels Indien*. Later, the *Itinerario* printed was also published in English in 1598, in German between 1598 and 1600, in Latin in 1599, and in French in 1610. François Pyrard de Laval published his *Voyages* in France in 1611. All these works give accounts not only of the nature of the Portuguese settlement in the East, but of oriental customs, trade, politics and civilization.

Similarly, from the end of the sixteenth century the cartographic representations of these areas multiplied in Dutch atlases. The best examples are the *Theatrum Orbis Terrarum*, by Abraham Ortelius (1579); the *Civitates Orbis Terrarum*, by George Braun and Franz Hogenberg (1572); the *Speculum Orbis Terrarum* (Amsterdam, 1578); and Gerardus Mercator's *Atlas,* published for the first time in 1595—all of which were republished repeatedly throughout Europe.

To sum up, the foreign printing of what might be termed Portuguese travel literature, alongside the published works by other Europeans, seems to have been relevant particularly in Italy, Germany and The Netherlands. Judging from the number of printed editions, more was known in Europe than in Portugal, in the sixteenth century, of Portuguese expansion and the worlds the Portuguese had recently discovered and told the Europeans about. This conclusion, accurate to the overall printed representations of the new worlds, can be applied particularly to the narratives centred on the East and Far East.

Even if they were actively published in Portugal and thus roused the interest of the common citizen, they would mainly circulate in elitist circles and be primarily consumed by an elitist public: those who could read and who could afford to buy those printed editions. Other representations would have been able to guarantee a more widespread diffusion. Indeed, apart from the conventional printed versions in book form, other types of material, in loose pamphlets, perhaps illustrated, were issued, printed by small typographers, and not by the large, well known printers, containing accounts of shipwrecks, fantastical descriptions of events and monsters.[25] At the same time, manuscript copies of the travel narratives, side by side with oral accounts, by navigators, sailors, merchants, travellers and adventurers, surely filled the imagination of large audiences in taverns, marketplaces and public squares, avid for news, real or fantasized, of these new worlds. These representations were undoubtedly responsible for the manifold and massive fantastical constructions and reconstructions of these wonderful, mysterious worlds, whose configurations could not be controlled by any official version. These personal narratives were the result of a blend of realities and fantasies, lived experiences and invented episodes.

Alongside these written and oral representations of that world, other more palpable testimonies bore witness to the global dynamics involved in these transferences and exchanges. Oriental people, mostly slaves, but also illegitimate children fathered by the Portuguese, were some of the faces of that reality. Wealth and fortune arriving from the East; the new smells and tastes brought by the spices, but also by the exotic perfumes; the jewellery, chinaware, tapestries, furniture, textiles, pictures and ornaments—they all introduced an oriental-based material culture which penetrated Portuguese daily life. In order to understand the potential impact and significance of these transferences, one should look at the dynamics, the agents, and the circuits by which those exchanges were operated.

Connecting Different Worlds: Agents and Networks

The availability of contacts and interactions between Europe, particularly Portugal, and the East and Far East depended on the regular operation of formal and informal networks connecting those worlds.[26] Among the formal and institutional Portuguese networks in the East, there are, in the first place, all the administrative, financial and military structures which represented the *Estado da Índia* ('State of India') which included a wide range of officers, from viceroys, judges, clerks, bailiffs, captains to tax collectors or notary officers. Those officers implicated in the logistics of the Cape Route, the maritime spice route governed from the *Casa da Índia*, involving a large number of nautical officers, mostly captains, ships' masters, sailors and soldiers recruited to serve as crew should also be considered. The institutional framework provided by the missionary activities of the Franciscans, Jesuits, Dominicans, and even Benedictines and, later on, Augustinians, should not be forgotten either. Those organizations, together with the ecclesiastical networks sustained by the structures of the bishoprics founded in the overseas territories—both integrated in the Portuguese *Padroado* in the East, ruled by the Portuguese Crown, all provided flows of information and goods.

Last, but not least, the framework provided by the *Misericórdia* Houses, present in the Portuguese colonial settlements, should also be considered. These were civil confraternities which duplicated and emulated the organization of their metropolitan counterparts. Ruled by the same status, each almost a copy of the other, all based on the mother *Misericórdia* in Lisbon, these institutions provided not only spiritual and social assistance to

Portuguese settlers and their descendants, but also provided ways of transferring news, goods and money. From *Misericórdia* to *Misericórdia*, Macau was connected to Malacca; both to Goa; Goa to Lisbon, and Lisbon to all the houses throughout the metropolitan territory. Intense flows of news, goods, fortunes, wills and other official documents were maintained by this institutional framework, parallel to, and frequently more efficient, than the State itself.

Besides this institutional framework, providing formal and institutionalized networks, the individual connections between agents also have to be considered. In order to characterize the typology of agents involved in overseas expansion, mainly connected with the East, three main types can be pointed out: seamen, covering an entire range of categories, from pilots to cabin-boys, merchants and adventurers. Boundaries have not necessarily to be created between them, since involvement in multiple activities seemed to prevail. The concept itself of nobleman/merchant is widely accepted in Portuguese historiography. To this one could add the pilot or sailor/merchant or even clergyman/merchant,[27] the latter being a secular priest or a missionary. The overlapping of administrative, military, fiscal, religious and sailing activities with overseas trade is a historically proven fact, with numerous implications. One example is the monopoly the Jesuits held in Japan, dealing with trade, which provided them with a dominant commercial activity and sustained a long-lasting mercantile flow between the ports of Nagasaki, Macau and Goa, for instance. The overall consequences of these dynamics in terms of interference of the Jesuits in the internal politics of Japan, or their conflicts with the Portuguese merchants, who depended on their permission to trade, are well known.[28]

The overlapping status which interests us the most, considering our aim to identify cultural transfers which can be projected on the universe of common people and on the daily life of maritime communities, is certainly the one that involves the seamen. In a global perspective, the concept of pluri-activity and pluri-functionality are extremely accurate when applied to these professional categories. Seamen are mainly known for their skills as nautical technicians, but they were also quite often, at least in the Portuguese case, shipowners, trade agents, commercial intermediaries and individual connectors in important networks and circuits of goods, money and information flows.

This pluri-activity was widespread throughout the kingdom's seaports involved in overseas navigation and was recognized, in fact, in other European countries.[29] It was most obviously manifested in the navigation/trade linkages. In the Portuguese case, the seamen's wage scheme for royal or private voyages established that a part of the payment was to be made in cash and another (in some cases, the most significant or, at least, the most attractive one) resulted from the possibility of transporting merchandise in the ships they served, on which there were further tax exemptions or discounts. The 'quintalada' system paradigmatically confirms this in the domain of the Indian trade route.[30]

The very circumstance that the seamen were also sometimes shipowners, involved in maritime routes other than the Cape, opened up new opportunities in the trade business, as shipowners and shipmasters. A larger portion of the ships' cargo capacity was assigned to them.

Their frequent trips overseas, performing technical or commercial functions, also made them very important, at times even indispensable, intermediaries, in the service of large-scale merchants, who made use of their services as commercial agents and loan collectors. This strategy implies the existence of networks of individuals and the existence of trade and financial networks, based on trust and the reputation of individual agents, rather than on official contracts or formal trade companies.[31]

Even in more informal circuits, in the absence of a communications system established and maintained by the state, individual agents, mostly seafarers, became responsible for the transfer of news, information, goods and capital to the families remaining behind and guaranteed a flow unable to be assured by the administrative system.

The agents mentioned connected the universe under study on a temporary basis, whether during the time of their voyage, or during a military campaign or over an administrative mission. Other, more permanent agents guaranteed these connections on a more regular basis: the emigrants located in the settlements of the East and Far East, whether official or not. Their profiles, activities and wealth varied along a very heterogeneous and differential scale, as the examples given later will confirm. They acted alongside traders and merchants, within legal and illegal settings in what related to their inclusion in the structures and the rule of the *Estado da Índia*.

In order to understand their profile and activity, it has to be stressed that some of the spice traders were not, in fact, merchants, but noblemen who had access to trade activities by royal privilege, frequently as a means to reward their administrative and/or military performances, obeying the logic of a redistributive mechanism of 'mercies' and privileges, which characterized the Iberian monarchies and their overseas settlements. The nobleman/merchant, along with the captains and administrators of the Portuguese factories, are thus, dominant as legal and official representatives of the Portuguese Crown in the East and Far East. However, as stressed by Luís Filipe Reis Thomaz, the presence of the Portuguese in the East went far beyond the control of the *Estado da Índia*. According to Thomaz, in general terms, this concept points to the interests which were officially governed by the Crown, but it does not coincide with nor does it exhaust the much broader notion of 'Portuguese Expansion in the Indian Ocean', which also covers the non-official modes of settlement all over the Indian ocean, regardless of the State and, in some cases, even against the State.[32]

The same author highlights the importance of a sub-colonization phenomena, the creation of sub-colonies from the main colonies, which escaped the control of the central power, whether in administrative or in economic terms. In fact, apart from the modes of settlement as organized by the Portuguese State in the Indian Ocean, spontaneous colonies of Portuguese traders also arose. These colonies proliferated throughout the Indian seaboard, in places like Pattani (in southern Siam); Negapatan; Saint Thomas of Mylapore (São Tomé de Meliapor, Coromandel Coast), and most particularly Macau. Macau began as a territory in which the State was only represented by the Captains-General of the Goa Route to Japan, comprising a type of mercantile republic, which developed in connection with the establishment and consolidation of municipal power, through the *Leal Senado.* It is a good example of the unofficial dynamics under analysis.[33] In fact, the consolidation of Portuguese sovereignty over the territory took place only later on, sustained by concessions from the emperors of China.

Self-organizing networks were bound to be successful, even in contexts where the Portuguese Crown should have had a more forceful presence in economic, financial and administrative domains, as happened in the East.[34] In this overall picture, the State frequently tried to incorporate the spontaneous and informal colonies when, later on, they had become successful enough to draw the state's attention, as happened with Macau.

Besides the groups whose performances were briefly characterized, the presence of women should also be considered. Even if European expansion tends to be analysed almost exclusively from a male point of view, the fact is that emigration flows included women agents, who departed through the Cape Route, with a legal or, more often, an illegal status. Some were crucial agents in the Crown's strategies to spread and consolidate Portuguese settlements, as happened with the 'king's orphans'.

Indeed, from the very beginning of the maritime expansion, European women could be found in overseas regions colonized by the Portuguese. Their presence was much more widely known than most of the literature would allow the researcher to believe. A stricter assessment of the presence of women overseas requires the examination of documentary sources other than chronicles, in which women only appear very occasionally; the travel literature, where the absence of women is almost total; censuses, especially military ones, where they naturally do not figure at all, or the registers of residents, where there are no women unless they are heads of households or unless the clerk was rigorous enough to signal the presence of some who sustained themselves by selling their bodies: the prostitutes.[35]

Possibly the most striking feature is that Portuguese womens' status and numbers in the settlement drive varied considerably according to the different overseas territories. Different situations were in place when one considered their status on the Moroccan garrisons in North Africa, those in Madeira and the Azores, those in the African archipelagos and the west coast of Africa, in Brazil and in India. The distance, the political and economic goals to be achieved, the climate and health conditions played a crucial part in the strategies followed and the trends established.

Even if registers, or the lack of them, suggest a lesser number of families migrating to India, the Crown did encourage marriage with women sent out from the kingdom. The presence of Portuguese women was, thus, also widespread, especially in Goa and other Eastern urban centres. Coercive family migrations, such as those of the New Christians', also nourished the flow of family women to the East, who became settlers in the new territories. In fact the Inquisition records for Goa show that there were a significant number of such households there in the sixteenth century.[36] The example of the Garcia da Orta family, living in Goa, could be a case in point.[37]

At the same time, single women became important agent of the colonization strategies implemented by the Portuguese Crown, with special reference to the East. This is the case of the so-called 'orphans of the king', young women who were accommodated in various institutions throughout the kingdom, notably the *Recolhimento do Castelo* (Castle Refuge), in Lisbon, who were then bestowed by the Crown for marriage in overseas settlements.[38] It is not their numerical significance that should be stressed here, since, according to Timothy Coates, in the two hundred years from 1550 to 1755, only between 615 and 1025 female orphans would have been sent to India. This is clearly a trivial number when compared to other indicators of the Portuguese female population in India.[39] In fact, their importance lies in their use as a basis for a settlement strategy which was not exclusive to Portugal. Significantly, the Portuguese model of state colonization, which incorporated convicts, orphans, prostitutes and other ethnic and marginal religious groups, such as gypsies and 'New Christians' as reluctant settlers, served as a basis for other European nations.

The colonization strategies orchestrated by the Portuguese government embraced not only the virtuous orphans, some daughters of the lower rung of the nobility, but also those housed in the various Refuges of Santa Maria Madalena scattered around the country; these were former prostitutes or marginalized women who would have been converted to regular, standard, social behaviour.[40] Coming from different walks of life, these women fit into distinct social circles overseas, but shared the same fate: marriages, which local institutions were striving to organize. By this means, they were to be transformed into reluctant instruments of settlement strategies in which they were essential elements.

The first question that should be asked concerns the possible repercussions on the mental representations of the women resulting from contact with women from other, especially Eastern cultures. How would the different status of these other women influence, as a model or as a peculiarity, the status of the European woman? In the absence of consistent studies on these questions, the results of research in anthropology should not be forgotten, with its emphasis on the prevalence of an ethnocentric—or more precisely, Eurocentric—attitude among the European discoverers/colonizers. This would have precluded the admission of diverse civilizational, religious or cultural patterns by the colonial societies. What may have prevailed is the co-existence of separate models and functions, according to their status of European women or local women. It is difficult to conceive of European men incorporating distinct civilizational notions into Western matrimonial and female standards, even though they themselves could enjoy the advantages of assimilating with freer customs and lesser social and religious control of their sexual behaviour. They enjoyed liaisons with local women frequently and openly, maintaining strong emotional ties with them. Moreover, they also legally adopted some of the children resulting from such unions and included the women in their family structure, whether as concubines or lawful wives. Take, for example, the strategy of miscegenation promoted in India by Afonso de Albuquerque through mixed marriages. Nonetheless, they certainly did not change their mental representation of the ideal female status.

In the East, maintaining the standards of behaviour identical to those back home was documented in the accounts of seventeenth century travellers, notably by Tavernier,[41] J. Albert de Mandelslo[42] and François Pyrard de Laval.[43] Tavernier says that '... the Portuguese living in India are the most vengeful and jealous in the world. If they have the slightest suspicion about their wives, they get rid of them without the least scruple, with either poison or the knife'.[44] And Mandelslo observes that 'You do not see many Portuguese or half-caste women wandering around the city, and when they do go out, it is to church or to pay any visits they need, they are carried in closed litters or accompanied and watched over by so many slaves that it is impossible to speak to them'.[45]

These views, relating to the high social levels of Europeans in Goa, contrasted to some degree with the roles women played as identified by several historical accounts. One of these was a poetic narration by Francisco de Andrade about the first and second sieges of Diu, in which female characters were exalted for their heroic deeds, albeit of a warlike nature,[46] and the same happened in times of war in the Moroccan garrisons. Women were, thus, important agents of colonization and should also be recognized as agents of connection between different worlds, even if usually forgotten by historiography.

Sailors, pilots, captains, priests and bishops, missionaries, merchants, adventurers and women thus took part in this heterogeneous world. Some stayed and died in that same universe which took them in and absorbed them, some returned, bringing with them material and mental representations.

The Vila do Conde case study confirms precisely this framework, with particular emphasis on the protagonist role of seamen and merchants. However, captains and soldiers, administrative, financial and judicial officers, as well as missionaries, also provide well-documented examples of Vila do Conde agents responsible for the transference of cultural and material representations of the East into the Western world. Among them, the performances of Fr. João de Vila do Conde, a famous Franciscan monk, as well as those of priests and bishops, namely D. João Ribeiro Gaio, bishop of Malacca, can be highlighted.[47] The dominance belongs, however, to the community of seafarers. In Vila do Conde, a famous example is Gaspar Manuel, a major pilot on the India route, but there are many other references in local documents. They were prominent and seemingly wealthy members of the community, though exceptions were also shown.[48]

The settlement of people from Vila do Conde in the East arose not only from individual presence and temporary stays, but also from emigration dynamics, although not necessarily on a large scale. The difficulties of studying Portuguese overseas emigration in the sixteenth and seventeenth centuries result from a lack of consecutive, consistent documentation. In spite of these limitations, some references persist. One could take the example of Amador Carvalho, a resident of Cochin. He was the illegitimate son of a cleric, Father Aires de Carvalho, and he emigrated as a young, unmarried man. By the time of his death, however, he had built up a large family in Malabar, where he had set up business.[49]

Even when they never returned, these men were all involved in material and cultural transference, processes with significant impacts on local societies, such as Vila do Conde, namely through their donations, letters and wills. Some of those testimonies in this town, which was deeply involved in overseas dynamics through navigation, trade, emigration and evangelization, will be examined. The profile of this micro-cosmos will also be characterized, as connected to a macro-cosmos, a global world, through networks and mechanisms of connection and transference of people, goods, information and wealth. This is one singular paradigmatic example of how these dynamics structurally framed the Early Modern Age in Portugal and Europe, giving real meaning to the expression 'First Global Age'.

People, Commodities, Material Culture and Aesthetical Patterns: The East and the Far East in Vila do Conde

The community under study, despite its almost insignificant territorial and demographic dimensions, achieved prominent projection and visibility during the fifteenth and sixteenth centuries, based on the processes and dynamics of private initiative and self-organized networks. The village, a seaport located 30 km. north of Porto, was characterized by a limited number of people. The population fluctuated between 3,600 and 5,000 inhabitants in the period between 1500 and 1640, corresponding to 0.32 per cent of the national population estimate in the 1527/1532 census. With a negligible territorial implantation and authority (the municipality did not possess practically any agricultural landscape, did not exceed 8 sq. km. in administrative boundaries and had only 0.5 sq. km. of effective urban occupation), this community had minimal financial resources and economic power; a socio-economic structure in which maritime and merchant groups prevailed (in 1568 almost 60 per cent of the population was involved in overseas trade and transportation, shipbuilding and other associated industries, according to a municipal tax roll), and in which the presence of the nobility was not allowed, and thus, was exceptional. Surrounded by a river of limited navigability, and by three of the most important municipalities in north-west Portugal, which enabled its hinterland projection, the sea became its geographical and economic way of life.[50]

This small world, lacking significant human, political or financial resources, achieved national and international prominence, taking advantage of highly favourable conjunctural dynamics. In fact, the particular conditions created by Portuguese overseas expansion in the fifteenth and sixteenth centuries were bound to have a significant impact on seaside communities, expanding their role and participation, at the same time as they shaped and structured their internal dynamics.

From an economic point of view, one can report the prevalence of naval logistics and industries in Vila do Conde: shipbuilding, rope and sail industries, a significant naval fleet (one of the most important in terms of transportation capacity at a national level) and a maritime community (in the sixteenth century, 1,664 seamen were identified in the period analysed: 1,109 sailors and 555 pilots and shipmasters). It was also a village where a socio-professional structure linked to maritime transport and trade prevailed; an economic universe dominated by capital flow, imbued with capitalist mentalities and mechanisms, albeit operating on a small scale; a business system governed by small capital investments, small partnerships in which even women figured as investors.[51]

Overseas emigration also emerged as a structuring dimension, from the last quarter of the sixteenth century, figuring as an answer to local difficulties which resulted from the failure of traditional investments in navigation and maritime transportation, at a time when the overseas Portuguese empire was affected by a structural crisis, and facing new and aggressive European competitors.

In order to measure, on a Portuguese scale, the relative weight of this community, whether in human resources or maritime logistics, a comparison can be attempted between the weight of the village in demographic and maritime terms, taking into consideration the number of seamen, and the naval fleet (see Maps 11.1 to 11.6). The representation of its main destinations of navigation, trade and emigration (see Maps 11.7 to 11.9) also indicates an overall prominence overseas, whether in the Atlantic Islands, Africa, Brazil or the Spanish Indies. Even if the East and Far East are included among the destinations mapped, their representativeness would, nevertheless, be underrated due to a lack of sources able to identify the real involvement in those circuits. In this domain, the major impact of the devastation of the archive of the *Casa da Índia*, as a result of the Lisbon earthquake of 1755 has to be stressed. The effects of the destruction of these sources on the lack of data regarding the navigation and trade to the East and Far East are undeniable. As those circuits of navigation and trade were under the absolute control of the *Casa da Índia*, an administrative, logistic, technical, customs and financial centre, controlled directly by the Crown, the municipal documental corpora only cover a partial and very fragmentary dimension of this reality. Nevertheless, those cannot be excluded from the study of global connections between the village under study and those different worlds.

The projection of Vila do Conde overseas through navigation, trade, emigration and evangelization was bound to have a major impact on this community, not only at an economic level, but also at the social, cultural and psychological ones.

Some specific references can be identified, in this small world, to the distant world that was to the Portuguese, 'India', or 'the Indias'. In the first place, this expression points to a vast and undetermined spatial universe which covered, without defined boundaries, the range of territories that were administered, managed or governed by the Portuguese Crown in the Indian Ocean and neighbouring seas, and the coastal territories from the Cape of Good Hope to Japan.[52] This territorial imprecision prevails throughout the data sources, only slightly reduced in accounts by those who knew, in fact and in person, those territories, and were able to mention, with precision, Bengal, Malacca, Goa, Kochi, China, Japan, Siam, Macau, or other territories. This is also the case of wills, notary records or other documents which required accuracy for official reasons. These references are, however, a minority in our sources, when compared to the perception of that global universe known as the 'Indias'.

This mental perception of the area contrasts with a very precise image of the East: it emerges as the utopian and wonderful world of wealth, fortune and prosperity. From India, money was supposed to arrive for dowries, funding to avoid family bankruptcies, donations to build churches, hospitals, chapels. A journey to India was usually taken as an opportunity to increase wealth and fame, even when it ended, as was often the case, in death. In the second half of the sixteenth century, particularly from the 1570s on, the number of compulsory recruitments for the India-bound 'armadas', the repeated cases of desertion, the cruelty of the punishments dealt to deserters, and the exceptional measures taken by royal orders to guarantee the constitution of crews on that route, which even included suspending criminal sentences during a round trip to India, are eloquent testimony to the difficulties, the risks and the resistance of seamen to embarking for the East, seen as a journey of increasing dangers, which were aggravated by Dutch and British privateering. Despite the inherent danger, during this period, the 'Indias' were mostly seen as lands of opportunity, from whence came highly valued products onto the market.

Actually, Vila do Conde received textiles from the East, particularly drapery,[53] along with spices,[54] precious stones and gold and silver items.[55] There was also musk from Macau and China—a good indicator of the reach of the trade engaged in by merchants from the town in places as distant as the Far East.[56] Mention of goods from the East in the town's daily life went beyond these references, however, and its material culture was infused with invocations to that distant world. A simple inventory of occurrences identified in large and heterogeneous documental corpora will suffice to point out the multiple reflections of that distant world in Vila do Conde.

Undertaking a painstaking diagnosis of the true extent of this phenomenon is not an easy task. Three sources were mainly used for this purpose, the results of which are necessarily fragmentary: notary records referring to trading ventures, wills and *post-mortem* property inventories.

The first group gives testimonies mainly related to circulating products. In the first place, these were dyestuffs, widely used in the textile industry, with pastel and saffron as the most important. Cotton, as a raw material for the same industry, was an essential part of cargoes from Brazil, but it also came from the East, as tissue, especially from the second half of the sixteenth century onward.[57]

Spices could also be found and were frequently mentioned. Pepper, cinnamon and mustard were, along with Brazilian sugar, essentials. The presence of seamen from Vila do Conde on the crews of the Cape Route assured them parcels of eastern spices, according to the 'quintalada' system.[58] Even though these were mostly sold in Lisbon, in the 'Casa da Índia', some still found their way to the crews' hometowns. Also identified as items sent to people in Vila do Conde, and eventually traded by them, were precious stones from the East—rubies, crystals, as well as musk, a highly prized perfume, regarded as genuine treasure, considering the high price it fetched in Western markets.[59]

And then, there were the silks, china, drapery and tapestries, all of them being traded by the townspeople, as well. These, along with exotic woods and oriental furniture, were repeatedly recorded in wills and post-mortem inventories. It is easy to perceive their social and economic value, which explains why they were so sought after, to the point of being subject to dispute in the division of property. One inventory states that '. . . the taker did not choose any of the items that they had inventoried and only asked the experts to put in his pile one of the two existing bedsteads from India…'.[60] The same record says that one person '… took the finest pieces on the inventory such as the hunting blanket made from Indian tapestry and its banner….'.[61]

After the death of Antónia de Oliveira, the wife of a seaman and merchant, a bedspread from China valued at 8,000 *reais* was found among the goods that belonged to her.[62] Among the many items that she bequeathed, Maria da Costa left two chairs and a porcelain salt-cellar, both from India, to the *Misericórdia.*[63] A bedstead and two chests, all from India, were among the property inventoried of João Gonçalves Marinho, a pilot.[64] Among the many items inventoried after the death of Manuel Barbosa de Sá, one can find a banner, a finely-embroidered hunting blanket, a silk tapestry, two large chests, a bedstead and half a dozen plates, all of which were said to have come from India.[65]

There are more references to articles of everyday use, which came from overseas, in the inventory taken after the death of Catarina Henriques, the daughter of a merchant. They range from allusions to actual precious and semi-precious stones to textiles, pottery and even to the furniture. But the items most often mentioned are textiles, grouped as garments for personal use and those for domestic wear. Among the semi-precious stones one finds jasper, set in gold or silver, and corals, which could have come from either the Atlantic or Eastern oceans. Their listed worth clearly show how much they were valued in Portugal.[66] In terms of textiles, there are references to towels from India and mention of damask mantillas and doublets.[67] Finally, this vast trousseau was kept in three large chests and one small one, all from India.[68]

The same variety, but in items of furniture, household and personal garments and crockery, can be found among the property left on the death of Luísa Correia, widow of Francisco Rodrigues Correia, a pilot on the India Route. It was this link to the Cape Route that surely must have determined the huge list of articles from the East, which is by far the longest of all those examined. Towels, bedspreads, banners and fabrics that were said to have come from India, as well as an Indian cloth headdress, stand out from the articles mentioned. The list of furniture is also long. There was a bed, a bedstead, three large chests and a small one, three high-backed chairs, a safe, and two mats. Two vases, maybe from China, and finally 20 porcelain bowls round off the references.[69]

The inventory of Simão Afonso de Faria, another pilot on the same route, included a bedstead and tapestry, which was said to be from India.[70] Finally, going back to the articles of public usage, it was mentioned that, among the goods left to the *Misericórdia* by Antónia Machada de Castro, wife of João Carneiro, another pilot, were '... a banner of Indian cut that the deceased used to borrow to cover the image of Christ of the Stations of the Cross...'.[71]

An unusual information, included in an Inquisition proceeding, relating to a New Christian from the town, who hanged herself, in despair at her imprisonment, using a piece of cloth from India, could also be noticed.[72]

References to items coming from 'India' clearly predominate the list of goods, 'India' being synonymous with the East in the sixteenth century economic mindset. This generic designation was applied, also, to wider areas which included China or even Japan. This was especially true in the case of tapestry/drapery and porcelain.

Other 'commodities' were also evocative of these other anthropological worlds. We identify a son of Manuel Ribeiro and grandson of the bishop of Malacca, D. João Ribeiro Gaio, who was identified as a 'balo'. He was, most probably, a young man of Malayan ancestry, almost certainly the offspring of a relationship between Manuel Ribeiro, the bishop's son, and a Malay woman. Alongside this freeman, who nonetheless had always to carry a letter of freedom, required because of his skin colour, so that he would not be confused with and treated as a slave,[73] there were references to actual slaves. Those coming from the East were, nevertheless, a minority in the overall number of slaves in the town. However, from the ethnic point of view, the details found are sufficient to show that many Eastern ethnic groups were among the slaves who came to Portugal, although black Africans clearly predominated.[74]

The contact with other civilizations and the valourization of the materials or aesthetic values of these various regions led to the introduction of items of personal, household and public utility into the daily life of the town, leaving a permanent mark on its material culture. But, on the other hand, living the risks linked to the overseas experience, maritime voyages, storms and piracy left an indelible mark on devotional and religious practices as well. In addition to the specific religious manifestations of the seafarers, like *ex-votos*, votive panels whose maritime nature evoked miracles that happened on sea voyages, especially those associated with storms and shipwrecks,[75] there are other manifestations to be mentioned. Practices of devotion to Our Lady, celebrated on the behalf of men that were absent overseas, are striking evidence with of this social universe.[76]

Other displays of devotion, exacerbated by the dangers of overseas journeys can be documented too: the bequests and the building of chapels by individuals involved in maritime expeditions, trade and emigration in the East deserves mention. These legacies played an active part in the town's architectural framework. The building of a chapel in the church of the *Misericórdia*, for instance, dating from 1578, was paid for by Sebastião Álvares da Fonseca, '... who was a resident in this town and died in India ordered his money and wealth be used to build it',[77] as well as its rebuilding; this budgeted in 1599 at 7,00,000 *reais,* was paid with capital coming in from India.[78] The church of the *Misericórdia* was itself largely funded by donations from Jerónimo Veloso, Prior of Seixo Amarelo, a cleric who saw his savings grow through commercial investments related to the East.

The substantial legacy of Amador Carvalho, who lived in Cochin with his family, is another example of generous assets amassed in the East. He left his property, the Quinta do Torno, to the town's Misericórdia, and various sums of money to relatives living in and around Vila do Conde.[79] Carvalho left an enormous fortune. In addition to real estate, including the above-mentioned, there were donations to religious institutions amounting to around 400 *xerafins*, 300 *patacões* and 10 *pardaos*, besides bequests to lay people, family members and servants, totalling 300,000 *reais* and 100 *xerafins*. Among his assets in Cochin were four houses, a large amount of silver, jewels, gold pieces and nine or ten slaves.[80] Finally there is the donation, made during his life by Belchior de Figueiredo, coming from India 'where he spent many years', to the sum of 900,000 *reais*. This latter donation suggests the acquisition of a vast fortune— a fact confirmed by a series of investments in real estate in the town and the countryside, which he looked after on his return.[81]

The circumstances portrayed indicate everyday practices, but also point to the regular sending of assets and legacies from the East, through transfer from one *Misericórdia* to another of the assets for remittance, with Lisbon being the epicentre.

Other significant legacies recorded include those for social purposes, especially through inheritances and dowries. But being in the East also meant drama and death: there are plentiful references to the deaths of mariners, alongside the many difficulties encountered in collecting their property. The many powers of attorney issued for this purpose, entered in notary records, are proof of this. Isabel Fernandes, wife of João Folgueira, a merchant, issued a power of attorney to residents in Goa so that they could receive from the treasury of the deceased all the property and wages left on the death of her father, Álvaro Fernandes Galhão, a pilot who died in Bengal.[82]

An entry from 1605 shows that Maria Álvares Sanches, widow of Pedro Álvares Pombeiro, a pilot on the India Route, issued a power of attorney to Manuel Cardoso, living in Cochin, to collect a rosary made of rubies worth 64,800 *reais*, which her late husband was bringing in the *Rosário*, the ship on which he had sailed from India to Lisbon.

In that same year, the administrator of the *Misericórdia* in Vila do Conde issued a power of attorney to Roque Godins Malafaia, so that he could collect 105,000 *reais* from the administrator and friars of the Lisbon *Misericórdia*. This sum had come from Cochin via Bartolomeu Veloso, a resident in that city. A power of attorney was also needed to collect the money left on the death of Manuel Teixeira, the son of a Vila do Conde resident.[83]

The same administrator, who held the power of attorney of residents of a farming hamlet in Vila do Conde, heirs of João Carvalho, who had died in Cochin, issued a new power of attorney so that he could receive the property left on the death of João Carvalho, of which the sum of 10,000 *reais* was to be given to the Misericórdia's poor.[84]

Another power of attorney was issued by the administrator and friars of the Vila do Conde Misericórdia, as heirs to the assets of Amador Carneiro, a pilot on the India Route, to the administrator and friars of the Cochin Casa da Misericórdia, to collect the belongings of the deceased pilot. The same power of attorney was issued to Francisca Carneira, his wife and heir of the other half of the property.[85]

Margarida Medela, widow of Francisco António, a shipbuilding officer, issued a power of attorney to the administrator and friars of the Malacca Casa da Misericórdia and residents in Cochin, for them to receive the assets left on the death of her husband, who was buried in Santo António de Malacca, leaving 100 *patacas*. Incidentally, the money was to be sent via the *Misericórdias* of Goa and Lisbon.[86]

Helena da Cruz, an avowed nun in the Santa Clara Monastery of Vila do Conde, widow, and her daughter, Maria Álvares da Costa, issued a power of attorney to the administrator and friars of the Goa Casa da Misericórdia, so that they could send to Portugal the money left by Manuel da Costa, who died in India. The money was to be sent through investment in goods and merchandise which were divided up and shipped on several vessels.[87]

Maria Jácome, wife of António Afonso, a blacksmith, issued a power of attorney to Manuel Fernandes Carneiro and Francisco Gonçalves, two pilots, so that they could collect 180,000 *reais* from the Goa or Cochin *Misericórdias*. This money had belonged to Pedro da Cunha who had died on a voyage from Malacca to India.[88]

These are just a few of the records of official deeds that united two distant worlds linked by pecuniary and material interests, embodied in the goods left there which reverted to the relatives of those who had died.

Another important social function was fulfilled by the dowries that relied on or made use of goods sent by people from Vila do Conde living overseas. In 1586 Beatriz da Costa, widow of Cristóvão Ribeiro, a pilot, issued a power of attorney to Amador Carneiro, a pilot on the India Route, so that he could collect, from the executors of the will or heirs of Amador Carvalho, her cousin, the 200 *cruzados* that he had left to her in his will for her daughters' dowries.[89]

Similarly, in 1591 Beatriz da Costa issued an identical power of attorney for the collection of the sum of 200 *cruzados* which Amador Carvalho had left her in his will.[90]

In 1596, Isabel de Mariz Pinheira, widow of Dr Francisco Carneiro da Costa, a former appellate judge from the crown, appointed her daughter, Margarida, in the factory of Malacca, which was granted by royal provision for three years after the death of her husband, to help with the marriage of one of her daughters.[91]

D. João Ribeiro Gaio, bishop of Malacca, was one of the main driving forces in this area. In 1580, Beatriz de Couros sought to collect 400 *cruzados* he sent as dowry for the wedding or entry into a religious life of one of her daughters.[92] And then again, in 1592, she gave Mecia Carneira, her daughter, 6,000 *cruzados*, 3,000 of which were donated by D. João.[93] He had also appeared as guarantor of another dowry in 1576, for Maria Folgueira, daughter of Manuel Gaio Folgueira, worth more than 700,000 *reais.*[94]

In all, these agents, whether absent or deceased in the East, allowed the interaction between local everyday life and the expectations of wealth acquired in this other world, the East, usually synonymous with India.

To conclude the discussion on the presence of the East in a community based on a maritime economy and on seafaring experiences, which were determining factors in the case studied, a final domain should be considered: that related to urban space and architectural features.[95] Since this village's rise to prominence was directly connected to the sea as well as to maritime capital and trade, the Vila do Conde of today is necessarily a reflection of its golden age: the era of sixteenth century overseas expansion.

If one walks through the centre of Vila do Conde, today, there are urban signs of that era at every turn: the town hall was built in that century, as were the customs house, the watermills, the quays; the defence structures—its maritime fortification; the *Misericórdia* House; the Hospital; as well as the most important manorial houses. Those which remain, characterize the urban fabric and bring out the aesthetic patterns of the Manueline style.

The design of the Chapel of Our Lady of Succour, dedicated to the Virgin of Safe Journeys (Nª Srª da Boa Viagem), was inspired by the pagodas in India and erected on the initiative of Gaspar Manuel, who paid for it all himself. His name was associated with the East, both as a pilot on the India Route and as an author of navigation route manuals, mentioned earlier. It is, in fact, symptomatic that he should have chosen Our Lady of Succour or Safe Journeys as a hagiographic referent for invocation, and that he should have introduced aesthetic standards from other places of worship—the eastern pagodas—into the religious architecture.

If one focuses on religious buildings, the cathedral, the church of *Misericórdia*, the São Francisco Monastery, the chapel of Socorro, built by a pilot on the India Route, the Seamen's Chapel or the São Roque Chapel emerge as detached examples. All were built in that golden age, with public and private capital provided by the maritime and overseas expansion, and

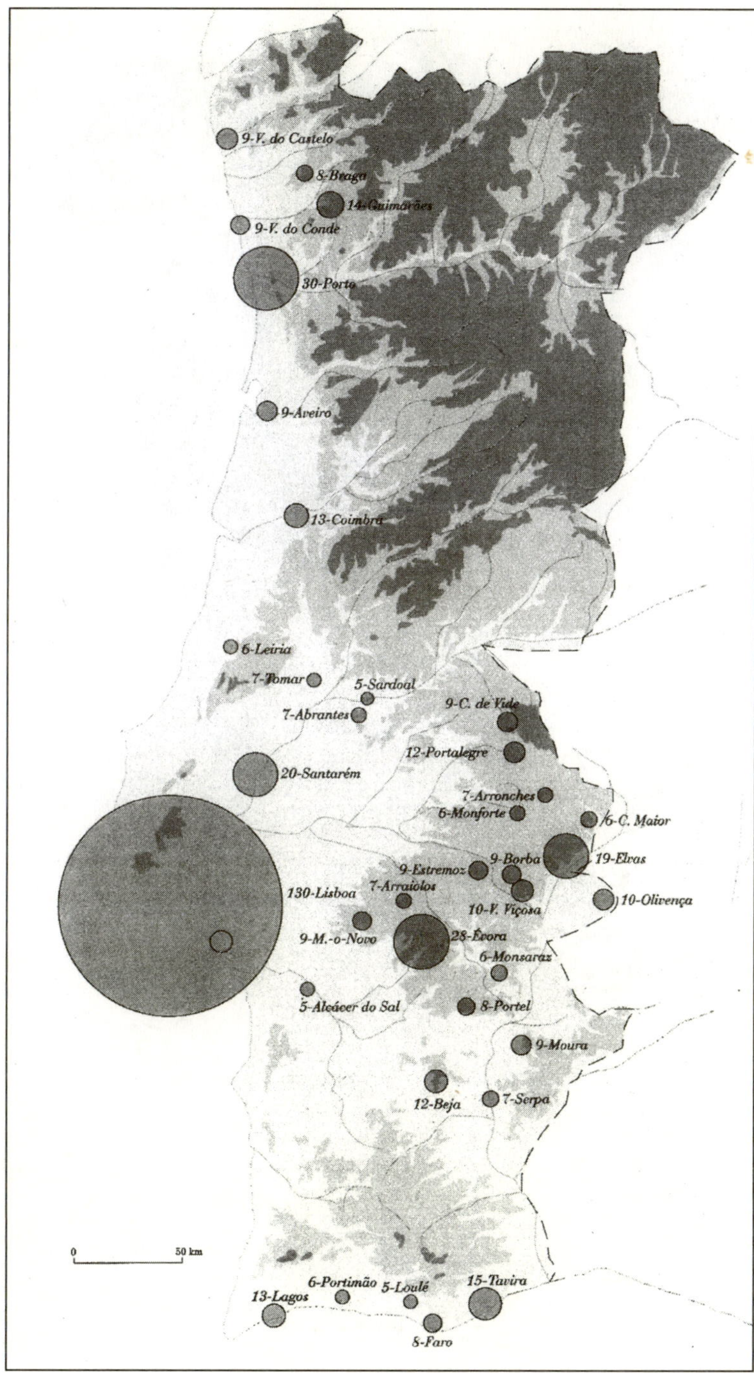

MAP 11.1: Population Distribution in main Portuguese Ports (1527-32)

Source: Mattoso, José, dir., *História de Portugal*, vol. III, Lisboa, 1993, p. 232.

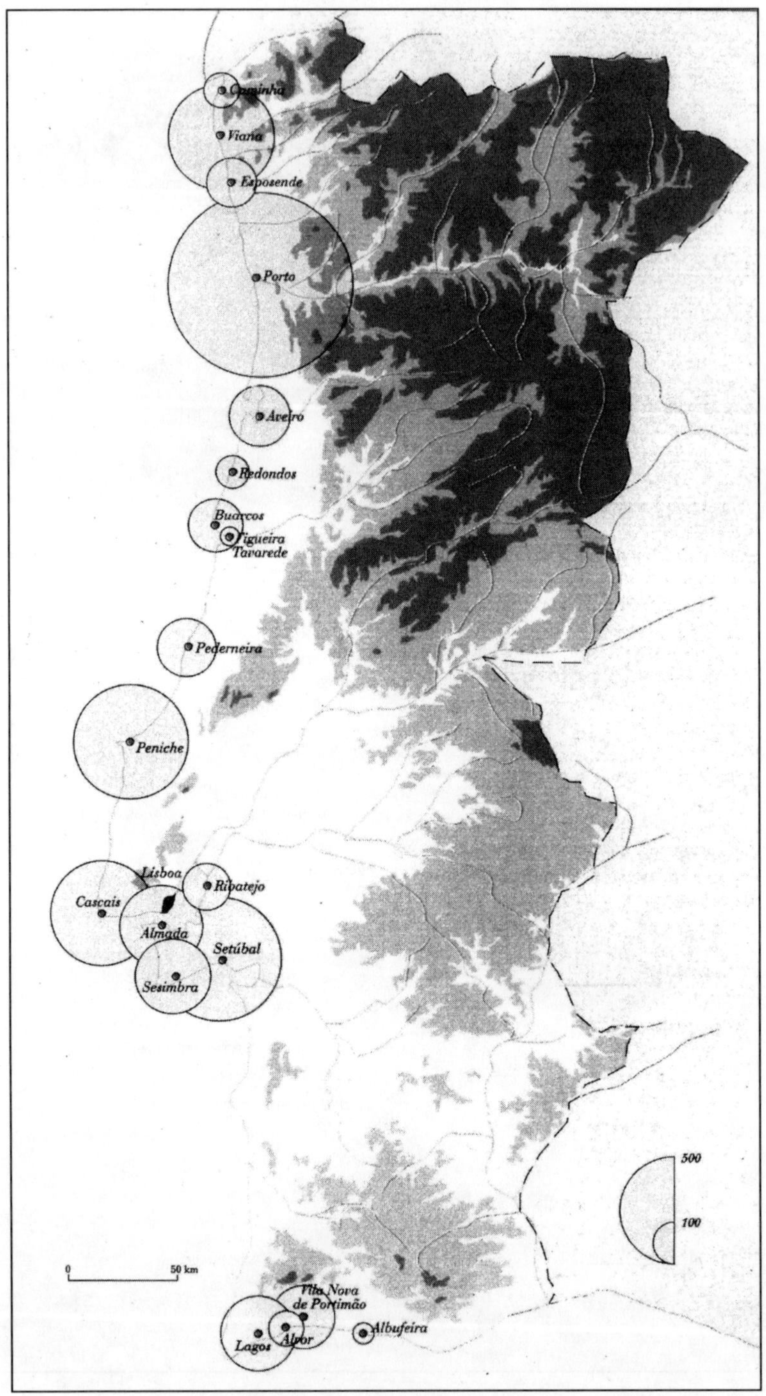

MAP 11.2: Distribution of Seafaring Communities in 1620

Source: Mattoso, José, dir., *História de Portugal*, vol. III, Lisboa, 1993, p. 239.

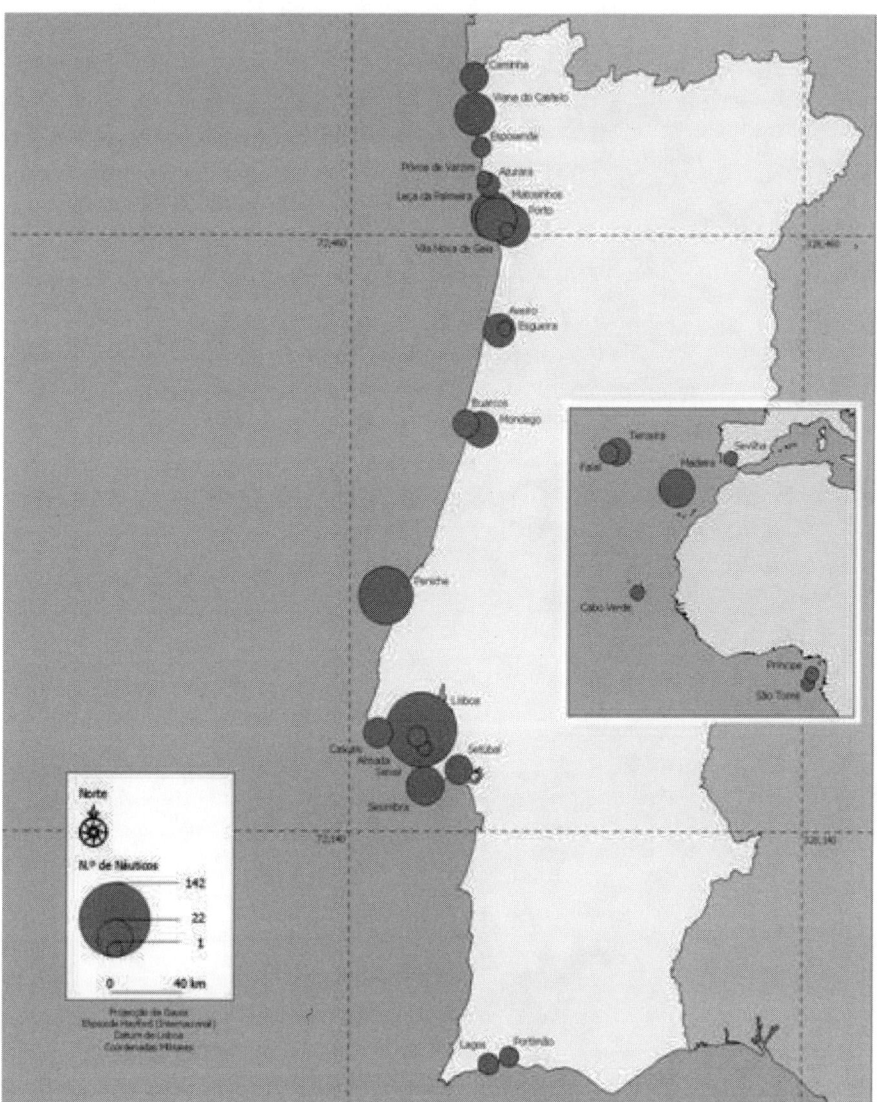

MAP 11.3: Nautical Examination of Pilots, 'Sotapilots' and Shipmasters between 1596 and 1648

Source: Polónia, Amélia, *Expansão e Descobrimentos numa perspectiva local. O porto de Vila do Conde no século XVI*, vol. 1, Lisboa, 2007, p. 442.

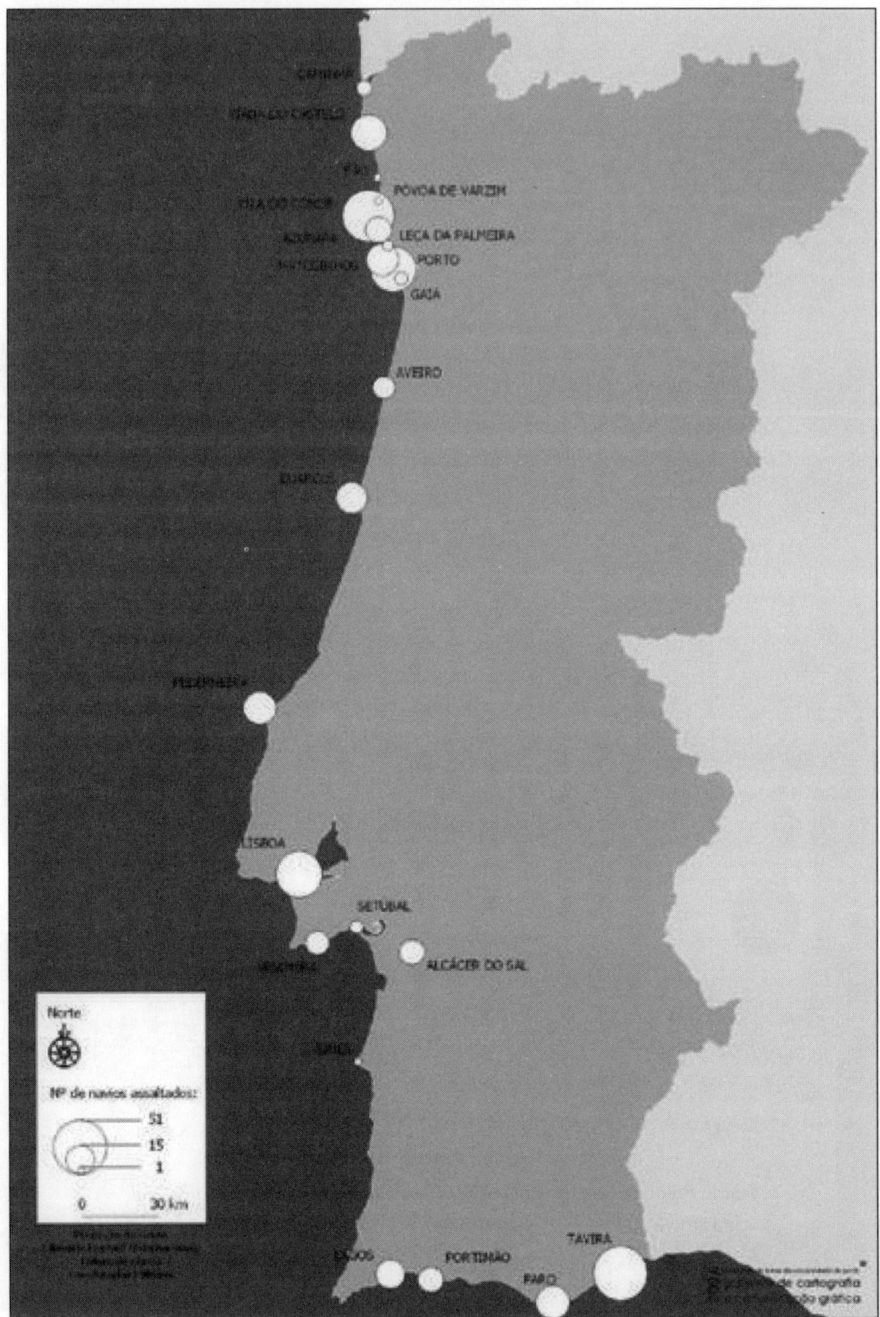

MAP 11.4: Ships Attacked by French Privateers (1508-38): Distribution by Seaports of Register

Source: Polónia, Amélia, *Expansão e Descobrimentos numa perspectiva local. O porto de Vila do Conde no século XVI*, vol. 1, Lisboa, 2007, p. 372.

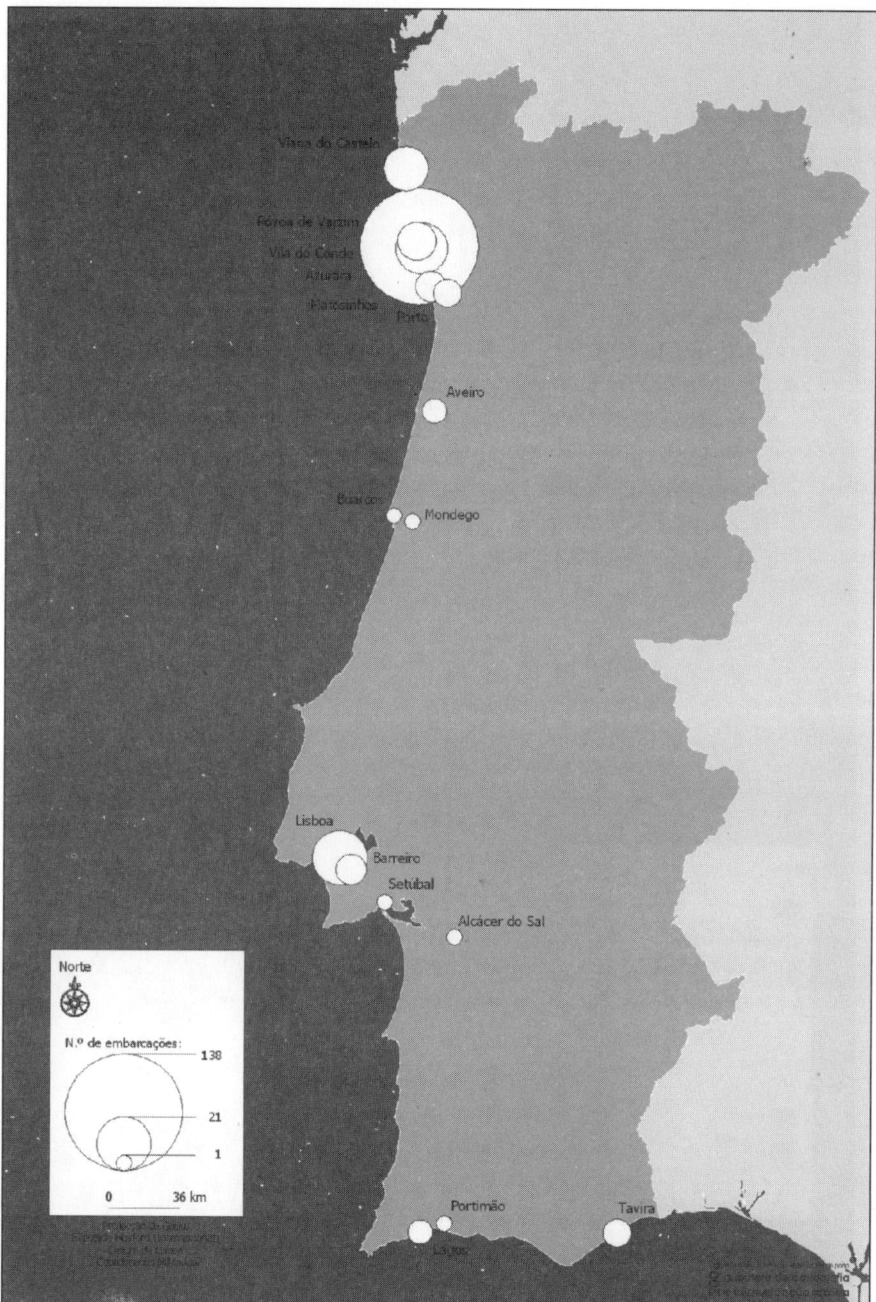

MAP 11.5: Portuguese Naval Fleet Registered in the Portuguese House of Antwerp (1535-51 and 1565-70): Distribution by Port of Origin

Source: Polónia, Amélia, *Expansão e Descobrimentos numa perspectiva local. O porto de Vila do Conde no século XVI*, vol. 1, Lisboa, 2007, p. 374.

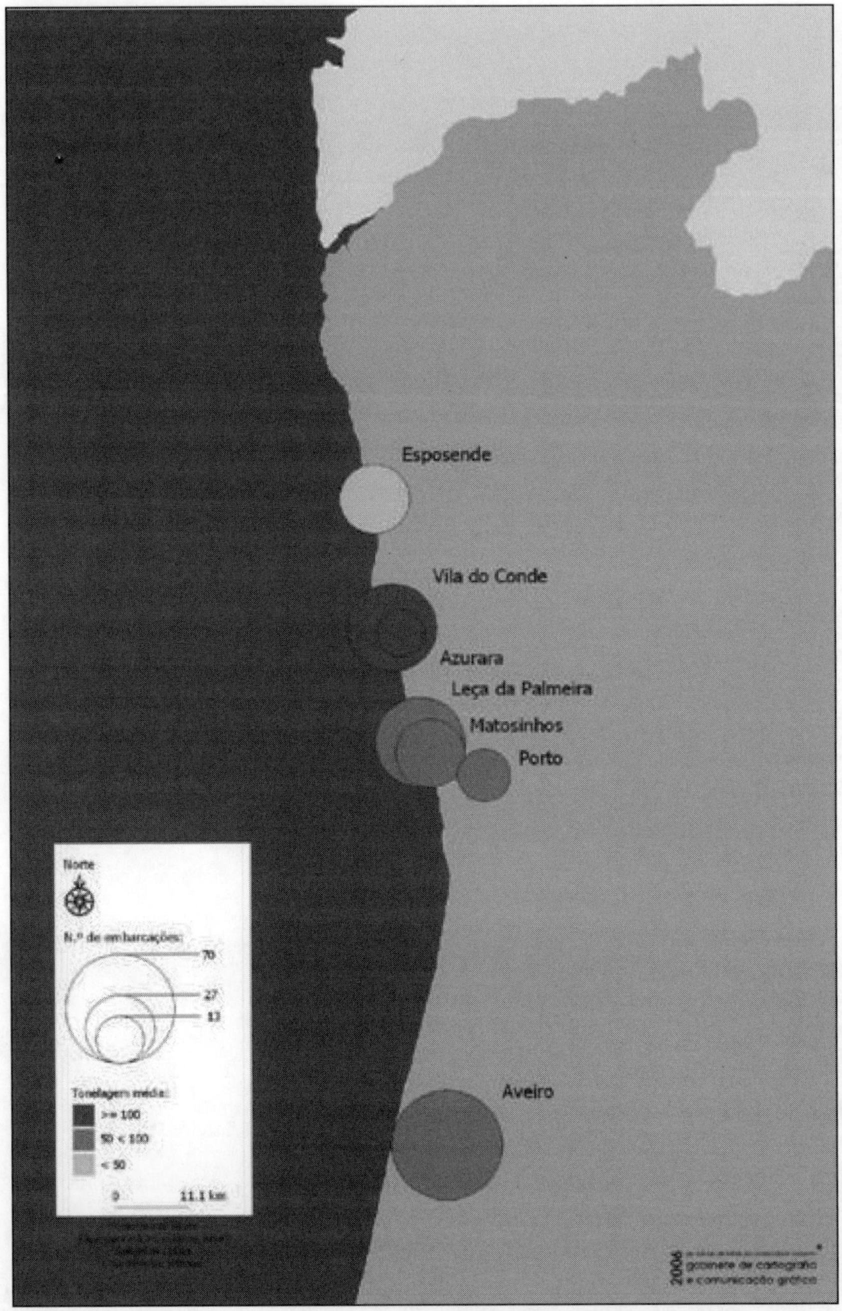

MAP 11.6: Portuguese Naval Fleet Registered in the Naval Census of 1552

Source: Polónia, Amélia, *Expansão e Descobrimentos numa perspectiva local. O porto de Vila do Conde no século XVI*, vol. 1, Lisboa, 2007, p. 387.

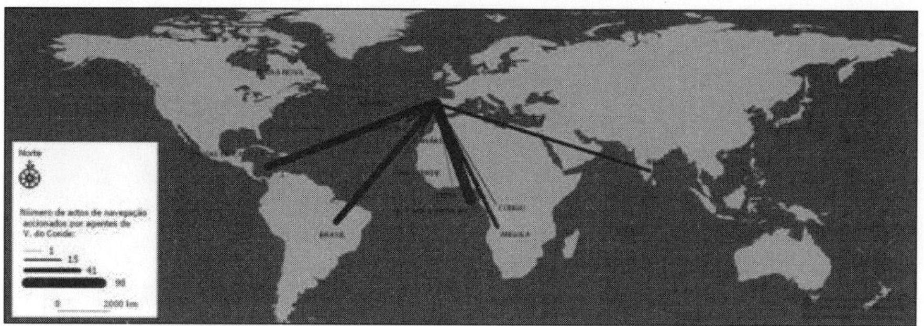

MAP 11.7: Vila do Conde: Navigation Destinations (1560-1620)

Source: Polónia, Amélia, *Expansão e Descobrimentos numa perspectiva local. O porto de Vila do Conde no século XVI*, vol. 2, Lisboa, 2007, p. 38.

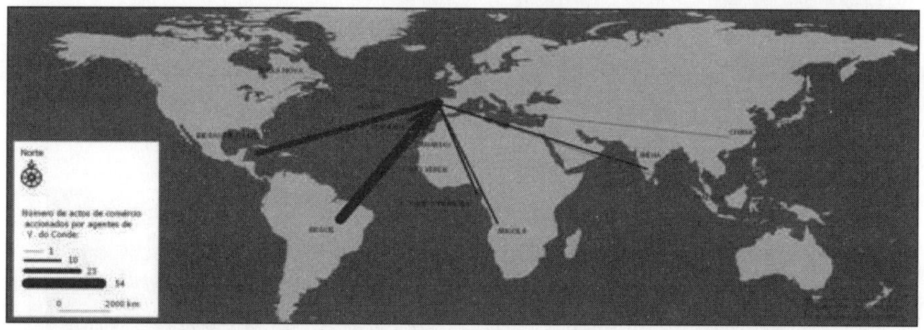

MAP 11.8: Vila do Conde: Circuits of Trade (1560-1620)

Source: Polónia, Amélia, *Expansão e Descobrimentos numa perspectiva local. O porto de Vila do Conde no século XVI*, vol. 2, Lisboa, 2007, p. 176.

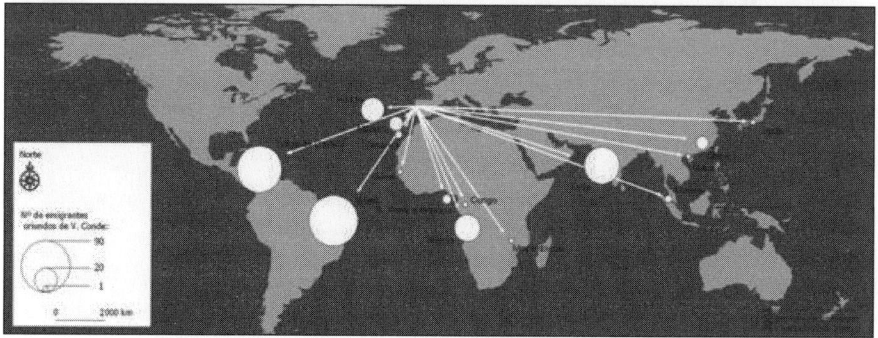

MAP 11.9(A): Vilo do Conde: Emigration Flows

Source: Polónia, Amélia, *Expansão e Descobrimentos numa perspectiva local. O porto de Vila do Conde no século XVI*, vol. 2, Lisboa, 2007, pp. 242-3.

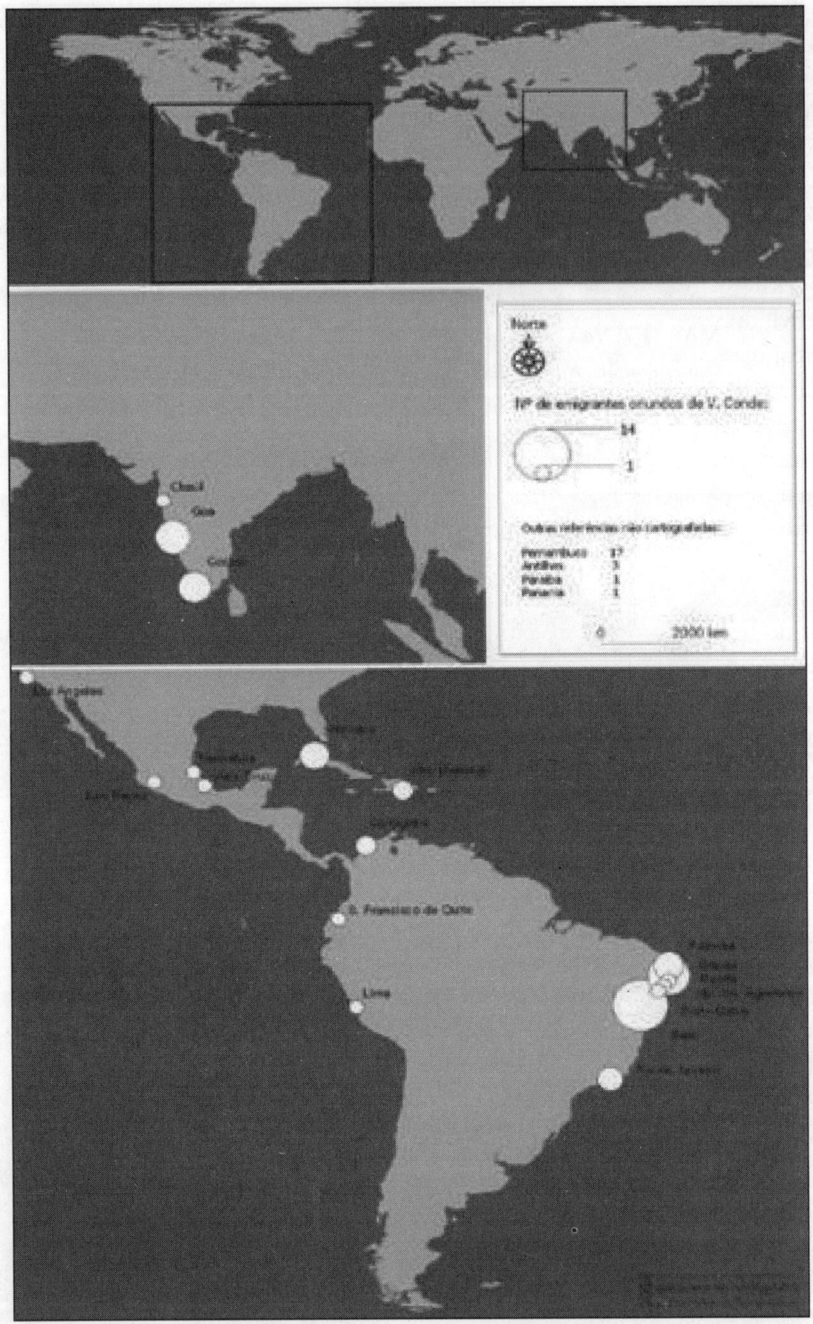

MAP 11.9(B): Vila Do Conde: Emigration Flows

Source: Polónia, Amélia, *Expansão e Descobrimentos numa perspectiva local. O porto de Vila do Conde no século XVI*, vol. 2, Lisboa, 2007, pp. 242-3.

by the enterprise of numerous agents of Portuguese shipping and overseas trade.

Vila do Conde's layout is thus the reflection of a lifestyle whose roots were deeply connected with maritime experiences and maritime financial resources, which proves the determinism of its overseas prominence in the development of this community.

To sum up, the East and Far East were seen in Vila do Conde through a special lens and filtered by the written and oral representations of people who knew and described these regions according to their own experience, knowledge and particular adventures. This 'other world', that was, for the Portuguese, the Indian subcontinent, South-East Asia and the Far East, located at various levels in the material, spiritual and religious antipodes of Westerners, was, indeed, present in the daily life of this, and many other small maritime communities in sixteenth century Portugal, through the actual, lived memory of people who had been in direct contact with that world and who were part of the formal and informal networks which established points and paths of connection and reciprocal cultural transfers. It was present in the artefacts which embodied palpable references to that world. It was present through the images constructed by those who, remaining behind, never ceased to connect themselves, from a local settlement, to a global world. This world was represented in very different, diverse, distorted and fanciful ways through distinct material and symbolic referents. This was the East of each individual, built according to the elements available in his or her own mental store of tools.

NOTES

1. For Europeans, the East (Near East) refers to relatively nearby lands of the Ottoman Empire, and Far East to countries along the western Pacific Ocean as well as along the Eastern Indian Ocean. Far East is a not term used in the sixteenth century documental corpora. On the other hand, the 'East' is a consensual categorization applied to territories placed east from the Cape of Good Hope. The East was mostly equivalent to India. The Far East not being used as a category, documents refer to China, Macau and Japan in a quite imprecise way when referring to the territories known as 'Far East' from the nineteenth century onward.
2. Robert Chartier, *A história cultural entre práticas e representações*, Lisboa: Difel, 1988.
3. *Misericórdias* were charitable institutions founded in Portugal at the end of the fifteenth century by laymen, and protected by the Crown, which became very important centres of social dynamics. They were established all over the Portuguese kingdom, as well as in overseas territories under the rule of the Portuguese Crown.

4. David Ringrose, *Europeans Abroad, 1400–1700: Strangers in Not-so-Strange Lands.* Available at <http://www.iga.ucdavis.edu/Research/All-UC/conferences/2006-fall/Ringrose.pdf>.
5. Fernão Mendes Pinto (1509-83) sailed from Portugal on 11 March 1537 bound for India. According to his own testimony in *Peregrinação*, Mendes Pinto claimed to have been shipwrecked, captured, and sold into slavery 16 or 17 times. The accuracy of his records is somewhat doubtful, the reality was a frequent mixture with fantastic and heroic narratives in his biography.
   Reaching the Portuguese headquarters of Goa, Mendes Pinto entered the service of the newly-appointed captain of Malacca on the coast of Malay. He arrived in Malacca in 1539 and worked for the captain of the fortress there as an emissary to the kingdoms of Sumatra and Malaya. He then went to Patani on the east side of the Malay Peninsula and started a thriving business trading with the Thais in Bangkok. Robbed by pirates, he and his partners got revenge by becoming pirates themselves. He then traded along the coast of Indochina. He was shipwrecked on the coast of China and sold as a slave to work on the Great Wall of China. Later, he became involved in the Burmese-Thai wars and wrote the first European account of Burmese history. From Thailand Mendes Pinto made his second trip to Japan where he landed in the port of Kagoshima. On his departure, he brought back a Japanese stowaway whom he handed over to St. Francis Xavier in Malacca and thus inspired Xavier's effort to travel to Japan and christianize the inhabitants. Sometime during these years in Asia, Mendes Pinto managed to accumulate a large fortune. He was a wealthy merchant when he made his third voyage to Japan in 1551, where Francis Xavier was installed at the court of one of the feudal lords of southern Japan. He gave Xavier the money to build the first Christian church in Japan.
   Mendes Pinto returned to Portugal on 22 September 1558. Sometime between the years 1569 and 1578 he wrote the book *Peregrinação* (*Peregrination*), unpublished until 1614. It was then translated into most Western languages and became a best-seller throughout Europe. However, it contained so many fantastic stories that it was considered to be a work of fiction. It was only as more information about the exotic lands he visited became available that the book was recognized to be largely (but not totally) factual. Mendes Pinto died on his estate on 8 July 1583, shortly after being awarded a small pension by the Portuguese government. Cf. <http://www.bookrags.com/biography/fernao-mendes-pinto/> and Pinto, Fernão Mendes in *Dicionário da Expansão Portuguesa*, vol. 2, Lisboa: Círculo de Leitores, 1994, pp. 904-6.
6. Luís de Camões, 1524?-80, a Portuguese poet, and one of the greatest figures in Portuguese literature. Born of a poor family, Camões gained wide familiarity with classical literature. Banished from court in 1546 because of a romance with an aristocratic lady, he served as a soldier in a Moroccan campaign, during which he lost an eye. After his return from Africa he was imprisoned in 1552 for wounding a minor court aide in a street fight. He was released the next year after consenting to serve in India. Apparently he had already begun his most celebrated work, *Os Lusiadas* (*The Lusiads*, sons of Lusus, i.e. the Portuguese), but this journey may have caused him to make Vasco da Gama's voyage over the

same route the central theme of his epic. After fighting in India, Camões was given an official post at Macao. In 1558 charges were brought against him for maladministration at Macao, and he was put aboard a ship for Goa in India. The ship was wrecked, but he managed to save his manuscript for *The Lusiads,* and he returned to Portugal in 1570 by way of Mozambique. The publication of his epic won him a small royal pension, and his work began to enjoy world fame. By 1655 it had appeared in English in a version by Sir Richard Fanshawe. The beauty of its poetry is enlivened by a vigorous and realistic narrative that embraces not only the voyage of Vasco da Gama but also much of Portuguese history. Apart from *The Lusiads,* however, Camões' flawlessly crafted sonnets and lyrics would have won him lasting fame. Cf. <http://www.encyclopedia.com/doc/1E1-Camoes.html> and Camões, Luís Vaz de in *Dicionário da Expansão Portuguesa,* vol. 1, Lisboa: Circulo de Leitores, 1994, pp. 182-3.

7. Garcia da Orta was born in Castelo de Vide, probably in 1501. His parents were Spanish Jews from Valencia de Alcántara who had taken refuge, as many others did, in Portugal at the time of the great expulsion of the Spanish Jews by the *Reyes Catolicos* Ferdinand and Isabella of Spain in 1492. Da Orta studied medicine, arts and philosophy at the Universities of Alcalá de Henares and Salamanca in Spain, graduated and returned to Portugal in 1523, two years after his father's death. He practiced medicine first in his hometown and from 1526 onwards in Lisbon, where he gained a professorship at the university in 1530. Perhaps fearing the increasing power of the Inquisition, and fortunately evading the ban on emigration of New Christians, he sailed for India in 1534 as Chief Physician aboard the fleet of the Viceroy Martim Afonso de Sousa. He travelled with the Viceroy on various campaigns, then, in 1538, settled at Goa, where he soon had a prominent medical practice. He was physician to Burhan Shah I of the Nizam Shahi dynasty of Ahmadnagar, and concurrently to several successive Portuguese Viceroys and governors of Goa: one of these granted him a lease of the island of Bombay, though he never lived there.

   In 1565 the Inquisition was introduced to the Indian Viceroyalty and a Tribunal (Inquisitorial Court) was opened in Goa. Active persecution against Jews, secret Jews, Hindus and New Christians began. Garcia himself died in 1568, apparently without having suffered seriously from this persecution, but his sister Catarina was arrested as a Jew in the same year and was burned at the stake for Judaism in Goa in 1569. Garcia himself was posthumously convicted of Judaism. His remains were exhumed and burned in an *auto da fé* (act of faith) in 1580.

   His remarkable knowledge of Eastern spices and drugs is revealed in his only known work, *Colóquios dos simples e drogas he cousas medicinais da Índia* (*Colloquia on the simples, drugs and medicinal substances of India*), published at Goa in 1563. He was the first European to describe Asiatic tropical diseases. Garcia de Orta revealed in his writings an unusual independence in face of the usually revered texts of ancient authorities, Greek, Latin and Arabic. His work was soon recognized across Europe when translations appeared in Latin (then the scientific lingua franca) and other languages. Large parts of it were included in a similar work published in Spanish in 1578 by Cristóvão da Costa (Cristobal Acosta), *Tractado de las drogas y medicinas de las Indias orientales* (*Treatise of the drugs and medicines of the East Indies*, Burgos, 1578. Cf. Orta, Garcia da in *Dicionário da Expansão Portuguesa*, vol. 2, pp. 837-8, and <http://en.wikipedia.org/wiki/Garcia_de_Orta>.

8. Cf. José Manuel Garcia, *A historiografia portuguesa dos descobrimentos e da expansão (séculos XV a XVII): Autores, obras e especializações memoriais,* Porto: [s.n.], 2006, 2 vols., Unpublished Ph.D. thesis presented at the University of Porto; Amélia Polónia, 'Os Descobrimentos na literatura impressa portuguesa do século XVI a partir do fundo da BPM, Colóquio Livros Impressos em Portugal no Século XVI' Porto: Biblioteca Pública Municipal do Porto, 5-6 May 2006, unpublished paper; Ana Paula Avelar, *Visões do Oriente: Formas de sentir no Portugal de Quinhentos*, Lisboa: Edições Colibri, 2003; Ana Paula Avelar, *Figurações da alteridade na cronística da expansão*, Lisboa: Universidade Aberta, 2003; Ana Paula Avelar, *Fernão Lopes de Castanheda: Historiador dos Portugueses na Índia ou cronista do governo de Nuno da Cunha?*, Lisboa: Cosmos, 1997.
9. Accounts of shipwrecks abound. They have been analysed in numerous publications. For example: Giulia Lanciani, *Os relatos de naufrágios na literatura portuguesa dos séculos XVI e XVII*, Lisboa: Instituto de Cultura Portugues, 1979; Giulia Lanciani, *Sucessos e naufrágios das naus portuguesas*, Lisboa: Caminho, 1997 and, Paulo Guinote, Eduardo Frutuso and António Lopes, *Naufrágios e outras perdas da 'Carreira da Índia': Séculos XVI e XVII*, Lisboa: CNCDP, 1998.
10. From the route guide literature, with reference to the East, one can quote the *Colecção de Roteiros para a India com uma derrota do estreito de Meca para a Judea*, by Manuel Álvares, or the famous routes of D. João de Castro, *Roteiro de Lisboa a Goa; Roteiro de Goa a Suez ou Roteiro do Mar Roxo*, *Roteiro de Goa a Diu.*
11. Fernanda Alegria, João Carlos Garcia and Francesc Relaño, 'Cartografia e Viagens', in *História da Expansão Portuguesa*, ed. Francisco Bettencourt and Kirti Chaudhuri, Lisboa: Círculo de Leitores, 1998, vol. 1, pp. 26-60.
12. Garcia da Orta, *Colóquios dos Simples e Drogas da Índia*, 2 vols., rpt, Lisboa: Imprensa Nacional, 1987.
13. D. João de Castro, *Tratado da Sphaera da geografia, notação famosa, informação sobre Maluco*, Lisboa: Agência Geral das Colónias, 1940.
14. Francisco Faleiro, *Tratado del esphera y del arte del marear con el regimieto de las alturas cõ alguas reglas nueuamete escritas muy necessarias,* 2nd edn, Madrid: [s.n.], 1980.
15. Cristóvão da Costa, *Tractado de las drogas, y medecinas de las Indias Orientales con sus Plantas debuxadas al biuo por Christoual Acosta medico y cirujano que las vio ocularmente: en el qual se verifica mucho de lo que escriuio el Doctor Garcia de Orta,* Burgos: [s.n.], 1578.
16. This was acknowledged by João de Lucena, *História da Vida de S. Francisco Xavier: E do que fizeram na Índia os mais religiosos da Companhia de Jesus*, Lisboa: [s.n.], 1600, p. 356. See Garcia, *A historiografia portuguesa dos descobrimentos e da expansão,* vol. 2, pp. 581-9.
17. For example, the letters of D. Manuel, sent to various popes and Castilian monarchs, telling them about the finding of the sea route to India, the discovery of Brazil and a number of conquests in the East. A considerable number of letters circulated in print, mostly in Latin, during the reign of D. Manuel, having

been published in Portugal and abroad between 1505 and 1521. Cf. Garcia, *A historiografia portuguesa dos descobrimentos e da expansão*, vol. 2, pp. 579–89.

18. The embassy sent by King D. Manuel I to Pope Leo X solemnly entered Rome on 12 March 1514, with Tristão da Cunha at its head. It included exotic animals and plants, as well as blacks and Indians.
19. Gil Vicente (1465–1536) is regarded as Portugal's greatest playwright, while also considered a renowned poet. He is often alluded to as the father of Portuguese theatre, or even of Iberian theatre, since he also wrote in Castilian, sharing this paternity of Iberian drama with Juan del Encina. Vicente's work is viewed as a reflection of the changing times and the shift from the Middle Ages to the Renaissance. It includes explicit references to the changes in Portuguese life brought about by the experiences of the discoveries and maritime expansion, notably in his Autos.
20. Jorge Borges de Macedo, *Os Lusíadas e a História*, Lisboa: Editorial Verbo, 1979, pp. 36-48.
21. Valentim Fernandes, also known as the German Valentim Fernandes or Valentim Fernandes of Moravia, was a German printer and translator from Moravia, who came to Lisbon in 1495, where he remained for 23 years. He gained renown as editor and translator of several classics, among which were the works of Marco Polo. Maintaining correspondence with several intellectuals and artists, among them Albrecht Dürer and Hieronymus Münzer, he sent news of the Portuguese discoveries to Germany.
22. Luís de Matos, *L'expansion portugaise dans la littérature latine de le Renaissance*, Paris: FCG-CCP, 1991; António Alberto Banha de Andrade, *Mundos novos do Mundo: Panorama da difusão pela Europa de notícias dos descobrimentos geográficos portugueses*, Lisboa: Junta de Investigações do Ultramar, 1972, 2 vols.; Joaquim Barradas de Carvalho, *A la recherche de la spécificité de la Rennaissance Portugaise: L'Esmeraldo de situ orbis de Duarte Pacheco Pereira et lsa litterature de voyages a l'epoque des grandes decouvertes: Contribution à l'étude de la pensée moderne,* 2 vols., Paris: Fondation Calouste Gulbenkian, Centre Culturel Portugais 1983.
23. Analysis based on the bibliographic repertoire of António Joaquim Anselmo, *Bibliografia das obras Impressas em Portugal no século XVI*, Lisboa: Oficinas Gráficas da Biblioteca Nacional, 1926. The reference is to the total number of works published, in their several editions, and not to the number of titles published.
24. Cf. Garcia, *A historiografia portuguesa dos descobrimentos e da expansão*, vol. 2, pp. 454-62.
25. The existence of these pamphlets seems proven by the appearance of collections, such as those by Fr. Bernardo de Brito, in the eighteenth century (Fr. Bernardo G. de Brito, *História Trágico-Marítima*, Lisboa Ocidental: Officina da Congregação do Oratório, 1735); or those collected by Lanciani, *Sucessos e Naufrágios das Naus Portuguesas*, in which one can find the accounts of shipwrecks, particularly on the India Route, which occurred in the sixteenth and seventeenth centuries, material used again in Guinote, Frutuso and Lopes, *Naufrágios e outras perdas da Carreira da Índia.*
26. See, on this subject, Glenn Joseph Ames, *The Estado da Índia: 1663–1677: Priorities and Strategies in Europe and the East*, Lisboa: [s.n.], 1989; Glenn Joseph

Ames, *Renascent Empire: the house of Braganza and the quest for stability in portuguese moonsoon Asia, c. 1640-1683,* Amsterdam: Amsterdam University Press, 2000; James C. Boyajian, *Portuguese trade in Asia under the Habsburg, 1580-1640,* Baltimore and London: Johns Hopkins University Press, 1993; Frank Broeze, ed., *Brides of the Sea: Port Cities of Asia from the 16th-20th Centuries,* Kensington: New South Wales University Press, 1989; Om Prakash, *European Commercial Entreprise in Pre-Colonia India,* New York and Cambridge: Cambridge University Press, 1998; Om Prakash and Denys Lombard, eds., *Commerce and Culture in the Bay of Bengal: 1500-1800,* Delhi: Manohar, 1999; Catarina Madeira Santos, *Goa é a chave de toda a Índia: Perfil político da capital do Estado da Índia (1505-1570),* Lisboa: CNCDP, 1999; Lúcio Manuel Rocha de Sousa, *O Japão e os Portugueses (1580-1614). Religião, política e comércio,* Porto: [s.n.] 2007, 2 vols., unpublished Ph.D. thesis presented at the University of Porto; Sanjay Subrahmanyan, *O império asiático Português, 1500-1700: Uma história política e económica,* Lisboa: Difel, 1995; Luís Filipe Ferreira Reis Thomaz, *De Ceuta a Timor,* Lisboa: Difel, 1994; Xavier, Ângela Barreto, *A Invenção de Goa: Poder imperial e conversões culturais nos séculos XVI e XVII,* Lisboa: ICS (Imprensa de Ciências Sociais), 2007.

27. Amélia Polónia, *Expansão e Descobrimentos numa perspectiva local: O porto de Vila do Conde no século XVI,* Lisboa: INCM, 2007, vol. 1, pp. 285-495; vol. 2, pp. 269-75; Amélia Polónia, 'Evangelização e comércio: A figura do eclesiástico mercador', in *Estudos em homenagem a João Francisco Marques,* Porto: FLUP, 2001, vol. 2, pp. 297-310.
28. See, among others, João Paulo Oliveira e Costa, *O Japão e o Cristianismo no século XVI: Ensaios de História Luso-Nipónica,* Lisboa: Sociedade Histórica da Independência de Portugal, 1999; João Paulo Oliveira e Costa, *Portugal e o Japão: o século Namban,* Lisboa: INCM, 1993; Valdemar Coutinho, *O fim da presença portuguesa no Japão,* Lisboa: Sociedade Histórica da Independência de Portugal, 1999; Sousa, *O Japão e os Portugueses (1580-1614).*
29. Jacques Bernard, *Navires et gens de mer a Bordeaux (vers 1400-vers 1550),* Paris: S.E.V.P.E.N., 1968, vol. II, pp. 567-8.
30. Proportions of the merchandise (particularly spice 'quintais'—hundredweights—thus the term 'quintaladas') which were included in the wage system of crews on the Cape Route.
31. Amélia Polónia, 'Self-organising networks in the construction of the Portuguese overseas empire', in 5th International Congress of Maritime History, promoted by International Maritime Economic History Association (IMEHA) (Greenwich, 23-27 June 2008). Submitted to the *International Journal of Maritime History* by Amélia Polónia and Jack Owens as 'Cooperation-Based Self-Organizing Networks in Portuguese Overseas Expansion in the First Global Age, 1400-1800' (Submission in process).
32. Thomaz, *De Ceuta a Timor,* p. 207.
33. *Leal Senado* is Portuguese for Loyal Senate, the seat of Macau's government.
34. Amélia Polónia and Jack Owens, 'Cooperation-Based Self-Organizing Networks in Portuguese Overseas Expansion in the First Global Age, 1400-1800' (submitted to the *International Journal of Maritime History*).

35. In fact, with respect to other overseas settlements, the Crown even used prostitutes as agents to get male settlers to remain. See the case of the Mina factory or that of São Tomé. Cf. Amélia Polónia, 'Mulheres que partem e mulheres que ficam: O protagonismo feminino na expansão ultramarina', *O Estudo da História*, no. 4, 2001, pp. 79-98; Amélia Polónia, 'De Portugal a espaços ultramarinos: Inclusão e exclusão de agentes femininas no processo de expansão ultramarina, Século XVI', in *Historia, Género y Familia en Iberoamérica. Siglos XVI-XX*, ed. Dora Davila Mendonza, Caracas: Universidad Católica 'Andrés Bello'/ Konrad Adenauer Stiftung, 2004.
36. Ana Isabel Cannas da Cunha, *A Inquisição no Estado da Índia; Origens (1539-1560)*, Lisboa: ANTT, 1995.
37. António Baião, *A Inquisição de Goa: Correspondência dos inquisidores da Índia (1569-1630)*, 2 vols., Coimbra: Imprensa da Universidade, 1930.
38. Timothy J. Coates, *Degredados e órfãs: colonização dirigida pela coroa no império português: 1550-1755*, Lisboa: CNCDP, 1998.
39. In the 25 years between 1561 and 1585, just 205 women (mostly New Christians) passed through the Goa Inquisition process. Cf. Baião, *A Inquisição de Goa.*
40. Coates, *Degredados e órfãs.*
41. Jean Baptiste Tavernier, *Travels in India*, 2 vols., New Delhi: Oriental Books Reprint Corporation, 1977.
42. J. Albert de Mandelslo, *Mandelslo's Travels in Western India: 1638-1639*, London: Oxford University Press, 1931.
43. François Pyrard de Laval, *Voyage of Pyrard de Laval*, rpt, New York, Burt Franklin, s/d.
44. Tavernier, *Travels in India,* vol. I, p. 152.
45. Mandelslo, *Mandelslo's Travels in Western India*, p. 80.
46. Francisco de Andrade, *O primeiro Cerco que os turcos puserão há fortaleza de Diu nas partes da India defendida pollos portugueses*, Coimbra: João de Barreira, 1589.
47. Polónia, *Expansão e Descobrimentos numa perspectiva local*, vol. 2, pp. 221-83.
48. Ibid., pp. 423-31. The exception is, for instance, that of Amador Carneiro, who left his wife in total poverty when he died [Cf. her will in Vila do Conde Misericórdia's Archive (ASCMVC), Col.1ª, 18, fols. 28-33].
49. ASCMVC, Maço de Testamentos Antigos: Will of Amador Carvalho, (n+/fl).
50. Polónia, *Expansão e Descobrimentos numa perspectiva local,* vol. 1, pp. 47-281; Amélia Polónia, 'The sea and its impact on a maritime Community: Vila do Conde, Portugal, 1500-1640', *International Journal of Maritime History*, vol. XVIII, no. 1, June 2006, pp. 199-222.
51. Polónia, *Expansão e Descobrimentos numa perspectiva local,* vol. 1, pp. 285-495; vol. 2, pp. 9-220.
52. This perception was somewhat the same of the 'State of India', as conceived by the Portuguese Crown. Cf. Thomaz, *De Ceuta a Timor,* p. 207.
53. Porto District Archive (ADP), Notarial records, V. Conde, 1° cart., 1ª sr., lv. 33, fols. 20v.-23v.
54. Ibid., 3ª sr., lv. 6, fols. 102v.-105v.; lv. 7, fols. 57-57v.; lv. 15, fols. 116-118.

55. Ibid., 1ª sr., lv. 23, fols. 113-114v.; lv. 25, fols. 30v.-31; lv. 29, fols. 86v.-88; lv. 32, fols. 62v.-64.
56. Ibid., 1º cart., 2ª sr., lv. 4, fols. 107v.-109.
57. Cf. Afzal Ahmad, 'Portuguese Trade on the Western Coast of India in the Seventeenth Century (1600-1663)', Baroda, 1984, unpublished Ph.D. thesis, submitted to the Department of History of the Faculty of Arts of Maharaja Sayajirao University of Baroda.
58. Proportions of the merchandise (particularly spice 'quintais'—hundredweights—thus the term 'quintaladas') which were included in the wage system of crews on the Cape Route.
59. The high price of musk is confirmed by the net value it reached in Lisbon in 1569, for a small jar of the perfume, less costs and customs duties: 63,770 *reais*. Cf. Vila do Conde House of the Misericordia Archive (ASCMVC), Maço de Testamentos Antigos, n.n.
60. ASCMVC - Col. 1ª, mç. 48, fol. 75.
61. Ibid., fol. 75v.
62. Ibid., mç. 25, n/f.
63. Ibid., mç. 17, n/f.
64. Ibid., mç. 11. Inventário de bens, fols. 9v. to 12v.
65. Ibid., mç. 48. Inventário de bens de Manuel Barbosa de Sá, fols. 30v.-36.
66. Ibid., mç. 39. Inventário de bens, fols. 3-5.
67. Ibid., fols. 6-12.
68. Ibid., fols. 5v.
69. Ibid., mç. 10, fols. 147 and 206v.-211v.
70. Ibid., mç. 8, Inventário de bens de Simão Afonso, fols. 15-16v.
71. Ibid., Lv. 2º de Registos, fol. 179v.
72. 'Gracia de Medeiros christãa nova viuva de Vila do Conde estava enforcada vestida com sua saia e gibão e dependurada por huma toalha que parecia de pano da India', Instiitute of the Portuguese National Archives/ Torre do Tombo (IAN/TT), Inquisição de Coimbra, proc. 8026, fol. 5.
73. ADP, Notarial Records. V. Conde, 3ª sr., lv. 5, fols. 127v.-128v.
74. Polónia, *Expansão e Descobrimentos numa perspectiva local*, vol. II, pp. 371-84.
75. F. Boullet and C. Boullet, *Ex-voto marins*, [s.l.]: Editions Maritimes et d'Outre-Mer, 1986; Robert C. Smith, *Pinturas de ex-votos existentes em Matosinhos e outros santuários de Portugal,* Matosinhos: Câmara Municipal, 1966.
76. A testimony of the same is available in an Inquisition proceeding, for instance: IAN/TT, Inquisição de Coimbra, proc. 3821, fol. 27.
77. ASCMVC, Col. 1ª. Bens de Raíz, Pasta 1. Papéis pertencentes ao Casal de Ansêde.
78. Ibid., Pasta 1, mç. 1, fl 50-56 e 74-79; Ibid., Col. 1ª, mç 3 . Capela de Jerónimo Veloso.
79. ASCMVC, Lv. de Capelas e Obrigações (ano 1579), fols. 86-89 and *Maço de Testamentos Antigos*.
80. ASCMVC, Maço de Testamentos Antigos: Will of Amador Carvalho. (n/fl).
81. ADP, Notarial Records, V. Conde, 1ºcart., 4ª sr., lv. 1, fols. 25v.-27.

82. Ibid., 1° cart, 1ª sr., lv. 23, fols. 113-114v.
83. Ibid., 1° cart, 1ª sr., lv. 23, fols. 137-138.
84. Ibid., 1° cart, 1ª sr., lv. 25, fols. 37-38; 1° cart., 1ª sr, lv. 26, fols. 132-5.
85. Ibid., 1° cart, 1ª sr., lv. 26, fols. 135v-136 and 136v-137.
86. Ibid., 1° cart, 1ª sr., lv. 27, fols. 72v-73v.
87. Ibid., 1° cart, 1ª sr., lv. 32, fols. 48v-52v.
88. Ibid., 1° cart, 3ª sr., lv. 11, fols. 75-77.
89. Ibid., 1° cart, 1ª sr., lv. 12, fols. 118v-120.
90. Ibid., 1° cart, 1ª sr., lv. 17, fols. 70-72.
91. Ibid., 1° cart, 1ª sr., lv. 19 fols. 164v-166.
92. Ibid., 1° cart, 1ª sr., lv. 9, fols. 211v.-212v.
93. Ibid., 1° cart, 1ª sr., lv. 18, fols. 140-145v.
94. Ibid., 1° cart, 1ª sr., lv. 9, fols. 152v.-154.
95. Amélia Polónia, 'Vila do Conde no século XVI: Reflexão sobre alguns índices de desenvolvimento urbano', *Boletim Cultural da Câmara Municipal de Vila do Conde*, II Série, vol. 14, December 1994, pp. 47-64.

PART V

Systemic Theories and the Pitfalls of Comparative History Writing

CHAPTER TWELVE

A 'World System' Stretched? The Case of the 'Eurasian and African World Systems'

Srijan Sandip Mandal

THIS ESSAY REVISITS THE CONCEPT OF the 'world system' and discusses the various theories that appropriate it to construct what is understood in academia as 'world history'. This attempt is made through an examination of the 'Eurasian and African world systems'—put forth by Philippe Beaujard in the *Journal of World History*—as a cautionary tale to the allure and optimism associated with the 'world system' as a 'grand unified theory' of the social sciences, not unlike the one of particle physics. It also hopes to serve as a deterrent to those who accept the 'world systems' theory and then work backwards to explain changes over a millennium or more in other parts of the globe.

While the recent trend to criticize the assumptions underlying the primacy of western Europe in the 'world systems' theory undoubtedly opens up new avenues of research, to argue for earlier existing 'world systems' with their cores in non-European societies, sometimes, perpetuates an ahistorical enterprise. This exercise works against the very notion of time, space and contingency, which are fundamental to any study of earlier societies and systems. Therefore, working backwards to reinforce this theory becomes damaging to the discipline of history itself. Hence, the case against metanarratives that tend to obscure the dynamism of various components within a system, and an attempted counter-argument for a plurality of systems—some of which are visible in the networks that the other essays in this volume discuss. It is only after having made such an attempt can the many faces of the First Global Age be understood and not, as convention would dictate, by concentrating on the early modern period with Europe at its core and the rest relegated to the status of peripheries.

'World System' Theory

The 'world system' theory is a macro-sociological approach that attempts to explain the dynamics of the 'capitalist world economy' as a 'total social system'.[1] Immanuel Wallerstein, the pioneer and most famous practitioner of this theory, defined it as:

> a social system, one that has boundaries, structures, member groups, rules of legitimation, and coherence. Its life is made up of the conflicting forces, which hold it together by tension and tear it apart as each group seeks eternally to remould it to its advantage. It has the characteristics of an organism, in that it has a lifespan over which its characteristics change in some respects and remain stable in others. . . . Life within it is largely self-contained, and the dynamics of its development are largely internal.[2]

However, this theory has its intellectual predecessors, too, in the Annales school, in Marxism, and in dependency theory, all of whom have come together to fashion this theoretical paradigm. Its historical approach and bias toward geography owes a great deal to the ideas of Fernand Braudel, one of the leading thinkers of the Annales school, who insisted upon looking at history in the long- term, or more famously *la longue duree*, and who used geographical regions as units of analysis. Marxism offered to it the fundamental reality of social conflict among material-based human groups, the concern with relevant totality, the transitory nature of social forms and theories about them, the centrality of the accumulation process and competitive class struggles that result from it, and a dialectical sense of motion through conflict and contradiction.[3] Dependency theory provided the intellectual blueprint upon which the 'world system' is built with its focus on the unequal relation between the core and periphery.[4] Beyond these, the works of Karl Polanyi and Joseph A. Schumpeter have also contributed to the further refinement of the 'world systems' theory.[5]

The 'multi-cultural territorial division of labour'—characteristic of any 'world system'—refers to the forces and relations of production of the world economy as a whole that, eventually, leads to the existence of two interdependent regions: the *core* and the *periphery*, which are geographically and culturally different, one focusing on labour-intensive and the other on capital-intensive production. This creates a relationship between the two that is asymmetrically structural with the semi-periphery acting as a buffer zone in the middle. Also characteristic of the system is the regular cyclical rhythm that every state within it experiences, and that too, in relative unison.[6]

However, like every other intellectual exercise, this theory, too, has invited criticism from several quarters across the ideological divide for being fuzzy about the very definition of the term 'system', for the Eurocentric view that it propagates, and the bias for the modern era that is implicit in its every elucidation. This backlash ensures that this approach—the most renowned of its kind in the sub-discipline of 'world history'—remains decidedly 'European' and 'modern' with no space in its framework for alternative avenues of exploration. Beaujard takes this very line of criticism against the theory, yet seems as enamoured as many critics with its 'holistic perspective "that looks for an explanation of the whole"'.[7] According to Beaujard, a suitable modification to the theory such as a definition established for the term 'system', a search for alternative spaces—in both land and sea—that exhibit the same characteristics as the 'modern world system', and turning back the clock beyond the 'modern' into the 'ancient' or even earlier would make it less susceptible to critics like himself.[8] Thus, the 'Eurasian and African world systems', one better than A.G. Frank's and B.G. Gills' 5,000-year-old 'world system' alternative,[9] feels Beaujard, for the former has more 'available actual data' at its disposal while the latter is significantly dependent on the inductive leap of faith.[10]

'Eurasian and African World Systems'

Beaujard believes that his 'system'—which is complex and dynamic and a source for both order and disorder, unity and diversity—shares the twelve characteristics enumerated by Wallerstein for his 'modern world system', namely the 'ever increasing capital accumulation, a division of labour, growing imbalances of power between cores and peripheries, phases of hegemony—within a given core—that alternate between a single power exercising control and several rival powers vying for control, and the existence of cycles'.[11] Therefore Beaujard opines that it can be perceived of as a viable alternative to it. This position, however, forces me to question the objective of this attempted shift to a different spatial and temporal unit of analysis when the ideas that govern it remain the same as that of the Eurocentric 'modern world system', whose very limitations are the reasons for such an attempt and whose negation is the very purpose of such an exercise. With this explicit nod to Wallerstein, Beaujard represents the first wave of Eurocentrism that eventually mars his theory and makes it redundant, in spite of claims to the contrary, haunted as it is by the spectre of European ideological hegemony and, therefore, unable to break out of its shackles.

From its origins in the first century CE, Beaujard writes, 'the Eurasian and African world system developed and was restructured following the rhythm of economic cycles that lasted several centuries (periods of growth followed by periods of decline) . . . [that] largely corresponded with cycles of political and religious events . . . [and] probably [even] to cycles in solar activity'.[12] Beaujard identifies four such cycles represented by 'four ascending waves—on an upward curve—with a corresponding growth in population, production, the volume and rapidity of trade, and urban development';[13] the first, from the first to the sixth century AD; the second, from the sixth to the tenth; the third, from the tenth to the fourteenth century; and the fourth from the fifteenth to the sixteenth century after which the 'system' began to shift Westward in the search of a new core due to the withdrawal of the Mings and, therefore, 'China', from it in 1433, and the development of capitalism in the West throughout the same century.[14]

Critique

Beaujard identifies 'China, India, western Asia, and Egypt' as the four permanent cores of this 'world system' and attributes this status to the high 'agricultural productivity in Mesopotamia, the Nile valley, the Ganges, the Yellow River, and the Yangzi . . . [and] the ensuing high rates of urbanization and extension of trading networks'.[15] Yet he confesses that one of them, namely 'India', appears to exhibit development 'sometimes out-of-sync with the rest of the world system', especially during recessions, such as the Gupta empire that emerged during a period of recession or the vibrant trade between India and South-East Asia that survived the economic downturns of the ninth and tenth centuries as well as that of the fourteenth century without suffering any setbacks.[16] It, thus, seems quite ironic that Beaujard's plea for the 'Eurasian and African world systems' is punctured by a spatial unit, i.e. the Bay of Bengal or the eastern Indian Ocean world that refuses to comply with the systemic rise and fall of the very system it is a core of—a prerequisite, one would imagine, of a core in particular and a 'world system' in general. Of course, it could be argued that the basis for such a critique is the national framework conventionally deployed to understand spaces on land, ironically at a time when these so-called nations were not understood as such, but were rather considered territories of individual and hereditary sovereigns. Thus, this exposes the critique itself to accusations of anachronism which would not altogether be unfounded had Beaujard's own use of the national framework—probably for the convenient availability and recognizability of labels—not deprived him of the privilege of this countercharge.

Each one of the four permanent cores in Beaujard's 'Eurasian and African world systems' also functions as a 'core' to its individual 'subsystem' which operates under the aegis of this larger 'world system': 'China' for the China Sea, 'India' for the eastern Indian Ocean, and western Asia and 'Egypt' for the western Indian Ocean, further stratified into the Persian Gulf for the former and the Red Sea for the latter.[17] Hence, the earlier thesis of the 'Indianization' of South-East Asia[18] as also the names China Sea, Indian Ocean, and Persian Gulf for the bodies of water around these 'cores' indicating the localized, albeit anachronistic, nature of their influence over the waters around them. Beaujard further states that '[recessions] do not affect . . . all parts of the system to the same degree, either because of the partial integration of certain subsystems or, more often, because of particular local conditions'.[19] Even 'trade was divided into [these] three zones or subsystems . . . with the exception of Persian and Arab ships, which plied the entire route from China to the Persian Gulf from the seventh to the ninth centuries'.[20] These excerpts, thus, seem to indicate that there is a case to be made, and probably a stronger one at that, for the 'subsystems' within this 'world system' than for the 'world system' itself as evinced from the varying degrees of assimilation experienced by these 'subsystems' vis-à-vis the 'world system' and the unsystemic nature of their trade.

The much-touted permanence of the four cores, too, seems contrived as their exploitation of the (semi)peripheries, meant to perpetuate their primacy in the system, does not seem to have succeeded in protecting them from frequent conquest by the latter 'as was the case for the Arab semiperiphery in the creation of the Muslim empire, for a Central Asian semiperiphery in the emergence of the Kushan empire in India (first century), and for the Mongol invasions of Mesopotamia and China (thirteenth century) and later of Mesopotamia and India (from the end of the fourteenth through the early fifteenth century)'.[21] In other words, the efficient extraction of surplus from the peripheries continued unabated for the supposed benefit of the cores. Yet the cores remained only marginal beneficiaries of it themselves as this extraction was now directed by the (semi)peripheries for the benefit of the (semi)peripheries themselves. Thus, one is forced to question the notion of the core, periphery, and semiperiphery presented in this theory and the justification for assigning these labels to one spatial unit and not the other, especially when a so-called core, for all its pre-eminence in a 'world system', falls prey to a semiperiphery it is meant to exploit and not be exploited by.

Beaujard notices two fundamental transformations in the nature of his 'system'; the first 'from 3500 to 2400 BCE in western Asia and Egypt and in the second millennium in China' and the second, 'toward the middle of the eighteenth century during the Industrial Revolution'.[22] Incidentally, the time frame he fixes for his 'system' excludes the era of either transformation as the origins of his 'world system' can be traced to the first century CE and its demise, sixteen centuries later, thus qualifying his statement that 'any changes that do occur do not affect the structure or the nature of the system.'[23] Was it, then, a world unchanging and static in nature, frozen in time and space?

Keeping that in mind, one observes that Beaujard also maintains that 'the state created favourable conditions for economic development through investments in public works such as the digging of canals and the improvement of roads', provided security 'as trade could only hope to flourish in a peaceful and relatively predictable setting', and even played 'a role in the redistribution of wealth, and so indirectly contribute[d] to production and social equilibrium'.[24] In other words, the State was responsible for the departments of finance, public works, and war—mostly paid for by the merchant class for whose benefit it was originally conceived, who extracted it as surplus, and efficiently so, from the peripheries all along the exchange networks and helped, in turn, to maintain the power relations between the core and the periphery and preserve the 'inequalities between regions and within the interconnected societies'.[25]

The arguments thus surmised represent the second wave of Beaujard's Eurocentrism that has infiltrated this non-European 'world system', however not as explicitly as his enunciation of the first one but rather tacitly and implicitly as a cultural stereotype that the Western mind is burdened with while analysing non-European societies like this one. In a nutshell, it is the concept of the Asiatic mode of production—introduced and developed by Karl Marx—that believed in the static and ahistorical nature of the so-called Asiatic societies represented here by the unchanging nature of the 'system'. In this the state was headed by an oriental despot as in Karl A. Wittfogel's thesis,[26] whose name changed with passing decades and centuries without any significant difference in the lives of the people s/he ruled and who was responsible for the departments of finance, public works, and war just like the states in the 'world system'.[27] The despot, in turn, appropriated surplus from the masses s/he lorded over, thus perpetuating the permanence of the 'village system' and 'hydraulic societies' seen here in the fate of the littoral societies that constituted the core-periphery power relations in the 'Eurasian and African world systems'.[28] As Marx saw it, this framework could be broken only by the advent of colonialism, however miserable an experience it was for the colonized coinciding, incidentally, with Beaujard's identification of the second 'fundamental transformation' with the Industrial Revolution in eighteenth-century Europe.[29]

From the themes discussed, it would seem that the 'Eurasian and African' world system is one that has been stretched too far, so much so that I am bound to conclude that it collapses under its own sheer weight, burdened as it is with inductive leaps of faith which, ironically, it accuses others of indulging in. It is littered with contradictions inherent in the 'system', which it acknowledges and yet fails to grasp the significance of. More damaging, however, is the ideological hegemony of Eurocentrism identified in two waves here that Beaujard represents and propagates tacitly while promising a framework outside of it, and even more so, the colonial stereotypes that are implicit in the text and colour of every argument made, consciously or subconsciously, in its defence. Beaujard, thus, emerges as a case in point for understanding the difficulties, nay near impossibility, of thinking outside European frames, or even national ones for that matter—also modelled on Europe—that have permeated the pores and interstices of contemporary intellectual or scholarly minds. There is a need, and a very real one at that, to think outside the box. However, attempts to do so have unearthed the omnipresent nature of the box, which refuses to entertain any thought of escape from its four walls. The autonomy of non-European societies in scholarship as in other arenas remains, therefore, only a pipe dream.

Returning to the seductive nature of the world system alluded to earlier in this essay, one is forced to ask if it is not, for all its critical acclaim, only another example of 'pigeon-holing', as R.G. Collingwood had remarked over 60 years ago—a manifestation of the 'impulse towards arranging the whole of history in a single scheme' as an enterprise of 'raising history to the rank of science'.[30] If it is so, then not only is the autonomy of non-Europeans in history in danger but the autonomy of the very discipline, too, is in peril and one fears that, like in the case of the former, it might already be too late to do anything.

Notes

*I would like to thank the volume editor for the risk that she has undertaken in giving me the opportunity to contribute an essay to this book. Moreover, this essay—the product of a presentation I gave in a course conducted by Rila Mukherjee, 'The World of Indian Ocean'—would not have been possible without her insistence on such presentations in class and on the critical reading of texts, whatever they may be.

1. Carlos A. Martinez-Vela, 'World Systems Theory', *ESD*, vol. 83, 2001, p. 1.
2. Immanuel Wallerstein, *The Modern World-System I: Capitalist Agriculture and the Origins of the European World-Economy in the Sixteenth Century*, New York: Academic Press, 1974, p. 347.

3. Martinez-Vela, 'World Systems Theory', pp. 2–3.
4. Daniel Chirot and Thomas D. Hall, 'World-System Theory', *Annual Review of Sociology*, vol. 8, 1982, pp. 90–3.
5. Karl Polanyi, *The Great Transformation: The Political and Economic Origins of Our Time*, Boston: Beacon Press, 1944; Joseph A. Schumpeter, *Business Cycles: A Theoretical, Historical and Statistical Analysis of the Capitalist Process*, New York: McGraw-Hill Book Company, 1939.
6. Walter L. Goldfrank, 'Paradigm Regained? The Rules of Wallerstein's World-System Method', *Journal of World-Systems Research*, vol. XI, no. 2, 2000, pp. 168–74.
7. Philippe Beaujard, 'The Indian Ocean in Eurasian and African World-Systems before the Sixteenth Century', *Journal of World History*, vol. 16, no. 4, 2005, pp. 412–3.
8. Ibid.
9. A.G. Frank and B.K. Gills, eds., *The World System: Five Hundred Years or Five Thousand?*, London: Routledge, 1993.
10. Beaujard, 'Indian Ocean', pp. 413–4.
11. Ibid., p. 413.
12. Ibid., pp. 413, 421, 434.
13. Ibid., p. 421.
14. Ibid., pp. 421–4.
15. Ibid., p. 437.
16. Ibid., p. 435.
17. Ibid., p. 413.
18. Ibid., pp. 421, 435, 441.
19. Ibid., pp. 434-5.
20. Ibid., p. 437.
21. Ibid., p. 445.
22. Ibid., p. 446.
23. Ibid.
24. Ibid., p. 457.
25. Ibid., p. 437.
26. Karl A. Wittfogel, *Oriental Despotism: A Comparative Study of Total Power*, New Haven: Yale University Press, 1957.
27. Karl Marx, 'The British Rule in India', in *Karl Marx & Frederick Engels: Collected Works*, vol. 12, Marx and Engels: 1853–54, Moscow: Progress Publishers, 1979, p. 127.
28. Ibid., p. 128.
29. Karl Marx, 'The Future Results of the British Rule in India', in *Karl Marx & Frederick Engels: Collected Works*, vol. 12, Marx and Engels: 1853–54, Moscow: Progress Publishers, 1979, pp. 217–22.
30. R.G. Collingwood, *The Idea of History*, revd edn, ed. Jan Van Der Dussen, Oxford: Clarendon Press, 1993, p. 264.

CHAPTER THIRTEEN

Networks of Production and Circulation in South Asia, 1500–1700 An Indian Ocean Perspective

Alex M. Thomas

> Traders exchanged goods and sailors manned the boats that carried along the coasts of the north-west Indian Ocean from at least about 2000 BCE.
>
> —Edward A. Alpers, 'Imagining the Indian Ocean World', Opening Address to the International Conference on Cultural Exchange and Transformation in the Indian Ocean World, UCLA, Los Angeles, USA, 2002.

This essay will discuss some of the multiple networks and cooperative strategies prevalent in South Asia from 1500 to 1700; a period coinciding with the mercantilist period in Europe. The scholarship in this essay departs from that of usual historical narratives by placing these networks within an Indian Ocean world. Beginning with an exploration of the meaning of an Indian Ocean world, subsequent sections look at the 'early modern' as a pathway to globalization,

*I thank Professor Rila Mukherjee, Department of History, University of Hyderabad for her constructive suggestions on earlier drafts of this essay.

mercantilist practices in Britain at the time when mercantilism burst in upon the Indian Ocean world and finally, some of the important South Asian networks which facilitated trade. Characteristics of the trade between the Indian and British merchants will also be studied. The essay concludes by delineating the merits of visualizing South Asian networks and strategies within an Indian Ocean framework.

Can we Talk of an Indian Ocean World?

Histories *of* and *in* the Indian Ocean have increased in frequency, especially, in the last ten years. A paradigmatic shift from the 'land' to the 'sea' has occurred owing to the hope that the latter might provide a better optics for studying history and that this also might 'transcend spatial and temporal categorizations'.[1] Such a research area opens up various modes of understanding 'history' and also aids in comprehending the multiplicity of historical entities. For instance, when studying how the globe has been mapped, we understand that the demarcation of various water spaces are mere intellectual constructs. Moreover, a history of mapping can also reveal embedded power structures and changing cultures. It also reflects 'the strategic interests of contemporary global capitalism'.[2]

Let me try and answer in this section the following questions: Does an Indian Ocean world exist? If it does, how do we study it? The first question is not only an ontological one, but also a politico-cultural one. This is so because the 'existence' of the Indian Ocean world helps the associated nations to understand their history, their present and hence, offers them an opportunity to reformulate and strengthen their identities. For, a look at the history of the Indian Ocean will completely undermine the notion that capitalism is a European invention.[3] And like many other constructs, a region's representation and public image are often products of status and power. Power determines the contours of a landscape; and every landscape contains notions of territory and territoriality.[4] Similar notions apply for water spaces as well. The second question concerns the method of studying the Indian Ocean world. Do we study it as a whole or as an aggregate of its constituent units? Do we give it territorial boundaries, cultural limits or linguistic borders? Do we demarcate the Indian Ocean according to space, time or both?

Fernand Braudel's *The Mediterranean* initiated a large corpus of history-writing on Asian waters, mainly owing to his emphasis on the sea but also because of the manner in which he divided time. Historians who study water spaces have more or less used a Braudelian model; however, Sutherland calls for caution here as Braudel's model suffers from 'conceptual confusion and analytic evasion'.[5]

Immanuel Wallerstein also drew his inspiration for the 'world system' from Braudel. Although the historians of the Annales school attempted an interdisciplinary approach in their scholarship, abandoned theories of linear time and questioned the (Western) notion of progress, Wallerstein (despite his radical departure) asserted that the Indian Ocean Basin was an 'external arena', outside the early modern world economy until 1750, thereby anticipating the period of the Industrial Revolution in Europe.[6] Also, and more significantly for our purposes here, Wallerstein's idea of South Asia being an external arena might be taken to suggest the presence of another world system of which India and the Indian Ocean were a part of earlier. Largely then, the present historiographies of the various 'oceans' may help in constructing a polycentric world system.

There was frequent movement of goods between the Bay of Bengal and the South China Sea, which formed part of the wider Indian Ocean trading system.[7] So, the question that arises is: can we talk of an Indian Ocean World based on the trading circuits that prevailed? Here, the trade zone could define the geographic entity, based upon the density of connections, which would further be a function of trade routes, the sailing patterns, number of voyages made, and so on. The density of connections could be represented qualitatively through a descriptive and analytical account. Or, a quantitative element could be added by making use of the 'science of networks'.[8]

How one studies the Indian Ocean depends on the lens we adopt and the perspective(s) we take on.[9] This is so because the identity of a geographical (or for that matter, any entity) is 'dependent on the definitions, on the observer's time-frame, and location in space'.[10] And *pace* Michel Foucault and Kurt Godel, we have seen that classificatory items lack universal meanings independent of the historical context. In the following paragraphs, I shall briefly survey some of the perspectives regarding the Indian Ocean.

For M.N. Pearson, the characteristics of littoral societies provide for the element of unity in the Indian Ocean world, where littoral refers to 'the coastal sea zone, the beach, and some indeterminate frontier on land'.[11] The characteristics are an 'openness to distant and "foreign" markets, diets largely derived from the sea, housing structures using materials such as coral available on the shore, a rhythm of life geared to the monsoons, ship architecture characterized by the use of lateen sails, the spread of certain lingua franca (including "nautical Portuguese"), and a functionally distinct folk religion'.[12]

A.N. Tucker's work is an important contribution to the histories of the Indian Ocean. From his linguistic analysis of Swahili, he identified that the greatest number of foreign words are of Arabic origin, though Persian, Hindustani, Portuguese, and English are also well represented.[13] This piece of work corroborates the hypothesis that a certain commonality characterized the Indian Ocean. Tucker's essay shows that the people of the Swahili coast were accommodative of 'foreigners', while also pointing to the fact that Africa was well represented in global trade. This also reinforces our notion of an Indian Ocean world in which Africa was a robust participant. However, eurocentric histories suggest that India and Africa were marginal and 'less developed'[14] before the Europeans began their world-colonization tour.

Anthony Reid analyses Asian history by taking up 'hybridity' as a category.[15] Reid argues that the hybridization of language, food and culture was a phenomenon that took place prior to the impact of European colonization, hence, making it an indispensable tool for understanding the history of the First Global Age.

André Wink proposed that 'Indian Ocean cities were characteristically fragile, lacking in continuity, and relatively undifferentiated from an overwhelmingly agrarian context.'[16] In order to argue on these lines, he analysed the role of rivers, river plains and deltas in the Indian Ocean region. These geographical entities provided immense support to the political economy of exchange. But, these entities were hydrologically unstable. Hence, 'environmental change associated with river instability, soil erosion in alluvial plains, earthquakes, and delta formation, was pervasive' in the Indian Ocean region.[17]

In the 2006 forum of the *American Historical Review* (*AHR*), Karen Wigen identified the five common perspectives of the ocean-oriented histories that were surveyed: (a) maritime regions were demonstrated to be modern cultural constructs, (b) there were investigations into emic conceptions of the sea, (c) maritime regions everywhere were understood to be fractured, fragmented worlds, (d) maritime regions were understood to be intrinsically unstable, and that (e) oceans connected at a global as well as at a regional level.[18]

Ironically, present-day maps give the impression of well-defined boundaries. The advances in cartography have only extended these stringent notions of boundaries. But, a significant characteristic of an ocean space is the fact that its boundaries keep changing. One reason for this is because 'major states emerged on the mainland, while maritime polities tended to fragment'.[19] At this juncture, it would be worthwhile to quote Braudel: 'To draw a boundary around anything is to define, analyse, and reconstruct it, in this case to select, indeed adopt, a philosophy of history.'[20]

However, drawing boundaries is central to all level of politics. For, boundaries are intimately linked to notions of sovereignty, identity and agency. And in the construction of boundaries, an in-depth understanding of both history and geography is crucial. In this light, one could talk of the 'Indian Ocean World' as a *heuristic* for understanding the history of the neighbouring countries, as well as those who traded frequently in that 'world'. Also, such a construction would help in the reconstruction of identities and hence, might be able to impart more 'power' to the concerned nations.

The Indian Ocean can be studied as a whole as well as from the vantage point of its constituent parts. And its history can be written within either a spatial or a temporal framework. Therefore, it is possible to visualize the Indian Ocean world as an entity—but an entity that was linguistically heterogeneous, multi-cultural, environmentally unstable, etc. The task of the oceanic-historian is to explain instability in the oceanic-space, keeping the borders of the space, fixed, yet fuzzy. Alpers mentions that Arjun Appadurai's notion of 'imagined worlds' will prove helpful as it provides a conceptual tool for understanding spaces which have fluid boundaries.[21] Another very interesting line of research Mukherjee suggests would be to pursue chorography as opposed to geography. In chorography, the *sense* of the place, as it is sometimes evinced in topography, is different from geographical representations of space. Geography reduces places to points or sites, while chorography retains the richness of topography by locating the *region* in that place.[22]

It is clear that various historians have adopted different concepts, frameworks or strategies to understand the dynamics of the Indian Ocean world. Different accounts of religion, folklore, languages, boat making practices, etc., have travelled within the world of the Indian Ocean. The apparent contradictions and complexity of movements are due to the interaction between the physical and mental domains.[23] And it is only by broadening the horizon of imagination that a rich historiography of the Indian Ocean can be constructed.

Conceptual problems, therefore, become glaringly evident when dealing with a new 'scholarly' and spatial entity—the ocean world. The emergence of this new scholarship requires novel methods, as well as new tools.

Pathways to Globalization

In her article, Sutherland points out another significant problem which is true of history writing in general. In the First Global Age, European mercantile activity generated substantial documentation, which in time came to be considered as a benchmark for measuring progress. Erickson and Bearman have utilized these extensive resources to support their hypothesis of English private traders having laid down the path for 'early' globalization.[24] Like any comparison, the results obtained from a comparative exercise largely depend on the benchmark that is used. And, history writing abounds with comparison exercises. Also, most of the historical analysis that is conducted takes place in the domain of the intellectual; the Indian Ocean is a mental construct which possesses sense but cannot be verified.[25]

Apart from problems such as these, any history of South-East Asia is incomplete if external influences by way of colonization are not considered. Therefore, any intelligible writing of Indian Ocean history must be able to accommodate the fall of the great empires of India and China wherein the imperial enterprise played a significant role. Such histories have direct implications in the construction of an Indian Ocean identity and, thus, indirectly aid in the rewriting (if necessary) of South Asian history as well.

At present, the volume of academic discussions pertaining to globalization have skyrocketed; this has had an adverse impact, with respect to the utility of constructing a history of Asia. Globalization has rendered identities indeterminate and they are prone to become fuzzier with time—due to the rise of English as a global language and owing to the extent of 'internationalization' of several countries! It is here that oceanic-historians can aid other disciplines by providing theoretical apparatuses to better comprehend movements across time and space of people, objects and ideas. And in this way, the history of globalization[26] can be documented from as early on as 2000 BCE; that is, 'ever since traders exchanged goods and sailors manned the boats that carried along the coasts of the north-west Indian Ocean'.[27] For, we are here not equating globalization with the capitalism that arose in Europe in the 'modern age', we are discussing instead globalization as the result of the world of exchange, what Braudel termed the 'Wheels of Commerce'.

The First Global Age is also regarded as the crucible of mercantilism in Europe and historians of South Asia have laboured to locate a burgeoning mercantilism in India. An investigation into the networks that were prevalent in South Asia roughly during what is known as the mercantilist era can capture the distinguishing features of South Asian trade and economy not within the continent but within the Indian Ocean World. However, before entering into the world of South Asian networks, let us take a look at some of the main characteristics of mercantilism.

On Mercantilism

Mercantilism is said to have existed roughly between 1498 and 1776. Incidentally, a school of thought that called itself mercantilism never existed.[28] Mercantilism is the term used to denote the 'state making' activities that the European nations pursued. The activities can be classified mainly as political and/or economic in nature. Adam Smith was the first person to use the term 'mercantile system' in his book *An Enquiry into the Nature and Causes of Wealth of Nations*. Smith elucidated the central tenets of mercantilism so that he could point out the demerits of the system. Mercantilism is also seen as the precursor to commercial capitalism. Hence, accounts of mercantilism are usually explained using capitalist terms and tendencies.

Britain's geography limited the extent of the market and thereby restricted the amount of surplus it could produce by carrying out trade within its territories and along the Silk Route. Also, the Silk Route could not provide British merchants with huge profits owing to the fact that the route passed through different countries. The extent of the market determined the demand for commodities and services while also providing opportunities for growth. The only other available solution to this quandary was to venture into the seas with the intention of increasing trade. Thus, the Britishers' aim was to establish trade in regions which they could dominate and thereby acquire windfall gains. The creation of the English East India Company was effected in accordance with these intentions. Thus, the mercantile era was a time when powerful national economies were built on the basis of extensive colonial possessions.[29]

In order to attain their economic goals, the British carried out the following policies: they acquired gold and silver through a favourable balance of trade, colonies and conquest; imported raw materials and exported finished goods; imposed strong regulations on international trade; centralized the government and ensured their goods were transported *via* ships by flying Britain's flag.[30] The public policy reflected the merchant's vices.[31] Ambirajan puts forth an interesting point regarding the merchants' attitude towards colonization, namely that, colonization was welcomed because of the belief that surplus capital in Britain would bring down the rate of profit in Britain. Therefore, the British would have had to find avenues for deploying their 'excess' capital.

Another significant outcome during the mercantilist period was the fusing of the merchants and the state—a process that gave immense power to Britain and led to the creation of the empire.[32] The state framed policies that were conducive to the merchants and the merchants in turn supplied financial resources for the state mainly to improve their defences. Trade was carried out with the national interest in mind and this required a licence from the government. These licenses ensured that the other countries knew who they were trading with, consequently setting up a system that also offered protection while on the seas from attackers.[33] Mercantilism thus had firm roots in national defence and aggression.

I will discuss some of Thomas Mun's policy prescriptions so as to reinvigorate the discussion on mercantile policies of the dominant merchants in Britain. Thomas Mun seems best suited as he is considered to have represented the mercantilist mentality in his book *England's Treasure by Foraign Trade, or our Foraign Trade is the Rule of our Treasure.*

Mun suggested measures such as: the stoppage of the importation of hemp, tobacco, flax, etc., as imports impoverished the nation and instead asked the state to cultivate these items; to aim for the reduction of imports by refraining from excessive consumption of foreign wares; to see that trade in foreign lands was undertaken in British ships to enjoy higher gains; to fish extensively in the seas of England, Scotland and Ireland as the only cost incurred would be the wages; to ensure the importation of corn, indigo, spices, raw silks, cotton wool and other such essential commodities so that they could be exported when the need arose; to 'esteem and cherish' the remote trade which took place in its colonies; to export commodities without imposing customs duties so that they would fare better in comparison to the Italian and Dutch products; and to effect a reduction in restrictions on trade and allowances.[34]

It is clear from the preceding discussion that mercantilism in England was characterized by a few actors, namely the State and the English East India Company. In this sense, it was monopolistic in nature. This is contrasted with the presence of multiple networks that were prevalent in the Indian economy during the same time. But there exists a different understanding of the nature of English trade in the Indian Ocean where, it has been argued, the private traders of the English East India Company behaved in a self-interested fashion, thereby laying down the foundation for an integrated global market.[35] The authors argue that these private traders transformed simple trade routes into 'complex multilateral networks of exchange'.[36] In other words, they argue that a situation resembling intense competition was prevalent during the time of the English East India Company. A critique of this position will be provided in the concluding section of this essay.

Networks and Strategies in Mughal India: 1500-1700

I will emphasize those prominent trade networks and strategies[37] during the period 1500–1700 which are significant to our understanding of how the South Asian economy functioned in the First Global Age. This section highlights some of the important networks/actors in the Mughal trade scene—the Mughal state, the north Indian *banjaras*, the maritime merchants, the peasants, the moneylenders and the inland 'Indian' merchants. The last group mainly exported textiles, gems and good quality artisanal products from sword-steel to hardwood furniture.[38] The Indian subcontinent played a significant role in world trade during the sixteenth to the eighteenth centuries.

BANJARAS[39]

The *banjaras* are today's gypsies whose primary occupation then was to transport commodities across different places (mainly in north India). *Banjara* groups consisted of people from different religions, caste, customs and origins. They transported goods primarily on cattle, and almost held a monopoly in the transportation of commodities. Though the movement of the goods was slow, the cost was reasonable. They provided valuable support to the Mughal army. The *banjaras* were guaranteed a proper livelihood by the Mughal state in return for which they supplied the State with the necessary supplies when the latter was far from their agricultural base. The *banjaras* also transported goods, mainly grain, when the Mughals were far from their political base, as for example, when they led campaigns in different parts of the subcontinent.

The *banjaras* were considered to be neutral in wars and enjoyed a right of transit through all the countries. The implications of this is the presence of some sort of mechanism whereby this network was granted access everywhere. The community owned enormous herds, a particularly hardy breed of oxen, and was willing to spend a large amount of time travelling. They organized themselves in a way so as to facilitate trade, possessed acumen for transactions and were also renowned for their toughness, military strength and cunning which were necessary tools of the trade.

Thus, the *banjaras* could be considered an indispensable transportation network which facilitated South Asian trade to a great extent because it enabled an almost continuous circulation of goods and commodities within and across the Mughal Empire.

MARITIME MERCHANTS

Amongst primary agents of seaborne trade in Mughal India, there existed various kinds of maritime merchants. They comprised the Indian ship-owning merchants, *nakhudas* (captains) who were experienced in navigation and sailing, powerful bankers and financiers, inland suppliers and the *mansabdars*, who were distinguished noblemen of the Mughal Empire dabbling in trade. Trade and politics went hand-in-hand in India. Philippe Beaujard quotes M. Gaborieau in this regard: 'the lack of a dividing line between the merchant and the soldier-administrator' was visible.[40]

Besides these, there were 'poor' itinerant merchants who travelled across markets with their goods. These were individuals who did not have a constant base of operation.[41] Those who kept to their shore base were 'merchants in general trade; they were merchants of particular commodities; they were the money merchants and, above all, they were the brokers of the port towns'.[42] According to Ashin Das Gupta, the maritime merchants provided a valuable service to India which was to be later filled by the British merchants in the eighteenth century.

The merchants relied on State protection from the royal ships while at sea. The importance of the royal ships as actors in trade and in protection declined after the entry of the Europeans[43] into the Indian Ocean. This could have been one of the reasons for the displacement of the maritime merchants from the Indian Ocean in the course of the eighteenth century.

The Indian Ocean did not just witness varied trade from China to Europe to Africa; it also witnessed an exchange of cultures. It witnessed long-distance trade in both bulk commodities and luxury goods. It saw a high volume of trade in which merchants from various cultures participated, this facilitated an exchange of people, cultures, religions, and also determined the dominance of specific actors. This process also accentuated an inter-regional division of labour.[44] Studies *into* the Indian Ocean world have resulted in hypotheses which claim that there were strains of mercantilism or early capitalism in Mughal India and in adjoining regions.[45] Such hypotheses further provide merit for classifying history into ancient, early modern and modern periods. This issue will be taken up in the last section of this essay.

PRODUCERS

Under this label, I place the farmers (cultivators), weavers, spinners, barbers, carpenters, tanners, sweepers, goldsmiths, etc. Among these, the role of the weavers alone will be discussed.[46] In this context, the role of the caste system will also be studied. Seventeenth-century India was the 'graveyard of gold and silver', according to Francois Bernier.[47] This was due to the Indian export of textiles, especially to Europe. Indian printed cloth—known as *Pintados*, were commonly seen in Britain, and these challenged the English textiles with their low cost, quantity and quality.

The weavers did not weave throughout the year. Likewise, farmers did not carry out farming activities all the time; 'Rather they mixed farming with other activities—weaving, labouring, soldiering and, often, robbing. Moreover, even as farmers, they rarely planted a single field with a single crop: crop mixes (for example, cotton and millet) guaranteed that, if one failed, the other might survive, to provide something to sell as much as eat'.[48] The underlying logic behind the production activities was to 'guarantee community reproduction, not the maximization of profits'.[49] The farmers exchanged their produce at huge *melas* (religious and other fairs) and at temples. There was thus a mingling of two networks: of agriculture and commercial production.

Historians have multiple views regarding the bargaining power of the weavers. Parthasarathi argues that weavers enjoyed more power than the middlemen—the merchants. Moreover, the weavers had the right to break a contract with the merchant by returning the advance—indicative of the fact that the merchants' profits were dependent on the weavers' decisions. Given such a scenario, one could infer that the Mughals gave more importance to the actual producers than to the middlemen.[50] However, Parthasarathi's views do not hold for other parts of South Asia—as, for example, Bengal, as Mukherjee's study demonstrates.[51]

However, according to the proto industrialization thesis, a conflict between weavers and merchants was inevitable at a certain point, and we do not know which group the State supported. Weavers who were primarily agriculturists were only interested in weaving to supplement their income, i.e. they functioned as part-time weavers. For the merchants, trade was a full-time activity, and they were consequently interested in a greater volume of *assured* production which would enable them to plan, so as to provide for distant markets at a time when transport networks were slow, costly and inefficient compared to our world today. The world of the merchant, which was determined by surplus value, clashed with the world of the weaver, which was primarily determined by use value. This conflict was natural as long as the basic income of the weavers came from agriculture; they were not interested in producing for the market beyond a certain point, while the merchant was interested in ever greater production for ever greater trade in order to amass ever greater profits.

Neeraj Hatekar, therefore, states that 'farmers were entering markets on unfavourable terms, middlemen usually creaming off all the profits. Peasants are also seen as crucially dependent on the State for recovery from adversity'.[52] What role did caste play in production? The caste system had both positive and negative effects on the Mughal economy.[53] The adverse effects were mainly with respect to the exploitation of the lower castes by the higher castes. Washbrook attributes the legendary skill of the Indian artisan to the specialization which arose from the Hindu caste system.[54] Thus, the caste system, in some sense, led to directed investment in human capital. This is considered one of the primary reasons for the fineness of Indian muslins, the intricacy of the chintz prints and the fastness of their dyes. The Hindu caste system provided an institutional set-up which facilitated production by carrying out caste-based production.

INLAND MERCHANTS

Neils Steensgaard points out that the Indian exports towards the West reached significant proportions in the sixteenth and seventeenth centuries.[55] The main mode of transportation were camel-driven caravans.[56] He also points out how the Quandahar route was one among the many expanding trade routes in the long sixteenth century. The trade routes were not laid down arbitrarily, they were dynamic in nature and determined by the consumption patterns. The caravan trade also connected to the sea routes, and thus connected with the Indian Ocean through the ports of Gujarat and Bengal to the west and east of the Mughal Empire. The Mughals built roadways so as to connect all the ports in their empire, they established a postal system and built *serais* or rest houses for travellers at regular intervals on roads. These *serais* were places where food could be cooked, horses changed and a bed bought for the night. The *serais* were part of intricate logistics and transport networks.

It therefore becomes evident as to how the Mughals built infrastructure to facilitate administration and transportation.[57] There was a substantial increase in trade, both inland as well as foreign, during Mughal rule. Additionally, one notes the emergence of an integrated national market as well.[58] By the seventeenth century, money started becoming institutionalized as well as more mobile with the evolution of the *hundis* and the *hawalas* network. These infrastructural undertakings, as well as more trade resulted in an increased mobility of labour; though it is debatable as to how much mobility it gave them owing to the constraints imposed by the caste system.

MONEYLENDERS

This group constitutes an important part of any trading activity simply because money is necessary for carrying out production and trade. According to the caste system, it was the *vaishyas* who could lend money apart from investing in trade, agriculture and attendance on cattle.[59] But, in practice, persons from all castes lent money. And the Mughals chose not to interfere with the Hindu law of moneylending.

On the whole, the Mughal administration seemed sympathetic and interested in the workings of their political economy. It can be safely said that they carried out support activities which their subjects preferred, such as both overland and seaborne trade, though it appears that the Mughals themselves were not very keen about the latter. An immediate example would be that of the support maritime merchants received from the Mughal state.

From the preceding discussion, it can safely be said that the Mughal trade scene functioned smoothly as a result of the cooperation that was necessary between the various networks of actors—the Mughal State, the north Indian *banjaras*, the maritime merchants, the peasants, the moneylenders and the inland 'Indian' merchants. These networks provided the necessary infrastructure that was required for production, for self-consumption as well as for exchange.

Thus, as evidenced from the study, the Mughal economy indeed functioned efficiently with the State machinery and the network of actors coexisting more or less peacefully. There were no reasons for the Mughals to change the nature of their operations drastically. It has been argued that Mughal India would have become capitalistic with time. It has also been convenient to argue the case for capitalism in Mughal India by positing that strains of capitalism or capitalist tendencies were prevalent in Mughal India. The utility of this counterfactual seems limited. For, if the structure and core of the Indian Ocean world was different from that of the Europeans, talking about capitalism in the European sense would be a futile exercise. The Indian ocean was a polycentric realm, rather than one driven by hierarchy as happened later. For instance, the Indian merchants traded as local communities at a global level, but the British merchants traded as a 'nation' at a global level.[60] The activities of the Indian merchants were community-driven rather than 'nation'-driven. This explains the presence of multiple actors in trade, resulting in a multiplicity of networks comprising *banjaras*, inland merchants, moneylenders, itinerant traders and maritime merchants and so on.

History and other disciplines have witnessed a surge in the literature pertaining to globalization or late capitalism. The oft-discussed theories are intrinsically European and economic in nature. The discipline of Economics plays a large and important role in the structure and argument of these theories. For one, there is the repeated mention of surplus, convergence of prices, information asymmetries, competition, and so on. How far these 'notions' aid in recovering/understanding the past of non-Western societies and nations remains debatable.

Reverting to the argument that proposed the beginnings of globalization and integrated markets to be an outcome of free-riding private traders of the English East India Company at the start of the seventeenth century,[61] a restatement of the meaning of globalization is necessary. One must remember that 'individual liberty' is an important feature of capitalism. It is a feature in the sense that capitalism was advertized as a system that gave utmost priority to individual freedom. Ironically, it is exploitative as well, as Karl Marx points out in his first volume of *Das Kapital*. Such notions of liberty were never prevalent among the subjects or the rulers of Mughal India.

Erikson and Bearman's argument depends crucially on the nature of data they used and on their definition of globalization. Their dataset is compiled from ships logs, journals, factory correspondence, ledgers and reports that provide information regarding the voyages taken by English traders of the East India Company. The lack of reliable data prior to the period between 1601 and 1833 poses problems in establishing the argument that these English traders paved the way for 'globalization before globalization'. Also, if globalization is defined as the interaction of all heavily populated land masses in a manner that deeply and permanently linked them,[62] then Erikson and Bearman's argument does not hold.

Nomenclatures like ancient, early modern, modern, medieval, etc., play a significant role in the writing of history. Hence, there is the need to re-view and re-look[63] these seemingly harmless labels, which has been the objective of this volume. For example, the words 'Asia' and 'Asian' require the prior conception of 'Europe' as a category to make sense.[64]

The purpose of this essay was to depict the various networks that were prevalent in South Asia and how through cooperative strategies, South Asia was able to become one of the greatest trading nations in the world before 1800. To conclude, I emphasize that it is necessary to visualize the South Asian past from the perspective of an Indian Ocean world. In this way, it is possible to identify the various traits of South Asian economy, culture, society and so on. These lend more weight to the assertion that the subcontinent had been an active player in the Indian Ocean world much before her connection with Europe.

Notes

1. Heather Sutherland, 'South-East Asian History and the Mediterranean Analogy', *Journal of South-East Asian Studies*, vol. 34, no. 1, 2003.
2. Martin W. Lewis, 'Dividing the Ocean Sea', *Geographical Review*, vol. 89, no. 2, 1999, p. 210.
3. P. Beaujard, 'The Indian Ocean in Eurasian and African World-Systems before the Sixteenth Century', *Journal of World History*, vol. 16, no. 4, 2005.
4. Rila Mukherjee, 'The Indian Ocean in the "New Thalassology"', *ARCHIPEL*, vol. 76, 2008.
5. Heather Sutherland, 'South-East Asian History', p.1.
6. Immanuel Wallerstein, *The Modern World-System I: Capitalist Agriculture and the Origins of the European World-Economy in the Sixteenth Century*, New York: Academic Press Inc., 1974, p. 301.
7. Heather Sutherland, 'South-East Asian History', p. 8.
8. See Duncan J. Watts, 'The "New" Science of Networks', *Annual Review of Sociology*, vol. 30, 2004, for a discussion of the merits of the 'new' science of networks for dynamical social studies.
9. See K.N. Chaudhuri, *Asia Before Europe: Economy and Civilization of the Indian Ocean from the Rise of Islam to 1750*, Cambridge: Cambridge University Press, 1990.
10. Ibid., p. 21.
11. M.N. Pearson, 'Littoral Society: The Concepts and the Problems', *Journal of World History*, vol. 17, no. 4, 2006.

12. Markus Vink, 'Indian Ocean Studies and the "New Thalassology"', *Journal of Global History*, vol. 2, 2007, p. 53.
13. A.N. Tucker, 'Foreign Sounds in Swahili', *Bulletin of the School of Oriental and African Studies*, University of London, vol. 11, no. 4, 1946, p. 854.
14. See also R.J. Barendse, 'Trade and State in the Arabian Seas: A Survey from the Fifteenth to the Eighteenth Century', *Journal of World History*, vol. 11, no. 2, 2000.
15. Anthony Reid, 'Hybrid Identities in the Fifteenth-Century Straits of Malacca', *Working Paper Series 67*, National University of Singapore: Asia Research Institute, 2006.
16. Andre Wink, 'From the Mediterranean to the Indian Ocean: Medieval History in Geographic Perspective', *Comparative Studies in Society and History*, vol. 44, no. 3, 2002, p. 439.
17. Ibid.
18. Karen Wigen, 'Oceans of History: Introduction', *American Historical Review*, vol. 111, no. 3, June 2006.
19. Sutherland, 'South-East Asian History,' p. 4.
20. Fernand Braudel, *The Mediterranean and the Mediterranean World in the Age of Philip II: Vol. I*, California: University of California Press, 1995, p. 18.
21. Edward A. Alpers, 'Imagining the Indian Ocean World', Opening Address to the International Conference on Cultural Exchange and Transformation in the Indian Ocean World, UCLA, 2002, p. 15.
22. Mukherjee, 'The Indian Ocean in the "New Thalassology"'.
23. Chaudhuri, *Asia Before Europe*.
24. E. Erikson and P. Bearman, 'Routes into Networks: The Structure of English Trade in the East Indies, 1601-1833', *ISERP Working Paper*, Columbia University: Institute for Social and Economic Research and Policy, 2004.
25. Chaudhuri, *Asia Before Europe*.
26. Here, I do not use globalization as is usually defined by economists. Globalization here is defined as the interaction of all heavily populated land masses in a manner that deeply and permanently linked them. For this conception of globalization, see D.O. Flynn and A. Giraldez, 'Born Again: Globalization's Sixteenth Century Origins (Asian/Global versus European Dynamics)', *Pacific Economic Review*, vol. 13, no. 3, 2008.
27. Alpers, 'Imagining the Indian Ocean World', p. 2.
28. J.K. Galbraith, *A History of Economics: The Past as the Present*, London: Hamish Hamilton, 1987. Galbraith writes that merchant capitalism of mercantilism was anything but a system. According to him, it is said to have prevailed for about 300 years from the middle of the fifteenth century to the middle of the eighteenth century. He identifies the end of mercantilism as the period when the Industrial Revolution began and to the publishing of Adam Smith's *Wealth of Nations*.
29. S. Ambirajan, *Classical Political Economy and British Policy in India*, Delhi: Vikas, 1978.
30. L. Reynolds, 'Mercantilism: An Outline, History of Economic Thought', 2000, available at <http://www.boisestate.edu/econ/lreynol/web/pdf_het/mercantilist.pdf> (last accessed on 8 May 2009).

31. Galbraith, *A History of Economics*.
32. Frank in *On Capitalist Underdevelopment* argues that mercantilist expansion is related to the crown and the consolidation of the national state and its power at home. See A.G. Frank, *On Capitalist Underdevelopment*, Bombay: Oxford University Press, 1975.
33. At that time, pirates and smugglers were not viewed as illegal groups of individuals and their activities were not qualified as legal or illegal by the State (the rulers). Note that the legal system has mainly evolved as an appendage to the ruling powers. The law was instituted to reduce hassles during the collection of money from the subjects and for the 'rulers' to maintain law and order. Concomitantly, the notion of 'justice' has also been biased towards the ruling authorities.
34. Thomas Mun, *England's Treasure by Foreign Trade, or our Foreign Trade is the Rule of our Treasure*, London, printed by J.G. for Thomas Clark, 1664.
35. Erikson and Bearman, 'Routes into Networks'.
36. Ibid., p. 2.
37. This is not in any way an exhaustive list.
38. David Washbrook, 'India in the Early Modern World Economy: Modes of Production, Reproduction and Exchange', *Journal of Global History*, vol. 2, 2007.
39. The details regarding *banjaras* are taken from R.G. Varady, 'North Indian Banjaras: Their Evolution as Transporters', *South Asia: Journal of South Asian Studies,* vol. 2, no. 1, 1979.
40. Beaujard, 'The Indian Ocean in Eurasian and African World-Systems', p. 458.
41. Ashin Das Gupta, 'The Maritime Merchant and Indian History', *South Asia: Journal of South Asian Studies*, vol. 7, no. 1, 1984.
42. Ibid., p. 28.
43. In parallel, the number of individual shipowners considerably increased. In accordance, 'the shipping at Surat expanded six fold to ten fold in the middle 17th century as the emperor Aurangzeb withdrew the large royal marine deployed on the Red Sea run'. See Das Gupta, 'The Maritime Merchant and Indian History', p. 32.
44. Vink, 'Indian Ocean Studies and the "New Thalassology"'.
45. For such a comment, see Washbrook, 'India in the Early Modern Economy', p. 98 where he writes 'Marxist commentators, such as Chicherov, saw in early modern India a classic situation in which a transition to capitalism was "immanent"'.
46. One primary reason for this is that, data relating to the rest are not readily available.
47. Michel Morineau, 'The Indian Challenge: Seventeenth to Eighteenth Centuries', in *Merchants, Companies and Trade: Europe and Asia in the Early Modern Era*, ed. Sushil Chaudhury and Michel Morineau, Cambridge: Cambridge University Press, 1999.
48. Washbrook, 'India in the Early Modern Economy', p. 96.
49. Ibid.

50. P. Parthasarathi, *The Transition to a Colonial Economy: Weavers, Merchants and Kings in South India, 1720–1800*, Cambridge: Cambridge University Press, 2001.
51. Rila Mukherjee, *Merchants and Rulers in Bengal: Kasimbazar and Jugdia in the Eighteenth Century,* New Delhi: Pragati Publications, 2006.
52. Neeraj Hatekar, 'Farmers and Markets in Pre-Colonial Deccan: The Plausibility of Economic Growth in Traditional Society', *Past & Present*, no. 178, 2003, p. 117.
53. See the chapter 'Caste in Indian History' regarding the adverse effects like limiting the mobility of labour, oppression, information and power asymmetries arising from sanskritization, etc., in Irfan Habib, *Essays in Indian History: Towards a Marxist Perception,* New Delhi: Tulika Publishers, 1995.
54. Washbrook, 'India in the Early Modern Economy', p. 101.
55. Neils Steensgaard, 'The Route through Quandahar: the Significance of the Overland Trade from India to the West in the Seventeenth Century', in *Merchants, Companies and Trade: Europe and Asia in the Early Modern Era*, ed. Sushil Chaudhury and Michel Morineau, Cambridge: Cambridge University Press, 1999.
56. Ibid. In terms of pure transport costs, maritime trade cost 27 per cent while overland/inland/caravan trade cost 20 per cent in Central India.
57. See also Washbrook, 'India in the Early Modern Economy', p. 104 who states that 'in terms of internal trade, the Mughal Empire made major efforts to protect the roads and regulate (if never stop) brigandage'.
58. Stephen F. Dale, *Indian Merchants and Eurasian Trade, 1600–1750*, Cambridge: Cambridge University Press, 1994.
59. See I.B. Sen, 'Moneylenders in India', *Journal of the Society of Comparative Legislation*, n.s., vol. 11, no. 1, 1910.
60. Claude Markovitz, *The Global World of Indian Merchants 1750–1947: Traders of Sindh from Bukhara to Panama,* Cambridge: Cambridge University Press, 2000.
61. Erikson and Bearman, 'Routes into Networks: The Structure of English Trade in the East Indies, 1601-1833'.
62. Flynn and Giraldez, 'Born Again: Globalization's Sixteenth Century Origins (Asian/Global versus European Dynamics)'.
63. It is with a similar motive that Ludden reviews history outside 'civilization'. See David Ludden, 'History Outside Civilisation and the Mobility of South Asia', *South Asia: Journal of South Asian Studies*, vol. 17, no. 1, 1994.
64. Chaudhuri, *Asia Before Europe*.

Bibliography

Primary Sources

ARCHIVO GENERAL DE INDIAS, SEVILLE, SPAIN

Philippines 7-R-7-N-88,'Memoria de las mercancías del embajador japonés'.

ARCHIVO GENERAL DE SIMANCAS, SPAIN

Escribanía Mayor de Rentas, box. 186-1*EMR*, leg. 177; leg. 177; leg. 191-3.
Cámara de Castilla, leg. 139, nº. 218; *1ª Ép.*, leg. 382, leg. 131, nº. 10.
Estado Génova, leg. 1362, nº 145; leg. 1362, nº 43, nº 142 and nº 144; leg. 1369, nº 38; leg. 1365, nº 239-41; leg. 1375, nº 21; leg. 1365, nº 243 and nº 239; leg. 1369, nº 5 and nº 10; leg. 1369, nº 38.
Madrid, 5 March 1567, fol. 88, 1567-March, Registro General del Sello.

ARCHIVO HISTÓRICO PROVINCIAL, CUENCA, SPAIN

Protocolo (henceforth P) 170, 1559, fols. 231r-231v, Protocolos Notariales.
P 170, 1559, fols. 377r, 379v, and 381v.
P 176, 1565-66, fols. 578r-578v.
P 170, fol. 383v.
P 170, fols. 332r-332v.
P 170, fol. 378r.
P 170, fols. 230r-230v.
P 170, fol. 371r.
P 170, 22 June 1559, fol. 368r.
P 170, fol. 367r.
P 170, fol. 369r.
P 170, fol. 348v.

P 170, fol. 362r.
P 170, fol. 378v.
P 170, fol. 381r.
P 170, 21 January 1559, fol. 351r.
P 170, 20 September 1559, fol. 379r.
P 170, fols. 236r-236v.
P 170, fols. 478r-478v.
P 170, fols. 480r-480v.
P 170, fols. 330r-330v.

ARCHIVUM ROMANUM SOCIETATIS IESU, ROME, ITALY

Opp. NN. 17, Colecção de Varias Receitas e Segredos Particulares das Principais Boticas da Nossa Companhia de Portugal, da India, de Macao e do Brazil (1766), fols. 1-688.

ARQUIVO DISTRITAL DO PORTO (PORTO'S DISTRICT ARCHIVE), PORTO, PORTUGAL

Cabido (Cathedral's chapter records), *Sentenças*, liv. 768, fols. 297-306.
Contadoria da Comarca do Porto (Royal Administration in Porto), liv. 2 (0007), fols. 196-196v.

Notary records, Porto, Portugal

Po1º, 3ª série, liv. 1, fol. 129v.
Po1º, 3ª série, liv. 2, fol. 106v.
Po1º, 3ª série, liv. 6, fol. 94.
Po1º, 3ª série, liv. 8, fols. 17-18v.
Po1º, 3ª série, liv. 13, fol. 94.
Po1º, 3ª série, liv. 14, fol. 34.
Po1º, 3ª série, liv. 14, fols. 70-1.
Po1º, 3ª série, liv. 14, fols. 147-8v.
Po1º, 3ª série, liv. 21, fol. 144v-6v.
Po1º, 3ª série, liv. 31, fols. 22-22v.
Po1º, 3ª série, liv. 41, fol. 193.
Po1º, 3ª série, liv. 41, fol. 198.
Po1º, 3ª série, liv. 43, fol. 160.
Po1º, 3ª série, liv. 50, fol. 117v.
Po1º, 3ª série, liv. 63, fols. 98v-100v.
Po1º, 3ª série, liv. 63, fol. 99.
Po1º, 3ª série, liv. 76, fols. 45-6.
Po1º, 3ª série, liv. 77, fols. 91v.
Po1º, 3ª série, liv. 80, fols. 93-5.

Po1º, 3ª série, liv. 96, fol. 122v.
Po1º, 3ª série, liv. 100, fols. 58v-62v.
Po1º, 3ª série, liv. 105, fol. 14v.
Po2º, 1ª série, liv. 5, fols. 183v-5.

Notary records, Vila do Conde, Portugal

1º cart., 1ª sr, lv. 9, fols. 152v.-154; 211v.-212v.
1º cart., 1ª sr, lv. 12, fols. 118v-120.
1º cart., 1ª sr, lv. 17, fols. 70-2.
1º cart., 1ª sr., lv. 18, fols. 140-5v.
1º cart., 1ª sr, lv. 19, fols. 164v-166.
1º cart., 1ª sr, lv. 23, fols. 113-14v.; fols. 137-8.
1º cart., 1ª sr, lv. 25, fols. 30v.-1; fols. 37-8.
1º cart., 1ª sr, lv. 26, fols. 132-5; fols. 135v-136; fols. 136v-137.
1º cart., 1ª sr, lv. 27, fols. 72v-73v.
1º cart., 1ª sr., lv. 29, fols. 86v.-88.
1º cart., 1ª sr., lv. 32, fols. 48v-52v.; fols. 62v.-64.
1º cart., 1ª sr., lv. 33, fols. 20v.-23v.
1º cart., 2ª sr., lv. 4, fols. 107v.-109.
1º cart., 3ª sr., lv. 5, fols. 127v.-128v.
1º cart., 3ª sr., lv. 6, fols. 102v.-105v.
1º cart., 3ª sr., lv. 7, fols. 57-57v.
1º cart., 3ª sr., lv. 11, fols. 75-7.
1º cart., 3ª sr., lv. 15, fols. 116-18.
1º cart., 4ª sr., lv. 1, fols. 25v.-27.

ARQUIVO HISTÓRICO MUNICIPAL DO PORTO (PORTO'S HISTORICAL ARCHIVE), PORTUGAL

Livro do despacho das naus (Ships dispatch book), fols. 24-24v.
Provisões, liv. 1, fols. 8 and 339.
Vereações, liv. 7, fol. 98.

ARQUIVO NACIONAL DA TORRE DO TOMBO (PORTUGAL'S NATIONAL ARCHIVE), LISBON, PORTUGAL

Gavetas, XV, maço 18, doc. 13.
Inquisição de Coimbra, proc. 8026, fol. 5; proc. 3821, fol. 27.

BIBLIOTHEQUE NATIONALE DU FRANCE, PARIS

Department of Manuscripts, Fonds Portugais no. 59, Breve compendio de varias receitas de medicina (1598), fols. 2-79v.

BIBLIOTECA NACIONAL DO RIO DE JANEIRO (NATIONAL LIBRARY), BRAZIL

Manuscripts division: nr. 1-15, 02, 026, Curiosidade; un libro de Medicina escrito por los Jesuitas en las Misiones del Paraguay en el año 1580 (1580), fols. 1-280.

CENTRE DES ARCHIVES D'OUTRE-MER, AIX-EN-PROVENCE, FRANCE

Entry nos. 2548, 2570, 2584, 22MI41.

CENTRAL LIBRARY OF PANAJI, INDIA

MS. 18: Notícias Particular do Commércio da Índia, fols. 2-58.

HISTORICAL ARCHIVE OF GOA, INDIA

MR 46A (1681-1682), fols. 96r-97v.
MR 52, fol. 191r/v.
MR 85, fol. 59v.
MR 115 (1742), fols. 88-9.
MR 135B, fol. 489v.
MR 169A, fols.305-7.
MR 173, fol. 227.
MR 173, fol. 168.
MR 176B, fols.436, 448.
MR 177A, fol. 218.
MR 175, fols. 219-30.
MR 178B, fols. 644-64.
MR 180B, fols.444-45v.
MR Nr. 181A, fols.9-45, 65.
MR Nr. 181B, fols.370-98.
MR Nr. 212A, fol. 200v.
Monções do Reino 178B, fols. 644-664.
Vol. 646, fol. 39.
Vol. 831 (Livro da Receita e Despeza de Medicamentos do Hospital do Convento de São João de Deus), fol. 3r (18 May 1733); fol. 72r (27 July 1735); fol. 2r (6 May 1733).
Vol. 865, 'Doentes do Hospital Real do Baçaim'.
Vol. 4508, 'Pessoal do Hospital Militar' (1777-1779), fol. 5r.
Volume 7887 ('Despezas do Convento do São João de Deus'), fol.197r, fols.2v, 7r, 9v and 40-3.
Vol. 7926, fols. 56r-56v, 'Relação de Medicamentos que vão da Botica do Hospital Real [de Goa] para a Fortaleza de Diu'.
Vol. 8030, fol. 28 (November 1832).
Vol. 8032, 'Botica do Convento do Santo Agostinho'.

INDIA OFFICE LIBRARY, LONDON, UK

Bayley, H.B. (Chairman of Board of Directors), *Letters to John Hob House president of the company's Board of Control,* on 11 January 1841, Research Dept., Miscellaneous Correspondence, no. 836, pp. 184-5 (unpublished document).
Kasimbazar Factory Records.
Bengal Public Consultations.

NATIONAL ARCHIVES OF INDIA, NEW DELHI, INDIA

Foreign Department, *Political Consultation,* 10 October 1823, nos. 23-5 (unpublished document).
———, 12 September 1851, nos. 151-2, pp. 465-87; no. 154 (unpublished document), pp. 546-50.
Foreign Department, Political A, 9 September 1876.
———, *Ladakh Diary,* 1880, nos. 67-77 (unpublished document).
———, March 1882, nos. 149-50, *Diary of British Joint Commissioner* (unpublished document).
Foreign Political Proceedings, 26 July 1822, no. 56 (unpublished document).
Foreign Secret Proceedings, 27 December 1850, no. 629, pp. 1567-8 (unpublished document).
IOR/G/21, 'East India Company, Records of Java'.
IOR/G/40/25 (4) 'Richard Welden at Banda to George Muschamp at Amboina', pp. 17-19.
IOR/G/12/17, p. 300.
Ladakh Trade Report A, pp. 1-47 (unpublished document).

SHEMBAGANUR PROVINCE ARCHIVES, SACRED HEART COLLEGE, KODAIKANAL, TAMIL NADU, INDIA

Annual Jesuit Missionary Letters of the Malabar Province, shelf 211, book 34 (1606-43), pp. 30-44, 47-50, 52-3 and 78; shelf 211, book 102 (1655-66), pp. 87-91 and 221-27.

VILA DO CONDE MISERICÓRDIA'S ARCHIVE, PORTO, PORTUGAL

Maço de Testamentos Antigos: Testamento de Amador Carvalho.
Col. 1ª, mç. 48, fol. 75, fol. 75v, mç. 25, n/f, mç. 17, n/f.; mç. 11.
———, Bens de Raíz, pasta 1, Papéis pertencentes ao Casal de Ansêde.
———, Pasta 1, mç. 1, fol. 50-6 e 74-9.
———, Mç 3, Capela de Jerónimo Veloso.
Inventário de bens, mç. 11, fols. 9v. to 12v.
———, mç. 48, fols. 30v.-36.
———, mç. 39, fols. 3-5v; fols. 6-12.
———, mç. 10, fols.147 and 206v.-211v.

———, mç.8, fols.15-16v.
Lv. 2º de Registos, fol. 179v.
Livro de Capelas e Obrigações (ano 1579), fols. 86-9.
Maço de Testamentos Antigos.

PRIMARY PRINTED SOURCES

Alburquerque, Luís de, ed.,*Dicionário da Expansão Portuguesa*, vol. 1, Lisboa: Circulo de Leitores, 1994, pp. 182-3.

Andrade, Franciscode, *O primeiro Cerco que os turcos puserão há fortaleza de Diu nas partes da India defendida pollos portugueses*, Coimbra, 1589.

Santo António, Frei Caetano de, *Pharmacopea Bateana*, Lisbon: 1713.

As gavetas da Torre do Tombo, vol. VII, Lisboa: Centro de Estudos Históricos Ultramarinos, 1968.

Azevedo, Frei Manuel, *Correcçam de Abusos*, vol. III, Lisbon: 1680.

Baldaeus, Philip, *A True and Exact Description of the Most Celebrated East-Indian Coasts of Malabar and Coromandel, and also of the Isle of Ceylon*, facsimile edn, New Delhi: Asia Educational Services, 2000.

Barbosa, Duarte, *The Book of Duarte Barbosa*, tr. M.L. Dames, London: Hakluyt Society, 1921.

Barbuda, C.L.M.de, *Instruçoes com que El-Rei D. José mandou passar ao Estado da Índia o Governador, e Capitão General, e o Arcebispo Primazdo Oriente no ano de 1774*, published and annotated by Lisbon: Imprensa Nacional, 1903.

Bell, Sir Charles, *The People of Tibet*, Oxford: Clarendon Press, 1928.

Biker, J.F.J., *Colecção de Tratados*, Lisboa: Imprensa Nacional, 1880.

Bombelles, Marquis of, *Journal d'un ambassadeur de France au Portugal 1786-1788*, Paris: Editions PUF, 1979.

Bowrey, Thomas, *A Geographical Account of the Countries Around The Bay of Bengal 1669-1679*, ed. R.C. Temple, Cambridge: Hakluyt Society, 1905.

Burnell, Arthur Coke, and P.A. Tiele, eds., *The Voyage of John Huyghen Van Linschoten to the East Indies*, vol. I, London: The Hakluyt Society, 1885.

Castro, D. João de, *Tratado da Sphaera da geografia, notação famosa, informação sobre Maluco*, Lisboa, 1940.

Colecção S. Lourenço, vol. II, preface and notes by Elaine Sanceau, Lisboa, 1975.

Correia, Gaspar, *Lendas da Índia*, 4 vols., Porto, 1975.

Costa, Cristóvão da, *Tractado de las drogas, y medecinas de las Indias Orientales con sus Plantas debuxadas al biuo por Christoual Acosta medico y cirujano que las vio ocularmente: en el qual se verifica mucho de lo que escriuio el Doctor Garcia de Orta*, Burgos, 1578.

Diogo do Couto, *Década 8ª da Ásia*, 2 vols., ed. Maria Augusta Lima Cruz, Lisboa, 1993.

Faleiro, Francisco, *Tratado del esphera y del arte del marear con el regimieto de las alturas cõ alguas reglas nueuamete escritas muy necessarias*, 2nd edn, Madrid, 1980.

Foster, William, *The English Factories in India, 1618-1669*, vol. 5, Oxford: Clarendon Press, 1906-27.

Gordon, Lt. Col. T.E., *The Roof of the World: Being a Narrative of a Journey over the high plateau of Tibet to Russian Frontiers and the Oxus; sources on Pamir*, Edinburgh, 1876.

De Graaf, Voyage de Nicolas de Graaf aux Indes Orientales, etc. (1639–87), Amsterdam: J.F. Bernard, 1719.

Grose, John Henry, *A Voyage to the East Indies*, 2 vols., London, 1772.

Hakluyt, Richard, *The Principal Navigations*, ed. Edmund Goldsmid, FRHS, 2006.

Hamilton, Walter, *East India Gazetteer*, 2 vols., London: Parbury Allen & Co., 1828.

Hedges, William, *Diary of William Hedges During His Agency in Bengal: 1681-87*, 2 vols., ed. R. Barlow and H. Yule, London: Hakluyt Society, 1880.

Khan, Shafaat Ahmad, ed., *John Marshall in India: Notes and Observations in Bengal (1668-1672)*, rpt, Read Books, 2006.

Knight, E.F., *Where Three Empires Meet*, London, 1895; Longmans, Green, and Co. 1905; rpt, Asian Educational Services, 1993.

Laval, François Pyrard de, *The Voyage of François Pyrard of Laval to the East Indies*, vol. II, London, 1888.

———, *Voyage of Pyrard de Laval*, rpt, 2 vols., New York, s/d.

Luillier, *Voyage du sieur Luillier aux Grandes Indes, avec une instruction pour le commerce des Indes orientales*, Paris: Claude Cellier, 1705.

Lyall, J.B., *Kangra Settlement Report*, Lahore, 1889.

Mandelslo, J. Albert de, *Mandelslo's Travels in Western India: 1638-1639*, London, 1931.

Markham, C., *Narratives of the mission of George Bogle to Tibet and of the journey of Thomas Manning to Lhasa*, London, 1876.

Ministério do Reino, Maço 469 (no date), cited in José Pedro Sousa Dias, Inovação Técnica e Sociedade na Farmáci da Lisboa Setecentista (doctoral dissertation of the Universidade de Lisboa, Faculdade de Farmácia, 1991), vol. II, pp. 638-9.

Moorcroft, William, Letters to Traill, *Asiatic Journal*, vol. XXI, no. IV, 1836, p. 217.

———, and George Trebeck, *Travels in Himalayan Provinces of Hindusthan and the Punjab, in Ladakh and Kashmir, in Peshawar, Kabul, Kunduz and Bokhara, 1819-1825*, 2 vols., London, 1841.

Mun, Thomas, *England's Treasure by Foraign Trade, or our Foraign Trade is the Rule of our Treasure,* London, Printed by J.G. for Thomas Clark, 1664.

Orta, Garcia da, *Colóquios dos Simples e Drogas da Índia*, Goa: Rachol Seminary and Ioannes de Endem, 1563; 2 vols., rpt, Lisboa, 1987.

Pinto, Fernão Mendes, in *Dicionário da Expansão Portuguesa*, vol. 2, Lisboa: Círculo de Leitores, 1994, pp. 904-6.

Pires, Tome, *Suma Oriental of Tome Pires, An Account of the East, From the Red Sea to China, written in Malacca and India in 1512-1515 and the Book of Francisco Rodrigues, Pilot Major of the Armada that Discovered Banda and the Moluccas*, ed. Armando Cortesao, London: Hakluyt Society, 1944.

Ramsay, H.L., *Western Tibet: A Practical Dictionary of the Language and Customs of the Districts included in Ladakh Wazaret*, Lahore, 1890.

Relação das naus e armadas da Índia, ed. de Maria Hermínia Maldonado, Coimbra, 1985.

Ribeiro, Luciano, Registo da Casa da Índia, 2 vols., Lisboa, 1954-5.

Santos, H.M. dos, *Catálogo dos documentos secretos do extinto Conselho de Guerra*, vol. 4, Lisboa, 1963.

Sinclair, W.F., and D. W. Ferguson, eds., *The Travels of Pedro Texeira, etc.*, London: Hakluyt Society, 1902.

Tavernier, Jean Baptiste, *Travels in India*, 2 vols, New Delhi, 1977.

———, *Les six voyages*, Paris: Gervais Clouzier, 1681/2.

Temple, R.C., ed., *The Diaries of Streynsham Master 1675-1680 and Other Contemporary Papers Relating Thereto*, 2 vols., London: John Murray, 1911.

Turner, S., *An Account of An Embassy to the Court of Tessholame in Tibet*, 1800.

Vargas, José Manuel, 'Almíscar', in *Dicionário de História dos Descobrimentos*, vol. I, Lisboa, 1994, pp. 56-7.

Varthema, Ludovico, *The Itinerary of Ludovico Varthema*, tr. R.C. Temple, London: Hakluyt Society, 1928.

Venkof, M., *A Brief Sketch of English Dominion in Asia* (Russian), St. Petersburg, 1875; English translation by F.L. Dankes, Simla, 1876.

Vogel, J.P., *Archaeological Survey of India Report*, 1906.

Wilson, C.R., *The Early Annals of the English in Bengal being the Bengal Public Consultations for the First Half of the Eighteenth Century*, vol. 1, London: Thacker, 1900.

Secondary Sources

Abreu, Laurinda, 'O papel das Misericórdias dos "lugares de além-mar" na formação do Império Português', in *História, Ciência, Saúde: Manguinhos*, vol. VIII, no. 3, September-December 2001, pp. 591-611.

Acero, Beatriz Alonso, *Orán-Mazalquivir, 1589-1639*, Madrid: CSIC, 2000.

Ahmad, Afzal, 'Portuguese Trade on the Western Coast of India in the Seventeenth Century (1600-1663)', Baroda, 1984, unpublished Ph.D. thesis, submitted to the Department of History of the Faculty of Arts of Maharaja Sayajirao University of Baroda, India.

———, *Os Portugueses na Ásia*, Lisbon: Imprensa Nacional/Casa da Moeda, 1997.

Albert, Réka, Hawoong Jeong, and Albert-László Barabási, 'Attack and Error Tolerance in Complex Networks', *Nature*, vol. 406, 2000, pp. 378-82.

Alden, Dauril, *The Making of an Enterprise: The Society of Jesus in Portugal, Its Empire, and Beyond, 1540-1750*, California: Stanford University Press, 1996.

Alegria, Fernanda, João Carlos Garcia and Francesc Relaño, *'Cartografia e Viagens'*, in *História da Expansão Portuguesa*, ed. Francisco Bettencourt and K.N. Chaudhuri, Lisboa: Círculo de Leitores, 1998, vol. 1, pp. 26-60.

Alonso, Hilario Casado, ed., *Castilla y Europa: comercio y mercaderes en los siglos XIV, XV y XVI*, Burgos: Diputación Provincial, 1995.

Alonso, María M., and Milagros Flores, *El Caribe en el siglo XVIII y el ataque británico a Puerto Rico en 1797*, Puerto Rico: National Park Service, Department of the Interior, 1998.

Alpers, Edward A., 'Imagining the Indian Ocean World', Opening Address to the International Conference on Cultural Exchange and Transformation in the

Indian Ocean World, UCLA, 2002, http://www.alamo.edu/sac/history/keller/indiano/alpers_ioworld.pdf (accessed on 13 January 2011).

Alvarez, L. Alonso, *Comercio colonial y crisis del Antiguo Régimen en Galicia, 1778-1818*, La Coruña: Xunta de Galicia (Consellería da Presidencia), 1986.

Amaro, A.M., *Introdução da Medicina ocidental em Macau e as receitas de segredo da botica do Colégio de São Paulo*, Macau: Instituto Cultural de Macau, 1992.

Ambirajan, S., *Classical Political Economy and British Policy in India*, Delhi: Vikas Publishers, 1978.

Ames, Glenn Joseph, *The Estado da India (1663–1677): Priorities and strategies in Europe and the East*, Lisboa, 1989.

———, *Renascent Empire? The House of Braganza and the quest for stability in Portuguese Monsoon Asia, c. 1640-1683*, Amsterdam: Amsterdam University Press, 2000.

Andrade, António Alberto Banhade, *Mundos novos do Mundo: Panorama da difusão pela Europa de notícias dos descobrimentos geográficos portugueses*, 2 vols., Lisboa: Junta de Investigações do Ultramar, 1972.

Andrews, Kenneth R., *Trade, Plumber and Settlement: Maritime Enterprise and the Genesis of the British Empire, 1480-1630*, Cambridge: Cambridge University Press, 1984.

Anselmo, António Joaquim, *Bibliografia das obras Impressas em Portugal no século XVI*, Lisboa: Bibliotheca National, 1926.

Arasaratnam, S., *Merchants, Companies and Commerce on the Coromandel Coast, 1650-1750*, New Delhi: Oxford University Press, 1986.

Araújo, Maria Benedita, 'A Medicina Popular e a Magia no Sul de Portugal', doctoral thesis presented to the Universidade de Lisboa, Faculdade de Letras, 1988, vol. III.

Arlachi, Pino, *Mafia Business: The Mafia Ethic and the Spirit of Capitalism*, tr. Martin Ryle, London: Verso, 1986.

Arrighi, Giovanni, *The Long Twentieth Century: Money, Power, and the Origins of Our Times*, London: Verso, 1994.

Ashworth, William J., *Customs and Excise: Trade, Production, and Consumption in England, 1640-1845*, Oxford: Oxford University Press, 2003.

Aslanian, Sebouh, '"The Salt in a Merchant's Letter": The Culture of Julfan Correspondence in the Indian Ocean and the Mediterranean', *Journal of World History*, vol. 19, no. 2, 2008, pp. 127-88.

———, 'Social capital, "trust" and the role of networks in Julfan trade: informal and semi-formal institutions at work', *Journal of Global History*, vol. 1, 2006, pp. 383-402.

———, 'Trade Diaspora versus Colonial State: Armenian Merchants, the English East India Company, and the High Court of Admiralty in London, 1748–1752', *Diaspora: A Journal of Transnational Studies*, vol. 13, no. 1, 2004, pp. 37-100.

Avelar, Ana Paula, *Fernão Lopes de Castanheda: Historiador dos Portugueses na Índia ou cronista do governo de Nuno da Cunha?* Lisboa: s.n., 1997.

———, *Figurações da alteridade na cronística da expansão*, Lisboa: Universidade Aberta, 2003.

———, *Visões do Oriente: Formas de sentir no Portugal de Quinhentos*, Lisboa: Colibri, 2003.

Azarian, G. Reza, *The General Sociology of Harrison C. White: Chaos and Order in Networks*, New York: Palgrave Macmillan, 2005.

Bacigalupe, Miguel Ángel Echevarria, 'Sistemas productivos y espacios económicos: Los Países Bajos en la España Imperial, 1500-1621', in *España y las 17 Provincias de los Países Bajo,* vol. 1, ed. Ana Crespo Solana and Herrero Sánchez Manuel, Cordoba: Universidade de Cordoba, 2002.

Baião, António, *A Inquisição de Goa: Correspondência dos inquisidores da Índia (1569-1630)*, 2 vols., Coimbra: Academia das Sciencias, 1930.

Bak, Per, *How Nature Works: The Science of Self-Organized Criticality*, New York: Copernicus Press for Springer-Verlag, 1996.

Baker, Wayne E., and Robert R. Faulkner, 'The Social Organization of Conspiracy: Illegal Networks in the Heavy Electrical Equipment Industry', *American Sociological Review*, vol. 58, 1993, pp. 837-60.

Balbi, Giovanna Petti, *Negoziare fuori patria: nazioni e genovesi in età medievale*, Bologna: CLUEB, 2005.

Balkrishna, *Commercial Relations between India and England, 1601-1757*, London: George Routledge and Sons, 1924.

Ball, J.N., *Merchants and Merchandise: The expansion of trade in Europe, 1500-1630*, New York: St. Martin's Press, 1997.

Ballard, Roger, 'Coalitions of Reciprocity and the Maintenance of Financial Integrity within Informal Value Transmission Systems: The Operational Dynamics of Contemporary *Hawala* Networks', *Journal of Banking Regulation*, vol. 6, no. 4, 2005, pp. 319-52. See also http://www.casas.org.uk/papers/hawala.html (accessed on 17 June 2010).

Barabási, Albert-László, *Linked: The New Science of Networks*, Cambridge, Massachusetts: Perseus, 2002.

Barendse, R.J., 'Trade and State in the Arabian Seas: A Survey from the Fifteenth to the Eighteenth Century', *Journal of World History*, vol. 11, no. 2, 2000, pp.173-225.

Barney, Warf, and Santa Arias, eds., *The Spatial Turn: Interdisciplinary Perspectives*, Routledge, 2008.

Barrett, Ward, '"World Bullion Flows", 1450-1800', in *The Rise of Merchant Empires: Long-Distance Trade in the Early Modern World, 1350-1750*, ed. James D. Tracy, Cambridge: Cambridge University Press, 1990.

Barros, Amândio, *A naturalidade de Fernão de Magalhães revisitada*, Porto, Ed. Afrontamento, 2009.

———, *Construção naval e cronologia das embarcações do Rio Douro*, Ílhavo: Museu Marítimo, 2009.

———, *Porto: a construção de um espaço marítimo nos alvores dos tempos modernos*, 2 vols., Porto: Faculdade de Letras, 2004.

Basto, A. de Magalhães, *História da Santa Casa da Misericórdia do Porto*, 2nd edn, 2 vols., Porto: Santa Casa da Misericórdia, 1997.

Beaujard, P., 'The Indian Ocean in Eurasian and African World-Systems before the Sixteenth Century', *Journal of World History*, vol. 16, no. 4, 2005, pp. 411-65.

Beerbühl, Margrit Schulte, and Jörg Vögele, eds., *Spinning the Commercial Web: International Trade, Merchants, and Commercial Cities, c. 1640-1939*, Frankfurt am Main: Peter Lang, 2004.

Beltrán, María Teresa López,'Fiscalidad regia en los puertos españoles del reino de Tremecén: Datos para su estudio', *Baética: Estudios de arte, geografía e historia*, no. 5, 1985, pp. 301-10.

Ben-Porath,Yoram, 'The F-Connection: Families, Friends, and Firms in the Organization of Exchange', *Population and Development Review*, vol. 6, 1980, pp. 1-30.

Benton, Lauren,'From the World-Systems Perspective to Institutional World History: Culture and Economy in Global Theory',*Journal of World History*, vol. 7, no. 2, 1996, pp. 261-95.

Bernard, Jacques,*Navires et gens de mer a Bordeaux (vers 1400-vers 1550)*, Paris: S.E.V.P.E.N., 1968, vol. II.

Bethencourt, Francisco and Diogo Ramada Corto, eds.,*Portuguese Oceanic Expansion, 1400-1800*, Cambridge:Cambridge University Press, 2007.

Bethencourt, Francisco and K.N. Chaudhuri, eds., *Nova História da Expansão*, vol. I, Lisboa: Círculo de Leitores, 1998.

Bhattacharya, Bhaswati, 'Making money at the blessed place of Manila: Armenians in the Madras-Manila trade in the eighteenth century',*Journal of Global History*, vol. 3, 2008, pp. 1-20.

Bilham, Roger, 'The 1737 Calcutta Earthquake and Cyclone evaluated', *Bulletin of the Seismological Society of America*, vol. 84, no. 5, 1994, pp. 1650-7.

Boerner, Lars, and Dan Quint, 'Medieval Matching Markets', Mimeograph, 2007.

Bol, Peter, *'This Culture of Ours': Intellectual Transitions in T'ang and Sung China*, Stanford, California: Stanford University Press, 1992.

———, 'Neo-Confucianism and Local Society, Twelfth to Sixteenth Century: A Case Study', in *The Song-Yuan-Ming Transition in Chinese History*, ed. Richard von Glahn and Paul Smith, Cambridge, Massachusetts: Harvard University Asia Center, 2003.

———, 'The Rise of Local History: History, Geography, and Culture in Southern Song and Yuan Wuzhou', *Harvard Journal of Asiatic Studies*, vol. 61, no. 1, 2001, pp. 37-76.

Booker, Jackie Robinson, *Veracruz Merchants, 1770-1829: a mercantile elite in late Bourbon and early independent Mexico,* Boulder: Westview Press Co., 1993.

Borges, Charles J., *The Economics of the Goa Jesuits, 1542-1759*, New Delhi: Concept Publishing, 1994.

Botin, Jacques,'Négoce et circulation de l'information au debut de l'Époque Moderne', in *Histoire de la poste:De l'administration à l'enterprise*, ed. Michel Le Roux, Paris: Éditions Rue d'Ulm, 2002.

Boullet, F., and C. Boullet, *Ex-voto marins*, [s.l.], 1986.

Boxer, C.R., 'Asian Potentates and European artillery in the sixteenth-eighteenth centuries',*Journal of the Malayan Branch of the Royal Asiatic Society*, vol. 38, 1965, pp. 156-72.

———, *O Império colonial português, 1415-1825*, Lisboa: Edicões 70,1981.

———, *Realções raciais no império colonial português 1415-1825*, Porto, ed. Afrontamento, 1977, 1988.

———, *Portuguese Society in the Tropics*, Madison: University of Wisconsin Press, 1965.

Boyajian, James C., *Portuguese trade in Asia under the Habsburgs, 1580-1640*, Baltimore and London: The Johns Hopkins University Press, 1993.

Braudel, Fernand 'La economía del Mediterráneo del siglo XVII', *Mediterráneo e Historia Económica*, no. 7, 'Colección Mediterráneo Económico', 2005.

———, *Civilization and Capitalism: 15th-18th century*, 3 vols., translated from French by Sian Reynolds, New York: Harper and Row, 1974-84.

———, *La dinámica del capitalismo*, México: Fondo de Cultura Económica, 1986.

———, *The Mediterranean and the Mediterranean World in the Age of Philip II: vol. I*, California: University of California Press, 1995.

Broeze, Frank, ed., *Brides of the Sea: Port Cities of Asia from the 16th-20th Centuries*, Kensington, 1989.

Brotton, Jerry, *Trading Territories: Mapping the Early Modern World*, London: Reaktion Books, 1997.

Bruner, Jerome, *Actual Minds, Possible Worlds*, Cambridge, Massachusetts: Harvard University Press, 1985.

Bueno, Idelfonso Pulido, *Almojarifazgo y comercio exterior en Andalucía durante la época Mercantilista, 1526-1740,* Huelva, 1993.

———, *La familia genovesa Centurión (mercaderes diplomáticos y nombres de armas), al servicio de España*, Huelva, 2004.

Bunes Ibarra, Miguel Ángel de, 'Relaciones económicas entre la Monarquía Hispánica y el Islam', *Revista de Historia Económica*, año XXIII, Extraordinary Issue, 2005, pp. 161-77.

Burgess, James, 'Extracts from the Journal of Col. Colin Mackenzie's Pandit on his Route from Calcutta to Gaya in 1820', *Indian Antiquary*, vol. 31, 1A, 1902, pp. 65-75.

Cabourdin, G., and G. Viard, *Lexique historique de la France d'Ancien Régime*, Paris: Armand Colin, 1978.

Cadenas y Vicent, Vicentede, *El protectorado de Carlos V en Génova: La 'Condotta' de Andrea Doria*, Madrid, 1997.

Callon, Michel, 'The Sociology of the Actor-Network: The Case of the Electric Vehicle', in *Mapping the Dynamics of Science and Technology*, ed. M. Callon, J. Law, and A. Rip, London: Macmillan, 1986.

Camman, S., *Trade through the Himalayas,* Princeton: Princeton University Press, 1951.

Capel, Horacio, *Geografía humana y ciencias sociales*, Barcelona: Editorial Montesinos, 1987.

Carande, Ramón, *Carlos V y sus banqueros. 3. Los caminos del oro y de la plata*, Barcelona: Crítica, 1990.

Carreira, Ernestine, 'From decline to prosperity: shipbuilding in Daman, 18th–19th centuries', in *Indo-Portuguese encounters: Journeys in science, technology andculture*, vol. 2, ed. Lotika Varadarajan, New Delhi: Indian National Science Academy, Aryan Books International, 2006.

———, 'O estado português no Oriente, aspectos políticos (1660-1815)', in *Nova História da Expansão Portuguesa*, Lisboa: Editorial Estampa, 2006.

———, 'Portuguese India in the reign of Tipoo Sultan', *Moyen Orient & Ocean Indien*, vol. 6, 1989, pp. 111-14.

———, 'Un empire à vendre: stratégies d'appropriation des ports de l'Estado da India par les compagnies britannique et française', in *L'empireportugaisface aux autres empires*, Paris: Maisonneuve et Larose, 2008, pp. 80-5.

Carrington, Peter J., John Scott, and Stanley Wasserman, eds., *Models and Methods in Social Network Analysis,* Cambridge, UK, and New York: Cambridge University Press, 2005.

Carvalho, Joaquim Barradasde, *A la recherche de la spécificité de la Rennaissance Portugaise: L'Esmeraldo de situ orbis de Duarte Pacheco Pereira et la litterature de voyages a l'epoque des grandes decouvertes: Contribution à l'étude de la pensée moderne*, 2 vols., Paris: Fondation Calouste Gulbenkian, Centre Culturel Portugais, 1983.

Carvalho, R., 'O recurso a pessoal estrangeiro no tempo de Pombal', in *O Marquês de Pombal e o seu tempo*, vol. 1, *Revista de História das ideias*, Lisboa: Faculdade de Letras, 1982.

Casalilla, Bartolomé Yun, 'Entre la economía mundo y el crecimiento polinuclear (los rasgos generales de la economía europea en el tránsito del siglo XVI (1490-1530)', in *De la unión de coronas al Imperio de Carlos V*, ed. E. Belenguer, Madrid: Sociedad Estatal, 2001, vol. 1, pp. 29-46.

Castillo, Guillermo Céspedesdel, *América Hispánica (1492-1898)*, Madrid: Marcial Pons, 2009.

Cavillac, Michel, *Pícaros y mercaderes en el Guzmán de Alfarache*, Granada: Universidad de Granada, 1994.

Chakrabarty, Dipesh, *Provincializing Europe: Postcolonial Thought and Historical Difference*, Princeton: Princeton University Press, 2000.

Chartier, Robert, *A história cultural entre práticas e representações*, Lisboa: Difel, 1988.

Chase-Dunn, Christopher, and Andrew Jorgenson, 'Regions and Interaction Networks: a World-Systems Perspective', paper presented at 'Interactions: Regional Studies, Global Processes, and Historical Analysis', Library of Congress, Washington D.C., 28 February–3 March 2001.

Chase-Dunn, Christopher, and Kelly M. Mann, *The Wintu and Their Neighbors: A Very Small World-System in Northern California,* Tucson, Arizona: University of Arizona Press, 1998.

Chatterjee, Kumkum, *Merchants, Politics and Society in Early Modern India, Bihar 1733-1820*, Leiden: Brill, 1996.

Chaudhuri, K.N., *The Trading World of Asia and the English East India Company, 1660-1760*, Cambridge: Cambridge University Press, 1978.

———, *Asia before Europe: Economy and Civilisation of the Indian Ocean from the Rise of Islam to 1750*, Cambridge: Cambridge University Press, 1990 and 1991.

Chaudhury, Sushil, 'International Trade in Bengal Silk and the Comparative Role of Asians and Europeans, circa. 1700-1757', *Modern Asian Studies*, vol. 29, no. 2, 1995, pp. 373-86.

———, 'The Inflow of Silver to Bengal in Global Perspective *c.*1650-1757', in *Global Connections and Monetary History, 1470-1800*, ed. Dennis O. Flynn, Arturo Giraldez and Richard von Glahn, Ashgate, 2003, pp. 159-68.

———, 'Trading Networks in a Traditional Diaspora: Armenians in India circa 1600-1800', in *Diaspora Entrepreneurial Networks: Four Centuries of History*, 2nd edn, ed. Ina Baghdiantz McCabe, Gelina Harlaftis and Ioanna Pepelasis Minoglou, Berg Publishers, 2005.

———, *Trade and Commercial Organisation in Bengal, 1650-1720*, Calcutta: Firma KLM, 1975.

Chaunu, Pierre and Huguette Chaunu, *Seville et l'Atlantique (1504-1650)*, Paris: S.E.V.P.E.N., 10 vols., 1955-6.

Chaunu, Pierre, *Sevilla y América: Siglos XVI y XVII*, Seville: Universidad, 1983.

Chenaye, Desbois and Badier de la, *Dictionnaire de la Noblesse*, vol. 15, Chez Schlesinger Frères, 1869.

Chirot, Daniel and Thomas D. Hall, 'World-System Theory', *Annual Review of Sociology*, vol. 8, 1982, pp. 81-106.

Chorley, R.,and P. Haggett, eds., *La geografía y los modelos socio-económicos,* Madrid, 1967.

Clossey, Luke, 'Merchants, migrants, missionaries, and globalization in the early-modern Pacific', *Journal of Global History*, vol. 1, London, 2006, pp. 41-58.

Clutton-Brock, Tim, *Meerkat Manor: Flower of the Kalahari*, New York et al.: Simon and Schuster, 2008.

Coase, Ronald, 'The Nature of the Firm', *Economica*, n.s., vol. 4, November 1937, pp. 386-405; *The Nature of the Firm*, Oxford, UK: Oxford University Press, 1991.

Coates, Timothy J., *Convicts and Orphans: Forced and State-Sponsored Colonization in the Portuguese Empire, 1550-1755*, Stanford: Stanford University Press, 2002.

———, *Degredados e órfãs: colonização dirigida pela coroa no império Português, 1550-1755*, Lisboa: CNCDP, 1998.

Coca, José Enrique Lópezde, 'Orán y el comercio genovés en la transición a los tiempos modernos', *Anuario de estudios medievales,* no. 24, 1994, pp. 275-98.

———, 'Relaciones mercantiles entre Granada y Berbería en época de los Reyes Católicos', *Baética: Estudios de arte, geografía e historia,* no. 1, 1978, pp. 293-311.

Coelho, Manoel Rodrigues, *Farmacopeia Tubalense Chimico-Galenica*, Lisbon: Officina de Antonio de Sousa Sylva, 1735.

Cohn, Bernard S., 'The Role of the Gosains in the Economy of Eighteenth and Nineteenth Century Upper India', *Indian Economic & Social History Review*, vol. 1, no. 4, 1964, pp.175-82.

Collingwood, R.G., *The Idea of History*, revd edn, ed. Jan Van Der Dussen, Oxford: Clarendon Press, 1993.

Constable, Olivia Remie, *Trade and Traders in Muslim Spain: the commercial alignment of the Iberian Peninsula, 900-1500*, Cambridge: Cambridge University Press, 1994.

Constant, David, Lee Sproull, and Sara Kiesler, 'The Kindness of Strangers: On the Usefulness of Weak Ties for Technical Advice', *Organizational Science*, vol. 7, 1996, pp. 119-35.

Corrales, Eloy Martín, *Comercio de Cataluña con el Mediterráneo musulmán (siglos XVI-XVIII), El comercio con los 'enemigos de la fe'*, Barcelona: Bellaterra, 2001.

Correia, Alberto C. Germano da Silva, *La Vieille-Goa*, Bastora: Rangel Press, 1931.

Cosgrove, Denis, 'Landscape And Landschaft', lecture delivered at the 'Spatial Turn in History' Symposium, German Historical Institute, 19 February 2004, *GHI BULLETIN*, no. 35, Fall 2004, pp. 57-71, available at http://www.ghidc.org/publications/ghipubs/bu/035/35.57.pdf (accessed on 10 May 2009).

Costa, Leonor F., *Naus e galeões na Ribeira de Lisboa: A construção naval no século XVI para a Rota do Cabo*, Cascais: Patrimonia, 1997.

Coutinho, Valdemar, *O fim da presença portuguesa no Japão*, Sociedad Historica da Independencia de Portugal: Lisboa, 1999.

Crespo Solana, Ana, 'La Gran Guerra del Norte y el comercio holandés con Cádiz y el Báltico en un período de crisis (1699-1723)', *Investigaciones de Historia Económica*, vol. 8, 2007, pp. 45-76.

———, 'The Iberian Peninsula in the First Global Trade: Geostrategy and Mercantile Network interests (XV to XVIII centuries)', in *Global Trade before Globalization (VIII-XVIII)*, ed. Federico Mayor Zaragoza, Madrid: Fondo Cultura de Paz, 2006.

———, 'El comercio marítimo entre Amsterdam y Cádiz (1713-1778)', *Estudios de Historia Económica*, no. 40, Madrid: Banco de España, 2000.

———, *Entre Cádiz y los Países Bajos: una comunidad mercantil en la ciudad de la Ilustración*, Cádiz: Fundación Municipal de Cultura, Cátedra Adolfo de Castro, 2001.

———, *La Casa de la Contratación y la Intendencia General de Marina de Cádiz (1717-1730)*, Cádiz: Universidad de Cádiz, 1996.

Cruz, Rafael Gutiérrez, *Los Presidios españoles del norte de África en tiempo de los Reyes Católicos*, Melilla: Consejería de Cultura, 1997.

Cunha, Ana Isabel Cannas da, *A Inquisição no Estado da Índia: Origens (1539-1560)*, Lisboa: Arquivos Nacionais/Torre do Tombo, 1995.

Cunningham, A., *Ladakh: Physical, Statistical and Historical*, London, 1854.

Curtin, P.D., *Cross-Cultural Trade in World History*, Cambridge: Cambridge University Press, 1984.

———, *The World and the West: The European Challenge and the Overseas Response in the Age of Empire*, New York: Cambridge University Press, 2000.

Dale, Stephen F., *Indian Merchants and Eurasian Trade, 1600–1750*, Cambridge: Cambridge University Press, 1994.

Das Gupta, Ashin, 'The Maritime Merchant and Indian History', *South Asia: Journal of South Asian Studies*, vol. 7, no. 1, 1984, pp.27-33.

———, *Indian Merchants and the Decline of Surat 1700-1750*, Wiesbaden: Steiner Verlag, 1979.

———, *Malabar in Asian Trade, 1740-1800*, Cambridge: Cambridge University Press, 1967.

Davies, John, Rudi Studer, and Paul Warren, *Semantic Web Technologies: Trends and Research in Ontology-Based Systems*, Chichester, UK, and Hoboken, New Jersey: John Wiley & Sons, 2006.

Davis, R., 'English Foreign Trade 1700-74', in *The growth of overseas trade in the Seventeenth and Eighteenth Centuries*, ed. W.E. Minchinton, London, 1969.

———, *Rise of the English Shipping Industry in the Seventeenth and Eighteenth Century*, London, 1962.

———, *The Industrial Revolution and British Overseas Trade*, Leicester, 1979.

Denucé, Jean, ed., *Inventaire des Affaitadi: Banquiers italiens a Anvers de l'année 1568*, Anvers: Éditions de 'Sikkel' and Librairie Ernest Leroux, 1934.

Deb-Ther-Son-Po, *Gos-lostba* (Tibetan), English translation by G.N. Roirich, *The Blue Annals*, pt.I, Calcutta, 1947.

Deheja, Vidya, 'The Collective and popular basis of Early Buddhist patronage: Sacred Monuments 100 BC-250 AD', in *Powers of Art*, ed. Barbara Staler Miller, New Delhi: Oxford University Press, 1992.

Deleuze, Gilles and Félix Guattari, *Rhizome: Introduction*, Paris: Éditions de Minuit, 1976.

Deloche, Jean, 'Boats and ships in Bengal Terracotta Arts', *Bulletin de l'Ecole Français ed' Extrême-Orient*, vol. 78, no. 1, 1991, pp. 1-49.

Dias, José Pedro Sousa, 'O Odor e o Sabor da Farmacologia Galénica', in *A Epopeia das Especiarias*, ed. Inácio Guerreiro, Lisbon: Instituto de Investigação Científica Tropical and Edições, INAPA, 1999.

———, and Rui Pita, 'A Botica de S. Vicente e a Farmácia nos Mosteiros e Conventos da Lisboa Setecentista', in *A Botica de São Vicente de Fora*, Lisbon: Associação Nacional das Farmácias, 1994.

Domingues, Francisco C., *Os navios dos Descobrimentos*, Lisboa, 1991.

———, 'Os navios de Cabral', in *Oceanos*, no. 39, July-September 1999, pp. 70-80.

Doria, Giorgio, 'Comptoirs, foires de changes et places étrangères: les lieux d'apprentissage des nobles négociants de Gênes entre Moyen Âge et Âge Baroque', in *Cultures et formations négociantes dans l'Europe Moderne*, ed. F. Angiolini and D. Roche, Paris: Editions de l'EHESS, 1995.

Drew, Frederick, *The Jammu and Kashmir Territories*, London, 1875.

Duchesne, Ricardo, 'Between Sinocentrism and Eurocentrism: debating Andre Gunder Frank's *ReORIENT: Global Economy in the Asian Age*', *Science & Society*, vol. 65, issue 4, Winter 2001, pp. 428-63.

Dutta, C.L., *Ladakh and Western Himalayan Politics (1819-1847)*, Delhi, 1972.

Edney, Matthew, *Mapping an Empire: The Geographical Construction of British India, 1765-1843*, Chicago: University of Chicago Press, 1997.

Edwards, Herbert Benjamin, and Herman Merivale, *Life of Sir Henry Lawrence*, 2 vols., London: Smith Elder and Co., 1872; 3rd edn in single volume, 1873.

Ehrenberg, Richard, *Le siècle des Fuggers*, Paris: S.E.V.P.E.N., 1955.

Eliade, Mircea, *Encyclopaedia of Religion*, vol. 16, New York, 1987.

Erikson, E., and P. Bearman, 'Routes into Networks: The Structure of English Trade in the East Indies, 1601-1833', *ISERP Working Paper*, Columbia University: Institute for Social and Economic Research and Policy, 2004; Columbia University Press, 2004.

———, 'Malfeasance and the Foundations for Global Trade: The Structure of English Trade in the East Indies, 1601–1833', *American Journal of Sociology*, vol. 112, no. 1, July 2006, pp. 195–230.

Fagel, Raymond, 'España y Flandes en la época de Carlos V: Un imperio político y económico?', in *España y las 17 Provincias de los Países Bajos: Una revisión historiográfica*, ed. Ana Crespo Solana and Herrero Sánchez, Córdoba: Universidad de Córdoba, Fundación Carlos de Amberes, Ministerio de Asuntos Exteriores, 2002.

Fernández, Nélida García, *Comerciando con el enemigo: El tráfico mercantil anglo-español en el siglo XVIII (1700-1765)*, Madrid: CSIC, 2006.

Fernández-Armesto, Felipe, *Before Columbus: exploration and colonisation from the* Mediterranean *to the Atlantic 1229-1492*, 1st edn, London: Houndmills, Hamsphire, 1987.

Figueiredo, João Manuel Pachecode,'The Practice of Indian Medicine in Goa During the Portuguese Rule, 1510-1699', *The Luso-Brazilian Review*, vol. IV, no. 1, June 1967, pp. 51-60.

Fisher, Margaret W., Leo E. Rose and Robert Huttenback, *A Himalayan Battleground*, New York: Frederick A. Praeger, 1963.

Flynn, Dennis O., and A. Giraldez, 'Born Again: Globalization's Sixteenth Century Origins (Asian/Global versus European Dynamics)', *Pacific Economic Review*, vol. 13, no. 3, 2008, pp. 359-87.

———, 'Cycles of Silver: Global Economic Unity through the Mid-Eighteenth Century', *Journal of World History*, vol. 13, no. 2, Hawai, 2002, pp. 391-427.

———, and Richard Von Glahn, eds., *Global Connections and Monetary History, 1470-1800*, Aldershot: Ashgate Publishing, 2003.

Flynn, Dennis O., and A. Giraldez, 'Born with a "Silver Spoon": The Origin of World Trade in 1571', *Journal of World History*, vol. 6, no. 2, 1995, pp. 201-21.

———, *World Silver and Monetary History in the 16th and 17th centuries*, Aldershot: Ashgate/Varorium Press, 1996.

Fonseca, Quirino da, *Os Portugueses no Mar*, Lisboa: Tipografia do Comércio, 1926.

Fontaine, Laurence, 'Pouvoir et cultures dans les circulations financières sous l'Ancien Régime', in *Pourvoir les finances en province sous l'Ancien Régime*, Paris, ed. Françoise Bayard, Comitè pour l'histoire économique et financière de la France, 2001.

Fontán, Antonio, and Jerzi Axer, eds., *Españoles y polacos en la Corte de Carlos V: cartas del embajador Juan Dantisco*, Madrid: Alianza, 1994.

Francke, A.H., *Ladakh: The mysterious land, History of Western Tibet*, London, 1907.

Frank, A.G., On *Capitalist Underdevelopment*, Bombay: Oxford University Press, 1975.

———, *ReORIENT: Global Economy in the Asian Age*, Berkeley-Los Angeles-London: University of California Press, 1998.

———, *Asian-Based World Economy, 1400-1800: A horizontally integrative macrohistory*, Amsterdam, 1995.

———, *World Accumulation, 1492-1789*, New York: Monthly Review Press and London: Macmillan Press, 1978.

———, and Barry K. Gills, eds., *The World System: Five Hundred Years or Five Thousand?*, London: Routledge, 1993.

Freitas, Eugénio de Andrea da Cunha, *História da Santa Casa da Misericórdia do Porto*, vol. III, Porto: Santa Casa da Misericórdia, 1995.

Friman, H. Richard, 'The Great Escape? Globalization, Immigrant Entrepreneurship and the Criminal Economy', *Review of International Political Economy*, vol. 11, 2004, pp. 98-131.

Fuentes, Lutgardo García, *El comercio español con América, 1650-1700*, Seville: Diputación, 1980.

Fujita, M., P. Krugman and A. Venables, *Economía Espacial*, Barcelona: Ariel, 2000.

Galbraith, J.K., *A History of Economics: The Past as the Present*, London: Hamish Hamilton, 1987.

Gambetta, Diego, 'Mafia: the Price of Distrust', in *Trust: Making and Breaking Cooperative Relations*, ed. Diego Gambetta, New York: Basil Blackwell, 1988.

García, David Alonso, 'Los *Fornari* y las rentas de Orán a comienzos del siglo XVI: Financiación del rey y negocio familiar', in *Los extranjeros en la España Moderna*, ed. M.B. Villar and P. Pezzi, Málaga: Universidad de Malaga, 2003, vol. II, pp. 101-12.

———, *El erario del reino. Fiscalidad en Castilla a principios de la Edad Moderna, 1504-1525*, Valladolid: Junta de Castilla y León, 2007.

Garcia, José Manuel, 'A historiografia portuguesa dos descobrimentos e da expansão (séculos XV a XVII): Autores, obras e especializações memoriais', Porto: [s.n.], 2006, 2 vols., unpublished Ph.D. thesis presented at the University of Porto.

Gelabert, Juan E., *La bolsa del rey: Rey, reino y fisco en Castilla (1598-1648)*, Barcelona: Crítica, 1997.

Ghosal, H.R., *Economic Transition in the Bengal Presidency (1793-1833)*, Patna: Patna University, 1950.

Gillard, D.R., *TheStruggle for Asia, 1828-1914: A Study in Russian and British Imperialism*, London, 1977.

Giraldo, Manuel Lucena, 'Tres décadas que cambiaron el mundo (sobre "El Imperio español de Colón a Magallanes" de Hugh Thomas")', *Revista de Occidente*, no. 276, 2004, pp. 191-4.

Girvan, M., and M.E.J. Newman, 'Community Structure in Social and Biological Networks', *Proceedings of the National Academy of Sciences of the United States of America*, vol. 99, no. 12, 2002, pp. 7821-6.

Gladwell, Malcom, *The Tipping Point: How Little Things Can Make a Big Difference*, Boston: Little, Brown, 2000.

Godinho, Vitorino Magalhães, *Os Descobrimentos e a economia mundial*, 4 vols., Lisboa: Editorial Presença, 1987.

Goldfrank, Walter L., 'Paradigm Regained? The Rules of Wallerstein's World-System Method', *Journal of World-Systems Research*, vol. XI, no. 2, 2000, pp. 150-95.

Goldstone, Jack A., 'The Problem of the "Early Modern" World', *Journal of the Economic and Social History of the Orient*, vol. 41, no. 3, 1998, pp. 249-84.

Gomes, Bernadette, 'Ethnomedicine and Healing Practices in Goa', unpublished Ph.D. thesis, Department of Sociology, University of Goa, India, 1993.

Gonçalves, Iria, 'Uma realização urbanística medieval: o calcetamento da rua Nova de Lisboa', in *Um olhar sobre a cidade medieval*, Cascais: Patrimonia, 1996.

González, Antonio García-Baquero, 'Cádiz y su Tercio de Toneladas en las flotas de Indias: Contribución al estudio de la pugna Sevilla-Cádiz en el interior del complejo monopolístico andaluz', *Gades*, no. 1, 1978, pp. 107-20.

———, 'Comercio colonial y reformismo borbónico: de la reactivación a la quiebra del sistema comercial imperial', *Crónica nova: Revista de historia moderna de la Universidad de Granada*, no. 22, 1995, pp. 105-40.

———, *Andalucía y la Carrera de Indias (1492-1824)*, Granada: Universidad de Granada, 2002.

———, *Cádiz y el Atlántico, 1717-1778*, Cadiz: Diputación Provincial, 1976, 2 vols.

———, *La Carrera de Indias: Suma de contratación y océano de negocios*, Sevilla: Universidad de Sevilla, 1992.

González, Fernando Fernández, *Comerciantes vascos en Sevilla: 1650-1700*, Vitoria-Gasteiz, Sevilla: Diputación de Sevilla, Area de Cultura y Deportes, 2000.

Grabher, Gernot, 'Trading Routes, Bypasses, and Risky Intersections: Mapping the Travels of "Networks" between Economic Sociology and Economic Geography', *Progress in Human Geography*, vol. 30, 2006, pp. 163-89.

Gracias, Fátima da Silva, *Health and Hygiene in Colonial Goa, 1510-1961*, New Delhi: Concept Publishing, 1994.

Gracias, J.B. Amâncio, *Médicos Europeus em Goa e nas Cortes Indianas nos séculos XVI á XVIII*, Bastora: Rangel Press, 1939.

Gracias, J.A.I., *Catálogo dos livros de assentamento da gente de guerra que veiodo reino para a Índia*, Goa: Imprensa Nacional, 1893.

Grafe, Regina, *Entre el mundo ibérico y el Atlántico: Comercio y especialización regional, 1550-1650*, Bilbao: Diputación Foral de Bizkaia, Departamento de Cultura, 2005.

Granovetter, Mark S., 'The Strength of Weak Ties', *American Journal of Sociology*, vol. 78, 1973, pp. 1360-80.

Gredi, Edoardo, *La repubblica aristocratica dei genovesi: Política, carità e commercio fra Cinque e Seicento*, Bologna: Il Mulino, 1987.

Greif, Avner, *Institutions and the Path to the Modern Economy: Lessons from Medieval Trade*, Cambridge, UK, and New York: Cambridge University Press, 2006.

Guerra, Ana M. Azcona, *Comercio y comerciantes en la Navarra del siglo XVIII*, Pamplona: Gobierno de Navarra, 1996.

Guimarães Sá, Isabel dos, *Quando o rio se faz pobre: misericórdias, caridade e poder no Império Português*, Lisboa: CNCDP, 1997.

Guinote, Paulo, Eduardo Frutuso and António Lopes, *Naufrágios e outras perdas da 'Carreira da Índia': Séculos XVI e XVII*, Lisboa: CNCDP, 1998.

Habib, Irfan, *Agrarian System of Mughal India, 1556-1707*, Bombay, 1957.

———, *Essays in Indian History: Towards a Marxist Perception*, New Delhi: Tulika Publishers, 1995.

Haken, Hermann, *Advanced Synergetics: Instability Hierarchies of Self-Organizing Systems and Devices*, Berlin et al.: Springer-Verlag, 1983.

Hatekar, Neeraj, 'Farmers and Markets in Pre-Colonial Deccan: The Plausibility of Economic Growth in Traditional Society', *Past & Present*, no. 178, 2003, pp.116-47.

Hausberger, Bernd and Antonio Ibarra, eds., *Comercio y poder en América colonial: los consulados de comerciantes, siglos XVII-XIX*, Madrid, Frankfurt am Main: Iberoamericana, 2003.

Heers, Jacques, *Gênes au XVe Siècle: Civilisation méditerranéenne, grand capitalisme, et capitalisme populaire*, Paris: S.E.V.P.E.N., 1971.

Hexter, J.H., *The History Primer*, New York: Basic Books, 1971.

Hodson, George H., ed., *Hodson of Hodson's Horse*, London: Keagan Paul Trench and Co., 1883.

Hopkirk, P., *Foreign devils on the Silk Road: The Search for the Lost treasures of Central Asia*, Oxford: Oxford University Press, 1980.

Hunter, Ian, *Rival Enlightenments: Civil and Metaphysical Philosophy in Early Modern Germany* (Ideas in Context), Cambridge University Press, new edn, 2008.

Husnain, F.M., 'The Brokpa Dards of Dah, Hanor and Gakun', in *Ladakh: Life and Culture,* ed. K.N. Pandita, Srinagar: Central Asian Studies, University of Kashmir, 1986.

———, *The History of Jammu, Kashmir, Ladakh and Kishtwar,* Delhi, 1972.

Ingram, E., *The Beginning of the Great Game in Asia, 1828-34*, Oxford, 1979.

Jackson, Matthew O., and Brian W. Rogers, 'The Economics of Small Worlds', *Journal of the European Economic Association*, vol. 3, nos. 2-3, 2005, pp. 617-27.

Jain, S.K., *Medicinal Plants*, New Delhi: National Book Trust, India, 1999.

Jettmar, Karl, *Between Ghandhara and Silk Roads*, Wiesbaden, Germany, 1987.

Jina, Prem Singh, 'Monasteries in Economy of Leh-Ladakh', paper presented at the 'All-India Conference on Buddhist Monasteries of Himalayan Region: Various Aspects', Leh, 9-13 August 1988.

Jolden, E., *Harvest Festival of Buddhist Dards of Ladakh and other Essays*, Srinagar, 1985.

Kachow, Sikander Khan, *Kadeem-Ladakh-Ki-Tawarikh-va-Tamadun* (Urdu), 1987.

Kamen, Henry, *Imperio: La forja de España como potencia mundial*, Madrid: Aguilar, 2004.

Keay, John, *When Men and Mountains Meet: The Explorers of the Western Himalayas 1820-75,* London: John Murray, 1977.

Keninston, Hayward, *Francisco de los Cobos: secretary of the Emperor Charles V*, Pittsburg: University of Pittsburg Press, 1958.

Kent, H.S.K., *War and Trade in the Northern Seas: Anglo-Scandinavian Economic Relations in Middle Eighteenth Century*, Cambridge: The University Press, 1973.

Kirk, Thomas, 'The Apogee of the Hispano-Genoese Bond, 1576-1627', *Hispania*, vol. 65, no. 1, 2005, pp. 45-65.

Knaap, G., and H. Sutherland, *Monsoon Traders: Ships, Skippers and Commodities in Eighteenth-Century Makassar*, Leiden: KITLV Press, 2004.

Knoke, David, and Song Yang, *Social Network Analysis*, 2nd edn, Los Angeles: Sage, 2008.

Koenigsberger, H.G., *Politicians and Virtuosi: Essays in early Modern History*, London and Ronccevette: Hambledon Press, 1986.

Kogut, Bruce, 'The Network as Knowledge: Generative Rules and the Emergence of Structure', *StrategicManagement Journal*, vol. 21, no. 3, 2000, pp. 405-25.

Kokko, Hanna, 'Commentary, Cooperative Behaviour and Cooperative Breeding: What Constitutes an Explanation?', *Behavioural Processes*, vol. 76, 2007, pp. 81–5.

———, Rufus A. Johnstone and T.H. Clutton-Brock, 'The Evolution of Cooperative Breeding through Group Augmentation', *Proceedings of the Royal Society of London B*, vol. 268, 2001, pp. 187-96.

Kutsukake, Nobuyuki, and T.H. Clutton-Brock, 'The Number of Subordinates Moderates Intrasexual Competition among Males in Cooperatively Breeding Meerkats', *Proceedings of the Royal Society B*, vol. 275, 2008, pp. 209-16.

Labourdette, J.F., *La nation française à Lisbonne de 1669 à 1790: EntreColbertisme et Libéralisme*, Paris: Fondation Gulbenkian, 1988.

Lamb, A., *British and Chinese Central Asia: The Road to Lahore, 1767-1905*, London, 1960.

Lanciani, Giulia, *Os relatos de naufrágios na literatura portuguesa dos séculos XVI e XVII,* Lisboa: Biblioteca Breve, 1979.

———, *Sucessos e naufrágios das naus portuguesas*, Lisboa: Caminho, 1997.

Landes, David, *The Wealth and Poverty of Nations: Why Some Are So Rich and Some So Poor*, New York and London: W.W. Norton, 1998.

Lanza, Ramón, *La Población y el crecimiento económico de Cantabria en el Antiguo Régimen*, Cantabria: Universidad de Cantabria, 1991.

Latham, Alan, 'Retheorizing the Scale of Globalization: Topologies, Actor-Networks, and Cosmopolitanism', in *Geographies of Power, Placing Scale*, ed. Andrew Herod and Melissa W. Wright, Malden, Massachusetts: Blackwell, 2002.

Latour, Bruno, 'On Recalling ANT', in *Actor-Network Theory and After*, ed. John Law and John Hassard, Oxford, UK, and Malden, Massachusetts: Blackwell/Sociological Review, 1999.

———, *Reassembling the Social: An Introduction to Actor-Network-Theory*, Oxford and New York: Oxford University Press, 2005.

Lehmann, Laurent, Kevin R. Foster, Elhanan Borenstein, and Marcus W. Feldman, 'Social and Individual Learning of Helping in Humans and Other Species', *Trends in Ecology and Evolution*, vol. 23, no. 12, 2008, pp. 664-71.

Leonard, E.G., *L'armée et ses problèmes au 18e siècle*, Paris: Librairie Plon,1958.

Van Leur, J.C.,*Indonesian Trade and Society*, The Hague: W. van. Hoeve, 1955. Distributed by Institute of Pacific Relations, New York, 1955.

Lewis, Martin W., 'Dividing the Ocean Sea', *Geographical Review*, vol. 89, no. 2, 1999, pp. 188-214.

Lieberman, Victor, 'Local Integration and Eurasian Analogies: Structuring Southeast Asian History, *c.*1350-*c.* 1830', *Modern Asian Studies*, vol. 27, no. 3, July 1993, pp. 475-572.

———, ed., 'The Eurasian Context of the Early Modern History of Mainland South-East Asia', 1400-1800, *Modern Asian Studies*, Special Issue, vol. 31, no. 3, July 1997.

Little, J.H., *The House of Jagat Seth*, Calcutta: Calcutta Historical Society, 1967.

Liu, Xinru, *Silk and Religion: An Exploration of Material Life and the Thought of People in AD 600-1200*, New Delhi: Oxford University Press, 1996.

Llorente, Henar Pizarro, 'Francisco de los Cobos', in *La Corte de Carlos V*, ed. J. Martínez Millán and C. J. de Carlos, Madrid: Sociedad Estatal, 2000, vol. III.

Lombard, Denys, *Le Sultanat d'Atjeh au temps d'Iskandar Muda 1607-1636*, Paris: Ecole Francaise d' Extreme-Orient, vol. 61, 1967.

Lopes, Maria de Jesus dos Mártires, *Goa Setecentista: Tradição e Modernidade (1750-1800),* 2nd edn, Universidade Católica Portuguesa, 1999.

López, Enrique Giménez, 'Dos décadas de estudios sobre el comercio valenciano en la Edad Moderna', *Revista de Historia Moderna*, nos. 6-7, Alicante, 1986, pp. 93-206.

Lucena, João de, *História da Vida de S. Francisco Xavier: E do que fizeram na Índia os mais religiosos da Companhia de Jesus*, Lisboa, 1600.

Ludden, David, 'History outside Civilisation and the Mobility of South Asia', *South Asia: Journal of South Asian Studies*, vol. 17, no. 1, 1994, pp. 1-23.

Lughod, Janet Abu, *Before European Hegemony: The World System, AD 1250-1350*, Oxford University Press, 1991.

Luz, F. P. Mendes da,'Livro das Cidades', *Studia*, vol. 6, 1960, fn. 8.

Macedo, Jorge Borges de, *Os Lusíadas e a História*, Lisboa: Verbo, 1979.

Magalhães, Joaquim R., 'Açúcar e especiarias', in *Nova História da Expansão*, vol. I, Lisboa: Círculo de Leitores,1998, pp. 298-307.

———,'Articulações internacional-regionais e economias-mundo', in *Nova História da Expansão*, vol. I, Lisboa: Círculo de Leitores, 1998, pp. 308-37.

Markovitz, Claude, *The Global World of Indian Merchants, 1750–1947: Traders of Sindh from Bukhara to Panama*, Cambridge: Cambridge University Press, 2000.

Marshall, P.J., *East Indian Fortunes: The British in Bengal in the Eighteenth Century*, Oxford: Oxford University Press, 1976.

———, *The Making and Unmaking of Empires: Britain, India and America, c.1750-1783*,Oxford: Oxford University Press, 2005.

Martín, Alberto Marcos,*España en los siglos XVI, XVII y XVIII*, Barcelona: Crítica, 2000.

Martinez-Vela, Carlos A., 'World Systems Theory', *ESD*, vol. 83, 2001, pp. 1-5.

Marx, Karl,'The British Rule in India' and 'The Future Results of the British Rule in India', in *Karl Marx & Frederick Engels: Collected Works*, vol. 12, Marx and Engels: 1853-54, Moscow: Progress Publishers, 1979.

Marx, K.,'Three documents relating to the History of Ladakh',*Journal, Asiatic Society of Bengal*,n.s.,vol. LX, 1891, pt. I, pp. 97-134.

Matos, Artur T. de, 'Some aspects of the Portuguese trade in the Malabar Coast: Cochim and the "mercadorias meudas"', *Indica*, vol. 26, nos. 1-2, 1989, pp. 93-102.

Matos, Luís de, *L'expansion portugaise dans la littérature latine de le Renaissance*, Paris: Fondation Calouste Gulbenkian, Centre Culturel Portugais, 1991.

McCants, Anne E.C., 'Exotic Goods, Popular Consumption, and the Standard of Living: Thinking about Globalization in the Early Modern World', *Journal of World History*, vol. 18, no. 4, 2007, pp. 433-62.

Melgar, José María Oliva, 'Inmigración extranjera en la Andalucía del siglo XVII: la atracción de la plata americana' in *Mobilidade interna e migraçoes intraeuropeas na Península Ibérica: Proceedings of the European Symposium,* ed. Domingo L. González Lopo and Antonio Eiras Roel, Santiago de Compostela, 8-9 November 2001, 2002, pp. 281-98.

———,'Realidad y ficción en el monopolio de Indias: una reflexión sobre el sistema imperial español en el siglo XVII', *Manuscrits: Revista d'història moderna*, no. 14, 1996, pp. 321-58.

———, *El monopolio de Indias en el siglo XVII y la economía andaluza: La oportunidad que nunca existió*, opening lecture, academic year 2004-5, Huelva: Universidad de Huelva, 2005.

Mhamai, S.K., *The Sawants of Wadi and the Portuguese*, New Delhi: Concept Publishing Company, 1984.

Modelsky, George and William R. Thompson, *Seapower in Global Politics, 1914-1993*, London: Macmillan, 1988.

Mohsin, K.M., *A Bengal District in Transition: Murshidabad 1765-93*, Dacca, 1973.

Molesworth, G.L. 'Indian Currency', *Annals of the American Academy of Political and Social Science*, vol. 4, 1894, pp. 1-36.

Montojo, Vicente Montojo, 'Las oligarquías de Murcia y Cartagena en el reinado de Carlos V: formación y perpetuación de su memoria', in *Carlos V. Europeísmo y Universalidad*, ed. Juan Luis Castellano and Francisco Sánchez-Montes, Madrid: Sociedad Estatal, 2001, vol. IV.

———, 'Las relaciones comerciales entre el Sureste español y América a finales del siglo XVI y principios del XVII: el ejemplo de Cartagena' in *Murcia y América*, Murcia: V Centenario, ed. Juan Bta. Vilar, Comisión de Murcia, 1992.

———, 'Le Béarn et le Levant espagnol', *Revue de Pau et du Béarn*, no. 32, 2005, pp. 215-28, Proceedings of the 'Journées du Patrimoine: Échanges et rélations entre le Béarn et l'Espagne, Du Moyen-Âge à la Révolution Française', Oloron-Sainte Marie, 18 September 2004.

———, 'Mercados y estrategias mercantiles en torno a Cartagena en el siglo XVI y primera mitad del XVII: Un microanálisis', in *Cuadernos del Estero: Revista de Estudios e investigación*, nos. 7-10, 1992-5.

Morales, Carlos Javier de Carlos, 'Carlos V en una encrucijada financiera: las relaciones entre mercaderes-banqueros alemanes, genoveses y españoles en los asientos de 1529-1533', in *Carlos V y la quiebra del humanismo político en Europa (1530-1558)*, ed. José Martínez Millán, Madrid: Sociedad Estatal, 2001, vol. IV.

Moreira, Manuel A.F., *O porto de Viana do Castelo na época dos descobrimentos*, Viana do Castelo: Câmara Municipal, 1984.

Moreno, Manuel Espinar, 'Precisiones sobre el avituallamiento de la ciudad de Orán (1510-1512): La contratación de Diego de Espinosa, regidor de Almería', in *Actas del II Congreso Internacional "El Estrecho de Gibraltar"*, Madrid: UNED, 1995, vol. IV, pp. 5-70.

Morineau, Michel, 'The Indian Challenge: Seventeenth to Eighteenth Centuries', in *Merchants, Companies and Trade: Europe and Asia in the Early Modern Era*, ed. Sushil Chaudhury and Michel Morineau, Cambridge: Cambridge University Press, 1999.

Moura, H., 'Dois franceses, castelães de Diu', in *O Oriente Português*, vol. 2, Goa, 1905.

Mui, Hoh-Cheung, and Lorna Mui, 'Smuggling and the British Tea Trade before 1784', *American Historical Review*, vol. 74, 1968, pp. 44-73.

Mukherjee, Rila, 'The Indian Ocean in the "New Thalassology"', *ARCHIPEL*, vol. 76, 2008, pp. 291-329.

———, 'The Last Commercial Frontier: French and English Presence in South Eastern Bengal and Beyond', *Indian Historical Review*, vol. 35, no. 1, 2007, pp. 167-86.

———, 'The Nawab's Business: Agricultural and Commercial Practices in Eighteenth Century Bengal', in *Business History of India*, ed. Chittabrata Palit and Pranjal Bhattacharyya, New Delhi: Gyan Books, 2006, pp.137-60.

———, *Merchants and Companies in Bengal: Kasimbazar and Jugdia in the Eighteenth Century*, New Delhi: Pragati Publications, 2006.

———, *Strange Riches: Bengal in the Mercantile Map of South Asia*, Delhi: Cambridge India/Foundation, 2006.

Mukherjee, Tilottama, 'The Co-ordinating State and the Economy: The Nizamat in Eighteenth-Century Bengal', *Modern Asian Studies*, vol. 43, no. 2, 2009, pp. 389-436.

Muldrew, Craig, *The Economy of Obligation: The Culture of Credit and Social Relations in Early Modern England*, New York: St. Martin's Press, 1998.

Murdoch, Jonathan, 'The Spaces of Actor-Network Theory', *Geoforum*, vol. 29, 1998, pp. 357-74.

Nandy, S.C., *Life and Times of Canto Baboo: The Banyan of Warren Hastings*, 2 vols., Bombay: Allied Publishers, 1977.

Napier, William, *The life and opinions of General Sir Charles James Napier*, 4 vols., London: John Murray, 1857.

Nazarof, P.S., *Moved On*, London, 1935.

Newman, M.E.J., D.J. Watts and S.H. Strogatz, 'Random Graph Models of Social Networks', *Proceedings of the National Academy of Sciences of the United States of America*, vol.99, no. 3, 2002, pp. 2566-72.

Newman, Mark, Albert-László Barabási, and Duncan J. Watts, *The Structure and Dynamics of Networks,* Princeton, New Jersey: Princeton University Press, 2006.

North, Douglas C., *Institutions, Institutional Change, and Economic Performance*, Cambridge, UK, and New York: Cambridge University Press, 1990.

Norton, M.A., *D. Pedro Miguel de Almeida*, Portugal, Lisboa: Agência Geral do Ultramar, 1967.

O'Brien, Patrick, 'European Economic Development; The Contribution of the Periphery', *Economic History Review*, no. 35, 1980, pp. 1-18.

Oliveira e Costa, João Paulo, *O Japão e o Cristianismo no século XVI: Ensaios de História Luso-Nipónica*, Lisboa: Sociedade Histórica da Independência de Portugal, 1999.

———, *Portugal e o Japão: o século Namban*, Lisboa: Imprensa Nacional Casa de Moeda, 1993.

Ormrod, David, *The Rise of Commercial Empires: England and The Netherlands in the age of Mercantilism, 1650-1770*, New York: Cambridge University Press, 2003.

Osmaston, H., 'The productivity of agricultural and pastoral system in Zanskar (North West Himalayas),' in *Ladakh Himalaya Occidental Recent Research, Ethnology, Ecology,* no. 2, ed. Claude Dendaletche, France, 1985, pp. 75-88.

Otte, Enrique, 'Il ruolo dei Genovesi nella Spagna del XV e XVI secolo', in *La Repubblica Internazionale del denaro tra XV e XVII secolo*, ed. Aldo de Maddalena and Hermann Kellenbenz, Bologna: Il Mulino, 1986.

———, *Sevilla y sus mercaderes a fines de la Edad Media*, Sevilla: Diputación, 1996.

Owens, J.B., 'What historians want from GIS', *ArcNews*, vol. 29, no. 2, Summer 2007, pp. 4-6, and http://www.esri.com/news/arcnews/summer07articles/what-historians-want.html (accessed on 17 June 2010); also available in *GIS Best Practices: Essays on Geography and GIS*, Redlands, California: ESRI, 2008, pp. 35-46, and http://www.esri.com/library/bestpractices/essays-on-geography-gis.pdf (accessed on 17 June 2010).

———, 'The "Villena Cartel": Organized Crime and International Smuggling in Philip II's Spain', unpublished paper presented to the annual meeting of the Society for Spanish and Portuguese Historical Studies, Santa Fe, New Mexico, USA, April 2001.

———, 'A Multi-national, Multi-disciplinary Study of Trade Networks and the Domain of Iberian Monarchies during the First Global Age, 1400-1800', *Bulletin of the Society for Spanish and Portuguese Historical Studies*, vol. 33, no. 2, in press.

———, Emery Coppola Jr. and Ference Sidra Szidarovsky, 'Fuzzy Ruled-Based Modelling of Degrees of Trust in Cooperation-Based Networks: Close Research Collaboration among Domain Experts (Historians) and Mathematical Modellers', essay presented in 'Visualization and Space-Time Representation of Dynamic, Non-linear, Spatial Data in DynCoopNet and other TECT Projects', ESF EUROCORES Workshop, TECT Strategic Workshop in Madrid, Spain, 25-6 September 2008.

Owens, J.B., 'Graduate Education in Geographically-Integrated History: A Personal Account', *Journal of the Association for History and Computing*, vol. 13, no. 1, May 2010, http://hdl.handle.net/2027/spo.3310410.0013.105 (accessed on 17 June 2010).

———, 'Smuggling through Spain: A Neglected Sixteenth-Century Commercial Connection between the Mediterranean and the Atlantic', in *Comunicaciones del VIII Congreso de la Asociación Española de Historia Económica, 13-16 de septiembre de 2005, Galicia (Santiago, A Coruña, Vigo)*, Sesión B24; available at http://www.usc.es/es/congresos/histec05/b24.jsp (accessed on 14 March 2009).

———, 'The Political-Economic Anatomy of a Criminal Organization Connecting America and Philip II's Western Mediterranean Domains', unpublished paper presented as part of the session I organized, entitled 'Smuggling, Clandestine Political Economies, and Public Authority in the First Global Age: Iberian Monarchies, Sixteenth to Eighteenth Centuries', at the annual meeting of the American Historical Association, Washington D. C., 10 January 2004.

———, 'Toward a Geographically-Integrated, Connected World History: Employing Geographic Information Systems (GIS)', *History Compass*, vol. 5, no. 6, October 2007, pp. 2014-40.

———, 'Violence and Smuggling in Sixteenth-Century Eastern La Mancha', *Society for Spanish and Portuguese Historical Studies: Bulletin*, vol. 32, nos. 1 and 2, Fall 2007, pp.70-1.

———, *"By My Absolute Royal Authority": Justice and the Castilian Commonwealth at the Beginning of the First Global Age*, Rochester, New York: University of Rochester Press, 2005.

———, and Laura Woodworth-Ney, 'Envisioning a Master's Degree Program in Geographically-Integrated History', *Journal of the Association for History and Computing*, vol. 8, no. 2, September 2005, http://mcel.pacificu.edu/jahc/2005/issue2/articles/owenswoodworth.php (accessed on 17 June 2010).

Owens, J.B., and Amelia Polónia da Silva, 'Scientific Report: TECT Networking Workshop', at University of Porto, Portugal, 26-9 March 2008.

———, 'Trust, Reputation, Defectors, and Sustaining Social Norms: Studying spatially complex cooperative relationships in ways that connect TECT projects', prepared for the European Science Foundation's EUROCORES (European Collaborative Research) Scheme's programme 'The Evolution of Cooperation and Trading' (TECT), Strasbourg, France, 1 June 2008; available for download at http://idahostate.academia.edu/JBJackOwens/Papers (accessed on 17 June 2010).

Owens, Jack and Matthew Ciolek, 'Rutas: reuniendo datos sobre el tejido conector de una Monarquía Global', in *Estudios de Historia Iberoamericana I. XXXIIII Reunión Anual de la Society for Spanish and Portuguese Historical Studies* (SSPHS), ed. J.M. Bernardo Ares and S. Gómez Navarro, Córdoba: Universidad de Córdoba, 2003.

Pacini, Arturo, 'I mercanti-banchieri genovesi tra la Reppublica di San Giorgio e il sistema imperiale hispano-asburgico', in *L'Italia di Carlo V. Guerra, religione e politica nel primo Cinquecento*, ed. F. Cantù and M.A. Visceglia, Roma: Viella, 2003.

———, *La Genova di Andrea Doria nell'Impero di Carlo* V, Florence: Leo S. Olschki, 1999.

Pallis, Marco, *Peaks and Lamas*, London, 1939 and 1940.

Parthasarathi, P., *The Transition to a Colonial Economy: Weavers, Merchants and Kings in South India, 1720–1800*, Cambridge: Cambridge University Press, 2001.

Paulo, Eulália and Paulo Guinote, *Problemas de recrutamento para as armadas da* 'Carreira da Índia', available atw http://nautarch.tamu.edu/shiplab/01guifrulopes/Pguinotemilit96.htm (accessed on 13 January 2011).

Pearson, M.N., *Spices in the Indian Ocean World*, Sydney: Ashgate Varorium, 1996.

———, 'Littoral Society: The Concepts and the Problems', *Journal of World History*, vol. 17, no. 4, 2006, pp. 353-73.

———, 'The Portuguese State and Medicine in Sixteenth Century Goa', in *The Portuguese and Socio-Cultural Changes In India, 1500-1800*, ed. K.S. Mathew, Teotonio R. de Souza and Pius Malekandathil, Goa: Fundacao Oriente, 2001.

———, 'The Thin End of the Wedge: Medical Relativities as a Paradigm of Early Modern Indian-European Relations', *Modern Asian Studies*, vol. XXIX, no. l, 1995, pp. 141-70.

———, *The Portuguese in India*, Cambridge:Cambridge University Press, 1987.

Petech, L., 'The Tibetan-Ladakhi-Mughal War 1681-1683', *Indian Historical Quarterly*, no. 23, 1947, pp. 169-99.

———, *The Kingdom of Ladakh*, Roma, 1977.

Phillips, J.R.S., *La expansión medieval de Europa*, México: Fondo de Cultura Económica, 1994.

Picazo, Antoni, 'Comercio y colaboración en el Mar del Sur: El ejemplo del Patache San Buenaventura', in *X Reunión Científica de la Fundación Española de Historia Moderna,* Santiago de Compostela, 2008.

Pichon, Alain le, *China Trade and Empire: The Letters of William Jardine and James Mathesonand the Origins of British Rule in Hong Kong, 1827-43*, Oxford: Oxford University Press, 2006.

Pieper, Renate and Peer Schmidt, eds., 'Latin American and the Atlantic World/El mundo atlántico y América Latina (1500-1850)', *Essays in honour of Horst Pietschmann*, Köln: Böhlau–Verlag, 2005.

Pietschmann, Horst, ed., *Atlantic History: History of the Atlantic System, 1580-1830*, Göttingen: Vandenhoeck & Ruprecht, 2002.

Pike, Ruth, *Enterprise and Adventure: The Genoese in Seville and the Opening of the New World*, Ithaca: Cornell University Press, 1966.

———, Javier Alfayam and Barbara Mc Shane, *Aristócratas y comerciantes: la sociedad sevillana en el siglo XVI*, Barcelona: Crítica, 1978.

Pinto, Sara,*Caminha no século XVI: estudo sócio-económico, Dos que ganhão suas vidas sobre as águas*, Porto: Faculdade de Letras, 2009.

Podolny, Joel M., and James N. Baron, 'Relationships and Resources: Social Networks and Mobility in the Workplace', *American Sociological Review*, vol. 62, 1997, pp. 673-93.

Polanyi, Karl, *The Great Transformation: The Political and Economic Origins of Our Time*, Boston: Beacon Press, 1944.

Polónia, Amélia,'De Portugal a espaços ultramarinos: Inclusão e exclusão de agentes femininas no processo de expansão ultramarina, Século XVI', in *Historia, Género y Familia en Iberoamérica. Siglos XVI-XX*, ed. Dora Davila Mendonza, Caracas: Universidad Católica 'Andrés Bello'/ Konrad Adenauer Stiftung, 2004.

———, 'Evangelização e comércio: A figura do eclesiástico mercador', in *Estudos em homenagem a João Francisco Marques*, Porto: FLUP, 2001, vol. 2, pp. 297-310.

———, 'Mulheres que partem e mulheres que ficam: O protagonismo feminino na expansão ultramarina', *O Estudo da História*, no. 4, 2001, pp. 79-98.

———, 'Os Descobrimentos na literatura impressa portuguesa do século XVI a partir do fundo da BPM, Colóquio Livros Impressos em Portugal no Século XVI', Porto: Biblioteca Pública Municipal do Porto, 5-6 May 2006,unpublished paper.

———, 'Self-organising networks in the construction of the Portuguese overseas empire', in 5th International Congress of Maritime History, promoted by International Maritime Economic History Association (IMEHA), Greenwich, 23-7 June 2008, unpublished paper.

———, 'The sea and its impact on a maritime Community: Vila do Conde, Portugal, 1500-1640', *International Journal of Maritime History*, vol. XVIII, no. 1, June 2006, pp. 199-222.

———, *Expansão e Descobrimentos numa perspectiva local: O porto de Vila do Conde no século XVI*, , 2 vols., Lisboa: Imprensa Nacional-Casa da Moeda, 2007.

———, *Vila do Conde um porto nortenho na expansão ultramarina quinhentista*, 2 vols., Porto: s.n., Ph.D. dissertation,1999.

Pomeranz, Kenneth, and Steven Topik, *The World that Trade Created: Society, Culture, and the World Economy, 1400 to the Present*, Armank-London: M.E. Sharpe, 1999.

Postma, Johannes and Victor Enthoven, eds.,*Riches from Atlantic Commerce: Dutch Transatlantic Trade and Shipping, 1585-1817*, Leiden: Brill, 2003.

Potro, Betsabé Caunedo del, 'Comercio y hombres de negocios castellanos en tiempos de los Reyes Católicos. Técnicas y aprendizaje', in *Comercio y hombres de negocios en Castilla y Europa en tiempos de Isabel la Católica*, ed. H. Casado Alonso and A. García-Baquero, Madrid: Sociedad Estatal, 2007.

Prakash, Om, 'International Consortiums, Merchants Networks and Portuguese Trade with Asia in the Early Modern Period', in *XIV International Economic History*, Helsinki, 2006, available at http://www.helsinki.fi/iehc2006/papers1/Prakash.pdf (accessed on 13 January 2011).

———, and Denys Lombard, eds., *Commerce and Culture in the Bay of Bengal: 1500-1800*, New Delhi: Manohar, 1999.

Prakash, Om, *European Commercial Entreprise in Pre-Colonia India*, New York and Cambridge: Cambridge University Press, 1998.

———, *The Dutch East India Company and the Economy of Bengal, 1630-1720*, New Delhi: Oxford University Press, 1988.

Puu, Tönu, 'Introduction to Mathematical Economics', in *Mathematical Models in Economics: UNESCO Encyclopaedia of Life Support Systems*, ed. Wei-Bin Zhang, Oxford, UK: Eolss Publishers, 2007.

———, *Arts, Sciences, and Economics: A Historical Safari*, Berlin and Heidelberg: Springer-Verlag, 2006.

———, *Attractors, Bifurcations and Chaos: Non-linear Phenomena in Economics*, 2nd edn, Berlin and Heidelberg: Springer-Verlag, 2003.

Raab, Jörg, and H. Brinton Milward, 'Dark Networks as Problems', *Journal of Public Administration Research and Theory*, vol. 13, 2003, pp. 413-39.

Rafael, Valladares, 'Portugal y el fin de la hegemonía hispánica', *Hispania, Revista Española de Historia,* vol. 56, no. 193, 1996, pp. 517-39.

Ragin, Charles C., and Paul Pennings, 'Fuzzy Sets and Social Research', *Sociological Methods & Research*, vol. 33, no. 4, May 2005, pp. 423-30.

Ramos, L.A. de O., *Franceses em Portugal nos fins do século XVI*, Lisboa: Instituto de Alta Cultura, 1968.

Rap, R.T., 'The Unmaking of the Mediterranean Trade Hegemony: International Trade Rivalry and the Commercial Revolution', *Journal of Economic History,* vol. XXXV, 1975, pp. 499-525.

Ravina, Agustín Guimerá, *Burguesía extranjera y comercio atlántico: la empresa comercialirlandesa en canarias, 1703-177*, Santa Cruz de Tenerife, Madrid: CSIC, 1985.

Ray, Indrajit, 'Long Waves of Silk Price in Bengal during 16th-17th Centuries', pp. 1-33, at http://www.lse.ac.uk/collections/economicHistory/GEHN/GEHNPDF/PUNERay.pdf (accessed on 28 April 2009).

Ray, Indrani, *The French East India Company and the Trade of the Indian Ocean: a Collection of Essays by Indrani Ray*, ed. Lakshmi Subramanian, New Delhi and Calcutta: Munshiram Manoharlal and Centre for Studies in Social Sciences, 1999.

Reagans, Ray, and Bill McEvily, 'Network Structure and Knowledge Transfer: The Effects of Cohesion and Range', *Administrative Science Quarterly*, vol. 28, June 2003, pp. 240-67.

Reid, Anthony, 'Hybrid Identities in the Fifteenth-Century Straits of Malacca', *Working Paper Series 67*, National University of Singapore: Asia Research Institute, 2006.

Reynolds, L., 'Mercantilism: An Outline, History of Economic Thought', http://www.boisestate.edu/econ/lreynol/web/pdf_het/mercantilist.pdf (accessed on 8 May 2009).

Ringrose, David, *Europeans Abroad, 1400–1700: Strangers in Not-so-Strange Lands*. at http://www.iga.ucdavis.edu/Research/All-UC/conferences/2006-fall/Ringrose.pdf (accessed on 13 January 2011).

Ringrose, David, *Expansion and Global Interaction, 1200-1700*, Longman Worlds History Series, Series Editor, Michael Adas, Longman, 2001.

Rizvi, J., *Trans-Himalayan Caravans: Merchant, Princes and Peasant traders in Ladakh,* New Delhi: Oxford University Press, 1999.

Rodríguez, Manuel Bustos, 'De Sevilla a Cádiz: hacia el cambio de funcionalidad en el seno del monopolio andaluz con América (1600-1650)', in *Estudios de la Universidad de Cádiz ofrecidos a la memoria profesor Braulio Justel Calabozo*, Cadiz: Universidad de Cádiz, 1998.

———, 'España en el desarrollo capitalista mercantil europeo (siglos XVI-XVIII): Historia y estado de la cuestión', *Anales de la Universidad de Cádiz,* nos. 3-4, 1986-87, pp. 215-28.

———, *Cádiz en el sistema atlántico: la ciudad, sus comerciantes y la actividad mercantil (1650-1830)*, Madrid: Sílex, 2005.

Roitman, Jessica, 'Us and Them: Inter-cultural Trade and the Sephardim, 1595-1640', unpublished Ph.D. thesis, University of Leiden, 2009.

Romá, Alberola, 'La actividad comercial de los puertos de Valencia, Alicante y Cartagena durante la Edad moderna: Una aproximación historiográfica', in *La Storiografia maritima in Italia e in Spagna in etá moderna e contemporanea. Tendenze, orientamenti, linee evolutive*, A.di Vittorio and C. Barciela López, Bari: Caccuci, 2001.

Rosser, J. Barkely, Jr., *From Catastrophe to Chaos: A General Theory of Economic Discontinuities*, vol. I, 2nd edn, Boston: Kluwer Academic, 2000.

Saldanha, A. de S., and V. S. de Saldanha, *As cartas de Manuel de Saldanha, Conde da Ega e 47 Vice-Rei da India a Sebastião José de Carvalho eMelo e seus irmãos (1758-1765),* Lisboa: Gabinete Português de Estudos Humanistícos, 1984.

Samuel, Geoffrey, 'Tibet as Stateless Society and Some Islamic parallels', *Journal of Asian Studies*, vol. XLI, no. 2, February 1982, pp. 215-21.

Sanakrityayana, R., *History of Central Asia*, Delhi, 1964.

Sánchez, Manuel Herrero, 'La república de Génova y la Monarquía Hispánica (siglos XVI-XVII), 'Introducción', *Hispania*, no. 219, 2005, pp. 9-20.

Santana, Elisa Torres, *La burguesía mercantil de las Canarias Orientales, 1600-1625*, Las Palmas de Gran Canaria: Cabildo Insular, 1991.

Santos, Catarina Madeira, *Goa é a chave de toda a Índia: Perfil político da capital do Estado da Índia (1505-1570)*, Lisboa, 1999.

Santos, H.M. dos, *Catálogo dos documentos secretos do extinto Conselho de Guerra*, vol. 4, Lisboa, 1963.

Santos, Maria Emília Madeira, 'Afonso de Albuquerque e os feitores', in *II Seminário Internacional de História Indo-Portuguesa*, ed. Luís de Albuquerque and Inácio Guerreiro, Lisboa: Instituto de Investigação Científica e Tropical/Centro de Estudos de História e Cartografia Antiga, 1985.

Sarkar, Benoy Kumar, *Inland Transport and Communication in Medieval India*, Calcutta: Calcutta University Press, 1925.

Sarkar, Jadunath, *Bengal Nawabs*, Calcutta: Asiatic Society, 1952.

Saul, S.B., *Studies in British Overseas Trade, 1870-1914*, Liverpool, 1960.

Schaub, Jean-Frédéric, *Les juifs du roi d'Espagne: Oran, 1509-1669*, Paris: Hachette Litérratures, 1999.

Schumpeter, Joseph A., *Business Cycles: A Theoretical, Historical and Statistical Analysis of the Capitalist Process*, New York: McGraw-Hill Book Company, 1939.

Sen, I.B., 'Money-lenders in India', *Journal of the Society of Comparative Legislation*, n.s., vol. 11, no. 1, 1910, pp. 168-76.

Sensarma, A.K., 'The Great Bengal Cyclone of 1737: an enquiry into the legend', *Weather*,1994, pp. 90-6.

Sepulveda, C.A. de M., *História orgânica e politica do exército português*, vol.15, Imprensa da Universidade, 1928.

Seth, M.S., *The Armenians in India*, New Delhi: Oxford & IBH Publishing Co. Pvt. Ltd., 1983.

Sharman, Raj, Rajiv Kishore, and Ram Ramesh, eds., *Ontologies: A Handbook of Principles, Concepts, and Applications in Information Systems*, New York: Springer-Verlag, 2007.

Shaw, Carlos Martínez and José María Oliva Melgar, eds., *El sistema atlántico español (siglos XVII-XIX)*, Madrid: Marcial Pons, 2005.

Shaw, Carlos Martínez,*Cataluña en la Carrera de Indias, 1680-1756*, Barcelona: Crítica, 1981.

Sideri, S., *Trade and Power: Informal colonialism in Anglo-Portuguese Relations*, Rotterdam: Rotterdam University Press, 1970.

Silva, A.C.G.da, 'Os Franceses Na colonização portuguesa da Índia', in *Studia*, Lisbon: CEHU, 1959.

Silva, Francisco Ribeiro da, *O Porto e o seu termo (1580-1640): Os homens, as instituições e o poder*, 2 vols., Porto: Câmara Municipal/Arquivo Histórico Municipal do Porto, 1988.

Silva, Chandra Richard de, 'The Portuguese East India Company 1628-1633', *Luso-Brazilian Review*, vol. 11, no. 2, 1974, pp. 152-205.

Sircar, D.C., 'Text of Puranic list of peoples', *Indian Historical Quarterly*, no. 21, Calcutta, 1945, pp. 297-314.

Sircar, D.C., *Studies in the Geography of Ancient and Medieval India*, Calcutta, 1960.

Sivarajan, V.V., and Indira Balachandran, *Ayurvedic Drugs and Their Plant Sources*, New Delhi and Bombay: Oxford & IBH Publishing Co. Pvt. Ltd., 1994.

Smith, Robert C., *Pinturas de ex-votos existentes em Matosinhos e outros santuários de Portugal*, Matosinhos: Câmara Municipal, 1966.

Smithson, Michael, and Jay Verkuilen, *Fuzzy Set Theory: Applications in the Social Sciences*, Thousand Oaks, California: Sage, 2006.

Stark, David C., 'Heterarchy: Distributing Authority and Organizing Diversity', in *The Biology of Business: Decoding the Natural Laws of the Enterprise*, ed. John H. Clippinger III, San Francisco: Jossey-Bass, 1999.

Steensgard, Niels, 'The Route through Quandahar: the Significance of the Overland Trade from India to the West in the Seventeenth Century', in *Merchants, Companies and Trade: Europe and Asia in the Early Modern Era*, ed. Sushil Chaudhury and Michel Morineau, Cambridge: Cambridge University Press, 1999.

Solano, Francisco de, and Salvador Bernabeu, eds., *Estudios (Nuevos y Viejos) sobre la Frontera*, Madrid: CSIC, 1999.

Sousa, Ivo Carneirode, 'As Misericórdias de Lisboa a Manila: Muito poder e alguma caridade', *Campus Social*, no. 2, Lisboa, 2005, pp. 114-21.

Sousa, Lúcio Manuel Rochade, 'O Japão e os Portugueses (1580-1614): Religião, política e comércio', Porto: s.n., 2007, 2 vols., unpublished Ph.D. thesis presented at the University of Porto.

Stein, Stanley J., and Barbara H. Stein, *Silver, Trade, and War: Spain and America in the Making of Early Modern Europe*, Baltimore: Johns Hopkins University Press, 2000.

Strachy, H., *Physical Geography of Western Tibet*, London, 1854.

Subrahmanyam, Sanjay, 'Connected Histories: Notes towards a Reconfiguration of Early Modern Eurasia', *Modern Asian Studies*, vol. 31, no. 3, 1997, pp. 735-62.

———, and C. A. Bayly, 'Portfolio capitalists and the political economy of early modern India', *Indian Economic Social History Review*, vol. 25, no. 4, 1988, pp. 401-24.

———, *Comércio e conflito: A presença Portuguesa no Golfo de Bengala, 1500-1700*, Lisboa: Edições 70, 1994.

———, *O império asiático Português, 1500-1700: Uma história política e económica*, Lisboa: Difel, 1995.

———, and Luís F.R. Thomaz, 'Evolution of empire: The Portuguese in the Indian Ocean during the sixteenth century', in *The Political Economy of Merchant Empires*, Cambridge: Cambridge University Press, 1991, pp. 298-331.

Sutherland, Heather, 'South-East Asian History and the Mediterranean Analogy', *Journal of South-East Asian Studies*, vol. 34, no. 1, 2003, pp.1-20.

Svoboda, Robert E., *Ayurveda: Life, Health and Longevity*, New Delhi, London and New York: Penguin Books, 1993.

De Terra, 'Himalayan and Alpine Orogenies', *Report of the XV International Geological Congress,* vol. 2, 1936, pp. 859-72.

Thomas, Hugh, *El Imperio Español: De Colón a Magallanes*, Barcelona: Editorial Planeta, 2006.

Thomaz Luís Filipe Ferreira Reis, *De Ceuta a Timor*, Lisboa: Difel, 1994.

———, 'The Malay Sultanate of Melaka', in *South-East Asia in the early Modern Era: Trade, Power and Belief*, ed. Anthony Reid, Ithaca: Cornell University Press, 1993.

Thrift, Nigel J., 'Rhizome', in *The Dictionary of Human Geography*, ed. Ronald J. Johnston et al., Oxford, UK, and Malden, Massachusetts: Blackwell, 2000.

Tilly, Charles, *Trust and Rule*, Cambridge, UK, and New York: Cambridge University Press, 2005.

Torres, José Antonio Martínez, *Prisioneros de los infieles: Vida y rescate de los cautivos cristianos en el Mediterráneo musulmán (siglos XVI-XVII)*, Barcelona: Bellaterra, 2004.

Tracy, James D., ed., *The Rise of Merchant Empires: Long-Distance Trade in the Early Modern World, 1350-1750*, Cambridge: Cambridge University Press, 1990.

———, *Emperor Charles V, Impressario of War: Campaign Strategy, International Finance, and Domestic Politics*, Cambridge: Cambridge University Press, 2002.

Treguilly, Ph le, 'Les francais en Inde au temps de la guerre d'independance americain (1778-1788)', *These pour le doctorat de lettres*, Paris, 1992.

Tuc, Patrick J.N., *The East India Company*, 1600-1858, London: Routledge, 2001.

Tucker, A.N., 'Foreign Sounds in Swahili', *Bulletin of the School of Oriental and African Studies*, University of London, vol. 11, no. 4, 1946,pp.854-71.

Unali, Anna, *Ceuta 1415: los orígenes de la expansión europea en África*, Ceuta: Archivo Central, 2004.

Urban, Hugh B., 'The Marketplace and the Temple: Economic Metaphors and Religious Meanings in the Folk Songs of Colonial Bengal', *The Journal of Asian Studies*, vol. 60, no. 4, 2001, pp. 1085-114.

Uriarte, Aingeru Zavala, *La función comercial del País Vasco en el siglo XVIII. El comercio y tráfico marítimo del norte de España en el siglo XVIII*, San Sebastián: Diputación, 1983.

Van der Veer, Peter, 'The Global History of "Modernity"', *Journal of the Economic and Social History of the Orient*, vol. 41, no. 3, 1998, pp. 285-94.

Varady, R.G., 'North Indian Banjaras: Their Evolution as Transporters', *South Asia: Journal of South Asian Studies*, vol. 2, no. 1, 1979, pp.1-18.

Vasallo, Carmel,*Corsairing to Commerce: Maltese Merchants in XVIII Century Spain*, Malta: University Publishers, 1997.

Veronne, Chantalde la, 'Población del presidio de Orán en 1527', *Revista de Archivos, Bibliotecas y Museos*, vol. LXXVI, no. 1, January-June 1973, pp. 69-108.

Vester, Matthew,'The Political Autonomy of a Tax Farm: The Nice-Piedmont Gabelle of the Dukes of Savoy, 1525-1580', *The Journal of Modern History*, no. 76, 2004, pp. 745-92.

Villanueva, Ramón Maruri, *La burguesía mercantil santanderina, 1700-1850: cambio social* y *mentalidad*, Santander: Universidad de Cantabria, 1990.

Vink, Markus, 'Indian Ocean Studies and the 'New Thalassology'", *Journal of Global History*, vol. 2, 2007, pp.41–62.

Vohra, R., 'Sogdian Inscriptions from Tangtse in Ladakh', in *Tibetan Studies Proceedings of 6th seminar of the International Association for Tibetan Studies*, Fagernes, 1992, vol. 2, ed. P. Kvaerne.

Volckart, O.J., *The Influence of Information Cost on the Integration of Financial Markets: Northern Europe, 1350-1560*, Institute of Economic History, Humboldt University: Berlin, 2006; 'The Influence of Information Costs on the Integration of Financial Markets: Northern Europe, 1350-1560', in *Information Flows: New Approaches in the Historical Study of Business Information*, ed. Leos Mueller and Jari Ojala, Helsinki: Finnish Literature Society, 2007, pp. 31-62.

Walker, Timothy,'Acquisition and Circulation of Medical Knowledge within the Early Modern Portuguese Colonial Empire', in *Science, Power and the Order of Nature in the Spanish and Portuguese Empires*, ed. Daniela Bleichmar, Kristin Huffine and Paula De Vos, Stanford: Stanford University Press, 2009.

Wallerstein, Immanuel, 'Remembering Andre Gunder Frank While Thinking About the Future', *Monthly Review*, vol. 60, no. 2, June 2008, http://www.monthlyreview.org/080630wallerstein.php (accessed on 17 June 2010).

———, *O sistema mundial moderno*, 3 vols., Porto, 1974-99; *The Modern World-System*,New York and San Diego, California: Academic Press, 1974, 1980, 1989.

———, *World-Systems Analysis: An Introduction*, Durham, North Carolina, and London: Duke University Press, 2004.

Washbrook, David, 'India in the Early Modern World Economy: Modes of Production, Reproduction and Exchange',*Journal of Global History*, vol. 2, 2007, pp. 87-111.

Watts, Duncan J., 'Networks, Dynamics, and the Small-World Phenomenon', *American Journal of Sociology*, vol. 105, 1999, pp. 493-527.

———, 'The "New" Science of Networks', *Annual Review of Sociology*, vol. 30, 2004, pp. 243-70.

———, and Peter S. Dodds, 'Influentials, Networks, and Public Opinion Formation', *Journal of Consumer Research*, vol. 34, no. 4, December 2007, pp. 441-58.

Watts, Duncan J., *Six Degrees: The Science of a Connected Age*, New York and London: W.W. Norton, 2003.

———, *Small Worlds: The Dynamics of Networks Between Order and Randomness*, Princeton Studies in Complexity, Princeton: Princeton University Press, 2003.

———, 'Networks, Dynamics, and the Small-World Phenomenon', *The American Journal of Sociology*, vol. 105, no. 2, 1999, pp. 493-527.

Weber, Klaus, *Deutsche Kaufleute im Atlantikhandel 1680-1830: Unternehmen und Familien in Hamburg, Cádiz und Bordeaux*, Munich: C.H. Beck, 2004.

White, Harrison C., 'Social Networks Can Resolve Actor Paradoxes in Economics and in Psychology', *Journal of Institutional and Theoretical Economics*, vol. 151, 1995, pp. 58-74.

———, *Identity and Control: A Structural Theory of Social Action*, Princeton, New Jersey: Princeton University Press, 1992.

———, *Markets from Networks: Socio-Economic Models of Production*, Princeton, New Jersey: Princeton University Press, 2002.

Wigen, Karen, 'Oceans of History: Introduction', *AHR Forum, American Historical Review*, vol. 111, no. 3, June 2006, pp.117-21.

Williamson, Oliver E., *The Economic Institutions of Capitalism: Firms, Markets, Relational Contracting*, New York and London: Free Press and Collier Macmillan, 1985.

Wink, Andre, 'From the Mediterranean to the Indian Ocean: Medieval History in Geographic Perspective', *Comparative Studies in Society and History*, vol. 44, no. 3, 2002, pp.416-45.

Wittfogel, Karl A., *Oriental Despotism: A Comparative Study of Total Power*, New Haven: Yale University Press, 1957.

Xavier, Ângela Barreto, *A Invenção de Goa: Poder imperial e conversões culturais nos séculos XVI e XVII*, Lisboa: ICS (Imprensa de Ciências Sociais), 2007.

Xavier, Carlos, 'Daman Port and Shipyards, 1800-1875', in *Purabhilekh-Puratatva, Journal of the Directorate of Archives, Archaeology and Museum*, vol. III, no. 1, January-June 1985, Panaji, Goa, pp. 10-12.

Yang, Anand, *Bazaar India: Markets, Society and the Colonial State in Bihar*, Berkeley and Los Angeles: California University Press, 1988.

Yang, Bin, 'Horses, Silver and Cowries: Yunnan in Global Perspective', *Journal of World History*, vol. 15, no. 3, 2004, pp. 281-322.

———, *Between Winds and Clouds: The Making of Yunnan, Second Century* BCE *to Twentieth Century* CE, New York: Columbia University Press, 2008.

Yousefi, Shahriar, Ilona Weinreich, and Dominik Reinarz, 'Wavelet-based Prediction of Oil Prices', *Chaos, Solitons and Fractals*, vol. 25, 2005, pp. 265–75.

Yuan, May, 'Adding Time', in *Handbook of Geographic Information Science*, ed. John Wilson and A. Stewart Fotheringham, Malden, Massachusetts: Blackwell, 2007, pp. 169-84.

———, 'Dynamics GIS: Recognizing the Dynamic Nature of Reality', *ArcNews*, vol. 30, no. 1, Spring 2008, pp. 1, 4-5, and http://www.esri.com/news/arcnews/spring08articles/dynamics-gis.html (accessed on 17 June 2010).

Yun, Bartolomé, *Las redes del imperio: Élites sociales en la articulación de la Monarquía Hispánica, 1492-1714*, Madrid: Marcial Pons, Universidad Pablo de Olavide, 2009.

Zadeh, Lotfi A., 'Toward a Theory of Fuzzy Information Granulation and its Centrality in Human Reasoning and Fuzzy Logic', *Fuzzy Sets and Systems*, vol. 90, 1997, pp. 111-27.

Zorraquino, José Ignacio Gómez, *La burguesía mercantil en el Aragón de los siglos XVI y XVII: 1516-1652*, Zaragoza: Diputación General de Aragón, Departamento de Cultura y Educación, 1987.

Editor and Contributors

AMÂNDIO JORGE MORAIS BARROS teaches at the Escola Superior de Educação do IPP, Politecnico do Porto, Portugal. Researcher at CITCEM-University of Porto, Porto, Portugal, he has authored numerous articles in Portuguese and English on the Portuguese expansion in the First Global Age.

ERNESTINE CARREIRA has been Maitre des Conferences at the University of Provence, France since 1987, where she is also currently the Director of the Department of Portuguese and Brazilian Studies. Dr Carreira is a member of CEMAF, a research centre dedicated to African Studies at the University of Provence (associated with the CNRS, France and Sorbonne University, Paris). Her research interests include naval technology, economic history and the interaction between the Portuguese and French empires in India, Africa and South America—fields in which she has published several articles.

DAVID ALONSO GARCÍA teaches at the Department of Modern History at Universidad Complutense, Madrid, Spain. As a principal investigator in the DynCoopNet network project (managed by Professors J.B. Owens and A. Crespo), supported by European Science Foundation, he leads a research project using Geographic Information Systems (GIS) technologies in order to analyse the Castilian tax system between the fifteenth-sixteenth centuries. Professor Garcia has been a Visiting Fellow to the London School of Economics (2000), Università di Roma 'La Sapienza' (2001), University of California, Los Angeles (UCLA, 2006) and Università di Roma Tre (2010). His publications include *Una corte en construcción: Madrid en la hacienda real de Castilla (1517-1556)* (2005), *El erario del reino: Fiscalidad en Castilla a comienzos de la Edad Moderna (1504-1525)* (2007) and *Breve Historia de los*

Austrias (2008). Together with A. Crespo, he has co-edited *Merchant Networks in the First Global Age: Cooperation and Representation* (forthcoming).

RATTAN LAL HANGLOO is Professor of South Asia and Central Studies, and Dean, School of Global Relations and School of Languages, Literature and Culture, Central University of Punjab, Bhatinda, Punjab, India. Professor Hangloo is a specialist on Kashmir affairs and Central Asia. In his previous engagements, he was Head, Department of History and Chief Proctor at Hyderabad Central University, Hyderabad, India. He has also served as the Chair of Indian Studies at University of West Indies, Trinidad and Tobago. He has been awarded Fulbright (USA) and DAAD Fellowships (Germany). He has published over 70 papers in national and international journals. His publications include: *Agrarian System of Kashmir (1846-1900)* (1995), *State in Medieval Kashmir* (2000), and has edited *Situating Medieval Indian State* (1995), *Approaching Islam* (2005) and *New Themes in Indian History: Politics, Gender, Environment and Culture* (2007).

SRIJAN SANDIP MANDAL completed his Master of Arts in History at the University of Hyderabad, Hyderabad, India where he took a course on The World of the Indian Ocean. At present, he is pursuing a Master of Philosophy, for which he is writing a dissertation entitled 'Deconstructing discourse: a study of the "primary" and "secondary" sources on Tipu Sultan'. In the future, too, he hopes to work on topics pertaining to the Philosophy of History and Historiography.

RILA MUKHERJEE is Professor and Head, Department of History, School of Social Science, University of Hyderabad, Hyderabad, India. A partner in the DynCoopNet project of the European Science Foundation, she has been a Visiting Professor and Visiting Scholar in Tokyo, Kolkata, Shanghai, Berlin and Paris. Professor Mukherjee is the author of *Merchants and Companies in Bengal: Kasimbazar and Jugdia in the Eighteenth Century* (2006) and *Strange Riches: Bengal in the Mercantile Map of South Asia* (2006).

ANTONI PICAZO MUNTANER is Associate Professor, Universitat de les Illes Balears, Palma de Mallorca, Spain. Professor Picazo's research encompasses the Spanish Pacific and Atlantic worlds. He has recently published for the DynCoopNet project, two works on business systems in the Indian and Pacific oceans: *Compañías mercantilistas en el Indo-Pacífico,* vol. I and *El modelo hispánico*, vol. II.

J.B. OWENS is Guggenheim Fellow and Research Professor of Geographically-Integrated History, Idaho State University, USA. Named his university's centennial distinguished researcher in 2002, Professor Owens has held major fellowships from the US National Endowment for the Humanities and the John Simon Guggenheim Memorial Foundation. In addition to numerous articles, book chapters, and reviews, his major publication is a book *"By My Absolute Royal Authority": Justice and the Castilian Commonwealth at the Beginning of the First Global Age* (2005). Professor Owens' current research involves combining Social Network Analysis (SNA) and the dynamics of Geographic Information Systems (GIS) to study smuggling and other cooperation-based social networks in the First Global Age; the work is funded by the US National Science Foundation (NSF). At present, he is completing a book on the emergence of cooperation from an environment of seemingly endemic violence.

AMÉLIA POLÓNIA is Professor at the Department of History, Political and International Studies, University of Porto, Portugal. Her research interests are Early Modern History, Maritime History, Social Networks, Trade Networks and Overseas Diaspora. Vice-President of the International Maritime Economic History Association (IMEHA), she is also principal investigator of DynCoopNet, a TECT/EUROCORES/ ESF Collaborative Research Project. Professor Polonia authored *Expansão e Descobrimentos numa perspectiva local: O porto de Vila do Conde no século XVI* (2007) and co-edited *Maritime History as Global History* (2011) and *European Seaports in the Early Modern Age: A comparative approach* (2007).

ANA CRESPO SOLANA is Professor, Tenured Scientist, at the Institute of History, CCHS, Consejo Superior de Investigaciones Científicas (Spanish National Research Council) since 2001. Her specializations include Early Modern History, with specific reference to relations between Spain, the Low Countries and the Baltic in the eighteenth century, in the fields of Social and Economic History. Her scientific research includes significant studies of Flemish and Dutch merchant communities in the Atlantic world, in European port cities and in the Caribbean and its surrounding areas. Professor Solana has been research fellow, invited lecturer and associate professor at several universities and research centres, such as Universidad de Cádiz, Spain; Katholieke Universiteit Leuven, Belgium (1993); Universiteit Leiden (IGEER), The Netherlands (1994, 1995, 1996-7, 1998, 2000, 2002); Institute Maritieme Geschiedenis, Universiteit Gent, Belgium (2000); and London School of Economics, London, UK (November 2001). She has authored seven books and numerous essays. Some of her publications include: *El Comercio marítimo entre Cádiz y Amsterdam, 1713-1778* (2000), *Entre Cádiz y los Países Bajos: una comunidad mercantil en la ciudad de la Ilustración* (2001), *América desde otra frontera: La Guayana Holandesa (Surinam), 1680-1778* (2006), *Comunidades Transnacionales: Colonias de mercaderes extranjeros en el mundo atlántico, 1500-1830* (2010), and has co-edited with M. Herrero Sánchez, *La Monarquía y las 17 Provincias de los Países Bajos: una revision historiográfica (siglos XVI-XVIII)*, 2 vols. (2002).

ALEX M. THOMAS is a research scholar at the Department of Economics, University of Hyderabad, Hyderabad, India. He completed his Masters in Economics at the same university where he also took up interdisciplinary courses such as The World of the Indian Ocean and Economic History of India. His research interests include Indian Economy, Classical Political Economy, History of Economic Thought and Philosophy of Economics.

TIMOTHY WALKER is Associate Professor of History at the University of Massachusetts, Dartmouth, USA. In addition to serving as Fulbright Program Advisor at the university, he is Associate Director of the Center for Portuguese Studies and Culture; a member of the graduate faculty of the Department of Portuguese Studies; and an affiliated faculty member of the Center of Indian Studies. Professor Walker is also an Affiliated Researcher of the Centro de História de Além-Mar (CHAM), Universidade Nova de Lisboa, Portugal. From 1994 to 2003, he was a Visiting Professor at the Universidade Aberta in Lisbon as also at Brown University during Fall 2010. He is the author of *Doctors, Folk Medicine and the Inquisition: The Repression of Magical Healing in Portugal during the Enlightenment* (2005).

Index